Marrakech & the High Atlas Handbook

The travel guide

Footprint

Justin McGuinness

Awi iyyi d man mmimnin, a targa
Yawi d ugharas ahbib, ay yagm

O stream, bring sweet water to the cistern
So the path will bring the lover to draw water.

Traditional Tachelhit verse

Marrakech & the High Atlas Handbook
First edition

Published by Footprint Handbooks
6 Riverside Court
Lower Bristol Road
Bath BA2 3DZ. England
T +44 (0)1225 469141
F +44 (0)1225 469461
Email discover@footprintbooks.com
Web www.footprintbooks.com

ISBN 1 903471 12 5
CIP DATA: A catalogue record for this book is available from the British Library

Distributed in the USA by
Publishers Group West

Credits

Series editors
Patrick Dawson and Rachel Fielding

Editorial
Editor: Sarah Thorowgood
Maps: Sarah Sorensen

Production
Typesetting: Davina Rungasamy, Leona Bailey, Emma Bryers and Jo Morgan
Maps: Robert Lunn, Claire Benison and Maxine Foster
Colour maps: Kevin Feeney

Cover: Camilla Ford

Design
Mytton Williams

Photography
Front cover: Impact Photo Library
Back cover: B Bocarra
Inside colour section: D Whiting, Impact, Pictures Colour Library Ltd, B Boccara, ImageState, Eye Ubiquitous, James Davis Travel Photography

Print
Manufactured in Italy by LEGOPRINT

Marrakech and the High Atlas

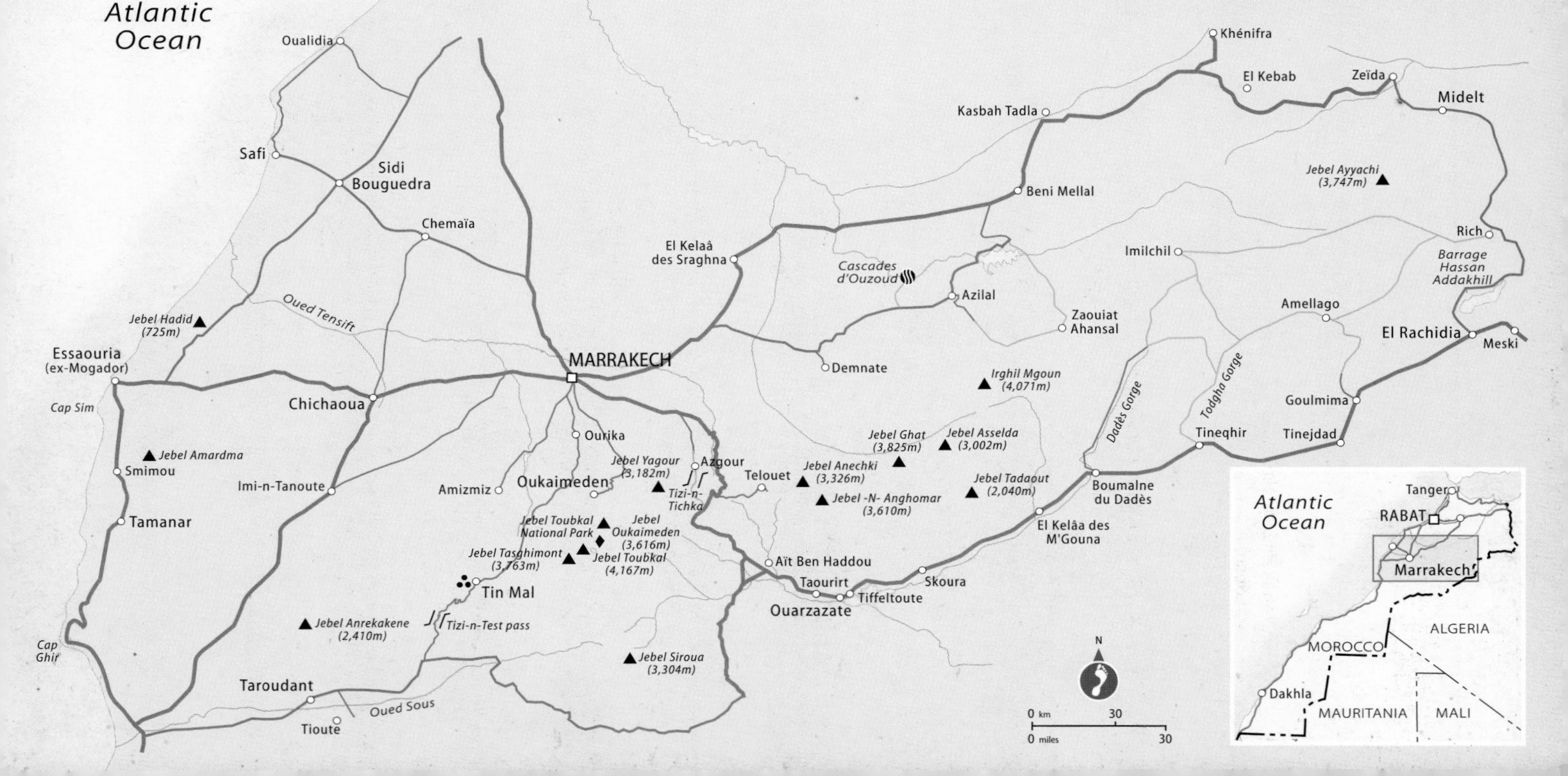

Atlantic Ocean
Oualidia
Safi
Sidi Bouguedra
Chemaïa
Oued Tensift
Jebel Hadid (725m)
Essaouria (ex-Mogador)
Cap Sim
Chichaoua
Jebel Amardma
Smimou
Imi-n-Tanoute
Tamanar
Cap Ghir
Taroudant
Tioute
Oued Sous
Jebel Anrekakene (2,410m)
Tizi-n-Test pass
Tin Mal
Jebel Tasghimont (3,763m)
Jebel Toubkal National Park
Jebel Toubkal (4,167m)
Jebel Oukaimeden (3,616m)
Jebel Siroua (3,304m)
Amizmiz
Oukaimeden
Ourika
Jebel Yagour (3,182m)
MARRAKECH
Azgour
Tizi-n-Tichka
Telouet
El Kelaâ des Sraghna
Demnate
Cascades d'Ouzoud
Azilal
Zaouiat Ahansal
Kasbah Tadla
Beni Mellal
Khénifra
El Kebab
Zeïda
Midelt
Jebel Ayyachi (3,747m)
Rich
Barrage Hassan Addakhill
Imilchil
Amellago
El Rachidia
Meski
Goulmima
Tinejdad
Tineqhir
Todgha Gorge
Dadès Gorge
Irghil Mgoun (4,071m)
Jebel Ghat (3,825m)
Jebel Asselda (3,002m)
Jebel Anechki (3,326m)
Jebel -N- Anghomar (3,610m)
Jebel Tadaout (2,040m)
Boumalne du Dadès
El Kelâa des M'Gouna
Skoura
Aït Ben Haddou
Taourirt
Tiffeltoute
Ouarzazate
N
0 km 30
0 miles 30

Atlantic Ocean
Tanger
RABAT
Marrakech
ALGERIA
MOROCCO
Dakhla
MAURITANIA
MALI

Contents

***Right**: carpet sellers keeping their cool in the souk.*

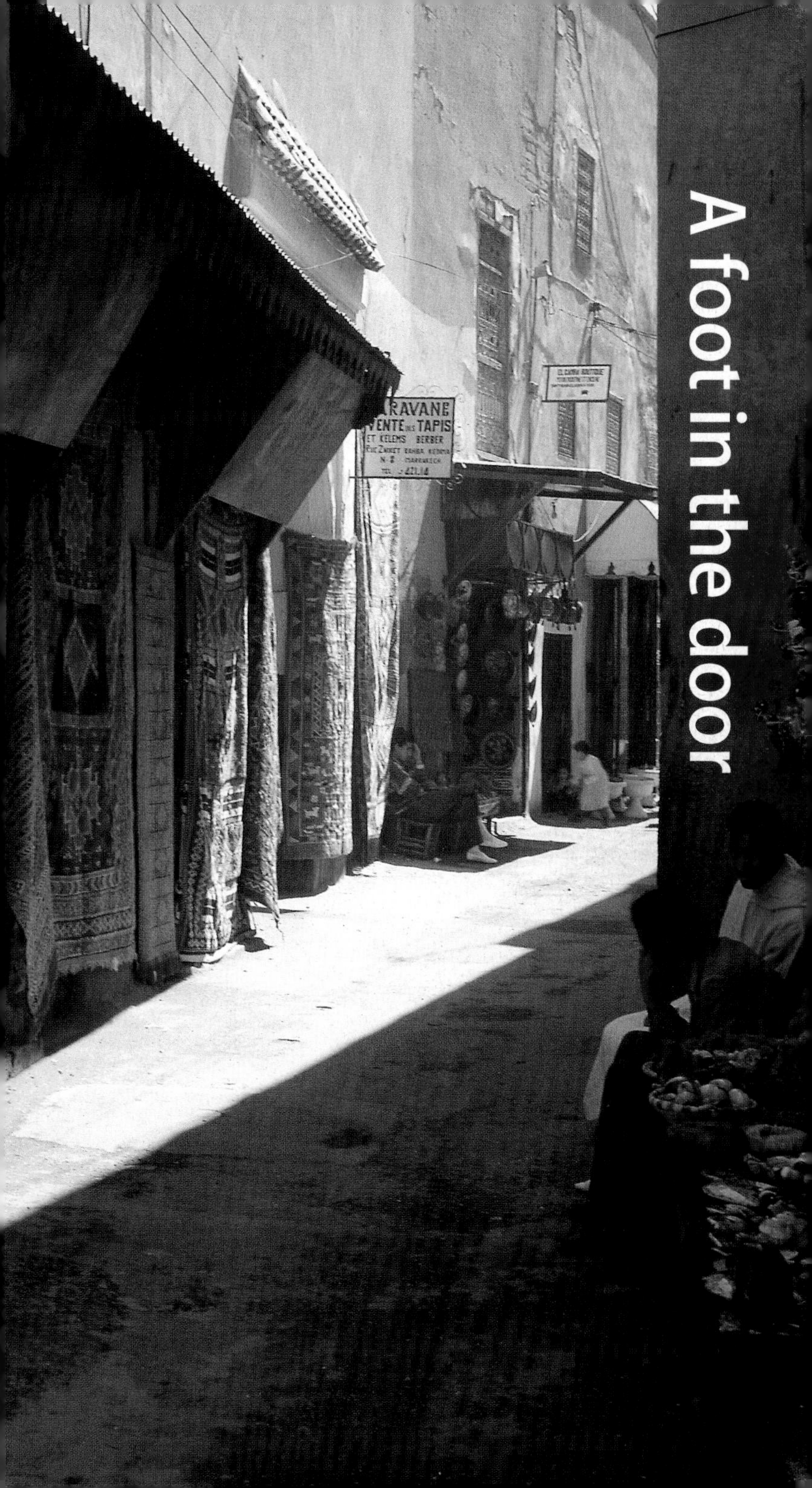

A foot in the door

__Right__: traditional beauty: a basket of dried rose buds to pound up for ghassoul shampoo.
__Below__: smiles in the streets of Marrakech.

__Above__: close shaves at an old-style barbershop.
__Right__: sea-going camels on Essaouira's sweeping Atlantic beach – not just a ships of the desert then...

Highlights

Indolent and overwhelming, often sensuous and occasionally illicit, with the odd patch of Disneyfication and too much traffic, Marrakech will never bore you. Long prized by travellers, this southern Moroccan city and its region have all the exoticism of the Indies or some other such sultry destination: the colour and press of souks, crumbling palaces and kasbahs, rugged mountains, the green splash of oasis vegetation in a rocky gorge. Just a couple of hours from the dry heat of Marrakech is a wild Atlantic coast and inland lie remote mountain valleys, only now just waking up to electricity and satellite television.

Southern Pearl

Marrakech, the strategic heart of southern Morocco, is a place with quite a past. Founded and fought over by dynasties from nearby mountain and distant desert, the city grew thanks to melt water from the Atlas mountains, flowing through long underground channels to irrigate date-palms and orchards. Oasis-city, garden-town, Marrakech pushed back the arid plain to become 'pearl of the South'. Within the walls, every quarter had its market gardens, every house a planted patio. Now on burning summer afternoons, orange and medlar trees provide shade and cardinal-purple bougainvillaea flower against pink-washed walls.

Once an imperial, if rather sleepy capital, ringed by terracotta-red ramparts and palm-groves, filled with great Islamic monuments and superb restaurants, Marrakech has well and truly woken up to international tourism.

Land & people

But apart from this engaging red-walled city, what makes this region of Morocco truly special are the landscapes: the High Atlas, with its shattered rock plateaux and green valleys, deep gorges, citadel villages and granaries, and the hundreds of kilometres of road snaking across stark and shimmering desertscapes south of the mountains. Here ancient adobe fortresses and oasis gardens have survived, telling of a time when people lived in better harmony with a harsh environment.

Ancient upheavals

It is no exaggeration to say that the Atlas is a providential range for western European hikers: after the Alps and the Pyrénées, they are the nearest high mountains, and in Africa to boot. Forming a great barrier cutting the northern, populated two-thirds of Morocco from the desert south, they have an addictive fascination. There are no soaring peaks, but rather massifs of rangey crests and expansive plateaux. Wide-floored valleys make easy walking, the canyons and their swift-flowing streams require basic climbing skills or wading. Dry precipitous paths lead to passes. On the heights, tumbled rock-falls and scree-beds can make the going difficult. Above 3,000 m, scanning the ochre and black rock austerity, you sense the ancient upheavals which shaped the earth's crust.

The Atlantic coast

Still just a couple of hours drive from Marrakech, ocean-side ports like Essaouira, Safi, and tiny Oualidia, have gradually by turns made their way into the guidebooks and the traveller's consciousness. An 18th-century citadel port, for all the world like an exotic St Malo, Essaouira was on the hippy-trail in the 1970s. In the 1990s, rediscovered by the surf-fraternity and sundry fashionistas, it became the in vogue destination. When Marrakech swelters, Essaouira has at least a pleasant breeze. Further north, Safi, sardine capital and phosphate port, is the macho version of Essaouira. Visit the potters' quarter, tour the ramparts, see how a small Moroccan town is managing in the modern world. And finally, still further north, is discreet Oualidia, known to some, with perhaps just a hint of irony, as Marrakech's St Tropez. You can enjoy the local oysters and out of season, the beach is perfect, if you like a little wind.

The Red City

Along with the green of the gardens, red is the defining colour of Marrakech. Local by-laws say that no one shall cut down a palm tree and that every façade shall be earth-red like the ancient ramparts. However, weathered by sun and the occasional thunderstorm, uniform terracotta gives way to graceful shades of pink, painters' mixes produce cinammon-brown, adobe-mauve, and sand-leather.

Monuments & crafts

After the initial colour-shock, the starting point for visitors to Marrakech is the esplanade of the Koutoubia Mosque. The minaret, an elegant four-square tower topped with a domed kiosk, is visible from across the city. Built in medieval times to mark the triumph of purifying Almohad Islam, it is to Marrakech what the Eiffel Tower is to Paris. Then there is the cloistered calm of the Saâdian Tombs, the cataclysmic ruin of the Palais Badi, the studious splendour of an ancient institute of learning, the Médersa Ben Youssef. For traditions and artefacts, take in the collections Dar Si Saïd.

Restoring the Red City

In the 1990s, refurbishing houses in Marrakech became quite the thing for a fringe of francophone Bohemia. (Architects and couturiers led the way, as is so often the case in decaying historic neighbourhoods.) A new haven of sun and authenticity, just three hours flight from Paris and Milan, had been found. But as second homes, palatial or otherwise, require upkeep, many were turned into holiday lets, exotic bolt-holes or pleasant guest houses. So, if you have the means, this is the sort of accommodation you should look for. Restored by local craftsmen, these *riads*, as the bijou garden-courtyard residences are called, are often very fine. Some keep to the most refined local building traditions, others are a turbulent decorative mix where Italy meets authentic Africa and Las Vegas.

Thanks in part to the vogue for *riads*, ancient crafts gained a new lease of life. *Zellige* and *zouak* (ceramic mosaics and painted woodwork), *gebs* and *tadelakt* (plaster arabesques and satin-smooth stucco rendering) became exportable commodities, too. The artisans' repertoires have been much expanded by contemporary artists, and any innovation quickly finds its way into the craftshops. Assiduous creation of detail has long been a Moroccan speciality, and not just in craftwork. Though the souks have a bewildering array of goods, in restaurants you will discover a mirrored profusion of dishes where sweet blends into savoury, slow-cooked fruit melting into meat and olive oil.

Marrakech, theatre of life

Though all this gentrification has grafted a cosmopolitan edge on Marrakech life, the city is old and wily enough to absorb such frivolities. Of pashas and their ménages, it has seen a few. Though the warm winter climate and the summer heat imply a daytime slowness, the Marrakchia are known as good-timers, as anyone who has been around for the annual festival of Achoura will know. And the Jemaâ el Fna, the great central square, is as theatrical an urban space as you could wish for. Here are acrobats, snake-charmers and fire-eaters, henna-tatoo artists, singers and storytellers working the crowd. Attractions change as the day advances. At nightime, the foodstalls present the world's biggest barbecue.

La Vie en Rose?

But Marrakech is of course changing. In Guéliz, the new town, dapper 1930s houses are giving way to new hotels, architectural slices of pink, post-modern cake. New resorts and chunky villas are going up in the Palmeraie. Meanwhile, however, continued drought on the plains makes the city a place of hope for country people. Here are factories and building sites, restaurants and hotels, places with jobs. Low living costs make imperial Marrakech, haven of the jet set, a 'city of the poor' as well.

Below: *reds and greeens on the right side of town: villas set among the shade of cypresses and palms.*
Left: *official architecture. Minaret of the Kasbah Mosque, with a façade of Almohad lozenge pattern and ceramic tiles.*

Left: Riad *blues, guesthouse courtyard in the médina.*
Above: *Barbary apes await the next photo-opportunity on Jemaâ el Fna, the great square and hub of Marrakech, as supple acrobats and tourists entertain the local crowd.*

Left: at Kasbah Aït Ben Haddou, children learn early on to keep an eye on the family livestock.
Below: in the High Atlas, while the walnut trees take on their early summer greenery, snow remains on the highest ground.

Above: the long and winding road...over the Tizi-n-Tichka. This link route over the High Atlas south of Marrakech finally reached Ouarzazate in 1928.
Left: new prosperity in the Atlas. Concrete villas replace older adobe buildings in the red-green landscape.

The High Atlas

Closest part of the High Atlas to Marrakech is the region centring on Africa's third highest mountain, Jebel Toubkal, rising to an easy 4,167 m. Further east, south of Azilal, is the area most prized by walkers, the Vallée des Aït Bougmez. From here you can trek east to Zaouiat Ahansal or south in the Massif du Mgoun. On the south side of the range are spectacular gorges where fast flowing streams cut down to the Dadès Valley. Still further east, the Imilchil High Atlas is a region of high plateaux. And then at the eastern end of the range, Midelt is the base for getting out to obscure corners like the abandoned mines of Ahouli.

Imazighen

For centuries, the Atlas valleys have been used by the hardy Imazighen, 'the free people', to extract a living. Referred to as 'the Berbers' by Europeans, they were the main population of North Africa before the eighth-century Arab invasions. Their warren-like villages and terraced fields cling to mountainsides, well clear of any seasonal torrent. You come across traces of their tenacity in extraordinary places: a fortified granary, fit to house a hobbit, up on a cone-shaped hill, cliff-face dwellings accessible only by ladder. In summer, on the remotest highland tract, you may come across a shoulder-high stone corral. A shepherd will be nearby, the sound of his flute floating in the vertiginous silence. In such wild places, traces of Neolithic forebears, mysterious solar wheels and daggers engraved on flat rocks can be found too.

Observers of the elements, the Imazighen have taken on the aura of the Atlas. Their language defends them from the city of the plain, giving them a strong community, outweighing differences of wealth. Though their women marry into urban families, their clan-structures stay paramount – tawdry display is not the thing. Your guide in plastic sandals will go skipping like a goat across a rocky slope and get a brasero going without complaint in the worst conditions. With their sparse, dry bodies, their generosity and hospitality, the Imazighen are like their landscapes, where the earth's bone structure goes revealed and where every spring fills the valleys with a smiling green.

An Atlas year

The seasons are part of High Atlas lives in a way few city dwellers can imagine and each season has sights and sounds which mark the visitor too. Beginning with an unexpected snowfall, winter is a quiet time. The Imazighen seem to hibernate. Snow covers the mountains, powders the roof terraces. In spring as the snow melts, there is water everywhere, the trees on the terraces awake with drifts of almond blossom and there is a new clarity in the mountains. It is time to repair irrigation channels and the rock-walls of the terraces, to plough and sow. In May, the barley turns golden, the walnut and fig-trees acquire their thick summer foliage. After shearing, the flocks head for the high pastures. And the tourists arrive, in need of mules and accommodation, a welcome source of extra income. High summer sees the harvest. The village threshing floor is cleared, terraces are covered with grain and maize laid out to dry, mules and donkeys tread the grain as they did centuries ago. If the harvest is good, there will be many autumn weddings, the villages resounding to the music of *ahouach* and *ahidous*.

The Atlas experience

Walking through the sunburned uplands of the Atlas, travelling through those light-filled landscapes are truly unforgettable experiences. In the evening, rock-falls lead the eye out to blue desert horizons. And when the mountain night takes hold, the starscapes, far from any baleful urban glow, are sublime. Returning to Marrakech after a trek, the world has taken on a new strangeness. But an envelope of photographs and the taste of Moroccan tea, that hit of gunpowder green enveloped in mint and glucose, may bring back the views from a mountain bivouac.

Essentials

Essentials

Planning your trip

Where to go

A journey to Marrakech and the High Atlas takes you to an unusual and challenging region just a few hours flight from Europe. However, as the distances are quite big and the mountain roads slow, some careful planning is necessary to make sure you get the maximum out of your trip. The question is, what can you reasonably expect to see, without over-tiring yourself, within the time you have for your trip? The following suggestions are based on circuits of a week, a fortnight and three weeks. Though Marrakech and Essaouira make a fine twin-centre break, it is really best to have 10 days to two weeks so you can switch off properly and appreciate Morocco at its own pace.

Bear in mind that sometimes flights to Marrakech are unavailable. If you fly into Casablanca, and plan to travel by public transport, note that the train service (shuttle to Casablanca, train on to Marrakech) could well take four to five hours, waiting time included. Agadir to Marrakech is less problematic, there being plenty of bus services.

For a week's break

All in all, given the distances, it is best to be selective - or have more than a week's break

If you have a week, the sleepy option is to hang out in **Marrakech**, perhaps doing an overnight up in the mountains at **Imlil** or **Moulay Brahim**. In Marrakech, you will see large palaces and small craft museums, go shopping and enjoy the atmosphere of the great square, Jemaâ el Fna. Eating options, apart from the little barbecue places on and around the square, include Moroccan palace restaurants, some good south European places and several superb French restaurants. If you have the means, then the chic thing to do is to stay in a restored courtyard house or riad for a few nights. The very chic option is a villa in the Palmeraie, with pool of course. There are plenty of big, pretty comfortable hotels, too, although these lack the personal touch of a riad. For those who like their golf, there are three courses (and more planned) in Marrakech which means sufficient entertainment for a week. Many hotels have tennis courts. If you are going in winter, however, check if your hotel has a heated or covered pool.

Basically, you need three nights to do Marrakech justice. You could have a day trip into the High Atlas, either up to the **Ourika Valley** to Oukaïmeden , to Imlil, Ouirgane and Tin Mal or up to the **Tizi-n-Tichka pass** and the fortress of Telouet. Or you could reduce the time in Marrakech and do a little **walking** in the Atlas, either from **Setti Fatma** or **Imlil**. Another easy day trip is east of Marrakech to the great cavern of **Imi-n-Ifri** and the **Cascades d'Ouzoud**. Finally, you could go to **Essaouira** on the coast for a couple of nights. Staying in an old restored house is a possibility here, too. For those on a honeymoon (or period of reconciliation, for that matter), then a few nights in the tiny Atlantic resort of **Oualidia** might be just the thing.

If you have an interest in things architectural (and a hire **car**), in a very energetic week you could cover Marrakech thoroughly, travel across the spectacular Tizi-n-Test pass to Taroudant for a night, then drive up to the 18th-century planned Atlantic port of Essaouira. From Essaouira, **Safi** (more ramparts and a médina) is an easy day trip, too.

For a two-week holiday

With two weeks, you could go for the relaxing option (a week in Marrakech and some side trips, followed by a week in Essaouira). However, a week in Essaouira might be a bit long, unless you are into surf-sports and/or watercolour painting. You could combine Marrakech and Essaouira in the first week followed by a trip over the Atlas to **Ouarzazate** and the **Dadès Valley** on the second week, either on an organized trip or with hire car. You could fit in a little off-roading (say the **Gorge to Gorge** route between the **Dadès** and the **Todgha** Gorges), or a short walking trip, say in the High Atlas of **Toubkal**. Keen walkers might prefer to do two weeks splendid hiking in the High Atlas (Toubkal or **Azilal** High Atlas), followed by a day tacked on the end to whizz round Marrakech.

Trekking in the High Atlas: some suggestions

Even though it may only last a week, a good trek in the High Atlas should really immerse you in the reality of the mountains, taking your mind away from your everyday existence. To help you choose your trek from a travel company catalogue – or discuss the options with a local guide – here, in brief, are some possible treks.

In one week:

***1. A Toubkal circuit**. Close to Marrakech, (trailhead village **Imlil**), this is one of the most visited regions of the High Atlas. Although Toubkal with its scree faces is not the most beautiful of mountains, it is the third highest in Africa and is very accessible. You will discover some beautiful valleys and their villages on a circuit which will include some cols over 3,000 m and around 5 to 6 hours' walking per day.*

***2. The Yagour Plateau**. Trailhead village is **Setti Fatma**, 2 hours' drive from Marrakech. See prehistoric rock art of the plateau and fine views over to the Toubkal Massif. Once on the plateau, walking is easier than the Toubkal circuit.*

***3. Zaouiat Ahansal circuit**. In the Azilal High Atlas, starting point **Zaouiat Ahansal**, a good day and a half day's journey from Marrakech, in practical terms. Four days' walking. The aim here is to trek in the high pastures of Ilemchane, dropping down to the village of **Taghia**. Harder, longer walking than the above with some big climbs, too.*

***In two weeks**:*

***1. From Imilchil to the Aït Bougmez**. Tough east-west trek to be undertaken with a good guide. Long day's transfer to **Imilchil** (eastern High Atlas, 360 km from Marrakech) to start the trek, return to Marrakech from Tabant via Azilal. Takes you along the gorges of the Assif Melloul, over high plateaux to the Cirque de Taghia, and Zaouiat Ahansal, then over two passes to Ifrane at the start of the Vallée des Aït Bougmez. Gentle walking from Tabant in this valley to end the trip.*

***2. Toubkal region**. With **Aremd** or **Imlil** as base point, two weeks would allow you to do two nice loops in this region, taking in the summit of Toubkal, on the first, and the ski resort of Oukaïmeden on the second.*

Essentials

For a three-week break

A three-week trip will enable you to get to know parts of Morocco really thoroughly: take a one or two week organized walking tour up in the **High or Anti-Atlas** (the latter in winter), and combine this with time out at one of the coastal resorts (**Essaouira**, possibly **Oualidia**), or travel by public transport all the way round the High Atlas (**Marrakech**, **Ouarzazate**, **Dadès Valley**, **Tineghir**, **Er Rachidia**, **Midelt** and across to **Beni Mellal**). And you would still have time to do some urban sightseeing. For the hardy, the highlight of a three-week trip might be five or more days walking in the middle of the trip in the **Vallée des Aït Bougmez**, south of Azilal in the east-central High Atlas.

On your fourth or fifth visit

By the time you've been to Morocco a few times, you don't really need to be told where to go. You probably have your favourite hotels and riads, and areas where you go walking that you tell all your friends about. At this point, you are ready to take in out-of-the-way sites like the abandoned mines of **Ahouli** near Mibladene or the **Kerrouchene** route between Zeïda and El Kebab. Really keen trekkers might be planning to take a month to do the long east-west walk along the top of the High Atlas (the famous *GTAM* or *Grande Traversée des Atlas Marocains*). Then there are parts of the **Tichka Plateau** in the western High Atlas which see few visitors, plus those out of the way prehistoric rock art sites (**Tizi-n-Tirghist** near Jebel Ghat) which you always meant to get to. Whatever, there will always be new valleys to discover. Happily, for both locals and visitors, the roads are constantly being improved, and parts of the country once accessible only to four-wheel drive are now open to the intrepid saloon car driver.

Handy hints for trekkers

Some treks in the Azilal High Atlas and Massif du Mgoun involve some wading. As well as your hiking boots, make sure you have with you a good pair of sports-shoes that will dry out in the sun. As your rucksack will be often be carried by mule, fleas sometimes find their way into your clothes. Have insect repellent, leave your sleeping-bag and clothes out in the sun (or use an insecticide spray). In the mountains, there is not generally any problem with theft, but all those pockets on your day-pack can be a temptation for little hands during a stop near a village. Regarding the 'donnez-moi un stylo' syndrome. Don't give out pens, dirhams or sweets. (Most villages have a hanout *with cheap sweets anyway.) Give to adults who have helped you, and not in front of children. And finally, your stomach. Don't drink from mountain streams, use purification tablets in your water bottle. In restaurants, wash hands well and try to avoid contact with door handles (difficult).*

Distances & journey times

When planning a trip in Morocco, remember that the distances are great, and that long trips on buses can be tiring. **Bus** journeys can be excruciatingly slow, even over short 200km journeys between fairly important towns. (Remember these vehicles are used mainly by people who travel a lot by mule and donkey cart, too.) To make maximum use of your time, if you don't mind dozing on a bus, take night buses to cover the longer distances. If you are trekking, and are setting up the trip yourself, remember to allow time for slow transfers by public transport, ie Marrakech to Azilal, then the minibus or Landrover taxi to your point of departure in the mountains, Azilal to Tabant or Zaouia Ahansal. All in all, if time is limited, it may be best to go with an organized group.

If you have sufficient funds, then there is always the option of taking **internal flights** – although these may not always fit in with your schedule. Public transport is very reasonably priced. **Car hire**, however, is expensive: although you may be able to get a small car for around 2500dh a week, you still have petrol or diesel costs on top of this. The advantage, of course, is the flexibility in getting to obscure places where the public transport is slow or rare.

When to go

Back in the 1900s, when resident general Maréchal Lyautey was trying to sell Morocco to the Paris bureaucrats, he coined various slogans like "Morocco is an Algeria where it rains" or "it's a cold country where the sun is hot." In the south, the rains come (irregularly) in the early autumn and late winter, and it is certainly true that the winter nights can be very cold. Thus with its bright sunshine, Marrakech is a good destination all year round, although in July, August and into late September it can be very hot. However, being a dry heat, the temperatures are bearable. Also, over the last couple of years, the summers have tended to be clement, a fall in temperature matched by warmer winters, too. It does rain (occasionally quite a lot) in Marrakech in the winter, turning the streets of the old town to mud. The pre-Saharan nights are chilly, which is not fun if the riad you are staying in doesn't have much in the way of heating. Note, too, that Essaouira has a much more temperate climate than Marrakech, warmer than the Red City in winter, cooler in summer when the Haouz Plain is baking at 35°C or more.

If you are driving down from Europe, note that routes from Tanger are busy in summer with returning migrant workers from Europe in overloaded cars. If you are going to do the southern routes such as the Dadès and Draâ Valleys, late February and March are magnificent. The blossom will be out, the days will be bright, and you won't suffer too much on public transport or driving.

For those coming to Morocco for an active sort of holiday, outside summer **golf** is very pleasant in Marrakech. For **mountain walking**, spring, summer and autumn are fine in the High Atlas, although the summer heat haze means the views from the summits are not as good a this time of year. In late summer, after the harvests have been gathered in, you may coincide with a traditional regional festival in some High Atlas village. The Jebel Siroua, east of Taroudant, the bridge between High and Anti-Atlas, is too dry to be a really pleasant summer walking destination. **Windsurfers**, based at Essaouira, will find winds stronger in summer, but the swell bigger in winter, when the resort is favoured by surfers. Oualidia, where **riding** is a possibility, is very quiet out of season, very busy in the height of summer. Stables can also be found attached to the *Palmeraie Golf Palace* in Marrakech and at Ouirgane in the High Atlas of Toubkal.

In short, the Atlantic towns are cold and damp in winter. Desert and pre-desert areas are obviously dry and hot, but from December to February are extremely cold at night. On the other hand, mountain areas can get quite hot during the summer days. Occasional but heavy showers occur turning the dry river beds into dangerous flash floods, and snow blocks the passes of the High Atlas in winter. The *Gendarmerie Royale* put up snow barriers to prevent people from driving themselves into drifts on the high passes.

Note also that Marrakech has increasingly high pollution levels due mainly to diesel vehicles and the petrol/oil mix used by the city's thousands of mopeds. The situation tends to be at its worst in mid-winter when there is little wind to shift the layer of pollution hanging over the city, and can make things a little difficult for those with asthma. (The situation is far worse in Casablanca, which adds in ocean humidity to the cocktail.)

Tours and tour operators

In the UK **Expensive** *Abercrombie and Kent*, T0207-7309600. *Morocco Made to Measure (CLM)*, 4a William Street, Knightsbridge, London, SW3 1JJ, T0207-2350123, F2353851. Made-to-measure itineraries, horse riding, trekking, bird-watching, cultural tours, golf, tennis. A reliable firm that knows its Morocco. **Mid-range** *British Airways*, T01293-723100. Moroccan city breaks. *Hayes and Jarvis*, T0208-7485050. Tours of Morocco's main cities. **Budget** *Moroccan Travel Bureau*, 304, Old Brompton Road, London, SW5 9JF, T0207-3734411. Reasonably priced flights and accommodation in main cities.

In the USA *Cross Cultural Adventure*, PO Box 3285, Arlington, VA 22203, T1-703- 237 0100. Custom crafted adventures for independent travellers and special interest groups. Some scheduled departures.

In Germany *Atlas Activ Tours*, Liebenhofen 42, D 88287 Grünkrant, T00-49-751-769340, F00-49-751-7693414, maroc@atlas-activ-tours.de, www.atlas-activ-tours.de

In Marrakech

When ringing from the UK, prefix 00 212 and remove the initial 0 from the nine-digit number. In Morocco all numbers have nine digits which includes the regional code

Atlas Sahara Trek, 6 bis Rue Houdhoud, Quartier Majorelle, T044-313901, F044-313905, sahara@cybernet.net.ma Highly recommended agency with 18 years experience of organizing treks in Morocco. Casablanca-born director Bernard Fabry knows the south-eastern desert really well. ***Complete Tours***, résidence Badr, 2nd floor, 220, Blvd Mohammed V, Guéliz, T061708036 (Tim Buxton), T06-8474943 (Aidan Webster). Arranges all sorts of excursions around Marrakech and Essaouira. Works with a number of well reputed British tour operators. Their Berber Trails four-wheel drive excursion is a firm favourite with visitors. ***High Country***, 31 Bab Amadil, Amizmiz, T044-454847, highcountry@cybernet.net.ma Agency based in Amizmiz in the foothills of the High Atlas. Organizes rock-climbing, off-roading, mountaineering, kayaking on the Lalla Takerkoust dam lake. Founded 1997, works with UK, US and Italian groups. ***Menara Tours***, 41 Rue Yougoslavie, T044-446654. Has English speaking staff, runs day trips and much used by English tour agencies. ***Pampa Voyages***, 203 Blvd Mohammed V, Guéliz. T044-431052, F044-446455, pampa@iam.net.ma

Special interest travel

There are a number of companies which specialize in holidays in Morocco. Some of the trekking companies have many years of experience

Alpinschule of Innsbruck In der Stille 1, A-6161 Natters, Innsbruck, Austria. Organize walking tours based on Taroudant. The walks are not too strenuous and participants are taken to and from. ***Atlas Mountain Information Service (AMIS)***, 26 Kircaldy Road, Burntisland, Fife, KY3 9HQ T01592-873546. Small agency run by Hamish Brown, who organizes treks and climbing trips. ***Cross Cultural Adventures***, PO Box 3285, Arlington, VA 22203, T1-703-237-0100. Custom crafted adventures for independent travellers and special-interest groups, from private Atlas treks to soft adventures by Mercedes cars. ***Dragoman***, Camp Green, Debenham, Stowmarket, Suffolk, IP14 6LA, T01728-861133, www.dragoman.co.uk ***Exodus Travels***, T0208-7723822, www.exodus.co.uk Well established worldwide operator. ***Explore Worldwide***, 1 Frederick Street, Aldershot, Hants GU11 1LQ, T0125-319448. Offers smallexploratory, accompanied travels. On offer are eight days in the Jebel Siroua including Taroudant; 15 days trekking in the High Atlas attempting an ascent of Mount Toubkal; 15 days in the sparsely populated Jebel Saghro; 15 days exploring the mountains, desert and coasts in winter. This group attempts to make the impact of tourism positive – by taking small groups, dealing with local suppliers for transport and food and controlling litter and waste disposal. ***Guerba – Africa in close-up***, Guerba Expeditions Ltd, Wessex House, 40 Station Road, Westbury, Wiltshire, BA13 3JN, T01373-826611. Tours and treks including 15 day High Atlas Trail, beginning in Marrakech with a climb of Mount Toubkal. ***Imaginative Traveller***, 14 Barley Mow Passage, Chiswick, London, W1 4PH, T0208-7428612, F7423045, www.imaginative-traveller.com Has well trained, motivated ground-staff who have worked in lots of countries. As you would expect, an imaginative choice of hotels. Main clients are experienced travellers with professional jobs who do not have the time to set up holidays for themselves. Lots of free-time built into schedules. ***Inspirations Morocco***, Inspirations East Ltd, Victoria House, Victoria Road, Horley, Surrey, RH6 7AD, T01293-822244, F3821732. Very reliable, offer special interest section birdwatching, trekking, sport, but their advertised tailor-made travels can only be made up from the areas/hotels they use. ***Morocco Bound Ltd***, Triumph House, 189 Regent Street, London W1R 7WE, T0207-7345307, F2879127. Guided tours, Land Rover tours, horse riding, short breaks. They can organize individual journeys using the hotels in their brochure. ***Nature Trek***, Chautara, Bighton, Hampshire, SO24 9RB, T01962-733051. Offer natural history and bird watching tours in South Morocco. Use good accommodation. ***Rambler Holidays***, Box 43, Welwyn Garden City, Herts, AL8 6PQ, T0207-7331133. ***Sarah Tours***, T800-2670036 (USA), F703-6199399, www.sarahtours.com Cultural tours of Morocco including visits to music festivals. ***Sunbird Tours***, PO Box 76, Sandy, Bedfordshire, SG19 1DF, T01767-682969. *Sunbird* and *Sunbirder* tours cater both for the keen birdwatcher happy to be out from dawn to dusk and also for those wishing to combine birds with other interests. ***Travel Bag Adventures***, 15 Turk Street, Alton, Hampshire, GU34 1AG, T01420-541007. Trekking holidays around Taroudant or in the Tafilalet, southeastern Morocco.

Finding out more

Moroccan tourist boards

Moroccan National Tourist Board (ONMT) offices overseas. **Australia**, 11 West Street, Sydney, NSW 2060, T9576711. **Belgium**, 66 rue du Marché-aux-Herbes, Brussels 1040, T027361100. **Canada**, 2 Carlton Street, Suite 1803, Toronto, Ontario M5B 1K2, T4165982208. **France**, 161 rue Saint-Honoré, Place du Théâtre-Français, 75001 Paris, T42604724. **Germany**, 59 Graf Adolf Strasse, 4000 Dusseldorf, T49211370551/2. **Italy**, 23 Via Larga, 20122 Milan, T392-58303633. **Japan**, Tokyo, T813-32517781. **Portugal**, rue Artilharia 7985, 1200 Lisbonne, T3885871. **Spain**, Calle Quintana 2 (2°e), Madrid, T5427431. **Sweden**, Sturegaten 16, Stockholm 11436, T66099. **Switzerland**, Schifflande, 5, 8001 Zurich, T2527752. **UK**, 205 Regent Street, London, T020-74370073. **USA**, 20 East 46th Street, Suite 1201, New York NY 10017, T2125572520.

Morocco on the web

A few sites to give you some background on Morocco. Many more can obviously be found by typing 'Morocco tourism' in your favourite search-engine

www.tourism-in-morocco.com Hotels, restaurants and crafts.
www.marrakech-medina.com For a look at some luscious houses for rent.
www.lexicorient.com/morocco Information on cities with photographs.
www.menic.utexas.edu/menic/countries/morocco Academic site with useful links.
www.maghrebnet.net.ma/artisanat Lots of information on Moroccan crafts.
www.festival-gnaoua.co.ma Details on the annual Gnaoua music festival in Essaouira.
www.ferrimaroc.com Information if you want to get the ferry to Morocco.
www.royalairmaroc.com For those wanting to fly to Morocco.
www.oncf.com.ma All about Moroccan rail services.
www.eudel.com Delegation of the European Union's site.

www.usembassy-morocco.org.ma As the name suggests, the US embassy site for the country. Provides useful links.
www.azure.net/alif For those wanting to study Arabic in Morocco.
www.ctm.co.ma Leading Moroccan bus company.
www.kelma.org French-based site with news and views from the gay community in the Maghreb, Belgium and France.

Language

See page 309 for lists of words and phrases

Arabic is the official language of Morocco, but nearly all Moroccans with a secondary education have enough **French** to communicate with, and a smattering of **English**. In the North, **Spanish** maintains a presence thanks to TV and radio. Outside education, however, Moroccan Arabic in the cities and **Amazigh** in the mountains are the languages of everyday life, and attempts to use a few words and phrases, no matter how stumblingly, will be appreciated. Those with some Arabic learned elsewhere often find the Moroccan Arabic difficult. It is characterized by a clipped quality (the vowels just seem to disappear), and the words taken from classical Arabic are often very different from those used in the Middle East. In addition, there is the influence of the Berber languages and a mixture of French and Spanish terms, often heavily 'Moroccanized'. In many situations French is more or less understood. However, you will come across plenty of people who have had little opportunity to go to school and whose French may be limited to a very small number of phrases.

Disabled travellers

Morocco really cannot be said to be well adapted to the needs of the disabled traveller. However, don't let this deter you. Some travel companies are beginning to specialize in exciting holidays, tailor-made for individuals depending on their level of disability. For those with access to the internet, a general site is provided by **Global Access - Disabled Travel Network Site** at www.geocities.com/Paris/1502 It contains useful information and includes a number of reviews and tips from members of the public. You might want to read ***Nothing Ventured*** edited by **Alison Walsh** (Harper Collins), which gives personal accounts of worldwide journeys by disabled travellers, plus advice and listings.

Gay and lesbian travellers

If there is no real public perception of what a lesbian might be in Morocco, foreign gays have long been a feature of life in towns like Marrakech and Tanger. The latter is long past its heyday of the fifties and sixties, while Marrakech continues to attract wealthy A-gays. However, according to the penal code, 'shameless or unnatural acts' between persons of the same sex can lead to short prison sentences or fines though this has never seemed to put anyone off. Note also that the body language is very different in Morocco. Physical closeness between men in the street does not indicate gay relationships. For the corruption of minors, the penalties are extremely severe.

Thanks to satellite television, there is an awareness among Moroccan gays that there is a certain 'international gay culture'. There is also an awareness of AIDS (le Sida in French), with an organization called the ***ALCS***, *Association de lutte contre le Sida*, founded by Prof Hakima Himmich, doing sterling service with its information campaigns and info-lines. Much still remains to be done, however.

In Marrakech, gay travellers (or rather their friends) have run into problems with the *Brigade Touristique*, see page 22.

Student travellers

Morocco is a good place for the budget traveller, as the costs are very reasonable. However, there are few student discounts of the sort available in Europe. The Youth Hostel network has been extended, and most hostels are clean and well run. Note that Moroccan Railways (ONCF) are included on the European under-26 Inter-Rail pass, which also gets you half-price tickets on the ferries from Algeciras to Tanger. (Note that Inter-Rail is not valid on coaches run by *Supratours*, the ONCF sister company). Youth rail tickets are also available to Morocco, valid for six months along a pre-arranged route.

Travelling with children

Moroccans love children. This trait of the culture is particularly understandable when you realise how difficult life is for many families and how many children die in childbirth or infancy in the rural areas, due quite simply to a lack of basic health education in the Amazigh languages and Moroccan Arabic.

Travelling with children, there are a few points to bear in mind. If you hire a car via an international agency, specifying the sort of child-seats you require, do not be surprised if your requirements get lost somewhere along the way. Most local car hire agencies will be unlikely to have child-seats.

Children from the lands of supermarkets and industrial agriculture will find Morocco fascinating. Daily life is lived in the open, all sorts of activities which take place behind closed doors can be seen. There are workshops spilling out into the street and butchers with carcasses hanging outside, markets with mule-parks, people ploughing with camels.

Children from formal European cities will probably enjoy all the excitement of Moroccan urban life – and the vast landscapes of the South. If doing a lot of driving, make sure you have things in the car to entertain them. You could provide them with a contrast by trying to stay in hotels with pools in Marrakech and Agadir. When you book, however, check whether there is a shallow children's pool and whether it is heated in winter (very often they are not). Though the sun is bright, the water will be damn cold.

On the **health** and safety front, make sure your children are up to date with all their vaccinations. Tap-water in major cities is safe to drink. In rural areas, give them sugary bottled drinks or mineral water. And on busy streets and squares, keep a tight hold, as the traffic is often very hectic.

Women travellers

Young women travelling with a male friend report few difficulties – and couples with small children will find that the little ones attract a great deal of kindly attention. However, a woman going out on her own from the hotel without male escort will soon notice the difference. For women travelling alone, the hassle and stares can be extremely tiring after a while. So what do you do? In towns, dress fairly smartly, look confident, busy, and as though you know where you're going. (Depending on your age, this may make hustlers think twice – is this person with an official delegation, do they have a Moroccan husband?.) Observe what smart Moroccan women are wearing, how they walk in public. Women from fairly traditional families will be wearing headscarves, others may be wearing expensive dark sunglasses.

Obviously you will want to strike up some acquaintances – and some women students waiting (say) for a grand taxi or in your train compartment will probably be delighted to have a chance to chat with an English speaker – as long as you don't look too outlandish by their modest standards of dress. Remember, a lot of importance is given to looking smart and respectable in Morocco. Many Moroccans lack the means to do this, and the unkempt European is really a bit of an extra-terrestrial to them, the object of all sorts of prejudices, and not worthy of much respect.

And the hassling males? One way to deal with them is to develop a schoolmarmish manner. Modestly dressed, you are interested in Roman ruins, architecture, birds, women's issues (but not local politics), you are a serious person. This may put your hassler off – or lead to some intelligent conversation. And if you do decide you want someone to show you around, then agree on the fee beforehand (official guides get 100dh). This can save you time and prove entertaining too, if the person is genuine.

Role-playing can be tedious, however. In fact, in many places, despite appearances, the visitor has the upper hand. Since 1995, the plain clothes ***Brigade Touristique*** has been in action in a number of the main holiday destinations. For a local observed giving a tourist a hard time, this can mean big problems, namely 1,000dh fine and/or a month in prison. Apart from Casablanca, Moroccan cities are really quite small provincial places where faces get known quickly. This is true even of Marrakech. The problem is then what happens if you are with a genuine Moroccan friend? You will have to convince the plainclothes policeman that you know the person you are with well and that there is no problem.

Working in the country

Morocco has a major un- and under-employment problem. University-educated young adults find it hard to get work, especially those with degrees in subjects like Islamic studies and literature. At the same time, industry and business are desperately short of qualified technicians and IT-literate staff. Low salary levels mean that the qualified are tempted to emigrate – and many do, fuelling a brain-drain which has reached worrying

Moroccan embassies and consulates

Australia *11 West St, North Sydney, T02-99576717.*
Canada *38 Range Rd, Ottawa, KIN 8J4,* ***Ontario****, T613-2367391.*
Denmark *Oregards Allé19, 2900 Hellerup, Copenhagen, T624511.*
Egypt *10 Rue Salah el Din, Zamalek, Cairo, T02-3409677.*
France *5 rue le Tasse, Paris 75016, T1-45206935.*
Germany *Goten Strasse 7-9, 5300 Bonn, T228-355044.*
Netherlands *Oranje Nassaulaan 1-1075, Amsterdam, T736215.*
New Zealand *See Australia.*
Norway *Parkveien 41, Oslo, T22556111.*
Spain *Serrano 179, Madrid, T1-4580950.*
Sweden *Kungsholmstorg 16, Stockholm, T8-544383.*
Switzerland *22 Chemin François-Lehmann, Grand Saconnex, Geneva, T22-981535.*
Tunisia *39 rue du 1 Juin, Tunis, T1-783801.*
UK *49 Queens Gate Gardens, London, SW7 5NE, T0207-5815001.*
USA *1601 21st St NW, Washington DC 20009, T202-4627979.*

levels. In cities, adults with a low level of skills find it hard to get work, basically as many simple jobs in small companies are done by badly paid, exploited adolescents. For the foreigner, this means that there are few opportunities for work, although international companies setting up in Morocco do employ foreign managerial staff, generally recruited abroad. Basically, the only opening if you want to spend time in Morocco is through teaching English, which is badly paid even with organizations like the British Council or the *American Language Centres*. It is your employer who will help you deal with the formalities of getting a *carte de séjour* (residence permit) in Morocco. For you to be able to work, your employer has to be able to satisfy the relevant authorities in Rabat that you are doing a job in an area which Morocco has a skills shortage. Anyone tempted to take up residence with the idea of doing a spot of Protestant conversion work should think twice. The authorities take a very dim view of potential missionaries.

Note that retired people (and others) from Europe can obtain residence relatively easily, providing they can prove that they have a regular source of income and that regular transfers of funds are being made into their Moroccan bank account. Towns where the police are used to processing the official paperwork for this sort of foreign resident include Agadir, Essaouira, Marrakech, Rabat and Tanger.

Before you travel

Getting in

Passports
Always carry photocopies of key pages of your passport with you

All visitors need a passport to gain entry into Morocco. Report the loss of your passport immediately to police giving the number, date and place of issue. The last hotel at which you stayed will have this information on the registration form. Getting fresh documents will probably entail a trip to Rabat and/or Casablanca. Probably the best idea is to send your passport details to a personal email address for easy retrieval.

Visas
From the point of entry travellers can stay in Morocco for 3 months

No visas are required for full passport holders of the UK, USA, Canada, Australia, New Zealand/Aotearoa, Canada, Ireland and most EU countries. Benelux passport holders require visas at the present time. On the aeroplane or boat, or at the border, travellers will be required to fill in a form with standard personal and passport details, an exercise to be repeated in almost all hotels throughout the country.

Visa extensions These require a visit to the **Immigration** or **Bureau des Etrangers** department at the police station in a larger town, as well as considerable patience. An easier option is to leave Morocco for a few days, preferably to Spain or the Canary Islands, or to one of the two Spanish enclaves, either Ceuta, close to Tanger, or Melilla, rather more remote in northeastern Morocco. People coming into Morocco from either of these Spanish enclaves for a second or third time have on occasion run into problems with the Moroccan customs. Given the large number of foreigners resident in Agadir and Marrakech, it may be easiest to arrange visa extensions in these cities. Approval of the extension has to come from Rabat and may take a few days.

Customs

Visitors may take in, free of duty, 400 g of tobacco, 200 cigarettes or 50 cigars and such personal items as a camera, binoculars, a portable radio, computer or typewriter. You may also take your pet to Morocco. It will need a health certificate no more than 10 days old and an anti-rabies certificate less than six months old. Foreign currency may be imported freely.

Prohibited items **Narcotics**: there are severe penalties for possession of or trade in narcotic drugs: three months to five years imprisonment and/or fines up to 240,000dh. You do not want to be involved in a Moroccan remake of *Midnight Express*. Morocco is under pressure from the European Union to reduce *kif* cultivation, and anyone caught exporting happy baccy will be turned into an example for others. **Wildlife**: be aware that wild animal skins and some other items openly on sale in Morocco cannot be legally imported into the EU. This includes products made of animal skins. The purchase of live animals for export from Morocco and their import into EU and USA is in most cases illegal and is punishable by large fines and confiscation.

Vaccinations

None required unless travelling from a country where yellow fever and/or cholera frequently occurs. You should be up to date with polio, tetanus, and typhoid protection. If you are going to be travelling in rural areas where hygiene is often a bit rough and ready, then having a hepatitis B shot is a good thing. You could also have a cholera shot, although there is no agreement among medics on how effective this is. If you are going to be travelling in remote areas of the far South, then a course of malaria tablets is recommended.

What to take

Always take more money and fewer clothes than you think you'll need

Travellers usually tend to take to much. Be ruthless! A travel-pack will survive the holds of rural buses and sitting on the roof-rack of a share taxi. If you acquire a carpet, there is plenty of cheap luggage on sale. If you are going to go trekking without the benefit of mule transport, then you'll need a good rucksack.

As for clothing, quite a few hotels have a reliable laundry service and clothes are cheap to buy should you need anything more. Outside summer you will need woollens or a fleece for evenings. It is advisable for women in particular to cover up in the country. Cotton trousers or skirts should therefore be packed. In the towns Moroccans like to dress well if they have the money. Many don't, so smart appearance is appreciated. In many areas, especially in the northern cities, a lot of grinding poverty is apparent.

If you are aiming to travel into the Atlas take a pair of decent walking shoes or boots as getting to some of the rock art sites requires some scrambling. If planning to bivouac out in the desert, you will need a warm sleeping-bag. The penetrating cold of the Sahara at night is a well known phenomenon, so bring some warm clothing. Layers of clothing in the winter are effective.

Air cushions for hard seating; earplugs; eye mask; insect repellant/cream, mosquito coils; neck pillow; International driving licence; photocopies of essential documents; plastic bags; short wave radio; spare passport photographs; sun hat; sun protection cream; Swiss army knife; torch; umbrella; wet wipes; zip-lock bags. If you're going for **budget accommodation** you may also need: a cotton sheet sleeping-bag or sheet; padlocks for luggage; shampoo; student card; toilet paper; towel; universal bath plug.

Checklists
This checklist might help you plan your packing

Health kit Anti-acid tablets; anti-diarrhoea tablets; anti-malaria tablets (chloroquin); antiseptic cream; condoms; contraceptives; mini first aid kit with disposable; syringes; sachets of rehydration salts; tampons; travel sickness pills; water sterilization tablets.

See page 64 for further health information

Money

The major unit of currency in Morocco is the **dirham** (in this Handbook: dh). In 1 dirham there are 100 **centimes**. There are coins for 1 centime (very rare), 5, 10, 20 and 50 centimes, and for 1, 5 and 10 dirhams, as well as notes for 10, 20, 50, 100 and 200 dirhams. The coins can be a little confusing. There are two sorts of 5 dirham coin: the older and larger cupro-nickel ('silver coloured' version), and the new bi-metal version, brass colour on the inside. The bi-metal ten dirham coin (brass colour on the outside), is replacing the rather scruffy red and pink ten dirham notes. There is a brownish 20 dirham note, easily confused with the 100 dirham note. The 50 dirham note is green, the 100 dirhams brown and sand colour, and the 200 dirham note is in shades of blue and turquoise.

Currency
Currency is labelled in Arabic and French. Most transactions are in cash. There is a fixed exchange rate for changing notes and no commission ought to be charged for this

You can sometimes buy Moroccan dirhams at *bureaux de change* at Gatwick and Heathrow airports. Dirhams may not be taken out of Morocco. If you have bought too many dirhams, you can exchange them back into French francs at a bank on production of exchange receipts. However, as European cash and Visa cards function in Moroccan cashpoints (*guichets automatiques*), in major towns it is possible to withdraw more or less exactly the amount one needs on a daily basis. However at weekends cashpoints both at airports and in the cities can be temperamental, so have cash and travellers' cheques to exchange. The most reliable cashpoints are those of the ***Wafa Bank*** (green and yellow livery).

Note that among themselves Moroccans will count in older currency units. To the complete confusion of travellers, many Moroccans refer to **francs**, which equal 1 centime, and **reals**, though both these units only exist in speech. Even more confusingly, the value of a real varies from region to region. A dirham is held to equal 20 reals in most regions. However, around Tanger and in most of the North, 1 dirham equals 2 reals. *Alf franc* (1,000 francs) is 10 dirhams. Unless you are good at calculations, it's obviously easier to stick to dirhams.

Exchange rates

Rates (November 2001) for buying dirhams:

Australian $	*5.88dh*
Canadian $	*7.37dh*
Euro	*10.32dh*
New Zealand $	*4.84dh*
South African Rand	*1.23dh*
UK£	*16.52dh*
US$	*11.95dh*
Yen (100)	*9.45dh*

The easiest way of staying in funds whilst travelling is by using a credit/debit card (but it's advisable to have a back up in the form of cash and/or travellers'cheques). They are widely accepted at banks, top hotels, restaurants and shops, but it is wise to check first. *American Express* are represented by *Voyages Schwartz* in Morocco, with limited services. Remember to keep all credit card receipts – and before you

Credit cards
Morocco has a problem with card fraud

Sample prices for basics

For comparison, 1dh = 06.5p, 10dh = 65p, 10dh = 1 euro, 10dh = US$1 approx.

Cafés and restaurants

Good meal with wine in a medium-range restaurant, 200dh to 250dh
Kefta sandwich with chips, 15dh to 20dh
Mini bastilla from a pâtisserie, 20dh
Coffee and croissant in a good café, say 10dh with tip
Cheap bottle of red wine 70dh

Food and drink

Litre of milk, 8dh
Litre bottle of Sidi Ali mineral water, 5dh
Litre of Coca Cola, 8dh90
Mid-range bottle of red wine, 40dh
Bottle of Flag beer, 5dh
4 natural yoghurts, 7dh60
Large round loaf of bread, 1dh10
Small tin of tuna, 7dh30
Kilo of tomatoes, 4dh
Kilo of onions, 3dh
Kilo of oranges, 5dh
Kilo of mandarins, 7dh
Kilo of beef, 55dh
Kilo of mutton, 60dh
(NB Meat prices higher in years when rain is good as more grazing for bigger flocks to be kept.)

Transport

A day's car hire, unlimited kilometrage, Fiat Punto, say 350dh to 500dh
Fill up (petrol) for the tank of a small car, say 350dh
First-class rail-ticket, Casablanca Voyageurs to Marrakech, 100dh
Second-class rail-ticket, Rabat to Casablanca Port, 27dh
CTM bus ticket, Marrakech to Fès, 65dh
Mercedes share taxi, Ouarzazate to Marrakech, 100dh
Marrakech, short daytime taxi ride Guéliz to Médina, say 10dh to 12dh
Marrakech, short ride on city bus, 3dh

Miscellaneous

Cheap mobile phone, 500dh
Small bottle of Cadum shampoo, 7.5dh
Small tube of toothpaste, 5dh
Men's haircut, 25dh to 35dh
Postcard, 3dh to 5dh
Stamp for letter to Europe, up to 20 g, 6.5dh

sign, check where the decimal marker (a comma in Morocco, as in Europe, rather than a dot), has been placed, and that there isn't a zero too many. You don't want to be paying thousands rather than hundreds of dirhams. To reduce problems with card fraud, common sense is to use your debit/credit card for payments of large items like carpets and hotel bills. If a payment is not legitimate, it is a lot less painful if the transaction is on the credit card rather than drawn from your current account.

Travellers' cheques Although somewhat time-consuming to change, travellers' cheques are probably the safest way to carry money (though unlike credit cards a small commission will be charged for changing them). They are usable in Morocco, although the traveller may be sent from bank to bank before the appropriate one is found. Use travellers' cheques from a well known bank or company, preferably UK, USA or European, although this is not an absolute rule. Some hotels and shops will exchange travellers' cheques. At the time of writing, the ***Banque Populaire*** and the ***Crédit Agricole*** (the one with the horse logo), did not charge commission on cashing travellers' cheques.

Banking hours Banking hours are 0830-1130 and 1500-1630. In the summer and during the month of fasting, Ramadhan, they are 0830-1400. There are also separate bureaux de change in the major cities, mainly of ***BMCE***, often open for longer hours (0800-2000), which in theory give the same rates of exchange but charge different amounts of commission. There are several different banks in Morocco, with ***BMCE, Crédit du Maroc (green and red livery), Wafa Bank*** and ***Banque Populaire*** all widespread. The ***BMCE*** and the ***Crédit***

du Maroc seem to have the best change facilities, while the ***Banque Populaire*** is often the only bank in southern towns. Banking in Morocco can be a slow, tortuous process, with several different desks for different purposes. The easiest way to get money is thus to use your Visa or cash card at a cash dispenser – always provided that this is in service.

Cost of travelling

As a budget traveller, it is possible to get by in Morocco for £20-30/US$30-40 a day. Your costs can be reduced by having yoghurt and bread and cheese for lunch and staying in an 80dh a night hotel. Accommodation, food and transport are all cheap, and there is a lot to see and do for free, however this budget does not allow much room for unexpected costs like a tip, stamps or a present. If you start buying imported goods, notably cosmetics and toiletries, foods and electrical goods, things can get expensive. Allowing £40/US$55 is more realistic.

In top quality hotels, restaurants, nightclubs and bars, prices are similar to Europe. Rabat, Casablanca and Agadir are the most expensive places while manufactured goods in remote rural areas tend to cost more. There are plenty of things to buy in Morocco, and the prices, if you bargain, can be quite reasonable. Prices for food and drink are non-negotiable, of course.

Cost of living

Although prices for many basics can seem very low indeed to those used to prices in European capitals, the cost of living is high for most Moroccans. At one end of the scale, in the mountainous rural areas, there is Morocco's fourth world, still on the margins of the cash economy. In these regions, families produce much of their own food, and are badly hit in drought years when there is nothing to sell in the souk to generate cash to buy oil, extra flour and sugar. Conditions are improving for the city shanty-town dwellers. Here families will be getting by on 2,000dh a month, sometimes much less. The urban middle classes, those with salaried jobs in the public and private sectors, are doing fairly well. A primary school teacher may be on 3,000dh a month, a private company employee at the start of their career will make around 3,000dh a month, too. This category has access to loans and is seeing a general improvement in living standards. Morocco's top-flight IT technicians, doctors, and business people have a plush lifestyle with villas and servants available to few Europeans. And finally, a very small group of plutocrats has long been doing very, very well, thank you.

To put the contrasts in perspective, there are parents for whom the best option is to place their pre-adolescent girls as maids with city families in exchange for 300dh a month. (You read that figure correctly.) The Amazigh-speaking boy who serves you in the corner shop may be given 50dh a week, plus lodging (of a sort) and board. His horizons will be limited to the shop, there will be a trip back to the home village once a year. He may never learn to read, his language is despised at official level. At the other, distant end of the scale, there are couples who can easily spend 40,000dh a semester to purchase an English-language higher education for one of their offspring at the private Al Akhawayn University in Ifrane.

Getting there

Marrakech and the High Atlas region are most easily reached by direct flights from Europe to either Ouarzazate (Taourirt) and Marrakech (Aéroport de la Menara). Agadir airport is also possible as an entry point, although less convenient than the previous two. Another option is to fly into Casablanca (direct flights from Europe, Middle East and North America) and then continue to Marrakech by air, train or road. There are ferries from France (Sète) and Spain (Algeciras, Almería) to northern Morocco. The most convenient route is Algeciras to Tanger or Ceuta, the northern Moroccan ports closest to Spain. From there you continue south to Marrakech by road or rail.

Discount flight agents in the UK and Ireland

Council Travel *28a Poland St, London, W1V 3DB, T020-74377767, www.destinations-group.com*

STA Travel *86 Old Brompton Rd, London, SW7 3LH, T020-74376262, www.statravel.co.uk They have other branches in London, as well as in Brighton, Bristol, Cambridge, Leeds, Manchester, Newcastle-Upon-Tyne and Oxford and on many university campuses. Specialists in low-cost student/youth flights and tours, also good for student IDs and insurance.*

Trailfinders *194 Kensington High Street, London, W8 7RG, T020-79383939.*

Usit Campus *52 Grosvenor Gardens, London, SW1 0AG, T0870 240 1010, www.usitcampus.co.uk Student/youth travel specialists with branches also in Belfast, Brighton, Bristol, Cambridge, Manchester and Oxford. The main Ireland branch is at 19 Aston Quay, Dublin 2, T01-6021777.*

Discount flight agents in North America

Air Brokers International *323 Geary St, Suite 411, San Francisco, CA94102, T01-800-883 3273, www.airbrokers.com Consolidator and specialist on RTW and Circle Pacific tickets.*

Council Travel *205 E 42nd St, New York, NY 10017, T1-888-COUNCIL, www.counciltravel.com Student/budget agency with branches in many other US cities.*

Discount Airfares Worldwide On-Line *www.etn.nl/discount.htm A hub of consolidator and discount agent links.*

International Travel Network/Airlines of the Web *www.itn.net/airlines Online air travel information and reservations.*

STA Travel *5900 Wilshire Blvd, Suite 2110, Los Angeles, CA 90036, T1-800-777 0112, www.sta-travel.com Also branches in New York, San Francisco, Boston, Miami, Chicago, Seattle and Washington DC.*

Travel CUTS *187 College St, Toronto, ON, M5T 1P7, T1-800-667 2887, www.travelcuts.com Specialist in student discount fares, IDs and other travel services. Branches in other Canadian cities.*

Travelocity *www.travelocity.com Online consolidator.*

Discount flight agents from Australia and New Zealand

Flight Centres *82 Elizabeth St, Sydney, T13-1600; 205 Queen St, Auckland, T09-309 6171. Also branches in other towns and cities.*

STA Travel *T1300-360960, www.statravelaus.com.au In Australia: 702 Harris St, Ultimo, Sydney, and 256 Flinders St, Melbourne. In New Zealand: 10 High St, Auckland, T09-366 6673. Also in major towns and university campuses.*

Travel.com.au *80 Clarence St, Sydney, T02-929 01500, www.travel.com.au*

Air

A number of airlines operate reasonably priced scheduled and charter flights to Morocco, and flights are fairly cheap. (They tend to be expensive when bought within Morocco.) There are over 50 travel companies' agents using scheduled flights to

Morocco. The state airline, ***Royal Air Maroc***, is a reliable and not overpriced company with an international network which includes main European cities, plus Montréal and, for the moment, New York. Main services all go through Casablanca. There are airports at Casablanca (Anfa and Mohammed V), Rabat/Salé, Tanger, Oujda, Fès, Al Hoceima, Marrakech, Agadir, Ouarzazate and Laâyoune. A rail shuttle links Aéroport Mohammed V with Casablanca and Rabat.

From the UK & Ireland

Charter flights Charter flights or package holidays bought here can be a cheap alternative, particularly to Tanger or Agadir. From **UK** by ***Cosmos***, Tourama House, Holcombe Road, Helmshore, Rossendale, Kent BR2 9LX, T0208-4643444, F4666640 from Gatwick and Manchester to Agadir; ***Goldenjoy Holidays***, 36 Mill Lane, London, NW6 1NR, T0207-7949767, F7949850 from Gatwick to Agadir; ***Inspirations***, Victoria House, Victoria Road, Horley, Surrey, RH6 7AD, T01293-822244, F821732 from Heathrow to Tanger, Fès, Casablanca, Agadir, Marrakech and Ourzazate, Gatwick to Agadir and Tanger and Manchester to Agadir; ***First Choice Holidays***, London Road, Crawley, West Sussex, RH10 2GX, T01293-560777, F3588680 from Gatwick or Manchester to Agadir. From **Dublin** to Agadir by ***Budget Travel***, 134 Lower Baggot Street, Dublin 2, Ireland, T00-353-1-6613122, F6611890 and ***Sunway Travel Ltd,*** Main Street, Blackrock, Co Dublin, Ireland, T00-353-1-28868828, F2885167.

Scheduled flights Most of the major European airlines fly to Morocco, including ***Air France***, ***Iberia*** and ***British Airways***. The most competitive from UK are normally ***KLM*** and ***Royal Air Maroc***, 205 Regent Street, London W1, T0207-4394361. The latter fly from Heathrow, Terminal 2, London-Casablanca daily except Wednesday with internal connections on domestic network; London-Tanger on Monday, Wednesday, Friday and Saturday. Departures from Heathrow, Terminal 1, to Agadir on Friday, Casablanca on Monday, Tuesday, Wednesday, Thursday and Saturday. ***British Airways*** offer daily scheduled services to Casablanca, twice weekly to Tanger and Marrakech and weekly to Agadir. All services depart from London's north terminal. For further information and reservations T0345-222111. Consult the following websites for scheduled flights to Morocco: www.british-airways.com, www.airfrance.com, www.royalairmaroc.com

Royal Air Maroc offices abroad: Amsterdam, T020-6530007, F020-5158956; London, T020-74398854, T020-74394361, F020-72870127; Montréal, T514-2851619, 514-2851689 or 2851937, resavations on T514-2851435, F514-2851338, New York, T212-7506071, F212-9807924. In Morocco, T090000800.

From Europe

Royal Air Maroc has flights from Amsterdam, Athens, Barcelona, Bastia, Bordeaux, Brussels, Copenhagen, Düsseldorf, Frankfurt, Geneva, Lisbon, Madrid, Málaga, Marseille, Milan, Munich, Nice, Paris, Rome, Stockholm, Strasbourg, Toulouse, Vienna and Zürich. Most flights are direct to Casablanca. ***Air France*** and ***Royal Air Maroc*** offer cheap flights from Paris. Charter flights or package holidays are also a cheap alternative worth investigating.

Fly-boat It is possible to get a flight to Gibraltar, Almería or Málaga, and then continue by boat to Melilla, Ceuta or Tanger. ***British Airways*** operate regular services to Málaga and Gibraltar.

From North America

Royal Air Maroc flies between Casablanca, Montreal and New York. (Flight time New York to Casablanca, six hours 40 mins.) Alternatively, travel to Europe with ***British Airways***, ***Air France***, ***Iberia*** or ***KLM***, all of which have flights to Moroccan destinations.

From Africa & the Middle East

In North Africa all the national carriers fly to Casablanca. ***Royal Air Maroc*** runs regular services between Casablanca and major cities in the other countries, including six a week from **Algiers**, eight a week from **Tunis** and four a week from **Cairo**. From the **Canary Isles** (Las Palmas) there are direct flights to Agadir and Laâyoune. There are two flights a week between Casablanca and **Nouakchott**. Elsewhere in Africa there are flights from Casablanca to **Abidjan**, **Bamako, Conakry**, **Dakar** and **Libreville**, and in the Middle East to **Abu Dhabi**, **Jeddah** and **Riyadh**.

Road

Bus

From London Victoria Coach Station there is ***Eurolines/Iberbus*** to Algeciras, which takes two days, T0207-7300202. It leaves every Monday and Friday, adult return, between £200-£240. Coach services use the Algeciras-Tanger ferry. *Eurolines* main UK office is on T01582-404511.There are regular coach services to Morocco from Paris and other French cities.

Consult ***CTM*** website for international services (www.ctm.co.ma) Departures from European cities include Alicante, Barcelona, Bolgna, Bordeaux, Brussels, Dijon, Frankfurt, Granada, Lille, Lyon, Madrid, Marseille, Paris, Rimini and Toulouse. The site is a bit slow.

Car

Import of private cars Foreigners are allowed temporary import of a private vehicle for up to six months in total (be it one or several visits) per calendar year. **Documents** required are car registration documents and a Green card from your insurance company, valid in Morocco, which will be inspected at the border along with International Driving Licence (or national licences). The car will be entered in the drivers' passport, and checked on leaving the country, to ensure that it has not been sold without full taxes being paid. It should be noted that some car hire companies do not allow customers to take cars into Morocco from Europe. The minimum age of driving is 21. Car entry is not possible from Mauritania. From Algeria, in more peaceful times, the crossing points are Oujda and Figuig.

Sea

Ferries
In the summer months, the ferries can be booked solid several days in advance

The many sea routes from Europe to Morocco provide relatively cheap travel. The principal passenger arrival point is Tanger. Other scheduled passenger services run to the Spanish enclaves of Ceuta and Melilla, as well as to Nador, near Melilla. Algeciras to Ceuta is the cheapest crossing, Algeciras to Tanger the most convenient. Sète to Tanger or Nador is a long sea journey, the latter taking a day and a half.

When you leave Spain for Morocco, you take an exit visa before boarding. Then, once on ship, you fill in a disembarkation form and have your passport stamped on board. Leaving Morocco, you fill in an embarkation form and departure card, which are stamped by the port police before getting on the boat. When you travel from Spain to Spanish enclaves Ceuta and Melilla, this does not apply, as you enter Morocco at a land border.

Contact ***Southern Ferries***, 179 Piccadilly, London W1V 9DB, T0207-4914968, F4913502. Details of ferries leaving Spain for Morocco can also be found on ***Transmediterranea***'s website, www.trasmediterranea.es (sic), click on South Straits zone.

From Algeciras to Tanger
This ferry service is booked solid in summer and around Muslim feast days

The main ferry route between Spain and Morocco is the Algeciras/Tanger passenger and car service, operated jointly by ***Trasmediterranea*** and ***Isleña de Navegación***. Algeciras has regular bus services from Gibraltar and Málaga, both towns having cheap flights from UK. Algeciras has a train service from Madrid, and tickets can be bought from London to Algeciras or Tanger. The ferry terminal, near the town centre, has a ticket office and money changing facilities. There are similar facilities in the Tanger terminal. The ferry takes two to three hours, and there are normally between six and 10 services a day, either way, with some seasonal variation. Although services usually leave late one should allow at least an hour to clear the police and customs, particularly in Tanger. Be cautious about scheduling onward journeys on the same day, in view of the delays.

The passenger fare one way is around 230dh, children from four to 12 years old are half price and under four year olds are free, cars from 320dh, motorbikes 215dh and bicycles are free. It is cheaper to buy a return in Tanger than two singles, if applicable. Tickets can be bought at either terminal or at numerous agents in both towns.

The ferries are often dirty and crowded. They have the usual bars, restaurants, cafés and lounges, as well as a *bureau de change*. When travelling from Algeciras to Tanger all passengers must have their passports stamped by Moroccan border police whilst on the boat. The conditions on board at that time would prevent any chance of escape in an emergency from overcrowded cabins where seats, aisles, corridors and exits are piled high with the passengers' unwieldy baggage.

The **hydrofoil service** runs Monday-Saturday and takes one hour. Contact ***Transtour***, T956-665200.

Train

Trains from London go via France and Spain and cross to Tanger. Rail entry from Europe is only through Tanger. Euro-Rail is valid in Morocco

Train travel to Morocco is a relatively cheap option for those under 26, and a convenient way to tie in a visit to Morocco with a short stay in Europe. For those under 26 an **InterRail** ticket bought in any participating European country includes the Moroccan train network, and a reduction on the Algeciras-Tanger ferry. Travelling through Spain often entails extra cost, as there are supplements to be paid on a number of trains. ***British Rail International***, London Victoria Railway Station, T0207-8342345 (enquiries), T0207-8280892 (tickets), only sell tickets to Algeciras, about £214 return. ***Eurotrain***, T0207-7303402, and ***Campus Travel***, their agents for people under 26, T0207-8284111, sell tickets from London Victoria to Tanger, including both ferry crossings. These are very reasonably priced from £265 return, and enable the traveller to stop off at any point on the fixed route for any length of time within the two month validity of the ticket. (If your route is to Morocco, then BIJ ticket validity is six months.)

Touching down

The vast majority of tourists arrive in Morocco by air at Casablanca, Marrakech or Agadir. Another way to Morocco is by ferry, as detailed above, arriving at Tanger, Ceuta or Nador. Information on onward travel from point of arrival is given here by destination.

Airport information

Aéroport Casablanca Mohammed V Casablanca's main airport is at Nouasseur, 30 km southeast of Casablanca, T022-339100. The airport terminal includes a restaurant, bar, post office, a *BMCE bureau de change,* and agencies for the larger hotels, tour companies and car hire companies. There are also cash dispensers on the main concourse, just after you pass customs. There is no hotel at this airport.

Onward travel is by shuttle train or taxi. The station is under the main airport concourse, and there are trains to Casablanca. If travelling on to a Moroccan destination other than Casablanca by train, you want Casa-Voyageurs station. Casa-Port is the station for down-town Casablanca. There are also regular bus services to both Casablanca (40 mins) and Rabat (90 mins). They drop and collect passengers at the *CTM* terminal in Casablanca, off Avenue des FAR, and in Rabat in front of the *Hotel Terminus*, on Avenue Mohammed V. Just outside the main door of the airport is the taxi rank. A grand taxi is 200dh to Casablanca city centre, 400dh to Rabat, non-negotiable. If you are in a hurry, this will be the preferable but expensive option, as there are only one or two trains an hour.

When it comes to leaving Casablanca, check train times and your departure time carefully. At one of the stations, they can give you a small ticket-sized printout with train times. Grand taxis for the airport may be found at the *CTM* bus station, behind the Tour Habous, on Avenue des FAR, or close to the Place des Nations Unies, on Avenue Moulay Hassan I.

Casablanca also has a second, smaller airport at Anfa, mainly for private traffic.

Aéroport Ouarzazate Taourirt Ouarzazate's airport, currently undergoing refurbishment, is just 3km from the town centre. You can get into town by petit taxi. Make sure you don't get overcharged. 20dh is quite enough for the (maximum) 5-minute hop into town, so try to have some change ready. Airport number is T044-882383, Royal Air Maroc number T044-882348 and T044-883236. Question: on an internal flight, do you fill in a landing form and go through passport control at this airport, even if your passport has been stamped at Casablanca? Expect this to be a possibility.

Aéroport Agadir Al Massira Agadir is the main destination in Morocco for large numbers of package tourists. This airport is a modern construction 28 km inland from the city, T048-839002, with connections by bus and grands taxis. Banks and car hire companies are open during office hours, closed on Sundays. The No 22 bus runs to Inezgane (3dh), a transport hub near Agadir, with buses and grands taxis to Marrakech, Taroudant and Agadir. Otherwise there are grands taxis, 150dh standard fare for up to six people, into Agadir (arrange to share costs in terminal building). Grand taxi drivers may accept foreign currency – make sure you have the rough equivalent of the dirham charge in notes. However you can now buy Moroccan dirhams at London airports.

Touching down

Business hours *The working week for businesses is Monday to Friday, with half day working Saturday. On Fridays, the lunch break tends to be longer, as the main weekly prayers with sermon are on that day. Any official business takes considerably longer in Ramadan.*
Banks*: 0830 to 1130 and 1430 to 1600 in winter, afternoons 1500 to 1700 in summer, 0930 to 1400 during Ramadan.*
Post offices*: 0830 to 1230 and 1430 to 1830, shorter hours in Ramadhan.*
Shops*: Generally from 0900 to 1200 and from 1500 to 1900, although this varies in the big towns.*
Museums*: Most close on a Tuesday. Hours generally 0900 to 1200 and 1500 to 1700, although this can vary considerably.*

Emergency services *Police: T19. Fire brigade: T15. Larger towns will have an SOS Médecins (private doctor on call service), and almost all towns of any size have a pharmacy on duty at night, the pharmacie de garde. Any large hotel should be able to give you the telephone/address of these. For most ailments, a médecin généraliste (general practitioner) will be sufficient.*

Directory enquiries *Dial 120 (business numbers) or 121 (personal numbers). For the operator dial 10, for information dial 16, for international calls when there is no direct line, dial 12.*

IDD code *212. Dialling out of Morocco, first 00, and wait for the tone before dialling the country code.*

Official time *Morocco follows GMT all year round, one hour behind the UK and two hours behind Spain in the summer.*

Weights and measures *Morocco uses the metric system.*

Essentials

Aéroport Marrakech Menara

Marrakech's airport, 6 km outside the city, is currently undergoing improvement work. The *BMCE* and the *Banque Populaire* have *bureaux de change*, closed outside office hours. For the optimistic, there is the No 11 bus to Jemaâ el Fna, at the heart of the médina and near the budget hotels. Otherwise, the quickest way into Marrakech is by petit or grand taxi. A grand taxi should not set you back more than 50dh (60dh at night), for the run from airport to Guéliz, the modern town, which also has reasonably priced hotels. Foreign currency may be acceptable to taxi drivers.

Aéroport Tanger Boukhalef

Although it is unlikely that you will fly into Tanger if you are planning a break in the High Atlas, you may just find a very cheap flight, making this information useful. Situated 15 km from Tanger, the Aéroport Boukhalef, T039-935720, has a couple of banks with *bureaux de change* but at the time of writing no cashpoint. Travel into Tanger either by bus or grand taxi. The taxi should cost 70dh for up to six people. Make arrangements with other travellers inside the terminal regarding taxi payment. Otherwise, the bus stop (Nos17 or 70) for the town centre is 2 km down the road from the airport.

Other airports

You may have to take a grand taxi to the **Aéroport Rabat-Salé**, 10 km from Rabat if you are going to take an internal flight down to Essaouira and its **Aéroport de Mogador**. Again, Essaouira is easily reached by grand taxi from the airport.

Airport tax

There are no airport taxes. On entry into Morocco vehicles and (just possibly) larger electronic equipment will be entered in the passport, to prevent resale without paying taxes.

Tourist information

Tourist boards
See individual towns for specific details

Most towns in Morocco have an *Office de Tourisme* and larger towns also have a Syndicat d'Initiative et de Tourisme (Information Office). The standard of information varies – often all they have available are the usual glossy pamphlets. They offer to find official guides, again of very variable standard. Fès in particular is a town where an official guide is probably a good thing, especially if you have limited time.

Maps

Of the road maps, the best is still probably the Michelin map, sheet 959, at scale 1/4,000,000, with insets at 1/1,000,000 and 1/1,600,000. You may find other maps in local bookshops.

If you are going to be hiking in the Atlas Mountains, and do not intend to engage the services of a guide, then you will want maps. These can be obtained from the Division du Cadastre et de la Cartographie, Ministère de l'Agriculture, 31 Avenue Moulay Hassan, Rabat, (T033-705311, F033-705191), open Monday-Thursday 0830-1100 and 0230-0530. Toubkal maps are readily available, others have to be ordered. The orders take two working days to process. At the last count, the 1:100,000 scale maps cost 80dh. In Marrakech, maps can be obtained from the cybercafé at the back of the *Hotel Ali* next to the Jardin Foucauld, Jemaâ el Fna, at the vastly inflated price of 140dh (you might get 10dh knocked off). The Toubkal 1:100,000 scale map is generally available, other sheets useful for the High Atlas of Azilal (Skoura, Tineghir, etc) are subject to availability.

If you can't get to Rabat before you travel, you could contact Hamish Brown at AMIS Atlas Mountain Information Service, T01592-873546, which produces useful map guides to certain regions of the Atlas popular with trekkers. In London, you could also try *Stanfords*, 12-14 Long Acre, WC2E 9LP, T0207-8361321.

The following maps may be available for the mountain areas

High Atlas of Azilal There is now a handy 1:100,000 scale colour map, ref. STR HTA99, Maroc Haut Atlas, Carte des randonnées de Zaouiat Ahançal, produced by the Division de la Cartographie in Rabat (also available from the *Hotel Ali*, Marrakech). Although not strong on mountain relief, it does show a number of good circuits. The five-colour 1:100,000 maps for the Azilal and Mgoun High Atlas include: Beni Mellal, Imilchil, etc, the rare 1:50,000 include Beni Mellal, Taghzirt. For the whole Azilal/Imilchil region, a very useful map is the 1:250,000 scale Khénifra map, sheet, NI-30-13 which covers the whole region from Khénifra in the top northwest corner right across to Midelt and Rich in the east. **High Atlas of Toubkal** 1:100,000: A pack of four maps for the Toubkal region, (including Amizmiz, Oukaïmeden-Toubkal, Tizi-n-Test and Taliouine) may be available from Stanfords in London. The rarer 1:50,000 maps include: Tahanawt (usually spelt Tahanoute), Larbat Tighdiwine. **Maps available for Jebel Toubkal** 1:100,000, Amizmiz, Oukaïmeden Toubkal, Telouat; 1:50,000, Tahanawt, Larbat Tighdiwine, Had Zaraqtane, Azgour, Amizmiz, Toubkal, Tala Yacoub, Taliwien, Assarag.

Unofficial guides

It is quite likely that you will be hassled by guides often posing as 'students' or 'friends', and extreme caution should be taken in accepting help from these people, as it can lead to considerable expense (whatever the initial fee). Actual physical danger is a risk, too, for women. In Marrakech, the *Brigade Touristique* seems to have cooled the ardour of the most enthusiastic *faux guides*, mainly by a mixture of fines and short term prison sentences. Travellers will be well advised to use an official guide from the tourist office or manage without.

Rules, customs and etiquette

Clothing & conduct

Morocco is more relaxed than many Muslim countries and therefore it is possible to wear clothing that exposes arms and legs in coastal resorts. However, to minimize hassle, women are advised to cover themselves away from the hotel compounds, at social occasions and visits in traditional rural areas. Full coverage of limbs and head is recommended when travelling in the heat. Winter temperatures can be low and night temperatures in the desert and at altitude are low all the year round so carry extra clothes.

Eating

Moroccan families may eat from a communal dish, often with spoons, sometimes with the hands. If invited to a home, you may well be something of a guest of honour. Depending on your hosts, it's a good idea to take some fruit or pâtisseries along. If spoons or cutlery are not provided, you eat using bread, using your right hand, not the left hand since it is ritually unclean. If the dishes with the food are placed at floor level, keep your feet tucked under your body away from the food. In a poorer home, there will only be a small amount of meat, so only take your fair share, or perhaps (better) wait until a share is offered. Basically, good manners are the same anywhere. Let common sense guide you.

Tipping

Can be a bit of a 'hidden cost' during your stay in Morocco

Tipping is expected in restaurants and cafés, by guides, porters and car park attendants, and others who render small services. Make sure you have small change at the ready for this. Tipping taxi drivers is optional. Do not tip for journeys when the meter has not been used, because the negotiated price will be generous anyway. For handling baggage in hotels, tip around 3dh, on buses 3dh-5dh, and 5dh on trains and in airports.

Religion

Sunni Islam is the religion of Morocco. The Gregorian calendar is used for all everyday matters, however. The Islamic or Hijra year, being a lunar year, is 10 or 11 days shorter. The Hijra calendar goes back to the seventh century AD, and year one corresponds to the Prophet Mohammed's emigration or *hijra* from Mecca to Médina in 622 AD. Friday is the Muslim holy day, when major sermons are given in mosques across the Islamic world. As a visitor, Islam won't affect you in the way it does on a visit to say, Saudi Arabia. In Ramadhan, however, the 11th hijra month, and a time of fasting during daylight hours, the pace of public life slows down considerably.

Prohibitions

Holy places Mosques in Morocco, except the Hassan II Mosque in Casablanca and the restored Almohad mosque at Tin Mal in the High Atlas, are off limits. Other Muslim religious buildings in use which you may visit are the very fine Medersa Bou Inania in Fès, the Tomb of Moulay Ismaïl in Meknès, and the Mausoleum of Mohammed V in Rabat. The remainder are strictly off the tourist track. People who are clearly non-Muslim will be turned away by door keepers from places where they are not wanted. Those who try to slip past the guardians should be sure they can talk their way out of trouble.

Narcotics *Kif* or marijuana represents a good source of income for small farmers in the Rif. However, the European Union has put pressure on Morocco to stop production. There is no serious attempt, however, to stop those Moroccans who so wish from having a gentle smoke. (*Kif* is also consumed in the form of *ma'joun* cakes, local variant of hash brownies, which have been known to lead to much merriment at otherwise staid occasions.) However, as a tourist, under no circumstances do you want to be caught by the police in the possession of drugs of any kind. Expect no sympathy whatsoever if caught trying to export cannabis resin or other substances. You have been warned.

Safety

For safety matters with regard to women travelling alone, see page 22

Morocco is basically a very safe country, although there is occasional violent street crime in Casablanca and (very rarely) Marrakech. Travelling on public transport, you need to watch your pockets. Do not carry all your money, cashcards, and travellers' cheques in the same place. A money belt and one of those small waterproof boxes (for credit cards or travellers' cheques) you wear round your neck are a very good idea. Never have more money than you can afford to lose in the pockets of your jeans. Thieves operate best in crowds getting on and off trains and at bus and taxi stations where they can quickly disappear into an anonymous mass of people.

One point is that you do need to be aware of the various skilled con-artists in operation in certain places. You need to be polite and confident, distant and sceptical – even a little bored by the whole thing. Some of the ruses, however, are pretty good, ie at Marrakech airport, 'would you like to make a contribution to the taxi drivers' football team fund?' Learn the values of the banknotes quickly (the yellow-brown 100dhs and the blue 200dhs are the big ones, a red 10dh is no great loss). Keep your wits about you. Remember, you are especially vulnerable stumbling off that overnight bus or strolling blithely around an unfamiliar street.

Should you be robbed, reporting it to the police will take time – but may alert them to the fact that there are thieves operating in a given place.

Where to stay

As anywhere, it's a good idea to take a look at a room before you take it

This area of Morocco has a good range of accommodation to suit all budgets. There are well appointed business hotels, luxurious places for the discerning visitor – and clean basic hotels to suit those with limited funds. Independent travellers appreciate the growing number of guesthouses (see Essentials section, Marrakech chapter), some very swish indeed, while in the mountain areas walkers and climbers will find rooms available in local people's homes. Modern self-catering accommodation is a rarity, although there are now a handful of places providing this in Marrakech. They tend to be very minimally equipped, however. This range of accommodation, growing constantly, is one of the main strengths of the Moroccan tourist industry.

So what should you expect of hotels in Morocco? Firstly, though there is an official star rating system, few hotels boast their membership of the one, two or even three star categories. There does not appear to be very tight central control on how prices reflect facilities on offer. There are considerable variations in standards, and surprises are possible. Note too that breakfast is generally not included in the room price.

Cheap At the budget end of the market are simple hotels, often close to bus or train stations, where you will pay between 30-60dh single, up to 90dh double for a small, simple room. There may be a washbasin, sometimes a bidet. Loos and showers (5-8dh), will be shared. The worst of this sort of accommodation will be little better than a concrete cell, stifling in summer. The best is often quite pleasant outside summer, with helpful staff and lots of clean, bright tiling. Rooms often open on to a central courtyard, limiting privacy and meaning you have to leave your room closed when out. Outside the big tourist cities, such hotels are almost exclusively Moroccan. Although such hotels are generally clean, it may be best to bring a sheet with you if you're planning to use them a lot. Water, especially in the southern desert towns, can be a problem. Generally, there will be a public bath (hammam) close by for you to take a shower after a long bus journey.

Mid-range More expensive (say 90-120dh for a single) are one-star-type hotels, generally in the new part of town (*ville nouvelle* neighbourhoods). Showers may be en suite, breakfast

Hotel classifications

This table explains the hotel classification system used in this book. Prices are based on double rooms, unless otherwise indicated, singles are marginally cheaper.

AL (1000dh and over) *Indicates an international luxury class hotel as found in Casablanca or Rabat, or one of the famous luxury hotels of Morocco. Extremely good management means that everything works to the highest standard.*

A (800-990dh) *Indicates a hotel with top class facilities and services.*

B (360-790dh) *Indicates a four-star hotel with all basic facilities, including air-conditioning and probably a pool.*

C (260-350dh) *Denotes a three-star hotel run to a good standard. This will be a clean hotel, with all basic facilities. Service may be a bit lacking on occasion, however.*

D (180-250dh) *A one- or two-star hotel, the best you may find in a small town. There may be a restaurant attached. Hot showers almost always available.*

E (120-170dh) *A one-star hotel, probably in an older area of a town. Will probably provide breakfast, but no restaurant. Shared WC and showers on corridor. Sometimes shower en suite. Hot water unavailable more often than not.*

F (60-110dh)

Essentials

(coffee, bread and jam, a croissant, orange juice) should be available, possibly at the café on the ground floor, for around 20dh. Next up are the two- and three-star places, where prices range from around 120-350dh a single. In this category again, most of the hotels are in the *ville nouvelle* areas. Rooms will have high ceilings and en suite shower and loo. Light sleepers need to watch out for noisy, street-facing rooms. Some of these hotels are being revamped, not always very effectively. Still in this price bracket, you have a number of establishments with a personal, family-run feel, including the *Gallia* in Marrakech and certain southern hotels which, despite aiming at tour groups, are rather pleasant.

Expensive

Happily, the days of amateurism in Moroccan hotel management seem to be numbered as foreign groups move in. ***Accor***, for example, has taken over a number of strategic hotels. Upmarket hotels in Morocco can either be vast and brash, revamped and nouveau riche, or solid but tasteful and even discreet with a touch of old-fashioned elegance. The main cities also have large conference hotels, including ***Mansour Eddahbi*** in Marrakech.

Hotel industry weaknesses

For years, many of the large tourist hotels in places like Marrakech were run as family businesses with little professional management. In the worst establishments, staff are poorly paid and generally on short-term contracts (at the end of which they are sacked and recruited again after a month). Hotel owners are also tempted to use *stagiaires* (trainees on placement from hotel management school) as free labour in summer. Staff motivation in many of Morocco's hotels is thus poor, even in pricey establishments. It is thus a nice gesture to leave any unwanted shampoo, toothpaste etc for the *femme de chambre*. She will be working long hours on a very small salary, maybe only 1,500dh a month.

Riads & guesthouses

The big phenomenon of the late 1990s in the Moroccan tourist industry was the development of the *maison d'hôte*. Wealthy Europeans bought old property in the médinas, the old towns, of Marrakech and Essaouira as second homes. Rather than leave the property closed for much of the year, the solution was to rent it out. A number of agencies specializing in the rental of riads (as these properties are generally called, after their garden courtyards or riads) were set up. Some riads are occupied for most of the year by their owners and so are more like guesthouses. If thinking of staying in a riad, you could make your first approach via a reliable agency like ***Riads au Maroc***, T044-431900. Certain UK travel companies – ***Cadogan***, ***Morocco Made to Measure***, for instance – now have riad accommodation in their brochures. Basically, they satisfy a growing demand in the hotel market with the benefit of offering something a little more personal. The welcome and service in a riad should be better than in a four-star hotel. Generally, riad charges cover accommodation and breakfast. Meals can be laid on at extra charge, and as they are prepared to order for a small number of people, will be of excellent quality. In a place like Marrakech, hygiene in a riad should also be far better than in one of the city's jaded four-star establishments. There is now guesthouse accommodation to suit medium to large holiday budgets. This sector of the hotel industry looks set to continue to expand in the near future, despite various rumours saying that Europeans will be banned from buying property in the médinas.

When reserving riad accommodation, you need to be clear on how you will be met (finding such houses in complicated médina streets is generally impossible for taxi drivers). Also check whether your accommodation is ground floor (damper in winter) or top floor (hot in summer) and the nature of the heating. Moroccan nights can be very chilly in winter. Check out **www.marrakech-medina.com**, **www.marrakech-riads.net** or **www.essaouiramedina.com**

Youth hostels (Auberges de jeunesse)

There are 11 hostels in all affiliated to the **IYHA**, located in the cities (Casablanca, Rabat, Fès, Meknès and Marrakech, Oujda and Laâyoune) as well as Azrou (Middle Atlas) and Asni (High Atlas). The HQ is in Meknès, on Ave Oqba ibn Nafi. Overnight charge between 20-40dh, use of kitchen 2dh, with a maximum stay of three nights and priority to the under-30s. Opening hours in the summer are 0800-1300, 1830-2400, winter 0800-1000, 1200-15000, 1800-2230. For further information try the **Moroccan Youth Hostel Federation**, Parc de la Ligue arabe, Casablanca, T022-220551, F226777. In practice, it is better to go for cheap hotels, more conveniently located and with better loos and showers. The Marrakech hostel, while convenient for the train station, is a long way from the main sights.

Mountain accommodation

When walking in the Atlas, you will note that many children and adults have to make do with lousy plastic shoes. Gifts of used, solid kids' shoes are always welcome, so pack a few pairs before you travel

In the mountains, you can easily bivouac out in summer or, in the high mountains, kip in a stone *azib* (shepherd's shelter). There are three main options for paying accommodation: floor space in someone's home, a *gîte* of some kind, or a **CAF** (*Club Alpin Français*) refuge. The latter are shelters where hikers may rest and use the basic basic dormitory and kitchen facilities. Rates depend on category and season but about 15-50dh per night per person is usual. The **CAF** can be contacted via BP 6178, Casablanca, T022-270090, F022-297292, also BP 4437 Rabat, T037-734442. In France, the **CAF** is at 24 Ave Laumière, 75019 Paris.

In accommodation terms, when walking in the Atlas, in certain villages often passed through by walkers you will find *gîtes d'étape*, simple dormitory accommodation, marked with the colourful *GTAM* (*Grande Traversée de l'Atlas Marocain*) logo. The warden generally lives in the house next door. Prices here are set by the **ONMT** (tourist board), and the *gîte* will be clean if spartan. The board also publishes an annual guide listing people authorised to provide *gîte* type accommodation.

In mountain villages where there is no *gîte*, you will usually be able to find space in people's homes, provided you have your own sleeping-bag. Many houses have large living rooms with room for people to bed down on thin foam mattresses. It is the custom to leave a small sum in payment for this sort of service. On the whole, you will be made very welcome.

Camping

There are campsites all over Morocco – the **ONMT** quotes 87 sites in well chosen locations. Few sites, however, still respect basic international standards. Security is a problem close to large towns, even if the site is surrounded by a wall with broken glass on top. Never leave anything valuable in your tent. As campsites are really not much cheaper than basic hotels, and as even simple things like clean toilets and running water can be problematic, cheap hotel accommodation is preferable. There are some notable exceptions however. In Tineghir, on the route up to the Todgha Gorge, there are some campsites popular with the campervan brigade (*Chez Bernard – Camping du soleil*, and at Ksiba, up in the hills near Beni Mellal, there is a simple and pleasant new site.

If you are going to camp in Morocco, bear in mind that many sites lack shade. The ground tends to be hard and stony, so pack suitably tough tent pegs. When choosing your tent pitch, bear in mind factors like proximity to where people dump their rubbish. You may not get much sleep if other campers have decided to spend the night with a sing-a-long to the rhythm of the *darbouka* drum.

Getting around

Travelling between Marrakech and Essaouira, Ouarzazate or Beni Mellal is fine. In the High Atlas, remember that the distances are great, and that long trips on buses can be tiring – though not nearly so tiring as travelling by Landrover taxi or lorry squashed in with locals and their sacks of flour. Bus journeys can be excruciatingly slow, even over say 200 km journeys between fairly important towns. Note too that grand taxi drivers have licences to cover only certain sections of major routes, ie Ouarzazate to Boumalne, and not Ouarzazate to Er Rachidia. If using public transport, you have to be patient and remember that rural buses are used mainly by people who travel a lot by mule or donkey cart, too. To make maximum use of your time, if you don't mind dozing on a bus, then take night buses to cover the longer distances, although this means that you will be missing out on the landscapes. Public transport is very reasonably priced. Car hire, however, is expensive: although you may be able to get a small car for between 1800dh and 2500dh a week, you still have petrol or diesel costs on top of this. The advantage, of course, is the flexibility in getting to obscure places where the public transport is slow or rare. And you can take photo-stops whenever you want.

Air

For the area covered by this guide, internal flights are only really of any use for doing the Casablanca to Essaouira or Casablanca to Marrakech hops. At present, there are no regular services between Marrakech and Er Rachidia at the eastern end of the Atlas, despite there being a good airport down there. As tourism grows in southeastern Morocco, services may well be set up. In early 2001, Casablanca to Essaouira flights were on Fridays and Sundays, Essaouira to Casablanca on Mondays and Saturdays.

Companies offering private plane rental include Airstar, 33 rue Loubnane, Guéliz, Marrakech T/F044-435502. Helicopter transfers by Hélisud Maroc, 2 Rue Ben Aicha, Guéliz, Marrakech T044-438438, heli-sud@iam.net.ma

Transport websites and phone numbers

Airlines: www.royalairmaroc.com
Airports: www.onda.org.ma
Bus: www.ctm.co.ma, T 022-458824, also SATAS (buses in the South) T022-404560
Train: www.oncf.co.ma
Ferry to Morocco: www.trasmediterranea.es, www.ferrimaroc.com, www.sncm.fr

For general information *Royal Air Maroc* (*RAM*) has internal flights from Casablanca to Tanger, El Hoceima, Oujda, Fès, Marrakech, Agadir, Ouarzazate, Laâyoune, and Dakhla. Note that Casablanca has two airports, Mohammed V at Nouaceur, outside the city, and the much smaller city airport at Anfa, generally used only for private flights. **Essaouira** has a tiny airport with flights from Casablanca and Rabat, and there are limited direct flights between **Marrakech** and **Fès**. As mentioned above, although **Er Rachidia** has an airport, demand is currently felt to be insufficient for regular flights to be started. **Zagora** has a military airport which might one day come on line for tourist flights. **Nador** will have an airport with regular flights shortly. For details of ***RAM*** flights, consult www.royalairmaroc.com, information available in English.

RAM head office is on T022-912000, F022-912397. All major towns have ***RAM*** agencies, generally on the main boulevard, as follows: Agadir, Ave Général Kettani, T048-840793, F048-839296; Al Hoceima, Aéroport Charif al Idrisi, T039-982063; Casablanca, 44 Ave des FAR, T022-311122, F022-442409; Essaouira, Aéroport Mogador, T044-476709, F044-476705; Fès, 54 Ave Hassan II, T055-620456, F055-626623; Laâyoune, Place Dcheira, T048-894071; Marrakech, 197 Ave Mohammed V, T044-446444, F044-446002; Meknès, 7 Ave Mohammed V, T055-520963/64, F055-523606; Nador, 45 Blvd Mohammed V, T056-606337, F056-605539; Ouarzazate, 1 Blvd Mohammed V, T044-885080, F044-886893; Oujda, Blvd Mohammed V, T056-683909; Rabat, Ave Mohammed V, T037-709766, F037-708076; Tanger, 1 Place de France, T039-935501; Tétouan, 5 Ave Mohammed V, T039-961260, F039-961577.

A small private airline company, ***Regional Airlines***, launched in 1998, has been slow to achieve any real presence on the internal flights market. Their small fleet of twin-prop planes flies to Agadir and Laâyoune, as well as Málaga, Las Palmas and Lisbon. Reservations on T022-53880, F022-538050. Their downtown Casablanca office is on Ave des FAR, near the *Hotel Royal Mansour*, almost opposite the *Hotel Excelsior*.

Flight prices In 2001, sample ***RAM*** prices were as follows: a single Casablanca to Marrakech 735dh, a return 1000dh. With ***Regional Airlines***, Casablanca to Málaga was 2338dh single, 2278dh return (special tarif).

Road

Bicycles & motorcycles
Theft from bikes is a problem

Mountain bikes, mopeds and sometimes small motorcycles can be hired in tourist towns. For exploring Marrakech and the Palmeraie, biking is quite a popular option, and there are hire-stands outside the hotels in Semlalia and Hivernage (at junction near *Hotel Safir Siaha*). There is no shortage of mechanics to fix bikes and mopeds. Trains, buses and even grands taxis will take bikes for a small fee. An increasingly popular option is the cycle tour holiday. A number of mainstream European companies now run such holidays, with bikes being carried on vans on the longer stretches. Off-road biking is popular in the Tafraoute area of the Anti-Atlas.

If you go touring with a bike or motorcycle, beware of the burning power of the sun. Wear gloves, cover those bits of exposed skin between helmet and T-shirt. For motorcyclists, helmets are compulsory, believe it or not, and gendarmes will be happy to remind you so.

Riding a motorbike in Morocco is even more testing than driving a car. Watch out for stray pedestrians, note that vehicle drivers will not necessarily show you much respect. Where flocks of animals are straying across the road, try not to drive between a single animal and the rest of the flock, as it may well try to charge back to join the rest. Use your horn. If you are going to go off road, wear boots, make sure your tyres are in excellent condition.

A number of cyclists and bikers have reported that theft from paniers was a problem. Anything loosely attached to your bike will disappear when you are being besieged by a horde of small kids in an isolated village.

Bus

There are plenty of domestic bus services in Morocco. While variations in price are small, for the visitor, the quality of service varies enormously. Broadly speaking, if the train, a ***Supratours*** bus or grands taxi run to your destination, don't bother with the small bus companies. For early morning services it's worth getting your ticket in advance, also at peak times when many Moroccans are travelling like the end of Ramadhan and around Aïd el Kebir (two months after the end of Ramadhan). Information on whether you have to reserve or not will be conflicting. As you bring your luggage to the bus, you will find that there is a man who helps stow luggage on roof or in hold, so have a couple of dirham coins handy for him.

Inter-railers note: the pass is not valid with Supratours

Supratours, CTM and ***SATAS*** In southern Morocco, undoubtedly the safest and most comfortable service is with ***Supratours***, an off-shoot of the **ONCF** (see above). Next best is the ***CTM***, *Compagnie de Transport Marocain* (white buses with blue and red stripes). Very often (but not always) their services run from stations well away from the main *gare routière* (inter-city bus station). This is the case in Casablanca, Fès and Marrakech, for example. For Tanger, the *CTM* station is just outside the port zone gates. For information (*renseignements*) on *CTM* services try T022-458881. Both ***Supratours*** and ***CTM*** buses **usually** run on time, and do not dawdle en route. As an example of prices, a single Marrakech to Essaouira costs 48dh with ***Supratours***. Note that *CTM* services seem to be being reduced. There is no longer any Casablanca to Beni Mellal service, nor a Marrakech to El Jadida. Check the company's quadrilingual website on www.ctm.co.ma Another good option if travelling in the South are the ***SATAS*** buses which run between major cities like Casablanca, Agadir and places south of the Atlas. Info line is Casablanca-based, ring T022-404560.

Local bus companies Other private bus companies are generally much slower, apart from a few *rapide* services with videos and the like. There are regional companies, like the *SATAS*, which serves much of the south, and all sorts of minor companies with names like ***Pullman du Sud***. While such buses get to parts that the ***CTM*** cannot reach, they are often slow. Bus terminals have a range of ticket windows (*guichets*), displaying destinations and times of departure. Several companies may serve the same destination, and as you head into the bus station, you may be approached by touts who will urge you to prefer one company to another. The main Casablanca bus station functions on this basis, to the extent that the ticket windows are practically out of business.

Safety Vehicles used by many private bus companies do not conform to high safety standards. In recent years, there have been some horrible bus accidents in Morocco. The deaths and serious injuries meant they were given high media coverage. Royal visits to hospitals indicated the level of official concern. The reason for this is that bus drivers are severely underpaid. To make up for their low wages, they leave half-full, aiming to pick up extra passengers (whom they won't have to declare to their employers) en route. This makes for a slow, stop/go service. On routes worked by several companies, drivers race each other to be first to pick up passengers in the next settlement. Given the poor condition of the vehicles and the often narrow roads, accidents are inevitable.

Although inter-city buses can be very slow (and you may even see the road surface under your feet) for many of the people who use them speed is not an issue. Pack mules link mountain villages to the rest of the world, while on the coastal plains, mule and donkey-drawn buggies provide transport to the weekly souk.

City buses Most towns have city buses which, when crowded, provide great opportunities for local pickpockets. The orange ***Alsa*** buses in Marrakech are fine. Note that there is no longer any bus service from Rabat or Casablanca to the Aéroport Mohammed V, Casablanca.

Hiring a car

Sample prices (per week) for car hire in Morocco, in 2001, low season and high season.

Group A	*Fiat Uno (Fiat Palio slightly more expensive)*	*2,100dh/2,800dh*
Group B	*Peugeot 205 JR*	*2,450dh/3,150dh*
Group C	*Peugeot 309 Renault 19*	*3,500dh/4,900dh*
Group D	*Renault Clio with a/c Renault 21 (rare)*	*5,000dh/6,000dh*
Group E	*Mercedes 190 E (rare)*	*5,600dh/7,000dh (cost can reach 1,200dh per day)*

Car hire

See individual city and town directories for details of companies

There is huge demand for hire cars during the Christmas and Easter breaks

As distances are great, having a car makes a huge difference to the areas of the country you can cover. All the main hire car companies are represented, including ***Europcar***, ***Hertz***, and ***Sixt-car***, and there are numerous small companies which vary hugely in reliability. Arriving at Casa-Mohammed V Airport, you will find hire-car companies on the main concourse to your left as you come out through the frosted-glass doors. The smallest car available is generally a Fiat Uno, more rarely a Renault 4. A large number of agencies now have Fiat Palios in their fleets. The Peugeot 205 is felt to be a more reliable small car, with slightly higher clearance and better road holding. A good deal would give you an Uno for 500dh a day, unlimited mileage, although certain Marrakech agencies (***Imzitours***, T044-433934/36, imzi_tours@usa.net for example) can be considerably cheaper. Four-wheel drives available in Morocco include the Suzuki Gemini (2 persons) and the Vitara (4 persons), at around 800dh per day; long-base Mitsubishi Pajeros (6 persons) are hired at 900dh to 1,000dh per day. Toyotas are said to be the best desert four-wheel drives. Landrovers are very uncomfortable for long cross-country runs on road, especially in summer without a/c.

Remember that you are responsible for damage if you take a car unsuited to the *piste* into areas suitable only for four-wheel drive vehicles. Regarding insurance, the best agencies will provide all-risk insurance. As a matter of self preservation, do not agree to take a hire car other than in the daylight. Check such for tyre condition (this includes spare tyre), presence of jack and warning triangle, working lights and safety belts. When hiring an all-terrain vehicle, try to ascertain that the agency you are hiring from has a reliable, well maintained fleet. Make sure that the vehicle will go into four-wheel drive easily and, as for ordinary cars, check the spare tyre. Look at the tyres closely – there should be no cuts on the sides.

In general, you will need dirhams to pay, as only the larger agencies take credit cards. They will probably want to take an imprint of your credit card as a guarantee.

Always try to have the mobile phone number of an agency representative in case of emergency

Car insurance In terms of car insurance and damage to vehicle, there are several possibilities. A good agency will have agreements with garages across Morocco for repairs. The garage will talk to the agency about the nature of the repairs, and the matter will be handled. If the damage is your fault, that is because you have taken the car onto rough tracks in breach of contract, you will be responsible for covering the cost of repairs. In the case of accidents, you have to get a *constat de police* (a police report), which is a document drawn up by the police stating whose fault the accident is. Depending on the type of insurance, the client pays a percentage of the cost of repairs. You can have a *sans franchise* (rental contract) which means that you will have nothing to pay, or with a franchise

No rules of the road

Driving in Morocco is hazardous. Grands taxis, buses and lorries thunder along, forcing oncoming lesser vehicles onto the hard shoulder, if it exists. Sometimes there is a tyre-splitting gap between tarmac and dusty edge. Pedestrians wander out into the road and cyclists stray into the fast lane. On poor roads, you will see Moroccan drivers holding a palm up to their windscreens. This is to reduce the risk of shattering due to stones shooting up from the wheels of oncoming cars.

People also seem to overtake in the most suicidal of places. Does the single continuous line have no meaning? In fact, driving in Morocco, you find yourself wondering how such a generally polite people manages to produce such appalling drivers. The answer lies in the fact that you can basically buy yourself a driving licence. The accident figures are appalling: 25.6 deaths per 1,000 accidents per annum in Morocco, as against 2.6 deaths per 1,000 accidents in France. The Gendarmerie royale is having a crackdown, however, especially on speed limits, and 400dh fines may be levied on the spot.

Do not rush, go with the flow and take your time. Apart from Casablanca, Morocco's cities are not large, and you will soon be out on the calmer country roads. Here you will share the roads with numerous animal-drawn carts and pack animals. This makes for slow driving but can also be hazardous at night. Most roads lack cats-eyes and most agricultural vehicles and mule carts drive without lights.

set at a certain level, that is a 50% franchise means that you pay 50% more than rental cost, so that if there is an accident, you pay only 50% cost of repairs.

A good agency will have you sign a *fiche technique* (a technical details form) after you have viewed the car before hire, in daylight, and checked that everything, including tyres, spare tyre, jack, lights, windscreen etc are in good order. It is important to check these things as there have been cases of unscrupulous hire-car agencies sending clients out with sub-standard vehicles which have broken down. Clients, in the lurch in remote towns, have then paid for repairs, which the agency has then refused to pay for. Pay attention to jack and spare tyre. It is best if the spare tyre is in the boot. If under the car, unpadlocked, it runs the risk of being stolen.

Most cars do not as yet use unleaded petrol

Petrol and other costs You may have to pay for the petrol already in the tank of your hire car. Usually, the car will be almost empty, and you fill up yourself. In early 2001, diesel in Morocco was 5dh per litre, petrol (*essence*) was at 10dh. Hire cars in Morocco generally run on petrol (*super*) rather than diesel. In early 2001, a fill-up (*le palin*) for a Fiat Uno cost around 350dh. In such a car, 200dh does the four-hour trip on winding mountain roads from Marrakech to Ouarzazate. A fill-up with diesel for a Pajero four-wheel drive costs 500dh, and on this the vehicle will do the 800km trip Marrakech to Zagora and back.

In remote areas, remember to fill up whenever possible. Fuel up at one of the larger petrol stations (***Shell***, ***Mobil***, ***CMH***, in most cities, ***Ziz*** in the south). There have been cases of petrol being watered down, with unfortunate results, in certain places. New looking service stations are best, in towns.

Should you need tyre repairs, prices vary. Expect to pay upwards of 50dh as a foreigner in a hurry in a small town, and less if you have time to wait in some rural outpost.

Always drive more slowly than you would in Europe

Risky roads There are a number of dangerous stretches of road which you may have to deal with in your hire car. Much concentration is needed on the four-hour drive on the winding, mountainous P31, Marrakech to Ouarzazate, via the Tizi-n-Tichka. Fog and icy surfaces are possible in winter. There are roads which seem excellent, you drive fast, and then meet sudden dips and turns. Note in particular the Ouarzazate to Skoura road. The P7, Casablanca to Marrakech, is dangerous on Friday evenings as holidaymakers hasten towards the Red City, competing with lorry traffic (watch out for the final stretch through the Jebilet after Sidi Bou Othman). Drivers are also tempted to go far faster than necessary on the straight stretches of the P24 between Marrakech and El Kelaâ des Sraghna. In the High Atlas barriers are put down on routes between Kasbah Tadla and Midelt and over the Tizi-n-Tichka and Tizi-n-Test when snow blocks roads.

Highway code The Moroccan highway code follows the international model. Speeds are limited to 120 kph on the autoroute, 100 kph on main roads, 60 kph on approaches to urban areas and 40 kph in urban areas. Watch out for the speed signs, which do not always follow a logical sequence. There are two types of police to be met on the roads: the blue-uniformed urban police and the grey-uniformed gendarmes in rural areas. The latter are generally stationed outside large villages, at busy junctions, or under shady eucalyptus trees near bends with no-overtaking markings.

The wearing of seat belts is compulsory outside the cities, and the gendarmes will be watching to see you're wearing them. (Many Moroccans who know the check point locations well seem to think that seat-belts are worn just for the gendarmes.) It is traditional to slow down for the gendarmes, although as a foreigner driving a hire car you will generally be waved through. They will not, on the whole, ask for 'coffee money' from you. Note however that the police are empowered to levy on the spot fines for contravention of traffic regulations. Fines are now quite severe in response to the high number of fatal accidents due to careless driving.

Other highway code tips. Red and white kerb markings mean no parking. Warning triangles are not compulsory – but highly useful, and if needed should be placed 10 m behind-broken down vehicle. In the case of an accident, report to nearest gendarmerie or police post to obtain a written report, otherwise the insurance will be invalid.

Remember that 4WD vehicles, designed for rough tracks, donot perform as well as standard saloon cars on normal roads

Off-road driving In addition to well over 10,000 km of surfaced road, Morocco has several thousand kilometres of unsurfaced tracks, generally referred to as pistes. Some of these can be negotiated with care by an ordinary car with high clearance. Most cannot however, and four-wheel drive vehicles are increasingly popular to explore the remote corners of Morocco. In south-central Morocco, a breathtaking but tough route is the 'Gorge to Gorge' piste from Msemrir at the top of the Gorges du Dadès round to Tamtattouchte at the top of the Gorges du Todgha. Another option in the High Atlas is the Telouet – Kasbah Anemiter – Aït Ben Haddou route, not however to be attempted after rain. Though the Azilal to Aït Bougmez and Rich to Imilchil routes are now easily accessible in ordinary vehicles with good drivers, there are plenty more difficult routes to follow in the east and central regions of the High Atlas, including Imilchil to Anergui and Ouaouizaght to Zaouiat Ahansal.

Four-wheel drive adepts should plan their trips carefully, noting that bad weather can impede travel. Snow blocks mountain tracks in winter, rain and melt-water can make them impassable. Ask locals about conditions. In many areas, pistes are being upgraded – or are no longer well maintained, as they have been made superfluous thanks to the presence of a new tarmac road. However, not all road improvement works are of very high quality. A hard winter can leave mountain tarmac partly destroyed, or wash large quantities of rubble and clay on to the road surface.

If you are driving into remote areas, it is highly advisable to go with two vehicles. The mountains are a hostile environment to trippers from outside, and if things go wrong, there is nobody to get you out if you are by yourselves. If you are unused to off-road vehicles, employ the services of a driver (around 300dh a day). He will know the routes well and be able to chat to locals and other drivers about the state of the tracks. If you don't have a driver and get a bit lost, you can always pick up a local hitchhiker who will show you the way. Outside the main tourist towns, he is unlikely to be a 'fake' guide.

Always check the weather beforehand when venturing off-road in winter

When out in wild country, never take an unknown piste if a storm is on its way or as night is falling. Before you leave, check the names of villages on the way and remember that some tracks lead to abandoned mining operations rather than helpful hamlets. Do not go full tilt into a ford without checking the depth of the water first by wading in. You do not want to be stranded in an oued in full flood, a very real risk in late spring and in the late summer, when thunderstorms over distant mountains can turn small rivers into torrents only hours later. In winter, if venturing into isolated valleys and sites like the Jebel Ayyachi and Jebel Azourki, always do a weather check and have plenty of supplies. You might have to extend your holiday if you are cut off by snow. As a general rule, remember that progress will be slow, and that after wet weather you may have to dig/pull vehicles out. Distances tend to be measured in hours rather than in kilometres.

Car parking In towns, parking is fairly easy. Parking meters rarely function and instead a sort of watchman, identified by blue overalls and a metal badge, will pop up. Give him some spare change, say 5dh, when you return to your undamaged vehicle. At night, it is essential to leave your vehicle in a place where there is a night-watchman (*le gardien de nuit*). In practice, all good hotels and streets with restaurants will have such a figure who will keep an eye out for eventual marauders.

Hitchhiking

Definitely unadvisable for women travelling on their own

It is possible to hitchhike in Morocco. There are lorries which go to and from Europe, and drivers can sometimes be persuaded to take a passenger. In remote areas, hitching is one of the ways to get around, although it will usually involve some sort of payment. (Vehicles in remote areas have high maintenance costs.) Vans and lorries may pick up passengers for a negotiated price. In remote mountain areas, do not count on hitching. Vehicles operating here are moving in difficult terrain with a purpose. Landrover taxis (jeeps) and Mercedes Transit are public transport with a price and will be packed on souk days.

Taxi

Taxi drivers' foreign language skills are highly variable

Long distance **grand taxis**, generally Mercedes 200 saloon cars, run over fixed routes between cities, or within urban areas between centre and outlying suburbs. There is a fixed price for each route and passengers pay for a place, six in a Mercedes, nine in a Peugeot 504 estate car. Taxis wait until they are full. You may however, feel rich enough to pay for two places in order to be comfortable at the front (and be able to wear a safety belt). In a Peugeot estate, the best places are undoubtedly at the front, or, if you are quite small, right at the back. The middle place in the middle row is probably the worst.

Between towns, grands taxis are quicker than trains or buses, and normally only a little more expensive. Each town has a grand taxi rank, generally, although not always, next to the main bus station. The drivers cry out the name of their destination, and as you near the taxi station, you may be approached by touts eager to help you find a taxi. (This is especially true of Essaouira.) The standard of driving sometimes leaves a little to be desired.

In mountain areas, the same system applies, although the vehicles are Mercedes transit vans (where there is tarmac) or Landrovers, which have two people next to the driver and ten in the back. Grand taxis also serve Casablanca Mohammed V airport, leaving downtown Casablanca from a taxi rank almost opposite the *Hotel Hyatt Regency*.

Petits taxis are used within towns, and are generally Fiat Unos and Palios. They are colour-coded by town (red for Casablanca, khaki for Marrakech, orange for Beni Mellal). Officially they are metered, with an initial minimum fare, followed by increments of time and distance. There is a 50% surcharge after 2100. A petit taxi may take up to three passengers. In Marrakech, Rabat and Casablanca, drivers use the meters, in Tanger they try to charge what they like. Note that taxi drivers in some cities (notably Rabat and Casablanca, where taxis are in short supply) allow themselves to pick up other passengers en route if they are going the same way, thus earning a double fee for part of the route. No doubt this practice does not feature in the petit taxi driver's code of practice. In any case, taxi drivers welcome a tip – many of them are not driving their own vehicles, and make little more than 100dh a day. In terms of price, a short run between old and new town in Marrakech will set you back 10dh. Casa Port station to Casa Voyageurs is almost 10dh too.

Train

ONCF timetables are available at all main stations and can be accessed on their website

The **ONCF** (Office national des chemins de fer), see www.oncf.co.ma, runs an efficient though fairly slow service between major cities. There are 1,900 km of railway line, the central node being at railway town Sidi Kacem, some 46 km north of Meknès. Coming into Casablanca airport, the traveller can take the shuttle train to Casa-Voyageurs station on the **main north-south line**. This runs from Tanger to Marrakech with significant stations being Kénitra, Sidi Kacem, Salé, Rabat, Casa-Voyageurs, Settat, and Benguerir. The ONCF's **main west-east route** does Casa-Voyageurs to Oujda, main stations on this route being Rabat, Sidi Kacem, Meknès and Fès. A second fast *navette* (shuttle) serves commuters in the Casblanca-Rabat region, doing Casa-Port to Kénitra. Note that this service **does not** run via Casa-Voyageurs. A new two-tier Casablanca to Fès shuttle train is scheduled to come into service in late 2002, they say. Very handily, at the ticket windows of most ONCF stations they can print out mini-timetables for you if you ask.

Prices & journey times

Prices on the railways are reasonable. A first-class single ticket, Marrakech to Casa-Voyageurs is 100dh, services between Casablanca and Rabat, depending on station and class, around the 35dh mark. Casa-Voyageurs to Tanger is 157dh first class. In terms of time, by way of example, Casablanca to Marrakech generally takes 3 hours, Casablanca to Rabat just under an hour, while Rabat to Tanger is 4¾ hours.

Branch lines

For railway enthusiasts, there are a number of moderately obscure branch lines, mainly developed to serve the needs of the phosphate industry. There is a line from **Benguerir to Safi** via phosphate town Youssoufia (ex-Louis Gentil) with a daily passenger service. Another branch line takes trains from **Casablanca to Khouribga** and Oued Zem, up on the Plateau des Phosphates. On Morocco's eastern flank, there is a weekly freight train from **Oujda to Bouarfa**. Most of the network is single track, apart from on the section Casablanca to Kénitra. In 2002, delays are expected to continue on the Settat to Marrakech line due to improvement works on the tracks.

Train-bus link

Supratours run buses to connect with trains from a number of stations. From just outside Marrakech station, ***Supratours*** has connecting buses to Ouarzazate, Essaouira, Agadir, Laâyoune and Dakhla. Sample prices in early 2001 as follows: Marrakech to Agadir 70dh, Agadir to Laâyoune 190dh, Marrakech to Ouarzazate 60dh. Note also that *Supratours* has a Khouribga to Beni Mellal service. The bus station numbers are as follows: Agadir T048-841207; Casa-Voyageurs T022-404299; Essaouira T044-475317; Laâyoune T048-894891; Marrakech T044-435525; Nador T056-607262; Ouarzazate T044-887912; Tetouan T056-607262.

Train classes

On the trains, first-class compartments are spacious and generally quieter than second class. Second-class rail fares are generally slightly more expensive than the *CTM* buses. You gain, however, in time saved, reliability and safety. Second class is perfectly acceptable. Trains normally have a snacks trolley, a sandwich costing 12dh, a small coffee 5dh.

At Marrakech station

All the drivers of Marrakech's khaki-coloured taxis know when the trains come in, so there is never any shortage of onward transport, as the heaving mass of vehicles outside indicates. All taxis have working meters, and to get to your hotel, if it's in the city limits, you need a *petit taxi*, not a large Mercedes. It seems to be unofficial local practice for people to double up if they're headed in the same direction. You still pay the same fare as on the meter. If you are headed for the médina, you could cross the road outside the station and try to flag down a Mercedes grand taxi headed for either Bab Doukkala, or, more practical for the cheap hotels, Jemaâ el Fna.

On leaving Marrakech, try to arrive early, especially if leaving the city on a Sunday evening. (You can board the train about 20 mins before departure.) First-class compartments in particular can fill up very quickly. The west (left-hand) side of the train gets the sun in the afternoon, and is therefore hotter if the a/c is off. Note that there is a small *buvette* (café with sandwiches and yoghurt), just to the right of the big newsagents in the station concourse. As you leave the building, left-luggage is on your left, as is a small pharmacy. *Supratours* coach services is accessible from the platform as you arrive. As you stand outside facing the station building, go left and the main *Supratours* entrance is a few metres down the road on your right. Again, for the popular Marrakech to Essaouira run, try to arrive early to be sure of a place.

Keeping in touch

Communications

Internet

See individual city and town directories

Cybercafés can be found in city centres and even quite out of the way places like Azrou, Ouaouizaght, and Zagora. Generally, you can get on line for as little as 30dh for half an hour. If you are going to be in Morocco for a longer period, you can get yourself an email address for as little as 100dh basic fee a month.

Post

Letters to or from Europe can take up to a week

Posting letters is relatively easy, with the *PTT Centrale* of each town selling the appropriate stamps. Postage costs to Europe are 6dh for a letter and 6.5dh for a postcard. Post offices are open 0800-1200 and 1500-1800 Monday-Friday in the winter, 0800-1500 in the summer. It is best to post the letter in the box inside or just outside this building as these are emptied more frequently than those elsewhere. For those without a contact address to receive letters, instruct that they should be addressed clearly, with the surname underlined, to: Poste Restante, *PTT Centrale*, name of town, Morocco. Each *PTT Centrale* will have a post restante section, where letters are kept for a number of weeks. There is a small charge on collection. Some travellers use ***American Express*** offices to collect mail; in Morocco this is c/o *Voyages Schwartz*.

Telephone

The international code for Morocco is 212

See inside front cover for more details of telephone numbers in Morocco

In this book, all telephone numbers are written out in full, including the first three digits, which must always be dialled

Phoning is easy, as every town has a number of public phone shops or *téléboutiques*, clearly marked in distinctive blue and white livery. These are always supervised, with change available and (generally) telephone directories (*annuaires téléphoniques*). Generally there is more than one téléboutique even in a small town. The machines are sometimes old French coin phones, and international calls are no problem. For internal calls put in several 1dh coins and dial the region code (even if you are in the region), followed by the number (a zero plus eight figures). For overseas calls, put in at least three 5dh coins, dial 00 and wait for a musical sequence before proceeding. Most call boxes only accept the 'silver all over' coins, although this is changing. Calls can also be made at the ***PTT Centrale***, or the ***Cabines Téléphoniques*** where generally the number is given to the telephonist who dials it and then calls out a cabin number where the call is waiting. It is simpler but significantly more expensive to phone from a hotel.

Fax facilities are available from luxury hotels and the main PTT offices. Many téléboutiques also have fax machines.

If you going to be in Marrakech for a couple of weeks, it might be worth investing in a local chip for your phone. There are two main mobile phone service providers with the pay-as-you-go option: the Jawal service, run by Maroc-Télécom, and a similar service provided by competitor company Méditel. Both are agressively marketed and there are Méditel shops in all the major towns. Mobile calls can be expensive, however. Still, a local phone number does mean you can be reached in any city in the country – if that is what you want. The mobile (*le portable*) has certainly revolutionised a lot of young urban Moroccans' private lives.

Media

The press

Moroccan newspapers are produced in Arabic, French and Spanish. The main political parties all have their newspapers. From the mid-1990s, the general tone of the press became increasingly critical, with issues once taboo, such as corruption, the fate of political prisoners and illegal emigrants, being discussed. Of the daily newspapers, ***Le Matin du Sahara*** and ***Maroc Soir*** are the most pro-government, whilst ***L'Opinion***, ***Libération*** and ***Al Bayane*** are more independent. These newspapers are cheap and give an insight into Morocco and its politics. Coverage of overseas news is limited, but sheds interesting light on attitudes to major international issues. For the business visitor, the daily ***L'Economiste*** is essential reading for some insight into the general economic climate.

More interesting, and generally better written, are the weekly newspapers, which include ***Maroc-Hebdo***, and ***La Vie économique***. The best discussion of contemporary issues is provided by ***Le Journal***, which also provides major economic and business coverage. Morocco also has a number of magazines, including ***Le Temps du Maroc*** (official in tone) and ***Téléplus*** (some cultural events coverage). Aimed at a sophisticated urban audience, the glossy monthlies ***La Citadine*** and ***FDM*** (***Femmes du Maroc***), have articles on issues concerning Moroccan women (the Moudawana or Family Code, polygamy, etc), alongside the fashion features. ***Maisons du Maroc*** will give you an idea about what an upmarket Moroccan home looks like. ***Au Maroc*** is a new, luxuriously produced arts and urban living magazine, not as yet widely distributed. (Try the bookshop in *Riad Temsna* in Marrakech.)

Foreign newspapers are available in larger towns and cities. ***The Guardian*** and ***Herald Tribune*** (International editions) and ***Le Monde*** and ***Libération*** reach Rabat and Casablanca in the evening. They are available, along with other European titles, at town centre news kiosks.

Television & radio

Radio Télévision Marocaine, the *RTM*, is the state service, predominantly in Arabic and French. The news is given in Arabic, French and Spanish, with early afternoon summaries in the three main Berber languages. *RTM* broadcasts a mixture of Egyptian soaps, South American soaps dubbed into standard Arabic, old Egyptian films, US films dubbed in French, Moroccan théâtre de boulevard, and the usual sports events – with pride of place given to football, golf and showjumping. Ramadhan viewing is characterized by concerts of traditional music and the *Causeries hassaniennes*, sermons given by leading Islamic scholars in the presence of the monarch.

Morocco's second TV channel, ***2M***, started life as a pay station, mainly broadcasting North American and European feature films. Recently taken over by the State, it looks set to return to the private sector in the near future. *2M's* news broadcasts are generally more lively than those on the *RTM*. ***Canal Horizons***, a branch of the French pay channel *Canal Plus*, is expanding in Morocco, and is popular in cafés due to its sports coverage. Satellite television is increasingly popular, even in the poorest neighbourhoods: satellite dishes can be seen on the roofs of villas and bidonvilles.

The Tanger-based commercial radio station ***Médi 1*** gives news and music in Arabic and French. Northern areas can pick up broadcasts from Spain, Portugal, and Gibraltar.

Food and drink

Moroccan cuisine

The finest of the Moroccan arts is undoubtedly its cuisine. There are the basics: *harira* and *bessera* soups, kebabs, *couscous* and *tagine* – a sort of stew – and the famous pastilla, pigeon, egg and almonds in layers of filo pastry. And there are other dishes, less well known, gazelle's horns, coiling m'hencha and other fabulous pâtisseries. The Moroccans consider their traditional cooking to be on a par with Indian, Chinese and French cuisine – though the finest dishes are probably to be found in private homes. Today, however, upmarket restaurants, notably in Marrakech, give the visitor an idea of what fine Moroccan food can be. Moroccan cuisine is beginning to get the international respect it deserves, with new restaurants opening in European capitals. However, the spices and vegetables, meat and fish, fresh from the markets of Morocco, undoubtedly give the edge to cooks in old médina houses.

The climate and soils of Morocco mean that magnificent vegetables can be produced all year round, thanks to assiduous irrigation. Although there is industrial chicken production, in many smaller restaurants, the chicken you eat is as likely to have been reared by a small-holder. Beef and, of course, lamb come straight from the local farms.

In addition to the basic products, Moroccan cooking gets its characteristic flavours from a range of spices and minor ingredients. Saffron (*zaâfrane*), though expensive, is widely used, and no Moroccan kitchen is without its saffron-substitute, the famous yellow *colorant*. Turmeric (*kurkum*) is also much in evidence. Other widely used condiments include a mixed all spice, referred to as *ra's el hanout* ('head of the shop'), cumin (*kamoun*), black pepper, oregano and rosemary (*yazir*). Prominent greens in use include broad-leaved parsley (*ma'dnous*), coriander (*kuzbur*) and, in some variations of couscous, a sort of celery called *klefs*. Preserved lemons (modestly called *boussera*, 'navels', despite their breast-like shape) can be found in fish and chicken *tajines*. Bay leaves (*warqa Sidna Moussa*, 'the leaf of our lord Moses') are also commonly employed. Almonds, much used in patisserie, are used in *tajines* too, while powdered cinnamon (Arabic *karfa*, *cannelle* in French) provides the finishing touch for bastilla. In pâtisserie, orange-flower water and rose water (*ma ouarda*) are essential to achieve a refined taste.

Eating times vary widely in Morocco. Marrakech gets up early – and goes to bed early, too, so people tend to sit down to dine around about 2000. (Casa-Rabat have a more reasonable rhythm, while Tanger takes a Spanish line, rising late, taking a siesta, and eating late.) Small towns south of the Atlas tend to rise early, snooze the afternoons away, awaking for some intensive promenading once the sun has gone down. Across the country, the big meal of the week is Friday lunch, a time for people to gather in their families. The main meal of the day tends to be lunch, although this varies according to work and lifestyle. As anywhere, eating out in plush eateries is a popular upper-income occupation. Locals will tend to favour restaurants with French or southern European cuisine, while Moroccan 'palace' restaurants are patronized almost exclusively by tourists – with some notable exceptions.

Starters *Harira* is a basic Moroccan soup, ingredients vary but include chick peas, lentils, veg and a little meat. Often eaten accompanied with hard-boiled eggs. *Bissara* is a pea soup, a cheap and filling winter breakfast. *Briouat* are tiny envelopes of filo pastry, something akin to the Indian samosa, with a variety of savoury fillings. Also come with an almond filling for dessert.

Snacks Cheaper restaurants serve *kebabs* (aka brochettes), with tiny pieces of beef, lamb and fat. Also popular is *kefta*, minced-meat brochettes, served in sandwiches with chips, mustard and *harissa* (red-pepper spicey sauce). Tiny bowls of finely chopped tomato and onion are another popular accompaniment. On Jamaâ el Fna in Marrakech, strong stomachs may want to snack on the local **babouche** (snails).

Main dishes *Seksou* (couscous) is the great North African speciality. Granules of semolina are steamed over a pot filled with a rich meat and vegetable stew. Unlike Tunisian couscous, which tends to be flavoured with a tomato sauce, Moroccan couscous is pale yellow. In some families, couscous is the big Friday lunch, an approximate equivalent of old-fashioned English Sunday lunch.

Tagines are stews, the basic Moroccan dish. It is actually the term for the two-part terracotta dish (base and conical lid) in which meat or fish are cooked with a variety of vegetables, essentially, carrots, potato, onion and turnip. *Tajine* is everywhere in Morocco. Simmered in front of you on a brasero at a roadside café, is always good and safe to eat. Out trekking and in the South, it is the staple of life. For *tajines*, there are four main sauce preparations: *m'qalli*, a yellow sauce created using olive oil, ginger and saffron; *m'hammer*, a red sauce which includes butter, paprika (*felfla hlwa*) and cumin; *qudra*, another yellow sauce, slightly lighter than m'qalli, made using butter, onions, pepper and saffron, and finally *m'chermel*, a red made using ingredients from the other sauces. Variations on these base sauces are obtained using a range of ingredients, including parsley and coriander, garlic and lemon juice, *boussera* (preserved lemons), eggs, sugar, honey and cinnamon (*karfa*).

In the better restaurants, look out for *djaj bil-hamid* (chicken with preserved lemons and olives), sweet and sour *tajine barkouk* (lamb with plums), *djaj qudra* (chicken with almonds and caramelised onion) and *tajine maqfoul*. Another pleasant little dish is *tajine kefta*, basically fried minced-meat balls cooked with eggs and chopped parsley. In eateries next to food markets, delicacies such as *ra's embekhar* (steamed sheep's head) and *kourayn* (animal feet) are a popular feed.

A dish rarely prepared in restaurants is *djaj souiri*, aka *djaj mqeddem*, the only *plat gratiné* in Moroccan cuisine. Here, at the very last minute, a sauce of beaten eggs and chopped parsley is added to the chicken, already slow-cooked in olives, diced preserved lemon, olive oil, and various spices.

All over Morocco, lamb is much appreciated, and connaisseurs reckon they can tell what the sheep has been eating (rosemary, mountain pasture, straw, or mixed rubbish at the vast Mediouna tip near Casablanca). Lamb is cheaper in drought years when farmers have to reduce their flocks, expensive when the grazing is good, and is often best eaten at roadside restaurants where the lorry drivers pull in for a feed.

Desserts

A limited selection of desserts is served in Moroccan restaurants. In the palace restaurants, there will be a choice between *orange à la cannelle* (slices of orange with cinnamon) or some sort of marzipan pâtisserie like *cornes de gazelle* or *ghrayeb*, rather like round shortcake. *El jaouhar*, also onomatopoeically known as *tchak-tchouka*, is served as a pile of crunchy, fried filo pastry discs topped with a sweet custardy sauce with almonds. Also on offer you may find *m'hencha*, coils of almond paste wrapped in filo pastry, served crisp from the oven and sprinkled with icing sugar and cinnamon, and *bechkito*, little crackly biscuits.

Most large towns will have a couple of large pâtisseries, providing French pastries and the petits fours essential for proper entertaining. See *Pâtisserie Hilton*, rue de Yougoslavie, Marrakech. Here you will find *slilou* (aka *masfouf*), a richly flavoured nutty powder served in tiny saucers to accompany tea. You won't find *maâjoun*, the Moroccan equivalent of hash brownies, made to liven up dull guests at wedding parties. On the more disastrous effects of *maâjoun*, see the 1952 Paul Bowles' thriller, *Let it Come Down*.

In local *laiteries*, try a glass of yoghurt. Fresh fruit is excellent, and cheap, in season. Oranges (*limoun*) and mandarins (*tchina*) are particularly cheap, as are prickly pears, sold off barrows. In winter in the mountains, look out for kids selling tiny red arbutus berries (*sasnou*) carefully packaged in little wicker cones. Fresh hazelnuts are charmingly known as *tigerguist*.

Regional specialities

The speciality of Marrakech is *tanjia*, a tall ceramic pot in which lamb or kid is baked in butter, spices and olives for hours, normally in the embers of the fire at the local hammam. This is a dish made by men before they go to work or sometimes when they have something to celebrate. In each *houma* in Marrakech, there will be one or two guys in a gang of friends who are famed for their ability to knock up a good *tanjia*.

Bastilla is a sweet and sour dish, made from layers of fine filo pastry, pigeon, eggs and pounded almonds. A hint of saffron, cinnamon and icing sugar provide the finishing touch.

On the south central Atlantic coast, the argan tree, a survival of the tropical forest that once grew all over the region, produces an oil highly valued for salads and cooking. Better still is *amlou*, an argan version of Nutella, to be found in specialized shops in Essaouira. Try to visit an argan co-operative to see how the women go about extracting the oil from the argan nuts.

Dishes for Ramadhan

At sunset the fast is broken with a rich and savoury *harira* (see above), *beghrira* (little honeycombed pancakes served with melted butter and honey) and *shebbakia* (lace-work pastry basted in oil and covered in honey). Distinctive too are the sticky pastry whorls with sesame seeds on top.

Cafés and restaurants

Most Moroccan towns have cafés, some of which offer croissants, petit-pain and cake, occasionally soup and basic snacks. Restaurants basically divide into four types: snack eateries, in the médina and *ville nouvelle*, generally cheap and basic. Some are modelled on international themed fast-food restaurants. (Marrakech even has a drive-in McDonalds. *Astaghfir Allah!*, what is happening to the Moroccan gastronomic tradition?) Also handy are the laiteries selling yoghurt and fruit juices. They will make up sandwiches with triangular cheese portions, salad and *kacher* (processed meat).

Full-blown restaurants are generally found only in larger towns, and some are very good indeed – '*vaut le détour*' ('worth going out of your way for') as French guides say. There are long-established restaurants with interesting atmosphere, too (*Au Sanglier Qui Fume* in Ouirgane). And finally, in Marrakech you have the great palaces of Moroccan cuisine, restaurants set in old, often beautifully restored private homes. These can set you back 500dh or even more. Some of these restaurants allow you to eat à la carte (*El Fassia* in Marrakech), rather than giving you the full banquet menu (and late night indigestion).

Eating out cheaply If you're on a very tight budget, then there are plenty of food stalls and open-air restaurants in every village, town and city serving various types of soup, normally the standard broth (*harira*), snacks and grilled meat. The best place for the adventurous open-air eater is the Jemaâ el Fna square in Marrakech, which is full of stalls in the evening. Another good place is near the port in Essaouira, where fresh fish are grilled. Obviously there is a greater risk of food poisoning with this type of food, so it is better to go for dishes that are cooked as one waits, or that are on the boil. The open-air restaurants near the port in Essaouira are another good bet for a fish snack.

Vegetarian food Vegetarians will find that Moroccan food (unlike Indian cooking, for example) is not terribly interesting for them. They should be aware that 'vegetarian cuisine' in many cases means taking the meat off the top of the couscous or *tajine*. The concept is really quite alien to most Moroccans, as receiving someone well for dinner means serving them a *tajine* with good chunk of meat. There are some excellent salads, however. Be prepared to eat lots of Kiri cheese and omelettes.

Food markets Local food markets are lively and colourful. Each city will have a central market, generally dating back to the early years of this century, stuffed with high quality fresh produce. Good food markets include the Guéliz market in Marrakech, on Ave Mohammed V, on your left after the intersection with Rue de la Liberté as you head for the town centre. Just off the main drag in Essaouira is a pungent fish market (complete with small fish fry places). Visiting food markets like this gives you an idea about everyday life – and is the time to stock up for a picnic or a hike.

Drinks

Tea All over Morocco the main drink apart from water is mint tea (*thé à la menthe/attay*) a cheap, refreshing drink which is made with green tea, fresh mint and masses of white sugar. The latter two ingredients predominate in the taste. If you want a reduced sugar tea, ask for *attay msous* or *bila sukar/sans sucre*. In cafés, tea is served in mini-metal tea pots. In homes it is poured from high above the glass to generate a froth *(attay bi-rizatou*, 'tea with a turban') to use the local expression. Generally, tradition has it that you drink three glasses. To avoid burning your fingers, hold the glass with thumb under the base and index finger on rim. In some homes, various other herbs are added to make a more interesting brew, including *flayou* (peppermint), *louiza* (verbena) and even *sheeba* (absinthe). If you want a herb tea, ask for a *verveine* or *louiza*, which may be with either hot water or hot milk (*bil-halib*).

Coffee Coffee is commonly drunk black and strong (*kahwa kahla/un exprès*). For a weak, milky coffee, ask for *café au lait/kahwa halib*. A stronger milky coffee is *café cassé/kahwa mherza.*

Other soft drinks All the usual soft drinks are available in Morocco, as street advertising shows. If you want still mineral water (*eau plate*) ask for *Sidi Harazem* or *Sidi Ali*. The main brands of fizzy mineral water (*eau pétillante*), are Oulmès and Bonacqua, a new water produced by *Coca Cola*. You may want either *une grande bouteille* or *une petite bouteille*.

The better cafés and local laiteries (milk-product shops) do milkshakes, combinations of avocado, banana, apple and orange, made to measure. Ask for a *jus d'avocat* or a *jus de banane*, for example.

Wines & spirits

Despite its Islamic status, Morocco is fairly relaxed about alcohol. One hopes this situation won't change should the Islamists take some of the local councils in the coming municipal elections. In the top hotels, imported spirits are available, although at a price. The main locally made lager beers are ***Flag***, ***Flag Spécial***, ***Stork***, ***Castel*** and ***Heineken***. In the spring, look out for the extremely pleasant ***Bière de Mars***, made only in March with Fès spring water. (The best beer in Morocco?)

Morocco produces wine, the main growing areas being Guerrouane and Meknès. Reds tend to prevail. ***Celliers de Meknès*** (CdM) and ***Sincomar*** are the main producers. At the top of the scale (off-licence prices in brackets) are ***Médaillon*** (90dh) and ***Beau Vallon*** (CdM, 90dh, anything up to 185dh in a restaurant). A ***CdM Merlot*** will set you back 45dh. Another reliable red is ***Domaine de Sahari***, Aït Yazem; a pleasant claret, best drunk chilled in summer (30dh). The whites include ***Coquillages*** and ***Sémillant***, probably the best (40dh). At the very bottom of the scale is rough and ready ***Rabbi Jacob***, or, cheaper and still cheerful, ***Chaud Soleil***. The local fig fire-water is ***Mahia la Gazelle***.

If you want to buy alcohol outside a restaurant, every major town will have a few licensed sales points, eg in the main food market in Guéliz in Marrakech. Often they are very well stocked with local and imported wines. The ***Marjane*** hypermarket chain, now represented in all major cities, also has an off-licence section. ***Asouak Essalam,*** the main competitor, does not stock alcholol, however. In Ramadhan, alcohol is on sale to non-Muslim foreigners only and many of the off-licences shut down for the month. At *Marjane*, towards the end of Ramadhan, you may well be asked by locals to buy a few bottles for their end of fasting booze-up.

Shopping

Marrakech has all manner of things to buy: carpets, lamps, jewellery, slippers, pottery. The list is endless. (One jaded European resident was heard to remark that there is nothing to do in Marrakech but shop.) Indeed the Red City seems to produce craft items by the ton, and lots of goodies are brought in from other areas of the country. Prices are very reasonable compared with what you might be paying for the same thing in arts and crafts shops in a European capital. Also interesting are the markets which are held on a daily or weekly basis in large villages and towns in the countryside, as well as specialist markets in larger urban centres. Note that tourist towns like Marrakech and Ouarzazate have fixed-price shops, although some of these can be negotiated despite the label. Most of the historic towns have special government run craft centres, referred to as *ensembles artisanal*. (There is a good one on Ave Mohammed V, Marrakech, on your left as you approach the Koutoubia from the Guéliz direction.) Such craft centres can give you a good indication of the range of products available, although they tend to be a bit expensive. The best bargains, and the more authentic experiences, are to be had in the *souks*, the areas of traditional shops found in most historic cities.

Bargaining

Bargaining is expected in a lot of shops, and can prove a tedious business, on occasion ending with tantrums on the part of the seller, and a line of argument running something like "you don't want to buy from me because you're a racist" and ending with "you're not my friend any more because you didn't buy from me." You are on holiday, so you don't need this sort of stuff. To avoid hassle, don't express interest unless you are actually interested. Be polite – but not apologetic. Think – do you really need that blue and white ceramic bowl? that little wooden box? The answer is generally no. There are more interesting things to do than arguing over a 25dh price difference. If the item really pleases you, think whether you can afford it, and how much it would cost you back at home. Then go for a price which suits your pocket. Voices should on no account be raised. Remember, the salesman is on home ground, can shout louder, and unless you're the souk hound from hell, knows his clientele and profit margins very well. In any case, whether you buy or not, he's probably going to do well, as the goods are bought in cheaply thanks to the young workforce in some dank workshop elsewhere in the médina.

Different nationalities react in different ways to playing at bargaining. The Moroccans and the French know each other well, the Germans play it serious, the Italians can give any souk vendor as good as they get, and with plenty of humour to boot. Above all, bargaining for souvenirs is not a life-and-death business, and should not be treated as such.

Getting taken in Sometimes visitors do get badly taken in, however. One disappointing little story, heard in particular in Essaouira, tells how young Americans, a bit lost after several weeks travelling in Morocco, are befriended by a local student. A relaxed friendship develops over a few days. One afternoon, the little group goes off to visit an uncle, who is (a) in need of money, and (b) happens to have a few fairly attractive touristy gift items to sell. Young American obliges, and is too polite to negotiate much. (After all, these are friends.) Then a few days later, a bit further on around Morocco, aforesaid American realizes that he has been ripped-off severely, having paid well over the odds for gift items. Faith in spontaneous friendship is thus destroyed. So in all circumstances, when travelling in a country where many have very little, one must be develop a bit of a carapace to survive.

Commissions In Marrakech, tourist guides – and in particular the portly, official ones – tend to make a good living from commissions. An agency guide will be paid around 300dh for showing a group round Marrakech for half-a-day, around 700dh for a day trip up into the mountains. If offered the choice, they will always take the first option. Why? Because a large carpet shop will automatically pay 1,000dh to a guide for taking a group through, there will be commission paid to the guide on any sales, often of the order of 20% – which means the price you are paying for your carpet is automatically inflated. So if possible, go to a carpet shop unaccompanied – or with someone you like whom you don't mind getting commission. In Marrakech, a number of the palace restaurants also operate on a similar basis, paying commission to hotel reception staff making the reservation or to taxi drivers bringing clients.

What to buy ***Babouches*** *Babouches* is the tourist name for the traditional slippers referred to by Moroccans as *belgha*. These come in a range of shapes and qualities. You can get a cheap pair for as little as 80dh. A good solid pair of yellow men's *belgha* can set you back 120-160dh, fashionably embroidered pair of women's slippers, with this season's motif, can cost even more. Best places to buy: médinas of Marrakech (for leather *belgha*) and Essaouira (for rather fetching raffia-work slippers).

Basketwork Splendid baskets in a range of shapes and sizes in the médina of Marrakech, go through the entrance opposite the Résidence de la Place and wind your way round.

Clothing Obviously there are the usual souvenir t-shirts. However, if you have the right sort of physique, you may want to invest in an item of traditional clothing. A *jallabah* (for men), or a caftan of some kind can be handy for sloping off down to the pool. High quality traditional clothing is beautifully made by specialized tailors who can be seen at work in some of the médinas. Men wear hooded tunics over their work clothes on Fridays when they go to the mosque to pray. Regarding women's traditional dress, note that there are top caftan stylists, an annual caftan fashion show, and that there are regular changes of style. The caftan is still required dress for women at court receptions.

Carpets and weavings Buying a carpet could be the major expense of your holiday – and Moroccan carpets are very fine indeed. The wealthy will want to look into some of the specialized shops in the médina of Marrakech. Those with time will head off for for places like Chichaoua and Taroudant. When buying a carpet, it is worth inspecting the weave closely. Note that the age of the carpet is not linked to how faded it is. Also, vegetable dyes do not make a carpet necessarily older – sometimes chemical dyes were cheaper in the past than natural dyes. Good buys include saddle bags and decorative strips from tents, sold as *couloirs* (corridors) by carpet merchants. The *Maison Berbère* shop in Ouarzazate has a good name for carpets. If you have £120/US$170 dollars to spare, you should be able to get yourself a very nice flat weave rug or *klim*.

The very best Moroccan carpets resemble contemporary western art (Rothko?) in their abstraction and use of colour. See in particular older pieces from Boujaâd. From the Marrakech region, Haouz carpets from the Ouled Bou Sba, Chiadma and Rhemna tribes are often magnificent expanses of orange strewn with faintly mysterious signs. Making such pieces was clearly an immense opportunity for artistic expression for the women who made them in isolated rural settlements. But now the country girls are increasingly going to school, so things will no doubt change. Glaoua carpets have an interesting mix of pile and flat weave, while certain regions of the High Atlas produce creamy blankets with fluffy strips and lots of sequins.

Ceramics Safi and Fès ceramics are found all over the country. The artisans of Safi have adapted to modern sub-Ikea taste, producing lots of cheap and cheerful pots in bright colours. Ceramics are also produced at Oulja craft centre near Salé (Rabat the capital of Morocco's twin town). Fès ceramics include large bowls, inkwells and dishes. Go for the more authentic, rougher, blue and white or yellow, green and cream pottery. The big innovation of recent years is Fès ceramic pieces set in decorative metalwork. This is often a bit too elaborate. For the wholesalers, it means that Fès pottery is exportable in large quantities. Despite its chunky appearance, it is actually quite fragile.

Leatherwork Morocco has long had a reputation for leatherwork, and *maroquinerie* is French for high quality leather goods. Top European names manufacture here, creating a skilled labour-force. Look out for top of the range leather goods in Guéliz, Marrakech. You might even want a gilt embossed leather *dossier* to take home for your desk.

Metal items Here you should look out for the lanterns which are available in a variety of metals, from shiny brass to rustic (and slightly rusty) iron. For tin lanterns, try ***Place des Ferblantiers*** near the Badi Palace, Marrakech.

Painted wood Look out for mirror frames and small boxes painted with arabesques. Often very reasonably priced.

Thuya wood Beautiful items, including jewel boxes, trays and ornaments in a wonderful walnut-like wood from Essaouira and region. Wood smells of a mixture of cedar and pencil sharpenings. Sometimes inlaid with mother of pearl or yellow citrus wood marquetry. There is so much thuya work produced now, that it's a wonder that there are any thuya trees left.

The beauty of a bath

A ritual purification of the body is essential before Muslims can perform prayers, and in the days before bathrooms, the 'major ablutions' were generally done at the hammam (bath). Segregation of the sexes is of course the rule at the hammam. Some establishments are only open for women, others only for men, while others still have a shift system (mornings and evenings for the men, all afternoon for women). In the old days, the hammam, along with the local zaouia *or saint's shrine, was an important place for women to gather and socialize, and even pick out a potential wife for a son.*

Very often there are separate hammams for men and women next to each other on the ground floor of an apartment building. A passage leads into a large changing room-cum-post-bath area, equipped with masonry benches for lounging on and (sometimes) small wooden lockers. Here you undress under a towel. Hammam gear today is football or beach shorts for men and knickers for women. If you're going to have a massage /scrub down, you take a token at the cash desk where shampoo can also be bought.

Next step is to proceed to the hot room: five to 10 minutes with your feet in a bucket of hot water will have you sweating nicely and you can then move back to the raised area where the masseurs are at work. After the expert removal of large quantities of dead skin, you go into one of the small cabins or mathara *to finish washing. (Before doing this, catch the person bringing in dry towels so that they can bring yours to you when you're in the mathara.) For women, in addition to a scrub and a wash there may be the pleasures of epilation with* sokar, *an interesting mix of caramelized sugar and lemon. Men can undergo a* taksira, *which, although it involves much pulling and stretching of the limbs, ultimately leaves you feeling pretty good. And remember, allow plenty of time to cool down, reclining in the changing area.*

Wrought iron work Candle holders in various trendy and original shapes. Larger items a little difficult to carry home, but worth the trouble.

Entertainment and nightlife

As society is in many ways still highly gender-segregated, Western style nightlife is not really a major feature of life in Morocco. People tend to be very family orientated, which means that engagement parties and weddings, generally held in summer, are the big social events of the year. Also important for socialising is the month of Ramadhan. The BIG occasion is ***Aïd el Kebir***, the 'Festival of the Sheep', which comes round once a year, two months after the end of Ramadhan. Extended families gather in their home towns or villages to sacrifice a sheep of some description, or a calf, in commemoration of how Allah sent down a lamb to Ibrahim so he wouldn't have to sacrifice his son.

Despite all this family-centred activity, at least in Marrakech you will find a little 'nightlife' to amuse yourself for a short stay.

Cinemas & theatre

In Marrakech, ***La Colisée*** in Guéliz does the usual over-advertised Hollywood block-busters, dubbed into French. The ***Rif*** in Daoudiate, a venue for the Marrakech Film Festival, occasionally shows the odd interesting film. There are quite a few small cinemas in the médina, notably the ***Mabrouka*** on Rue Bab Agnaou and the ***Eden*** on Riad Zitoun Jedid. Most of these smaller picture palaces show Hindi and karate films, generally sub-titled in Arabic and French. Film buffs in the country for any length of time will want to look out for special film events at the ***Institut Français de Marrakech***, Route de Targa, just a 10 minute walk from central Guéliz. The ***IF*** programmes theatre and, more rarely, contemporary dance. Moroccan films, with a few exceptions, tend to have very short runs. Consult the local press. Outside Marrakech, Safi has a small picture house at the ***Hotel Atlantide***. Basically, you go to southern Moroccoto take your own video footage, not for multi-screen lifestyle cinema experiences.

Nightlife

Marrakech has a small range of bars and nightclubs ranging from the plush to the rough. The average nightclub (if there is such a thing), will have a socially mixed clientele. There will be students and ordinary funsters, businessmen out for a night, even sex-workers of various kinds. Do not be surprised if the stylish person you meet expects a financial contribution. On the music front, there will be western club music, depending on the DJ's contacts. Main floor-fillers will be Egyptian pop, *raï*, and even some Latino. Not too surprisingly, Moroccans have a liking for reggae.

Clubs in Marrakech *New Feeling* (posh, out at the *Palmeraie Golf Palace*, Casablanca *jeunesse dorée* lets its hair down here at the weekend), ***Paradise*** (at the *Hotel Mansour Eddahbi*, a bit stuffy, said to have the best dance-floor), ***Le Diamant Noir*** (not too rough; interesting basement club with lots of opportunities for gazing down on the dance-floor; a good night out if you're not too choosy); ***Star House*** (more dodgy, if we're honest, near the fountain roundabout on Ave Mohammed V), ***Shahrazade*** (often closed due to various scandals). Not really for dancing, but definitely fine for drinks and food at the start of a long night out is ***Le Comptoir*** in the Hivernage district, very stylish and almost opposite the Hotel Impérial Borj. Outside Marrakech, the upmarket Ouarzazate hotels have small nightclubs. In Essaouira, the new *Sofitel* on the ocean front has a nice bar.

Holidays and festivals

Religious holidays

Religious holidays are scheduled according to the Hijna calendar, a lunar based calendar. Given the clear night skies of Arabia, it is easily comprehensible that the Muslims should have adopted a year based upon the cycles of the moon. The lunar year is shorter than the solar year, so the Muslim year moves forward by 11 days every Christian year. Thus in 10 years' time, Ramadhan, currently in the winter, will be at the height of summer. The start of Ramadhan can vary by a day, depending on the *ru'ya*, whether the crescent moon has been observed or not.

The main religious holidays are as follows:
1 Muharram First day of the Muslim year
Mouloud Celebration of the Prophet Mohammed's birthday
Ramadhan A month of fasting and sexual abstinence during daylight hours
Aïd els Seghir (the Lesser Aïd) Two-day holiday ending the month of Ramadhan
Aïd el Kebir (the Great Aïd) One-day holiday which comes 70 days after Aïd es Seghir. Commemorates how God rewarded Ibrahim's faith by sending down a lamb for him to sacrifice instead of his son. When possible, every family sacrifices a sheep on this occasion.

During ***Ramadhan***, the whole country switches to a different rhythm. Public offices go on to half-time, and the general pace slows down during the daytime. No Moroccan would be caught eating in public during the day, and the vast majority of cafés and restaurants, except those frequented by resident Europeans and tourists, are closed. The cities are lively at night however, with shops opening, especially in the second half of the month. Ramadhan is an interesting time to visit Morocco as a tourist, but probably to be avoided if possible if you need to do business.

Public holidays

New Year's Day 1 January.
Fête du Trône 3 March: Commemorates the present king's accession.
Fête du Travail 1 May: Labour Day.
Fête de la Jeunesse 9 July.
Anniversaire de la Révolution 20 August.
Marche Verte/El Massira el Khadhra 6 November: Commemorates a march by Moroccan civilians to retake the Spanish-held Saharan territories of Rio de Oro and Saguiet El Hamra.
Independence Day 18 November: Commemorates independence and Mohammed V's return from exile.

Festivals

Morocco also has a number of regional and local festivals, often focusing around a local saint or harvest time of a particular product, and are fairly recent in origin. The *moussems* or traditional local festivals have on occasion been banned in local years, the authorities giving as a reason the health risks created by gatherings of large numbers of people in places with only rudimentary sanitary facilities. The decision has been regretted, however, as the *moussems* are such an important part of Moroccan rural life. The main Moroccan festivals come in two categories: firstly, the more religious festivals, the timing of which relates to the lunar Islamic year, and secondly the annual festivals with relatively fixed dates.

Movable religious holidays, 2002

Dates for the main religious holidays in 2002(AH or Anno Hegirae 1422 to 1423) are as follows, give or take a few days:
Ras el 'Am or New Year 1423 15 March
Mouloud (Prophet Mohammed's birthday) 25 May
Beginning of Ramadhan 6 November
End of Ramadhan 6 December
Aïd el Kebir 23 February 2003

Fixed -date festivals

April *Honey festival* Immouzer des Ida Outanane, between Essaouira and Agadir;
May *Rose festival* El Kelaâ des Mgouna, Dadès Valley;
June *Symphonies du Désert* Ouarzazate; *Festival of Folk Art and Music* Marrakech;
August *Moussem of Setti Fatma* Setti Fatma, Ourika. Large crowds from the Red City gather at the top of the cool Ourika Valley to escape the heat of the plain;
September *Marriage Festival* Imilchil in the last week of September/first week of October. A much photographed festival which has not always been held in recent years, for the reasons indicated above regarding *moussems* (seasonal festivals) in general. The festival does not actually take place in Imilchil itself, but at a location not far from that village, clearly signposted off the main Rich to Imilchil road.
October *Festival du cinéma de Marrakech* First held in early October 2001, in the rather unfavourable context of the Anglo-American bombing of Afghanistan. Nevertheless, attracted a good showing of African and European directors and their films, looks set to continue.

Sports

Morocco's resort hotels will have swimming pools and tennis courts. The Atlantic coast resort of Agadir has all the usual things to do on the beach, camel and horse rides, and beach buggies too. Elsewhere on the Atlantic coast – and especially at Essaouira - you will meet members of the **surfing** and **windsurfing** fraternity. Morocco is also known as a **golf** destination, and this, along with **mountain trekking**, is an area of tourism which is expanding rapidly. **Horse riding** is quite popular too. Moroccans themselves are keen on football and proud of their country's success in middle and long distance running, and **Marrakech** regularly hosts cross-country events. Down in the desert, the annual Marathon des Sables, a gruelling cross-desert trek in which contestants must carry all their own food, grabs plenty of media-space.

Ballooning

There is a small Marrakech-based company, ***Ciel d'Afrique***, T044-303135, F044-303136, www.aumaroc.com/cieldafrique, which can organize hot-air balloon flights most anywhere in the country – at a price. The basic excursion involves leaving Marrakech very early for a flight over the Jebilet, the hills north of Marrakech. Four-wheel drive vehicle necessary to get to take-off point.

Camel trekking

This activity saw a real growth in popularity in the 1990s with beasts being brought up from Mali to satisfy the growing demand. In the area covered by the present guide, treks through magnificent scenery along the Atlantic coast around **Essaouira** are the main option. For completeness sake, information is provided here on camel trekking in the desert, **Merzouga** (the Erg Chebbi) and **Zagora** being the two main camel trek bases. Apart from the quick camel ride into the dunes (especially popular at Merzouga) there are two options: the *méharée* and the *randonnée chamelière*. The **méharée** actually involves you riding the camel, the **randonnée chamelière** (camel hike) means you walk alongside the camels, used essentially as pack animals. Obviously, in the former option, you can cover a lot more territory. You will ride for about 4 to 5 hours a day, the only difficulty is getting used to the movement of the camel. Average daily cost is about 300dh per person. A good organizer will lay on everything apart from sleeping-bags, although blankets are generally available. Best times of year for the south are Oct to Apr. (NB sandstorms a possibility between Nov and Feb.) A good 6-night camel hike out of Zagora would enable you to see a mix of dunes and plains, palm groves and villages, taking you from Zagora down to the dunes of Chigaga, with an average of 5 hrs walking a day (4 hrs in morning, 1 hr afternoon). For more on camel trekking in the south, contact the ***Hotel Zagour***, BP 17, 45900 Zagora, T044-847451, F044-846178. In the Essaouira area, try the ***Auberge de la Plage – Club Equestre***, T044-476600, F044-473383, aubplage@iam.net.ma.

Flying

Moroccan Federation of Light Aviation and Aerial Sports can be contacted at Complex Sportif Prince Moulay Abdellah, Rabat, T037-708347, F037-706958. There are Royal Aero Clubs at Marrakech, T044-447764 and Beni Mellal, T023-482095.

Gliding (vol à voile)

This is possible at the *Centre Royal de Vol à Voile* at Beni Mellal, T023-482095. The club is essentially run for *Royal Air Maroc* staff, but outsiders have been let in.

Golf

Introduced at the beginning of the 20th century, golf was the late King Hassan II's favourite sport. Major competitions such as the Trophée Hassan II attract international attention and much RTM television coverage. There are currently 15 courses designed by masters of the art and plans for more. All have superb facilities and settings are as varied as the courses themselves. The High Atlas forms a backdrop to the courses at Marrakech, and more are planned. All courses are open to the public though evidence of handicap is required.

Check locally for regulations, green fees and opening hours. The Royal Moroccan Golf Federation is at the *Royal Dar es-Salam Golf Course* in Rabat, T037-755960, F037-751026. Note that from the UK, *Best of Morocco* (T0044-1380-828533) produces a specialized golf holiday brochure.

The Marrakech Royal Golf Club, BP 634, Ancienne Route de Ouarzazate, T044-444341, F044-430084. 18 holes, 6,200 m, par 72. A beautiful course with lots of

Sporting Heroes

Morocco is proud of its reputation as a sporting nation. Athletics and football are its strengths, as the following dates and records indicate.

***1970**. Morocco is the first country to represent the African continent at the Mexico World Cup.*

***1984**. 8 August. Nawal el Moutawakil wins a gold medal in the women's 400m hurdles at the Los Angeles Olympics.*

***1992**. Saïd Aouita, Olympic 5,000m champion, takes the world indoor 3,000m title.*

***1995**. March. Hichem el Guerrouj wins the 1,500m at the World Athletic Championships in Barcelona.*

***1996**. August. Salah Hissou breaks the 10,000m world record in Brussels.*

***1999**. Morocco participates in the World Cup held in France.*

***2000**. Abdelkader Mouaziz, seventh in the marathon at the Sidney Olympics, wins the New York Marathon. Moroccan fails in its bid to be the first African country to host the 1996 Mundial.*

shade trees, it was built in the 1920s by the Pasha of Marrakech. One of the longest established clubs in the country, it has been frequently renovated and improved.

The Palmeraie Golf Club, Marrakech, Les Jardins de la Palmeraie, PB 1488, T044301010, F044302020. 18 holes, 6,214 m, par 72. Opened 1993, designed by Robert Trent Jones Snr, this course has thousands of palm trees, seven lakes, and Mauresque-style club house.

Golf d'Amelkis, Marrakech, the newest of the Red City's courses, said to be one of the most striking in Morocco, 6,657m, par 72, designed by C.B. Robinson, set with palm groves and water traps. Located close to the Amanjena Resort.

The Ouarzazate Royal Golf Club, T044-882653, F044-883344, nine holes, 3,150 m, par 36 is located east of Ouarzazate to the south of the P32 Boumalne du Dadès road near waters of the Barrage Mansour Eddahbi. Low rainfall of late means that the course is barely maintained. The nearby villa development, once on the shores of the lake, is now quite a way from the water.

Hunting & fishing Morocco has long been a destination for French and Italian hunters. In the Marrakech region, there are wild boar in the countryside around Asni and Amizmiz, partridge and quail in the Ourika valley. All foreigners wishing to hunt in Morocco must produce a valid hunting permit and permit to carry firearms from country of origin, and three photographs. A permit to hunt will be given which lasts 30 days and cannot be extended. It is compulsory to take out an insurance by a Moroccan company for this visit.

Keen fishers may find trout in the fast flowing but remote rivers of the High Atlas of Azilal. Licences for freshwater fishing can be obtained from the Ministry of Water and Forests, 11 Rue du Devoir, Rabat (also offices in most large towns) on a daily or annual basis for fishing in the rivers. A special licence must be obtained for fishing in the reservoirs and other artificial lakes. Fishing is not permitted anywhere between sunset and sunrise. Information regarding restrictions such as closed seasons, catch limits, sale of catch and forbidden areas will be provided with the permit. In recent years, drought has had an effect on fish populations in both storage barrages and natural lakes, including notably the Barrage Lalla Takerkoust, Marrakech, the Barrage Ben el Ouidane near Beni Mellal and the great reservoir east of Ouarzazate

Quad-biking This is another of the expensive sports currently taking off in Morocco as tourism expands. Roar around on chunky-tyred quad-bikes especially designed to destroy the peace of the palm groves. Available in Marrakech and Ouarzazate. Try the ***Hotel Palma-Riva***, T044-305854, T061-153250 in Marrakech and in Ouarzazate. ***Kart Aventure***

Ave Moulay Rachid, between the hotels *Berbère Palace* and *Kenzi Belère*, T044-886374, F044-886216, half-day rental around 1,200dh, full day 1,700dh.

Riding

The horse is the object of a veritable cult in Morocco. Fantasias, spectacular ceremonies where large numbers of traditionally dressed horsemen charge down a parade ground to discharge their muskets a few metres away from tentsful of banqueting guests are an occasion to see Moroccan riding skills. The late King, Hassan II, assembled one of the world's finest collections of rare black thoroughbred Arabian horses. Many towns have riding clubs, the television covers national show-jumping events, and the wealthy are keen to have their offspring learn to ride.

In Marrakech and region, the following can provide riding: ***La Roseraie*** at Ouirgane, on the Taroudant road, T044-439128, F044-439130, roseraie@cybernet.net.ma, the well managed stables at ***Palmeraie Golf Palace***, Marrakech, also ***Club Boulahrir***, km 8, route de Meknès, T044-329451, F044-329454. South of Essaouira, at Sidi Kaouki, try the ***Auberge de la Plage – club équestre***, T044-476600, F044-473383, aubplage@iam.net.ma (also do camel treks). Based in Ouarzazate, ***North Africa Horse***, contact Joël Proust, T/F044-449464, T044-886689, F044-886690, can set up 6-day treks.

Skiing

The Marrakech region has one ski resort often mentioned in the tourist literature: **Oukaïmeden**, an hour's drive up in the High Atlas south of the Red City. The up-and-coming winter sports would seem to be ski-climbing and ski-trekking. In all honesty, however, irregular and decreasing snowfall over the last decade or so has got the better of Morocco's reputation as a ski destination. Whereas 25 years ago, the ski season in Oukaïmeden lasted several months, today falls of snow rarely exceed 20 cm and tend to melt very quickly in the bright sun, only to refreeze leaving a brittle surface. Essentially, one cannot count on good snow for an Alpine-style skiing holiday. Skiers in Morocco tend to be locals who, as soon as snow is announced on the news, rush down from Casa-Rabat for a weekend at one of the resorts. Hopefully, climatic change has not put paid to what could be a major supplementary attraction.

Further details of skiing might be available from the Royal Moroccan Federation of Skiing and Mountaineering, Parc de la Ligue Arabe, BP 15899, Casablanca, T022-203798, F022-474979. Another source of information might be Mountain Information Centre of the Ministry of Tourism, 1 Rue Oujda, Rabat, T073-701280. The best book is Claude Cominelli's 1984 *Ski dans le Haut Atlas de Marrakech* (Andorra: Cominelli ed), available from the *Librairie Chatr* on Ave Mohammed V in Marrakech.

For the record, Oukaïmeden (alt. 2,600m) in the High Atlas, 74 km south from Marrakech is Morocco's premier ski resort. There is a good range of accommodation from 3-star hotel to mountain lodges, and numerous chalets owned by wealthy locals. The *Hotel Kenzi Louka* (T044-319080/86, F044-319088) and the refuge managed by the *Club Alpin Français* (T044-319036, F044-319020) should be able to advise on skiing conditions. The summit above the plateau is Jebel Oukaïmeden (3,270m). There is a télésiège, and pistes ranging from black to green. The ski station infrastructure is managed by the ONEP, the Moroccan national water board, and is to undergo a major refit in the near future.

Skiing in the **High Atlas of Azilal** remains the preserve of the hardy and initiated for the moment. An enterprising soul has yet to open ski hire in the Aït Bougmez. Older mountain guides to this region suggest wilderness ski-touring possibilities. The **Jebel Azourki** (3,050 m), between Tabant and Zaouiat Ahansal is held by many to be one the best mountains for off-piste skiing. The track to the bottom of this mountain, running south from Aït Mhamed (the old main track for Tabant, before the road was opened on the Oued Lakhdar / Agouti route coming in from the west), is not easy in winter. Ski trekkers could also use the Aït Bougmez as a base for short excursions to nearby mountains. More difficult of access in winter conditions, the **Irghil Mgoun** also provides ski trek opportunities. Basically, these are late season options, as with heavy snow you could be cut off in an isolated village for quite some time. The problem with late season skiing is that the snow surface can be 'corrugated' by wind erosion and melting. In recent years, as in the Toubkal High Atlas, snow cover has declined according to some locals with long memories. Take local advice or go through an agency if you want to ski-trek this region. You will almost certainly have to bring all your equipment with you. There is simple *gîte*-type accommodation in Tabant.

Further east, in the **High Atlas of Imilchil**, the Jebel Ayyachi (3,747m) has some good ski descents. Here again, this is terrain for the committed wilderness-ski fraternity. The Auberge Timnay, T055-583434, F055-360188, timnay@iam.net.ma, at Aït Ayach near Midelt may be able to provide information.

Swimming

Large towns have municipal pools but these can be crowded and grubby at the end of the summer season. They also tend to be all-male affairs. Marrakech has a small public pool near the Koutoubia, plus larger pools in the Daoudiate and Sidi Youssef Ben Ali neighbourhoods.

In the summer the pools of the luxury hotels are very tempting, and non-residents can on occasion use these pools for a fee. (The best pool in Marrakech is said to be at the Club Sangho.) Note that very few hotels have heated pools (check on this when you book a winter break) and what actually constitutes the definition of 'heated' can vary. Beware of strong currents on the Atlantic beaches. On many of them, bathing is prohibited outside the summer season when a coastguard is present.

Surfing & wave sports

Surfing and windsurfing are popular in Morocco with both locals and visitors. Foreign surfers first arrived in the 1960s, and the sport caught on in a small way. Today, the weekends see lots of enthusiasts out surfing. On chill, bright winter afternoons, even the rather polluted waters of the Bouregreg Estuary up in capital city Rabat have their share of keen amateurs. In 2000, Dar Bouazza south of Casablanca hosted a stage of the European Bodyboard Tour. Fly surf has arrived, too. Essaouira, 'Wind City, Afrika', is the capital, but there are surf spots all along the Atlantic coastline. North of Rabat, surfing is possible at Moulay Bouselham, Mehdia Plage (famed for its powerful waves, not for beginners) and Plage des Nations. Between Rabat and Casablanca, Rabat Estuary, Oued Cherrat and Bouznika Plage are all popular. Things get more serious south of Casablanca in the El Jadida area, Dar Bouazza (difficult, lots of sea-urchins) and Jack Beach (used for competitions) being popular. South of El Jadida, Oualidia is ideal for beginners. Essaouira has surfing and windsurfing facilities. The surfers are around in the winter months, while from April to October the alizé winds bring the windsurfers in. A few kilometres south, Sidi Kaouki is popular with windsurfers due to persistently strong winds. Still further south, Taghzaoute, north of Agadir is popular with the winter surf set. Mirhleft and Sidi Ifni are popular destinations, too.

For further information on surfing, try the following: ***Océan Vagabond***, Blvd Mohammed V, Essaouira, right on the bay, T061-728340 (Bruno), T061-883013 (Catherine), bruno_erbani@yahoo.fr, oceanvagabond@hotmail.com. Have good, recent equipment for rent and provide tuition. Also see the *UCPA*, also nearby on the bay, although they may have to move soon, T044-472972, F044-473417. South of Essaouira, at Imessouane, try the ***Auberge Kahina***, T048-826032 (unreliable line), where Valérie and Hichem will do their best to provide wave-sport information and accommodation.

Tennis

Morocco has an international tournament in Agadir. The big cities have tennis clubs and all the larger hotels will have a few courts. The country also now has a handful of male tennis stars playing to international standards.

Trekking

See each individual chapter for details of all these trekking areas

There are considerable opportunities for hiking in Morocco. The most popular area is the Toubkal National Park in the High Atlas. However, as roads improve and inveterate trekkers return for further holidays, new areas are becoming popular. Starting in the west, to the south of the High Atlas, the **Jebel Siroua**, east of Taroudant, is a plateau with pleasant spring walking. The **Toubkal High Atlas** is best from late April to October, with various loops up into the mountains, staying in Amazigh villages possible. You will probably want to climb North Africa's highest peak, Jebel Toubkal, altitude 4,167m. The only problem is that the mountain has become almost too popular. South of Azilal, the beautiful **Vallée des Aït Bougmez** is becoming popular. For weekend trekkers, there are gentle walks along the flat valley bottom. The Aït Bougmez also makes a good departure point for tougher treks, including the **north-south crossing of the west-central High Atlas** to Bou Thraghar, near Boumalne and El Kelaâ des Mgoun. On this route, you have the chance to climb the region's second highest peak, Irghil M'goun, 4,071m. Still in the west-central High Atlas, there is a tough 4- or 5-day circuit to taking in the **Canyons of Joro, Ouandras and Arous**. Further east, there is magnificent trekking into the high pastures around **Zaouiat Ahansal**. Even less visited is the east-central High Atlas where Midelt and Imilchil are the main trek bases. From Midelt, you can access the **Cirque de Jafar** and the **Jebel Ayachi**. Imilchil is famous for its kasbah and glacier lakes, also the *moussem* des fiancés, the 'wedding festival' which generally takes place every year in late summer. There is a fine trek to be made from **Imilchil** via **Anergui** to **Zaouiat Ahansal**, too.

Really hardened trekkers will want to take on the challenge of a Grande traversée du Haut Atlas, say east to west from the **Aït Bougmez to Toubkal**, or a looping route west to east from **Demnate to Tilouguite**, a 20-day walk in the west-central part of the High Atlas taking in Jebel Ghat, Megdaz, the villages of the Assif Tessaout, the north side of the Mgoun and then via the Aït Bougmez and the canyons of Ahansal to the cathedral rocks of Tilouguite and then on up the gorges of the Assif Melloul to the village of **Anergui**. From here the course of the Melloul can be followed east-north-east on to **Imilchil**.

Though not covered by the present guide, the **Middle Atlas**, much less well known to walkers, merits a few words. Certain parts are quite a Hobbit-land, especially between Azrou and the source of the Oum er Rabi river, where there is beautiful walking in the **cedar forests**. Despite its proximity to the rich farmlands of Meknès and the Saïs Plain, this is an extremely poor region which would benefit from increased ecologically friendly tourism.

For **walking** in Morocco, you can either book through a specialized trekking operator in your home country or hope to find a guide available when you arrive. In popular trekking areas such as Toubkal, guides are available in trailhead settlements. Not all will have trained at the CFAMM, the mountain guide training school in Tabant, Aït Bougmez. For walking the best period is April to October, but in the high summer keep to the high valleys which are cooler and where water can be obtained. Note too that the views are not as good in the High Atlas at the height of summer because of the haze. Tents or bivouacking is fine in summer but indoor accommodation is necessary in autumn in refuges, shepherds' huts or locals' homes. The use of mules/donkeys to carry the heavy packs is common. Specialist maps and guides are useful and can be obtained via the ***Hotel Ali*** in Marrakech. Note that classified guest rooms in rural areas now have the GTAM (Grande traversée des Atlas Marocains) label of approval. The ***Club Alpin Français*** has five refuges with dormitory type accomodation in the High Atlas, reservations necessary on T022-270090 F022-297292. Places where trekking guides can be arranged include the *Hotel Ali* (T044-444979) in Marrakech (High Atlas), at the *Auberge Tinmay* (T/F055-583434) near Midelt (Middle Atlas and Djebel Ayyachi), and the Auberge Souktana, (T048-534075), Taliouine, near Taroudant (Jebel Siroua).

If you are setting up a trek yourself, note that a good mule can carry up to 100kg, i.e., the rucksacks of three trekkers. A mule with muleteer comes at around 120dh/day, a good guide should be paid 250dh/day, a cook around 150dh. When buying food for the trek with your guide, you will have to buy enough for the muleteers, too. Generally, trekkers will consume about 100dh-worth of food and soft drinks a day. If you do not do a loop, you will generally have to pay for the 'mule-days' it takes to get the pack animals back to their home village.

Trekkers soon discover the beauties of the Atlas – and the secrets of ensuring that the walking is as comfortable as possible, ways of dealing with dehydration and fatigue. As on any hill trek, a steady, regular pace should be maintained. At higher levels, ensure you pause if a dizzy feeling sets in. A good trip leader will ensure you make an early start, to enjoy walking in the cool morning. Vehicle pistes look alluring to walk on but are in fact hard on the feet. Keep to the softer edges or go for footpaths when possible. Gorges are not the easiest places to walk in, so your local guide should know of the higher routes, if there is one which is safe. Pay particular attention if your route involves some scree running. You don't want to leave the mountains on a mule because of a sprained ankle. If you are not used to walking at altitude, try to avoid high routes in the early stages of your trip. In villages which see a lot of tourists, the kids will be on the look out, ever ready to scrounge a dirham or a bonbon. They can, however, be useful in showing you the way through to the footpath on the other side of the settlement. Always be nice to them (but make sure your rucksack pockets are well zipped up if you pause). And after all, they never have holidays at the seaside. A smile and a wave never hurt.

Avoid giardia: always put your steritabs in your water bottle when you fill up from a stream

There are few books on trek routes in English. For the central High Atlas, there is a seriously detailed work, André Fougerolles' 1982 *Le Haut Atlas central, guide alpin* (Casablanca: CAF). Walking and scrambling tours in the Mgoun are described with small maps in the handy 94 page *Randonnées pedestres dans le Massif du Mgoun* (Casablanca: Belvisi, 1989). Both books are generally available at the Librairie Chatr, Ave Mohammed V, Marrakech.

Spectator sports

The major cities have arenas with basketball, handball, athletics and football all popular. Check the local press for details. The main sports stadium in Marrakech is Jnène el Harti, near the Hivernage. Football (*koura*) is seriously popular, with kick-arounds in the most remote locations, and an excellent standard of play on beaches and on town pitches. If you're watching a beach football game, and are a bit of a player, you may well be asked to join in.

Health

Staying healthy in Morocco is straightforward. With the following advice and precautions you should keep as healthy as you do at home. Most visitors return home having experienced no problems at all beyond an upset stomach. However, in Morocco the health risks are different from those encountered in Europe or the USA. It also depends on how you travel and where. Often, you will have to make your own judgement on the healthiness or otherwise of your surroundings.

Medical facilities

There are French, or English, speaking doctors in the major cities who have particular experience in dealing with locally occurring diseases. Any pharmacy or large hotel will be able to give you the name of a good *médecin généraliste* (GP). Major cities also have a private SOS Médecins service on night duty (will generally do hotel visits, cost between 300dh and 500dh). The SAMU is the emergency service. If you do fall ill and cannot find a recommended doctor, try the outpatient department of a hospital. In practice, this means getting a pharmacy, hotel or a taxi driver to take you to the best local clinique privée (small private hospital), which offers an acceptable standard of care to Europeans. They can, however, be expensive, and on occasion try to provide more health care than is strictly necessary. The likelihood of finding good medical care diminishes very rapidly as you move away from the big cities. Generally, however, there will be a dispensary or *infirmière* (district nurse) able to provide very basic care. Especially in the rural areas there are systems and traditions of medicine wholly different from the western model and you may be confronted with less orthodox forms of treatment such as herbal medicines, not that these are unfamiliar to most western travellers.

Before travelling

Take out medical insurance. Make sure it covers all eventualities especially evacuation to your home country by a medically equipped plane, if necessary. You should have a dental check up, obtain a spare glasses prescription, a spare oral contraceptive prescription (or enough pills to last) and, if you suffer from a chronic illness (such as diabetes, high blood pressure, ear or sinus troubles, cardio-pulmonary disease or nervous disorder) arrange for a check up with your doctor, who can at the same time provide you with a letter explaining the details of your disability in English and French. Check the current practice in countries you are visiting for malaria prophylaxis (prevention). If you are on regular medication, make sure you have enough to cover the period of your travel.

Medicines

There is very little control on the sale of drugs and medicines in Morocco. You may be able to buy any and every drug in pharmacies without a prescription. Be wary of this because pharmacists can be poorly trained and might sell you drugs that are unsuitable, dangerous or old. Many drugs and medicines are manufactured under licence from American or European companies, so the trade names may be familiar to you. This means you do not have to carry a whole chest of medicines with you, but remember that the shelf life of some items, especially vaccines and antibiotics, is markedly reduced in hot conditions. Buy your supplies at the better outlets where there are more refrigerators, even though they are more expensive, and check the expiry date of all preparations you buy. Immigration officials occasionally confiscate scheduled drugs (Lomotil is an example) if they are not accompanied by a doctor's prescription.

Children

More preparation is probably necessary for babies and children than for an adult and perhaps a little more care should be taken when travelling to remote areas where health services are primitive. This is because children can become more rapidly ill than adults (on the other hand they often recover more quickly). Diarrhoea and vomiting are the most common problems, so take the usual precautions, but more intensively. Breastfeeding is best and most convenient for babies, but powdered milk is available in the cities, as are a few baby foods. Bananas and other fruits are all nutritious and can be cleanly prepared. The treatment of diarrhoea is the same as for adults, except that it should start earlier and be continued with more persistence. Children get dehydrated very quickly in hot countries and can become drowsy and unco-operative unless cajoled to drink water or juice plus salts. Upper respiratory infections, such as colds, catarrh and middle ear infections are also common and if your child suffers from these normally take some antibiotics against the possibility. Outer ear infections after swimming are also common and antibiotic eardrops will help. Wet wipes are always useful and can be found in the major cities as can disposable nappies.

Medical supplies

You may like to take some of the following items with you from home: sunglasses; earplugs; high protection factor suntan cream; insect repellent – containing DET for preference; mosquito net – lightweight, permethrin-impregnated for choice; travel sickness tablets; tampons – can be expensive in some countries in North Africa; condoms; water-sterilizing tablets; antimalarial tablets; anti-infective ointment eg Cetrimide; dusting powder for feet etc – containing fungicide; antacid tablets – for indigestion; sachets of rehydration salts plus anti-diarrhoea preparations; painkillers; antibiotics – for diarrhoea etc; first aid kit – small pack containing a few sterile syringes and needles and disposable gloves. The risk of catching hepatitis etc from a dirty needle used for injection is very low in Morocco, but some may be reassured by carrying their own supplies – available from camping shops and airport shops.

Vaccination & immunization

Smallpox vaccination is no longer required anywhere in the world and cholera vaccination is no longer recognized as necessary for international travel by the World Health Organisation – it is not very effective either. A yellow fever vaccination is not required either although you may be asked for a certificate if you have been in a country affected by yellow fever immediately before travelling to North Africa.

Vaccinations against the following diseases are recommended: Typhoid; Poliomyelitis; Tetanus; Infectious hepatitis.

Further information

Further information on health risks abroad may be available from a local travel clinic. If you wish to take specific drugs with you such as antibiotics these are best prescribed by your own doctor. Beware, however, that not all doctors can be experts on the health problems of remote countries. More detailed or more up-to-date information than local doctors can provide are available from various sources. In the UK there are hospital departments specializing in tropical diseases in London, Liverpool, Birmingham and Glasgow and the Malaria Reference Laboratory at the London School of Hygiene and Tropical Medicine provides free advice about malaria, T0891-600350. In the USA the local Public Health Services can give such information and information is available centrally from the ***Centres for Disease Control*** (CDC) in Atlanta, T404-3324559. ***Travax*** in Glasgow, T0141-9467120, ext 247. General advice is also available in the UK in "Health Information for Overseas Travel" published by the Department of Health and available from HMSO, and "International Travel and Health" published by WHO Handbooks on First Aid are produced by the British & American Red Cross and by St John's Ambulance (UK).

On the road

Intestinal upsets

The thought of catching a stomach bug worries visitors to North Africa but there have been great improvements in food hygiene and most such infections are preventable. Travellers' diarrhoea and vomiting is due, most of the time, to food poisoning, usually passed on by the insanitary habits of food handlers. As a general rule the cleaner your surroundings and the smarter the restaurant, the less likely you are to suffer.

Foods to avoid Uncooked, undercooked, partially cooked or reheated meat, fish, eggs, raw vegetables and salads, especially when they have been left out exposed to flies. Stick to fresh food that has been cooked from raw just before eating and make sure you peel fruit yourself. Wash and dry your hands before eating – disposable wet-wipe tissues are useful for this.

Shellfish When eaten raw, shellfish is risky and at certain times of the year some fish and shellfish concentrate toxins from their environment and cause various kinds of food poisoning. The local authorities notify the public not to eat these foods. Do not ignore the warning.

Heat treated milk (UHT pasteurised or sterilized) Becoming more available in North Africa as is pasteurized cheese. On the whole matured or processed cheeses are safer than the fresh varieties. Fresh unpasteurized milk from whatever animal can be a source of food poisoning germs, tuberculosis and brucellosis. This applies equally to ice-cream, yoghurt and cheese made from unpasteurized milk, so avoid these home-made products – the factory made ones are probably safer.

Tap water Rarely safe outside the major cities, especially in the rainy season. Stream water, if you are in the countryside, is often contaminated by local communities. Filtered or bottled water is usually available and safe, although you must make sure that somebody is not filling bottles from the tap and hammering on a new crown cap. If your hotel has a central hot water supply this water is safe to drink after cooling. Ice for drinks should be made from boiled water, but rarely is, so stand your glass on the ice cubes, rather than putting them in the drink. The better hotels have water purifying systems.

Travellers' diarrhoea

This is usually caused by eating food which has been contaminated by food poisoning germs. Drinking water is rarely the culprit. Sea water or river water is more likely to be contaminated by sewage and so swimming in such dilute effluent can also be a cause. Infection with various organisms can give rise to travellers' diarrhoea. They may be viruses, bacteria, eg Escherichia coli (probably the most common cause world-wide), protozoa (such as amoebas and giardia), salmonella and cholera. The diarrhoea may come on suddenly or rather slowly. It may or may not be accompanied by vomiting or by severe abdominal pain and the passage of blood or mucus when it is called dysentery.

How do you know which type you have caught and how to treat it? If you can time the onset of the diarrhoea to the minute ('acute') then it is probably due to a virus or a bacterium and/or the onset of dysentery. The treatment in addition to rehydration is Ciprofloxacin 500 mg every 12 hrs; the drug is now widely available and there are many similar ones. If the diarrhoea comes on slowly or intermittently ('sub-acute') then it is more likely to be protozoal, ie caused by an amoeba or giardia. Antibiotics such as Ciprofloxacin will have little effect. These cases are best treated by a doctor as is any outbreak of diarrhoea continuing for more than three days. Sometimes blood is passed in amoebic dysentery and for this you should certainly seek medical help. If this is not available then the best treatment is probably Tinidazole (Fasigyn) one tablet four times a day for three days. If there are severe stomach cramps, the following drugs may help but are not very useful in the management of acute diarrhoea: Loperamide (Imodium) and Diphenoxylate with Atropine (Lomotil). They should not be given to children.

Any kind of diarrhoea, whether or not accompanied by vomiting, responds well to the replacement of water and salts, taken as frequent small sips, of some kind of rehydration solution. There are proprietary preparations consisting of sachets of powder which you dissolve in boiled water or you can make your own by adding half a teaspoonful of salt (3.5 g) and four tablespoonful of sugar (40 g) to a litre of boiled water.

Thus the lynch pins of treatment for diarrhoea are rest, fluid and salt replacement, antibiotics such as Ciprofloxacin for the bacterial types and special diagnostic tests and medical treatment for the amoeba and giardia infections. Salmonella infections and cholera, although rare, can be devastating diseases and it would be wise to get to a hospital as soon as possible if these were suspected.

Fasting, peculiar diets and the consumption of large quantities of yoghurt have not been found useful in calming travellers' diarrhoea or in rehabilitating inflamed bowels. Oral rehydration has on the other hand, especially in children, been a life saving technique and should always be practised, whatever other treatment you use. As there is some evidence that alcohol and milk might prolong diarrhoea they should be avoided during and immediately after an attack. So should chillies!

Diarrhoea occurring day after day for long periods of time (chronic diarrhoea) is notoriously resistant to amateur attempts at treatment and warrants proper diagnostic tests (cities with reasonable-sized hospitals have laboratories for stool samples). There are ways of preventing travellers' diarrhoea for short periods of time by taking antibiotics, but this is not a foolproof technique and should not be used other than in exceptional circumstances. Doxycycline is possibly the best drug. Some preventatives such as Enterovioform can have serious side effects if taken for long periods.

Paradoxically **constipation** is also common, probably induced by dietary change, inadequate fluid intake in hot places and long bus journeys. Simple laxatives are useful in the short-term and bulky foods such as rice, beans and plenty of fruit are also useful.

Purifying water There are a number of ways of purifying water in order to make it safe to drink. Dirty water should first be strained through a filter bag (camping shops) and then boiled or treated. Bringing water to a rolling boil at sea level is sufficient to make the water safe for drinking, but at higher altitudes you have to boil the water for longer to ensure that all the microbes are killed.

There are sterilizing methods that can be used and there are proprietary preparations containing chlorine (eg Puritabs) or iodine (eg Pota Aqua) compounds. Chlorine compounds generally do not kill protozoa (eg giardia).

There are a number of water filters now on the market available in personal and expedition size. They work either on mechanical or chemical principles, or may do both. Make sure you take the spare parts or spare chemicals with you and do not believe everything the manufacturers say.

Altitude Mountain sickness is hardly likely to occur, even in the High Atlas. A not-too-rapid ascent is the sure way to prevent it.

Insects These are mostly more of a nuisance than a serious hazard and if you try, you can prevent yourself entirely from being bitten. Some, such as mosquitoes are, of course, carriers of potentially serious diseases, so it is sensible to avoid being bitten as much as possible. Sleep off the ground and use a mosquito net or some kind of insecticide. Preparations containing pyrethrum or synthetic pyrethroids are safe. They are available as aerosols or pumps and the best way to use these is to spray the room thoroughly in all areas and then shut the door for a while, re-entering when the smell has dispersed. Mosquito coils release insecticide as they burn slowly. They are widely available and useful out of doors. Tablets of insecticide which are placed on a heated mat plugged into a wall socket are probably the most effective. They fill the room with insecticidal fumes in the same way as aerosols or coils.

You can also use insect repellents, most of which are effective against a wide range of pests. The most common and effective is diethyl metatoluamide (DET). DET liquid is best for arms and face (care around eyes and with spectacles – DET dissolves plastic). Aerosol spray is good for clothes and ankles and liquid DET can be dissolved in water and used to impregnate cotton clothes and mosquito nets. Some repellents now contain DET and permethrin, an insecticide. Impregnated wrist and ankle bands can also be useful.

If you are bitten or stung, itching may be relieved by cool baths, antihistamine tablets (care with alcohol or driving) or mild corticosteriod creams, eg hydrocortisone (great care: never use if any hint of infection). Careful scratching of all your bites once a day can be surprisingly effective. Calamine lotion and cream have limited effectiveness and antihistamine creams are not recommended – they can cause allergies themslves.

Bites which become infected should be treated with a local antiseptic or antibiotic cream such as Cetrimide, as should any infected sores or scratches. When living rough, skin infestations with body lice (crabs) and scabies are easy to pick up. Use whatever local commercial preparation is recommended for lice and scabies.

Crotamiton cream (Eurax) alleviates itching and also kills a number of skin parasites. Malathion lotion 5 (Prioderm) kills lice effectively, but avoid the use of the toxic agricultural preparation of Malathion, more often used to commit suicide.

Sunburn

The burning power of the tropical sun, especially at high altitude, is phenomenal. Always wear a wide brimmed hat and use some form of suncream or lotion on untanned skin. Normal temperate zone suntan lotions (protection factor up to seven) are not much good; you need to use the types designed specifically for the tropics or for mountaineers or skiers with protection factors up to 15 or above. These are often not available in Morocco. Glare from the sun can cause conjunctivitis, so wear sunglasses especially on tropical beaches, where high protection factor sunscreen should also be used.

Other risks and more serious diseases

Rabies

Remember that rabies is endemic throughout North Africa, so avoid dogs and cover your toes at night from vampire bats, which also carry the disease. If you are bitten by a domestic or wild animal, do not leave things to chance: scrub the wound with soap and water and/or disinfectant, try to have the animal captured (within limits) or at least determine its ownership, where possible, and seek medical assistance at once. The course of treatment depends on whether you have already been satisfactorily vaccinated against rabies. If you have (this is worthwhile if you are spending lengths of time in developing countries) then some further doses of vaccine are all that is required. Human diploid vaccine is the best, but expensive: other, older kinds of vaccine, such as that derived from duck embryos may be the only types available. These are effective, much cheaper and interchangeable generally with the human derived types. If not already vaccinated then anti-rabies serum (immunoglobulin) may be required in addition. It is important to finish the course of treatment whether the animal survives or not. Dogs and other domestic animals also carry hydatid disease – keep away from them. A pocketfull of stones to throw at attacking animals is useful as you approach a mountain hamlet.

AIDS

AIDS is increasing its prevalence in North Africa but at nothing like the rate of sub-Saheran Africa. It is not wholly confined to the well known high risk sections of the population ie homosexual men, intravenous drug users, prostitutes and the children of infected mothers. Heterosexual transmission is now the dominant mode of infection and so the main risk to travellers is from casual sex. The same precautions should be taken as when encountering any sexually transmitted disease. The AIDS virus (HIV) can be passed via unsterile needles which have been previously used to inject an HIV positive patient, but the risk of this is very small indeed. It would, however, be sensible to check that needles have been properly sterilized or disposable needles are used. The chance of picking up hepatitis B in this way is more of a danger. Be wary of carrying disposable needles. Customs officials may find them suspicious. The risk of receiving a blood transfusion with blood infected with the HIV virus is greater than from dirty needles because of the amount of fluid exchanged. Supplies of blood for transfusion are supposed to be screened for HIV in all reputable hospitals so the risk should be small. Catching the virus which causes AIDS does not necessarily produce an illness in itself; the only way to be sure if you feel you have been put at risk is to have a blood test for HIV antibodies on your return to a place where there are reliable laboratory facilities. However the test does not become positive for many weeks.

Malaria Malaria is not prevalent in Morocco but remains a serious disease and you are advised to protect yourself against mosquito bites as above and to take preventative drugs if you are entering a malarial area. Check with your doctor before you go for current advice on malaria in the Marrakech and Atlas region. Start taking the tablets a few days before exposure and continue to take them six weeks after leaving the malarial zone. Remember to give the drugs to babies and children, pregnant women also.

Infectious hepatitis (Jaundice) The main symptoms are pains in the stomach, lack of appetite, lassitude and yellowness of the eyes and skin. Medically speaking there are two main types. The less serious, but more common is hepatitis A for which the best protection is the careful preparation of food, the avoidance of contaminated drinking water and scrupulous attention to toilet hygiene. The other, more serious, version is hepatitis B which is acquired usually as a sexually transmitted disease or by blood transfusion. It can less commonly be transmitted by injections with unclean needles and possibly by insect bites. The symptoms are the same as for hepatitis A. The incubation period is much longer (up to six months compared with six weeks) and there are more likely to be complications.

Typhus Can still occur carried by ticks. There is usually a reaction at the site of the bite, and a fever. Seek medical advice.

Intestinal worms These are quite common and the more serious ones, such as hookworm, can be contracted from walking barefoot on infested earth or beaches. Some cause an itchy rash on the feet "cutaneous larva migrans". Various tropical diseases can be caught in some areas, usually transmitted by biting insects. An example is leishmaniasis. **Leishmaniasis** is present in all countries around the Mediterranean, Sudan and Kenya especially in rural areas. It is transmitted by sandflies, that tend to bite at dawn and dusk. The cutaneous form causes a crusty sore or ulcer that persists for several months. The rare but more serious visceral form causes a persistent fever. Protect against sandfly bites by wearing impregnated long trousers and long sleeved shirt, and DET on exposed skin. Sleep under an impregnated bed net.

Leptospirosis Various forms of leptospirosis occur throughout North Africa, transmitted by a bacterium which is excreted in rodent urine. Fresh water and moist soil harbour the organisms which enter the body through cuts and scratches. If you suffer from any form of prolonged fever consult a doctor.

Dengue fever This is increasing world-wide but is not a significant problem in Morocco. It can be completely prevented by avoiding mosquito bites in the same way as malaria. No vaccine is available. Dengue is an unpleasant and painful disease, presenting with a high temperature and body pains. There is no specific treatment – just pain killers and rest.

Snake bite This is a very rare event indeed for travellers but if you are unlucky (or careless) enough to be bitten by a venomous snake, spider, scorpion or sea creature, try to identify the creature, without putting yourself in further danger. Snake bites in particular are very frightening, but in fact rarely poisonous – even venomous snakes bite without injecting venom. What you might expect if bitten are: fright, swelling, pain and bruising around the bite and soreness of the regional lymph glands, perhaps nausea, vomiting and a fever. Signs of serious poisoning would be the following symptoms: numbness and tingling of the face, muscular spasms, convulsions, shortness of breath or a failure of the blood to clot, causing generalized bleeding. Victims should be taken to a hospital or a doctor without delay. Commercial snake bite and scorpion kits are available, but are usually only useful for the specific types of snake or scorpion. Most serum has to be given intravenously so it is not much good equipping yourself with it unless you are used to making injections into veins. It is best to rely on local practice in these cases, because the particular creatures will be known about locally and appropriate treatment can be given.

Treatment Reassure and comfort the victim frequently. Immobilize the limb by a bandage or a splint or by getting the person to lie still. Do not slash the bite area and try to suck out the poison because this sort of heroism does more harm than good. If you know how to use a tourniquet in these circumstances, you will not need this advice. If you are not experienced, do not apply a tourniquet.

Precautions Avoid walking in snake territory in bare feet or sandals – wear proper shoes or boots. If you encounter a snake stay put until it slithers away, and do not investigate a wounded snake. Spiders and scorpions may be found in the more basic hotels. If stung, rest and take plenty of fluids and call a doctor. The best precaution is to keep beds away from the walls and look inside your shoes and under the toilet seat every morning.

Marine bites & stings

When trodden upon, certain tropical sea fish inject venom into bathers' feet. This can be exceptionally painful. Wear plastic shoes when you go bathing if such creatures are reported. The pain can be relieved by immersing the foot in extremely hot water for as long as the pain persists.

When you return home

Remember to take your antimalarial tablets for six weeks after leaving the malarial area. If you have had attacks of diarrhoea it is worth having a stool specimen tested in case you have picked up amoebas. If you have been living rough, blood tests may be worthwhile to detect worms and other parasites. If you have been exposed to schistosomiasis by swimming in lakes etc. check by means of a blood test when you get home, but leave it for six weeks because the test is slow to become positive. Report any untoward symptoms to your doctor and tell the doctor exactly where you have been and, if you know, what the likelihood of disease is to which you were exposed.

Further reading

In the anglophone countries, good bookshops will generally carry coffee table books on Moroccan cooking, interiors and crafts. You'll certainly find novels by Paul Bowles or other Tangerine writers set in Morocco, and maybe stories by Bowles' Moroccan protégés. For those who read French, there is masses of reading material, much of it coming out of Casablanca and Rabat. Leading publishers include Abdelkader Retnani's ***Edif*** and Leïla Chaouni's ***Le Fennec***, which has a good name for its collections of essay and contemporary fiction. The annual book awards, the ***Prix Grand Atlas***. established in the 1980s, attracts a fair bit of media attention. Morocco also has a tradition of beaux livres, fine albums of art photography on Morocco's cities and traditions. In southern Morocco, there is not much choice in terms of bookshops. Marrakech has the ***Librairie Chatr*** on avenue Mohamed V, Guéliz plus another small but well stocked bookshop in the line of shops where the rue Bab Agnaou (Le Prince) starts on Jemaa el Fna. Try also the small but well-stocked bookshop (posters, cards, artbooks, some novels) at ***Riad Temsna*** at 23 Riad Zitoun el Jadid, T044-385272, see Marrakech chapter. Another literary stronghold in the South, some would say, is the ***Café-Restaurant Taros*** on rue de la Skala, Essaouira (T044-476407) which has a good collection of art books.

Nevertheless, real bibliophiles will have to head north to the country's intellectual centres, capital Rabat (best bookshops: ***Kalila wa Dimna***, ***Le Livre Service***) and the Maârif neighbourhood, Casablanca (***Le Carrefour du Livre***) to look at what's going on in Moroccan publishing. The ***Maghreb Bookshop*** in Bloomsbury (45 Burton St, London WC1) carries a range of Morocco-related literature.

Arts & crafts There are now plenty of illustrated titles in English, one of the most accessible being **James F. Jereb**'s ***Arts and Crafts of Morocco*** (London: Thames and Hudson, 1995).

Cooking With Moroccan cuisine trendy in London for a while in the late 1990s, a spate of cookbooks was published, many being of the sort that leave you wondering when it comes to the unlikely ingredients – and preparation times, for much Moroccan cooking is highly labour intensive. Avoiding the more lavish titles, (which really tend to be about someone or other's trendy restaurant) try ***North Africa, the vegetarian table*** by **Kitty Morse** (San Francisco: Chronicle Books, 1996) and the serious ***Traditional Moroccan Cooking*** by **Mme Guinaudeau** (London: Serif, 1994) which is thorough and completely free of poncey photographs.

Cultural background: Marrakech A couple of coffee table books to recommend, namely ***Médersa de Marrakech*** by **Y. Pochy and Hamid Triki** (Paris: EPA, 1990), a superb photo portrait capturing the austerity of one of the Red City's most venerable buildings, and ***Jardins de Marrakech*** by ***Mohamed El Faïz***, a historical introduction to the gardens and palmgroves that give the town so much of its atmosphere.

Cultural background: the Atlantic coast There are now a good number of coffee table books on Essaouira, its sights and painters. **On Safi, T'hami Ouazzani**'s ***La colline des potiers*** (Casablanca: Editions LAK International, 1993) is a superbly illustrated introduction to that city's pottery – and could well become a collector's item).

Cultural background: the High Atlas If your treks in the Azilal High Atlas left you in acute need of more than just a few souvenir photos, **K. and T. Lamazou**'s ***Sous les toits de terre*** (Casablanca: Belvisi/Publication, 1988) is a must. The fine line and watercolour illustrations portray a year in the life of the village of Imelghas, up in the Vallée des Aït Bougmez.

Ethnography *Morocco has attracted a good deal of scholarly interest from anthropologists based in US universities.* There is some good work now appearing in essay form in Morocco itself. Try for example **Mounia Bennani-Chraïbi**'s ***Soumis et rebelles, les jeunes au Maroc*** (Casablanca: Editions Le Fennec, 1994). Good, readable account, based on interviews, on what it feels to be young and aspiring in Morocco today. Also excellent (and in English) is **Vincent Crapanzano**'s ***Tuhami, story of a Moroccan*** (Chicago University Press, 1980). Based on fieldwork in Meknès, this is an account of the life and times of an illiterate Moroccan tilemaker – and a great storyteller. 'Probes the limits of anthropology' says the blurb. Worth reading. In terms of contemporary Moroccan sociologists available in English look out for translations of works by the prolific, polemical but methodologically chaotic **Fatema Mernissi**. See for example her autobiographical ***The Harem Within. Tales of a Moroccan Girlhood*** (New York: Bantam Books, 1994).

Fine art Good bookshops in Rabat and Casablanca will also stock books on contemporary Moroccan painters like Cherkaoui, Chaïbia and Belkahia. If you are a fan of Orientalist painting any of the ACR coffee table books are well worth looking out for. See for example **Liz Thornton**'s ***Les orientalistes, peintres voyageurs, 1828-1908*** (Paris: ACR, 1983) and ***La femme dans la peinture orientaliste*** (Paris: ACR Editions, 1985).

History The essential work on North African history in English is **J. Abun-Nasr** 's scholarly and dense***History of the Maghreb in the Islamic Period*** (Cambridge: CUP, 1987). More difficult to find will be **W. Blunt**'s ***Black Sunrise*** (London: Methuen, 1951), an account of the life and times of Moulay Ismaïl, Emperor of Morocco 1646-1727. On the Imazighen,

On the way to Marrakech: five titles for the airport lounge

Running from the light to heavy(ish) reading, five books for your trip to Marrakech

Hideous Kinky by Esther Freud (London: Penguin, 1992)
The Tatooed Map (San Francisco: Chronicle Books, 1995)
Love for a Few Hairs by Mohamed Mrabet
The Voices of Marrakech by Elias Cannetti(London: Marion Boyars, 1967, numerous reprints).
The Garden of Secrets by Juan Goytisolo (London: Serpents Tale, 2000).
If you read French, look out for anything by Mahi Binebine or Rachid O., or (a bit depressingly) Ahmed Marzouki's Tazmamart, Cellule 10.

there is now a good general history in English by ***Michael Brett*** and ***E. Fentres***, ***The Berbers*** (Oxford: Blackwell, 1996), which ranges over the history of the Tamazight-speaking peoples of North Africa from earliest times to the present.

Fiction: Moroccans on Morocco

There is a growing amount of contemporary fiction in Arabic and French. If you read French, look out for ***Lotfi Akalay*** (***Les nuits d'Azed***) and ***Fouad Laroui*** (*Les dents du topographe*). **Rachid O.** (***L'enfant ébloui***, ***Plusieurs vies***) and ***Paul Smaïl***'s short and angry ***Vivre me tue***. (See also his recent ***Ali le Magnifique***). Both Smaïl and Rachid O, are published in France, but write with a vigourous spoken-language style. **Mohammed Zezaf** is perhaps the most highly regarded of the Arabic language novelists.

Back to French, and there is a lot of women's writing in that language published in Morocco. The first novel by a woman was **Halima Ben Haddou**'s 1982 ***Aïcha la Rebelle***. Contemporary women writers include **Nadia Chafik** and **Bahaa Trabelsi**. The best contemporary novelist is probably **Mahi Binebine**, whose most recent novel ***Cannibales*** takes a look at the harsh realities facing the *harraga*, the desperately poor who will do anything to cross the Straits of Gibraltar in search of a better life in Spain. The most successful book of 2000 was undoubtedly ***Tazmamart, cellule 10***, (Casablanca: Editions Tarak, 2000, now published in France by Gallimard), an account of 18 years imprisonment in inhuman conditions in the Moroccan outback by former detainee **Ahmed Marzzouki**. Of 58 officers, soldiers and pilots accused of participating in the failed coups of 1971 and 1972 and imprisoned at Tazmamart only 28 survived.

Fiction: Moroccans in English translation

The most translated writers include **Tahar Ben Jelloun**, **Mohammed Choukri** and **Driss Chraïbi**. In all honesty, ***Ben Jelloun***'s spare (oniric?) prose does not always go into English very easily. **Choukri**'s storytelling, through the Bowles translation-filter is very accessible, while **Chraïbi**'s dense ***Le Passé simple*** is outstanding autobiographical writing (English translation long out of print). You will probably easily find ***Paul Bowles***' translations of stories by **Mohammed Mrabet** (***Love for a Few Hairs***) and **Driss Ben Hamed Charhadi** (***A Life full of Holes***, Edinburgh: Rebel Press, 1997). In translation from Literary Arabic, look out for **Mohammed Berrada**'s ***The Game of Forgetting*** (London: Quartet, 1997, translation Issa Boullata), which contains some fine pages on life in Rabat and Fès.

Well known in Morocco, much less so elsewhere but still translated into English are ***Brick Ousaïd*** and ***Abdelhak Serhane***. And finally, new arrivals in English include **Abdelkader Benali** (***Wedding by the Sea***, London, Phoenix, 1999, described as 'a magical realist tale in which an immigrant from Holland returns to deserted seaside village for his sister's wedding') and **Hafid Bouazza** (***Abdullah's Feast***, London, Hodder, 2000, 'memories of a lively village with its own mosque and idiot'.

Fiction: Europeans on Morocco In London, Daunt's Travel Bookshop has a small but good selection of Moroccan fiction in English. Numerous European writers have written fiction set in Morocco, including Jean Genet, Paul Morand, Paul Bowles and Joseph Kessel. In a light vein, try **Aldo Busi**'s ***Sodomies in Elevenpoint*** (London: Faber and Faber 1992). The title sets the tone for this account of the adventures of an Italian novelist in Agadir and Taroudant. Marrakech's star European writer must be **Juan Goytisolo**, responsible in part for Jemaâ el Fna's oral heritage being added to the Unesco-sponsored World Heritage List. One of his most readable novels, ***Makbara*** (London: Serpent's Tail, 1993) is a surreal tale shifting between genders and cities, between Morocco, Paris and imagined otherwheres. In his most recent work published in English, ***The Garden of Secrets*** (London: Serpent's Tail, 2000) a Decameron-like gathering recount the multiple lives of a mysterious writer settled in Marrakech.

Photography Given the wealth of colour and texture of the Morocco's cityscapes and countryside, it is hardly surprising that there are some superb photography books, of which one of the finest is **William Betsch**'s ***The Hakima, a tragedy in Fez*** (London: Secker and Warburg, 1991). Text and image work very well together. Well worth looking for – a collector's item. **Gérard Rondeau**'s ***Figures du Maroc*** (Casablanca: Eddif, 1997) portrays Morocco's intellectuals, musicians, writers and painters in black and white, creating a veritable visual Who's Who of the country's artistic life. In European or North American bookshops, look out for a quixotic bijou of a photo book entitled ***The Tatooed Map*** (San Francisco: Chronicle Books, 1995).

Poetry Here there is practically nothing translated into English. If you read French, look out for anything by the Morocco's senior poet, survivor of the militant 1970s, **Abdellatif Laâbi** (most recent collection: ***Spleen de Casablanca***).

Travel writing One of the most read 20th century travel accounts of Marrakech must be ***The Voices of Marrakech*** by **Elias Cannetti** (London: Marion Boyars, 1967, numerous reprints). Also in this category, two demi-classics come to mind. **Gavin Maxwell**'s ***Lords of the Atlas*** (London 1966, recently reissued in an overwrought coffee table version). Maxwell, drawing heavily on earlier writers like the Tharaud brothers, provides a good account of French and the Glaoui family's rule in Marrakech. No clue is given, however, as to Maxwell's motives for writing such a book. **Edith Wharton** was guest of the French Residency just after the First World War and thus produced ***In Morocco*** (London: Macmillan, 1920, republished since). You could also look out for writing by **Antoine de St Exupery** (***Wind, Sand and Stars*** or ***Southern Mail***). **Rom Landau** writing in the 1950s and 60s, something of an apologist for the Morocco he found. There are some memorable descriptions of Marrakech in some of his books. At the same period, the likes of **William Burrough**'s and miscellaneous members of the Beat Generation (Jack Kerouac, Alan Ginsberg et al) were holed up in Tanger doing a spot of writing when not indulging that cosmopolitan city's many delights.

Post-beat travel writing After the Beat Generation, Anglo-Saxon literary interest in Morocco rather died off. However, look out for **Esther Freud**'s short novel ***Hideous Kinky*** (London: Penguin, 1992), a child's view of travels with a hippy mother in search of primal religious experience. Some good sequences as mum strives to understand soufi Islam while kids muck in with the street urchins of Jemaâ el Fna in Marrakech. (See also late 1990s film with Saïd Tangeaoui in the role of Moroccan lover). For the worst of Morocco, see **Sylvia Kennedy**'s ***See Ouarzazate and Die*** (London: Abacus Travel, 1992), journeys with a jaded former EFL teacher. A travelogue in which the *kif* sellers are always swarthy, the German blondes spaced out and looking for a cause for tears and confrontation. Sample sentence: "Abdul and his friends still sat at the café... shades clamped on their noses, baying about Arab dignity". Nevertheless, some powerful insights, too (see description of Safi).

Trekking

Here there is little available in English, apart from: **Matt Dickinson**'s ***Long Distance Walks in North Africa*** (Crowood Press 1991) and **Karl Smith**'s excellent ***The Atlas Mountains, a walkers' guide*** (Milnthorpe: Cicerone, 1989) which describes treks in the Toubkal and Mgoun areas in great deal, and also provides coverage of the Jebels Siroua and Saghro.

In Marrakech, especially at the Librairie Chatr in Marrakech, (Ave Mohamed V, half-way between Shell Station and Café La Renaissance) you could look out for books on trekking in French, including **André Fougerolles**' ***Le Haut Atlas central, guide alpin*** (many good diagrams and maps), and **Michael Peyron's** ***La grande traversée de l'Atlas marocain***, (also available in a well translated English version published by Westcol Publications of Goring, Berks, first edition 1990). Vol 1 of their Great Atlas Traverse does the Moussa Gorges to the Ayt Bou Wgemmaz, while vol 2 does the Ayt Bou Wgemmaz to Midelt, with some supplementary treks in the Middle Atlas and the Jebel Saghro. Unfortunately, this sort of guide needs very regular updating as paths in remote areas like the Assif Melloul gorges are prone to land-slips. Both books are useful but no substitute for a good local guide. There may be material available on ski trekking at the Librairie Chatr too, or at one of the Oukaïmeden hotels.

Wildlife

P. and F. Bergier's *A Birdwatcher's Guide to Morocco* (Perry: Prion Ltd) is a slim but useful guide to the best localities in Morocco for bird observation, with good site maps and fairly comprehensive species list. Generally available from Stanfords in London. For flora, go for **M. Blamey and C. Grey-Wilson**'s *Mediterranean Wild Flowers* (London: Harper Collins, 1993), which is both beautifully illustrated and comprehensive, though focused on coastal localities and not particularly easy for the non-specialist to use. Many Moroccan endemics are not described. Difficult to obtain is **J. Cremona and R. Chote**'s *Alternative Holiday Guide to Exploring Nature in North Africa* (Ashford) which is a very good general introduction to the flora and fauna of North Africa but insufficiently detailed for the specialist, however. The definitive guide to the birds of the region is **PAD Hollom, PAD et al**'s *Birds of the Middle East and North Africa* (1988). It is best used along with a guide covering birds in Europe such as **Peterson, Mountford et al's** *A Field Guide to the Birds of Britain and Europe*.

Road maps

The late 1990s saw a spate of road improvement schemes across Morocco. The road maps available in 2000 had not kept pace. The **Michelin 959** was probably the most accurate, although not much cop for *pistes* (unsurfaced roads). The **Geo Center World Map**, 1:800,000 scale, is another option, although inaccurate for the region south of Azrou, for example, while the heading 'other minor roads' includes both tarmac surfaced road and difficult piste – see for example the region of the Atlas north of Skoura, El Kelaâ des Mgouna and Boumalne du Dadès. Maps identify roads by letters and numbers (P = *parcours*, ie main road, S = *route secondaire*, generally tarmac surface). Road signs, bilingual in Arabic and Latin letters, rarely show route numbers at all. Note that Morocco does not use the Arabic numerals in use in the Middle East. If you need more detailed maps, try the **Institut géographique national** (IGN), 107 rue de la Boétie, Paris 75008 which may supply 1:100,000 scale maps with latitude and longitude, useful if you are working with a GPS system.

Film

Unfortunately, Moroccan films are hard to find in their country of origin. Those with a real interest in North African film might try to coincide with the annual Festival cinématographique de Marrakech, first held in late September 2001. Film buffs should also note an annual film festival in the phosphate town of Khouribga, plus occasional film events in the northern city of Tetouan. The bookshop at the *Institut du monde Arabe* (IMA), Quai St Bernard,near the Jussieu Faculty, on the Left Bank in Paris (Metro: Jussieu, intersection lines 7 and 10)has a small selection of Moroccan and other Arab films on video. The IMA also runs occasional Arab film seasons.

Since the early 1990s, Moroccan filmmakers have taken an increasingly critical stance. The following are worth looking out for: Abdelkader Lagtaâ's ***Un amour à Casablanca***, sharp portrait of patriarchy in a city family, and Mohamed Abderrahman Tazi's ***A la recherche du mari de ma femme***, which portrays the venerable but ridiculous Fassi, Hadj Ben Moussa running after his various wives in some archetypal médina. Back to the Great White City, Lagtaâ was also hailed for his ***Les Casablancais***, a horribly accurate portrait of the urban neuroses brought on by political repression in 1980s Morocco. More focused social critique is increasingly present in films, too – see Hakim Noury's ***L'enfance volée (Stolen Childhood)***, about the plight of the child maids who work in upper class Moroccan families, ***Saâd Chraïbi***'s ***Femmes et femmes***, and more recently, ***Lagtaâ***'s taboo-breaking ***La Porte close***, which finally reached the screen in May 2000 after a year's delays because of censorship. Films by Tangerine director Farida Belyazid are also definitely worth looking out for. On a more quirky note, ***Adieu Forain***,an art-photographer's portrait of a failing itinerant funfair in the Moroccan south is aesthetically pleasing if a little depressing.

Of the up-and-coming directors, **Nabil Ayyouch** is definitely one of the most interesting. His 1997 ***Mektoub*** combines film noir quotes with road-movie. More recently, Ayyouch's ***Ali Zaoua*** portrays the lives of a couple of Casablanca urchins as they seek to give a decent burial for one of their number. Made with international actor Saïd Tangeaoui and a group of kids, the film was a huge success in Morocco in 2000 and won prizes in European festivals. Still on the street kids theme, ***El Hafa/La Falaise***, shot in black and white, is one of the best shorts of recent years.

Many foreign films have been shot in Morocco. A good chunk of Hollywood blockbuster ***Gladiator*** was shot at the Atlas Studios in Ouarzazate. But foreign directors have also portrayed Morocco in a sensitive light – see in particular André Téchiné's recent (2001) feature set in Tanger, ***Loin***, which through an account of three days in the lives of group of young people in Tanger, manages to touch upon drug smuggling, illegal immigration, the status of women and education in Moroccan society – and the pains of love.

Marrakech مراكش

Marrakech

__Marrakech__, pleasure town, has long been a draw for travellers. Both place of myth and tourist metropolis, it is a delicious city, a city to be tasted with all its colours and smells.

Surrounded by palms and olive groves, arid plains and sprawling concrete suburbs, it is within easy reach of cool mountain valleys. One of the great Islamic cities of North Africa, Marrakech is also the only oasis north of the High Atlas mountains which, snow-capped until April, form a dramatic backdrop to the city. In town, Marrakech has a memorable beauty, with its palm-lined streets and earth walls, surrounding a huge médina of red houses. The focus points are the 12th-century __Koutoubia Mosque__ and the __Jemaâ el Fna__ 'square', with its grillstalls, traders and entertainers and the vast network of souks, where people come to buy and sell from all over the surrounding plains, the High Atlas and the Sahara. Around these, the médina stretches away with its narrow streets, flat-roofed houses and minarets.

The souks are stuffed with merchandise of all kinds, for the artisans of Marrakech are most adept at producing bijou items of Eastern inspiration. Marrakech also has a reputation as a garden city. As the sun goes down, visit the great gardens of the __Agdal__ or the __Menara__ to enjoy the cool of the early evening.

Ins and outs

Getting there
Colour map 2, grid B4

See page 124 for further details

Marrakech is easily accessible by air, road and rail. There are direct flights from French and some other European cities to Marrakech-Menara airport, and 7 trains a day to Casablanca (journey time 3½ hrs), with onward connections to the rest of Morocco. There are also good bus and grand taxi connections with all major cities – although the journey times are long (around 8 hrs to Fès, for example). For car drivers, once out of Marrakech, the roads are rarely crowded. However, the Marrakech-Casablanca road is reputed for the high number of accidents, so drive carefully. Marrakech makes an excellent point of arrival in Morocco because of its centrality, situated at the meeting point of routes for Essaouira (Atlantic coast), Ouarzazate (key to the gorges south of the Atlas), and the northern imperial cities.

Getting around The airport is a short taxi ride from the city (50dh during the day, 60dh at night, have change ready). From the railway station to Guéliz, the heart of the *ville nouvelle*, is a 15-min walk; the Jemaâ el Fna area, where most of the budget hotels are located is a further 20-min walk on from Guéliz. It is best to get a taxi into the city (say 10dh). Alternatively, take bus No 3 or 8 from outside the station along Ave Hassan II and Ave Mohammed V, to the médina. Inter-city buses arrive at Bab Doukkala, a 15-min walk from Jemaâ el Fna. Marrakech is a spread out city, built on a plain – hence the large number of mobylettes and bicycles – and rental of a 2-wheeler is an option. (There are numerous agencies.) Upmarket travellers may find themselves in hotels out in Semlalia, which run shuttle services to the centre. Taxis in Marrakech do not generally seem to bother with meters: remember to have change handy. A short ride from Jemaâ el Fna to Guéliz should not be more than 10dh. Finally, the most picturesque way to drive around Marrakech is in a *calèche*, a horse-drawn carriage. The energetic, however, will want to do most of their exploring on foot.

Hassle The 'hassle' which deterred some visitors in the past is reduced a little thanks to the unseen but ever-vigilant *Brigade touristique*. The predominant atmosphere is relaxed, best appreciated from a café terrace beside Jemaâ el Fna.

Background and history

The city In some early European maps Marrakech appears as 'Morocco city', although 'Maraksh' is the Arabic name. The origins of the name are obscure: some see it as a corruption of 'aghmat-urika', the name of an early town. The city is surrounded by extensive palm groves, into which areas of villas and hotels are gradually spreading. Yet there are also sandy, arid areas near, and even within, the city which give it a semi-Saharan character. And then there are the mountains. Arriving from Fès or Meknès one runs alongside the bald arid **Jebilet** 'the little mountains', or cross them at Sidi Bou Othmane as one runs in from Casa-Rabat. (Perhaps the most beautiful approach to Marrakech is on the P9, from Casa and Sidi Bennour, which crosses the Plateau des Gantours and the end of the Jebilet.) However, from most points in Marrakech, cloud and heat haze allowing, it is the **High Atlas**, the Adrar (literally 'the mountains'), in Tachelhit, which dominate. At times the optical illusion is such that the snow-covered mountain wall appears to rise from just behind the city.

Marrakech covers a large area, with distinct zones separated by less populated areas. For the visitor this will entail long walks between the main points of interest in the médina, **Guéliz** (the *ville nouvelle*), and the two olive groves

Things to do in Marrakech

- In the médina, explore chic, urban enclave **Mouassine**.
- Trawl the fondouks, the old merchant's hostelries on **Place Bab Ftouh** behind the *Café Argana*, and purchase camel litter, nomad couscous bowls or other antiquities.
- Join the crowds on **Jemaâ el Fna** in the early evening. Watch the locals watching the entertainers and other tourists.
- Eat out in a **palace restaurant** in the médina.
- Enjoy, *mini-bastilla, cornes de gazelle* and other Moroccan **sweet delights** from the *Pâtisserie Hilton*, opposite the *Café Renaissance*, Gueliz.
- Take a bike ride out onto the **Circuit de la Palmeraie**.

of the **Agdal** and the **Menara**, or more probably reliance on taxis, *calèches*, buses or your own transport. The long, wide tree-lined boulevards of the *ville nouvelle*, a number of which are focused on the beautiful **Koutoubia Mosque**, give the city an impressive feeling of spaciousness, which contrasts with the equally impressive density of the médina.

Marrakech is Morocco's fourth largest city. The official population in 1993 was 550,000, although today the figure is probably nearer the 800,000 mark. Its people are a mix of Arab and Amazigh; many are recent migrants from surrounding rural regions and further south. For centuries important as a regional market place, Marrakech now has a booming service economy. There is still a wide range of handicraft production and small-scale industry, particularly in the médina. Out in the western suburbs are factories, with food processing and garment manufacture important. Increasingly, tourism is being seen as the mainstay of the city's economy. Marrakech is one of the major tourist attractions of Morocco and many of the city's large unemployed or under-employed labour force supplement their incomes by casual work with tourists, their unwanted attentions having in the past given the city a bad name.

Almoravid origins & role

Although Marrakech has probably been occupied since Neolithic times, it was first founded properly in 1062 by one Youssef ben Tachfine, the Almoravid leader, as a base from which to control the High Atlas mountains. A kasbah, Dar al-Hajar, was built close to the site of the Koutoubia Mosque. Under Youssef Ben Tachfine Marrakech was an important capital and marketing centre, with the building of several mosques, palaces and the city's famous walls, as well as the development of extensive gardens and an irrigation system. The population was probably a mixture of haratine or blacks from the Oued Draâ, Berbers from the Sous Valley and the nearby Atlas, and Jewish Berbers. The city attracted leading medieval thinkers from outside Marrakech.

In 1147 Marrakech was taken by the Almohads, who almost totally destroyed and then rebuilt the city, making it the capital of their extensive empire. Under the Almohad Sultan Abd el Moumen, the Koutoubia Mosque was built on the site of Almoravid buildings, with the minaret added by Ya'qub al Mansur. Under the latter Marrakech gained palaces, gardens and irrigation works, and again became a famous centre for musicians, writers and academics, but on his death it declined and fell into disarray.

Merinid neglect & Saâdian revival

Whilst the Merinids added several *medersa* to Marrakech, Fès received much of their attention, and was preferred as the capital, although from 1374 to 1386 Marrakech was the centre of a separate principality. Marrakech was revitalized by the Saâdians from 1524 with the rebuilding of the Ben Youssef

Water for the Red City

How does Marrakech, a city with well over 1,000,000 inhabitants (recent estimate) set on a dry and dusty plain, manage for water? Historically the site was probably chosen because the water table was near the surface, so homes could have wells. And then came the khettaras*, the tunnels which brought water from the foot of the High Atlas, across the gently sloping Haouz Plain, to great reservoirs such as the Menara, just outside the Red City. From this* sahrij *or basin, the water was drawn off to the different parts of the city through open channels and terracotta piping. Each neighbourhood had a sort of cistern or* ma'da *(literally stomach), and each house or set of houses had a right to so many hours of water from the local* ma'da *each day, timed with a water clock, just as in an oasis. The best houses were those closest to the cistern.*

In the early 20th century, this system fell into disuse. The open channels were no longer properly maintained; carrion and rubbish polluting them were a source of epidemics. The French introduced a modern water distribution system, as the community was no longer willing to pay for the upkeep of the khettaras*. Today, details of the pre-modern distribution system have largely been lost – although when there is heavy rainfall, people with* khettaras *in their gardens suddenly find the waters gushing. Two-thirds of Marrakech's water now comes along the canal from the Barrage Si Driss near Demnate, some 120 km away. The remaining water needs are pumped out of the ground near the city. But the water table is falling fast. Whereas 20 years ago there was water 20 m below ground, the aquifers are now between 40 and 50 m down. This may be linked to increased consumption – or a major climatic change. Within living memory, there would be hail in Marrakech in the winter and snow in the Ourika Valley. Today, the snow lasts a few weeks only, and it hasn't rained consistently on the Haouz Plain for four years.*

Happily, water prices remain (broadly speaking) acceptable. Households using under 24 m^3 a month pay 3dh per m^3. Users of up to 60 m^3 pay 5dh per m^3, close to the cost price of water. And those using over 60 m^3 are charged 8dh per m^3.

Mosque, and the construction by Ahmed al Mansour Ad-Dahbi of the El Badi Palace and the Saâdian tombs. Marrakech also became an important trading post, due to its location between the Sahara and the Atlantic.

Alaouite Marrakech

The Alaouites took control of Marrakech in 1668. In the early 18th century the city suffered from Moulay Ismaïl's love of Meknès, with many of the major buildings, notably the El Badi Palace, stripped to glorify the new capital, and a significant shift in power and wealth. The destructive effects of this period were compounded by the civil strife following his death. However, under the Alaouite Sultan Moulay Hassan I, from 1873, and his son, Marrakech gained a number of important buildings and re-established its prestige. A number of fine palaces that can still be visited date from this time.

Early 20th century: Glaoui rule

From 1898 until independence, Marrakech was ruled by the Glaoui family. The French took control of Marrakech and its region in 1912, crushing an insurrection by a claimant to the Sultanate. Their policy in the vast and rugged southern territories was to govern through local rulers, rather as the British worked with the rajahs of India. With French support, Pacha T'hami el Glaoui extended his control over all areas of the South. His autonomy from central authority was considerable, his cruelty notorious. And of course, there were great advantages in this system, in the form of profits from the new

The Generous Glaoui

In Paris in the 1930s, to be chic was to know about Coco Chanel and cubist painting, to be familiar with jazz and trans-Atlantic steamers – and to know the latest gossip about the Glaoui. As Indian maharajahs travelled to London and sent their sons to public schools and Oxbridge, so T'hami el Glaoui, Pacha of Marrakech and effective ruler of southern Morocco allowed his sons a French education and would spend part of every year in Paris, Vichy and the Riviera. T'hami's appetite for women was legendary, as was his generosity. Sometimes the two characteristics met with strange results – as in the following anecdote recounted in Gavin Maxwell's story of the House of Glaoua, Lords of the Atlas. With his usual hospitality, T'hami had invited some French residents of Marrakech to dine. With them was a young Parisian woman new to the ways of the Orient. When the high point of the meal arrived, a whole roast lamb, T'hami, in the best local tradition, removed a choice morsel from the bone and held it out to her. La parisienne, unaware that her host was both cosmopolitan and sophisticated, remarked to her friends that the pacha was nothing more than a pig, adding to that she wouldn't mind an emerald ring like the one he was wearing. After the meal was over, T'hami found a moment to take the upstart aside. In perfect French, he remarked: "Madame, a gemstone like this emerald was clearly not made for a pig like me. Allow me to make a present of it to you."

French-developed mines. In the 1930s, Marrakech saw the development of a fine *ville nouvelle*, Guéliz, all wide avenues of jacarandas and simple, elegant bungalow houses. Acquiring a railway line terminus, Marrakech reaffirmed its status as capital of the South. And it was at this time, when travel for pleasure was still something reserved for the privileged of Europe, that Marrakech began to acquire its reputation as a retreat for the wealthy.

Capital of the south

In recent decades Marrakech has grown enormously, its population swelled by civil servants and armed forces' personnel. Migrants are attracted by the city's reputation as 'city of the poor', where even the least qualified can find work of some kind. (For many rural people, the urban struggle is hard, and as the Tachelhit pun puts it, Marrakech is *ma-ra-kish*, 'the place where they'll eat you if they can'.) North of the médina, new neighbourhoods like Daoudiate and Issil have grown up next to the Université Cadi Ayyad and the mining school. South of the médina, Sidi Youssef Ben Ali, referred to in Marrakchi slang as SYBA, is an extension of the old town with a reputation for rebellion. West of Guéliz, north of the Essaouira road, are the vast new housing areas of Massira, part low-rise social housing, part villa developments. The most upmarket area is on the Circuit de la Palmeraie, however. Little by little, the original farmers are being bought out, and desirable homes with lawns and pools behind high walls are taking over from vegetable plots under the palm trees. East of the médina is the vast Amelkis development, a gated community complete with golf course and the discrete Amenjana 'resort'. Here the money and privilege are accommodated in an area equal to one third of the crowded médina. It is a tribute to Morocco that enormous wealth and intense deprivation can sit so close to each other without street crime of the Latin American kind being a problem.

Future of Marrakech

The late 1990s saw Marrakech in an upbeat mood. The *Brigade Touristique* set up in the mid-1990s had managed to reduce the hassling of tourists. All forms

24 hours in the city

Marrakech has so many visitors these days that the main historic sites are at visitor saturation level.

Before the rush, start your day with lots of walking in the southern part of the old town to take in the museums, maybe the **Dar Si Said**, *the* **Palais Bahia** *(19th century), and the* **Palais Badi** *(a vast 16th-century ruin). The* **Saâdian Tombs** *are a must but get very, very crowded.*

Next, whizz over to the small but perfectly planted **Jardin Majorelle** *in a petit taxi. From here you could get another petit taxi over to Guéliz for a spot of light shopping (area around Rue de la Liberté) and then on to lunch at a restaurant like* Les Cépages *(excellent, expensive), or* La Bagatelle *or* La rotisserie du Café de la Paix, *on Rue de Yougoslavie (all have outside terraces, latter two the best).*

After a quick siesta at your hotel, you can soldier back to the médina for more monuments (area north of Jemaa el Fna, Ben Youssef Medersa, Musée de Marrakech) and even some shopping.

Sundown will see you on Jemaa el Fna, having your photo taken with gnaouas*/snake charmers/acrobats and retiring for a mint tea and pâtisserie at the* Café Argana *or perhaps the* Café CTM *(more locals than tourists).*

*Marrakech sits down to dinner relatively early. Choose one of the more discreet restaurants in the Mouassine/Bab Leksour area of the old town (*Ksar Saoussan, Le Tobsil, *possibly* Dar Moha*). Or go for brochettes at one of the eateries on the great square, (the largest open-air barbecue in the world?). The scene here will entertain you for hours.*

Marrakech

of tourist activity were on the up, with hotels reporting record booking levels. According to one report, there were over 80 private guesthouses in the médina, many owned and run by Europeans. The problem was how to deal with the influx. Certain monuments had reached saturation point: the exquisite Saâdian tombs were home to a permanent people jam. On the drawing boards is a major new tourism zone of over 1,000 ha, the *Oliveraie de Marrakech*, to be located on land southwest of the old city. The avenue de France is to be extended for a few more kilometres. The plan's opponents worry whether this will be the final blow for what remains of the city's rural character, destroying working olive groves and the open approach to the southern side of the city. On a positive note, the airport is to be moved further out, probably to Sidi Bou Othmane on the future Casablanca to Marrakech autoroute. There remains the problem of transport in the central areas. At peak times, the area around Jemaâ el Fna is a seething mass of vehicles and mopeds, bicyles, carriages, buses and humanity. One rumour has it that the square is to be dug up to create an immense underground car park.

Still the 'Venice of Morocco'?

Whatever decisions the planners take, Marrakech will continue to draw the visitors in. Thanks to public relations campaigns like the 1998 *Année du Maroc* in France, the city continues to have its hold on the Western imagination. The setting is undeniably exotic, eccentricities are tolerated, and (rather less honourably) domestic help is cheap. Features in international decoration magazines fuel the demand for property; major monuments are being restored. Yves St Laurent, a long-term occasional resident, even dubbed Marrakech 'the Venice of Morocco'. The Red City remains the closest Orient one can find within a few hours flight of the grey north European winter, and provided the city authorities can keep vehicle pollution in check, it looks set to maintain its popularity.

Orientation in Marrakech

Apart from the labyrinthine souks, Marrakech is actually quite easy to find your way around. There are two main centres, ***rond-point Abd el Moumen*** *in Guéliz, and the great square on the western side of the Médina, the* ***Jamaâ el Fna****. The long straight Ave Mohamed V links the two. If you need to meet people in Guéliz, the* Café Les Négociants *and the Café Renaissance are easily located on rond-point Abd el Moumen. On Jamaâ el Fna, the easiest landmarks for meeting people are the* Café Argana *(big red sign on roof) and the* Café-Hotel de France. *At the Jamaâ el Fna end of pedestrian Rue Bab Agnaou is a big café with a terrace, known as the* Café Lipton *on account of the advertising on its awning.*

Regarding explorations of the ***médina****, there are two major areas: souks around Medersa Ben Youssef, and the Palaces. The Medersa Ben Youssef is reached after a long but more or less straight trek down Souk Semarine and Souk el Kebir. The palace museums are also fairly easily reached, off Rue Riad Zitoun el Jedid (Dar Si Saïd, Palais de la Bahia and Maison Tiskiouine), and between Bab Agnaou and Bab Berrima (Saâdian Tombs and Palais Badi'). Detailed itineraries are given under sights.*

Sights

Main areas of interest

Marrakech is clearly divided into the large historic city, the médina, and the *ville nouvelle*, Guéliz. The focal point of the médina, and indeed of the whole city, is the **Jemaâ el Fna**, an open place full of street entertainers and food sellers, adjacent to which are the most important souks. Handily for the tourist, it is located between the two main areas of historic sights. **North of Jemaâ el Fna** are the souks and the Sidi Ben Youssef Mosque, the city's main mosque after the Koutoubia. On a walk in this neighbourhood, you can visit the Almoravid Koubba, the Ben Youssef Medersa, and the Museum of Marrakech. **South of Jemaâ el Fna**, down Riad Zitoun el Kedim, you have an area of palaces, the Saâdian Tombs and a tiny ethnographic museum, the Maison Tiskiwine. If you are staying in a riad, you may well be in the **Bab Doukkala** or **Leksour/Mouassine** neighbourhoods, the former on the Guéliz side of the médina. The latter is very central, just north of Jemaâ el Fna, and is fast becoming the 'chic enclave', home to bijou gallery places like the Ministero del Gusto (sic) and Dar Chérifa. Bab Doukkala is handier for the bus station. For visitors with more time, the cheap goods market at **Bab el Khemis** is busy on a Sunday morning. The tanners at **Bab Debbagh** are also interesting.

Another popular feature of a visit to Marrakech is a tour of the gardens. This will include the **Jardin Majorelle**, quite close to Bab Doukkala, the **Menara**, a large square pool set in a vast olive grove south of Guéliz, and the **Agdal**, another pleasant olive grove close to the Sidi Youssef Ben Ali neighbourhood. To the east and north of Marrakech, across the Oued Issil, is the **Palmeraie**, increasingly built up but with a narrow road for intrepid bike riders. Close to the médina, the gardens between Koutoubia and Mamounia have been totally replanted with roses – and may well open soon. For the time being, **Arset Moulay Slimane**, opposite the Municipality on your way to Jemaâ el Fna, has been left to its own devices.

Most visitors will spend some time in **Guéliz**, the suburb laid out by the French in the 1920s. Despite all the new apartment buildings and traffic, it has a pleasant enough atmosphere with its cafés, upmarket boutiques and food market. The main thoroughfare is Ave Mohammed V and the evening promenade here is popular.

The **Festival national des arts populaires** brings together music and dance troops from all over Morocco, along with other folklore displays. The dates of this annual festival vary (it used to be in June), so you might try to coincide with this by checking with the Moroccan tourist office in your home country. A recent royal initiative is Marrakech's **Festival cinématographique**, probably to be held annually in the early autumn.

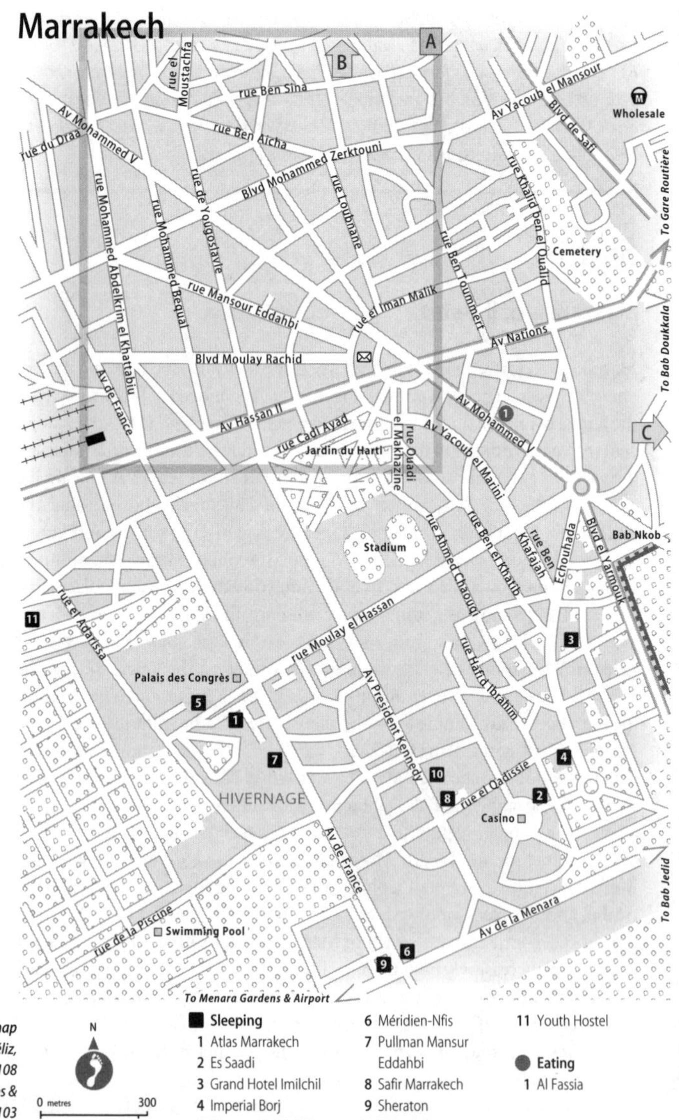

Jemaâ el Fna

The Jemaâ el Fna, unique in Morocco, is perhaps the greatest pull for tourists, yet is still a genuine social area for the Marrakchi people and those flooding in from the surrounding regions, with much aimed solely at Moroccans. It is a large irregular space full of people hawking their goods or talents and others watching, walking, talking and arguing. Its activity never seems to finish, and at each point of the day has a distinctive character. It is particularly memorable during Ramadan when the day's fast ends. Whatever the time of day or year, Jemaâ el Fna is somewhere that the visitor will return to again and again, responding to the magnetic pull that affects locals as much as tourists, to mingle with the crowd or watch from the terrace of the *Café de France* or *Café-Restaurant Argana*.

History

Jemaâ el Fna means 'assembly of the dead', and may refer to the traditional display of the heads of criminals, executed here until the 19th century. In 1956, the government attempted to close down the square by converting it into a corn market and car park, but it soon reverted to its traditional role. In the late 1980s, the bus station was moved out to Bab Doukkala. In 1994, the square was fully tarmacked for the GATT meeting. The food stands were reorganized, and the orange juice sellers issued with smart red fezzes and white gloves. Today, Jemaâ el Fna, despite the pressures of tourism and poverty, or perhaps because of them, retains its attraction.

At 'la Place'

During the day you can explore the stalls and collections of goods spread out on the ground: fruit, herbs and spices, clothes, shoes, alarm clocks and radios, handicrafts too; there are snake charmers and monkey tamers, watersellers and wildly grinning gnaoua musicians with giant metal castanets, all too ready to pose for photographs. Sheltering from the sun under their umbrellas, the fortune tellers and public scribes await their clients. In the evening, the crowd changes again, a mix of students and people pausing on the way home from work, smart tourists strolling to exclusive patio restaurants in the médina – and backpackers ready for hot tagine or harira soup at one of the foodstalls. You may see Ouled el Moussa tumblers or a storyteller enthralling the crowd. Sometimes there are boxers, usually groups of musicians: after much effort to extract a few dirhams from the crowd, an acoustic band will get some Berbers dancing, while around a hissing gas lamp a group will perform a song by Jil Jilala, an activist group popular in the 1970s. There may be *nakkachat*, women with syringes full of henna, ready to pipe a design onto your hands, rather as if they were cake decorating. Modern innovations include a fairground game of 'hook the ring over the coke bottle', while a lad with a dumb-bell improvised from two old millstones will let you do some exercises for a dirham or two. You may find an astrologist-soothsayer tracing out his diagram of the future on the tarmac with a scrubby piece of chalk. A modern variation on the traditional halka or storyteller's circle touches harsh social reality: local people listen to a true tale told with dignity by the relatives of a victim of poverty or injustice. And should you need an aphrodisiac, there are stalls with tea urns selling cinnamon and ginseng tea and little dishes of black, powdery *slilou*, a spicey sweet paste.

Remember to watch your wallet and have change handy for entertainers and orange juice. The hassling of tourists which marred visiting Jemaâ el Fna in the 1980s is a thing of the past: the plain clothes *Brigade Touristique* is watching, and the penalties for hassling are severe. And finally, apparently there are proposals afoot for Jemaâ el Fna to receive some sort of international recognition for its contribution to humankind's oral heritage.

The Koutoubia Mosque

As this is a place of prayer, and in every way the most important mosque in the city, dress decently if you are going to approach the site to view it at length. Behind the mosque are gardens, and some good photo opportunities

The Koutoubia is to Marrakech what the Eiffel Tower is to Paris and the Statue of Liberty is to New York (or so the publicity for the recent restoration of the minaret would have it). There is no doubt about it, the 65-m high **minaret** of the Koutoubia dominates the whole of Marrakech. Visible from afar, it is the landmark which provided the focal point for urban planner Henri Prost when he laid out the modern neighbourhood of Guéliz. The Koutoubia is clearly visible as, unlike the Qarawiyin Mosque in Fès, it is set apart from the dense building of the old town. A fairly unlikely legend (of orientalist inspiration?) goes that as this structure overlooked the harem, only a blind muezzin was allowed to climb it to call the faithful to prayer. The name Koutoubia derives from the Arabic *kutub* (books) and means the 'Booksellers' Mosque', no doubt reflecting the fact that the noble trade of selling manuscripts was conducted in a souk close to the mosque.

History Unusually, the Koutoubia is a **double mosque**, both parts dating from the reign of the second Almohad ruler, Abd el Moumen (1130-63). Standing on the esplanade facing the minaret, the ruins of the first Koutoubia are behind railings to your right (first excavated in the late 1940s, and re-explored recently). The bases of the prayer hall's columns, and the cisterns under the courtyard, are clearly visible. The ground plan of the second Koutoubia, still standing, is the same as that of the ruined one (17 naves). The Almohad mosque at Tin Mal, visitable for non-Muslims, has a similar plan.

So why, back in the 12th century, did the Almohads go to the trouble of building not one but two mosques? Why bother destroying the Almoravid mosque? The site of the mosque is itself historic, originally occupied by a late 11th-century kasbah, the Almoravid **Dar al-Hajar**.

The successful Almohads destroyed much of the Almoravid city, and in 1147 built a large mosque, close to the fortress. In all likelihood they had to do this because, puritan as they were and considering the Almoravids to be heretics, they could not pray in a tainted building. Unfortunately, the orientation of the new Almohad mosque was not quite right – the focal point in a mosque is the direction of Mecca, indicated by the *mihrab*, or prayer niche. The solution was to build a second mosque – the present Koutoubia – even though the faithful at prayer can correct this directional problem themselves, under the direction of the imam, once the right direction has been worked out.

Thus two mosques existed for some time side by side, the first probably functioning as a sort of annexe. Given Almohad religious fervour, the congregations were no doubt large. Today, the bricked-up spaces

The Koutoubia Mosque in the 1930's

on the northwest wall of the Koutoubia Mosque indicate the doors which connected them. However, the complex was excessive in size and the older structure fell into disrepair and eventual ruin. The excavations of 1948 also revealed a *maqsura,* or screen, in front of the *mihrab,* which could be wound up through the floor to protect the Sultan, and a *minbar,* or pulpit, which was moved into position on wooden rollers. The two cisterns in the centre may have been from a previous Almoravid structure. On the eastern flank of this mosque was an arcade of which a niche and the remains of one arch remain.

Existing Koutoubia Mosque

It's fully illuminated on Friday, the Muslim holy day

The existing Koutoubia Mosque was built by Abd el Moumen in 1162, soon after the building of the first mosque. The minaret is 12.5 m wide and 67.5 m to the tip of the cupola on the lantern, and is the mosque's principal feature, rightly ranked along with later Almohad structures, the **Hassan Tower** in Rabat and the Giralda in Sevilla. The minaret, a great feat of engineering in its day, was to influence subsequent buildings in Morocco.

The minaret is composed of six rooms, one on top of the other. The cupola on top of the minaret is a symmetrical, square structure topped by a ribbed dome and three golden orbs. These are alleged to have been made from the melted down jewellery of Yaqoub al Mansour's wife, in penance for having eaten three grapes during Ramadan. The cupola has two windows on each side, above which is a stone panel in the *darj w ktaf,* 'step-and-shoulder' motif. (For a close-up view of the top of the mosque and this design feature, consult your 100dh banknote.) The main tower has a band of coloured tiles at the top.

The Koutoubia, a vast structure for its day, had to be a mosque equal to the ambitions of the western caliphate. It is held to be the high point of Almohad art, a cathedral-mosque of classic simplicity. It is here that the innovations of Hispano-Moorish art – stalactite cupolas, painted wooden ceilings – reach perfection. There are perspectives of horseshoe arches, no doubt an aid to contemplation. (Although the prayer hall is off-limits to the non-Muslim visitor, an idea of what it is like can be gained at the Tin Mal mosque in the High Atlas.) The unique *minbar* (preacher's chair), set against this apparent simplicity, is all decoration and variety – and very much in keeping with the elaborate taste of Ummayad Spain. (The *minbar,* also recently restored, can be viewed at the Badi Palace.) Both prayer hall and chair were to be a source of inspiration for later generations of builders and decorators.

Ultimately, the Koutoubia is striking because it is the work of one ruler, Abd el Moumen. Comparable buildings in western Islam – the Great Mosque of Cordoba and the Alhambra – were built over a couple of centuries.

Behind the mosque, on Rue Sidi Mimoun, is a small tomb to the Almoravid Sultan Youssef Ben Tachfine, the founder of Marrakech.

The northern médina

The souks

Many of the souks of Marrakech retain their original function and the presence of both craftsmen and traders means that they are worth at least a morning to explore. It is, however, far from a relaxing experience, with traders continually besieging tourists with pleas of 'just for looking' or similar. It's worth getting an idea of prices before choosing a reasonable trader and getting down to serious bargaining, if souvenir buying is your thing. An unofficial guide is likely to be more trouble and expense than he is worth, and certainly one should not believe the 'Berber market, only open today' line, which is used everyday.

Paul Pascon – the French Moroccan

Explaining the Moroccan way of life and economy, especially the problems of modern development they face, is not easy either to the Moroccans themselves or to Westerners. Morocco is geographically so close to western Europe, has such great potential of natural resources yet is in many ways distant from the conventional norms of living standards and administrative skills of Europe. The cultural and historical processes that have contributed to this great gap between apparent neighbours need a plausible exposition.

Perhaps the one person best qualified to do this task was the French Moroccan, Paul Pascon. He was born in Fès of French colonist farmer stock in 1932 but was never part of the French establishment – his parents being anti-Vichy during the Second World War. He grew up in a local Moroccan school system and was as much at home in the Arabic as French languages. His advanced education was likewise shared between the University in Rabat and at the Sorbonne in France. He opted for Moroccan citizenship when Morocco became independent in 1956.

Pascon was a rigorous man intellectually. He never sold himself to any single 'ism' but worked himself on research into the nature and direction of development of the native Moroccans in the Marrakech region to show how all the components of the rural Moroccan communities – based in soil, water, kinship, culture and politics – work together to make up a singular and intense society. His book Capitalism and Agriculture in the Haouz of Marrakesh (KPI, London, 1986) is a classic for those who want to get deeper into the Moroccan way of life. He explains in incisive language the 'hows' and 'whys' of Morocco as neither Moroccan alone dare nor European could.

Paul Pascon died in a car accident in 1985.

The main souks lie to the north of Jemaâ el Fna. The entrance to them is to the left of the mosque. Follow this round to the left and then turn right in the main thoroughfare of the souks, **Souk Semmarine**. Alternatively, enter through the small tourist pottery market, further round to the left on Jemaâ el Fna. Souk Semmarine is a busy place, originally the textiles market, and although there are a number of large, expensive tourist shops, there are still some cloth sellers. To the left is a covered *kissaria* selling clothes. The first turning on the right leads past **Souk Larzal**, a wool market, and **Souk Btana**, a sheepskin market, to **Rahba Kedima**, the old corn market, now selling a range of goods including traditional cures and cosmetics, spices, vegetables and cheap jewellery, and with some good carpet shops. Walk back onto the main souk via a short alley with wood-carved goods. Here the souk forks into **Souk el Attarine** on the left and **Souk el Kebir** on the right.

To the right of Souk el Kebir is the **Criée Berbère**, where carpets and *jallabahs* are sold. This was where slaves, mainly from across the Sahara, were auctioned until 1912. Further on is the **Souk des Bijoutiers**, with jewellery. To the left of Souk el Kebir is a network of small alleys, the *kissarias*, selling Western goods. Beyond the *kissarias* is the **Souk Cherratine**, with leather goods, somewhere to bargain for camel or cowhide bags, purses and belts.

Continuing back on the other side of the *kissarias* is the **Souk des Babouches**, a far better place to buy slippers than in the tourist shops. This feeds into **Souk el Attarine**, the spice and perfume souk, which itself leads back into Souk Semmarine. West of the Souk el Attarin is the carpenters' **Souk Chouari**. From here walk on to a Saâdian fountain and the 16th-century **Mouassine Mosque**. South of Souk Chouari is the **Souk des Teinturiers**, or dyers' market, where wool recently dyed is festooned over the walkways, the most picturesque area of the médina. Nearby are the blacksmiths' and coppersmiths' souks.

Islamic monuments

Once you have threaded your way up Souk Semmarine, onto Souk el Kebir and past Souk Cherratine, you are in the neighbourhood of some of a selection of the city's most important Islamic monuments, the **Almoravid Koubba** and **Ben Youssef Medersa**. With the **Museum of Marrakech** and the **Fondation Belarj**, there is also much evidence of private money creating new heritage sites.

Ben Youssef Medersa

Now protected by elaborate neo-Versailles wrought iron railings, the **Almoravid Koubba** (**Koubba el Baroudiyine**) dates from the 11th century, and is a rare example of the architecture of this period, the only complete Almoravid building surviving. It dates from the reign of Ali ben Youssef (1107-43), and perhaps formed part of the toilet and ablutions facilities of the mosque that at the time existed nearby.

At first glance it is a simple building, with a dome surmounting a square stone and brick structure. The dome is quite decorated, however, with a design of interlocking arches, and a star and chevron motif on top. The arches leading into the *koubba* are different on each side. Climb down the stairs to look at the structure close up. Inside, the ceiling below the dome is intricately carved. It includes an octagon within an eight-pointed star, and the use of a range of Almoravid motifs, including the palmette, pine cone and acanthus. Around the corniche is a dedicatory inscription in cursive script. Set into the floor is a small, almost square, basin.

Marrakech souqs

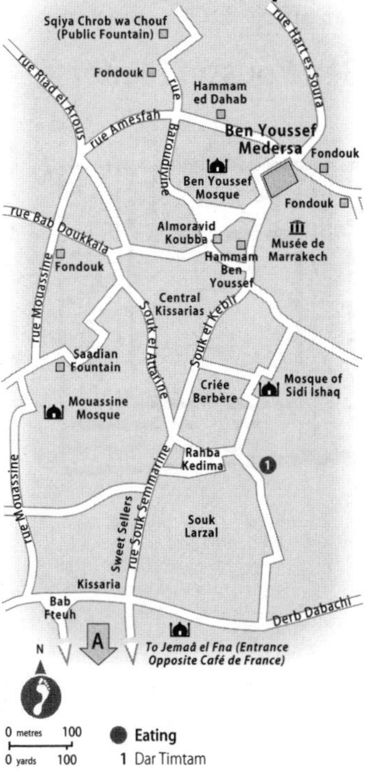

● Eating
1 Dar Timtam

The entrance to the **Musée de Marrakech** is clearly in evidence just off the open area in front of the Almoravid Koubba. The museum is housed in Dar M'nebhi, the early 20th-century palace of a former Moroccan minister of war. ■ *0900-1800, closed Mon. 20dh. T044-390911.* After the entrance courtyard (good café and clean loos on left, bookshop on right), a narrow corridor takes you into the exhibition areas proper. The simple whitewashed walls of the domestic wing shelter temporary exhibitions of contemporary art. Off the main courtyard, now entirely paved and protected by a plexi-glass roof and a brass chandelier as big as a small UFO, are rooms with exhibits of Koran manuscripts, coins, ceramics and textiles. Note the Portuguese influence in the elaborate wooden façades to the rooms on the left. A small passageway to the left of the main reception room takes you through to the restored *hammam*, now home to a small collection of early engravings on Morocco.

Seven saints for a city

Seven is the all-sheltering number at Marrakech. The city has seven spiritual masters, the seb'atu rijal. *A Berber tale runs that in the beginning seven brothers were born of the same mother at the same time – and they all died at the same time. When they were born, they were presented to the prince of the city on a silver plate in the form of 'seven fried fish'. In the seventeenth century, the powerful Alaouite Sultan Moulay Ismaïl, keen to remove any threats to his rule, is said to have promoted the cult of seven saints in Marrakech – to counterbalance the cult of seven saints in the Regrega region which had led to the overthrow of the preceding dynasty, the Saâdians. Four of these saints guard the city gates, Sidi Bel Abbes es-Sebti (Bab el Khemis), Sidi Youssef Ben Ali (Bab Aghmat), Sidi Qadi Ayyad (Bab Ailan), and Imam es-Soheili (Bab er-Ruh). The other saints are Sidi 'Abd el Aziz, Moul Leqsour and Sidi Ben Slimane. The Marrakchis say that their city has seven gates opening onto the cemeteries protecting the town. (In fact there are 11 gates in all. Of the four extra, there are three giving access to the kasbah, plus the West Gate). The important thing in the old days was the protective presence of the dead at the city gates, thresholds of the wider world.*

Standing with the Almoravid Koubba behind you, the minaret of the large 12th-century **Ben Youssef Mosque**, rebuilt in the 19th century, is clearly visible. Turning right out of the Museé de Marrakech, follow the street round and you will come to the entrance to the city's most important Islamic monument, the 16th-century **Ben Youssef Medersa**. One of the few Islamic buildings open to the general public, it is currently being restored by the Fondation Ben Jelloun. Founded in 1564-65 by the Saâdian Sultan Moulay Abdellah, on the site of a previous Merinid *medersa*, it functioned as a boarding school for students of the religious sciences and law. The *medersa* is centred around a square courtyard containing a rectangular pool, and with arcades on two sides. Each student had a separate cell with a sleeping loft and a window looking onto the courtyard. Note the much worn but still fine cedar wood of the upper façades around the courtyard. You will see fine *zellij* tiling on the arcade floor, walls and pillars. Inscriptions are in Kufic and cursive lettering, interwoven with floral patterns.

At the far end is the **prayer hall** covered with an eight-sided wooden dome. Beneath the dome plaster open-work windows illuminate the very attractive tilework. In the *qibla* wall is a five-sided *mihrab*. Note the stalactite ceiling of the *mihrab*, and the carved stucco walls with pine

Ben Youssef Medersa

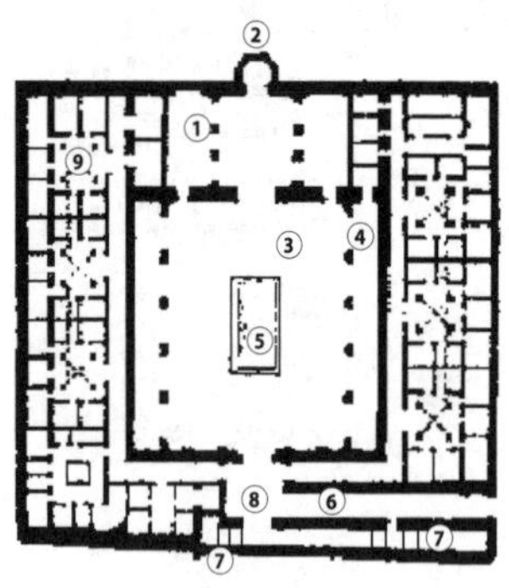

1 Marble pillars
2 5-sided mihrab
3 Open courtyard paved with marble
4 Marble pillars with wooden lintels to support two galleries
5 Marble pool
6 Entry
7 Stairway to students' cells
8 Vestibule
9 Individual students' cells around courtyard

Marrakech

cone motif. (Why did they go for pine cones?) The inscription here, dedicated to the Sultan, has been translated as: "I was constructed as a place of learning and prayer by the Prince of the Faithful, the descendant of the seal of the prophets, Abdellah, the most glorious of all Caliphs. Pray for him, all who enter here, so that his greatest hopes may be realized." Note also the massive Carrara marble columns.

On the way out of the *medersa*, the smelly toilets on the right of the vestibule have an elaborate stalactite design on the ceiling. There is also a 10th-century Andalucían ablution basin in the vestibule, decorated with eagles and Cordoban floral designs. ■ *0900-1200 and 1430- 1800, closed Fri.*

Turning right out of the *medersa*, then left under a covered street, you will come to the entrance of **Dar Belarj**, 'the House of Storks', on your left. The building, restored recently by a couple of Swiss artists, dates from the 1930s. Prior to this there was a *fondouk* on the site which housed the only hospital for birds in North Africa. Here there dwelt a wise man who had the gift of curing wounded storks. Today, the building, austerely but simply refurbished, is used primarily as gallery space. It is definitely worth calling in. Recent events have included an exhibition on the earthen architectures of the Draâ Valley. If director Susan Biederman is on hand she may have time to explain the house and its restoration.

North of the Ben Youssef Medersa

North of the Ben Youssef Medersa, you can wander through residential neighbourhoods. Much of the housing is recent, built on the site of former orchards and market gardens. You begin to realize the contrast with Fès. Whereas Morocco's spiritual capital has steep and narrow streets, accessible only by pedestrians and mules, flat Marrakech is teeming with bicycles and mopeds, mini-taxis and handcarts. Eventually, your wandering might take you to the open square of **Bab Taghzaoute** and on to **Zaouia of Sidi Bel Abbes**, one of the seven saints of Marrakech. Born in Ceuta in 1130 (some authorities say 1145), he championed the cause of the blind in Marrakech and was patronized by Sultan Yaqoub al Mansour. The shrine, recently restored, is strictly closed to non-Muslims. Nearby is the **Zaouia of Sidi Ben Slimane el Jazouli**, a 14th-century Sufi.

Kasbah quarter

Bab Agnaou, meaning the gate of the blacks, marks the entrance to the kasbah quarter. To get to it, follow Rue Bab Agnaou from Jemaâ el Fna, or enter the médina at Bab Rob. The kasbah quarter dates from the late 12th century and the reign of the Almohad Sultan Yaqoub al Mansour. Bab Agnaou is also Almohad. The gateway itself is surrounded by a series of arches within a rectangle of floral designs, with a shell or palmette in each corner and an outer band of Kufic inscription.

The road from the gate leads to Rue de la Kasbah, turn right along here and then take the first left. On this road is the much restored **Kasbah Mosque**, dating from 1190. The minaret has Almohad *darj w ktaf* and *shabka* (net) motifs on alternate sides, with a background of green tiles, above which is a band of coloured tiles. Though not as impressive as the tower of the Koutoubia Mosque, the minaret is a notable landmark en route to the Saâdian Tombs. The entrance to these lies directly to the right of the mosque.

The late 16th-century **Saâdian Tombs** are the mausoleums for the dynasty's Sultans and their families, and were only discovered in 1917, having been sealed off by Moulay Ismaïl in the 17th century. A series of chambers around a small garden, decorated with carved cedar and plaster, is the final, and ultimately rather moving, resting place of the Saâdian family. The *mihrab* of the first main burial chamber is particularly impressive. Here lies the prince Moulay Yazid. The second room contains the tomb of Ahmed al Mansour. The second and older mausoleum was built for the tombs of Ahmed al Mansour's mother, Lalla Messaouda, and Mohammed esh Sheikh, founder of the Saâdians. In the garden and courtyard are the tombs of numerous other

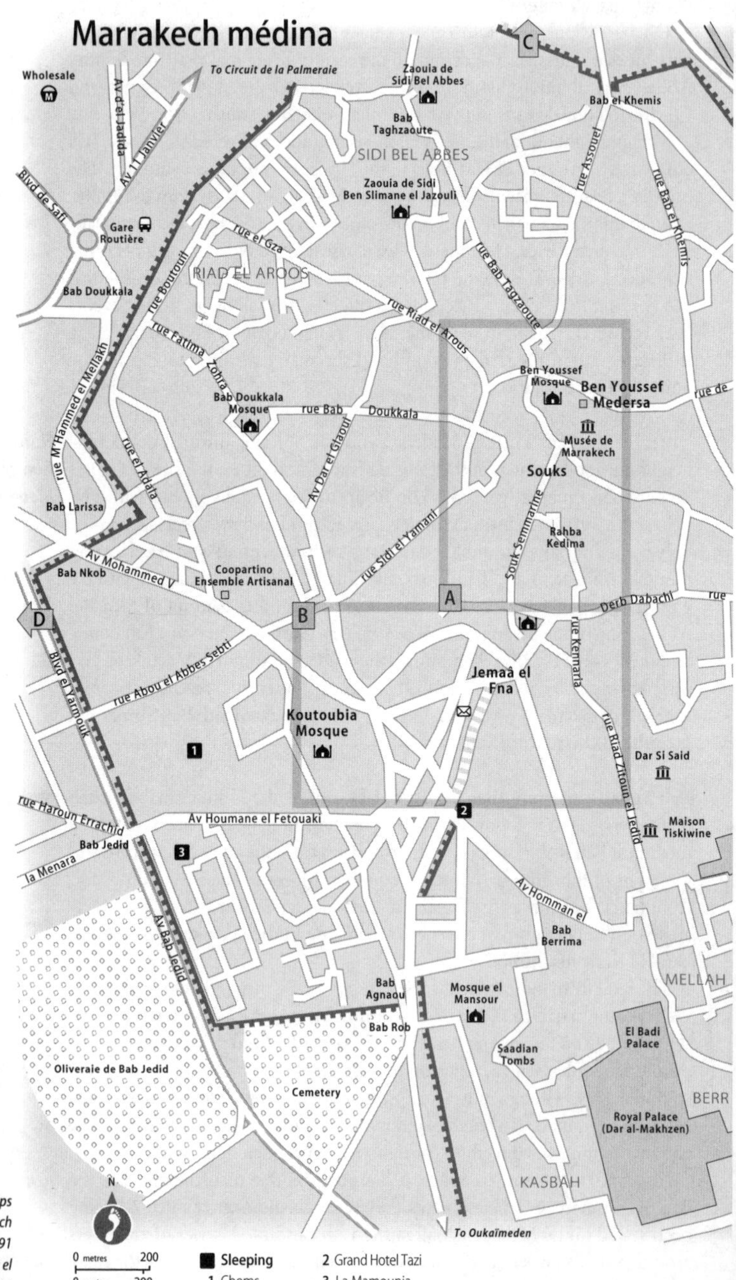

Related maps
A Marrakech souks page 91
& B Jemaâ el Fna page 104

princelings and followers. Try to visit early in the day as the place gets horrendously crowded with tour groups. ■ *0800-1200 and 1400-1800.*

El Badi Palace was built by the Saâdian Sultan Ahmed al Mansour ed-Dahbi (the Golden) between 1578 and 1593, following his accession after his victory over the Portuguese at the Battle of the Three Kings, at Ksar el Kebir in northern Morocco. To get there return to the Bab Agnaou and head right inside ramparts, and then take the second right. Road leads more or less directly to Place des Ferblantiers, a square with a number of workshops where they make lanterns and other items in tin. Pass through Bab Berima, the gate on the southern side. The entrance to the palace is on the right, between high pisé walls. ■ *0900-1200 and 1430-1730.*

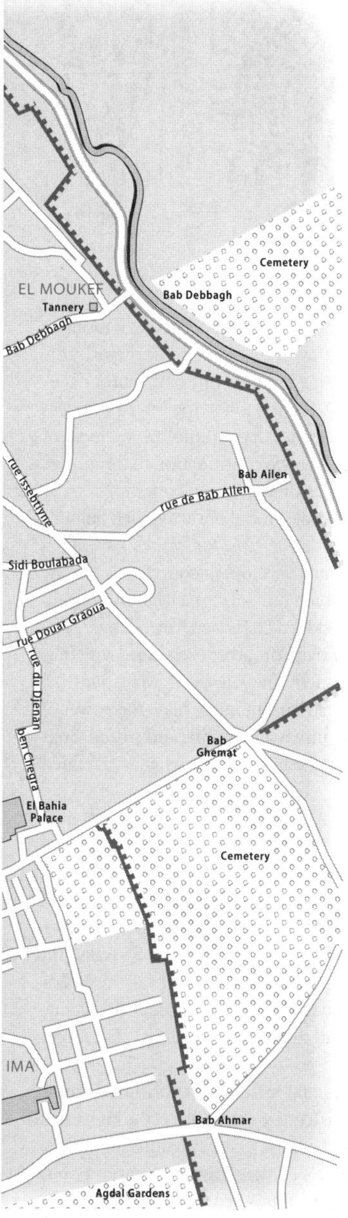

The 16th-century palace marks the height of Saâdian power, the centrepiece of an imperial capital. It was a lavish display of the best craftsmanship of the period, using the most expensive materials, including gold, marble and onyx. Today only the great walls have survived as a reminder of one of the periodic royal re-foundations of Marrakech. The palace was largely destroyed in the 17th century by Moulay Ismaïl, who stripped it of its decorations and fittings and carried them off to Meknès. No austere royal fortress, the Badi was probably a palace for audiences – and it was at one of these great court ceremonies that the building's fate was predicted: "Among the crowds taking part at the banquet was a visionary who, at the time, enjoyed a certain reputation for his saintliness. 'What do you think of this palace?' asked the Sultan Al Mansour in jest. 'When it is demolished, it will make a big pile of earth,' replied the visionary. Al Mansour was lost for words at this answer. He felt a sinister omen." El Ifrani, a historian writing in the early 18th century, noted the inauspicious numerical meaning of the palace's name. The value of its letters is 117 – exactly the number of lunar years the palace remained intact (from 1002 AH to 1119 AH, that is 1594-1708).

Bab Aguaou
Marrakech

The name El Badi ties in with the palace's once elaborate decoration. In Arabic, *'ilm el badi* is one of the main varieties of classical Arabic rhetoric, the art of stylistic ornament – and the palace was certainly one of the most decorated in its day. Above one of the main gates, the following inscription was placed in flowing Arabic calligraphy: "This gate is as beautiful as the eloquent beginning of a fine poem, and the palace is as the continuation of this poem. Thus it was named *badi*, using hyperbole, assonance and pleonasm."

In its day, the Badi Palace was the physical symbol of the Golden Sultan's glory. Al Mansour had conquered the Soudan (Arabic for 'blacks'), bringing them under Islamic rule. Deeply influenced by Ottoman court traditions, he no doubt hoped to establish the imposing ceremonial of the Istanbul court in Morocco. The palace drew in wealth and skilled craftsmen from all over. The colonnades were of marble, apparently bought, or rather exchanged with Italian merchants, for their equivalent weight in sugar. Al Mansour had sugar-cane presses built. Perhaps there is a visual message here, the power of the prince transforming crystalline sugar into white marble and stucco. Sugary sweets were distributed to the Sultan's guests – at a time when well refined sugar was a rarity.

The ill omens which had so frightened Al Mansour were realized: not only was the palace destroyed, but all its fine building materials were dispersed. The glory of the palace was dismantled, and in the words of one contemporary observer, "there was not a single city in Morocco which did not receive some debris of El Badi." The vaulting ambition and power of the great Moulay Ismaïl in turn had to find an expression in stone – or rather adobe – walls, but at Meknès, not Marrakech. Perhaps there was a political logic to all this building activity. Moulay Ismaïl is said to have declared: "If I have a sack full of rats, I must move the sack constantly to prevent them from escaping." The moral of the tale? 'Keep your subjects busy.'

In June, El Badi comes alive for the annual **festival of traditional dance and music**. Most of the year, however, it is a quiet sort of place, the high thick walls protecting the vast courtyard from the noise of the surrounding streets. The courtyard is divided by water channels connecting a number of pools. The largest of these even has an island. The ruins on either side of the courtyard were probably summer houses, the one at the far end being called the **Koubba el Khamsiniya** after the 50 pillars in its construction. The complex

El Atlal – laments for traces of the past

Sometime in the 16th century, Leo Africanus visited the ruined Almohad palace (on which El Badi Palace was later to be built) of Marrakech: "Despite the slight remains of the past which have survived in this town," he wrote, "they still bear witness to the pomp and grandeur which reigned at the time of Yaqoub al Mansour. Today only the palace of the royal family and the palace of the archers are inhabited. In the latter are housed the porters and muleteers of the present sovereign. All the rest is home to rock doves, crows, owls and birds of this sort." The palaces of old Morocco – like the kasbahs of the southern regions – were built of pisé, a sort of earth, lime and gravel mix. With heavy rains and wind, they were eroded away, and needed constant repair and rebuilding. When a dynasty disappeared, its capital would often disappear with it, sometimes for good. Across the Arab world, there are abandoned royal capitals – legendary Samarra in Iraq, the ruined cities of Islamic Andalucía, Raqqada near Kairouan in Tunisia, Chellah outside Rabat, and Tin Mal in the High Atlas, of which only the mosque has survived.

In poetic descriptions of such remains, Arab and other writers would draw their moral conclusions about the ruins, meditating on the rise and fall of dynasties, and the hubris of domineering builder-rulers. Contemplating remains of the past, reliving better days goes right back to the earliest days of recorded Arabic poetry in the 6th century AD. Nomad poets wrote of the emotions aroused as they looked at the charred remains of a campfire, the only trace of the encampment of the departed loved one. El Atlal (The Remains), sung by 20th-century Egyptian diva Um Kalthoum, opens with just such a lament. If there is one Arab song you should try to discover while you are in Morocco, it is El Atlal, perhaps the most famous piece of 20th-century Arab music.

contains a small museum which includes the movable *minbar*, a sort of pulpit, from the Koutoubia Mosque. The scattered ruins of the palace, with odd fragments of decoration amidst the debris, also include stables and dungeons.

To the south of the El Badi Palace is the **Dar el Makhzen**, the modern-day Royal Palace, now one of King Hassan II's favourite residences. Marrakech is especially animated when the court is in residence, generally for a couple of months in the winter.

Nearby, the **Musée Dar al Funoun ash Shaâbia** has audio-visual displays on various themes of Moroccan arts including dance, theatre and the marriage ceremony, each lasting between 20 and 45 minutes. ■ *154 Derb Sahrige, Rue Arset Moussa, Riad Zitoun el Kedim, T044-426632.*

The southeastern médina

Museum of Moroccan Arts and Crafts

To get to the southeast area of the médina follow Rue des Banques from just past *Café de France* on the Jemaâ el Fna. This leads into Riad Zitoun Jedid. Off to the left is the **Dar Si Said**; the Museum of Moroccan Arts and Crafts is on Riad Zitoun Jedid. This palace was built by Si Said, Vizier under Moulay El Hassan, and half-brother of Ba Ahmed Ben Moussa. The museum includes pottery, jewellery, leatherwork from Marrakech and a collection of beautiful carpets from Chichaoua. It is particularly strong on Amazigh artefacts such as curved daggers, copperware, jewellery of silver, ivory and amber. The first floor has been made into an elegant salon with Hispano-Moorish decoration and some very elegant cedarwood furniture. The palace itself is small but with a cool and pleasant courtyard, where a remarkable collection of old window and door frames are on display. Items to look out for include a marble basin, unusually decorated with heraldic birds, from Islamic Spain, and a primitive four-seater wooden ferris wheel of the type still found in *moussems* (country fairs) in Morocco. Those particularly interested in traditional Moroccan artefacts will want to continue to the neighbouring Maison Tiskiwine. ■ *0900-1200, 1600-2100 in the summer, 1430-1800 in the winter, closed Tue. T044-442464.*

Maison Tiskiwine

Don't miss the beautiful Saharan leatherwork

Between the Palace and Dar Si Said is the Maison Tiskiwine ('the House of the Horns'), home to a fine collection of items related to Moroccan rural culture and society. This small museum was put together by the Dutch art historian Bert Flint. There is an exhibition of craftsmen's materials and techniques from regions as far apart as the Rif, High Atlas and the Sahara, including jewellery and costumes, musical instruments, carpets and furniture. The building itself, around a courtyard, is an authentic and well maintained example of traditional domestic architecture. Flint was also instrumental in setting up another collection of traditional Moroccan craftwork for the City Council in Agadir. ■ *T044-443335. 8 Rue de la Bahia.*

See plan over page

Further to the south is the **Bahia Palace** (Bahia means 'brilliant'). It was built in the last years of the 19th century by the Vizier Ba Ahmed Ben Moussa, or Bou Ahmed, a former slave who exercised considerable power under Sultans Moulay Hassan and Abd el Aziz (see map). Generally packed with tour groups, the palace is a maze of corridors, passageways and empty chambers with painted ceilings. The story goes that Bou Ahmed was so hated that, on his death in 1900, his palace was looted and his possessions stolen by slaves, servants and members of his *harem*. The visit concludes with a marble paved courtyard of 50 m x 30 m, and the guides will tell you that each wife and concubine had a room looking onto the patio. Enjoy the pleasant garden planted with fruit trees and flowers. ■ *0800-1200 and 1430-1800.*

The Jewish quarter

The *mellah* was created in 1558. This lies south of the palace and to the west of the El Badi Palace. It's an extensive quarter reflecting the community's historic importance to the city, when they were involved in the sugar trade and banking, as well as providing most of the jewellers, metalworkers and tailors. There were several synagogues, and under the control of their rabbis, the area had considerable autonomy. There are now few Jews left, but the quarter is still distinct in the cramped houses and narrow streets. Conditions here remain worse than in much of the médina, with unpaved roads and insanitary drainage. It is worth asking around to be let into one of the synagogues. There is a small one down an alley as you face the restaurant *Dar Douiria*, on your right as you leave Place des Ferblantiers behind.

The walls and gates

The extensive ramparts of Marrakech (20 gates and 200 towers stretching for 16 km) are predominantly Almoravid, excepting those around the Agdal Gardens, although extensively restored since. The reconstruction is a continual process as the pisé-cement walls, made of the distinctive earth of the Haouz plains, gradually crumble. The ramparts and gates are one of the distinctive sights of Morocco. A ride in a horse-drawn *calèche* will allow you to see part of the ramparts. In places, there has been much beautification going on of late, with fancy wrought iron railings and rose gardens taking the place of the dust on the Hivernage side of town.

Bab Rob, near the buses and grands taxis on the southwest side of the médina, is Almohad, and is named after the grape juice which could only be brought through this gate. **Bab Debbagh** (the Tanners' gate), on the east side, is an intricate defensive gate with a twisted entrance route and wooden gates, which could shut off the various parts of the building for security. From the top of the gate there would be a good view of the tanneries (see below) if one were allowed up. It is possible to look around the tanneries. Note that hides are often laid out to dry on the banks of the nearby Oued Issil – where a large social housing development is going up replacing the local bidonville. **Bab el Khemis**, on the northeast side, opens into the **Souk el Khemis** (Thursday market) and an important area of mechanics and craftsmen. Stop in to check out the junk-market on a Sunday morning. There is a small saint's tomb inside the gate building. **Bab Doukkala**, on the northwest

Bahia Palace

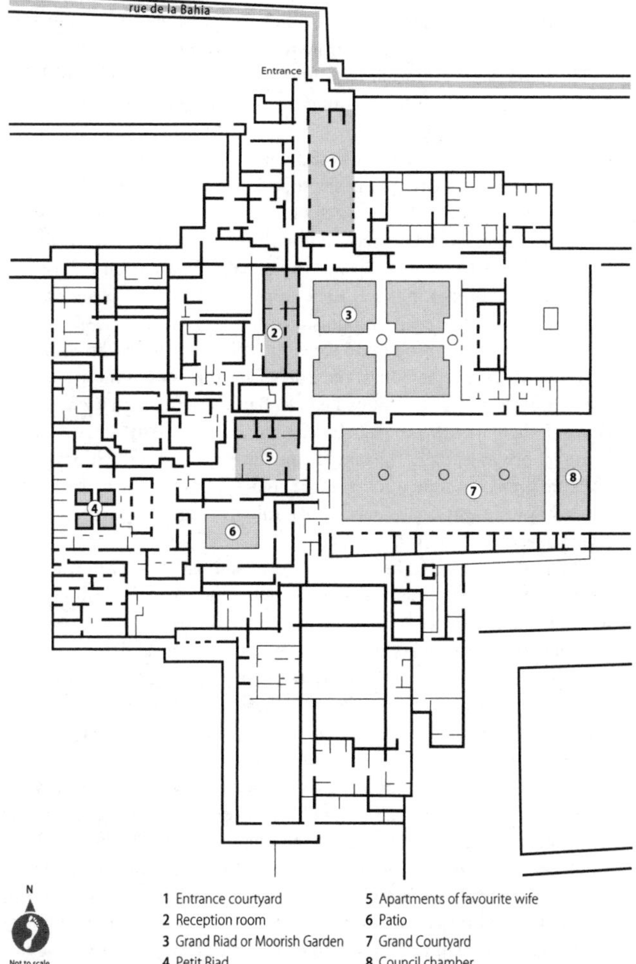

1 Entrance courtyard
2 Reception room
3 Grand Riad or Moorish Garden
4 Petit Riad
5 Apartments of favourite wife
6 Patio
7 Grand Courtyard
8 Council chamber

side by the bus station, is a large gate with a horseshoe arch and two towers. The médina side has a horseshoe arch and a cusped, blind arch, with a variation on the *darj w ktaf* (step and shoulder) motif along the top. There are occasional exhibitions in the guardroom inside the gate. The esplanade has been badly neglected, the orange trees have died off...but then few wealthy visitors to Marrakech see this gate. At night, this is the place to locate a black-market booze merchant. A road is being opened up running across the palm grove north of Bab Doukkala, to complete the circuit of the ramparts.

Tanneries near Bab Debbagh

The tanneries near Bab Debbagh (literally Tanners' Gate) are some of the most interesting sights in Marrakech. You may want to get a view of the area from the leather shop terrace next to Bab Debbagh. Wandering towards the tanners' area, you will in all likelihood be approached by some lad who will offer to show you the tanneries (20dh is a very reasonable tip). Through a small metal door, you will be shown an area of foul-smelling pits, where men tread and rinse skins in nauseous liquid. In small lean-to buildings, you will find other artisans scraping and stretching the skins. Located close to the seasonal Oued Issil, the tanners were on the edge of the city with plenty of water and space to expand away from residential areas.

The tanners are said to have been the first to settle in Marrakech at its foundation and a gate is named after them, the only one to be named for a craft corporation. 'Bab Debbagh, bab deheb' – 'Tanners' Gate, gold gate' – the old adage goes, in reference to the tanners' prosperity. One legend runs that seven virgins are buried in the foundations of the gate (sisters of the seven protector saints of Marrakech) and women who desire a child should offer them candles and henna. Another legend runs that Bab Debbagh is inhabited by Malik Gharub, a genie who dared to lead a revolt against Sidna Suleyman, the Black King, only to be condemned to tan a cowhide and cut out *belgha* soles for eternity as punishment.

The tannery was considered a dangerous place – as it was the entrance to the domain of the Other Ones, and a beneficial one, since skins were a symbol of preservation and fertility. Bab Debbagh was the eastern gate into the city, and there was a symbolism based on the sun rising in the east and skin being reborn as leather. The tanners, because they spend their days in pits working the skins, were said to be in contact with the unseen world of the dead; they were also seen as masters of fertility, being strong men, capable of giving a second life to dry, dead skin.

The tanneries used to be regulated by an annual cycle, with work more intensive in summer, when the skins can be cleaned in the fermenting water more quickly and dried on the walls and river banks. In the winter, the tanners of country origin would return to their fields to plough and sow.

In the old days, the complex **process of tanning** would start with soaking the skins in a sort of swamp – or *iferd* – in the middle of the tannery, filled with a fermenting mixture of pigeon guano and tannery waste. Fermenting would last three days in summer, six in winter. Then the skins would be squeezed out and put to dry. Hair would be scraped off. Then the skins would go into a pit of lime and argan-kernel ash. This would remove any remaining flesh or hair, and prepare the skin to receive the tanning products. The lime bath lasts 15-20 days in summer, up to 30 in winter. Then the skins are washed energetically, trodden to remove any lime, and any extra bits are cut off. Next the skins spend 24 hours in a *qasriya*, a round pit of more pigeon dung and fresh water. At this stage the skin becomes thinner and stretches. (This is a stage to be undertaken with care, because a djinn lives in the pit, and skins can be ruined

Hedgehogs and porcupines

The kunfud *or hedgehog is traditionally a crafty little character, rather like the fox in western European folk legends. It is said that this little spiny animal was once a man who prostituted his daughter, and in punishment was transformed into a hedgehog. Its near relative, the porcupine, has a similar legend attached to it. The porcupine is said to have been a Jewish blacksmith who made faulty arrows to sell to the Muslims. God cursed him and turned him into a bequilled creature. As the porcupine can see at night, it is said to have supernatural powers. Both animals are hunted by the tanners (who are said to be great hunters), and hedgehog skins are cured and sold to the herbalists or to women who may use them in magic rites, notably as part of a cure for male impotence or baldness. Melted hedgehog fat is said to be an aphrodisiac, while hedgehog paws – on account of their resemblance to human hands – are used to ward off the evil eye.*

if left too long.) There follows soaking in wheat fibre and salt, for 24 hours, to remove any traces of lime and guano.

Then begins the actual tanning process. The word *debbagh* actually means tannin. Traditional tanneries used only plants – roots, barks and certain seeds and fruits. In Marrakech, acacia and oak bark are used, along with *takkut*, the ground up fruit of the tamarisk. A water and tannin mix is prepared in a pit, and the skins get three soakings.

After this, the skins have to be prepared to receive the dye. They are scraped with pottery shards, beaten and coated with oil, alum and water. Then they are dyed by hand, with the dye traditionally being poured out of a bull's horn, and left to dry in the sun. (The characteristic yellow of leather for *belgha* slippers came from pomegranates.) Finally, the skins are worked to make them smoother and more supple, stretched between two ropes and worked on smooth pottery surfaces. Skins were sold at auction.

The process of tanning skins is strongly symbolic – the tanners say that the skin eats, drinks, sleeps and 'is born of the water'. When the skin is treated with lime, it is said to be thirsty; when it is treated with pigeon dung, it is said to receive *nafs*, a spirit. The *merkel* (treading) stage prepares the skin to live again, while the *takkut* of the tanning mixture is also used by women to dye their hair. At this point, the skin receives *ruh* (breath). Leather is thus born from the world of the dead and the *ighariyin*, the people of the grotto, and is fertilized in the swampy pool, the domain of the dead – who are also said to have the power to bring rain.

In Marrakech, you will probably be told that there are two tanneries: one Arab, the other Berber. In all likelihood, the workforce is ethnically mixed today. Certainly there are specialities, with one set of tanners working mainly on the more difficult cow and camel skins, and the others on goat and sheep skins. For the record, the tanners were known to be great nocturnal hunters, doing a trade in hedgehog skins for magic. They were also known as big *kif* smokers: working in such difficult conditions with the foul odours and the presence of spirits would have been difficult without a daily pipe of *kif*.

The interesting thing is to see a pre-industrial process, still alive and functioning not far from the heart of the médina – even though the traditional dyes have been replaced with chemical products. If walking precariously between pools of nauseous skins and liquid is too much, you could always take a carriage to one of Marrakech's gardens.

Gardener's words

With Marrakech being such a garden city, it is hardly surprising that the city's Arabic has so many words to name gardens: agdal *and* arsat, boustan *and* buhayra, jnene *and* riad. *Some of the terms are of Persian origin, hardly surprising given the Iranians' love of flowers:* boustan *is an amalgam of* bou *(perfume, odour) and* stan *(place). Also of Persian origin is the European term paradise, which derives from* firdaous. *For the foreign visitor,* riad *will be the most immediately familiar garden term.* Riad, *also the name for the capital of Saudi Arabia, is a plural form of* rawda, *meaning a 'fine watered garden'. In Morocco,* riad *has come to signify a house with a garden courtyard, generally divided symmetrically into four equal sections, planted with shade-giving fruit trees and divided by walkways of* bejmete *(terracotta bricks) or* zellij, *ceramic mosaic. In Marrakech, a* jnene *(plural of* janna, *which term also designates paradise in Arabic), is a market-garden, as is an* arsat. *As the population of Marrakech grew, old market gardens were divided up for building homes. The word* arsat *still survives in the names of certain neighbourhoods. The terms* agdal *and* buhayra *denote large irrigated areas outside the city walls, focusing on a large central irrigation basin or* sahrij. Buhayra *in fact means 'little sea', while* agdal *(also spelt* aguedal *) is a term of Amazigh origin, meaning a walled meadow. In Marrakech – and elsewhere in Morocco for that matter – the term* agdal *came to be used for the private walled gardens of His Cherifian Majesty. The first gardens of this type, equipped with huge square artificial lakes and elaborate water supply systems, were created by the Almohad sultans in the 12th and 13th centuries in their power centres across northwest Africa and Andalucía. Even today, in the age of air-conditioning, both the urban* riad *and the vast* agdal, *outside the ramparts, create marvellous micro-climates where one can take refuge from the overwhelming heat of summer.*

The gardens

Agdal Gardens The Agdal Gardens, stretching south of the médina, were established in the 12th century under Abd el Moumen, and were expanded and reorganized by the Saâdians. The vast expanse, over 400 ha, includes several pools, and extensive areas of olive, orange and pomegranate trees. They are in the main closed when the king is in residence, but are worth visiting at other times. Of the pavilions, the **Dar al Baida** was used by Sultan Moulay Hassan to house his *harem*. The largest pool, **Sahraj el Hana**, receives its coachloads of tourists, but in-between times is a pleasant place to relax, although not to swim.

Menara Gardens From the médina and the Agdal Gardens, Avenue de la Menara leads past the **Oliveraie de Bab Jedid** to the Menara Gardens. This is an olive grove, and in itself not very interesting but, with its shelter from the sun, a good place for a picnic. At the centre is a rectangular pool with a good view of the Atlas Mountains, a picture on numerous postcards and brochures. The green-tiled pavilion alongside was built in 1866. Inside, above the small display of carpets and other Amazigh artifacts, is an impressive, painted cedarwood ceiling.

The Jardin Majorelle The Jardin Majorelle, also called the **Bou Saf-Saf Garden**, is off Avenue Yaqoub al Mansour. This is a small tropical garden laid out in the inter-war period by a French artist, Louis Majorelle, scion of a family of cabinet-makers from Nancy who made their money with innovative Art Nouveau furniture. Majorelle portrayed the landscapes and people of the Atlas in large, strongly coloured paintings, some of which were used for early tourism posters. His garden reflects his love for contrast and strong colour. The buildings are a vivid cobalt blue, the cactuses huge and sculptural. Bulbuls sing in the bamboo thickets and flit between the Washingtonia palms. The garden belongs to Yves St Laurent, who has a house close by. A green-roofed garden pavilion houses a small **Musée d'Art Islamique** with a fine and easy digestible collection of objects. Sensitive souls tempted to try Majorelle Garden blue in decorating schemes back home in northern climes should beware – the result depends on bright sunlight filtered by lush vegetation. ■ *0800-1200 and 1400-1700 in the winter, 0800-1200 and 1500-1900 in the summer.*

The Palmeraie

Marrakech is surrounded by extensive palm groves. In the original Prost development plan, no building was to be higher than a palm tree – and it is illegal to cut down a palm tree – hence palms have been left growing in the middle of pavements. In recent years the Palmeraie has suffered as the urbanized area round Marrakech has expanded, and certain areas have been divided up for

Northern suburbs & Palmeraie

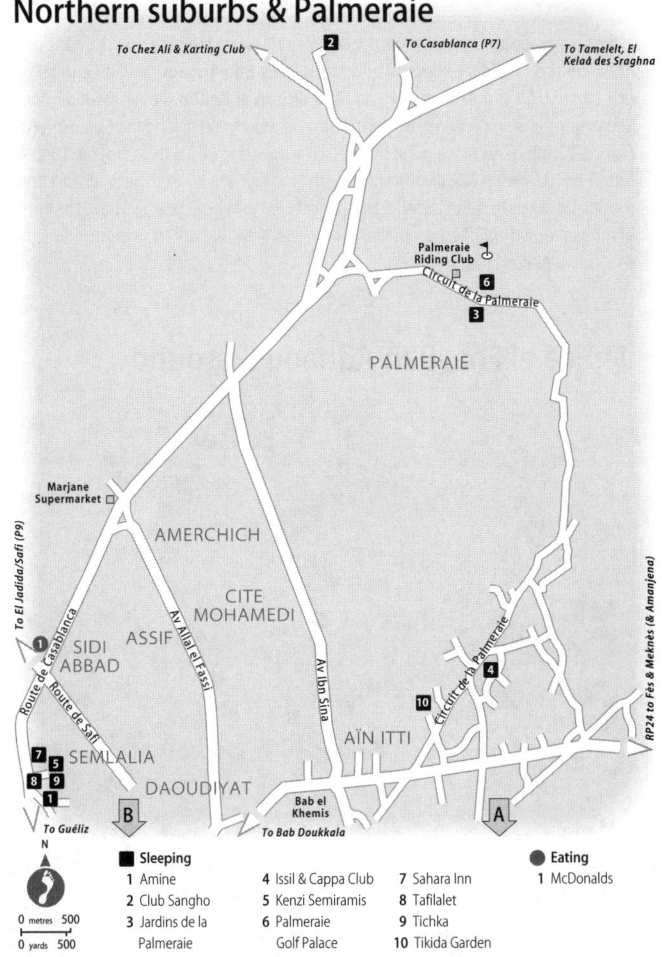

up market holiday development. Nevertheless, it is a good place for a drive or a *calèche* tour. Take the Route de la Palmeraie, off the P24 to Fès, to explore it.

Essentials

Sleeping

■ on map
Price codes:
see inside front cover
If visiting at peak times (winter holidays, spring) you should reserve rooms – demand far outstrips supply

The upmarket hotels are located in three areas, in the **Hivernage** garden city area and along the neighbouring Ave de France, in a development on the Casablanca road in the **Semlalia** neighbourhood, and in the **Palmeraie** east of the city. L'Hivernage is close to **Guéliz**, and a short taxi ride into Jemaâ el Fna in the old town. Upmarket guesthouse-type accommodation is located in the médina (favoured locations: Bab Doukkala and Bab Leksour) and the Palmeraie. Medium price hotels tend to be located in Guéliz, with quite a few along Ave Mohammed V and Blvd Mohammed Zerktouni. Hotels ***Toulousain***, ***Moutamed*** and ***Oasis*** are all OK, a step up from médina traveller hotels. More expensively, there is some good city-tour type accommodation here, see hotels ***El Kebir***, ***Nassim***, ***Oudaya***, ***du Pacha***, ***Tachfine*** and ***Tafoukt***.

In terms of cheap accommodation, the vast majority of small hotels are 5-10-mins walk from Jemaâ el Fna, in the alleys off pedestrian street **Bab Agnaou** (hotels *Central Palace*, *Ichbilia*, *Ali* and *Arset el Bilk*), off **Riad Zitoun el Kedim** (hotels *Essaouira* and *Sherazade* for example), and the **Kennaria** neighbourhood behind the *Café-Hotel de France*. (Coming by rail and *CTM* buses, you will need to take a petit taxi, say 10dh to Jemaâ el Fna/Arset el Bilk. If your rucksack isn't too heavy, it is just about walkable from the Bab Doukkala bus and taxi station.) To get to Jemaâ el Fna, you also have the number 1 bus down Ave Mohammed V from near the tourist information service on rond-point Abd el Moumen.

Jemaâ el Fna, Bab Agnaou & around

■ Sleeping
1 Ali
2 Badr
3 Chella
4 CTM
5 de Foucauld
6 Essaouira & Médina
7 Gallia
8 Ichbilia
9 Kennaria
10 La Gazelle
11 Mabrouka
12 Mimosa
13 Mounir
14 Résidence de la Place & Café-Hotel de France
15 Sherazade

● Eating
1 Al Baraka
2 Café Restaurant Argana
3 Palais Gharnatta
4 Riad Temsna

The médina

AL *La Mamounia*, Ave Bab Jedid, T044-444409, F044-444660. Now part of the ***Leading Hotels of the World*** network. A Marrakech institution, one of the first hotels in the city, built just within the walls a couple of mins walk from the Koutoubia. Originally owned and run by Moroccan railways, it was patronized by the rich and famous back at its beginnings in the 1930s. The major 1980s refit was undertaken by royal decorator André Paccard and was in its turn revamped in the late 1990s by Alberto Pinto. Although the Art Deco-Arabesque mix is a little overwhelming in places, there is much perfection. Prices start at around 2,000dh for a double in low season (excluding petit déjeuner, for which add 190dh). 171 luxurious rooms, 49 normal suites, 8 themed suites, 3 villas, outstanding service, 5 restaurants serving stunning menus of the highest standard, 5 bars, casino, conference room, business centre, boutiques, fitness and beauty centre, hammam, pool, tennis, squash, 5 ha of gardens. All in all, kind of nouveau riche. **AL** *La Maison Arabe*, 1, Derb Assehbe, Bab Doukkala, T044-391233, F044-443715. A restaurant now converted into very swish accommodation, run by the Prince Ruspoli and Pierre Cluzel. Private house atmosphere – which may soon be destroyed by the addition of a further floor. 10 rooms, including 6 suites with private terraces covering 2 courtyards. Price includes breakfast and afternoon tea. Evening meal available by arrangement.

Good selection of cheap hotels in the streets off the pedestrian Rue Bab Agnaou, off Jemaâ el Fna. Also very handy for banks and other services

Rue Bab Agnaou (aka Le Prince) and around **C** *Hotel Chems*, Ave Houmane El Fetouaki (listed here for convenience), BP 594, T044-444813. Small, restaurant, bar and nightclub. **D** *Hotel de Foucauld*, Ave el Mouahidine, T044-445499. 33 rooms, a good hotel with restaurant and bar, same management as the *Tazi*. Easily located just opposite the well planted square de Foucauld, aka Arset el Bilk. Used by trekking groups. **C/D** *Hotel Gallia*, 30 Rue de la Recette, T044-445913. Clean, conveniently located. Head down Rue Bab Agnaou from Jemaâ el Fna, the Gallia is at the end of a narrow street on the left. A 1930s building with beautifully planted courtyard. Had a rather sulphurous reputation a couple of decades ago, but has been considerably smartened up. Very popular, so reserve well in advance. Some very good rooms, plenty of hot water. **D** *Grand Hotel Tazi*, Rue Bab Agnaou, T044-442787, F044-442152, at the far end of pedestrian Rue Bab Agnaou from Jemaâ el Fna. Prices: 1 person 280dh room only (300dh B&B). 2 persons 320dh room only (360dh B&B). Memorable rooms with extravagantly painted ceilings and furniture, one of the few bars close to the médina, reasonable Moroccan restaurant at average prices, pool closed. Though convenient for the sights and services, expensive for what it is. Reception pretty unpleasant. **E** *Hotel Ali*, Rue Moulay Ismaïl, T044-444979, F044-440522. Especially recommended for those intending to go climbing/trekking in the Jebel Toubkal region as the guides are here; clean, comfortable and friendly, good Moroccan cuisine, adjacent to Jemaâ el Fna. **E** *Hotel La Gazelle*, 13 Rue Beni Marinine (the street through the arch to the right of the post office), T044-441112, F044-445537, 2 persons 110dh, showers on corridors. Well managed, small terrace. **E** *Hotel Ichbilia*, on a street linking Rue Beni Marinine and Rue Bab Agnaou (turn left off the latter just before Cinéma Mabrouka), T044-390486. Street-facing rooms noisy. Fine for a night. Cyber-café in basement of building. **E** *Hotel Central Palace*, T044-440235, F044-442884. Well signed in an alley off Rue Bab Agnaou, on your left as you come from Jemaâ el Fna. 40 rooms, 120dh for a twin room. One of the best cheapies. Also has an annexe to house overflow. **E** *Hotel Afriquia* 45, Derb Sidi Bouloukat, T044-442403. Close to *Hotel Central Palace*. With a patio and roof terrace. 80dh for 2 persons, washbasins in rooms. **E** *Hotel Ed Dakhla* 43, Derb Sidi Bouloukat, T044-442359. Keep going down alley after *Hotel Afriquia*. 40dh persons. Prefer the *Afriquia* or the *Central Palace*. **F** *Hotel Azhar*, T044-445955, down the alley to the left of the *Hotel CTM*, with lots of other sleeperies, 40dh,1 person. Clean and cheap. **F** *Hotel Mabrouka*, on Rue Bab Agnaou, just opposite Cinéma Mabrouka, 40dh single. 10 cell-like rooms off 2 tiny courtyards, hot showers 5dh. Acceptable, good location if not much else. **F** ***Hotel Nouazah***, on the 1st left off Rue Bab Agnaou; and **F** ***Hotel el Atlas***, a friendly, efficient place on Rue de la Recette.

Riad Zitoun el Kedim and around **C** *Hotel Sherazade*, 3 Derb Djama (3rd narrow street on your left as you come up Riad Zitoun el Kedim from Jemaâ el Fna, big awning over door), T/F044-429305, sharazade@iam.net.ma, also reservations via Herr Khan in Germany on T06-21771633. Germano-Moroccan management. Spotlessly clean. Varied accommodation around large, pleasantly decorated courtyards. Rooftop terraces. Can organize excursions and car hire. **E** ***Hotel Chella***, T044-442977, heading down Riad Zitoun el Kedim from Jemaâ el Fna, take third narrow side street on your right. Small, clean establishment, showers extra, 40dh, 1 person. **E** ***Hotel Essaouira***, 3 Derb Sidi Bouloukat, down an alley left off Riad Zitoun el Kedim as you come from Jemaâ el Fna (just before the left turn for the *Hotel Sherazade*). T044-443805, 50dh, 1 person. Fine for a couple of nights. **E** ***Hotel Médina***, 1 Derb Sidi Bouloukat, T044-442997. Similar but smaller to *Hotel Essaouira*. 50dh, 1 person, breakfast extra. **E** *Hotel CTM*, on the Jemaâ el Fna, T044-442325. Good and clean rooms, some with a view of the square (noisy), often full. Note that *CTM* buses now go from Blvd Mohammed Zerktouni in Guéliz. **E** ***Hotel de France***, 197 Riad Zitoun el Kedim. Another cheapie, with be-rucksacked figure striding out on sign.

Marrakech

Kennaria and around There is a small selection of cheap hotels in the side streets behind the *Café de France*, on Riad Zitoun Jedid, aka Kennaria. To get into this area, take Rue des Banques, the road that runs straight ahead of you as you face the *Café de France*; this intersects with Rue el Kennaria, which then turns into Rue Riad Zitoun Jedid. **E** ***Hotel-Résidence de la Place***, right on Jemaâ el Fna, the one next to *Café-Hotel de France*, T06-1776169. 1 person 100dh, 2 persons 125dh, with shower and WC, 16 rooms, number 25 the best. Best classified as *un hôtel de passe*. How they got planning permission for this is anyone's guess. Good views of the square from the indifferent café-restaurant. **F/E** ***Hotel Kennaria***, 10 Rue el Kennaria, T044-390228. 23 rooms off a courtyard, clean but spartan. Single 40dh, double 80dh (washbasin and bidet, no shower), single with shower 50dh. Nice management. **F** ***Hotel Badr***, Rue des Banques, down a long alley. 1 person 30dh, 2 persons 60dh, 3 persons 75dh. Quiet during the day. Cold showers only. **F** ***Hotel Mimosa***, Rue des Banques, T044-426385. Built 1997, 1 person 50dh, 2 persons 80dh, 3 persons 120dh. 16 rooms with washbasin and cupboard. Shower free, terrace. Tiles everywhere. **F** ***Hotel Mounir***, Rue el Kennaria, T044-444356, 13 rooms, 1 person 40dh, 2 persons 70dh. Hot showers. Slightly better than *Hotel Kennaria*, rooms less cell-like and look outwards onto street.

L'Hivernage **AL** *Sheraton Marrakech*, Ave de la Menara (at south end of Ave de France), T044-448998, F044-437843. 291 comfortable a/c rooms and suites, Moroccan and international restaurants, pizzeria, heated pool, tennis, shops, salon, very friendly atmosphere. Has a well established American Jewish clientèle. **A** ***Hotel Atlas Marrakech***, Ave de France, just across from the Palais des Congrès, T044-339900, F044-433308, atlasmrck@cybernet.net.ma Huge, impersonal building, all facilities revamped 1998-99. 304 rms, 18 luxury suites, 2 pleasant pools, 1 for adults, 1 for kids, with poolside restaurant and lawns. Souvenir shops, etc. **A** ***Hotel el Andalous***, Ave President Kennedy/Jnene el Harti, T044-4448226, F044-447195, www.elandalous-marrakech.com 200 double rooms each with 2 queen size beds, bath, a/c, balcony, telephone and radio, authentic Andalucían style, 2 restaurants (Moroccan and international), pool, tennis, sauna, fitness centre. Service poor for this category. **A** ***Hotel Es Saadi***, Ave Kadissia, T044-448811, 044-447010, F044-447644, www.essaadi.com Luxurious hotel built in 1950s style and set in large and pleasant gardens (best feature), with a fair restaurant, bar, nightclub, tennis and pool. Popular with older clients of up market tour companies, but generally felt to be in need of a refit. Service poor. **A *Impérial Borj***, 5 Ave Echouhada, T044-447322. 187 rooms, modern, conference centre, restaurant, bar and popular nightclub. Houses overspill from the palace when the court is in residence. Popular for small conferences. Almost opposite chic piano bar and restaurant *Le Comptoir*. **A *Hotel Mansour Eddahbi***, Ave de France, T044-448222. 450 rooms, restaurant, pool, tennis. Vast hotel next to Marrakech's (and indeed Morocco's) largest conference centre. OK if you're in Morocco for a conference, too impersonal for real holidays. Currently managed by *Accor* – but for how long? Ownership disputes mean that the hotel is long overdue for a refit. **A *Hotel Safir Marrakech***, Ave President Kennedy, T044-447400, F044-448730. 280 rooms. Facilities include disco, 2 tennis courts, bar, restaurant, shops, hammam and a pool surrounded with palm trees. **C *Hotel Menara***, Ave des Remparts, T044-436478, F044-447386. Typical Moroccan-style hotel, situated half way between the médina and the European Centre, views over the ramparts to the High Atlas, 100 rooms with bath, balcony, a/c, and central heating, telephone, Moroccan and French cooking, bar, TV room, garden, pool, tennis, free parking. A bit rundown. **C *Hotel Siaha Safir***, Ave President Kennedy, T044-448952, F044-448730. 243 rooms, pool and hammam. **C *Grand Hotel Imilchil***, Ave Echouhada, T044-447653, F044-446153. 2 persons 360dh, excluding breakfast. 96 rooms with a/c in hotel on a quiet street with pool, restaurant and bar. Used by tour groups. Location good for both Guéliz and the médina.

Guéliz

See map next page

Quite a good mix of accommodation here, city hotels with pocket-size swimming pools plus 1 or 2 cheapies. Without wishing to cast aspersions, avoid the *Hotel Boustane*.

B *Hotel Agdal*, 1 Blvd Mohammed Zerktouni, Guéliz, T044-433670. Ugly block of a hotel with 129 rooms and 4 apartments, all with a/c, balcony, telephone, radio, bath, pool heated in winter, bar, restaurant, breakfast room with panoramic view. Very handy for the train station, *CTM* bus offices and services near rond-point Abd el Moumen in Guéliz. Used by tour groups. **B/C *Hotel Kenza***, Ave Yacoub al Mansour, T044-448380, F044-435386. Expensive for what it is. Small pool. Marrakech low-life to be found in the hotel's nightclub, the *Shehrazade*, provided it hasn't been raided by the police recently.

C *Hotel Nassim*, 115 Blvd Mohammed V, T044-446401, F044-436710. Centrally located city hotel, practically next to tourist office on rond-point Abd el Moumen. All rooms with a/c, TV and bath.1 person 600dh, 2 persons 800dh, breakfast extra 60dh. Tour groups and people on business only. **C *Hotel Myriem***, 154 Rue Mohammed el Beqal. Rooms have a/c, TV, direct telephone and radio, 2 restaurants, pool and safe parking. **C *Hotel Amalay***, Ave Mohammed V, just next to the *Café Renaissance*. City hotel with noisy street facing rooms and lousy a/c. Prefer the *Tachfine* or the *Oudaya* in this area. **C *Hotel el Harti***, 30 Rue Cadi Ayad, T044-448000, F044-449329. A recent hotel close to the Jnene el Harti stadium, on a street parallel to the Ave Hassan II. Double around 400dh, a/c. Used by young male Marrakchis and their women friends? Pretty close to the train station. **C *Hotel Ibis Moussafir***, Ave Hassan II, right next to the train station, T044-435929, F044-435936. Major renovation work early 2001. Has soundproofing of rooms been improved? Ought to be a good hotel but wasn't. **C *Hotel Koutoubia***, 51 Blvd Mansour Eddahbi. At present closed, this small hotel was one of the best in Guéliz. Site no doubt earmarked for redevelopment. **C *Hotel Résidence le Grand Sud***, 25 Blvd Mansour Eddahbi. 1990s block with small self-catering flats close to Guéliz centre. Small unheated pool. Fine for a short stay. **C *Hotel Oudaya***, 147 Rue Mohammed el Beqal, T044-448512, F044-435400. As you face the Cinéma Le Colisée, go left and take 1st right. City hotel, typical of those built in the 1990s. Used by *Panorama* and other tour operators. 15 suites, 77 rooms, small unheated pool, restaurant and bar. Very clean. Pool-side rooms quietest. Fine for a couple of nights. 1 person

368dh, 2 persons 482dh. **C** ***Hotel du Pacha***, 33 Rue de la Liberté (left turn off the Ave Mohammed V, just before the market, as you head médina-wards), T044-431327, F044-431326. Just about creeps into the **C** category. Small hotel which could be loads better. Some rooms with a/c, lousy breakfast. **C** ***Hotel Tachfine***, Blvd Zerktouni/Rue Mohammed el Beqal, next to the Cinéma Le Colisée, T044-447188, F044-437862. 2 persons 350dh. 50 rooms with small balcony, TV, a/c. Adequate city hotel, have breakfast at nearby café.

E ***Hotel Farouk***, 66 Ave Hassan II, near the main post office, T044-431989, F044-433609. Double 120dh. A long established Marrakech address, same management as *Hotel Ali*. Acceptable. **E** ***Hotel Toulousain***, 44 Rue Tarak ben Ziad, Guéliz, T044-430033. Handily located behind the Guéliz food market, this is the best cheap option in the *ville nouvelle*. Rooms open onto courtyards – so not too much privacy. Nevertheless, a reliable choice.

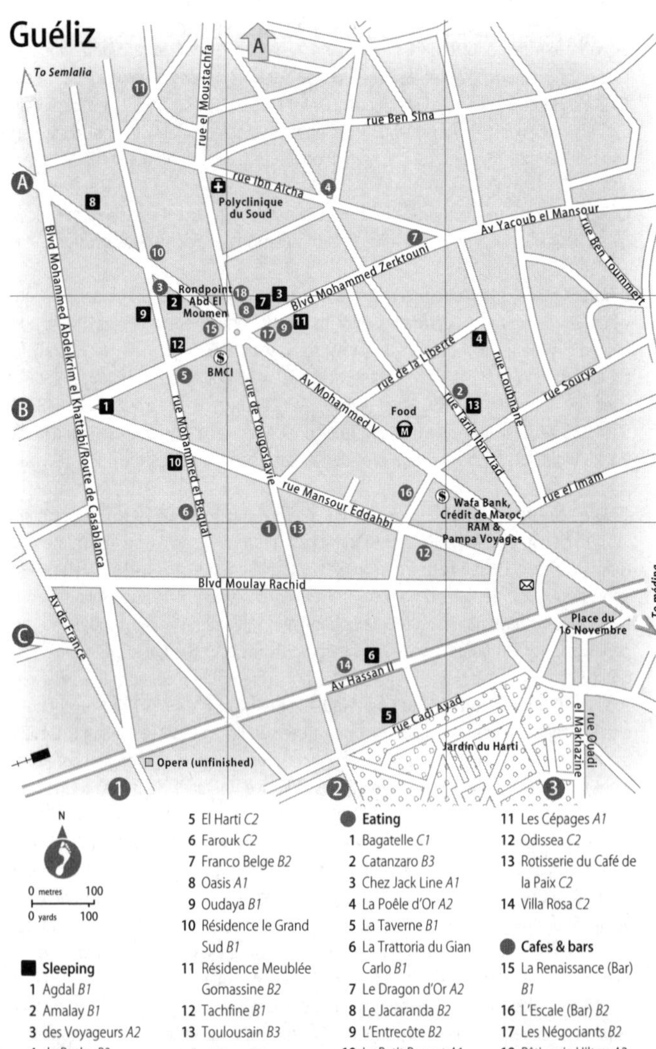

In summer, go for ground floor rooms as 1st floor rooms can be extremely hot; in this area also try ***Hotel Oasis***, 50 Ave Mohammed V (same side as *Hotel el Moutamid*), T044-447179, good but noisy, with restaurant and bar, clean, large rooms, some with shower. ***Hotel des Voyageurs***, 40 Blvd Mohammed Zerktouni, T044-447218, almost opposite *Café Les Négociants*. Reasonable and central but *Oasis* is better choice. ***Hotel Franco Belge***, 62 Blvd Mohammed Zerktouni, just down from *Restaurant Le Jacaranda* on rond-point Abd el Moumen. T044-448472. Old-style traveller's hotel which has seen better days. Pleasant courtyard planted with orange trees, old furniture. Quiet – if people in next room are quiet. Clean, but could do with a bit of attention. Rooms cold in winter. 1 person with en suite shower 100dh, 2 persons with en suite shower 130dh. Entrance, almost exactly opposite *Somepi* petrol station and *Europcar*, is easily missed.

Palmeraie (east & north of city)

Some interesting new options in this area, including the rather pleasant *Kasbah des Roses*. Look out for a new development, *Le Caravanserail*, Ouled Ben Rahmoun, scheduled for completion late summer 2001, contact M Lawrence on T044-432749.

AL ***Amanjena Resort***, route de Ouarzazate km 12, T044-403353, F044-403477. Up market complex centring on a large reflecting pool (*bassin*). Four types of accommodation, all luxuriously appointed with TV/DVD and CD players and nice big beds. Prices per night for 2 persons: pavilion, 6,950dh; pavilion with view of bassin, 8,000dh; maison with private pool 15,000dh; maison jardin, also with private pool 18,000dh. (The master bedrooms in the maison category are upstairs.) This is the first *Aman Resort* in Africa. Amanjena (says the blurb) comes from the Sanskrit *aman*, meaning peace, and the Arabic *jena*, meaning paradise. For the moment, it's all a bit new. Grounds – few mature trees – are disappointing. Handy for golf courses on eastern side of Marrakech. If you can afford these prices, you can stay in a riad (or have your own). Popular with Saudis entertaining starlets and others in need of a certain discreteness (ie well out of town). 2 restaurants with stratospheric prices, 1 doing Asian food. On top of the prices you have a 10% service charge and 10% government tax. **AL** ***Palmeraie Golf Palace***, T044-301010, F044-305050, in Les Jardins de la Palmeraie. 77 ha site, 314 rooms. Accommodation includes 6 senior suites, 2 royal suites and 24 suites with sitting room, all rooms have balcony, a/c, direct dial telephone, satellite TV, 24-hr room service, restaurants, bars, baby sitter, crèche, travel agency, bank, hairdresser, laundry/dry cleaning, car rental, 15 km from airport and 10 km from train station, gardens, tennis, 18-hole golf course, mini-golf, bowling, squash, horseriding (recommended), fitness centre with hammam, sauna, etc, 5 pools (2 heated), conference centre with variety of meeting rooms, shopping arcade. Hotel good for golf enthusiasts. On the down side, it is all a bit overblown. If paying this sort of money, why not go for an upmarket riad and make sure they can lay on transport to the golf courses. Fine for conferences, but a bit industrial in scale. Pool is accessible for day fee of 200dh.

A ***Les Deux Tours***, out at Douar Abiad in the Palmeraie, about 1 km from the *Hotel Issil Club*, T044-329525, F044-329523, www.deux-tours.com Pick-up at Marrakech airport. Taxis will have difficulty finding this place, off a piste leading off the Palmeraie Circuit. Double room starts at about 1,750dh a night, breakfast extra. Out in the palm groves, this small development was originally designed by local architect Charles Boccara as second homes for Casablancans (and others) tired of the big city. The small houses, built in the vernacular tradition, are surrounded by palms, and each has its own plunge pool. Beautiful bathrooms with slightly dodgy plumbing. Nice swimming pool, though flies can be a problem in summer. You are in the middle of a working oasis here, however. Meals available to order. In short, recommended. **A/B** ***Tikida Garden***, Circuit de la Palmeraie, T044-329595, F044-329599. Despite the corny name, pretty good if you can't get into a riad or *Les Deux Tours*. Good pool, generally heated in winter.

B/C ***Kasbah des Roses***, km 9 route de Ouarzazate, T044-329305, F044-329303. Recommended. Upmarket guesthouse on a 35 ha flower farm east of the city.

Semlalia (Casablanca road) There is a small area of 5 large upper-middle range hotels on the Casablanca road, here called Ave Abd el Karim el Khattabi. No particular advantages to staying here, apart from relative closeness to *McDonalds*! The hotels *Semiramis* and *Tichka* are at the back of the development. Coming from *McDonalds* direction, turn left down private road between *Sahara Inn* and *Hotel Tafilalet*.

AL ***Hotel Kenzi Semiramis***, route de Casablanca, T044-438226, F044-447127. Once part of the *Méridien* chain. Prices: 1 person 1,300dh, 2 persons 1,600dh. Nice (but small) grounds with lawns and mature palm trees. Tennis, pool with paddling area for kids, conference rooms for anything up to 300 people. Free gold shuttle bus to Amelkis course (green fees 450dh). Rooms redone in 1996 and 1999. Despite all this, vastly overpriced for what's on offer. Service good 'if they know you'. At this price, a more convenient hotel could be found in L'Hivernage or the médina. **A** ***Hotel Tichka***, route de Casablanca, Semlalia, T044-448710, F044-448691. Prices: 1 person 950dh, 2 persons 1,250dh, breakfast extra at a weighty 90dh. 138 rooms, beautifully decorated, restaurant, international and Moroccan menus, bar, nightclub, tennis, heated pool in which you can just about do lengths, shop, conference rooms for 20 and 150 people. Credit cards accepted. Used by companies for incentive trips. Likes to call itself 'the little Mamounia'. **B** ***Hotel Amine***, route de Casablanca, T044-436376, F044-438143. 1 person 500dh, 2 persons 700dh, a/c and heating, TV. Small pool in garden area which has constant noise from nearby busy road. West-facing rooms have view of back of *Total* petrol station and poor neighbourhood built in a quarry over the road. Handy for *Société générale bank* and *Le Diamant Vert Café-Glacier* next door. Tour groups only. **B** ***Hotel Tafilalet***, route de Casablanca, T044-449818, F044-447532. The first hotel in this area, dating from the early 1970s. Consists of 2 kasbah-like blocks. Rooms small but pleasant. Grounds too small, pool with terrace restaurant. Now belongs to the *CIH*, the national hotel and housing development company. Nothing special. **C** ***Hotel Sahara Inn***, route de Casablanca, T044-438334, F044-434610. 1 person 402dh, 2 persons 512dh, 3 persons 622dh. The cheapest of the bunch, works mainly with Spanish and French tour groups. Bedrooms recently redone in salmon-pink. Pool and terrace with piped music. Staff pleasant, anxious to please, but not really very able.

Maisons d'hôte A relatively recent form of accommodation in Marrakech, the *maison d'hôte* (riad or guesthouse) gives you the experience of staying in a fine private house, generally in the médina. The prices, however, are often high – and in keeping with the luxurious standards of these houses. The riads, often restored and converted, are managed either directly by their owners or via an agency which deals with everything from reservations to maintenance. Clients are generally met at the airport, and the rental fee will include breakfast and cleaning. Evening meals can generally be prepared in the riad to order. Prices vary enormously, and some are extremely luxurious indeed. Client reactions to this type of accommodation are generally positive. The riads have created a lot of work for locals (and pushed property prices up), so many feel they have a stake in the guesthouse system. With regard to tipping, err on the generous side.

When booking a stay in a riad, there are a few details you should check. What sort of mattresses do they have (foam mattresses are very hot in the summer)? How is the shower water heated (electric water heating will provide plenty of hot water, a gas *chauffe-eau* providing water for several rooms is inadequate if more than 1 person is having a shower)? Note that ground floor rooms are preferable in summer, 1st floor rooms in winter. Note too that in winter it can rain heavily in Marrakech, turning streets in the old town to muddy tracks.

Buying an ideal Oriental home?

It had long been the fashion for foreigners with an artistic bent to own property in Marrakech. In the early 1990s, property prices in the old town were cheap as the rural poor crowded citywards, fleeing drought in the countryside, and decent Marrakchi families sought to get rid of their old family homes. Although tourism in Marrakech was at an all time low (due to the Gulf War and the constant hassling of visitors by faux guides*), the médina was 'rediscovered' by a fringe of the Euro-French intelligentsia who began to buy and restore crumbling old properties. At about the same time, the general climate for tourism began to improve: Marrakech successfully hosted the GATT meeting in 1994, while the new plain-clothes* Brigade Touristique *ensured that visitors could cross Jemaâ el Fna unmolested. Then the rumour got round that labyrinthine houses with cool and sexy rooms and courtyards full of orange trees could be acquired for a handful of dirhams. Decoration magazines like* Côté Sud *and* Maisons du Maroc *spread the word, and then in 1998 French TV documentary series* Capital *did a piece on foreigners restoring property in Marrakech. All of a sudden, riads were the fashion. The ideal Oriental home had become an accessible dream for an averagely wealthy European professional.*

Since the mid-1990s, a huge variety of property has been restored, for use as private homes and restaurants, maisons d'hôte *and exhibition space. Latest estimates give between 50 and 80 guesthouse type places in the médina. Styles range from minimalist elegance (*Dar Belarj *and* Dar el Kadi*) and Marrakech chic (*Riad Temsna*) to designer Orient (*Restaurant Yacout*) and extreme Los Angeles-meets-the-Orient camp (*La Rotonda*). The fashion for Marrakech has taken off, pushing houses prices up – much to the delight of existing local owners, who can now sell off their decaying property and buy themselves comfortable modern apartments. Once the paperwork has been done and title deeds have changed hands, the new owners begin the restoration process – which often means all sorts of hidden costs and surprises. Specialized restoration companies have emerged, and houses brought round to new uses by the likes of Abdellatif Aït Ben Abdellah and architect Quentin Wilbaux are very beautiful indeed. Unfortunately, not all the new investors are interested in traditional building and authentic decoration: in 2000, Marrakech lost one of the largest unrestored palaces,* Dar Louarzazi, *unscrupulously demolished by a private developer. The site was reconstructed as the* Hotel Jardins de la Koutoubia *(sic).*

AL ***Dar Temsna, Palmeraie***, for reservations contact owner Meryanne Loum-Martin (speaks perfect English), T06-1242717. Same management as the beautiful *Ryad Tamsna* eatery boutique in the médina. Well away from the bustle of down-town Marrakech, the twin villas (10 suites) of Dar Temsna make an ideal base for the up market visitor. Close to the Palmeraie golf course. Highly personalized service. One of the best in Marrakech – at a price. Highly recommended. **AL** ***Riad el Ouarda***, 5 Derb Taht es Sour, Zaouia el Abbasia, T044-385714, F044-385710. Located in the northern side of the médina, beautifully decorated. 2 suites and 4 rooms. Prices are steep: suite for 2 persons is 1,850dh, 1,700dh for 1 person; rooms clock in at 1,200dh for 1 person, 1,300dh for 2. Breakfast included. **AL** ***Villa des Orangers***, 6 Rue Sidi Mimoun, T044-384638, F044-385123, www.orangers.com Close to both L'Hivernage and médina. Near the new royal palace and the kasbah area. Expensive and very chic haven. Outside the streets are snarling with traffic. **A/B** ***Magesor SARL***, Villa Le Grillon, Rue Oumou el Banine, Marrakech – Guéliz (managers Florence and Jean Marie Milicent), T06-3040104, F044-436997, www.magesor.com Small agency with 2 properties for rent in Marrakech: a villa in Guéliz with large suites at 600dh per day for 2 people and a riad in the Bab el Khemis neighbourhood, close to the new Museum of

Five good, cheap and cheapish hotels in Marrakech

- *Hotel Le Toulousain*, Rue Tarak ben Ziad, Guéliz. Very popular, T044-430033, F044-431446. 170dh per person.
- *Hotel Sherazade*, Riad Zitoun el Jedid, Médina. Cheapest simplest double at 180dh, more expensive rooms too. Charming. T044-429305.
- *Hotel Ali*, Rue Moulay Ismaïl, nr Jemaâ el Fna. Old favourite with hikers. T044-444979, F044-440522. Double 120dh. Linked with *Hotel Farouk* in Guéliz, T044-431989, F044-433609.
- *Hotel Central Palace*, off Rue Bab Agnaou, Médina, T044-440235, F044-442884. A good cheapie, easy to find, in area of lots of cheap hotels, 100dh per person.
- *Hotel Mimosa*, Rue des Banques, Médina, behind *Café Hotel de France*, T044-426385. 80dh per person. Very good value.

Marrakech, which can sleep up to 12 people for 7,200dh per day. Prices include maid service, breakfast and all taxes.

A, B, and C *Agency Marrakech-Médina SARL*, 79 Derb El Kadi, Azbest. Offices at 2 Derb Tizogarine, near Dar el Pacha, Bab Doukkala, médina, T044-429133, F044-391071, www.marrakech-Médina.com From Paris, reservations on T00-33-143259877 or a range of self-catering accommodation from this Belgo-Morocco-Canadian partnership. A very personalized service. Houses are classified by 'palm trees' according to the standard of accommodation. For example, rental prices in a 2 palm tree home start at 300 French francs a night, plus daily service charge of 60 francs a head for a riad sleeping 5 people in the low season. Airport transfer charges 100FF a head. The agency has much larger and more luxurious riads on offer as well. They also act as agents for self-catering holiday accommodation in Essaouira, Telouet and (in the near future) Oualidia.

A, B, and C *Riads au Maroc*, 1 Rue Mahjoub Rmiza, Guéliz, T044-431900, F044-431786 (manager Serge Meadow). The offices are located in a small modern block just off Ave Mohammed V. Heading towards the médina, just before Bab Nkob, go left and then left again; office is on your left. *Riads au Maroc* functions as a centralized reservation service for both rooms in riads and whole riads. Highly personalized service. A small but choice range of homes for rent, including the elegant *Villa Hélène* in Guéliz (with pool) and the exquisite Dar Tchina. Properties rated by lanterns (1 to 5). Rooms are available as in a hotel for short periods. Cheapest room is 300dh. An average property, 3 lanterns, ie *Dar Nimbus*, sleeping 8, costs 2,400dh a night. ***Riad al Kadi***, Derb Debbachi is the most spectacular property. Great attention paid to bathrooms and mattresses. Meals can be cooked in-house to order, average cost 100dh a head.

A *Riad Enija*, 9 Derb Mesfioui, Rahba Lakdima, T044-440926, F044-442700. A truly jungle-like courtyard and absolutely fabulous artistic beds ('remarkable fabrics, darling'). You too can slip under the gloss of a décor magazine. Best visited with one's personal photographer. Not all rooms have en suite bath and shower. Blue room is coolest, the Suite Harem has roof terrace. **A** *Dar Moha*, 81 Rue Dar el Bacha, T044-386400, F044-386998. Very accessible for both médina and Guéliz in Rmila neighbourhood. 3 double rooms at 1,700dh (with breakfast), 1 single room at 1,300dh. Fine decoration, but downstairs functions as a restaurant (with piped music), so this is not as private and exquisite as it should be for the price. Tiny pool is in the restaurant courtyard downstairs at the back. **A** *Dar Zina*, 4 Jnene Brika, Targa, T044-346645, F044-495653, tajm@iam.net.ma www.darzina.com Out on the Targa (west side of town), a relatively new venture which has a regular clientele. Small pool, attentive service. 4 rooms and 3 suites, named after the heroines of the 1001 Nights. **A** ***Riad Noga***, 78 Derb Jedid, Douar Graoua, T044-377670, F044-389046. From 1,100dh to 1,600dh, 2 persons with breakfast, tea and coffee. TV and internet access from most rooms. Not the most traditional of riads, but very comfortable. **A** ***Palais Rhoul***, reservations via French office on T00-33 145721200 or 145721307, Marrakech office T044-329494, F044-329496, www.palais-rhoul.com A unique, rather glitzy property out in the Palmeraie, northeast of the city. Features include high-columned dining area, hammam and suites with rooms opening directly onto round swimming pool. The building is in fact modelled on a Roman consul's villa in Galilee (owner-manager Chahine Rhoul's mother bought the plans at auction). Accommodation is in the form of 12 suites, each 140 m². Reserve well in advance. **A** ***Sublime Ailleurs***, T044-329644, F044-329645, T061-249816. Beautifully appointed villas, some with small pool, for rent out in the Palmeraie. Exclusive. Used by English Morocco specialist *Morocco Made to Measure*. Prefer this to the Amanjena if you are looking for discrete luxury. **A/B** ***Dar el Kadi***, 59 Derb el Kadi, Azbezt, Derb Debbachi. (Mail to BP101 Marrakech-Médina.) Definitely 1 of the best riads in the médina. 4 patios, plunge pool, cool and simple decoration. Living room with fireplace and books. Highly recommended. Advance reservations essential, T044-378655, F044-378478, riyadelcadi@iam.net.ma

B ***Riad el Arset***, 10 bis Derb Chemaâ, near Dar Glaoua, Arset Loughzail, T044-387567. Around 700dh, 2 persons with breakfast. Fine colonnades and a beautiful suite in the summer house. **B** ***Riad Catalina***, 21 Derb Abdallah Ben Hssaine, Bab Leksour, T044-426701, F044-426702. More of a small hotel than a riad, despite the courtyard. Accommodation for up to 35 people – might suit a group holiday. Fully a/c, satellite TV, and diminutive roof-terrace swimming pool accessible to all. Accommodation for 2 people starts at 750dh per night. Clean, located in a part of the médina close to Ave Mohammed V and Guéliz, but is to a traditional home what Paris Disneyland is to Chambord. **B** ***Riad Cais***, T044-440141. In the Riad Zitoun el Kedim area, close to the Badi Palace, about 10-mins walk from Jemaâ el Fna. (Owner-manager, architect Christian Ferré, lives on premises.) Named after Cais, the Romeo of early Arabic poetry (Leila was his Juliet). One of the finest riads, beautifully decorated, full of nooks and crannies. Open fires everywhere in winter. Garden patio with tall, mature trees. Lots of staff to look after you. Difficult to fault in fact. (Used by UK agency *Simply Travel*.) **B** ***Dar el Borj***, hidden away at 63 Derb Moulay Abd el Kader, Derb Debbachi, just 10-mins walk from Jemaâ el Fna, T/F391223, P061675942, www.riyads.com Manager: Rachid Bouabid. One of the most reasonably priced riads. Good central location and good value in low season with it. Double room 600dh low season, 750dh high season. Roof terraces and a small, pleasantly planted courtyard. Week's rent for 8 people: low season 13,000dh, high season 21,500dh. **B** ***Dar el Farah***, Arset Bouachrine, Riad Zitoun el Jedid, T044-441019, F044-427522. Close to Jemaâ el Fna. Can sleep up to 12 people. Weekly rent for full house party in high season, breakfast included, about 1,750dh. Pleasant terrace and plunge-pool in main patio. French owned and managed. **B** ***Dar el Hana***, T/F429977, very small riad which would suit a (well heeled) family. Sitting room with fireplace. 7 rooms. **B** ***Riad Malika***, 29 Derb Arset Aouzal, Bab Doukkala, T044-385451, from 900-1,400dh for 2 persons with breakfast. Features many nice old chairs and Art Déco bits. **B** ***Riad l'Oasis***, Arset el Baraka, T044-428080, F044-427777. Located on the east side of the médina, near Bab Aïlen. Kind of gaudy and on the wrong side of the médina. Will do if all other riad addresses are full. **B** ***Villa Occitane***, 3 Rue Nador, T/F448319. Situated in a quiet corner of l'Hivernage. 6 rooms. Prices include breakfast and laundry. 1 person 500dh, a little extra for half-board. Has an Oscar Wilde touch.

B/C ***Dar Mouassine***, 148 Derb Snane, Mouassine, T/F445287, T06-1341784. Contemporary styling, all rather sleek, 3 suites and 2 rooms, prices 600-900dh double. Recommended. **B** ***Les Yeux bleus***, near the *Maison arabe* at 7 Derb el Ferrane, Bab Doukkala, T044-378161/061422682, owner Mme J Despin. 1,500dh, 2 persons with breakfast. Luxurious and tasteful. **B** ***Riad Noor***, 31 Derb el Kebir, Ben Salah neighbourhood, T044-386095, F044-386931. Pleasant small French-run riad. Highly recommended. **B/C** ***Marrakech Riads***, 8 Derb Charfa Lekbir, Mouassine, T044-385858, F044-385708, M061163630. Small agency managed by Abdellatif Ait Ben Abdallah. Properties available include the simple *Dar Sara* and the beautiful *Dar Zellije* (Sidi Ben Slimane), double rooms between 1,200-1,500dh per night. The agency's headquarters, the beautiful *Dar Cherifa*, a 17th-century house converted with gallery space on the ground floor, are worth a visit in their own right. **B/C** ***Riad Ifoulki***, 11 Derb Mqqadem, route Arset Loughzail, médina, T044-385656. Manager: Abdelhak Ait el Haraj. Located close to Derb Debbachi, 10-mins walk from Jemaâ el Fna. 1,500dh per double room. Expensive as compared with other riads. No English spoken. Prefer one of the agencies or a home with a real host. **B/C** ***La Maison Alexandre-Bonnel***, 4 Derb Sania, Bab Leksour, near the restaurant *Ksar Es Saoussan*, T/F044-429833. Double room 500dh (3 rooms available). Personable small house in a central neighbourhood. Owners Christophe and Valérie Crouzet live on the premises and know the region really well. Can set up excursions, advise on restaurants, etc. An excellent address. **B/C** ***Riad Nisrine***, Mouassine, T06-1341357, also via France on T0033-148780273. 2 persons about 600dh. Beautiful garden courtyard, fine roof terrace. **B/C** ***Dar Zerqa***, 30 Derb Kaâ Akhij, Sidi Ben Slimane, T06-1340463. Attractive small riad. 1st floor with 2 double rooms, living room downstairs with couches. Would suit a family. Located between Sidi Bel Abbès and Dar el Bacha. Ably managed by M Gelmane, who with a French partner is restoring *Dar Warda* at 266 Derb Sidi Bou Amor, Riad Laârous (2 double rooms, beautifully finished, terrace room with a/c, 1st floor room with fireplace). Highly recommended. *Dar Warda* to be ready late spring 2001. **C** ***Riad Zina***, 38 Derb Assabane, Riad Laârous, T044-385242, F06-1249197. Well managed small riad, 3 rooms only, with an agreeable laid-back feel. Recommended.

Self-catering flats Simple self-catering accommodation in the form of sparsely equipped holiday flats is also available in Marrakech. Such *résidences*, generally blocks of flats of a few storeys, are located in Guéliz and the newer residential area Daoudiyet. Many flats are run with hotel-type facilities. This sort of accommodation, modern, clean but a bit lacking in charm, tends to be favoured by Moroccan families down from Casablanca for the weekend. If you have the money, try to go for a riad instead. **B** ***Résidence el Bahja***, corner of Rue Ben Aicha and Rue Mohammed el Beqal, T044-448119, F044-346063. 13 spacious self-catering flats, but not within easy walking distance of the médina. Moroccan meals to order. Street-facing rooms noisy. **B** ***Résidence Zahia***, route de Casablanca, T044-437815, F044-430028. 44 self-catering flats and studios able to sleep 4 people. Avoid street-facing accommodation. Pool. **C** ***Résidence Meublée Gomassine***, 71 Blvd Mohammed Zerktouni, Guéliz, Marrakech, T044-433086, F044-433012. Facing the *Café Les Négociants*, go left, this apart-hotel is about 70 m down the street on your right. Brand new in 1999. Very clean. Prices: 300dh 1 person, 400dh 2 persons, 460dh 3 persons, 700dh 5 persons. Larger flats have living rooms. Fully equipped kitchens and a/c. Large café with good cakes on ground floor.

Youth hostel Rue el Jahed, Quartier Industriel, off Ave de France, T044-447713. 80 beds, kitchen, meals available, bus 200 m, train 700 m, overnight fee 30dh, hot showers, IYHF cards only, open 1200-1400 and 1800-2200 in winter, 0600-2400 in summer. A long way from the sights – and there is plenty of cheap accommodation in the médina for a few extra dirhams.

Five special restaurants in Marrakech

- ***Ksar Essaoussan***, Leksour, Médina, chic and elegant Moroccan cuisine. T044-440632, F044-426075.
- ***Les Cépages***, Guéliz, for refined French cooking in a converted villa. T044-439426, F044-438981. Sublime chocolate deserts. Not cheap.
- ***Dar Moha***, Dar el Bacha, Médina. Where well healed locals might go to enjoy Moroccan food. T044-386400, F044-386998.
- ***Bagatelle***, Rue de Yougoslavie, Guéliz. Pleasant dining in gardened courtyard. Very reasonably priced. T044-430274.
- ***Le Tobsil***, Leksour, Médina. Most elegant Moroccan food. T044-444052, 044-441523, 044-444535, F044-443515.

Camping *Camping Municipal*, off Ave de France, 5 mins south of the railway station, with shop, showers and café, site of 2 ha, bar, laundry, first aid, electricity for caravans, petrol at 800 m, quiet, clean and pleasant.

Eating

Guéliz
● *on map*
There is a good selection of places to eat in Guéliz

The older bar restaurant places tend to be located on the main Ave Mohammed V. There is a small selection of restaurants, including *Pizzeria Niagara*, at the end of the avenue farthest from the médina. More interesting (and slightly more expensive) are the European-style places, located in the side avenues, such as *L'Entrecote*, *Odissea*, the *Trattoria di Gian Carlo* and *Les Cépages*. Guéliz also has some smart cafés (notably *Les Négociants* on rond-point Abd el Moumen). For a panoramic drink, take the lift up to the mirador of *Bar La Renaissance*, also on aforesaid rond-point. ***Al Fassia***, 232 Ave Mohammed V, T044-434060. Reservations recommended, an excellent Moroccan restaurant which allows you to dine à la carte and avoid the surfeit of Moroccan food you automatically get in the 500dh a head palace restaurants. Recommended (and easy to find on Ave Mohammed V, about halfway between rond-point Abd el Moumen and Jemaâ el Fna). ***Les Cépages***, 9 Rue Ben Khaldoun, T044-439426, F044-438981. To locate: from rond-point Abd el Moumen, go straight ahead down Rue de Yougoslavie between *Shell* station and the *Pâtisserie Hilton*. Going over the first major intersection – Polyclinique du Sud on your right – take the first left. ***Les Cépages*** and its superb food is almost straight ahead in a small villa. Proper French chef. Open for lunch and dinner, closed Mon. Leave enough room for dessert. ***Le Jacaranda***, 32 Blvd Mohammed Zerktouni (opposite *Café Les Négociants*), T044-447215. Long-standing restaurant with good reputation. Elaborate French food, strong on fish and creamy sauces, closed Tue and Wed lunch time, bar. Eating à la carte, expect to pay 250dh. The menus are much cheaper. Terrace very noisy, sit upstairs inside for quiet. ***La Trattoria du Gian Carlo***, 179 Rue Mohammed el Bequal, T044-432641. To locate, find *La Taverne* (opposite Cinéma Le Colisée near rond-point Abd el Moumen), which is on corner of Blvd Mohammed Zerktouni and Rue Mohammed el Bequal. *La Trattoria* is 2 blocks down, next to *Café L'Amandine*. It had a very good reputation as the city's best Italian restaurant. Excellent selection of wines, superb desserts. The Milanese owner recently died and the restaurant stayed closed for a while. Hopefully, the new team can maintain standards. ***Le Dragon d'Or***, 10 bis Blvd Mohammed Zerktouni, T044-433341. Chinese food. ***Villa Rosa***, 64 Ave Hassan II, T044-430832. A small Italian restaurant specializing in pasta and fish. Full meal anything between 200dh and 300dh. A good address, easily located by taxi drivers. Best to eat out on patio, if possible.

Ramparts of Marrakech

Lots of places in the medium-price bracket, many of which are very good

Mid-range Look out for new Basque restaurant *La Concha* (opening early summer 2001), on Rue Loubnène, not far from the Guéliz food market, T044-44436471. ***Rotisserie du Café de la Paix***, 68 Rue Yougoslavie, T044-433118, there is a garden in the summer, and reasonable grilled food all the year round; just opposite is ***Restaurant Bagatelle***, 101 Rue Yougoslavie, T044-430274, good French food served in the restaurant and vine shaded courtyard, open 1200-1400 and 1900-2300. Very pleasant lunch stop in summer. Try the *salade fermier*. Recommended – good light lunch for around 100dh, the full whack for 200dh. Closed on Wed. ***Catanzaro***, Rue Tarak ben Ziad, behind the market in Guéliz, next to the *Hotel Toulousain*, T044-433731. Excellent Italian food. Full meal for around 150dh, though you can spend far less. A very popular lunchtime address. Try to reserve for the evening. ***Chez Jack'line***, 63 Ave Mohammed V, T044-447547. Atmospheric, in a 1950s bistro sort of way. Meat beautifully cooked. French and Italian cuisine. Ideal for a European meal when you've just spent 2 weeks up in the mountains eating tagine. There is a resident parrot, too. The lion cub has long gone, sadly, as has the monkey. ***La Poêle d'Or***, Rue Allal ben Ahmed, on a square behind the *Hotel Boustane*. (To get there, starting with *Les Négociants* on your right, take 1st left on Rue Tarak ben Ziad, after *Hotel Boustane*.) A reliable little address. Franco-Moroccan cooking, small shaded outside dining areas. Nice lunch for 160dh. Recommended. ***La Taverne***, 23 Blvd Mohammed Zerktouni (opposite Cinéma Le Colisée), T044-446126. Fixed standard menus and a bar. Lighting on the bright side, fine for a beer and cheap eat out. ***L'Entrecote***, 55 Blvd Mohammed Zerktouni, T044-49428. (Manager Abdel Ghani Khatir's T06-1245042.) To locate: start at rond-point Abd el Moumen, facing *Les Négociants*. Go left. *L'Entrecote* is on your right, about 20 m from roundabout, in the ABN Amro building, at back of small mall. Recommended. Meat particularly good. Menu 120dh, lunchtime quick menu 70dh, 150dh for a good feed. ***Le Jardin des Arts***, 6/7 Rue Sakia el Hamra, T044-446634, F044-446649. Near *Hotel Amine* and *Café le Diamant Vert*. In Semlalia rather than Guéliz but included here for convenience. A new (Apr 2001) French restaurant that fills the gap in the Semlalia hotel zone. Promising. ***Odissea***, 83 bis Blvd Mansour Eddahbi, T044-431545, F044-449921. To get there, coming from the médina on Ave Mohammed V, locate the main *RAM* agency and *Wafa Bank*. Go left, and left again. *Odissea* is a few metres down on your right. The decor of this Italian-run restaurant is molto Versace, with impeccable

waistcoated waiters and giant paintings of leopards. Excellent pizzas. Highly recommended, pizza and wine for 2 will work out at about 200dh. ***Pizzeria Niagara***, Route de la Targa (take a taxi), T044-449775. Good pizzas. Covered terrace. Gets crowded in the evenings with chic locals, so reservations essential. Recommended.

Cheap Top of the cheap range in the *ville nouvelle* is ***Brasserie du Regent***, 34 Ave Mohammed V, T044-448749; also try ***Badr***, Rue de la Liberté, Guéliz. ***Le Petit Poucet***, Ave Mohammed V, T044-448238. Bar and restaurant with basic but good French dishes. ***Tiffany***, under the arcade on Ave Mohammed V, near the post office. Basic meals and breakfasts, good service, stays open during the day in Ramadan; or ***Café Agdal***, 86 Ave Mohammed V, T044-448707, good for chicken, no alcohol. Highly recommended is the ***Bar L'Escale***, almost opposite the main market in Guéliz. Coming from the médina, go left at the *Wafa Bank* and it is a few doors along on your right. The eating area is at the back. Go for charcoal grilled *coquelet* and chips with your Flag beer. Not really for unaccompanied women.

L'Hivernage

Although a quiet district of villas and large hotels, there are now a few restaurants

Expensive Although not exactly in L'Hivernage, the famous *Hotel Mamounia*'s restaurants are nearby in easy walking distance of the area's hotels. ***Le Comptoir***, Ave Echouhada (almost opposite the *Hotel Impérial Borj*), T044-437702, F044-447747. An stylish establishment with much muted lighting and elegant waitresses in kaftans. The place for a pre-dinner drink perhaps. They also have a little boutiquey place at the back. Dinner will set you back around 400dh. Trendissimo. (The same management also has a ***Comptoir*** on 37 Rue Berger, 75001 Paris, T00-33-1400262666.) ***Restaurant La Calèche***, in the *Hotel Mamounia*, Ave Bab Jedid, T044-448991, French food with a view over the hotel's famous gardens. ***Restaurant marocain de l'Hotel Mamounia***, also in the *Hotel Mamounia*, Ave Bab Jedid, T044-448991. Reservations recommended, lavishly decorated restaurant introducing élite Moroccan cuisine. Expensive for what it is.

Mid-range ***L'Amandier***, on the corner of Rue de Paris and Ave Echouhada, T044-446093. Quiet near hotels *Impérial Borj* and *Saâdi* and *Polyclinique Koutoubia*. French cuisine. ***Safran et Cannelle***, T044-435969, F044-434274, 40 Ave Hassan II. Close to Jnene el Harti on a busy main avenue. A trendy popular place. Apart from restaurant on ground floor, there is a noisy bar in the basement and the karaoke bar *L'Hacienda* on 1st floor. Not for those in search of a quiet night out. Lots of beer for 20dh a go.

The médina

These listings are generally in the expensive category

The upmarket Moroccan restaurants in restored houses with garden courtyards are part of the Marrakech experience. Reservations are essential. Generally, they are indicated by a discreet wall plaque – taxi drivers know where they are, or someone from the restaurant will come to accompany you. You make your reservation, and they will give you a place to tell the taxi driver to drop you off. There you will be met by the restaurant doorman, generally togged up in traditional gear. Most of the traditional restaurants are located in one of three districts: **Riad Zitoun el Kadim and la Kasbah**; **Bab Leksour** (*Ksar Saoussen, Stylia, Tobsil*); or **Dar el Bacha and Bab Doukkala** (*Dar Moha* and the *Marjana*). Note that the médina restaurants vary greatly in size and style. The profits to be made by catering for large groups means that not all can offer intimate courtyard dining. Indeed, behind discrete doors in alleyways are some big restaurant operations – for example, the *Stylia* in Leksour or the vast *Dar Haj Idder* off Derb Debbachi. Here you will be eating in the company of jolly coach parties from Agadir or *IBM* employees on their convention spree.

Close to the Koutoubia *Dar el Baroud*, 275 Ave Mohammed V, T044-426009, F044-311443. A good address for refined Moroccan food and not excessively expensive at 400dh per head. Easily located down an alley opposite the Koutoubia, on your left as you come from Guéliz. ***Restaurant Relais Al Baraka***, Jemaâ el Fna, near the police station, T044-442341. Moroccan meals around a courtyard with fountain, convenient after sightseeing, reservations recommended.

Riad Zitoun el Kadim and Kasbah *Dar Douiriya*, 14 Derb Jedid Hay Essalem, off Ave Houman el Fetouaki (and very close to the Place des Ferblantiers and the Badi Palace), T044-403030, F044-403055. 4-course dining at around 380dh a head. Dining in slightly gaudy surroundings with the usual trimmings (live music, belly dancer doing her brief bit). Ideal for an air-conditioned lunch stop after doing the palace museums. Main plus points: easy accessibility by taxi, nice service. A good if unexciting introduction to Moroccan food. Can seat up to 120 but has intimate corners. ***Restaurant Palais Gharnatta***, 56 Derb el Arsa, Riad Zitoun el Jedid, T044-445216, near the Bahia Palace. Moroccan dishes at high prices, clients paying for the supposedly 16th-century palatial surroundings. Reservations essential. ***Restaurant Riad***, Rue Arset el Maach, T044-425430. Expensive Moroccan meals accompanied by folklore entertainment. ***Ryad Temsna***, Riad Zitoun el Jedid, 23 zanka Daïka,T044-385272, F044-385271, in the Kennaria district, down an alley on the right after the old cinema (see map or call, they'll send someone to meet you at the *Café de France* on Jemaâ el Fna). Beautifully restored riad open for lunch, about 200dh. Lebano-Moroccan cuisine. A fine eating experience. Highly recommended. Occasional exhibitions of painting, too. No booze.

Bab Leksour area *Ksar es Saoussan*, T044-040632, F044-426075. Dinner only, seats up to 40. Three fixed-price menus, 300dh, 400dh and 500dh. Prices include an aperitif and half bottle of wine. An early 17th-century house with a new function as a restaurant, located next to one of the oldest houses in Marrakech, the ruined Dar el Messaoudiyine. Red-robed porter will meet guests at the entrance to Rue Leksour. Small by médina restaurant standards but highly recommended. Food excellent. Manager, Jean-Laurent Graulhet. ***Le Pavillon***, 47 Derb Zaouia, T044-387040. Near *La Maison arabe*, opposite the mosque at Bab Doukkala, at the end of an alley. One of the first of this kind, originally restored by a French decorator, now under new management. Dinner only, closed Tue. Good wines, around 300dh per head. Recommended. ***Restaurant Stylia***, 36 Rue Ksour, T044-443587. One of the largest traditional palace restaurants, reservations required, with all the usual Moroccan traditional dishes. Unfortunately, hasn't been able to maintain the original quality. Service is poor. Works mainly with groups (can cater for up to 700 people, they say), as the restaurant consists of several inter-linked houses. Easy access – torch-bearers will show you the way. Around 400dh per head. For information, *stylia* means 'bucket-makers'. ***Le Tobsil***, 22 Derb Abdallah ben Houssein, Ksour district, T044-444052, 044-441523, 044-444535, F044-443515. A safe bet. Elegant Moroccan cuisine. Reservations absolutely essential as there are not very many tables. 550dh a head, wine and spirits included. *Tobsil* means plate. Highly recommended.

Bab Doukkala and Dar el Bacha *Dar Marjana*, 15 Derb Sidi Ali Tair, T044-385110, F044-385152. Down an alley almost opposite the entrance to Dar el Bacha, currently the royal residence when the king is in Marrakech. Lunch for groups, dinner for all-comers. Choice of 3 5-course menus: 600dh (tagine and couscous), 650dh includes *tlaâ* (succulent shoulder or lamb), 700dh includes *mechoui* (barbecued lamb). Prices include aperitifs and alcohol. Recommended. If the manager has had too much to drink, female guests may get a little hassle! ***Dar Moha***, 81 Rue Dar el Bacha, reservations on T044-386400, F044-386998. Easily located by a taxi as on the busy Rue Dar el Bacha. On foot, if heading towards Jemaâ el Fna, turn back left at 20 mins to the hour just opposite the Koutoubia minaret. Follow busy Rue Rmila for some 200 m. It curves round to right, becoming Rue Dar el Bacha. The smooth, clean façade of Dar Moha is on your left after 100 m. Originally restored by Pierre Balmain, the house now functions partly as an exclusive guesthouse (upstairs). In summer, try to get a table in small patio out back. One of the better médina restaurants, digestible Moroccan nouvelle cuisine.

Arset Ihiri/Riad Laârous *Dar Fès*, 8 Rue Boussouni, Riad Laârous (car park Arset Ihiri), T044-382340. Not as chic as some of the old city restaurants, but pleasant nonetheless. Comfy blue velvet sofas in a garden patio. ***El Yacout***, 79, Derb Sidi Ahmed Soussi, T044-382929, F044-382538, closed Mon, dinner only. Reservations essential. 600dh a head. The full Moroccan culinary experience. Atmospheric, but has been enlarged and in the process totally lost the intimate touch. (*Une usine à bouffe*, as the French say.) Caters for large groups – popular with the American market. Terrace is pleasant for drinks.

Close to Jemaâ el Fna (Mid-range and cheap) ***Restaurant de Foucauld***, in the *Hotel de Foucauld*, Ave el Mouahidine, good couscous and tagines near the Jemaâ el Fna. ***Restaurant Tazi***, in the *Grand Hotel Tazi*, Rue Bab Agnaou, similar restaurant run by the same management, the cheapest licensed establishment in the médina. Buffet dinner in ***Hotel Ali***, Rue Moulay Ismaïl, good choice and very reasonably priced. ***Café-Restaurant Argana***, Jemaâ el Fna, food with a view. Popular with locals and tourists. Gets very busy at sundown. Café on ground floor is a strategic meeting place, as no-one can miss the large red Argana sign atop the restaurant. ***Restaurant Etoile de Marrakech***, Rue Bab Agnaou, good value set meals with view of Jemaâ el Fna from the roof.

Near Rahba el Kadima *Dar Timtam*, 44 Rue Rahba el Kedima, T044-391446, near the square of the same name. Turn right off the square on the far side from the *Wafa Bank*. A funny sort of place that looks as though it is waiting to be turned into yet another large Moroccan banquet restaurant. Lighting and décor all wrong, patio roofed over. Currently does light meals for about 150dh, excluding drinks. No booze. Handy as a tea-stop if you are in the central souks.

In the médina the most popular option is to eat at the open-air restaurants on the Jemaâ el Fna

On 'la Place' Piles of salads and steaming tagines are set up under hissing gas lamps. Each stall has a different variety of cooked food. Conditions are pretty sanitary. However, in summer it is best to go for the food cooked to order whilst waiting. The salads always look pretty fresh, however. Another possibility is ***Chez Chekrouni***, on Jemaâ el Fna, left of the *Café de France* in the Derb Debbachi direction, the one with the counter seating overlooking the square (packed at lunchtimes). There is a series of cheap restaurants, often packed with locals, along Bani Marine (the one which runs behind the Cinéma Mabrouka, parallel and between Rue Moulay Ismaïl and pedestrian Rue Bab Agnaou), such as ***Casse-Croûte des Amis***. Also, behind the souvenir stalls opposite the nut sellers, you have a covered area of cheap restaurants.

Cafés On Jemaâ el Fna try ***Café-Restaurant Argana***, with a good view from the top terrace. Good lemon tartlettes. Another good meeting place is the ***Café de France***, with several levels and an excellent panorama over the square and the médina beyond. In Guéliz, the rond-point Abd el Moumen has lots of popular cafés on each side, including the ***Café Les Négociants*** and ***Café La Renaissance***; ***Boule de Neige***, on Rue de Yougoslavie, just off this roundabout, is a trendy place for pricey but excellent drinks, ice-cream and breakfasts; next door is ***Pâtisserie Hilton***, with a full range of Moroccan sweets and cakes. For late-night coffees or ice-creams (most places close by 2130), try ***Café-Glacerie Siroua***. ***Café Zohor***, Rue de la Liberté, gets crowded in the early evening (try also the neighbouring ***Pâtisserie Zohor***). ***Café Firdaous***, Ave Mohammed V, also has a local clientele. ***Café Caruso***, on the corner of Rue el Malik and Ave de France, is an upmarket address.

Bars The trendiest address in town, perhaps too trendy for its own good, is ***Le Comptoir Paris-Marrakech***, on Ave Echouhada, opposite the *Hotel Impérial Borj*. More conservatively, there is the ***Piano Bar***, at the *Hotel Mamounia*, Ave Bab Jedid, 1800-0100, drinks not cheap. More cheaply, for a beer with a view, you have ***La Renaissance***, Ave Mohammed V. Go up the lift to the rooftop bar with the best view of the Guéliz. (You pay for your 1st drink at the counter downstairs.) For a beer, chicken and chips, go for ***L'Escale***, just off Ave Mohammed V, after the *Wafa Bank*. ***Le Petit Poucet***, 56 Ave Mohammed V, has fairly cheap drinks. Reaching further downmarket, the ***Ambassadeurs***, 6 Ave Mohammed V, must have been a good address years ago. In summer 2001, ***Le Fondouk***, a tapas-type bar, will be opening near the Ben Youssef Medersa, filling the gap between indigestible traditional-banquet restaurants and low-life bars.

Entertainment

Casinos ***Grand Casino de la Mamounia***, at the *Mamounia Hotel*, Ave Bab Jedid, T044-444570. Open from 2000 or 2100. ***Hotel Es Saadi***, Ave Kadissia, T044-448811.

Cinemas The major cinemas showing films in French are the ***Colisée***, Blvd Mohammed Zerktouni and the ***Regent***, Ave Mohammed V. Try also the ***Centre Culturel Français***, Route de Targa, Guéliz, T044-447063.

Nightclubs ***Disco Paradise***, at the *Hotel Pullman Mansour Eddahbi*, Ave de France, T044-448222. Admission 80dh, 2200-0700, a large disco with the latest equipment. ***Cotton Club***, at the *Hotel Tropicana*, Semlalia, T044-433913. Admission 60dh, 2100-0500. Also try ***L'Atlas***, ***Le Flash*** and ***Le Diamant Noir*** at the *Hotel Marrakech*, both on Ave Mohammed V.

Folklore & fantasia The ***Cappa Club*** at the *Hotel Issil*, the ***Hotel le Marrakech***, Ave Mohammed V, and the ***Club Méditerranée*** all have large folklore displays but can be difficult to get into. The best bet is the ***Restaurant Riad***. For fantasia, drive or take a taxi to: ***Chez Ali*** in the

Palmerie, after the Tensift bridge, T044-448187; ***El Borj***, after the Tensift bridge, T044-446376; ***Zagora***, Route de Casablanca, T044-445237; and ***Ancien Casino de Marrakech***, Ave Kadissia, T044-448811. Food and extravagant displays from 2100, admission 100dh. ***Restaurant Chaouia***, near the airport, T044-442915. Displays of horsemanship, sword play, dance and music.

Sports

Ballooning Take off behind *Oasis Restaurant*, 2,000dh for 1 hr. **Flying** *Royal Flying Club*, Aéroport Marrakech Menara, T044-431769. **Go-Karting** At *Kart Hotel*, Sud Quad. **Golf** The ***Royal Golf Club***, 6 km south off the Ouarzazate road (P31), T044-444341, T044-430084. Is a large 18-hole course set in orchards, 6,200 m, par 72, fee per round 300dh, club hire 100dh, open every day. ***Palmeraie Golf Palace***, 18-hole, par 72, 6,214 m, fee 350dh, 15 km south of town. **Riding** At ***Club de l'Atlas*** (Haras Régional), Quartier de la Menara, T044-431301. Or there is ***Club royal équestre***, 4 km along the road to Asni, T044-448529. Most suitable for children are the stables at the ***Palmeraie Golf Palace***. **Skiing** The best site is 76 km from Marrakech at Oukaïmeden (see page 176). Snow has been irregular in recent years. **Swimming** At the municipal pool in the ***Moulay Abd es-Salam Garden***, Rue Abou el Abbes, near the Koutoubia Mosque. Open summer only, and crowded too. The water gets a little mucky at the end of the season. Not really for ladies. There are other municipal pools for SYBA, Daoudiate and the Menara, the best being the one in Daoudiate, a short taxi ride from the centre. The large hotels have pools, not always heated, however ***Sheraton***, ***Ticka*** and ***Méridien-Nfis*** are. The best pool in Marrakech is said to be at the ***Hotel-Club Sangho***, off the Casablanca road. **Tennis** *Royal Tennis Club de Marrakech*, 8 courts, central location at Jnene el Harti, Rue Oued El Makhazine, T044-431902. 30 tennis courts in hotels. **Trekking** *Atlas Sahara* ***Trek***, 6 bis Rue Houdhoud, Quartier Majorelle, T044-313901, F044-313905, (may change soon). One of the best trekking agencies in Marrakech with 18-years experience. Moroccan-born founder Bernard Fabry knows his deserts well. Did the logistics for the Eco-Challenge. Also runs upmarket accommodation in the Vallée des Aït Bougmez. ***Erg Tours***, 22 Ave Mohammed V, T044-438471, F044-438426. Landrover hire. ***High Country***, 31 Bab Amadil, Amizmiz, T044-454847 (manager Matthew Low). Agency based in Amizmiz in the foothills of the High Atlas. Organizes rock-climbing, off-roading, mountaineering, canoeing. Recommended. ***TTM-Trekking Tour Maroc***, 107 Rue Saâd ben Errabia, Issil, T044-4308055, F044-434520, offer ski trekking in Toubkal from 15 Jan-30 Apr, camel trekking by the Atlantic coast, mountain walking guides, meals and all camping equipment provided. ***Pampa Voyage (Maroc)***, 203 and 213 Blvd Mohammed V, Guéliz, T044-431052, F044-446455. Another agency with a good reputation. Small groups will find English-speaking ***Mohammed Nour***, T/F302189, very helpful for setting up treks.

Spectator sport The *Kawkab* (KACM) football club of Marrakech, one of the best in Morocco, can be seen at the Stade al Harti, Rue Moulay El Hassan, Hivernage.

Shopping

Handicrafts

Marrakech is something of a shoppers' paradise. Since the early 1990s, craft production has taken off in a big way, with a range of new products, notably in metal and ceramic, being added to classic leather and wood items. The influence of the international decorator set can clearly be felt. Close to the Dar El Pacha, in the Bab Doukkala neighbourhood, are a number of antique dealers, and in Guéliz, the keen shopper will find a number of chic boutiques with upmarket clothing, fine leather and other items. Prices in Guéliz are fixed, and more expensive than the médina. A feel for prices can also be gained by visiting the workshops in the large craft training centre (the *Coopartim Ensemble Artisanale*), on your left as you go from Guéliz to the médina. Here again prices are non-negotiable, and slightly more expensive than in the old city. However, in a very short time you can see people at work at practically all the main crafts, including embroidery, ceramic mosaic and basketry, felt hats, wood painting and slipper making. In the médina, there is so much on offer that you begin to feel a little dazed – craftwork overdose, or something like the *syndrome de Stendahl*, the result of seeing too many souks rather than too many Italian paintings.

In the médina, prices are of course negotiable. Remember, you are buying non-essential articles for decoration – so it really doesn't matter if you have them or not. Keep a sense of humour (remember how absurd it all is when some salesman whom you met 5 mins ago reasons that "you are not my friend because you don't want to buy from me." Always be polite, and you may just come away with some bargains. The price you pay for that bijou plate or mirror is really only what a decorative item is worth to you.

Good items to buy in Marrakech include thuya wood boxes and trays, painted wood mirrors, ceramics and *belgha* (leather slippers). You can also find very nice wrought ironwork mirror frames, and if you are feeling strong, you could go for a small (but heavy) zellij table top. A particularly good buy are the baskets, available from stalls in the Guéliz food market.

Guéliz There are quite a few souvenir shops and shops selling clothes and luggage on Ave Mohammed V. There are number of little boutique-type places on Rue de la Liberté, which cuts across Ave Mohammed V just after the main food market in Guéliz, on your left as you come up from the médina. Also have a quick trawl along Rue Mohammed Bequal (turn left just after the restaurant *La Taverne*, which itself is almost opposite the Cinéma Le Colisée).

Rue de la Liberté *Côté Sud*, 4 Rue de la Liberté (as you come from the médina on Ave Mohammed V, turn left after *Place Vendôme* clothes shop; *Côté Sud* is about 30 m along on right). Boutique owned by craft specialist Sabine Hmami-Bastin. A fine choice of items, including embroidery, ceramics and small paintings and attractive frames. Also does perfumes, candles and incense. Many articles made especially for the shop. ***Intensité Nomade***, corner Ave Mohammed V/Rue de la Liberté. A tasteful selection of clothes and leather goods for style gurus. ***L'Orientaliste***, 15 Rue de la Liberté. A good selection of ceramics and perfumes, paintings and semi-antiques. ***Place Vendôme***, 141 Ave Mohammed V, almost opposite the food market. High quality leather and maroquinerie. ***Yves Rocher***, Rue de la Liberté. For the lotions and potions you forgot to buy before you left home.

Rue Mohammed Beqal *Chic Caftan*, immeuble 100, no 2, T044-435093. Almost opposite the Galerie Bikenmeyer. As the name suggests, a good choice of upmarket traditional women's gear. Beautiful babouches with a modern touch.

The médina It can be terribly confusing for shopping. Originally each souk specialized in a given item. This system has largely broken down, however, on the main tourist drag (Souk Semmarine and its continuation, Souk el Kebir) up to the area round the Ben Youssef Medersa. Basically, there are shops specializing in slippers, traditional gear, wood and ceramics, and a number of large antique shops.

You could make your way into the médina at the 'entrance' just opposite *Résidence de la Place*. You will wind round and eventually come through an arch into the wide, paved **Souk Semmarine**. There are some big antique shops and carpet emporia here, some of them very expensive. At the end of Souk Semmarine, you come to another arch, the street rises slightly, and you are in Souk el Kebir (good choice of babouches and jellabahs). **Rahba el Kedima**, off to the right, also has some interesting small shops. Further on, Souk el Kebir successively becomes Souk el Najjarine, the Carpenter's Souk. You pass under a sort of wooden lintel, and the street becomes Souk Chkaïria, The Bag Makers' Souk.

Near the Ben Youssef Medersa ***Chaussures Ben Youssef***, Kaâte Bennahi, 6 Souk Ahl Fès, T044-377810. Small workshop, easily missed, behind the *medersa*. (Go straight on instead of turning left for Dar Belarj, the workshop is on your right.) The place to buy the best babouches, prices between 200-280dh, materials used include old flat weaves and modern silks. Beautiful presents.

Leksour and Mouassine neighbourhoods ***Au Minaret Mouassine***, 56 Fhal Chidmi, Mouassine, T044-441357/06-1181194. Owner Hassan Errijaji is an English-speaking carpet dealer. Good place to buy. ***Beldi***, a maison de haute couture at 9-11 souikat Leksour, T044-441076. Fine selection of traditionally tailored clothes, mainly for women. Waistcoats and flowing shirts for men. ***D'Altro 1***, 21 Fhal Chidmi, Mouassine, T044-444289, owner Abd el Moumen Mhaidi. Minimalist decorative goods. Lamp bases in tadelakt, simple wood picture frames. A surprising little shop. ***Dar Bou Ziane***, 20-21 Rue Sidi el Yamani, Leksour, T044-443349, F044-443367. Asiatic, Syrian and Moroccan antiques on premises which used to be a flour mill. The place to buy your marble fountain or Damascene mother-of-pearl love seat. Everything for the ideal oriental home including wild wrought iron and ram-horn chandeliers by designer Med. But who knows how many kasbahs were pillaged to stock their antique door section. ***Trésorie du Sud***, Rue el Mouassine, T044-440439. Small jewellers.

Books

Despite the presence of the Université Cadi Ayyad, Marrakech is not the most intellectual of towns. Nevertheless, there are a few book shops where you can stock up on large coffee table books, maps and recent Moroccan fiction in French. Foreign newspapers can be bought from the stands along Ave Mohammed V, and in the large hotels.

Guéliz ***Librairie d'Art ACR***, 55 Blvd Mohammed Zerktouni, Guéliz (in the ABN Amro arcade, to find it, go left as you face the *Café Les Négociants*). Expensive art books and a variety of other reading material, including guides and a few books in English. ***Librairie Chatr***, under the arcades at the top end of Ave Mohammed V, near the *Shell* station and the intersection with Rue Abd el Karim el Khattabi. Best choice of books in the city. At the back of the shop, coffee table books and in the far right hand corner, novels in English. Also stocks Atlas Mountain guidebooks (in French). The ***Librairie Gilot***, almost opposite, is not as well stocked.

The médina ***Librairie-Papeterie el Ghazzali***, 51 Bab Agnaou, next to *Café Lipton* just off Jemaâ el Fna. North African novels in French, some maps and guide books, also newspapers.

Food & wines

On the Casablanca road, the vast but rather appalling ***Hypermarché Marjane*** stocks just about everything. Importantly, Europeans can buy alcohol here in Ramadhan. Otherwise, the central food market in Guéliz stocks just about everything. In this market, ***Hassan Oumlile*** (shop 19, sort of in the middle, to the right as one goes through the main entrance) has a good range of booze. More importantly, he will deliver wine to riads in the médina, telephone your order on T044-433386 (shop opening hours 0800-1400, 1600-late, Fri and Sun 0800-1400). Another, a couple of doors left of the *Hotel Nessim* on Ave Mohammed V, is the ***Entrepot alimentaire*** which has a good selection of imported wines and alcohols. Further up the Ave Mohammed V, just after the restaurant ***Le Petit Poucet***, a good *épicerie* on the corner of Rue Mohammed Beqal sells wine and beer. The best known stock-everything shop in Guéliz is ***Achkid*** (which is Tachelhit for 'come along'), coming from the médina, turn left at the *Wafa Bank* on Ave Mohammed V, shop is on your left about 30 m on after the junction.

Country markets

A look in at a country market can be fitted in with an excursion out of Marrakech

Such markets serve local needs, although there are inevitably a number of persistent trinket pushers. Men from the mountain villages come down on mule, bicycle and pick-up truck to stock up on tea and sugar, candles and cigarettes, agricultural produce, maybe have a haircut or a tooth pulled. This is the place to sell a sheep, discuss emigration or a land sale. There may be some Islamists peddling cassettes of sermons, perfumes and religious texts. At such markets, just how different living standards in the countryside are really hits home. The markets are dusty, rough and ready sorts of places, people are paying with the tiny brass coins hardly seen in the city. You really feel that people are living from the land, how hard drought can hit them. Country market days as follows: **Ourika** (Mon), **Amizmiz** (Tue), **Tahanaoute** (Tue), **Ouirgane** (Thu), **Setti Fatma** (Thu), **Asni** (Sat) and **Chichaoua** (Sun).

Tour operators

Menara Tours, 41 Rue Yougoslavie, T044-446654. Has English speaking staff, runs day trips and much used by English tour agencies. Also try ***Atlas Tours***, 40 Ave al Mansour Eddahbi, T044-433858. ***Sahara Tours***, 182 Ave Abdelkrim El Khattabi, T044-430062. ***Comanov Voyages***, 149 Ave Mohammed V, T044-430265. ***Atlas Voyages***, 131 Ave Mohammed V, T044-430333. ***Wagons Lits Tourisme***, 122 Ave Mohammed V, T044-431687. ***Royal Air Maroc***, 197 Ave Mohammed V, T044-436205.

Transport

Local

Bus Enquiries, T044-433933. Can be caught from Rue Moulay Ismaïl, just off the Jemaâ el Fna, and elsewhere along Ave Mohammed V and Ave Hassan II. No 1 is the most useful, running from Jemaâ el Fna along Ave Mohammed V, No 3 and 8 run from the railway station to the bus station, via Jemaâ el Fna, No 10 from Jemaâ el Fna to the bus station, No 11 from the Jemaâ el Fna to the Menara Gardens.

Bicycle/motorcycle hire *Hotel de Foucauld*, Ave El Mouahidine, T044-445499. ***Peugeot***, 225 Ave Mohammed V, several cheaper places in Bani Marine, the road in between Rue Moulay Ismaïl and Rue Bab Agnaou.

Calèche Green-painted horse-drawn carriages, can be hailed along Ave Mohammed V, or from the stands at Jemaâ el Fna and Place de la Liberté. There are fixed prices for tours around the ramparts, other routes are up for negotiation, but they are not normally prohibitively expensive, and this is a pleasant way to see the city.

Car hire 2,000dh for 3 days is a plausible rate. You should be able to do better, getting something like a small Fiat for 500dh per day, unlimited kilometrage. Avoid the lesser known firms if possible. ***Avis***, 137 Ave Mohammed V, T044-433727. ***Europcar Inter-Rent***, 63 Blvd Mohammed Zerktouni, T044-431228, and at the airport. ***Euro Rent***, 9 Ave al Mansour Ad-Dahbi, T044-433184. ***Hertz***, 154 Ave Mohammed V, T044-434680/044-434680, airport T044-447230. ***La Royale***, 17 Rue Mauritanie, T044-447548. A good bet is ***Imzi Tours*** off Rue de Yougoslavie, take 1st right after *Pâtisserie Hilton*, T044-433934, F044-438295. Lesser known firms with more competitive rates are ***Concorde Cars***, 154 Ave Mohammed V, T044-431114 (speak English), and ***SAFLOC***, 221 Ave Mohammed V, T044-433388. Avoid ***Set Car*** at 213 Ave Mohammed V. For 4WD vehicles, agencies with a good reputation include ***Imzitours***, T044-433934/36, imzi_tours@usa.net, ***Ballouty Trans***, T044-447377, F044-447315, and ***Lune Car***, T044-447743, F044-447354, lunecar@iam.net.ma

Taxi **Petit taxi**: The city's khaki-coloured petits taxis are much in evidence. As you get in, check the driver switches the meter on. From the médina to Guéliz should cost 8-10dh during the day, and 10-15dh during the late evening and night. A journey out to the ***Marjane*** supermarket from Guéliz will cost nearly 20dh. Few journeys should cost much more than this. Major ranks are to be found in Jemaâ el Fna, at the Gare Routière by Bab Doukkala, and outside the *marché municipal*, Guéliz. **Grand taxi**: Normally more expensive, can be found at the railway station and the major hotels. They also run over fixed routes, mainly to outlying suburbs, from Jemaâ el Fna and Bab Doukkala, most rides cost 3dh, 1 person when there are 6 people squeezed in.

Long distance

Air Aéroport Marrakech Menara, T044-447862, is 6 km west of the city, by the Menara Gardens, and clearly sign-posted from the centre. There are flights to Casablanca (2 a day), as well as to Brussels (Fri), Geneva (Sun), daily to Paris and almost daily to London and to Madrid.

Road **Bus**: Run from the Gare Routière at Bab Doukkala, T044-433933, which is easily reached by taxis and local buses. There is often a choice between a number of different companies, including *CTM*, with different prices and times. Long distance buses – when leaving Marrakech, as there is more than 1 bus company, make sure the number of the booth where the tickets are bought matches the bus stop number where you intend to catch the bus. Always be there in advance even if the bus does not leave on time. It is worth trying the bus driver with 10dh for a seat near the front. *CTM* departures are currently: **Ouarzazate** 0445, 0730, 1300 and 1700; **Er Rachidia** 0445; **M'Hamid** 0730; **Beni Mellal** 0630, 1900 and 2100; **Agadir** 0800 and 1830 (currently 60dh single fare); **Laayoune** 1900; and **Casablanca** 0630, 1230, 1630 and 1800. There are also private line services to **Beni Mellal**, **El Kelaâ des Sraghna**, **Rabat**, **El Jadida** (very slow), **Essaouira** (best service with *Supratours*), **Ouarzazate** and **Skoura**, **Agadir** (also very slow), **Safi**, **Taroudant** (2 a day), as well as to **Asni**, **Oualidia**, **Khouribga** and **Demnate**. It is wise to call at the station the previous day as some services, notably across the High Atlas to **Taroudant** and **Ouarzazate**, leave early in the morning. There are *CTM* services to **Paris** every day except Fri and Sun at 1700, cost 1,150dh. The private line alternative leaves at 1200. *CTM* services for **Agadir** and **Casablanca** can also be taken from Guéliz, in Blvd Mohammed Zerktouni, but places should be reserved a day in advance. Buses to the **Ourika Valley**, **Asni** and **Moulay Brahim** run from Bab Rob. **Taxi**: Grands taxis running over fixed routes, with fixed prices, leave from a variety of places around the city. For Ourika, Asni and Ouirgane, leave from Bab Rob. For most other destinations, including Chichaoua, Essaouira and Agadir, go to Bab Doukkala. For destinations east, check out Bab Doukkala or Bab el Khemis.

Train The railway station is in Guéliz, on Ave Hassan II, T044-447768. Although there are very long-term plans for an extension of the line south to Agadir and Laayoune, at present ONCF operates only bus services to the south, connecting with the arrival of the express trains. Express trains for **Casablanca** (3 hrs) and **Rabat** (4 hrs) leave at 0900, 1230, 1400 and 1900, and non-express services at 0700, 1705, 2050 and 0130. Timetable subject to modification during Ramadhan and major public holidays.

Directory

Airline offices *RAM* is at 197 Ave Mohammed V (T044-436205/044-446444; information on T044-4447865), opening hours 0830-1215/1430-1900. The ever helpful ***Menara Tours***, 41 Rue de Yougoslavie next to the *Café Atlas*, is the representative for *British Airways*, T044-446654. ***Airstar***, 33 Rue Loubnane, Guéliz, T/F435502, provides an excursion and transfer service in southern Morocco. Try also ***Maint'aero*** (Vincent Duroc/Patrick Simon), T044-300658. Has a small Cesna, subcontracts with other agencies. Helicopter transfers by ***Hélisud Maroc***, 2 Rue Ben Aicha, Guéliz, T044-438438, F044-420488, **Airport:** Marrakech Menara, information on T044-447862.

Banks The main concentrations of cashpoints are on Rue Bab Agnaou, on Ave Mohammed V next to the *RAM* agency and near the rond-point Abd el Moumen, Guéliz. As elsewhere in Morocco, cashpoints can go unpredictably off-line. If stuck at weekends and public holidays, then the *BMCI*, almost opposite the Cinéma Le Colisée on Blvd Mohammed Zerktouni, is open 0930-1130 and 1600-1900. Otherwise it opens 0900-1300 and 1500-1900. ***ABM***, 55 Blvd Mohammed Zerktouni, T044-448912. ***Banque Al Maghrib***, Jemaâ el Fna, T044-442037. ***Banque Populaire***, 69 Ave Mohammed V, T044-434851. ***BCM***, Blvd Mohammed Zerktouni, T044-434805. ***BMCI***, Blvd Mohammed Zerktouni. ***Credit du Maroc***, Ave Mohammed V, T044-434851. ***SGMB***, 59 Rue de Yougoslavie, T044-448702. ***Wafa Bank***, 213 Ave Mohammed V, T044-433840. **American Express**: ***Voyages Schwartz***, Immeuble Moutaouskil, Rue Mauritania, T044-433321.

Communications **Post office:** The Central PTT for post is normally very busy. For telegrams, poste restante and payphones outside, head for the big post office on Place du 16 Novembre, Guéliz, open till 1800. There is also a reasonable post/telephone office on the Jemaâ el Fna. There are now plenty of *télé-boutiques* scattered across the city – just keep your eyes open. Close to Jemaâ el Fna, there is one on Derb Debbachi (on your right, after the *Café-Hotel de France*). **Cybercafés:** Try those signed off the pedestrian Rue Bab Agnaou or in the building opposite the Cinéma Colisée in Guéliz. Also ***Cyberland***, 61 Rue de Yougoslavie, passage Ghandouri, No 46, T044-436977. Small and friendly, in centre of Guéliz. There is another close to the Jardin Majorelle.

Cultural and language centres *Institut français*, open 0830-1200 and 1430-1830 except Mon), Route de la Targa, Guéliz. With a recommended café, open-air theatre and pleasant garden, shows films, holds exhibitions and other cultural events. Library has small stock of books in French on Morocco-related subjects.

Embassies and consulates *The French Consulate*, Rue Ben Khaldoun, right next to the Koutoubia Mosque, T044-444006. Open 0830-1145.

Estate agents There are numerous unscrupulous *semsara* in the médina who will label any crumbling dwelling a riad and try to sell it to you, complete with tenants. Remember that anything you need to buy must have property deeds, and that restoration costs to bring a house up to your exacting standards will mean you spending 50% as much again. There are all sorts of pitfalls, so try to talk to others who have bought and restored. Sample prices in early 2001: riad with small upstairs, 230 sq m ground floor surface, priced at 750,000dh; riad with total ground floor area 180 sq m, patio 50 sq m, 3 rooms ground floor, 3 rooms 1st floor, terraces, good condition, 550,000dh. If you are serious about buying, contact a reliable estate agent's first: ***Agence Vernet Immo Services***, T044-200870, F044-433903. A reliable agency which also acts as a property rental agency. In UK, contact ***Morocco Made to Measure*** via www.morocco-travel.com They have a Marrakech-based property agency run by Max Lawrence, T044-432749.

Hairdressing Women: ***L'Univers de la femme***, 22 Rue Bab Agnaou, T044-441296, or ***Coiffure l'Image***, 8 Rue Imam Chafi, Centre Kawkab, Hivernage, T044-434208. Also hairdos at home by Khadija, T044-436004. **Men:** Barbers on Rue Riad Zitoun el Kedim, through the arch on your right as you come from Jemaâ el Fna. Massages by Mahjoub on T06-3171020, will visit riads.

Medical services Doctor on call: T044-404040 (ambulance service too), SAMU T044-433030. **Chemists:** ***Pharmacie Centrale***, 166 Ave Mohammed V, T044-430151. ***Pharmacie de Paris***, 120 Ave Mohammed V. At the Jemaâ el Fna, end of Rue Bab Agnaou, you have a couple of pharmacies, also next to ***Café de France***. The préfecture operates an all-night pharmacy, the ***Dépôt de Nuit***, which looks like a ticket window on Place Jamaâ el Fna (with the Koutoubia behind you, turn left after the stone wall of the Club Med compound). You may have to queue for some time. There is an all-night chemist, ***Pharmacie de Nuit***, at Rue Khalid ben Oualid, T044-430415. **Dentists:** Dr Hamid Laraqui, 203 Ave Mohammed V, T044-433216, and Dr E Gailleres, 112 Ave Mohammed V, both speak English. **Doctors:** Dr Ahmed Mansouri, Rue de Sebou, T044-430754, and Dr Perez, 169 Ave Mohammed V, T044-431030. Both speak English. **Private hospital:** *Polyclinique du Sud*, 2 Rue de Yougoslavie, T044-447999, F044-432424, green number T08002525. *Polyclinique Les Narcisses*, Camp el Ghoul, 112 Route de la Targa (behind the Petit Marché), T044-447575. Also try *Clinique Ben Tofail*, Rue Ben Abd el Malik, Quartier des Hôpitaux, Guéliz, T044-4387118, F044-438717, M061181370 (Dr Driss Bouyousfi).

Places of worship (Christian and Jewish) Catholic: ***Eglise des Saints-Martyrs***, Rue El Imam Ali, Hivernage, for information T044-430585. **Jewish:** ***Synagogue Bet-el-Guéliz***, Arset El Maash, for information T044-447832/044-447976. ***Protestant Church***, services in the library of the Catholic church, Pastor Deon Malan can be reached on T044-430865. Inter-denominational service in English, 1030 Sun.

Tourist offices ***Office du Tourisme***, Place Abd el Moumen ben Ali, T044-448889. ***Syndicat d'Initiative***, 176 Ave Mohammed V, T044-432097/044-434797. Rather sleepy.

Useful addresses Emergency services: **Private ambulance service:** 10 Rue Fatima Zohra, T044-443724. **Fire:** Rue Khalid ben Oualid, T16. **Police:** Rue Ben Hanbal, T19. If you are robbed or hassled, the *Brigade Touristique* is on the Mamounia side of the Koutoubia, near the *CMH* petrol station (blue and yellow livery), in a small building on a public square with a few trees. Believe it or not, if you are spending some time in the city, you may have to visit them to do the paperwork authorizing a Moroccan friend to accompany you so they don't have hassle with the *Brigade*. This seems to apply only if the Moroccan is not of a recognizably educated background. **Garages:** ***Peugeot***: Toniel S A, Rue Tarak ben Ziad. ***Renault***: CRA, 55-61 Ave Mohammed V, T044-432015. Others are ***Auto Hall***, Rue de Yougoslavie, and ***Garage Ourika***, 66 Ave Mohammed V, T044-430155. **Hammams:** Try one of those on Riad Zitoun el Kedim or ***Hammam Dar El Bacha***, Rue Fatima Zohra. This is a large hammam dating from the early 1930s. The vestibule has a huge dome, and inside are 3 parallel marble-floored rooms, the last with underfloor heating. The men's hammam on Souk el Bayadine, just off Derb Debbachi, is handy for the cheap hotels in Kennaria (but has a rather scurrilous reputation). The closest hammam to the Bab Agnaou hotels is the *Bain Polo*, on the same street as the *Hotel Gallia*. In the Sidi Ben Youssef area are 2 hammams. The bigger one is almost opposite the entrance to the Musée de Marrakech. As this is a poor neighbourhood, so is the clientele. The much older *Hammam ed Dahab* is almost opposite the entrance to the Fondation Dar Belarj. Outside the médina, there are more salubrious hammams in the Quartier Majorelle and close to the wholesale market near Bab Doukkala. One of the best hammams, outside weekends, is *Hammam ez Zohour*, located out in Massira III, about 20-mins drive out of the centre.

Central Atlantic coast

Central Atlantic coast

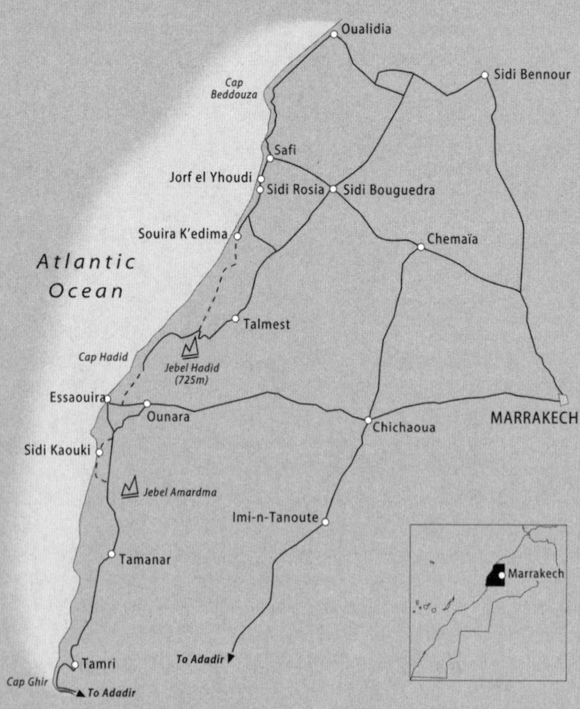

When Marrakech gets too hot and overwhelming, you can head west to the Atlantic coast. Just a couple of hours drive away is beautiful ***Essaouira****, equipped with elegant fortifications and araucarias, fishing port and palm trees. One-time hippy destination, rediscovered by Paris intellectuals in the 1980s, Essaouira became a happening destination in the late 1990s and now has an airport to prove it. Within its ramparts, it has quality guesthouse accommodation and plenty of reasonable eateries. In the early summer there is a festival of Gnaoua music. For wave-sports enthusiasts of all varieties, Essaouira (aka 'Wind City, Afrika'), with its long, wild beach is a must on the tour of Atlantic Morocco's surf spots. Further north,* ***Safi****, briefly a Portuguese bastion, is in many ways the antithesis of Essaouira. It is a tougher sort of place, resolutely untouched by mass tourism. Where Essaouira is bijou and boutiquey, its guesthouses the archetype of good taste, Safi is salt-of-the-sea and industrious. There is a busy port exporting fish and phosphates as well as a fair bit of poverty. Quality accommodation is limited, although there are some reasonable cheap options. And finally, just a short drive north of Safi lies* ***Oualidia****, tomato capital and home to oyster farms and flamingoes. It has also recently been dubbed by hipsters the 'San Tropez of Morocco' but the place only really wakes up in the summer months. However, a short, out-of-season visit here would be a great way to unwind and eat fish. Around its calm lagoon are some good restaurants and hotels, fine for a weekend* à deux *or a break from the exotic pressures of the Red City.*

Ins and outs

Getting there

Marrakech to Essaouira Oualidia, Safi and Essaouira are all accessible from Marrakech, most easily by hire car, although there is an excellent *Supertours* coach service on the Marrakech to Essaouira run. By road, Marrakech to Essaouira is a direct east-west run on the P10 via Chichaoua (a rug-making centre) and Ounara, an undistinguished sort of place a few kilometres outside Essaouira. Routes between Essaouira and Safi are described below.

Marrakech to Safi From Marrakech to Safi, there are rail and road options. For the train option (slow but safe), take the Marrakech to Casablanca train and change for Safi at Benguerir. The interesting road option is to take the P9 north for El Jadida out of Marrakech, up through the Jebilet and then northwest on the P12 via Chemaïa and Sidi Bouguedra to Safi. (A side-trip to exciting phosphate centre Youssoufia, ex-Louis Gentil might be an option.) Another, much slower, possibility is to head for Essaouira and fork right (north) at Ounara on the P8.

Marrakech to Oualidia Marrakech to Oualidia is as for Safi, from where you take the coast road north past Cap Beddouza to Oualidia. The public transport options here are slow and will mean a change of buses at Safi. Unfortunately, the fast buses doing the Agadir-Essaouira-El Jadida-Casablanca run by-pass Oualidia as they run on the inland P8 road. Still, there is always the grand taxi.

Oualidia الوليدية

Colour map 1, grid A3 Almost midway between El Jadida and Safi, Oualidia is a restful, unspoiled sort of place. Named for the Saâdian Sultan El Oualid, who built a kasbah there in the 1630s, the town is best known today for its oysters – and its restaurants. There is a small fishing port, a lagoon, safe swimming and ample amusement for twitchers, as the inlets and beaches are much appreciated by migrating birds in autumn and spring. Busy in summer, it's very tranquil for the rest of the year.

Ins & outs Oualidia is 78 km south of El Jadida – say 45 mins by car, and 66 km north of Safi. There is 1 slow bus a day (2 in summer) from El Jadida, taking well over an hour, and 3 from Safi, again taking around 1½ hrs.

Sights The village of Oualidia forms a crescent shape around a peaceful lagoon, entered by the sea through two breaches in a natural breakwater. Above the beach, the skyline on the wooded hillside is dominated by the **kasbah** built in 1634 by Saâdian Sultan El Oualid (a track to right off the S121 opposite the turning to Tnine Gharbia leads up to the building) to defend the pleasant and potentially useful harbour. Below it is the now disused **royal villa** built by Mohammed V as a summer palace. The town has a market (Saturday) for local agricultural produce. The lagoon and beach provide an ideal sheltered location for sailing, surfing, windsurfing and fishing, and riding may be a possibility, too. From late June to September, Oualidia is very busy, being referred to in some circles as 'le St Tropez de Marrakech'. The beach gets very crowded and the water none too clean. Off-season, you have the beautiful surroundings almost to yourself. The oyster beds came into production in the late 1950s, and annual production is of the order of 200 tonnes, mainly for

Five things to do on the Central Atlantic Coast

- View the wild Atlantic from the **Skala**.
- Stock up on healthy, nutty argan oil, wooly post-hippy cardigans or raffia Aladdin sandals.
- Take a camel ride (negotiate prices beforehand) or a long walk along the beach at Essaouira to the '**Castles in the Sand**'.
- Have lunch in the **fish souk** in Essaouira.
- Visit the **potter's quarter** in Safi.

local consumption. Early fruit and vegetables, and in particular tomatoes, are produced here under plastic for local and European consumption. (**NB** If you can't get to Oualidia to eat the oysters, they may be found in high quality Casablanca restaurants like *La Taverne du Dauphin* (200dh head), Avenida Houphouët Boigny, T022-221200 and the expensive but most gastronomic *A Ma Bretagne*, T022-36211, out at Sidi Abderrahmane on the Corniche.)

For a change of beach, you could head for Lalla Fatna, just 2 km outside the main village, signposted. For those with a car, a possible side-excursion is to the **Kasbah Gharbia** about 20 km to the southeast on the S1336. The kasbah is a huge enclosure, with a large white building in the centre, no doubt the home of a local notable in Protectorate times. The locals will be pleased to have a visit, and will no doubt show you round.

Sleeping & eating

Two of Oualidia's best known establishments are currently closed. However, change is in the air. The 30-room ***Hotel Le Lagon*** should be open by early 2002, and there are a couple of guesthouse places set to open, too. If a holiday home on the Moroccan Atlantic attracts you, contact www.oualidia.net and take a look at *Les Jardins de la Lagune* or contact their Casablanca office on T022-982332. By the time of going to press, *Marrakech-Médina SARL* (see under 'Sleeping, Maisons d'hôte', Marrakech), www.marrakech-medina.com, may have quality self-catering accommodation for rent in Oualidia.

B ***Hotel Hippocampe***, T022-366108, F022-366461. 20 rooms, small, very relaxed, good restaurant, bar, tennis and immaculate pool, beautiful setting above lagoon. **C** ***Hotel Auberge de la Lagune***, is currently closed due to internal management problems. **C** ***Complexe Touristique Chems***, in a wonderful location, but also closed, due to a legal dispute. Guests said to have been accidentally gassed, no less. **D** ***Motel-Restaurant à l'Araignée Gourmande***, T022-366447, F022-366144. 15 rooms all with balconies, 6 with ocean view (2 persons/290dh), good restaurant particularly for fish, street parking, welcoming staff, slight damp smell, dining room a bit gloomy but terrace views of the lagoon, royal villa. Recommended. Cheap menu 70dh, 200dh menu with lobster. Owner set to open another 25 room establishment. **D** ***Hotel-Restaurant l'Initiale*** T022-366246. Opened late 2000, 6 spacious rooms near ocean, 1 with ocean view, very clean, charming, 2 persons/200dh. Good Italian menu at 90dh, dear menu at 180dh. **D** ***Restaurant Ostréa II***, on your right as you come into Oualidia from the Casablanca direction. Oysters and white wine, nice lagoon view. (***Restaurant Ostréa I*** is in Casablanca.) For cheap eats, ***Les Roches*** has a good 80dh menu, nice service and air of the 1960s, while ***Tomato Beach*** with its little terrace does sea food, including a plate of fried fish for 40dh and a splendid *tajine de poisson*. WC none-too-clean and reserved for dwarves. ***Le Thalassa*** opened in 1999, has a restaurant and a few rooms. Nice terrace for dining, menu at 50dh.

El Jadida – Oualidia road **C** *Le Relais*,T022-345498, at Sidi Abed. Restaurant all year round (except Ramadhan), accommodation in summer. A handy coffee stop if you're on a long drive. **D** *Villa La Brise*, T022-346917. With bar and good cooking.

Camping *Camping Municipal* and *Camping International de Oualidia*, T022-366160. Site of 30 ha, bar, snacks, restaurant, grocery shop, hot and cold showers, laundry, petrol at 1 km, electricity for caravans in summer only 10dh per night, other charges per night: caravan 30dh, tent 30dh, car 2dh, person 3dh.

Southwards to Safi Travelling south from Oualidia, the S121 is elevated with the land falling away to the east towards a cultivated plain; to the west there are beautiful views of craggy coastlines, broad reaches of deserted beach and the Atlantic Ocean beyond. Despite the isolated nature of much of this route, you are unlikely to travel far before passing optimistic traders offering bead necklaces and other trinkets for sale. The landscape becomes more barren approaching the rocky headland and green-topped lighthouse at **Cap Beddouza** (ex-Cap Cantin), a dominating, fortress-style building. This remote promontory is believed to be where a shrine to the sea god Poseidon was built in the fifth century BC by the Carthaginian navigator Hanno. The final 30 km of the route into Safi has some splendid cliff scenery as the road follows the sweep of the bay towards **Cap Safi** and then beyond to **Sidi Bouzid** (see page 140). Make sure that you stop here to enjoy the extensive views of Safi, notably the commercial port and fishing harbour, the Portuguese fortress, médina and the new town on the hill above the old town.

Safi آسفي

Colour map 1, grid A3
Population: about 300,000

Safi is the largest of the five Atlantic coastal towns, with fortifications and other sights dating back to a Lusitanian past. It is also probably the least attractive to the tourist, with a good deal of industry and much poverty. Despite its médina and renown as a centre for fine, traditional pottery, it is probably for enthusiasts only. For those in search of architectural oddities, the médina contains a fragment of a cathedral in the Manueline Gothic style, all that the Portuguese had the time to build during their brief occupation in the 16th century. Unlike El Jadida to the north, Safi was an enclave where they stayed a mere 33 years.

Ins and outs

Getting there *See page 142 for further details*

Safi is easily accessible by bus from Casablanca (4¾ hrs), Essaouira (6 hrs) and El Jadida (2½ hrs). There is 1 daily train from Casablanca which goes via Benguerir on the Casablanca to Marrakech line. If driving, Safi is on the S121 coastal road from El Jadida and the P12 from Marrakech. Approaching on the main P8 from Casablanca and El Jadida to Essaouira and Marrakech, turn along the P12 from Tleta de Sidi Bouguedra.

Getting around The train station is south of the town centre – take a taxi to the médina. The bus station is southeast of the town centre, say 1½ km from the médina. Turning out of the bus station onto Ave du Président Kennedy, past the *Hotel Abda*. At the first main junction, place Idriss, bear right (north) and follow the road north for the place de l'Indépendence and the médina. Parallel to this street, further west, the Rue du Caïd Sidi Abderrahman, subsequently becoming Rue de R'bat, will also take you there. All the major sites in the old town are within walking distance of each other. Beaches are a different matter. South of the town, the coast is highly polluted by the chemical

Did the ancient Egyptians sail to America?

In his attempt to prove that ancient Egyptian navigators could have crossed the Atlantic to Central America and founded the Inca and Aztec pyramid cultures more than 4,000 years ago, the Norwegian ethnologist and explorer Thor Heyerdahl set sail from Safi in his papyrus reed boats Ra I (1969) and Ra II (1970). The first attempt failed after 2,800 miles but the second crossing in Ra II achieved a safe landing after 57 days at Bridgetown, Barbados. Heyerdahl named his craft after Ra, the sun god of Egyptian mythology, who was considered to be the creator and controller of the universe and was depicted with the head of a hawk and a human body.

industry. Local buses (numbers 10 and 15) run up to Lalla Fatna, a sheltered beach 15 km north of the town.

History

Safi is a port and an important industrial centre. Its harbour has been important since pre-Roman times and it was one of the first areas of Morocco to receive Islam. Later it was the site of a *ribat*, or fortress, held by ascetic Muslim warriors.

The Almohads surrounded the city with ramparts and built the **Zaouia of Sheikh Mohammed Saleh**. During their rule, Safi had an active intellectual and religious life. The first written mention of the town goes back to 11th-century geographer, El Bakri, who wrote that "... the ships sail up along the coast from the Oued Sous to Marsa Amegdoul (today's Essaouira) ... and then to Marsa Kouz (the mouth of the River Tensift), which is the port of Aghmat, and thence to Marsa Asafi". El Idrissi, writing in the mid-12th century, said that ships could load at Safi "when the Ocean of Shadows was calm".

The Portuguese had had a trading centre at Safi since 1481 and took control of the town in 1508, building a citadel, repairing the kasbah and building the distinctive **Dar el Bahar** (Castle of the Sea) in 1523, to defend the northern entrance of the port and to be the official residence of the governor. Some of the cannon, cast in Spain and the Netherlands, remain today, 'protecting' the town. The Portuguese left in 1541. Under the Saâdians in the later 16th century, Safi developed a role as the port for the sugar produced at Chichaoua and for Sous copper, a strategic raw material much in demand in the foundries of Europe. The Saâdians also built the **Grand Mosque** in the médina.

In the 17th century, European countries had a significant trading presence in Safi, and Moulay Ismaïl was instrumental in developing the city in the early 18th century. Under Sidi Mohammed ben Abdallah, trade intensified, with France, England, the Dutch Republic and Denmark all having agents. An indication of the effects of contact with Europe is given by one Dr Lempriere, an English visitor in 1789: "During the time I spent in the town, I lodged in a Jewish house where I saw two Arabs who had been to London, and who spoke a few words of English. They thought to please me greatly when they proffered a chair and a small table. Since I had left Tangiers, I had only seen this furniture, now completely indispensable to us, at the French consul's house in Rabat."

However, developments were cruel to Safi. Its position as the chief diplomatic port for the capital, Marrakech, was removed when Essaouira was rebuilt in the late 18th century. Between 1791 and 1883, no less than 18 natural catastrophes of various kinds hit the town. Nevertheless, not all was doom and gloom: in the mid-19th century, potters from Fès came to settle, bringing with them their craft skills. The Jewish community developed – it says much for the open-mindedness of Safi that there was never any walled-off *mellah* area – and a mixed Franco-Hispano-Portuguese commercial and fishing community gradually took root.

Safi was the base of a large sardine fishing fleet, which continues to this day, and, for many years, Safi was the biggest world sardine port. Large schools of sardines are present as a result of the currents of cold water bathing the coasts south of El Jadida in the summer, and more than 30,000 tonnes of fish now pass through the port annually – hence an important processing and canning industry, providing much employment for women.

Under the French, Safi was developed as a port for exporting phosphate rock, connecting it by rail to the mines around Youssoufia. In 1964 a new processing complex for Maroc-Chimie to the south of the town on the road to Souira Kédima came on line, allowing the export of phosphate fertilizers, as well as unprocessed phosphates, and established Safi as one of Morocco's largest ports.

The development of Safi has been rapid, with the population rising from 40,000 in 1960 to 400,000 today. The once bustling multi-national sardine port has become a provincial city where a combination of factors have produced rather negative results. Chemical products poured into the sea have had a bad effect on the fish population. There are no useable town beaches, and scant respect has been paid to the town planning regulations. There is a huge sub-standard housing problem, especially in the médina. A few years ago, a large number of the urban poor of Agadir and Marrakech were apparently relocated to Safi, creating a certain climate of insecurity – no doubt much exaggerated. A Safi lobby has yet to get together to 'do something', and many former Safiots who grew up there in the 1950s and 1960s prefer not to go back. This is all rather unfortunate, given the fact that the town does have

Safi

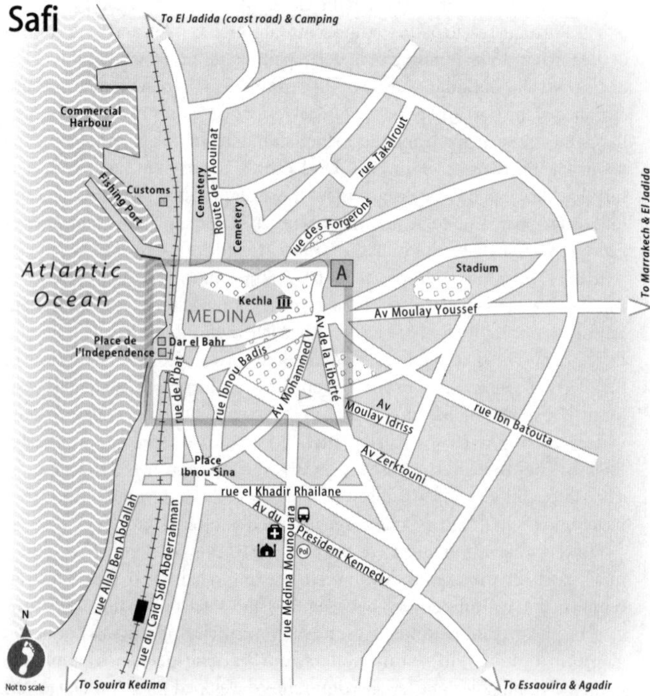

Related map
A Safi centre,
page 139

Lamali and the invention of art pottery in Safi

First French resident-general in Morocco, Hubert Lyautey had a great interest in all things Moroccan, and in particular in its traditional heritage. A special Service des Beaux-Arts was set up in Rabat to study traditional crafts. A ceramics unit was established and the director, on a visit to Paris to discuss plans, was introduced to one Boujemaâ Lamali, a master potter from Kabylia (Algeria). The result of this chance meeting was the birth of art-pottery in Safi.

Born in 1890, Lamali had wanted to be a potter from childhood. He studied under master-ceramicist Soupierau at the Fine Arts School in Algiers, and subsequently in Paris. After the First World War, he was sent to Fès to train apprentice potters to give new life to the local pottery industry – but preferred to settle in Safi, where things were less hidebound. From 1918 to 1935 he ran the Safi pilot workshop. Although there was some resistance from local potters at first, the tiny unit attracted some keen students, some of whom were later to become master potters. Under the influence of Lamali, the purest old shapes were revived, experiments were made with iridescent colours and turquoise-blue backgrounds, and new decorative motifs were introduced, including the khidous design, with its lozenges evoking weavings from the High Atlas. Safi firing techniques were applied to Rif-type pottery, traditionally hand-modelled with matt black decoration. Safi pottery was to win international fame at the universal exhibitions in the interwar period, leading to major orders from clients in Paris and elsewhere.

Today a number of potters continue the Lamali tradition, and pieces by Ben Brahim El Fakhkhari, Ahmed Serghini and the Laghriss family are much sought after by collectors. Although much contemporary Safi pottery is not to tastes used to Habitat minimalism, the visitor will find Safi production right across Morocco, such was the success of Boujemaâ Lamali in creating a recognizable style.

an interesting history and sights. Although it will never be a major destination, it would be a pity if Safi's tourist potential was totally neglected.

Sights

The médina

The médina, with its ramparts and large towers, slopes westwards towards the sea and can be entered by the main gate, **Bab Chaaba**. The main thoroughfare which runs from place de l'Indépendence to Bab Chaaba is Rue du Socco, around which are located the main souks. It is a busy, bustling area, with shops and street stalls selling all manner of food, jewellery, cheap toys and plastic goods. Close to the northern wall of the médina near Bab Chaaba is the pottery souk, a colourful alleyway and courtyard crammed with pots and plates displaying a wide variety of local designs. This leads on up some steps to an open courtyard with attractive archways housing some further pottery stalls. Just off the Rue du Socco is the **Grand Mosque** with a notable minaret, and behind it a ruined Gothic church built by the Portuguese, and originally intended as part of a larger cathedral. There is also an interesting old *medersa*. On the east flank of the médina is the **Kechla**, which houses the **National Ceramics Museum**, a large kasbah built by the Saâdians, clearly identifiable with its towers and green-tiled roofs. It offers some outstanding views over the médina and the potters' quarter at Bab Chaaba. The entrance opens out into the main courtyard, gardens and a terrace. Displays of ceramics here are divided into three sections: contemporary, local and ancient and, amongst these, are some very fine pieces of 20th-century Safi pottery. The visit might even inspire you to visit the local potters, where a cruder form of pottery is available and the construction can be observed. ■ *0830-1200 and 1400-1800. 10dh. T044-463895.* On the right of its entrance is a large round tower built by the Portuguese, and within the **Kechla** is the **Bahia Palace**, an 18th-century governor's residence flanked by gardens.

Dar el Bahar Just outside the médina ramparts, overlooking the sea, is the Dar el Bahar fort and prison built by the Portuguese in 1523. Used by them as the governor's residence, it was restored in the 1960s. It is worth entering the building, if only for the view. Entry is under an archway, inscribed 'Château de Mer', opposite the *Hotel Majestic*. Just to the left of the pay kiosk is a hammam and to the right is the prison tower. The dungeon area can be clearly seen but it is more interesting to climb the spiral staircase of the tower (narrow and dark in places) for the excellent views of the médina, Kechla and port from the top. After returning to the foot of the tower, access to the ramparts on the seaward side of the fortress is via a ramp. Here can be seen an impressive array of Dutch and Spanish cannon pointing out to sea; castings on two of these show 'Rotterdam 1619' and two others are marked 'Hague 1621'. From the top of the southwest bastion there is a further opportunity to enjoy a fine panorama, including the coast southwards towards Essaouira. ■ *0830-1200 and 1430-1800. 10dh.*

Town centre Away from the médina, activity is centred around the town's two main squares, the place de l'Indépendence and place Mohammed V. Located just to the south of the junction of Avenue Moulay Youssef and Boulevard du Front de Mer, place de l'Indépendence is a wide, bustling street with a central, tree-lined reservation, flanked by shops, banks, cafés and restaurants. Street markets are also to be found here and in the Rue de R'bat to the south. The impressive fortifications of the Dar el Bahar dominate the views at the northwest corner of the square. In contrast, on the hill high above the old town, place Mohammed V is a large, modern paved area somewhat lacking in character, acting as the focal point for the seven streets converging on it. The town hall is the main building here and the principal post office, the tourist office and the more expensive hotels are close by. However, some of the local cafés manage to add a little colour to an otherwise lacklustre street scene.

The Potters' Quarters These quarters at **Bab Chaaba** are well worth a visit. Bright children will be particularly fascinated, as they can see all the stages of the pottery process happen in and around tiny workshops. From the port side of the old town, you can cut straight through to the potters' area which centres on the marabout Sidi Abderrahman, Moula El Bibane, 'Protector of the city gates' and patron of the potters; the whole area was given official listing as being of historic importance in 1920. Safi once produced pottery with an international reputation (and also continues to make the green tiles found on many major buildings throughout Morocco). The recent development of the potteries is an interesting story, shedding light on French policy towards traditional crafts in Morocco.

The simplest pottery produced in the Safi area comes from Lamaâchate, on the north coast road, where amphorae are made. This manufacture is no doubt very ancient: Safi always had water shortages, and there were many springs at Lamaâchate. In the 12th century, the Andalucíans brought by Youssef ben Tachfine the Almoravid may have contributed to the development of pottery: glazed green water jars for the *haji*, the pilgrimage to Mecca, are said to have been made there. At the end of the 18th century, the *amine* or leader of the Potters' Corporation had a Fassi potter brought to Safi. In the

19th century, talented ceramic artists came from Fès to settle, and for many years, only blue pottery with Fassi motifs was produced. Blue was the cheapest colour, readily available as it arrived by sea, unlike the other colourants (iron oxide, chrome and manganese), which came from the remote Tafilalet and Fès. After the First World War, Safi pottery was hit by the sudden mass availability of cheap enamelled metal dishes. Local hand-modelled pottery was hard hit.

However, thanks to the energetic Boujemaâ Lamali, a master potter of Algerian origin (see box), the Safi pottery industry was to take a radical new direction in the 1920s and 1930s. In many ways a product of the Lyautey system, Lamali's reinvention of Safi pottery, in terms of both shapes and decoration, was to have a long-lasting impact.

Today, the techniques in the 140 or so workshops have changed little since the beginning of the century. The Safi potter's equipment is simple: potter's wheel, basin, reed, pot-shard and a few planks to leave pots drying in the shade are quite sufficient. The clay comes in the form of large chunks which need to be broken up and softened in water. On the second day of preparation, the clay is left in the sun before being kneaded with the feet in big round pats on a bed of ashes. After a secondary kneading with the hands and the removal of stones, it is ready for transformation. In dark workshops, well out of the bright daylight, the potters can be seen hard at work at their foot-operated wheels.

The kilns, essentially fired by *rtem* or brushwood, are designed to avoid huge leaps in temperature. On day one, the temperature does not rise above 200°C, and big pots stay three or four days at this temperature. (Clay, a highly

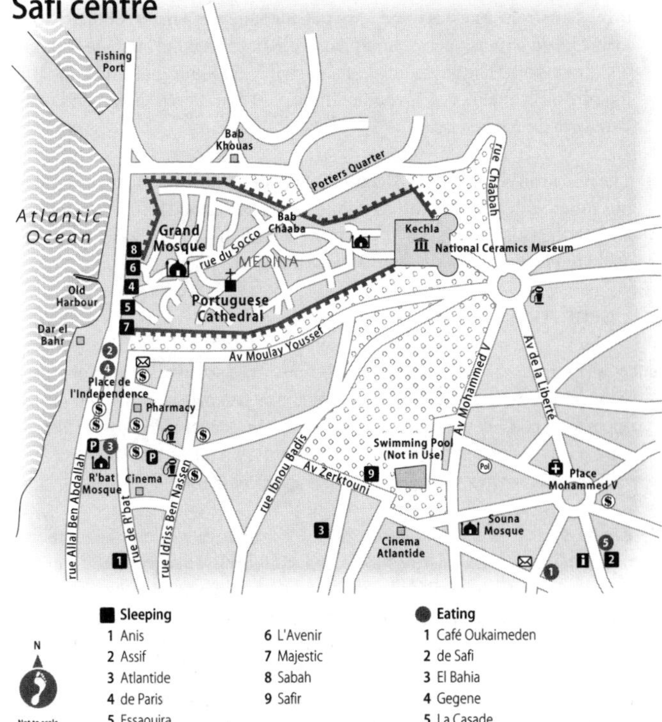

malleable substance, only really begins to change texture significantly at 600°C, and solidifies at 900°C.) During firing, a pot loses 15-20% of its volume, and imperfections due to poor technique during throwing become apparent. After the kiln has cooled fully, pots can be removed.

Painting and glazing were areas in which numerous experiments were conducted under Lamali. Before painting, the pot has to be dipped in a mixture of white clay and water, to cover the original clay colour. Traditionally, the glaze – a liquid composed of tin, lead and silicate – was applied before coloured designs. Pots must be extremely clean before glaze is applied. Generally five colours are used: white, blue, green, yellow and brown. (Lamali revived the old colours of Safi pottery, which had disappeared with the ease of producing Fassi blue and white designs.) The motifs are painted in outline by the *maâlem*, and the apprentice does the colouring in. Different chemical substances produce the colours: cobalt blue is the most highly valued, green is produced by copper oxide, while a lead oxide is used to produce the deep green roof tiles. Manganese is the base for the browns, deep purple brown being referred to as *zbibi*, from *zbib* (raisin).

The pot-painters, often women, are highly skilled workers. The pots are carefully piled in the kilns before re-firing. A small tripod or *chouka* is used to separate the bigger pieces so that air can circulate in the kiln. The three marks left after this second firing are painted in afterwards. The motifs have names like honeycomb, scorpion and *jnaweh boufertoto* (butterfly wing), olive kernel and bull's eye. However, many of the designs today are somewhat garish. Note that the best place to buy is not always the stalls below potters' hill. You could also try the pottery souk in the médina, off Rue du Socco.

Profits for the workshop owners are potentially very good. The clay brought in from quarries some 5 km outside Safi costs a mere 200dh the lorry load. Skilled potters operate on a piece work basis, making between 500dh to 600dh a month. The guys who do the carrying, clay-kneading and kiln-stoking obviously make less. If you had time, you could even design and order your own dinner service.

Beaches The best local beach is **Sidi Bouzid**, just north of the town and on the No 15 bus route, with cafés and the very good *Le Refuge* seafood restaurant. Further afield is the **Lalla Fatma** beach, just past Cap Safi. If they can, locals go further afield to **Plage Souiriya**, some 30 km to the south.

Essentials

Sleeping
■ *on map*
Price codes: see inside front cover

In Safi the budget traveller can find budget hotels at a fraction of the price of those in Essaouira. The cheap hotels are all concentrated in the southwestern side of the médina, opposite the port, just below the long, sloping place de l'Indépendence (where there are some good cheap eateries). They are a hefty, 2 km walk from the bus station. For those with nostalgia and more cash, the *Atlantide* is an Agatha Christie sort of place.

B ***Hotel Safir***, Ave Zerktouni, T044-464299, F044-464573. 90 rooms, restaurant, bar, nightclub, snack bar, conference room and small pool, a modern hotel, with well appointed rooms, some having fine views over city to the ocean. Suites available at 690/960dh, dinner menu 160dh, breakfast 50dh, parking, major credit cards, expensive and not entirely decorous – a reflection of the poverty of the town. **C** ***Hotel Atlantide***, Rue Chaouki, T044-462160/1, F044-464595. Close to the *Hotel Safir*, to which it is to be entirely preferred. 47 rooms, pleasant restaurant with terrace, nice pool. A pleasant, old-style hotel with an air of faded elegance not entirely wrecked by recent renovation work. Opened in 1920 by the Compagnie Paquet de Navigation as the *Hotel Marhaba*, the *Atlantide* now belongs to the Office Chérifien des Phosphates, and is mostly used by company personnel (lots of seminars). It has a quiet position overlooking the centre of Safi new town. Rooms are plain but comfortable, some have panoramic views. Next door is the *Cinema Atlantide* offering one daily afternoon film performance for hotel guests, parking in quiet street, no credit cards. **D *Hotel les Mimosas***, Rue Ben Zeidoun, T044-463208, F044-625955. 34 rooms, all with bath, 2 suites, restaurant, bar and snack bar, nightclub/discotheque, clean, simply furnished rooms. A hotel convenient for town centre and place Mohammed V. Not as quiet and decorous as it perhaps should be. **E *Hotel Abda***, Ave du Président Kennedy, near the bus station, T044-610202, F044-463868. New establishment, street-facing rooms noisy. ***Hotel Anis***, Rue de R'bat, T044-463078. 36 rooms, restaurant, close to the place de l'Indépendence and the médina. **E *Hotel Assif***, Ave de la Liberté, T044-622940, T044-462311, F044-621862. 26 rooms, restaurant, an old hotel, close to place Mohammed V, ie about 1 km north of bus station. Clean and comfortable rooms (250dh per 2 persons with shower), family rooms available, tourist dinner menu 79dh, breakfast 20dh, street parking in front of hotel, extension of further 40 new rooms, including more family rooms, due to open in summer 1996, with restaurant, lift, conference facilities, new rooms, estimated price category **D**, looks better equipped, including TV and telephone, and larger than the older part of the hotel, major credit cards. **F *Hotel Majestic***, place de l'Indépendence (corner of Ave Moulay Youssef), clearly visible from main square, T044-464011. 20 rooms, triple 110dh, shared showers 5dh, TV room, basic, quite friendly and clean, no breakfast, public parking 20 m. Round the corner and up a side street, try ***Hotel-Café de l'Avenir***, T044-462657, kind of gloomy, tiny restaurant at back, hot shower shared, 5dh, cold showers in rooms with WC. Further up the street, on the right, is ***Hotel de Paris***, T044-462149, 1 person/30dh, 2 persons/60dh, in an old house built round a courtyard. Spartan, clean accommodation, big, airy rooms. If stuck try ***Hotel Sabah*** in same street.

Camping *Camping de Sidi Bouzid*, 3 km north of Safi at Sidi Bouzid, T044-462871. Site of 6 ha, bar/snacks, grocery shop, pool, showers, laundry, petrol 2 km, electricity for caravans. ***Camping Balnéaire***, at Kédima 32 km south, site of 2 ha, beach 3 km, showers, laundry, electricity for caravans, petrol at 18 km.

Eating

• *on map*

Expensive Try the restaurant in the ***Hotel Atlantide*** which has a pleasant terrace. Also good is the ***Restaurant La Trattoria***, aka ***Chez Yvette***, a large Italian restaurant on Rue Aouinate, on an uphill road leading south of the médina, T044-620959. A good feed for 200dh, salad and fish main course for 150dh, pizza, lasagne, *osso bucco* and occasionally tiramisu. A good address. Centrally located and easily identified by bright displays of vegetables and plastic flowers are ***Restaurant de Safi***, 3 Rue de la Marine, T044-610472 and ***Restaurant Gegene***, 8 Rue de la Marine, T044-463369. Specializing in fish and Italian dishes; both are just off the place de l'Indépendence near the *Wafa Bank*. Cheaper places are to be found around the médina. Although out of Safi to the north (a petit taxi or car needed), also try ***Restaurant Le Refuge***, Route de Sidi Bouzid, T044-464354. Has a good reputation for French cuisine, particularly fish dishes (closed Mon) and ***Restaurant La Corniche***, also on Route de Sidi Bouzid, T044-463584. Moroccan food and shellfish. Often, restaurants in Safi do not display menus outside so check inside to be sure of prices and range of food on offer.

Cafés Try the ***Café-Restaurant El Bahia*** at the southern end of the place de l'Indépendence for a pause. In the area around place Mohammed V ***Café*** Oukaïmeden on Ave Zerktouni has a pleasant street terrace; other possibilities worth trying include ***Café al-Marjan***, also on Ave Zerktouni and ***Café La Cascade*** next door to *Hotel Assif* on Ave de la Liberté.

Entertainment **Sports** The beach at Sidi Bouzid is known for surfing. There is horse riding at ***Club Equestre***, Route de Sidi Ouassel. There are signs to a swimming pool from place Mohammed V along Ave Moulay Idriss. However, the pool site on Ave Mohammed V next to the public gardens looks distinctly neglected and certainly not used at present.

Shopping The best bargain in Safi is pottery (see above), for which the town is celebrated. In the médina, there are lots of stalls selling cheap shoes and clothes.

Transport **Local Bus**: No 7 takes you from main bus station into town centre, 2dh. **Car hire**: *Europcar*, place Ibnou Sina, T044-462935.

Long distance Train The railway station is to the south of the town, on Rue du Caïd Sidi Abderrahman, the continuation of Rue de R'bat, T044-464993. There is 1 train daily at 0815 to **Benguerir**, journey time approximately 1 hr, which connects with services to **Casablanca**, **Rabat**, **Kènitra**, **Meknès**, **Fèz**, **Marrakech**, **Asilah** and **Tanger**. The daily arrival at Safi from all these destinations is at 1846.

Road The bus terminal is on Ave Président Kennedy to the south of the town. *CTM* operates 6 buses daily to **Casablanca**, first bus is at 0430 and the last departure is at 1600. For **Marrakech** its service leaves at 0700 and there are 2 buses daily for **El Jadida** leaving at 0830 and 1430. *CTM* buses for **Agadir** leave at 1000 and 2300, for **Tiznit** at 1000 and **Essaouira** at 2100. *Chekkouri* offers 6 daily buses to **Marrakech**, first bus 0500 and last bus 1700, 6 **Agadir** services, first bus at 0100 and last bus at 2330. **Casablanca** is very well served by *Chekkouri* with 9 daily buses, first at 0200 and last at 2300, and they also have departures for **Taroudant** at 0400 and **Rabat** at 0130.

Directory **Banks** *BMCE*, place Ibnou Sina and *BMCE*, *BMCI* and *Banque du Maroc*, place de l'Indépendence. ***Bank Populaire***, Ave de la Liberté, close to place Mohammed V. **Communications** **PTT:** place de l'Indépendence and **Post Office:** Ave Abdallah, at junction of Ave Zerktouni. **Tourist offices** Ave de la Liberté, Ville Nouvelle. Open Mon-Fri 0900-1200 and 1500-1830. The office is in a small portacabin in a side street opposite the *Hotel Assif* and, although you will receive a friendly welcome and a willingness to help, only generalized tourist literature about Morocco seems to be available, so expect little by way of specific maps and information about Safi itself.

Routes from Safi

Safi to Agadir – via Chichaoua & the High Atlas This route is an alternative to the more direct option using the P8 via **Talmest** and **Ounara** and, later in the journey, provides a good opportunity to enjoy some of the fine scenery of the western High Atlas mountains. Leave Safi on the P12; beyond Sidi Bouguedra the road climbs steadily into the hills for the first part of the 42 km to **Chemaïa** and then levels out to give views of high plains in all directions. Petrol is available outside Sidi Tiji. In Chemaïa, where there is little of interest to detain the traveller, turn south on the S511 for **Chichaoua** (63 km). This is a very isolated section (no petrol), travelling across wide plains with flat-topped hills in the far distance, crossing the Oued Tensift after 35 km. Reaching the busy junction with the P10 road to Marrakech offers the chance to refuel and stop at one of the shops or cafés here. Chichaoua is noted for the distinctive animal designs of its good quality, brightly coloured carpets (see page 233). Travelling south on the P40 the impressive peaks of the High Atlas soon comes into sight on the way to **Imi-n-Tanoute**; a detour off the main road into this busy but unattractive town provides the chance to visit shops and banks but little else. Leaving Imi-n-Tanoute the route winds upwards through the pass of

Tizi Maachou (1,700 m) through some beautiful mountain scenery. Beyond the summit there are fine views of the higher peaks to the east before you reach the reservoir and **Barrage Abdelmoumen**; on the way you will pass many local traders offering bottles of argan oil for sale. A rapid descent to the viewpoint at **Ameskroud** then follows; it is worth stopping here to enjoy the extensive views southeast over the plain towards **Taroudant** before completing the remainder of the journey to Agadir.

Safi to Essaouira – on the coast road

After the beach resort of Sidi Rosia is **Jorf el Yhoudi** – also known as the Jew's Cliff. On the coast at **Souira Kédima**, 32 km south of Safi, is a rebuilt/restored Portuguese *ribat*, more or less open to the public. It dates from the 1550s. Guides say it was completed in 1521 and abandoned in 1525. Across the Oued Tensift, the ford having been replaced by a new road and bridge, and beyond Dar Caïd Hadji is the more recent **Kasbah Hamidouch**, built in the 18th century by Sultan Moulay Ismaïl to control this region. At one time the river surrounded the building as a moat. It is a splendid building, crumbling turrets and crenellations in abundance. This coastal area is very popular in summer. Good campsite here, see page 141.

The road continues through **Akermoud** with Jebel Hadid (Iron Mountain) to the east. In this region are a number of white shrines. That of Moulay Bouzerktoun set among the sand dunes is most striking.

Essaouira الصويرة

Colour map 1, grid B1

Essaouira, 'little picture', is one of those stage set places: you half expect to see plumed cavalry coming round the corner, or a camera crew filming some diva up on the ramparts. It is a beautifully designed 18th-century military port, and somehow hasn't been too much changed since. The walls are white, the windows and shutters are cracked and faded blue, while arches and columns are sandy camel-brown. Three crescent moons on a city gate provide a touch of the heraldic, while the surfers and the much exhibited local naïve school of artists hint at Essaouira's hippy days, a couple of decades ago. Tall feathery araucaria trees and palms along the ramparts add a Mediterranean touch. So far Essaouira's isolation (over six hours by road to Casablanca) has helped it avoid the fate of Agadir. There is now an airport, however, and large numbers of foreigners have bought picturesque property.

Ins and outs

Getting there

See page 155 for further details

Essaouira is accessible by bus from Agadir (3½ hrs), Marrakech (between 3 hrs and 4½ hrs), Casablanca (6 or 9 hrs, depending on route) and from Safi and El Jadida. Both *CTM* and private lines arrive at the bus station about 1 km from the town – say 20-mins walk with luggage. You might want to take a petit taxi in, around 7dh, 10dh at night. Grands taxis also run to the bus station, although arrivals will be dropped off next to Bab Doukkala. Drivers may want to use the car park (24-hr warden) close to the harbour next to Place Prince Moulay El Hassan. There are plans for flights from Rabat airport to Essaouira, making it a possible long weekend destination for the capital's wealthy.

Getting around

One of the most appealing aspects of Essaouira is that all the principal tourist sites can be comfortably reached on foot; cars can be left in the parking area to the south of Place Prince Moulay El Hassan. There are some good walks along the windswept beach to Borj El Baroud. The walk to Cap Sim is an all day excursion.

Fishpaste and imperial purple

On the subject of the colour purple, Pliny the Elder wrote: "In Rome, the fasces *part at its approach; this colour makes childhood majestic; it distinguishes the curia from the knights; it is worn to pacify the gods, and it gives style to all types of clothing; it is worn with gold in triumphal dress. Let us thus pardon the wild passions aroused by purple ..." Off the coast at Essaouira, the Iles Purpuraires are so-named for the dye production workshops located there in ancient days. Given the lack of islands along the Atlantic coast, the biggest island of the tiny rocky group was quickly developed by the ancients as a mini-industrial estate producing that most vital substance to Roman imperial prestige: purple.*

However, dye production was only really a second string to the tiny island's industrial bow. Fishing was the number one activity (as it still is today in Essaouira). Fish were plentiful, notably tuna, during seasonal migrations. Garum, a sort of fish seasoning/paste widely enjoyed in the ancient Mediterranean – black garum from Cadiz was a particular gastronomic treat – was produced there. As salt flats were close by, salt was readily available for preserving the catch. Sardine fishing was a spring time activity, reaching a peak in May. Tuna fishing took place from late May to July. Salt was gathered in late summer, when evaporation was at its height, and no doubt garum was manufactured as fish was salted. Shellfish, from which dye was extracted, could be gathered at other times. Thus there was no inactive part of the year for this ancient 'off-shore industrial zone'.

The purple dye industry was probably piloted by Mauretanian ruler Juba II, anxious no doubt to add a second luxury item to the island's production. Reared in Rome, husband of Cleopatra Selene, Juba II was well aware of the value of purple at court. Both the main shellfish species producing the dye were abundant in the area: Purpura Haemastoma *and* Murex Trunculus, *for the zoologically minded. Excavations on the island revealed shells of a size rarely seen today.*

Pliny, in Book I of his Natural History, gives us a fair bit of information about making purple. The ink-glands were removed from the shellfish, and macerated in salt. Then the briney mixture was heated at low temperature in lead-lined basins.

History

Essaouira is a quiet sort of place with a long history. There was a small Phoenician settlement at Essaouira, previously called Magdoura or Mogador, a corruption of the Berber word *Amegdul*, meaning 'well protected'. The Romans were interested in the purple dye produced from the abundant shellfish on the rocky coast, which they used to colour the robes of the rich (see box). Mogador was occupied in the 15th century by the Portuguese who built the fortifications around the harbour. The town was one of their three most important bases, but was abandoned in 1541, from which time it went into decline. Mogador was also visited by Sir Francis Drake, Christmas 1577. In 1765, the Alaouite Sultan Sidi Mohammed ben Abdallah transformed Mogador into an open city, enticing overseas businessmen in with trade concessions, and it soon became a major commercial port, with a large foreign and Jewish population establishing the town as a major trading centre. The Sultan employed the French architect Théodore Cornut to design the city and its fortifications. In his design, Cornut chose a rectangular layout for the main streets, resulting in a very uniform style, and constructed ramparts in the Vauban style. The fortifications were not always very effective, however.

From time to time, the tribesmen of the region would raid the town, carrying off booty and the merchants' wives – who it is said, were not always that happy to return. Perhaps life in the *bled* was more pleasant than listening to the wind in the damp counting houses of Mogador.

Orson Welles stayed here for some time, filming part of *Othello* at the **Skala du Port**. At Independence the town's official name became Essaouira, the local Arabiac name meaning 'little picture' – perhaps because Essaouira is 'as pretty as a picture'? In the 1960s Essaouira had a brief reputation as a 'happening place', which attracted hippies and rock stars, including Jimi Hendrix. Essaouira now seems to be emerging from several decades of decline, for on top of fishing, fish processing, a small market and handicraft industries, the town is attracting greater numbers of tourists, notably surfers – who refer to it as 'Wind City, Afrika'. Upmarket and activity tourism may yet bring some wealth to the inhabitants of this most relaxed town, without spoiling its gentle atmosphere. Essaouira has some useful friends in influential places, including André Azoulay, one of HM the King's special advisers, and there is an artistic lobby, too, including gallery owner Frederick Damgaard and Edmond Amran-Mellah, the writer. With luck and some planning, the charm will not fade under the impact of oversized hotel developments and day-trippers from Marrakech.

Sights

Essaouira does not have a lot in the way of formal sites (another reason perhaps for its failure to attract mainstream tourist investment), and it is more of a gently atmospheric sort of place than anything else.

The médina

Enclosed by walls with five main gates, the médina is the major attraction. Entering from **Bab Doukkala** the main thoroughfare is Rue Mohammed Zerktouni, which leads into Ave de l'Istiqlal, where there is the **Grand Mosque**, and just off, on Darb Laalouj, the **Ensemble Artisanal** and the **Museum of Sidi Mohammed ben Abdallah**, which houses the Museum of Traditional Art and Heritage of Essaouira and which has an interesting collection of weapons, as well as handicrafts such as woodwork and carpets. This house, once the home of a pacha, has examples of stringed instruments beautifully decorated with marquetry which were used by the musicians to accompany their dances. On display too are documents on Berber songs. Upstairs is the ethnographic collection which is well worth a visit. This collection features a wide range of signs and symbols which play an important role in the traditional craftwork of the artisans of the Essaouira region. These mystico-religious symbols appear in carvings and engravings, in finely crafted filigrees, tapestries and embroidery and on attractive forms of local jewellery. ■ *0830-1200 and 1430-1800, except Fri 0830-1130 and 1500-1830, closed Tue. 10dh. T044-472300.*

Avenue de l'Istiqlal leads into Ave Okba ben Nafi, on which is located the small **Galerie des Arts Frederic Damgaard**, at the end of the street a gate on the right leads into Place Prince Moulay El Hassan, the heart of the town's social life and although recently repaved and modernized, still with character. The town's souks are mainly located around the junction between Rue Mohammed Zerktouni and Rue Mohammed El Gorry, although there is an area of woodworkers inside the **Skala** walls to the north of Place Prince Moulay El Hassan, where some fine pieces can be picked up with some good-natured bargaining. At the northeast end of Rue Mohammed

Zerktouni, close to Bab Doukkala, is the ***mellah***, or old Jewish quarter, an area of significant size underlining the importance of the Hebrew population settling in Essaouira at the time of its foundation. Although the Jewish community no longer remains, it made a substantial contribution to the commercial and cultural development of the town.

The Harbour & Skala Off Place Prince Moulay El Hassan is the small but vibrant harbour, which principally supports a fishing fleet, and is worth a visit. It is still possible to see the work of traditional shipbuilders and repairers on the bustling quayside and nearby the lively fish market and open-air restaurant stalls serve many varieties of grilled fish, typically prices range from 10-25dh. The sea gate (the **Porte de la Marine**) which serves to link the harbour with the médina was built in 1769, it is said by an Englishman converted to Islam, during the reign of Sidi Mohammed ben Abdallah. The gateway is built of stone in the classical style and the year of its construction (1184 of the Hegira) is inscribed on the pediment. It is connected to the ramparts on the **Skala**, an old Portuguese sea defence and battery, by a bridge which spans small primitive dry docks. Entry to the **Skala du Port** (10dh) is via a kiosk close to the Porte de la Marine and from the top of the bastion there are extensive panoramic views of the harbour and the offshore islands, the **Iles Purpuraires**.

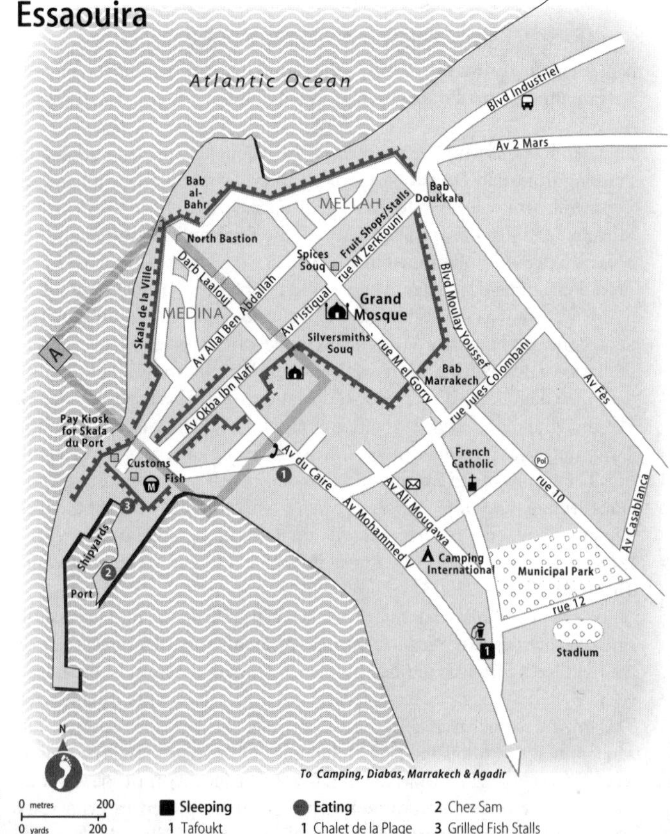

Related map
A Essaouira Médina, page 151

Sidna Boulal

Visiting a tourist site in some Moroccan town, as likely as not you will come across a couple of Gnaoua musicians. Wearing coloured tunics and cowrie-shell caps with tassels, clutching guenbri *string instruments or outsize metal castanets, they may offer to perform for a handful of dirhams. Despite present touristification, Gnaoua music is an ancient affair, the core of trance rituals and other psychotherapeutic rites which were so much a part of life in Morocco.*

The term Gnaoua (a plural) is thought to derive from Guinea – due to the sub-Saharan, slave origins of most of the adepts. Gnaoua trance rites combine ritual, divinatory and healing practices, bringing together musicians, soothsayer-therapists and followers. While the Gnaoua were important in Marrakech and Essaouira, the latter town is the only one today to have a specifically Gnaoua sanctuary – the Zaouia or shrine of Sidna Boulal close to the ocean ramparts in the old town. It is said that late in the 19th century, a rich Souiri family left a piece of land to the Gnaoua, where they built their zaouia, a simple building with a big courtyard and a couple of rooms, one for storing the drums and musical instruments, the other for the women where they could go into trance-dances out of sight of the men during gnaoua ceremonies. In the old days, the master musicians would meet at this zaouia to organize the ceremonies at followers' homes.

Twice a year, the Gnaoua of Essaouira would process through the town to collect funds, once in Chaâbane (the month before Ramadhan), and once after Aïd El Kebir, the Feast of the Sacrifice. In the mid-afternoon, the procession, led by the red and green standards of the Gnaoua, followed by a sacrificial animal, generally a heifer, and musicians with drums and qraqeb metal castanets, would move from the Great Mosque down the main street towards Bab Doukkala. They would salute the zaouias of the other brotherhoods on their way to the sanctuary of Sidna Bilal. After the sacrifice, the lila *(lit night) of different dance rites would take place in thezaouia, culminating in 'possession' dances.*

The name of the Gnaoua's patron, Sidna Bilal, is of course important. Bilal, sometimes called Ibn Hamma after his mother, was a black slave of Ethiopian origin born in Mecca. One of the first converts to Islam (the second adult convert, according to some sources), he was freed and became the Prophet Mohammed's assistant. When the Muslims took Mecca from the pagan tribe of Quraysh, he was the first to make the call to prayer from the roof of the Kaâba, the great square building at the heart of the holy city. The Gnaoua take great pride in tracing their group's pedigree back to the seventh century and the first muezzin *('prayer caller') of Islam.*

Skala de la Ville

Further to the north of Place Prince Moulay El Hassan it is possible to get on to the ramparts of the Skala de la Ville from Rue de la Skala close to its junction with Rue Darb Laalouj. Entry here is free and crenellated walls protect a 200 m long raised artillery platform and an impressive array of decorated Spanish and other European cannon. From the tower of the North Bastion there are fine views of the old *mellah*, the médina with its white buildings and blue shutters and the coastline to the north of Essaouira. The woodworkers' souks are situated here in arched chambers underneath the ramparts.

Cemeteries

Outside Bab Doukkala is the Consul's cemetery for British officials, who died there converting Mogador into a trading post with strong UK links. Behind the high wall on the road to the bus station is the Jewish cemetery. If you can find the man with the key, you may discover the resting place of Leslie Hore-Belisha, inventor of the first pedestrian crossing light.

Beaches Essaouira has fine beaches. The wind, known as the *alizée*, stirs up a lot of sand, and makes it cold for swimming, but ideal for surfing. The northern Plage de Safi is fine in the summer, but can be dangerous during windy weather. South of the town, the wide beach is great for football – surely Essaouira must be a school for soccer champions. Past the Oued Ksob, you will see the waves breaking against the remains of Borj El Baroud. When walking far along the beach it should be noticed that the incoming tide makes the Oued Ksob below the village of Diabat into an impassable river.

Diabat The ruined palace/pavilion below Diabat is worth a detour from a beach walk, just after the stream which crosses it, but the village of Diabat is dreadfully miserable. The building is said to have been swallowed by the sand after the people of the Sous put a curse on it as their trade was being ruined. The old fort was built by the Portuguese in the 18th century. A short walk up the road from Diabat will bring you to the *Auberge Tangaro*, one of Essaouira's most pleasant hotels. Half a kilometre further on, and you are at the crossroads with the P8 road from the south, which runs back into town.

Iles Purpuraires These islands to the southwest are a bird sanctuary, particularly for Eleonora's falcons. It is possible to see these falcons from the end of the jetty using a good telescope. One particular area frequented by the falcons is the mouth of Oued Ksob to the south of the town. This river mouth is also noted for a large colony of yellow-legged herring gulls and a variety of migrating seabirds including black, little, sandwich, whiskered and white-winged terns. The *oued* can be reached from a track off the P8 south of the town but access to the sea is not easy. The scrubland in the same vicinity provides sufficient sightings to satisfy any birdwatcher. It is possible to visit the main island, the Ile de Mogador, and the ruins of a prison, by contacting the Tourist Information Office on place Moulay Hassan. They will direct the visitor to the Province office off Ave Mohammed V where a permit can be obtained for 50dh, and will arrange a boat for transport for the 15-minute trip, for a negotiable price. The creation of a regular daily ferry service to the islands is hopefully only a rumour: nothing should be allowed to disturb the rare Eleonora's falcons when they are nesting – after all they are rare and have flown all the way from Madagascar.

Essentials

Sleeping
■ *on map*
Price codes: see inside front cover

Accommodation in Essaouira divides into four areas: the southwest side of town/Quartier des Dunes with a couple of big hotels and some guesthouses, the médina with upmarket guesthouses and damp cheap hotels, near the train station and finally the country guesthouses south in Diabat, Ghazoua and Cap Sim. Médina guesthouses are listed separately. For cheap hotels in Essaouira it is important to get a well ventilated room with windows, and preferably a view of the ocean. Staying in a restored old house is now an option. The typical Essaouira house rose up two storeys round a courtyard with rooms opening onto balconies round all four sides. If the courtyard is small, the result is often a bit gloomy to modern western taste. High ceilinged rooms and decoration schemes compensate.

The amount of accommodation is expanding. A large new upmarket place is going up on the site to the old *khayria* (orphanage) at Bab Marrakech. Still, it is important to ring ahead for the small *hotels de charme*, as these can be booked up well in advance. If you are looking for self-catering accomodation, you could try ***Jack's Kiosk***, at 1, Place Prince Moulay El Hassan, T044-475538, F044-476901, or, more upmarket, ***Essaouira***

Médina, T/F044-472396, www.essaouiramedina.com If you are interested in buying property, contact the latter as they have a good name. See Directory for further advice.

Quartier des Dunes/ Agadir road

A *Sofitel Essaouira*, Ave Mohammed V, T044-479000, F044-479037. Recently built by the *Groupe Accor*. Right opposite the beach. Very comfortable establishment indeed, just what the town needed. Nice bar (which could be anywhere, however), good restaurant. Recommended. **A** ***Hotel Ryad Mogador***, out of town on the Agadir road, T044-783555, F044-783556, www.net-tensift.com/mogador 650dh single, 800dh double, junior suite 2,000dh, buffet breakfast extra 80dh, lunch 170dh. Recent hotel built round a central pool, very quiet, immaculately clean. Rooms on small side, no alcohol allowed – is this why there are so few clients? There is much more interesting accommodation than this in Essaouira. Plus point: tennis courts. **B** ***Hotel des Iles***, Ave Mohammed V, T044-472329, F044-472472. 70 rooms of which 46 are bungalow-style around a central swimming pool, remaining rooms are in the older part of the hotel built in 1948. On the grim side – but then you're likely to be out most of the day, seafood and international restaurants (views of harbour and beach), bar, nightclub and secure parking, tourist menu 180dh (3 course), breakfast 55dh, convenient for beach. All major credit cards accepted. **B** ***Hotel Tafoukt***, 98 Ave Mohammed V, BP 38, T044-784504/05, F044-784416. 40 rooms, a reasonable hotel just across the road from the beach but an appreciable walk (about 1 km) from the centre of town, tea room, bar and restaurant but ask for a room with sea view. **C** ***Hotel Jasira***, 18 Rue Moulay Ali Cherif, Quartier des Dunes, T044-784403, F044-476074, aljasira@iam.net.ma 30 rooms and 4 small suites, pool, restaurant, but no booze. Prices in the 400-500dh bracket.

The médina

Hotels **A/B** *Hotel Palazzo Desdemona*, Ave Okba ben Nafi, T044-472227, F044-785735 (same management as *Auberge Tangaro*, see below). Prices run from 500dh for simplest room on terrace to 950dh for a beautiful suite. Excellent establishment, fireplaces in some rooms, plenty of hot water. Highly recommended. **B** ***Hotel Villa Maroc***, 10 Rue Abdallah ben Yassin, T044-476147, F044-475806, villamaroc@casanet.net.ma 17 rooms, around 650dh 2 persons. Converted merchant's house, beautifully decorated round a central court festooned with plants and greenery, roof terrace with superb views, apartment sleeping 4 available for 1,200dh, restaurant for guests only, dinner 150dh, breakfast included in room price, public parking (approximately 200 m) near Place Orson Welles, all major credit cards. A personable establishment but a victim of its own success. Hot water for showers (gas-fired water heaters) a problem if several people showering at same time. **B** ***Hotel Riad al Madina***, 9 Rue Attarine, T/F044-475727, F044-476695, www.riadalmadina.com Prices around 600dh 2 persons. A former hippy hotel which has been over-expanded to 30 rooms. Though the decorator's hand is much in evidence, rooms are very pokey. Too little privacy at this price as almost all suites and rooms open on to a central courtyard. **C** ***Hotel Le Grand Large***, 2 Rue Oum er Rabi, T044-472866, F044-473061, www.essaouiranet.com/legrandlarge Tastefully restored place on main street. Rooms individually priced, 2 persons about 350dh, 3 persons 450dh. Very clean, rooms on small side. Pizzeria on ground floor – noise rises to upper landings. Good for a couple of nights.

D ***Hotel Beau Rivage***, Place Prince Moulay El Hassan, T/F044-475925. 18 rooms, central, rooms available with and without showers, some with balconies overlooking main square (noisy), others with sea view, TVs in room may prove to be more decorative than functional, clean, basic and with friendly, helpful management, roof terrace, no restaurant but breakfast (14dh) available from café outside hotel. **D** ***Hotel Dar el Qdima***, 4 Rue Malek ben Rahal, T044-473858, F044-4874154. Just off main drag (ave de l'Istiqlal), on your right as come from port area, on same alley as Azurette the herbalist. 1 person 150dh, 2 persons 250dh. Old building restored, very pretty decor, if you like beige tadelakt you will love this place. Rooms around central court. Weak point: the hot water. Very, very good value. **D** ***Hotel Emeraude***, 228 Rue Chebanate, near the little gate of Bab Marrakech, T044-473494, www.essaouirahotel.com Small, attractive Franco-Moroccan-run hotel on the dry side of the médina, prices 200dh-350dh. Recommended. **D** ***Hotel Kasbah***, 4 Rue Tetouan, T044-475605. Close to Place Prince Moulay El Hassan, a large old house with craftwork on sale in the courtyard. Some rooms with views over the town. **D** ***Hotel Le Poisson Volant***, 34 Rue Labbana, T044-472150, F044-472152. 8 rooms, 260dh 2 persons. A bit damp, but otherwise fine. Windsurfer clientèle. **D** ***Hotel Shahrazad***, 1 Rue Youssef el Fassi, T044-476336. Small hotel, some rooms with bathroom, 200dh 2 persons. Acceptable.

E ***Hotel Cap Sim***, 11 Rue Ben Rochd, T044-785834. Clean and cheap, just round the corner from Place Prince Moulay El Hassan. **E** ***Hotel Majestic***, 40 Darb Laalouj, T044-474909. 70dh single. Nothing very majestic about this place. 18 rooms, cheap and charmless, youths hanging around outside. Nice views from terrace. For the record, this was the first French courthouse building in town, opened 1914. **E** ***Hotel Mechouar***, Ave Okba ben Nafi, T044-784828. 25 rooms, uninviting appearance, not the best value option in this price range, no breakfast, restaurant reported as open in the season. **E** ***Hotel des Remparts***, 18 Rue Ben Rochd, T044-475110. 27 rooms on 3 floors round a courtyard, a popular place with friendly staff and a spectacular view from the roof terrace. However, a bit rundown, rooms reported as dark and damp, no restaurant for evening meals, breakfast 17dh, public parking in a restricted area. **E** ***Hotel Sahara***, Ave Okba ben Nafi, T044-475292. 70 rooms, in the médina next door to the *Hotel Mechouar*, comfortable and central, range of rooms, some quite pleasant, cheaper rooms on inner courtyard are darker, less well ventilated but noisy, terrace, breakfast 20dh, no restaurant, public parking near Place Orson Welles 200 m. **E** ***Hotel Smara***, 26 Rue de la Skala, T044-475655. 17 rooms, just inside the ramparts in the woodworkers' *souk* north from Place Prince Moulay El Hassan, around 120dh 2 persons, clean and friendly, most rooms have wash basins, showers cost extra, WCs shared, make sure room has ocean view, others can be damp and dark, no restaurant, breakfast available. Roof terrace with a view as good as anywhere in Essaouira, very restricted parking in street, probably best cheap option. **E** ***Hotel Souiri***, 37 Rue Attarine, T/F044-475339. 20 rooms, cheapest 150dh 2 persons, 250dh 2 persons with shower. Central, clean. **F** ***Hotel du Tourisme***, Rue Mohammed ben Messaoud, at the southeast corner of the médina. Some rooms damp, not recommended.

The médina

Guesthouses This type of accommodation took off in a big way in Essaouira in the late 1990s, and by the time this goes to press, new addresses are sure to have appeared. The following is a small selection of the better ones. **A/B/C** ***Essaouira Médina***, 8 Rue Ben Rochd, Essaouira, just off Place Prince Moulay El Hassan, T/F044-472396, contact@essaouiramedina.com (Manager Abd el Fatah Mazouz). Traditional houses and flats to rent and buy. Very reliable, honest agency (welcome in a place full of sharks). **B** ***The Tea House***, 74 Darb Laalouj, La Skala. Despite its English name, this small and pleasant guesthouse is very much 'traditional Essaouira'. Two self-catering 5-room flats are available for rent, beautifully decorated, each comfortably accommodating 4 people. Each flat has kitchen, large bathroom, living/dining room with open fire (a definite draw) and 2 bedrooms. Breakfast included, along with firewood. Highly recommended, reservations on T044-783543, www.aescalon.demon.co.uk/teahouse (Owner-manager Alison McDonald.) **B** ***House of Caïd***, Rue Chebanate, close to Bab Marrakech, (ie good location on the dry side of the médina), T06-1708036, houseofcaid@joymail.com By the time of going to press, restoration works should have transformed a historic building into the House of Caïd *maison d'hôte*, although there was talk of a projected Moroccan cookery school. Original owners Tim and Aidan know the region well. Can set up excursions.

Highly recommended. **B** ***Villa Quiéta***, 86 blvd Mohammed V, T044-785004, F044-785006. Located at end of promenade, 15 mins from médina. Around 650dh double. Suites very nice, some rooms have a hint of British seaside resort. A former family house transformed into a guesthouse. Modern, a bit lacking in charm, but still one of the nicest places in Essaouira. **B** ***Riyad el Zahia***, 4 Rue Mohammed Douiri (a side street left off Darb Laalouj, as you head towards the ramparts), T06-1347131. 500dh 2 persons (including breakfast), 6 rooms and 2 suites, beautifully decorated. **C** ***Les Chandeliers***, 14 Darb Laalouj, opposite the museum, T044-476450, via *Restaurant Les Chandeliers*, you can rent a guest suite at 500dh or a simple room at 350dh. Good value in a historic building at the heart of old Essaouira. **E** ***Chez Brahim***, 41 Rue el Mourabitine, near Bab Marrakech, T044-472599. A very good budget option. Prices tend to be negotiable, around 80dh for a single, breakfast 15dh. Clean establishment, rooms around a courtyard, pleasant terrace for breakfast. One of Brahim's scouts meets likely guests at the *Supratours* bus stop or the *gare routière*. Room for surfboards on ground floor. No sign, you get the house keys to let yourself in. **Camping**: ***Camping d'Essaouira***, 2 km out of Essaouira on the Agadir road, well protected, clean loos.

Near the bus station

There is a sprinkling of small, reasonably priced hotels here, ideal if you are allergic to the ocean damp or have an early departure. **D** ***Hotel Palais d'Essaouira***, 5 Ave du 2 Mars, right opposite the *gare routière*, T044-472887, F044-472387. 29 rooms, some triples, opening onto central covered courtyard, no damp, very clean. Noisy at night if TV on in central area. Much Moroccan decoration, ground-floor restaurant. **D** ***Hotel el Andalous***, T044-472951. As you leave bus station, cross over main road towards pharmacy. The hotel is 3 storeys, café on ground floor, on this avenue on right. Preferable to *Palais d'Essaouira* if you need quiet. No damp, clean, much Moroccan decor. 1 person 150dh, 2 persons 250dh, 3 persons 300dh. **E** ***Hotel Marjane***, T044-476691, signposted just round corner from the *Andalous*. 10 rooms. 1 person 60dh, 2 persons 200dh,

Essaouira Médina

shower 5dh. A good cheap address, better than *Argana*. **E/F** ***Hotel Argana***, just outside the ramparts at Bab Doukkala, T044-475975. 50dh single, 5dh shower. Adequate travellers' hotel. Turkish loos. Go for newer 2nd-floor rooms some of which have view of ocean and Christian and Jewish cemeteries. Smell of urine on 1st floor.

South of Essaouira

Diabat The one-time favourite hippy destination of Diabat, about 5 km from Essaouira, is easily reached by petit and grand taxi, say 40dh. **B** ***Auberge Tangaro***, Diabat, T044-784784. Same management as *Hotel Palazzo Desdemona* (T044-472227) in town. Half-board compulsory. A pleasant farm-type place. No electricity, good food, hot water a bit dodgy sometimes. Has a local clientèle. Camping possible.

Ghazoua **C** ***Baoussala***, El Ghazoua, T044-474345, dchoupin@yahoo.fr Small guesthouse, 5 en suite rooms, peaceful location 10 km from Essaouira and 10 km from Sidi Kaouki, scheduled to open summer 2001. Prices 500dh per head.

Agadir road and Sidi Kaouki The turn off for Sidi Kaouki is some 15 km south of Essaouira on the Agadir road. **B** ***La Maison du Chameau*** , off the Agadir road some 13 km from Essaouira, take the left turn off for Marrakech, T044-785077, F044-476901, maisonduchameau@yahoo.fr Traditional whitewashed farm buildings converted into guest accommodation. **C** ***Dar Kenavo***, 13 km out of Essaouira on Agadir road, take the left turn for Marrakech, T06-1207069, F044-476867, around 300dh 2 persons, breakfast included. Out in argan country, a small house with rooms around a pleasant patio. **C/D** ***Auberge de la Plage***, Sidi Kaouki, T044-476600, F044-473383. Italo-German management, 11 rooms, 250dh-350dh double. Shared showers and loos. No electricity (yet). Also do horse riding and camel excursions. **D** ***Résidence Le Kaouki***, T044-783206, or via the *Villa Maroc* in town. Around 200dh double room, 10 rooms. Ideal for windsurfers – near the beach. **D** ***Auberge de l'Etoile de la Mer***, T044-472537. Tiny guesthouse close to the mausoleum of Sidi Kaouki. 3 rooms, 150dh-250dh double.

Eating
● *on map*

Expensive *Chez Georges*, probably the best food in Essaouira, near the Skala. Couscous on terrace under tents, small dining room in house. Doesn't advertise. ***Chez Sam***, T044-473513, in the harbour with fine views of the port, a fish and seafood restaurant and bar, with good food and drink and a distinctive atmosphere, particularly good lobster, although pricey, at 170dh for 3 courses, seafood platter at 100dh for two, main courses range from 45-70dh, *Amex* and *Diners Club* credit cards taken here. ***Les Chandeliers***, 14 Darb Laalouj, just opposite the museum, T/F044-476450. Pleasant surroundings for candlelit supper. Prices range from midday menu at 40dh right up to a large dinner at 250dh. Pizzas between 50 and 70dh. Excellent *magret de canard*, fish in a variety of sauces. Southwestern French dishes, as owners Patrick and Martine Dupeyrat from that part of the world. A rather good address. Recommended. Also have guest rooms over restaurant (see above). ***Riyad Bleu Mogador***, 23 Rue Benchtouf, T044-784128, F044-784583, down a side street off Rue Mohammed el Gorry, on your right as you head into the médina leaving Bab Marrakech behind you. Cheapest menu at 150dh, though you can pay anything up to 300dh per head. European and local cooking. Highly recommended if the chef is on good form.

Mid-range *Chalet de la Plage*, 1 Ave Mohammed V, T044-472972, F044-473419. Good fish dishes but also a wide ranging menu, main courses range from 50-90dh, with a set 4-course meal for 90dh, also open for lunch, if the wind isn't too severe, try for a table on attractive terrace directly overlooking the beach. ***Le Coquillage***, inside the port, T044-476655. Cheapest menu at 100dh, more expensive menus with lobster 250dh. Sometimes overrun with charabanc parties at lunchtime. ***Dar Baba***, 2 Rue de Marrakech, T044-476809. Top end of this category. Italian food, alcohol.

The Argan tree – the tree of the flying goats

Visitors to this particular area of Morocco might be forgiven for thinking that the trees are full of flying creatures. The creatures are goats, but though they are perched on the extended boughs of the argan tree they climb, they do not fly.

The argan tree is found today only in this small region of Morocco between Agadir and Essaouira, and eastwards along the Sous Valley beyond Taroudant and in parts of Mexico.

At first glance one could mistakenly think that the area was under olive cultivation. The trees are well spaced and the average height is the same, around 4 m, although some specimens reach 20 m. The short trunk, however, is thicker, perhaps 8 m in girth. In fact it is not one trunk but a fusion of stems, and the canopy of clumps of argan can spread to 40 m. The trees grow very slowly but live a long time, with an estimated average lifespan of 125 years.

The wood from the tree is extremely hard and makes excellent charcoal, and the small pale green leaves set among vicious spines make nutritious fodder. The small greenish flowers are produced in spring and sometimes in autumn, and the resulting fruit, something like a wrinkled yellow plum, appears between May and September. Don't be tempted to try one. The fruit is much prized. The fleshy cover makes a rich, longlasting cattle cake, while being particularly rich in sugar, the juice can be fermented to produce an alcoholic drink.

The oil from the kernels within the hard shell is used by the local population who have acquired the taste. It is honey coloured with a nutty flavour. It is used in cooking, in the preparation of sweets, and mixed with almond paste and honey it makes a delicious 'butter'. A bowl of argan oil into which hot bread is dipped is served at most meals.

The goat herders collect the fruit from the ground. Officially they are forbidden to beat the trees to make the fruit fall. Some fruit is dislodged by the feeding goats, in other cases the stones which are spat out by the goats that have eaten the pulp, and the stones that have travelled through the animal's digestive systems are collected. The nuts can be stored for years, providing food in times of scarcity. The women produce the oil in small quantities because it cannot be stored. They break the shell, roast the kernel often using the shell casing, grind the kernels into a paste which is mixed with tepid water, and from this squeeze the oil. The work is tedious and the yield is very low, estimated at about 2 kg of oil for every 100 kg of kernels. The oil's reputation as an aphrodisiac is widespread.

Recommended. Credit cards accepted. ***Pizzeria L'As Dos***, 34 Rue Lattarine, on left just after first arch on Ave de l'Istiqlal, as you come from port direction. T044-473553. Starters 30dh, pizzas 50dh, candlelit but no booze. ***Pizzeria Le Grand Large***, 2 Rue Oum er Rabi, perfectly adequate pizzeria in the heart of the médina. ***Restaurant El Khaima***, in a small square off Darb Laalouj, opposite the museum, a good licensed restaurant with Moroccan specialities, separate lobster menu at 180dh, alternative fixed-price menu at 80dh, individual main courses cost between 55-65dh. ***Restaurant Bab Lachouar***, at southwest end of Place Prince Moulay El Hassan. Fixed price menus at 50-60dh, main dishes 35-45dh. ***Restaurant La Licorne***, 26 Rue de la Skala, T044-473626, lalicorne_restau@yahoo.fr Traditional Moroccan food. Easily located – turn left at the ramparts end of Darb Laalouj. ***Restaurant L'Orange Bleue***, 18 Rue Zayan, T06-1581950. Attractive modern decoration, exhibitions upstairs on the terrace, an African room is being decorated, good food, alcohol. Attracts a young crowd. ***Café-Restaurant Taros***, 2 Rue de la Skala, T044-476407, F044-476408, closed Sun, open late. Easily located, up street on your left as you face Place Prince Moulay El Hassan with port behind you. Good food, lots of books and magazines in café area. Breton management. Recommended. *Taros* is the local name for the ocean wind.

Cheap By far the best cheap eating option is to sample the freshly caught fish grilled at open-air restaurants between Place Prince Moulay El Hassan and the port; accompanied by a tomato salad this makes a meal at a reasonable, negotiated price. The standard of hygiene has been upgraded. Make sure you are absolutely clear on the price when you order. Another cheap option is the little fish barbecue place in Souk El Hout, the fish market in the town centre (the one on the left as you come from the port area down Ave de l'Istiqlal). ***Laâyoune***, 4 bis Rue Hajjali, T044-474643, (close to Place Prince Moulay El Hassan), cheap and cheerful, young crowd some evenings. ***Les Alizés***, 26 Rue de la Skala, ground floor of *Hotel Smara*. Alcohol. A good little address. Cheap eateries off to the left of Rue Mohammed Zerktouni as you head for Bab Doukkala. Other good cheap options including ***Café-Restaurant Essalam*** on Place Prince Moulay El Hassan offering good value local dishes, couscous at 40dh, open daily from 1200-2300; and ***Mustafa's***, on Ave Mohammed ben Abdallah. The latter street has a number of cheap places.

Cafés The best places for breakfast are on Place Prince Moulay El Hassan, particularly ***Café L'Opéra*** and ***Chez Driss***, a good place to have breakfast, or watch the evening social life pass by. Breakfast here will be better value than in a cheap hotel, and no-one seems to mind if you bring your own cakes. There are several beachside cafés, too.

Bars Essaouira is not really the place for wild nightlife, although it livens up during the annual **Gnaoua music festival**. Try ***Chez Sam***, in the harbour; or ***Hotel des Iles***; and ***Hotel Tafoukt***, on Ave Mohammed V. The best upmarket bar is in the ***Sofitel***. For buying booze, the main off-licence is near the *Cinéma Rif*, (right out of Bab Doukkala, the off-licence is on your left, before cinema – it has black and white tiles and beer posters).

Shopping

In its own quiet way, Essaouira offers some rather good opportunities for spending surplus cash

The main tourist shops are sort of between Place Prince Moulay El Hassan and Darb Laalouj. Objects made in fragrant, honey-brown thuya wood are everywhere, from small boxes inlaid with lemon-wood to chunky, rounded sculptures. More expensively, you can pick up **paintings** by the local school of naïve and pointillist artists. Traditionally, the town's women wore all-enveloping **cotton/wool mix wraps**, in cream or brown, just the thing to keep out the ocean mists. Islamic fashions change, though happily, the weavers have found a new market providing fabrics for *maisons d'hôte* and their denizens. New colours and stripes have been added, and you can get a nice bedspread for 300dh. A visit to Essaouira is also a good opportunity to stock up on **argan oil** and **amlou**, a runny peanut-butter type product. In Essaouira, you can also find plenty of flowing shirts and pantaloons in greys, creams and beiges. However, the ultimate nouveau-hippy item must be the delicate, totally impractical **raffia-work sandals**, available direct from the cobbler in the odd dank workshop.

Chez Kabir, Raphia Mogador, on the central Souk des Grains, (the market square on your right off Ave de l'Istiqlal as you come from the port), is the ultimate supplier of *babouches* and raffia sandals, which in fact are made from doum-palm fibre. The best are the pointy-toed Aladdin ones. Can be ordered to suit your feet in colours ranging from natural cream to electric green and purple. Argan products can be picked up in quite a few places. Try ***Co-operative Amal***, Village de l'Arganier, Tamanar, T044-788141. Get to understand the production process by visiting this women's co-operative in the Essaouira region. Sample prices: 20 g bottle of amlou, 40dh, Arganati oil, 25cl for 80dh. Try also ***Essaouira Médina***, 8 Rue Ben Rochd, Essaouira. This property rental agency also sells argan products.

Sport

Cycling Bikes, including mountain bikes, can be seen for hire in the old town and from the *Hotel Shahrazad*, close to the tourist office. **Riding** *Cavaliers d'Essaouira*, 14 km inland from Essaouira on the Marrakech road, next to restaurant *Dar Lamine*,

T06-5074889. New stables which does riding by the hour and short treks in beautiful rolling countryside, all argan and olive groves and thuya plantations. Try also ***Auberge de la Plage***, at Sidi Kaouki, 27 km south of Essaouira, take bus no 5, T044-476600, F044-473383, aubplage@aim.net.ma Budding cameleers can take lessons at ***La Maison du Chameau***, off the Marrakech road, T044-785077, F044-476901, maisonduchameau@yahoo.fr Accommodation too – see above. **Surfing** Winter is the surfing season in Essaouira. From Apr to Oct, the wind is up and the windsurfers are out in force. If you don't have your own gear, you can rent. However, the problem with surf gear is that it gets such intensive use that it ages quickly. Check carefully when you rent. There are a couple of surf places, of which the best is probably ***L'Océan Vagabond*** right on the main beach, T06-1728340 (Mob), bruno-erbani@yahoo.fr Try also ***Palais d'Océan***. Gear is about a year old but in good condition, 60dh per hour for wave riding gear, 180dh per hour for windsurfer. They also do snacks and drinks. Surf-scene tends to focus here. ***UCPA***, a well managed surf centre close to ***L'Océan Vagabond***, T044-472972, F044-473417, was scheduled for removal as it got in the way of visitors to the new *Sofitel*. In town, ***No Work Team***, 7 bis Rue Houmane el Ftouaki, T044-475272, F044-476901, just off Rue Mohammed ben Abdallah, almost opposite. ***Maison du Sud*** does clothing and gear.

Transport

Air Flights with the ***RAM*** from Casablanca to the tiny new Aéroport de Mogador, reservations and information on T044-476709, F044-476705. Schedules spring 2001, Essaouira – Casa Mohammed V on Mon and Sat, 0700 depart, arrive Casablanca 0750. Casablanca – Essaouira, Fri at 2200 and Sun 2230.

Buses from Essaouira can get very full in summer and during the Gnaoua Festival in Jun. Check your departure times the day before you travel and try to reserve

Road Bus *CTM* and private line bus services operate from the terminal north of Bab Doukkala, with connections to Casablanca, Safi, Marrakech and Agadir. There are lots of touts competing for custom – go inside terminus and look at ticket windows where departure times are clearly posted. The best onward service is with ***Supratours*** (Essaouira office on T044-475317) service to **Marrakech**, to connect with onward trains to Casablanca-Rabat, depart at 0620 (48dh single), from the big square outside Bab Marrakech. Buy your ticket at the kiosk on the square the day before, as this is a popular bus.) ***CTM*** has departures for **Safi** at 1115 and 1500, **El Jadida** 1115, **Casablanca** 1115 and 2400, **Agadir** 1230 and 2030, **Tiznit** 1230. ***Pullman du Sud*** does a midnight departure for Casablanca, *guichet* 9 has frequent departures for Marrakech. **Taxi** Grands taxis operate from a parking lot beside the bus terminal. (You may have to wait a while for the vehicle to fill up if you are going to Marrakech.) There are frequent departures for **Diabat**, **Ghazoua**, **Smimou** and other places in the region, also for **Marrakech** and **Agadir**. Petits taxis are numerous, 5dh for a short ride in town. There are numerous *calèches* to be caught from the cab rank outside Bab Doukkala.

Directory

Banks Branches of ***Bank Commercial du Maroc***, ***Bank Populaire*** and ***Crédit du Maroc*** (you can change money here Sat morning in addition to normal banking hours) are in and around Place Prince Moulay El Hassan. Foreign residents say that ***Wafa Bank*** on Ave de l'Istiqlal (cashpoint, bureau de change) is the most practical when dealing with abroad. **Communications** The **PTT** is on Ave Lalla Aicha, back from the seafront and Ave Mohammed V. Stamps also available from telephone booths opposite *Restaurant Chalet de la Plage*. *Jack's Kiosk* will send a fax for you (30dh per sheet to England). **Internet** places clearly signed almost opposite *Hotel Agadir* on Ave de l'Istiqlal and on Rue Mohammed el Gorry. The best is probably ***Essaouira Informatique***, at 127 Rue Mohammed el Gorry, T044-473678, esinfo@iam.net.ma **Hammams** Several in the neighbourhood between Bab Doukkala and the bus station, easily identifiable by chimneys producing black smoke. At the time of writing, works on an expensive 'European hammam', the

Mounia Hammam Café (to have ambient music, plants, etc) were being completed. Ask for information at the restaurant *L'Orange Bleue*. **Medical emergencies** **Dentist**: Dr Elacham, 1 Blvd de Fès, T044-474727, also Dr Sayegh, on Place de l'Horloge, T044-475569. **Doctor**: Try Dr Mohammed Tadrart, opposite the post office, T044-475954. Also Dr Haddad, Ave de l'Istiqlal, close to the ***Wafa Bank***, T044-476910. **Hospital**: Outside the old town on Ave El Mouqawama (the one behind the *Sofitel*). Emergencies on T044-474627. **Pharmacies** In médina there are pharmacies on Ave de l'Istiqlal and on Place de l'Horloge. Several pharmacies on Ave Al Massira near Bab Doukkala. **Tourist offices** Ave du Caire, open Mon-Fri 0830-1200, but don't expect too much by way of useful information from this rather basic-looking office. In fact, they tend to send you to hotels which will pay them commission. **Useful numbers** **Police**: Main commissariat on T044-784880.

North from Essaouira to Safi via the coast road

For the journey northwards to Safi the main route travels east on the P10 to Ounara and then northwards on the P8 through the market village of Talmest to Sebt-des-Gzoula. Here there is the option to branch off northwest on the P120 or continue north to Tleta-de-Sidi-Bouguedra (126 km from Essaouira) and then west on the P12. If you are travelling by car, following the coastal route is a much more attractive alternative; make sure, though, that you have sufficient petrol for the 125 km drive as there are no service stations once you leave the main road. Leave Essaouira on the P10 to Marrakech and after about 6 km turn left on a new road (not yet marked on the Michelin map) signposted to Safi. For about 15-20 km this fast stretch of well metalled road travels through open scrub landscape before descending at Km 244 towards the sea near **Cap Hadid** to give superb views of Atlantic waves breaking on to a long, windswept beach. For much of the next 35 km there is plenty of opportunity to enjoy the wild, unspoiled beauty of the coastline and the mountains of the Chiadma region to the east. The highest peak in this range is **Jebel Hadid** (Iron Mountain), 725 m. At Km 221 there is a rough track to the left to Plage Bhibhab and, on an otherwise isolated route, *Café Voyageur* is passed just before Km 206. Before reaching the new bridge across the Oued Tensift at Khemis-Oulad-el-Hadj, look for the ruins of **Kasbah Hamidouch**, an 18th-century fortress built by hyperactive builder Sultan Moulay Ismaïl. The road narrows and deteriorates as it follows the river estuary northwards but improves again at **Souira Kédima** (see page 143) where the rather dreary looking *Café Echabab* is close to the beach. For the next 15 km the route becomes more elevated with some fine cliff-top scenery before the left turn at the *Café-Restaurant Essaouira*, 17 km from Safi. Much of the remaining journey is through a large industrial complex; on reaching the ring road, head for the centre of town as signposting is certainly not Safi's strong point.

Essaouira to Agadir

The road southwards runs some distance in from the coast. Although Essaouira has extended, there are remnants of the argan tree forest that once covered this area. At km 161 a track goes west to **Sidi Kaouki** on the coast. After a further 19 km another track leads west to more marabouts. At Smimou a road leads east by the side of Jebel Amardma to **Souk el Tnine** and **Sebt des Aït Daoud**, an interesting detour. The road then descends the side of Jebel Amsittene with many bends to cross the two parts of the Oued Iguezoulen, then climbs up the other side. **Tamanar** is built round a large kasbah. A winding road of 21 km leads down to the resort, shrine and viewpoint at Point Imessouane. A steep ascent leads up to **Tamri**, **Cap Ghir** (also spelt Rhir) which has some good views, Paradis Plage (not as pleasant as its name suggests), Taghazout, a fishing village, and then you come to sprawling Agadir.

5 The High Atlas of Toubkal

The High Atlas of Toubkal

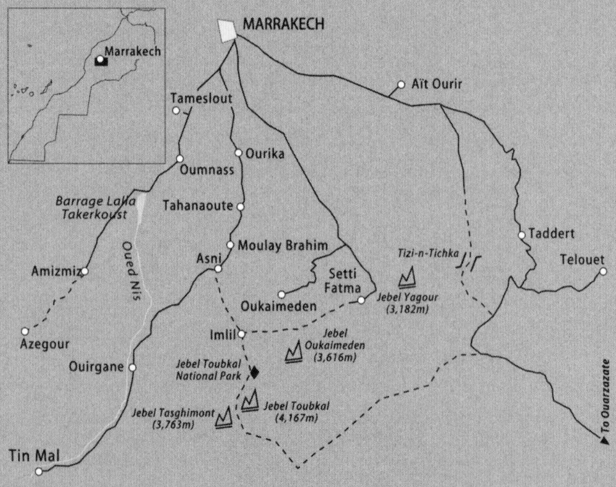

In easy day-trip distance of Marrakech, the ***High Atlas of Toubkal*** *has long been a draw for tourists. In addition to the* ***Toubkal National Park****, named for* ***Jebel Toubkal****, the highest peak in North Africa, the region also has some other worthwhile excursions, including the much-visited* ***Ourika*** *and the ski-resort of* ***Oukaïmeden****. Up the* ***Nfis Valley****, there are pleasant hotels at the mountain retreat of* ***Ouirgane****, and the striking, restored mosque of* ***Tin Mal****, on the spectacular road to the* ***Tizi-n-Test*** *pass. Heading south from Marrakech in the Ouarzazate direction – and still within day-trip distance – is another striking high pass, the* ***Tizi-n-Tichka*** *and the village of* ***Telouet*** *with its brooding Glaoui fortress. You can travel on south across the Atlas by road, or, in a four-wheel drive vehicle. Take the rough mountain tracks from Telouet down to* ***Tamdacht*** *and the famed kasbah of* ***Aït Ben Haddou****, just north of Ouarzazate.*

The region has plenty of bivouac and accommodation opportunities for trekkers and for the less energetic many interesting places can be visited as part of an organized four-wheel drive excursion from Marrakech. Particularly popular are trips up onto the ***Plateau du Kik*** *and across from the* ***Ourika Valley*** *to the* ***Asni/Imlil*** *road. The problem is that certain treks, including the ascent of Toubkal (referred to by one French climber as being a 'boulevard-type' hike), are almost too popular in the summer season. Nevertheless, there are plenty of alternative routes. If not hiking with a foreign-based tour company, you should be able to work out some sort of interesting route to suit your capabilities with an experienced local guide.*

Up the Amizmiz Road

For accommodation listings, see 'Sleeping' page 162

Take the main S501 road south out of Marrakech (straight over at the junction near the Hivernage). A few kilometres after the Club royal equestre, the road forks. You go left for Asni (S501), right for Amizmiz in the foothills of the Atlas. The road passes through a number of small settlements, including Tamesloht, and the Lalla Takerkoust Lake, where accommodation is available.

Tamesloht Tamesloht, 3 km to the west of the S507, is famous as the home of the man of '366 sciences', one Abdallah ben Hussein El Hassani, credited with working miracles. Today, it is a typical rural settlement on the Haouz Plain. Agriculture has been much affected by the drought, and those with the means to run a water pump are finding water at greater and greater depths. Some have abandoned their land as simply unprofitable. From the tourist's point of view, the village is home to a potters' co-operative. On the main road you will pass shops selling the large terracotta food storage jars now popular for plants in the tasteful houses of Marrakech.

Oumnass Oumnass is an attractive, small, sand-coloured settlement. A wealthy European has a discrete fortified retreat here, at the nearby village of **Tagadirt**. A British-Moroccan partnership is working on a new kasbah-retreat hotel. (Contact Max Lawrence at caravanserai@iam.net.ma, F 044-436993 for the latest on

Around Marrakech

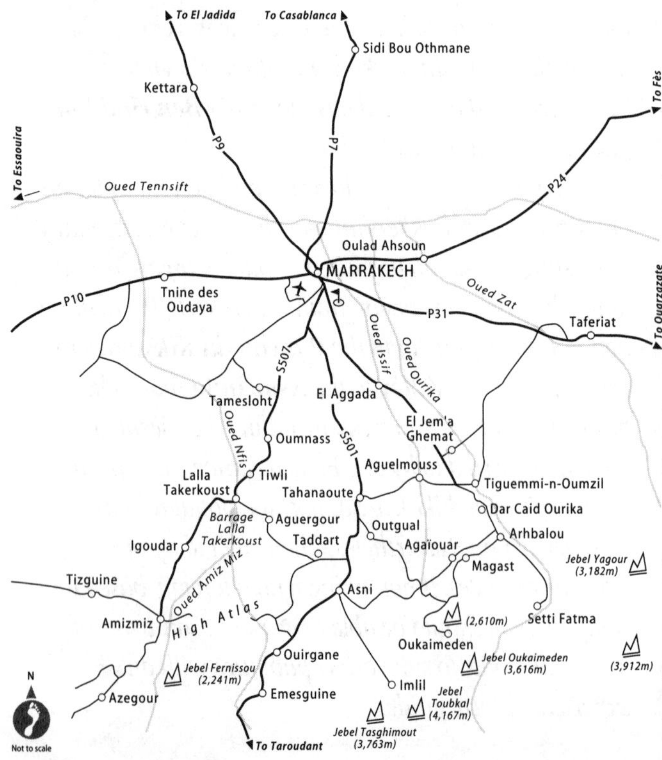

Five things to do in the High Atlas of Toubkal

- On a winter weekend, join the Marrakchis thronging up to **Oukaïmeden** to see the snow.
- Have mint tea and walnuts at the **Kasbah de Toubkal, Imlil**. (If you have the cash, stay the night and enjoy their famous fig tajine).
- Children might enjoy a short **mule**-back excursion through the **walnut woods** at Imlil.
- Drive out to **Amizmiz**, take a stroll in the mountains, then continue across to **Ouirgane** for lunch, then back to Marrakech via **Asni**.
- Visit the (heavily) restored Almohad mosque at **Tin Mal** on the Taroudant road, one of the few mosques in Morocco visitable by non-Muslims.

this venture.) A few kilometres further on, the road reaches the small gorges of the Oued Nfis below the Barrage Cavagnac, now renamed **Barrage Lalla Takerkoust**. A turn-off left takes you on a road round the shores of the 7-km long lake. In recent years water levels have been extremely low. Restaurants and camp sites, once right on the lake shores, now find themselves 100 m or more from the water. After this detour, going back down the lake shore road, you return to the main road which takes you on to Amizmiz, 21 km further on.

Amizmiz

Amizmiz, 55 km southwest from Marrakech at the end of the S507, has been known as the home town of acrobats since medieval times, and now trains many of the acrobats appearing in Marrakech and European circuses. It was founded by a *marabout*, one Sidi Ahmed. The town also has semi-ruined kasbah, a former *mellah*, and an important Tuesday morning souk. The **F** *Hotel de France*, with attached bar (still open?), is adequate. There are regular buses (2½ hours), and much quicker grands taxis, to and from Bab Rob in Marrakech. The post office, bank and cybercafé are all in a new district on the main road as you arrive from Marrakech.

Turning off right just after the 'administrative zone', you can wind up into the foothills to the *maison forestière*. Parking in the shade, there is some gentle walking along a track above the Assif Anougal, with views down over the villages. From Amizmiz, there is also a metalled road eastwards to **Ouirgane**. The road runs across rolling open land as far as the Oued Nfis, where there is a ford (*radier* in French on the detailed maps). Then you drive up to the Tizi-n-Ouzla (1,090 m), near which a sign suggests there is a reserve for mouflon. Here you have a splendid view of the Assif Amassine valley, with the Toubkal Massif as backdrop. There then follows a winding descent to the junction with the S501, where you can go right for Ouirgane (accommodation) or left for Asni and Marrakech. Note that in a wet year, clay hillside may crumble onto the upper sections of this Amizmiz to Ouirgane road.

Southwest from Amizmiz to Azegour

Amizmiz, or rather the region south and west of it, including the Jebel Erdouz (3,578 m) probably merits some further exploration. There is a four-wheel drive piste which continues southwest from Amizmiz to **Azegour** (19 km) via a col at 1,638 m. (From Azegour, possible excursion to the old copper mines.) After Azegour, the track continues across an arid plateau with the Jebel Erdouz to the south. (Check with locals about the state of the track.) Here again there were mines (lead and zinc) in the time of the Protectorate. To the north lies Jebel Tamrakht. After Azegour, Adassil, 47 km from Amizmiz is the next main village. From here, another track runs north along and above the Assif-n-Al Mal

Valley to join the road leading back to Amizmiz after Sidi Bou Othmane and Tafroukht. Again, check with locals about the state of the tracks.

Sleeping Before you reach Amizmiz, there are several options if you want to make an overnight stop. At **Tamesloht**, 100 m off the main road, there is a recently opened **D** ***Ferme d'accueil***, T06-1342837 (look out for yellow signs) run on a sustainable basis by Myriem and Mustapha Nassef. They have 2 small guest chalets and will be operating their venture as an educational farm. At **Lalla Takerkoust**, on the lake shore, is the country style **C** ***Relais du Lac***, T044-484924, which has accommodation for up to 20 people in small bungalows (370dh/pp b&b, 500dh full board). This would be ideal for children, combined with 3 nights in a riad in Marrakech. In the neighbouring restaurant area, the *Relais* also has 185 places in traditional tents and caters for weddings and incentive business groups. They can organize VTT, trekking and canoeing.

Excursions up the Taroudant road

Leaving Marrakech on the S501, **Tahanaoute** is the first main settlement. Its new administrative buildings and training college speak of the Moroccan state's efforts to extend its influence into the rural areas in the late 1990s. After Tahanaoute, the road winds upwards through gorges before dropping down to the turn off right for Moulay Brahim and the small market village of **Asni**, a few kilometres further on. **Drive with great care**. Though the approach is attractive with tall poplars and rustling cane, Asni has limited facilities (garage, telephone, police, post office, shops and youth hostel) and quite a lot of hustlers, generally selling small enamelled boxes and cheap necklaces. There are regular grands taxis from Bab Rob to Asni, as well as the Taroudant buses which leave from the *gare routière* at Bab Doukkala and call at Bab Rob. The bus takes 1½ hours from Marrakech, by car one hour is a realistic time.

Moulay Brahim

The road winding up to the village is narrow, so if driving, take care

Coming from Marrakech, there is a right turn-off for Moulay Brahim. With its numerous small hotels and eateries, Moulay Brahim is a popular weekend stop for the Marrakchis. The village gets particularly busy from June to September, with people coming to visit the shrine of Moulay Brahim, visible with its green-tiled pyramid roof in the middle of the village. Stalls selling various scraggy pelts, chameleons and incense indicate that all sorts of favours may be asked of Moulay Brahim. Indeed, he is said to be a dab hand at fixing women's fertility problems. There is a festive atmosphere, with whole families coming to rent small semi-furnished apartments. Nicely out of the way, but still close to the big smoke of Marrakech, the village also has a reputation as a place for illicit liaisons. Out of season, things are fairly quiet, so the guesthouse accommodation no doubt has to be kept busy somehow. Unmarried couples occasionally have problems. There are plenty of taxis and buses to/from Asni and Marrakech.

Asni

After the somewhat nerve-wracking drive through the Gorges of Moulay Brahim, the approach to Asni with its tall stands of cane and poplar and willow trees comes as something of a relief. If you arrive on Saturday, you will be able to see the souk, (located in a big dusty enclosure on your left as you come from Marrakech) with its accompanying chaos of grands taxis, mules and minibuses. The village is in fact quite extensive, with houses scattered in clusters in the valley. Asni is an acceptable place to stop en route to Ouirgane, Tin Mal or Taroudant, or on to the Toubkal National Park, if you can deal with the attentions of the jewellery sellers. All depends on how harassed you've been earlier in Marrakech. The Saturday market has become a tourist attraction but if you are there early it is pleasant to watch the day's events unfold. Watch the locals get an all-over headshave. Or try the open-air dentists if you need a tooth pulled.

There is good walking from here along the **Plateau du Kik** to the west of Asni, north to Moulay Brahim and southwest to Ouirgane. The lower slopes are forested and the higher limestone plateau is indicated by a rocky scarp. The spring flowers are a delight to behold. Walk up the Tizi-n-Test road to where a mule track goes off right beyond a distinctive conical hill. Continue aiming for the plateau edge. Here there is a choice of going northeast to Moulay Brahim or southwest to Ouirgane. As these are long distances, be prepared to take a taxi back to Asni for the return leg. For a possible long day walk, starting from Asni, you could take an early local minibus or grand taxi up to Imlil and then walk downhill back down the valley through Tinifine (about 8 km from Imlil). After the Assif Imenane joins from the right, cut across to Tansghart on the old mule track back into Asni. Total distance around 17 km. A popular four-wheel drive excursion takes you from Marrakech to Asni, up to Moulay Brahim and thence up above the village onto the Plateau du Kik (see local map Amizmiz NH-29XXII-2). From here you may drop down to the villages around Tiferouine before heading some 8 km northwest across country to the settlement of Lalla Takerkoust and its reservoir lake. Tourist agency trips tend to picnic at encampments near the receding lake shore. The return north to Marrakech is on the S507 Tizi-n-Test road.

Sleeping The main option used to be the **D** *Grand Hotel de Toubkal*, a converted kasbah, at the south end of the village. At the time of writing, the hotel was closed. If stuck, check out the small hotel opposite the entrance to the souk – although you will do best to carry on to Imlil. **Youth hostel**, T044-447713, on route d'Imlil, at far end of village where the road goes out left to Imlil. Take sleeping bags, blankets can be hired, can be cold in winter, 40 beds, quite spartan but beautiful setting, kitchen, overnight fee 20dh, open all year, open to non-members. Near Asni, on the road up to Imlil, the ***Kasbah Tamadoht***, super-kitsch Berber 'château' of an Italian antique dealer, has been acquired by Virgin Hotels. New rooms are being built: whether the original terrifying 'Beverly Hills plus Shangrila and the 1001 Nights' decorative concept will survive remains to be seen.

Eating Limited choice available. In the centre of the village are a number of stalls and cafés cooking harira soup and tagines. This is the last major place to stock up on basic supplies for a visit to the Toubkal region.

Transport Buses/taxis to Imlil go from just south of the youth hostel.

Ouirgane

Ouirgane is a beautiful village about one hour's drive (61 km) from Marrakech, located on the valley floor of the Oued Nfis on the S501. The almond blossom in spring is breathtaking. Ouirgane can be reached by bus from Marrakech (the Taroudant service), or by grand taxi from Asni. The three hotels in Ouirgane have good food and offer the opportunity to explore the valley in easy rambles.

Sleeping C *Le Val de la Roseraie*, BP 769, Marrakech 40000, T044-439128, F044-439130, www.cybernet.net.ma/roseraie Some 23 a/c rooms, is a peaceful hotel set in extensive gardens, with 2 restaurants, bar, hammam, hydrotherapy centre, tennis, horse riding, and outdoor pool and small indoor pool. The *Roseraie* has a well established clientele, but is said to be on the expensive side for the level of services on offer. Food variable. **D *Auberge Au Sanglier Qui Fume***, T044-485707/08, F044-485709, address CP 42150, Ouirgane, Marrakech. A small, country hotel run by a French couple, the Poucets, daughter and son-in-law of the Thévenins who founded the auberge back in 1945. It has 22 individually decorated chalet-style rooms, a restaurant serving excellent French country food, a bar, tennis and a pool in the summer, and would make a nice stop-off for a family. Mountain bikes are available for rent, and the management will put you in touch with guides should you wish to do some walking. Horseriding by arrangement with the neighbouring *Roseraie*. The campsite was swept away in the floods a couple of years ago, but it is hoped to make an area for camping available again soon. **D *La Bergerie***, about 2 km before Ouirgane village as you come from Marrakech, turn off right for Marigha, signposted, French management, T044-485716, F044-485718, postal address BP 64 Marrakech. Set in 5 ha of grounds in a valley away from the village. Around 450dh/2 persons with breakfast, meal without wine at 120dh. Eight nice rooms in a farm-type atmosphere. Highly recommended. Another, slightly overpriced possibility is **D *Résidence Ouirgane Adam***, postal address BP Asni 74, just outside the village, 10 rooms, doubles 300dh, menu 80dh. **E *Chez Momo***, T044-4485704, has reasonably priced rooms. Reservations difficult to make. Recommended. Finally, cheap rooms in private homes opposite the *Auberge Au Sanglier* have been recommended. For reasonably priced eating, on the Tizi-n-Test side of Ouirgane, you have the ***Restaurant Le Mouflon***, T044-485722. Tagines as per usual, between 60-75dh per head.

Tin Mal

Colour map 1, grid C4

Tin Mal is a small settlement high in the Atlas Mountains, off the S501 from Marrakech to Taroudant. Once upon a time, it was the holy city of the Almohad Dynasty. For the non-Muslim visitor, it offers a rare opportunity to see the interior of a major mosque, with examples of 12th-century Almohad decor intact amidst the ruins.

Getting there & around

Tin Mal is 100 km from Marrakech (about 1¾ hr drive, taking things easy), just past the village of Ijoukak. If you are not driving, you can take a Taroudant bus or a grand taxi as far as Ijoukak, where there are several basic cafés with rooms. Just after the village, on the right, is the Talat-n-Yacoub Kasbah, the home of the Goundafi clan, who formerly ruled the area, and a ruined summer pavilion with a ribbed dome, and further along, on the left, another kasbah of the Goundafi family. Carry on walking, and across the river to the right can be seen the square structure of the Tin Mal Mosque, built 1153-54. Cross the river on the next bridge (often impassable by car), and walk up past Tin Mal village to the mosque.

History

To appreciate Tin Mal, fast rewind back to the early 12th century. In 1122, one Ben Toumert, after much roaming in search of wisdom, returned to Morocco. He created too much trouble in Marrakech with his criticisms of the effete Almoravids, and shortly after, when the mountain tribes had sworn to support him and fight the Almoravids in the name of the doctrines he had taught them, he was proclaimed Mahdi, the rightly guided one. In 1125 Ben Toumert established his capital at Tin Mal, an anonymous sort of hamlet strategically situated in the heartlands of his tribal supporters. The rough and ready village was replaced with a walled town, soon to become spiritual centre of an empire, a sort of Muslim Lhasa. The first mosque was a simple affair. The building you see today, a low square structure, was the work of Ben Toumert's successor, Abd el Moumen – a student whom the future Mahdi had met in Bejaïa.

A 12th-century warrior dynasty from the mountains

Visiting remote Tin Mal, you need to imagine your way back to early medieval times, when Islam was not as stable as it is today – and when the narrow rocky valleys of the Atlas Mountains must have been very remote indeed. One Ben Toumert, a Masmouda Berber born around 1080 in the Anti-Atlas, was to found a religio-politico movement which was to overthrow dynasties and control the whole of North Africa. In 1106, Ben Toumert set out for Cordoba – and later the Middle East, in search of learning. On his return to his native Atlas in 1117, he had very definite ideas about what a good Muslim should be. His basic principle was that the true Muslim could not be satisfied merely with carrying out the religious obligations of Islam – he would take it upon himself to ensure that others did so too.

The year 1121 found Ben Toumert in Marrakech, the capital of the Almoravids, denouncing the use of musical instruments and other forms of pleasure... He raised an uproar in the capital by declaring that it was unbefitting for the Emir, Ali ben Youssef, to wear the litham *or veil of the men of the desert, and told him that the dyed mat on which he sat in the mosque was ritually unclean because of the droppings used in the dye. The Emir could not ignore these provocations, and summoned the troublesome Ben Toumert to a debate with the religious leaders. Needless to say, Ben Toumert got the better of them – and the court savants advised the Emir to put him to death. Unfortunately for the Almoravid dynasty, the Emir's great piety prevented him from doing this; he merely banished Ben Toumert from Marrakech, even though he had thrown the Emir's sister from her horse when he saw her riding along unveiled.*

Ben Toumert withdrew to the mountains to preach his doctrine of the unity of God – and the stage was set for a major rebellion, as our dour religious leader preached ardently to the Masmouda Berbers. In 1125 he settled at Tin Mal, and gradually built up a strong community whom he called el muwahhidoun *'unitarians', hence the term Almohad, a Spanish corruption of the Arabic name. Tin Mal was an ideal HQ, for the enemy Almoravid forces were composed of cavalry which could not operate along the twisting, dangerous mule tracks of the Nfis valley.*

In 1130 Ben Toumert died, but his work was carried on by his right-hand man Abd el Moumen, aged just 36. It is said that Ben Toumert's death was kept secret for three years, time enough for his successor to establish his authority. 1144 saw the final rout of the Almoravids near Tlemcen, and Marrakech fell in 1147. Abd el Moumen was to lead the Almohad movement for over 30 years, unifying North Africa under his rule. Perhaps the most impressive thing of all in this tale is the power of an austere set of ideas to give scattered tribes the drive to build an empire.

Looking across at the mosque from the Taroudant road, you need to imagine it surrounded by a walled town, with banners on the ramparts and smoke rising from the hearths. Tin Mal was the first *ribat*, as the austere Almohad fortresses were called – and subject to a puritan discipline. The Mahdi himself, the very infallible imam, was by all accounts a sobre, chaste person, an enemy of luxurious living. All his efforts went into persuading his followers of the truths of Islam – as he conceived them. In fact, his task was not unlike that of the Prophet Mohammed at Medina back in the early days of Islam: how to build a unified community out of a heterogeneous set of tribespeople. There was a council of 50 elders to represent the tribes – who cannot have willingly given up their independence.

Tin Mal was subject to a pitiless discipline. Prayers were led by the Mahdi himself and all had to attend. Public whippings and the threat of execution kept those lacking in religious fervour in line. As well as prayer leader, the Mahdi was judge, hearing and trying cases himself according to Muslim law – which had barely begun to penetrate the mountain regions.

Tin Mal Mosque Standing in the quiet mosque, today mostly open to the sky, looking down the carefully restored perspectives of the arcades, it is difficult to imagine what a hive of religious enthusiasm this place must have been. And after Ben Toumert's death, it was to remain so, as his simple tomb became the focal point for a mausoleum for the Almohad sovereigns.

The prototype for Tin Mal was the Great Mosque at Taza (near Fès), also built by Abd el Moumen. The Koutoubia at Marrakech (Almohad capital as of 1147) was in turn modelled on it. Completed in 1154, also under Abd el Moumen, the Tin Mal Mosque has a simple exterior. (Was there once an elaborate minaret?) The *mihrab* (prayer niche) is built into the minaret. To the left, as one stands before the *mihrab*, is the imam's entrance, to the right is a space for the *minbar*, the preacher's chair, which would have been pulled out for sermons. The decoration is simple: there are several cupolas with restored areas of stalactite plaster work and there are examples of the *darj w ktaf* and palmette motifs, but little inscription. The technique used, basically plaster applied to brick, is a forerunner of later, larger Almohad decorative schemes.

Essentially, the Tin Mal Mosque marks the firm establishment of Ben Toumert's doctrine under his successor, his long-standing follower and companion, Abd el Moumen, who was to lead the Almohad armies into Marrakech. But although the new empire acquired a fine capital well located on the plain, Tin Mal was to remain its spiritual heart – and a sort of reliable rearbase. It was to Tin Mal that Abd el Moumen sent the treasures of Ben Tachfine the Almoravid.

The tombs of Ben Toumert, Abd el Moumen, Abu Yaqoub and Abu Youssef were at Tin Mal as well, becoming venerated as a pilgrimage centre, even after the Merinid destruction of 1275-76. The tombs inspired deep respect – and Ben Toumert became a great saint – quite the reverse of what he would have wanted. The Almohad rulers, whenever they were to undertake a military expedition, would visit Tin Mal to seek success.

The end of the Almohads Eventually, the Almohads were to collapse in internecine struggles. The final act came in the 1270s. The last Almohads took refuge in Tin Mal, led by the Vizier Ben Attouch. However, the governor of Marrakech, El Mohalli (named by the rising Merinid sovereign), isolated the tiny Almohad group in their mountain retreat. In 1275 the Almohads made a last desperate attempt to retake Marrakech – without success. El Mohalli pursued them into their mountain fastness, and besieged and took the seemingly impenetrable town. The Vizier died in battle and the Almohad caliph and his followers were taken prisoner and executed. But the winners went even further. An adventurer, one Abu Ali (who after a failed revolt against the Almohads had taken refuge with the Merinids), decided to take his revenge. The great Almohad sovereigns, Abu Yaqoub and Abu Youssef, were pulled from their tombs and decapitated. The Merinid Sultan is said to have been scandalized. The Almohads, one time conquerors of the whole of the Maghreb and much of Spain, were destroyed in their very capital, barely 150 years after they had swept away the Almoravids.

Restoration of the mosque When Tin Mal was studied and surveyed by French art historians in the 1920s, the mosque was in an advanced state of decay. The tombs had long since disappeared, the rigour and puritanism of Almohad Islam belonged to the remote past. Strange cults has taken over in the abandoned sanctuary: the inhabitants of the region came to venerate the stone of Sidi Wegweg. The central authorities rejected the Caïd Goundafi's proposal to restore the mosque – fearing perhaps a revival of a long-vanished dynasty?

In the early 1990s, the state of the mosque came to the attention of a charitable foundation of the ONA, Morocco's largest conglomerate. Six million dirhams (circa £400,000) was put forward for restoration work. Only local materials were used, although a special lime for repairing the plasterwork came from Spain. Cedar from Azrou was used for the ceilings. No cement or concrete was used: the restoration is as ecological as can be. There remains, however, the question of the site museum. Will there eventually be a display of the unique square silver coins struck by the Almohads at Tin Mal? The spiritual heart of a medieval Muslim Empire has survived. The villagers, who for centuries had a decaying basilica-mosque at their disposal, now live next to what might one day become a major stop on the heritage tourism trail. Or alternately, the mosque may return to fully fledged religious use. As it is, it is used for Friday prayers.

Onward to Taroudant via the Tizi-n-Test

The S501 from Marrakech to Taroudant is one of the most spectacular routes in Morocco, winding its way up and then down through the High Atlas Mountains, above the beautiful valleys and past isolated villages, eventually reaching the Tizi-n-Test pass, with its breathtaking views across the Sous valley to the Anti-Atlas mountains. There are buses between the two cities, although check that they are *par Tizi-n-Test*. Driving has been feasible since the road, a traditional trading route, was formally opened in 1928, following the work of French engineers. Some of its sections are a bit scary, but it is a highly recommended experience, particularly when tied in with visits to Asni, Ouirgane and Tin Mal. Signs on the exit to Marrakech will indicate if the pass is open. The S501 joins the P32 from Taroudant to Ouarzazate.

For a lunch stop on this route, you have the cheap *Restaurant La Belle Vue*, about 1 km after the pass on the Taroudant side. Cheap rooms available, have sleeping bag ready – it gets cold at 2,100 m altitude.

Trekking in the Toubkal National Park

Ins and outs

Getting there

Toubkal National Park is reached by a road/track, which leads off left after the centre of Asni and the *Grand Hotel de Toubkal*. For those without transport either hike or negotiate a grand taxi, easy to find especially on market day. It is possible to walk from Asni to Imlil, or to Tacheddirt, which has a refuge run by the *Club Alpin Français*, information, T022-270090, F022-297292.

Getting around

Walking Options include the **Aremd circuit**, a refreshing hike through remote villages and past breathtaking views, and a hike to the **Lac d'Ifni**. Another is to walk to **Setti Fatma**, in the Ourika Valley. Much more challenging is to climb **Jebel Toubkal**, the highest mountain in North Africa at 4,167 m. It is necessary to break the walk at the *Club Alpin Français* **Toubkal Refuge** (ex-'Refuge Neltner', and stil referred to as such by most maps and walkers), a simple dormitory place with no meals at 3,106 m. In winter this is a difficult trek and full equipment is essential. A wise plan is to purchase specialist hiking books, such as Robin Collomb's *Atlas Mountains*, and maps, for the region,

The profitable mule

Since the late 1970s and the growth of trekking, the mule has become doubly important in the economies of trail-head villages. True, the mule is still vital to farmers: in harness with a donkey, it can be seen drawing the plough and walking endless circles on the threshing floor. An elegant mule is its owner's pride and joy when it carries him to the weekly souk. But trekkers and day-trippers need transport too, and mule-hire has become a source of ready cash for families in villages like Imlil. As most households have a mule or two, they can benefit from the summer influx of visitors.

In general, a mule going off on a trek will be accompanied by its owner or (more likely) a male relative. Though difficulties sometimes arise if there is irrigation or harvesting work to be done at the same time, most families have a spare male who can go off with the beast on a trek. Like humans, mules need to be well fed on such excursions. They go uphill for considerable distances, to areas above the tree-line where the grazing is poor. Near much-used bivouac sites, such pasture is likely to be heavily overgrazed. Thus the mule needs a 10 kg daily ration of barley to ensure that it returns to the village in good health. As local barley production is generally insufficient, such fodder has to be bought in.

In principle, mule-hire prices are established by the tourist authorities each year. However, unless you have a local guide to set things up for you, rates can vary. A wealthy-looking trekker on a first visit will be asked for more than someone who knows the country. At certain times of year, when demand is higher, prices will be higher. And as work with trekkers is seasonal, there is always the temptation to extract as much income as possible out of the busy summer months. In any case, the expansion of mule hire shows how effectively a conservative, once isolated community can react when a source of cash profits appears.

before arriving, ie the 1:100,000 scale Oukaïmeden/ Toubkal map, feuille (sheet) NH-29-XXIII-1, possibly available at the *Hotel Ali* in Marrakech. More up-to-date, with extremely detailed directions for walking in the Toubkal region, is Richard Knight's *Trekking in the Moroccan Atlas* (Hindhead: Trailblazer, 2001). Mules and guides can be hired in Imlil, most easily in the *Refuge* or at *Ribat Tours*.

Imlil

Colour map 1, grid C4, Altitude 1,790 m 17 km S-SE from Asni

Imlil is the most important village of the Aït Mizane Valley. It is the start of the walks in this area. In the centre of the village is the car park/taxi area with the stone built CAF hut at the corner of the road, guides hut and *Café du Soleil*. There are numerous small cafés and shops, a good baker and a travel agent. Mules are 'parked' to the south of the village, on the left, before the junction. There is a utilitarian concrete route indicator on the right, should you be unsure of your direction. When you arrive, you may be besieged by lots of underemployed blokes, keen to help you in some way or other. The souvenir sellers are not too persistent, however.

Sleeping & eating

In Imlil, the top option is the **C *Kasbah de Toubkal***, T044-485611, F044-485636. Contact also UK office: *Discover Ltd*, Timbers, Godstone RH9 8AD, T0044-1883744392, F0044-1883744913. The kasbah (which played the role of a Tibetan fortress in the recent film *Kundun*) has dormitory-type accommodation much used by student and British public school groups, and a couple of very nice rooms on the terrace. The building, one time HQ of the local caïd, has been well restored and for a 20dh contribution to the local development fund, you can have mint-tea and walnuts on the roof terrace.

More reasonably, try **D** ***Atlas Gîte***, T/F022-485609, manager Jean-Pierre Fouilloux. 3 double rooms, 2 larger rooms. Will advise on setting up treks. A good little address. 2 persons, 300dh. Cheaper options are **F** ***Café du Soleil***, a tiny and basic place; the **F** ***Et***oile de Toubkal (8 rooms), T044-449767, F044-434396; the **F** ***Hotel-Café El Aïne***, as you arrive in the village from Asni on your right (best rooms upstairs), or the ***Refuge du Club Alpin Français*** (no reservations), which provides clean but minimal facilities. 40 beds in dormitories, open all year round, more expensive if you aren't a CAF member. For **information** try T022-270090. The ***Café Aksoual***, opposite the CAF, also has some very cheap, rudimentary rooms.

The *Bureau des Guides*, in the centre of the village, can provide information on accommodation in local homes. The locals, who are used to walkers, are generally anxious to provide a floor or mattresses to sleep on. ***Aït Idr Mohammed*** in Targa Imoula, just through Imlil, has been recommended for accommodation and hire of mules and guides. **Information** is available through ***Ribat Tours***, the ***Café du Soleil*** and at the CAF refuge.

Climbing Toubkal

Colour map 1 grid C5

There are a number of routes up North Africa's highest peak. Imlil is often the departure point for groups heading for the mountain. The least technical route, which requires a little scrambling from the ex-Neltner Refuge to the summit is used by several thousand visitors each year. Other routes are rather more difficult, and therefore less frequented and consequently more peaceful. The following suggested routes require adequate preparation, good maps and the correct equipment for safe and complete enjoyment. A good guide and mules would remove the strain.

Best time to visit

The best time for walking is after the main snows, at blossom time in the spring. Mules cannot negotiate passes until Mar/Apr. For some, summers are too hot, visibility in the heat haze is poor. Nov-Feb is too cold and there is too much snow for walking, although frozen ground is often more comfortable than walking on the ever-moving scree. Deep snows and ice present few problems to those with ropes, ice axes, crampons and experience. Without these – stay away in winter.

Tours

Customized walking tours are organized by Hamish M Brown, ***AMIS***, 26 Kirkcaldy Rd, Burntisland, Fife KY3 9HQ, Scotland, who also provides maps, briefing sheets and sound advice. He has been walking in these mountains for over 30 years. Other recommended group walking tour operators are listed on page 124.

Imlil to Jebel Toubkal

Imlil is the end of the surfaced road but it is possible to reach **Aremd** (also spelt Aroumd) by car up the rough track. Takes about 45 minutes to walk. *Café Lac d'Ifni* makes a good stop here. **Sidi Chamharouchouch** is reached in another 2½ hours, going steadily uphill. It is important to bear right after the *marabout* to find the initially very steep, but later steady slope up to the ex-Nelter Refuge (3,207 m). Allow 4½ hours from Imlil. The *Refuge du Club Alpin Français*, with dormitory space for 30 persons, US$5 per night, is often crowded. On the plus side, the warden sells bottled water, soft drinks, and can do food for small groups. Campers using level site below the hut can use the facilities.

Jebel Toubkal by the South Cwm

This is the usual approach for walkers, a long day's walking and scrambling if you want to do up and back. The route is clearer on the map than it is on the ground – first observe the route from the rear of the Neltner refuge and the large boulders on the skyline. These are a point to aim for. Leave the refuge and go down to the river. Cross over, and up the other side is the main path to the foot of the first of the many screes. Take the scree path up to the boulders which can be reached in just over an hour. From there is a choice, the long scree slope to the north of the summit or the shorter, steeper slope to the south of the summit ridge. Either way, allow 3½ hours.

The summit is not in itself attractive, especially if people are making calls from their mobile phones. (Who carried up the pieces of iron for the strange pointed structure on the top?) The stone shelters make fairly comfortable overnight camping for a good view of sunrise. Views are excellent if there is no heat haze, to the Jebels Saghro and Siroua but as the summit here (4,167 m) is a plateau other views are limited. Be prepared for low temperatures at this altitude and for the bitter winds that blow three out of four days in the spring and autumn. The descent is quicker, allow between 2 and 2½ hours.

Jebel Toubkal region

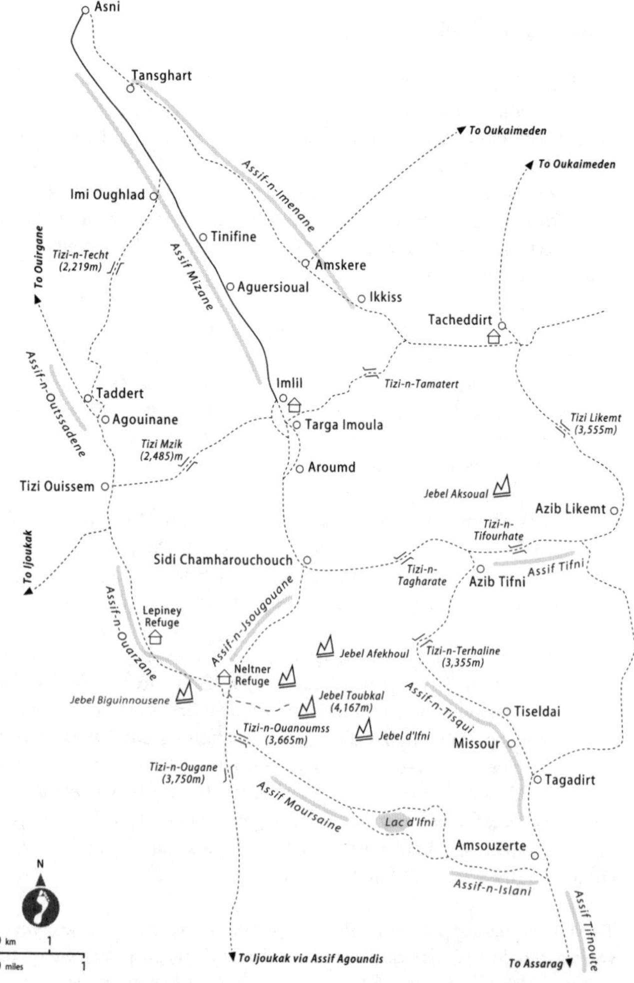

Refuges run by CAF in Casablanca

	height	*beds*
Refuge d'Imlil	*1,740 m*	*38*
Refuge du Toubkal	*3,207 m*	*30*
Refuge de la Tazarhart	*3,000 m*	*22*
Refuge de Tachddirt	*2,314 m*	*23*
Refuge de l'Oukaïmeden (restricted opening times)	*2,630 m*	*80*

Jebel Toubkal by the North Cwm

This route is certainly less congested but you will need a guide and/or a good map. Take the route north from the Neltner Refuge, crossing the river after about 1 km near the small ruined building. Hike up towards the north cwm. The screes move here and the path is not very distinct although the direction is clear enough. The way is up the back of the cwm to the left, to the break in the craggy skyline and a col. The summit then lies to the south along the ridge. It is a long hard climb. Allow at least 4 hours for the ascent.

The Toubkal Circuit

This circuit starts and ends at Asni The times are approximate and assume most equipment is carried by mule. Note that some of the high passes like Tizi-n-Ouanoumss may not be passable by mule until late June.

1 To **Amskere** (1,800 m) Arrange transport to Imi Oughlad or to Aguersioual (about another 5 km) and from there a gentle walk to Amskere (2 hours).

2 To **Tacheddirt** (2,300 m) This walk follows the Oued Imenane towards its source (5 hours). There is a CAF hut here with a helpful warden.

3 To **Azib Likemt** (2,650 m) This is not an easy day as the going is steep, the path winds and bends across the screes. The pass of Tizi Likemt (3,555 m) is a well earned rest with excellent views of the way already travelled. Downhill is quicker but no more comfortable (8 hours).

4 Azib Tifni (2,800 m) A shorter leg, again uphill by the Assif Tifni. Keep to the right of the *oued*. Just 1½ km out of Azib Tifni, a left-hand track leads south as an alternative route to Amsouzerte. Continue along the *oued* to the Amazigh village of Azib Tifni (4 hours).

5 Amsouzerte (1,740 m) This long leg leads up, out of the valley, to the pass of Tizi-n-Terhaline (3,355 m), the views as breathtaking as the ascent. The descent, also very steep, swings round south and southeast to Assif-n-Tisqui, by Tiseldaï (2,100 m) which gives its name to the valley, Missour and Tagadirt, down through more and more settlements and into the walnut groves around Amsouzerte (8 hours). The last section of this walk by the stream is particularly pleasant through the terraced fields. At Amsouzerte (1,797 m), rooms are available in some of the unusual three- to four-storey houses. There is also a gîte, a little difficult to find – ask (30dh a night), and landrover taxis back down to Marrakech. The village also has one or two shops and mule hire is possible. There is an option to spend a second night here and visit the market town of Assarag, about 2 hours south up the Assif Tifnoute, but only if it coincides with the Saturday market.

Fruit and nuts

The fine shade trees which surround Imlil are walnuts, an important cash-crop in the local economy. You will see lots of carefully constructed terraces where the local farmers go in for vegetable production. Fruit trees are increasingly grown, notably apples and cherries, in addition to the longer-established figs. At blossom time, the crop is sold for a lump sum to a local fruit wholesaler. Again, this is an important source of income for the locals. The stone walls which shore up the terraces need lots of work, however. Torrents of water can come down the valley after thunderstorms, carrying everything before them. In spring, you will see lots of blue-flag iris flowering on the terrace walls. The root systems of these plants stabilize the terrace walls. The bulbs are also harvested. When dried, they are sold on for a good profit, as they contain a natural scent stabilizer much in demand in the ecologically minded sectors of the perfume industry.

6 Lake Ifni (2,290 m) The route, gradually uphill, reaches Lake Ifni, which is not such an inviting area of water as it appears on the map. Overheated walkers can take a swim before setting up camp on the lake shore (4 hours). The lake once extended further west and there is a large area, about 1 km in length and 250 m wide of round boulders, once part of the lake bed. Circular patches in these are clearings made by previous campers. Round the lake is a series of tidemarks showing earlier levels of the water. Near the lake is a seasonal hut café which does warm soft drinks. Further away from the lake, as the trail up to the Tizi-n-Ouanoumss begins, is another hut selling soft drinks.

7 Neltner Refuge (Refuge Toubkal) (3,106 m) A slow steady ascent to Tizi-n-Ouanoumss (3,665 m) takes a long morning. There is time then to admire the views before the short steep descent, much of it scree, down to the Neltner Refuge (see page 169) (6 hours).

8 From this refuge the **ascent of Jebel Toubkal** is made. It is a very popular climb/walk with some very arduous screes and some stiffer slopes. Allow a long day for the ascent and return to this base (7 hours). See details above.

9 Aroumd (1,920 m), also spelt Aremd. There is a gentle downhill gradient alongside the **Assif-n-Isougouane** where the spring blossom on the walnut trees is magnificent, the steeper ascent being before the shrine of Sidi Chamharouchouch (2,340 m) and its tiny collection of stalls. At the time of the pilgrimage this shrine is very busy. Then on to Aroumd, quite a big settlement after the tiny Amazigh villages (3 hours).

10 Imi Oughlad (1,300 m) A last long stretching of the legs. The country is certainly more gentle though the mule track up to the pass of Tizi Mzik (2,485 m) is steep enough. You will head west from Aroumd up to the Tizi Oussem (1,850 m). Next you continue down to the Assif-n-Ourssadene which is followed north for 3 to 4 km. The track never reaches the *oued* bed but keeps along the contour and only gradually rises to go through the small settlements of Agouinane and Taddert before the last pass, Tizi-n-Techt (2,219 m) gives access to Imi Oughlad, a village on the road a few kilometres south-southeast from Asni. It is here one wonders if the arrangements made for collection and return to Marrakech were really understood.

Jebel Toubkal from Ijoukak

Ijoukak, on the S501, 94 km out from Marrakech, can be reached by bus – although grand taxi is more reliable. There are toilets and cafés and rooms may be rented. Taking the bus a little further permits a walk to historic Tin Mal about 5 km off the road, just before the largish settlement of Mzouzit. You can then do a quiet walk back downstream to Talat-n-Yacoub to Ijoukak, the track following the contours above the river most of the way.

Talat-n-Yacoub/Ijoukak can also be taken as trail-head villages for approaching Toubkal from the west. From Ijoukak, you head more or less east along the Assif Agoundis, with the plateaux of Tajgalt and Tazaghart to the north. (After the Toubkal climb, the return route takes you via Tizi Oussem with the same plateaux to the south.) The route up the Assif Agoundis is a steady climb and the walk along under the crests (provided the snow line is high enough) provides good views, and in spring a surprising number of flowers. The most commonly followed tracks lead eventually to the Neltner Refuge, allowing keen scree scramblers to reach the summit of Jebel Toubkal. After the descent, you continue north via Sidi Chamharouchouch to Aroumd and Imlil. After the section Imlil to Tizi Oussem, walked on most circuits, the route continues west over the Tizi-n-Ouarhou to Tizgui (1,930 m) and back to Ijoukak, passing over the Tizi-n-Iguidi to Aït Zitoun, about 6 km from the Nfis Valley road. Allow 10 to 14 days for this demanding circuit if taking in the Jebel Toubkal summit.

In terms of **maps**, this circuit runs through 3 1:100,000 scale maps: Tizi-n-Test (NH-29-XVI-4), Toubkal (NH-29-XXIII-1) and Amizmiz (NH-29-XXII-2). As usual, it is best to have a local, Tachelhit-speaking guide.

The Ourika Valley

Colour map 1, grid B4

The Ourika Valley is a beautiful area of steep-sided gorges and green, terraced fields along the winding Oued Ourika, about 45 minutes drive south of Marrakech. The beauty and accessibility of the Ourika Valley makes it a most popular excursion for Marrakechis and tourists alike, and in summer certain sections of the valley are crowded with campers and day-trippers happy to be away from the hot, dusty air of the plain. Just before Aghbalou, the S513 splits, with a right-hand road taking you up to the ski resort of Oukaïmeden. The trail-head village of Setti Fatma is reached by going straight ahead. With a very early start, it would be possible to visit both Setti Fatma and Oukaïmeden on a long day trip with a good, patient driver. In addition to the tagine stalls and small hotels at Setti Fatma, there are now quite a few accommodation and upmarket eating options along the valley.

Ins & outs

The valley has a problem with flash floods, which campers should bear in mind

Buses and grands taxis to Ourika leave from Bab Rob, Marrakech (20dh). It is worth going all the way to Setti Fatma, at the head of the valley. If driving head straight for the mountains on the S513, starting from the fountain roundabout just outside the city walls at Bab Jedid, next to the *Hotel Mamounia*. Once in Ourika, a possible means of transport is a lift in the open top vans and lorries which speed along the valley.

To Aghmat

After postcard views of the ramparts of Marrakech, the road heads out across flatlands, the monotony broken only by occasional olive groves and crossing the large concrete canal, which brings irrigation water from the Sidi Driss dam east of Marrakech to the Haouz Plain. The first minor side excursion, for enthusiasts of long-gone dynasties, would be to turn off left, 29 km from

Marrakech, to Aghmat (spelt Rghmate on some maps), first Almoravid capital of the region, now a small settlement set in verdant olive groves and plant nurseries. Here there is a mausoleum, built entirely in the early 1960s and dedicated to Youssef ben Tachfine, founder of Marrakech in 1062. The four-square domed building, modelled on the Almoravid Koubba el Baroudiyine in Marrakech, was no doubt built to affirm the ruling Alaouite Dynasty's links with the early Muslim past of the region. You may want to explore further to find the vaulted foundations of an early hammam building, all that remains of the once magnificent Almoravid town.

Dar Caïd Ourika

Despite the tourists, this is still a good opportunity to see rural Morocco

Some 35 km from Marrakech another left turn takes you down to the main market town at the foot of this part of the mountains, Dar Caïd Ourika, also referred to as Tnine Ourika, ie Monday souk on the Ourika. Thus on Mondays, the place is lively, local colour added to by giant tour buses and crowds of foreign visitors. Arriving on market day, look out for the mule and donkey park as you cross the bridge over the usually dry river bed. There are very few women at the market, an indication of what a gender-separated society this is. The men are here to have a haircut, listen to a story teller, buy and sell animals and produce, have the donkey re-shod, and buy a sickle or two for the harvest. Apart from the market, Tnine Ourika has few attractions apart from a *zaouia* and a ruined kasbah. Some buses terminate here, too. If you want to do a round trip, you can continue from the market along the track, currently being surfaced, to Aït Ourir on the Ouarzazate to Marrakech road. From Tnine Ourika to Setti Fatma, 50 minutes is a reasonable journey time.

As you head up into the foothills, the road winds past a large pottery on your left. Indeed, the whole road is lined with shops selling terracotta ware – it's surprising there's very much of the foothills left, so much clay must have been mined. After the pottery, there is a sign for the *Camping Amassine*, a woody (peach trees) and apparently secure site with room for camping cars. Charges, 9dh tent, 8dh person, 8dh hot shower. No restaurant. Drawback? Some traffic noise from the road above during the day.

After the right turn for Oukaïmeden, the next big village is **Aghbalou**, also spelt Arhbalou. From here on, there are a number of pleasant hotels along the roadside.

Sleeping and eating **C** *Hotel Ourika*, before the turn and Aghbalou, T06-1120999. A large, 1970s establishment. 27 a/c rooms, with restaurant, bar and pool, expensive breakfast at 35dh. About 1 km after that turn, look out on your right for **D** *Le Maquis*, T044-484531, just before the roadside settlement of Oulmès. With Franco-Moroccan management, *Le Maquis* has both proper guest rooms (1 person, 260dh with breakfast) and 6-sleeper bunk rooms. Accommodation here is bright and cheerful, the restaurant slightly less so (basic menus 55-120dh). After Aghbalou, you have the **D** ***Hotel-Restaurant Amnougour***, which has fantastic views, rooms at 200dh, 2 persons and a disappointing restaurant. (On this stretch are ***Restaurant le Lion de l'Ourika*** and ***Restaurant Kasbah de l'Ourika***, patronized by coach parties). Next along, at Km 50, try the **D** ***Auberge Ramuntcho***, T044-444521, F044-484522, T06-1165182, with a large (too large?) restaurant (pleasant outside terrace), bar and pool. They have 14 nice-sized rooms, 2 persons 300dh, 1 person 250dh, breakfast 40dh. Set up by a Basque – hence the name, Ramuntcho being 'king of the mountains' in a Pierre Loti novel. Some 5 km from Aghbalou, at **Oulmès** (not to be confused with Oulmès-les-thermes, between Meknès and Rabat, where the fizzy water comes from), on your left as you arrive, is the chintzy, cosy **D** ***Dar Piano***, T06-1121073 / 061342884 (MT), 4 rooms at 200dh/1 person, 250dh/2 persons, breakfast extra 40dh. They also

Sidi Chamharouchouch, Sultan of the Others

In Moroccan folklore, 'the Others' are the djnoun, *the unseen spirits, and Sidi Chamharouchouch is one of their seven mythical kings. His shrine is up in the High Atlas, just below Jebel Toubkal, at the head of the Aït Mizan valley near the village of Aremd. Local legend has it that Sidi Chamharouchouch converted to Islam at the time of the Prophet Mohammed, and became the judge of the* djnoun *– and thus appears to his followers dressed in the flowing robes of a great savant. The Gnaoua adepts of Marrakech visit his sanctuary in summer, when Sidi Chamharouchouch visits them in their dreams. The saint's name often figures in talismans, and in traditional Arabic magic he is the spiritual intermediary who ensures the effectiveness of a spell. However, he is only a potent force on a Thursday, each of the six other 'sultans' having another day of the week.*

Close to the meeting place of two streams, a few flags and a great whitewashed boulder indicate the shrine of Sidi Chamharouchouch. There is no actual tomb in the cavity in the boulder, for the saint is still alive. The local people nominate a moqadem *to organize the annual* moussem *or gathering held at the end of the summer in Aremd – on the first Thursday in September. There are traditional dances, a market and a mini-fair, and most importantly, the ritual sacrifice of a black calf. Sidi Chamharouchouch is also said to preside over a court where 'disputes' between the sick and the* djnoun *who torment them are settled.*

The cult of Sidi Chamharouchouch also has something of a political dimension, maintaining a form of ritual discrimination in the local rural community. Although the sacrificial beast is bought by the community, only a specific group of families, the Id Bel'id, can make the sacrifice, for long ago their ancestors lent Sidi Chamharouchouch a horse. The sacrificial meat is distributed to the men. Heads of household whose father is still alive receive small shares, while those whose father is deceased receive major shares. Thus the traditional social hierarchy is maintained and all share something of the saint's baraka *or blessing. For foreign visitors, the interest of this sort of* moussem *will be in the crowd: the women's colourful caftans, maybe a primitive wooden four-seater Ferris wheel, the stalls of teethpullers, trinket sellers and doughnut makers, and families picnicking under the walnut trees.*

have a small flat sleeping 4 for 400dh and are closed from Jun-Aug. The restaurant has a good menu at 150dh. In the village itself, the **E** ***Hotel Raha*** is probably the best of the cheapies. In spring 2001, Oulmès, like Setti Fatma, was awaiting the arrival of *Maroc Télécom* to put in phone lines.

Setti Fatma

By the time this goes to press, mobile and land phone lines may have reached Setti Fatma

The road ends at Setti Fatma, noted for its annual summer *moussem*, seven waterfalls and 100-year-old walnut trees. There is a small weekly market, a *Bureau des guides de montagne* and quite a choice of basic accommodation, as befits a popular summer tripper destination. Setti Fatma must once have been quite pretty. Today, the impression is of lots of new, breeze-block housing, set with satellite dishes, built among the older stone homes. The happy sound of the river saves the day, and after all, Setti Fatma could be a good starting/end point for a trek.

Up to the Cascades The main part of Setti Fatma, however, is further on, entailing a climb on the far side of the river to the road. At the main village, cross over to the boulders and grassy area where the youth of Marrakech picnic and relax. There are a number of café-restaurants along the bank, including **F** *Hotel-Café Bouche de la Source*, which provides basic rooms and cheap *tagines*; alongside, and marginally better, is **F** *Auberge des Routards/Restaurant les 7 Cascades*; beyond is the *Restaurant des Cascades*. The seven cascades are a 30-minute scramble up from Setti Fatma, following the path up behind the first café, and there are plenty of young men and kids who will help you find the way. There is a café perched up where the path ends, beside the first waterfall.

Walking from Setti Fatma Setti Fatma makes a good base for exploring the **Jebel Yagour**, a plateau region famed for its numerous prehistoric rock carvings. About 10 km from Setti Fatma is Tachedirt, where there is a *Refuge du CAF*. If you don't have much time in Morocco, it is feasible to do three-day treks up onto the plateau. To set up a trek, contact the *Bureau des guides de montagne*, on your right before the hotels. They have leaflets laying out details of itineraries and prices. The staff, including English-speaking Hassan Aït Brahim, are the same people who ran the Asgaour trekking office. Contact trained guide Abderrahim Mandili on T044-426113. By way of example, a three-day trip into the Yagour or the three-day hike from the Ourika Valley to the Toubkal Valley, possible from April to October, costs around 990dh per person for 2-3 people, less for larger groups, price includes guide, all meals, mules and cooks, and bivouac equipment. Day walks in the region cost between 110dh and 160dh per person, price includes guide, picnic and tea in a local house. Half-day walks up to the fifth cascade cost 50dh/per person, less if the group has more than four people.

Sleeping and eating **F** ***Hotel Tafoukt***, on your left as you approach Setti Fatma. 1 person/80dh. 6 rooms and 2 small flats. Run by the friendly Slimane Bouhliha. Lunch 70dh. Views over the valley. Wonderful location. Like much of the new building in the valley, the hotel is an aesthetic disaster. *Tafoukt* means sun. **F** ***Hotel Asgaour***, on your right, several hundred metres after the *Tafoukt*. 20 basic, clean rooms, 50dh/1 person. **F** ***Hotel Billa***, right at the top end of the village, on the right, after the crossing to the cascades, identifiable by green façade. 20 rooms, 60dh/1 person, breakfast 20dh, hot shower 10dh. Large *salon marocain* with river view. Probably the best of the cheapies. For reservations, contact Omar on T06-6186607. Still among the cheapies, if stuck try **F** ***Hotel-Café Atlas***, good rooms and **F** ***Hotel Zohour***.

Oukaïmeden

Colour map 1, grid B5

Oukaïmeden, 'the meeting place of the four winds', is Morocco's premier ski resort. It's some 2,600 m up in the Atlas and a two-hour drive from Marrakech, making it a fine day trip from the city. It is also possible to climb the Jebel Oukaïmeden in a day. In winter hotels and restaurants are open but in summer it is less busy and many places are closed.

Ins & outs Daily buses from Marrakech in the winter. Also reached via the S513 Ourika Valley road – but forking right 43 km out of Marrakech, instead of left for Setti Fatma. Another option is to walk the piste which leaves the road south of Oukaïmeden, and cross the hills to the S501 to south of Asni. See also routes below.

The resort & surrounding area The resort is open for skiing from December to March, with a high ski lift up the 3,273 m Jebel Oukaïmeden, though it's not always in service. The skiing is very variable and good skiable snow cannot be counted on for certain. The hot African sun means that the snow melts, only to freeze again at night.

Nevertheless, as soon as there is snow, people flock down from Casablanca with their gear. There are instructors working in the resort, plus a ski shop near the *Hotel de l'Angour*.

In summer visitors can walk, climb and even parasail. Look out for the prehistoric carvings on the rocky outcrop below the dam wall. Takes about 20 minutes with the right guide. There are further carvings on the flat rocks among the new chalets.

Altitude and vegetation at Oukaïmeden provide an interesting range of birds, including golden eagles (2 m wingspan) and the larger lammergeier. The smaller booted eagles are recognizable by their acrobatic displays. On the lower approaches, look out for black redstarts, noisy red-billed choughs, blue rock thrushes and black wheatears. Occasionally, magnificent Barbary sheep are sighted.

North of Oukaïmeden is Jebel Tizerag, 2,784 m, with an easy track almost to the top. It is only 200 m higher than the resort itself, but the views are magnificent. Sunset from the summit is an unforgettable sight.

Routes to Oukaïmeden

Although the villages and landscapes are beautiful, the villages are very poor, and small children are eager to cadge pens, notebooks and a few dirhams. When you pull away from a village, watch out that the bolder elements are not clinging onto the back of your vehicle for a thrilling (if dangerous) dare.

In a four-wheel drive vehicle, Oukaïmeden is accessible from the west by winding roads and tracks from Tahanaoute and Asni on the S501 Tizi-n-Test road. From Marrakech, take the S501 as far as **Tahanaoute** (34 km), then the piste (only the first few kilometres are surfaced) up to the Tassaft-n-Tizi, 1,807 m (say 22 km). Here you meet the track coming up from Asni. Go left

Oukaimeden

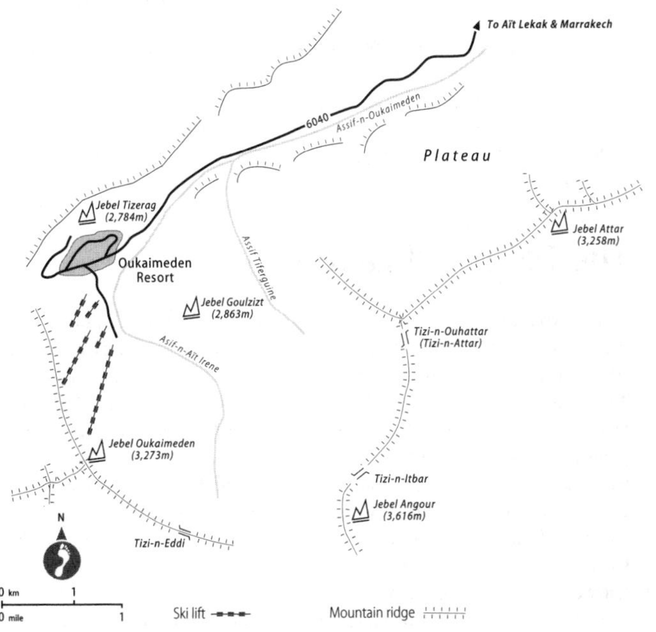

for Oukaïmeden. A few kilometres further on is a further junction, the left-hand track taking you down to Aghbalou, the right to the surfaced Oukaïmeden road (where you go right to climb up to the resort).

Details of this route are best seen on the 1:100,000 scale Oukaïmeden/Toubkal map, feuille NH-29-XXIII-1

An alternative, less frequented route starts at **Asni**, where you take the track leading southeast from near the souk. You drive up the east side of the valley past the villages of Tamassit and Tansghart before heading northeast and east up another valley to Sidi Fars, then past Tadamt on your left to the pass, the Tassaft-n-Tizi. Here you meet the track coming up from Tahanaoute. Go right, and then right to head for the tarmac road to Oukaïmeden.

Sleeping & eating

Oukaïmeden has a small but adequate supply of accommodation. In practice, the resort only gets crowded on snowy weekends, and many Moroccan visitors prefer to return to Marrakech to sleep. Out of season, rooms in mountain chalets can be found. Oukaïmeden has one or two local shops with expensive tinned goods for sale. In the restaurants, prices for tagines vary wildly according to the customer; 40dh is plenty to pay.

B ***Hotel Kenzi Louka***, T044-319080/86, F044-319088. Large, triangular-shaped hotel open all year round, comfortable rooms. Outside pool (generally heated), information and advice on skiing and trekking. **D** ***Hotel Imlil***, T044-319032, a comfortable place with restaurant and good bar. Tends to close in summer. Beautiful views from terrace. **D** ***Hotel de l'Angour*** (aka *Auberge Chez Juju*), T044-319005, information and reservations via Marrakech on T/F044-448378, open all year (except Ramadan). 8 rooms, fair restaurant with French cuisine, bar with cold beer, half-pension required (250dh), but fair prices for clean sheets and hot showers. ***Hotel Panoramique***, open all year has 14 rooms and a dormitory with 20 beds. ***Le Chouka***, only open in winter, 8 rooms and a dormitory with 30 beds, restaurant, modern and comfortable. **F** ***Refuge of the Club Alpin Français***, T044-319036, 60dh/1 person in winter, 35dh summer, has space for 100, but not bunks for all, often has spaces for non-members, restaurant with reduced prices for the CAF members, very comfortable considering position, skiing equipment, mountain bikes etc can be hired here, open all the year, bar room, games room, showers (sometimes with hot water), very clean. **F** ***Chalet de la Jeunesse et des Sports***, just before the CAF, T044-319004, 50dh/1 person winter, 30dh/1 person summer, sleeping bag required, no heating. ***Camping Oukaïmeden***, small site, is open only to caravans, has electricity and petrol 1 km. Self-catering chalets are available via a Marrakech-based company, ***Magesor SARL***, Villa Le Grillon, Rue Oumou el Banine, Marrakech – Guéliz. (Managers Florence and Jean Marie Milicent), T06-3040104, F044-436997.

The Tizi-n-Tichka route

Colour map 1, grid B5

Of the two mountain routes over the High Atlas to the southern side of the mountains, the P31 from Marrakech to Ouarzazate, and its **Tizi-n-Tichka** pass, is a larger road and safer option than the route over the Tizi-n-Test to Taroudant. Completed in 1936 by the Foreign Legion, the P31 gives stunning views. It runs through the full range of Atlas environments, from the Haouz plains, through the verdant *dir* foothills of the Oued Zat, to the barren peaks of the Atlas and the arid regions around Ouarzazate. Drivers need maximum concentration on this route, especially in the twilight when as likely as not you will meet donkeys and flocks of sheep wandering across the road, guided by small children. Clapped out local buses break down, and there are some very hairy bits leading up to the pass after Taddert. Don't cut corners. A further hazard is the fossil sellers who hang out at viewpoints and café stops. Also note that in winter, there can be heavy cloud cover, snow storms and icy rain, reducing visibility and making the road extremely slippery. In such conditions, the road is not much fun at night. If snow cuts the pass, then the snow barriers will be down.

Total distance Marrakech to Ouarzazate is nearly 200 km. You should pace yourself. Good places to stop include upper Taddert (very busy, 86 km from Marrakech), the Tizi-n-Tichka itself which is almost exactly half way, or Ighrem-n-Ouagal, about 118 km from Marrakech where there is an old agadir (granary) to visit. Driving carefully in good conditions, Marrakech to Taddert will take you 2 hours, while Taddert to Ouarzazate is about another 2 hours. You will need to stop for photographs of course, and may want to do side-trips to Telouet and/or Aït Ben Haddou.

To leave Marrakech, the best way out is on the Fès road. Then after 7 km, after a large service station, you go right onto the Aït Ourir and Ouarzazate road which runs through a sparse eucalyptus plantation and past olive and fruit tree groves. After 15 km, you intersect with the road coming out from the médina of Marrakech. At 22 km from Marrakech, you reach a possible accommodation option, the **D** *Complexe Touristique du Dadès*, on your right. The main advantage is they have a pool. At 36 km from Marrakech, you are on the **Aït Ourir** by-pass. (A turn-off left takes you into this rather undistinguished town.) On the right on a bend is a possible stopping place, the small restaurant *Le Coq hardi* which also has some accommodation. Then the road climbs through the foothills with some splendid views of the green valley of the Oued Zat.

Before the pass is the roadside village of **Taddert**, which now sprawls in two fairly unsightly parts. Pause for tagine, biscuits and drinks in upper Taddert. Hygiene in the cheap restaurants is fine in the colder months, the best being (perhaps) the last one on your right, as you head for Ouarzazate. Shortly after Taddert, on a hairpin bend before a steep climb up, is a further more peaceful café which should be open soon.

A few kilometres after the pass is a turning on the left leading to the **Kasbah Telouet** (see below). From the pass the road winds and sweeps down to Ouarzazate. At Ighrem-n-Ouagal (1,970 m) there is a fine fortified granary to visit. At Agouim, 126 km from Marrakech, a piste comes in from the west. Next point of interest is **Amerzgane**, where you have a turn-off right (west) for Taroudant and the neighbouring ruins of Tasgedlt. 167 km from Marrakech a track leads off east for Aït Ben Haddou. The next major junction is a right turn off for Taliouine and Taroudant. Then, about 176 km from Marrakech, at a fairly built-up junction, you have a left turn off onto the road for Aït Ben Haddou (see below). 191 km from Marrakech is a right turn off onto the road for Zagora which enables you to avoid Ouarzazate – and passes just by the spectacular Kasbah of **Tiffoultoute**. Or you can carry straight on into Ouarzazate, past the film studios (left, Egyptian temple décor) and the bus-station.

Telouet

Colour map 1, grid B6

An eagle's nest of a place, high in the mountains, Telouet is something of a legend. It has one of the most spectacular kasbahs in the Atlas, megalomaniac and decaying. The bloodstained history of the dynasty which built it is recounted in Gavin Maxwell's Lords of the Atlas. Today, it is on the tourist circuit, as the hordes of four-wheel drive vehicles which can be met there testify. Within living memory, however, its name was synonymous with the repressive rule of the Glaoui brothers. Easily accessible, it is one of the great sites of mountain Morocco, and is a good starting point for a four-wheel drive journey southwards to Aït Ben Haddou.

Ins and outs

A narrow road, rather in need of resurfacing and with some nasty tyre-splitting edges, takes you from the Tizi-n-Tichka road to Telouet (turn off left, 106 km from Marrakech, or turn off right 85 km after coming up from Ouarzazate). For those without their own vehicle, the trip is problematic, though there may be grands taxis up from Ighrem-n-Ouagdal. Adventurous four-wheel drive people may want to try to reach Telouet from the south by the piste which runs up from Aït Ben Haddou via Tamdacht, Tizgui-n-Barda and Animiter (see below for description of route in reverse).

History

The history of Telouet and its kasbah is short but bloodthirsty. It is the story of how two brothers of the Glaoui tribe, sons of an Ethiopian slave woman, by force of arms and character, managed to achieve absolute dominance over much of southern Morocco in the early 20th century. As it is a story in which neither of the main players, French and Moroccan, appear in an exactly glorious light, the main episodes of the Glaoui Empire's history have tended to be left alone by serious contemporary historians. For the English-speaking reader, Gavin Maxwell's 1965 *Lords of the Atlas* gives a vivid portrait of the turbulent times in Marrakech and the mountains as first the Moroccan monarchy and then the French skirmished with the southern tribal leaders to achieve dominance. The dénouement, which came shortly after Moroccan independence in 1956, was fatal to Glaoui power.

Rise of the Glaoui

If told in detail, the rise of the Glaoui 'dynasty' is one of Byzantine manoeuvrings in kasbahs and imperial cities and confused military skirmishes in the mountainous confines of the Sahara. All this was played out at a time when the European powers were glancing with increasingly greedy eyes at one of the last uncolonized corners of Africa, and certainly the closest unexploited region to Europe. The local context in the Atlas was one of tribal confederations living in relative isolation in the valleys, involved in occasional sporadic warfare when grazing rights were infringed upon. Tribes controlling the mountain passes would of course seek to extract tribute from passing caravans.

Simplifying hugely, in 1893, the tax-gathering caravan or *harka* of Sultan Moulay Hassan I, heading up from southern Morocco, passed via Telouet, which at that time was located on the most practicable north-south pass in the Atlas Mountains. The Sultan had been on a trip to the Tafilalelt, in the far southeast of his domains, where his family, the Cherifian Alaouites had its origins. However, as Gavin Maxwell puts it, the Sultan's return from the Tafilalelt was 'like the retreat of Napoleon's armies from Moscow'. The winter snows had fallen when the troops and mule trains began to climb into the Atlas, and what was left of the army was in a miserable state when the Tizi-n-Telouet was reached.

The lords of Telouet, however, Madani el Glaoui and his younger brother T'hami, had decided to save the Sultan's armies. They quickly raised enough food to feed the starving army from the tribal granaries and flocks. In thanks, the grateful Sultan named Madani his representative in the south, and left a present which was to change the history of southern Morocco: a 77 mm bronze Krupp cannon, the only piece of working artillery in the country outside the Cherifian army's possession.

Madani's rise to power

In 1894, the energetic Sultan Moulay Hassan I passed away. Thanks to the clever strategy of the Vizier Ba Ahmed, the throne went smoothly to one of his younger, more intellectual sons, Moulay Abd el Aziz. Ba Ahmed built himself the vast Bahia Palace in Marrakech, whence the capital was transferred. The Sultan was weak, too young to play an effective role in running the country and distracted by gadgets provided by foreign salesmen and advisors. During these years, Madani el Glaoui's influence spread in the mountains, due in no small measure to the devastating effects of the Krupp cannon. 1901 saw the subjugation of Tamdacht, the last major kasbah to resist. A form of feudal régime was taking root, bringing the deep-rooted, independent minded Amazigh communities under a new form of repression.

In 1907, the French landed in Casablanca in response to urban rioting which had left some European civilians dead. Madani el Glaoui and Moulay Hafid, one of the Sultan's brothers, marched north on Fès. In a confused battle, Moulay Abd el Aziz's army panicked, and Moulay Hafid was proclaimed Sultan. Madani el Glaoui, sultan-maker, was made minister of war. It was just 14 years since Hassan I's column had passed through Telouet. Glaoui power seemed unstoppable.

Madani's fall (and rise)

But Moulay Hafid grew jealous of his sponsor, and in May 1911, Madani was unceremoniously dropped. But the writing was on the wall for Moulay Hafid, too. French power was growing and in early 1912, the Sultan signed the Treaty of Fès, basically making Morocco over to foreign interests – ironically for a ruler who had come to power on the premise that he was defending the country against the Christians. Meanwhile, down south there was a rising led by one of those wild pretenders that early 20th-century Morocco seemed to spawn so frequently. T'hami el Glaoui, then in Marrakech, observed the different sides, and in an affair involving French hostages and the occupation of Marrakech in August 1912, managed to manoeuvre himself into the graces of the new protecting power. In 1913, T'hami, together with the leader of the Goundafi clan, drove the pretender El Hiba out of Taroudant.

Promoting the Grands Caïds

The Glaoui brothers had chosen the winning side. For his role in protecting foreign lives, T'hami was confirmed as Pacha of Marrakech. To Madani was restored the command of all lands and tribes he had lost on his fall from grace with Moulay Hafid. With French blessing and, for the region, sophisticated weapons, they were in a position to create a feudal despotism, which they proceeded to do, with no small measure of cruelty, blasting their way into kasbahs, seizing flocks and crops as they saw fit.

The French were in no position to allow things to happen otherwise. Liberty, fraternity and all the rest did not really apply too much outside metropolitan France. Important interests were at stake, and the so-called *politique des grands caïds* was adopted, according to which the regions which could not be occupied militarily would be managed by loyal local leaders. War in Europe was in the offing, and France, never exactly gifted for winning battles, could ill afford sustained armed conflict in the wild North African mountains. When the First World War finally came, the Glaoui brothers remained loyal (despite the anti-French pronouncements of nephew-in-law Hammou, Pacha of Telouet). German rule in Morocco would have led to their downfall, of course.

It was Madani, above all, who most impressed the French. He had a brilliant grasp of foreign affairs and strategy, and regularly had newspaper articles concerning Morocco translated for him. But in July 1918, unfortunately for the long term interests of the Glaoui clan, he died suddenly, just a few days

Camping in Morocco a century ago

In 1901, Lady Grove, wife of the first baronet, set out from Tanger on mule-back, accompanied by three English gents and a lady, to take a look a the wild interior of the Cherifian Empire. Through Caïd MacLean, military advisor to the sultan, she had managed to obtain an invitation to Telouet, to visit the Glaoui brothers' realm, in the off-chance of a spot of mouflon hunting. Happily, she found time on her return to Britain to write up an account of her trip, entitled Seventy-one Days' Camping in Morocco.

On 3 June 1900, Lady Grove's party arrived in Telouet where they were met by T'hami el Glaoui in person. After refusing the usual simple guest apartments, ("five human beings cannot live here for three or four nights; we are not sheep"), they were shown to apartments generally reserved for distinguished local guests: "My room was about sixty feet long, with a central doorway, over which was hung an embroidered curtain of Rabat work; on the floor were some beautiful rugs, which I longed to pack up and carry away".

The mouflon hunt failed to live up to expectations, however. The full might of the Telouet cavalry was assembled for a exhibition of horsemanship, with T'hami displaying his riding skills. Lady Grove failed to be impressed by this most authentic of fantasias. As the Berber riders left the kasbah, "… wild shrieks and yells burst from them, and they rushed around in an excited, inconsequent manner, meant to represent a mimic fight, the same kind of performance being gone through on horseback by the Khalifa, amid the delighted yells of his admiring followers". There was no hunting to be had that day, although one of the party had been attacked by a cigar-eating mouflon in the Sultan's gardens in Marrakech.

Lady Grove also found time to visit the women's quarters in Telouet, doing a little light medical work, distributing Eno's Fruit Salt for indigestion. One of the ladies showed her "a 'bad place', – thus momentarily transporting one in imagination to the cottages in one's own villages at home, – so having promised her something, I parted with some of my precious Crème-Simon".

Health services in the mountains remain primitive for most people, even if Morocco has otherwise changed a fair amount in a hundred years. But in many ways, Lady Grove's account of Morocco is more about the attitudes of the newly ennobled British to foreign cultures, some of which attitudes, dinosaur-like, are still at large today. The mouflon have not been so lucky. Although there are signs for a mouflon reserve off the Amizmiz to Ouirgane road, the poor beasts seem to have been hunted off the map.

after his favourite son Abd el Malek had been killed in battle. All agreed that it was of a broken heart.

T'hami rules alone Thus T'hami found himself at the head of the clan, albeit it with a thorn in his side in the form of the obstinately anti-French Hammou, husband of Madani's daughter. (In fact, the Tizi-n-Tichka route was built to by-pass Telouet because of Hammou's hostility to all things foreign.) Finally, in 1934 Hammou died and T'hami was full master of the south. An extravagant man, he rapidly developed business interests to cover his costly lifestyle. (Expenditure had to cover the construction of new palaces and kasbahs, tens of concubines and mistresses, and Marrakech's first golf course.) Happily, southern Morocco had plenty of minerals, and T'hami ensured he had a finger in every mining pie, including the Omnium Nord-Africain, the country's leading mining company. He also owned four of the five main newspapers and much property in Casablanca and Marrakech.

T'hami the Kingmaker

But in the 1930s, the Istiqlal, the movement for Moroccan independence, put the writing on the wall for the French protectorate – and its neo-feudal protégés. T'hami, seeing how the wind was blowing, was instrumental in having the popular Sultan Sidi Mohammed deposed in 1953 and replaced by an elderly uncle, son of Hassan I. But the immense resistance to Moulay Arafa's proclamation as Sultan led to urban riots. There would be no peace without the true Sultan, and French politicians, eager for a decent solution, decided that Sidi Mohammed had to return from exile in Madagascar. T'hami the Kingmaker, now an old man, sick with cancer, travelled to France to make his peace with the man he had had deposed. Then in January 1956, he passed away in his Marrakech palace. Sidi Mohammed had returned to his country to a fine welcome, the era of the lords of the Atlas was over.

The fall of the Glaoui clan

T'hami was buried, like his brother, in the shrine of Sidi Ben Slimane at the heart of Marrakech, the city which he had ruled for 43 years. Did he die thinking that his legacy was secure? Probably not. The freedom for rapacious action he had enjoyed was too dangerous for the infant independent Moroccan state. In 1957, a decree was issued confiscating the property of all those who had worked for the French-sponsored régime. Two leading families were targeted, those of T'hami el Glaoui and of the former Grand Vizier El Mokri. Senior brother Brahim el Glaoui was given 15 years exile, four other Glaoui brothers were imprisoned. By the time of their release, all their inheritance had been dismantled, and the family kasbahs pillaged or sold. Glaoui power had not even lasted a century: it was a mere 65 years since Hassan I had struggled up to Telouet, leaving on his departure a Krupp cannon.

Visiting Telouet

Surprisingly perhaps, we have few eyewitness accounts of Telouet in its heyday. None of the former inhabitants have written on their home, perhaps the foreign writers and intellectuals of the 1930s were too preoccupied with Marrakech to make it up to the mountains. Gavin Maxwell left a short description of the fortress in winter, just after a great blizzard which left thousands of goats suffocated on the mountainsides. As the snow melted, ravens, crows and kites gorged themselves on the carcasses. At sundown, "the air was dark with them as with a swarm of locusts; they homed for Telouet in their thousands, … till the branches of the trees broke under them, till the battlements of the castle were foul with their excreta".

Abandoned before completion, the Kasbah of Telouet as we see it today is in fact mainly the result of 20th century building schemes implemented by T'hami el Glaoui. Generally, as visitors arrive, someone will emerge to show one round. Although not exactly in splendid condition, the great reception rooms with their cedar ceilings and crumbling stucco, perfect transposition of late 19th century Moroccan urban taste to the mountains, are worth a visit. Some will see in it 'the labyrinth at whose heart one might expect the minotaur' described by earlier visitors. Others will be amazed at how such a display of quasi-medieval power was created in the 20th century.

Sleeping

With its towers and courtyards (and no doubt dungeons), the Kasbah of Telouet might make splendid guesthouse accommodation. For the moment, there is little on offer in terms of accommodation in Telouet, apart from a couple of cheap and insalubrious hotels. A better option, especially if you are in a group, is to look out for the man who has a couple of old French-built houses for rent (2 bedrooms, 300dh per night, no hot water, but still fairly charming). The better of the 2 houses is above the souk, but much less accessible. Key is with the hammam keeper, immediately north of the souk. Marrakech- Médina SARL, T044-442448, F044-391071, should soon have a property for rent here.

A four-wheel drive route from Telouet to Ouarzazate via Aït Ben Haddou

For those with four-wheel drive, Telouet is also the starting point for an 80 km excursion down to Ouarzazate. You need to ask for the road to Animiter, the first main village. Leaving Telouet, after a few km, a turn-off to the left, near the foot of Jebel Amassine, takes you up to the source of the Glaoui family's wealth, a salt mine. **Animiter**, some 9 km east from Telouet, was famous in the early days of Moroccan tourism as its kasbah, painted by Jacques Majorelle, was featured on an early poster. Here the surfaced road runs out. It should be possible to camp near the Oued Mellah. The next village, **Timsal**, lies a few kilometres to the south. After Timsal, follow the track along the Adrar Taqqat, used when they put in the electricity lines. You reach **Tioughassine** and the track follows the Ounila Valley. At **Assaka**, note abandoned granaries located under the cliffs. The track then follows up onto a sort of plateau above the canyon. Next, the main track drops steeply down to the valley bottom; **Tizgui-n-Barda** is the next main village, about 29 km from Telouet. Continue along the Assif Ounila to reach **Tamdacht**, meeting point of the oueds Marghene and Ounila and the start of the metalled road. **Aït Ben Haddou** is reached 50 km from Telouet.

In fact, this route was used in earlier times by caravans coming up from the south to pick up salt from the Telouet mine. Today, it is increasingly popular as an off-road excursion. The main difficulties are that in wet weather parts of the track turn to red-clay mud, extremely trying if you get stuck. As for other off-road adventures, it is to be tackled by vehicles in pairs because if you get stuck, you will definitely need someone to pull you out.

Off the Tizi-n-Tichka route: rock carvings at Tainant

Of minor interest, for those doing their Moroccan prehistory diplomas, are the rock carvings at Tainant, on the south side of the High Atlas, off the main Marrakech to Ouarzazate via Tizi-n-Tichka route. The site is less visited than the classic sites at Oukaïmeden, Jebel Ghat and Nkob, south of the Jebel Saghro, but if you are in Morocco for some time, might be worth a look. Coming down from the pass, the turn-off right for the site comes 4 km from the village of Ighem-n-Ouagal, 120 km from Marrakech. Some 4 km of rough track take you up to the village of Tainant. You then leave the vehicle in the village to continue on foot. To reach the carvings you will take about 2 hrs on foot. The best way to find them might be to take along a lad from the village, making sure you agree on his 'guiding fee' beforehand.

You eventually come to a set of sheep folds. Continue along the Assif-n-Ouaouzalt. In the distance, you will see the pass, the Tizi-n-Tainant. At the foot of the mountain is an expanse of grazing land. On some low red sandstone cliffs, the carvings can be found. A good description is provided in Susan Searight and Danièle Hourbette's *Gravures rupestres du Haut Atlas* (Casablanca: Editions Belvisi, 1992). All in all, this excursion could make a long and energetic day out from Ouarzazate.

getaway tonight on
www.exodus.co.uk

exodus
The Different Holiday
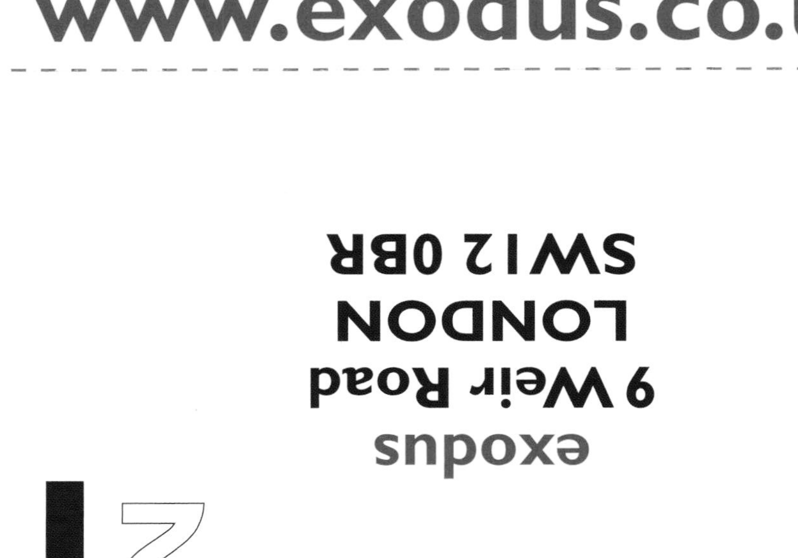
2
exodus
9 Weir Road
LONDON
SW12 0BR
BUSINESS REPLY SERVICE
Licence No SW4909

South of the High Atlas: Taroudant to Er Rachidia

South of the High Atlas: Taroudant to Er Rachidia

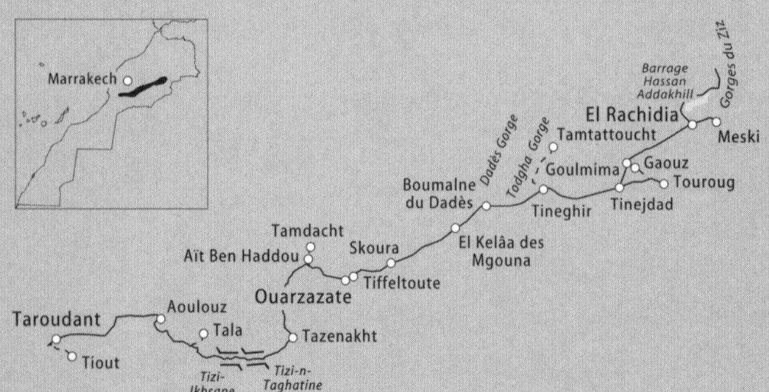

The region south of the High Atlas has some of the finest scenery in Morocco ranging from arid mountains to gentle oases, a volcanic massif and some splendid canyons.

The most spectacular drivable pass across the High Atlas is the **Tizi-n-Test***, taking you from Marrakech to its smaller southern relative,* **Taroudant***, a quiet old place within its ochre ramparts. East of Taroudant, the road takes you round the southern flanks of the* **Jebel Siroua***, a wild volcanic outcrop now being discovered by trekkers. And then you head on to legendary* **Ouarzazate***, legionnaire base turned tourist town.*

Travelling over the High Atlas via the **Tizi-n-Tichka***, your first point of call – after the famous kasbah of* **Aït Ben Haddou** *– will be Ouarzazate. East of here is the* **Dadès Valley***, kasbah land, a place where palm groves and startling earth fortresses stand against backdrops of arid hills. It is also a place where the intrepid can head up into sparsely populated mountains and plateaux, maybe discovering a primitive rock carving or two.*

From **El Kelaâ des Mgouna***, you can venture into the Mgoun Massif, while the gorges of the* **Dadès** *above* **Boumalne** *and the* **Todgha** *gorges above* **Tineghir** *make excellent starting points for treks up into the Atlas. East of Tineghir, the road rises to* **Goulmima** *and then* **Er Rachidia***, former Ksar es Souk, another legionary base and meeting of the ways. From Er Rachidia, those intent on completing an Atlas loop can head on north to* **Rich** *and* **Midelt***.*

Taroudant تارودانت

Colour map 1, grid C3

Taroudant is famous for its red-brown crenellated walls. Nicknamed by locals 'the grandmother of Marrakech', it has some of the character of its more famous neighbour across the Tizi-n-Test pass, albeit on a far smaller and sleepier scale. The médina is enclosed by impressive rammed earth ramparts. Inside are two largish squares, higgledy-piggledy streets and some souks. Much of the older building has been replaced by new concrete stuff, however. Taroudant makes a good overnight stop on an exploration of Southern Morocco. Agadir and the coast are a short hop westwards. Much farther afield are the pre-Saharan oases of Tata and Akka (rock carvings close by). North is the western High Atlas, while eastwards are routes to Ouarzazate and the Draâ, Dadès and Ziz valleys.

Ins and outs

Getting there

See page 192 for further details

Taroudant is easily accessible from Agadir and its transport hub, Inezgane, by bus and grand taxi. There are further bus and grand taxi links across to Ouarzazate and north across the mountains to Marrakech. If you are planning to visit the oases of Tata and Akka, there are grands taxis, plus onward connections to Tiznit. Buses and taxis arrive at Bab Zorgane. There are no longer any buses coming into the central squares. Note that the buses can be very slow - the *CTM* from Marrakech on the easy Chaouia route has been known to take a ridiculous 6 hrs for what is only a 223 km trip.

Getting around

The town centres on place Assarag (aka place des Alaouites) and place Talmoklate (aka place Ennasr). The sights, such as they are (basically the ramparts and souk), can be done on foot. You might hire a bike from an outfit on place Assarag to explore a bit more. From Taroudant, possible day trips include the old village of Freija, some 10 km from town, and the oasis of Tiout, which has an old kasbah. Pale-brown petits taxis do runs in the local area, and there are a few horse-drawn *calèches*, too.

History and background

An inhabitant of Taroudant is called a 'Roudani'

Located at the heart of the fertile Sous valley, Taroudant was always an important regional centre, and even managed to achieve national prominence on a few occasions. Taken by the Almoravids in 1056, it achieved a certain level of independence under the Almohads. Temporary fame came in the 16th century with the rise of the Saâdians (they of the beautiful hidden necropolis in Marrakech). From 1510, the first Saâdian leader, Mohammed el Qa'im, was based in Taroudant as the Emir of the Sous. Even after the Saâdians had gained control of the rest of Morocco, Taroudant remained their capital for a while. Later, in the 17th century, Taroudant supported Moulay Ismaïl's nephew in his rebellion. When the great Sultan took the town in 1687, he took his revenge by slaughtering the population and destroying much of the town. Decline set in, continuing into the 18th and 19th centuries. In the early years of the French Protectorate, Taroudant harboured the rebel Sultan el Hiba and was consequently sacked by colonial forces. Today, the town is a regional market. Two luxury hotels attract visitors. Most tourists, however, are day-trippers from Agadir or people over-nighting on their way to other southern destinations.

Possible routes

*With a car, there are some magnificent options for exploring this region from Marrakech. You could make it part of a **circular tour**. On a short trip, you would start by going from Marrakech to Taroudant via the **Tizi-n-Test**, taking in the much-restored mosque of **Tin Mal** on the way. The next day would take you from **Taroudant** to **Ouarzazate**. After a day of exploring kasbahs from Ouarzazate (Skoura, El Kelaâ des Mgouna), you would head back to Marrakech (via the Tizi-n-Test), taking in **Tiffoultoute**, **Aït Ben Haddou** and **Telouet**.*

*Another possibility would be to take in the region as part of a big **'round the Atlas' tour**, heading east from Ouarzazate for **Tineghir**, then **Er Rachidia**, before completing the circuit back to Marrakech via **Rich**, **Midelt**, **Beni Mellal** and **Azilal**.*

*Another option, if you are more of a **day walker**, is to take it a bit more easy and spend a couple of nights in (say) **Skoura**, **Boumalne** and **Tineghir** in order to explore the palm groves and gorges.*

Sights

The walls

The 16th- and early 17th-century Saâdian pisé walls, nicely crenellated and set here and there with chunky square towers, are Taroudant's best sight. You could follow the walls round the town, possibly in a *calèche* (horse-drawn carriage), generally available from outside the *Palais Salam* for around 40dh per hour. There were originally only five gates (running clockwise from the bus station, Bab Zorgane, Bab Targhount, Bab Oulad Bounouna, Bab el Khemis and Bab el Kasbah), and you can go up at least one of these for a look out over olive groves, orchards and much new building. En route you'll pass the kasbah, the most densely populated and poorest part of town. This in fact was a fortress rebuilt by Moulay Ismaïl in the 17th century. Outside the walls, you might try to visit the tanneries, left from Bab

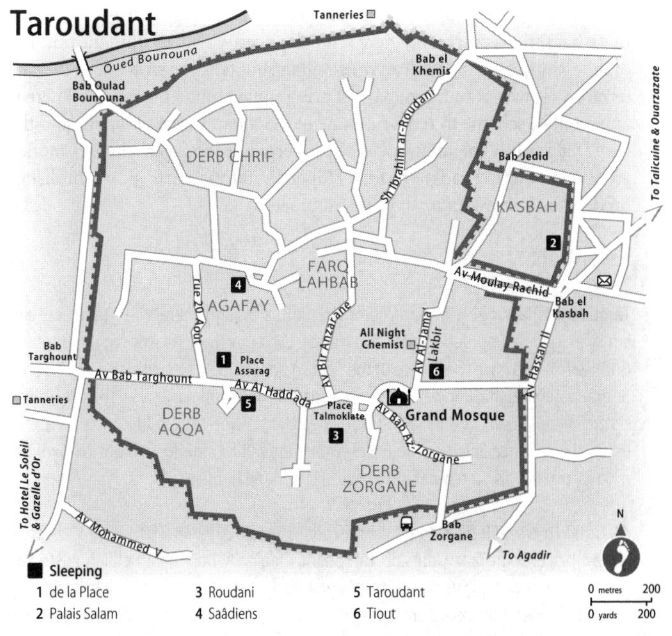

South of the High Atlas

Five things to do South of the High Atlas

- Buy polished **fossils** or ersatz **crystals** from vendors on the Tizi-n-Tichka road.
- Buy traditional, women's woven **belts** in Ouarzazate.
- Take a short side trip from Ouarzazate to the Kasbah of **Tiffoultoute**.
- Explore the kasbahs in the palm groves of **Skoura** or spend the night in the **Todgha Gorge**.
- Admire the wild landscapes of the **Gorges du Ziz**, north of Rachidia, on the way to Midelt.

el Khemis ('the Thursday gate'), where skins of a variety of animals are still cured using pretty traditional methods.

Souks Although nowhere near as extensive as those of Marrakech, the souks of Taroudant are fairly good. They are perhaps an easier, calmer place to look around for souvenirs than Marrakech, where handicraft indigestion sometimes sets in. Thursday and Sunday are busy days, with people coming in from the surrounding villages. The souks lead off from place Assarag, beside the bank. Notable specialities of the town include jewellery and mock ancient carvings in local limestone. Carpets can also be found. There are small stalls and a few bigger tourist shops. Off the far side of place Talmoklate (literally 'square of the Little Pot') is an area with little shop selling spices, herbs, medicines and pottery.

The town Apart from its walls, Taroudant is not the most picturesque of places by day. Originally, part of the area within the walls was devoted to orchards and market gardening. Much of this has now been built up, and the majority of the original low pisé buildings have long since been replaced by charmless concrete housing. In the evening, however, Taroudant takes on a more interesting air, and men stay up late socializing in the cafés in the centre. Essentially, this is a farming centre, and there is much poverty, evident from the number of shoe-shiners willing to clean your walking boots as you sit at one of the café terraces. However, tourism may yet bring some limited prosperity. There is apparently a scheme to redevelop one of the squares with fountains and the like. Deterred by the high prices of property in Marrakech, there is money around looking for riads to restore. Hopefully, the ramparts will not be disfigured by further restaurant-type developments.

Essentials

Sleeping
■ on map
Price codes:
see inside front cover

Taroudant is lacking in good accommodation, although there was talk of an Italian-managed riad opening in late 2001. If you can't pay the stratospheric prices of the *Gazelle d'Or*, you have the choice of the *Palais Salam* (should be better than it is), some unprepossessing mid-range places – or a spartan, noisy room in one of the very cheap central hotels (early morning call from nearby mosque). For budget-ish travellers, either the *Hotel Le Soleil* or the *Hotel Taroudant* will be fine for a night or two. For groups, there is also a self-catering type place, Jnène Remane.

AL ***Hotel La Gazelle d'Or***, route d'Amezgou, T048-852039/48, F048-852737. A truly 'toney' place, some 2 km outside Taroudant. Originally built by a Belgian aristocrat. Generally closed in summer. 100 ha of beautiful grounds, pool, tennis, hammam, riding and croquet. Half-board around 4,000dh in one of the garden houses. Suites much more expensive. Said to be one of the best hotels in Morocco. **A *Palais Salam***, built into the ramparts around the kasbah district, in a building which was the local pacha's palace, T048-852501, F048-852654. Prices start at around 650dh plus 70dh for breakfast. Two pools, including one in the shape of a Moroccan horseshoe arch (bit tacky, really). Is not in fact as classy as it likes to make out, witness the piped music at the poolside. The only place where you can get a beer (for the moment).

The best of this bunch? Difficult to say - possibly 'El Ouarda'

E *Hotel Saâdiens*, Ave du 20 Août, Borj Oumansour, T048-852589, F048-852118. Well signed, even though in the middle of the old town. Double 200dh, with breakfast. Small pool. All in all, not a very exciting deal. **E *Café-Hotel-Restaurant Le Soleil***, close to Bab Targhount, just outside the walls in the Agadir direction, T048-551707. Single 80dh, double 100dh. Pleasant place with a small garden and big rooms, old-fashioned bathrooms (baths Egyptian sarcophagus model) and hot water. Quiet by day. At night tends to be rather noisy: clients arrive from late buses, water trickles in unseen pipes. At the last count, management seemed to consist of 2, 14-year-old kids who, considering they kip on the kitchen floor, were doing a very good job. **E *Hotel-Restaurant Taroudant***, on place Assarag, T048-852416. Range of prices, from 55dh for the simplest rooms to 160dh for the best twin with shower and loo. Breakfast 10dh. As usual, prefer inward facing rooms, although these are noisy when the bar is in action. As the old licence holder had died, there was no alcohol in late 2000. (RIP the only ordinary bar in Taroudant?) Staff very nice. A good address, if a little basic with its linoleum and air of the 1950s. Try for room 14. **E *Hotel-Restaurant Tiout***, on Ave du Prince Héritier Sidi Mohammed, T048-850341, F048-854480. 37 rooms including 12 with tiny balcony, 200dh single, 265dh double, breakfast 35dh, lunch 65dh. Family rooms 350dh. Re-opened in Jan 1999 after 'major renovation work', ie much artistic paintwork to mask a basic concrete building as cheaply as possible. Ugly terrace ('solarium'). A false *bel hôtel*. **F/E** Creeping into the **E** category are a number of small hotels on place Assarag, including the hotels ***Les Arcades***, ***El Ouarda*** (literally 'the Rose') ***de la Place*** and ***Roudani***. Very basic, tiny and none-too-clean rooms for 60dh to 70dh.

Self-catering *Jnene Remane* (lit Garden of the Pomegranates). Well run small outfit with private flats and dormitory accommodation, located in the old town. Ecologically managed by a UK-based company, *Naturally Morocco Ltd*, based at Hill House, Llansteffan SA33 5JG, Wales, T/F0044-1267-241999. Locally based staff are very knowledgeable about the region. Bookings are made via the central offices in Wales. Vegetarian food a speciality. Highly recommended, have small car for hire, can set up informed tours of the region.

Elsewhere in the region **C *Palais Riad Hida***, Oulad Berhil, 40 km out of Taroudant on the P32 road to Aoulouz, T048-531044, F048-531026. Look out for the sign in the village centre. Around 300dh for a double. Small establishment in a restored pacha's country residence, 10 rooms, nice grounds. Invaded by tour groups some lunchtimes.

Eating

Expensive *La Gazelle d'Or*, route d'Amezgou, T048-852039. Restaurant of the hotel of the same name. Posh togs necessary. Restaurant at the *Hotel Palais Salam*, reservations via hotel reception on T048-852501 or numbers above. Menu at around 240dh, wine extra. In Jan 2001 this was the only place with alcohol. **Mid-range** ***Restaurant Jnene Soussia***, in a sort of tent just outside the ramparts near Bab Zorgane, T048-854980. Was it really necessary to put such an ugly establishment right next to the ramparts? Location handy for parked tour buses. Overpriced Moroccan fare. Restaurant at the ***Hotel Saâdiens***. Menu and à la carte. Acceptable. Restaurant at the ***Hotel Taroudant***. Simple menu at 70dh, no alcohol for the moment. **Cheap** Quite a lot of choice on place Assarag. If rushed, try the restaurant of the ***Hotel Les Arcades***, basic lunch for 40dh. Rather better is the ***Restaurant el Baraka***, between the 2 squares, where lunch for 2 (chicken portion, brochettes, chips and salads) will set you back 50dh.

Transport **Bus** The journey to Agadir, only 80 km, can take up to 2 hrs by bus - probably better to take a grand taxi. **Marrakech** can be equally slow. For distant towns (**Casablanca**, **Marrakech** via the Tizi-n-Test, **Ouarzazate** etc), buses leave early in the morning. Buses leave from the Bab Zorgane station. Regular buses to **Agadir** (4 per day), **Casablanca** (4 per day), **Inezgane** (on the hour), **Ouarzazate** (5 per day), **Tata** (3 per week). Early morning service to Marrakech via Tizi-n-Test takes 9 hrs. Sample bus prices 2001: Taroudant to Agadir with the *CTM*, 29dh, Taroudant to Marrakech, *CTM*, 70dh. **Driving** To **Agadir**, you can take the main P32 (straightforward but boring), or (for an insight into rural Morocco) a poorly surfaced minor road (P7016) along the northern side of the Oued Sous. This brings you onto the P40 from Chichaoua to the northeast of Agadir. For **Marrakech**, the quickest route is up the P40 to Chichaoua, followed by the P10 eastwards. **Taxi** Grands taxis for **Agadir** and **Inezgane**, need to change at Ould Teima.

Directory **Banks** There are several cashpoints, including ***Banque Populaire*** and ***Société Générale*** (SGMB) on place Assarag and the ***Crédit du Maroc***, opposite the *Hotel Taroudant*. Try also ***BMCI*** on Rue Bir Anzarane off place Talmoklate. **Bike hire** On place Assarag, opposite *Hotel Taroudant*. **Hammam** Near the *Hotel Taroudant*, also off place Assarag. **Medical services** Dr Ahmed ben Jedid, T048-852032 (clinic), T048-853626 (home). **Sports** Try the ***Hotel Palais Salam*** for tennis.

Excursion to Tiout

Just 7 km east of Taroudant, a road (7084) leaves the P32, and follows a 171-km route across the Anti-Atlas mountains and down into the Sahara to the oasis of **Tata**. Although most tourists do not find the time to get beyond **Tiout**, this is a fine journey, with views of some spectacular landforms and the palm groves of the **Akka Valley**. Definitely a trip for devotees of wilderness, and now that the road has been metalled it is easily done by car, although spare parts and petrol are none too plentiful. (Those with even more time will be able to get to the rock carvings at **Oum El Alek** near Akka.)

Ins & outs There are grands taxis and occasional buses doing the short run from Taroudant to Tiout.

Tiout

Souk day in Tiout is Wednesday

Tiout, 33 km from Taroudant on the road south, could be your first stop. It has a splendid palmery and a newly restored kasbah founded in the 16th century, overlooking the seven small villages. At this time, affluent merchants came from as far as Fès, Marrakech and the Sahara to trade. Just for the record, a version of *Ali Baba and the Forty Thieves*, starring French comic Fernandel (as Ali Baba in Berber gear with a Marseille accent) and the lush Egyptian dancer Samia Gamel, was made here in the early 1950s.

Restaurant Kasbah Tiout, T048-51048, is a possible lunch stop, although it has not done much for the kasbah in aesthetic terms. Rather more *sympathique* is *Chez Hmid* (T048-53582), a little restaurant in a street leading to the mosque with a wooden door and a blue surround.

Taroudant to Ouarzazate, via Taliouine and Tazenakht

Basically, there are two viable road routes south over the High Atlas from Marrakech: the western, tricky Tizi-n-Test route or the easier four hour drive via the Tizi-n-Tichka, which takes you down to Ouarzazate. Most people heading for the southern flanks of the Atlas will take the latter option. For those with a good head for heights, the Tizi-n-Test journey is a worthwhile option. Heading east out of Taroudant, you take the P31 to Ouarzazate. At Oulad Berrehil, where the road begins to leave the fertile **Sous Valley**, the road coming over the Tizi-n-Test intersects. The first useful settlement is, **Taliouine**, a good starting point for walking in the **Jebel Siroua**. It is also said to produce the best saffron in Morocco. The col of **Tizi-n-Taghatine** marks the end of the Sous basin and the beginning of the Draâ. At **Tazenakht**, there is a carpet-makers' co-operative (Ouzguita tribal weaving available), while just before Ouarzazate is the Taghdout Dam, a place to picnic for those with a car.

If you are driving east from Taroudant on the P31, the first major settlement is **Oulad Berrehil**. Coming over the Tizi-n-Test, you meet the junction for Ouarzazate 52 km east of Taroudant.

Further along the P31, **Aoulouz**, about 30 km east of the junction to Tizi-n-Test, is a beautiful spot. There is easy access to the Oued Sous. Take the track to the right when approaching from the west, which goes right down to the water's edge. There are good places to stop and view the surroundings, even stop and picnic. In good years there is water in the oued. Here, while the women use this water to wash the clothes, there may be an opportunity to see a rare bald ibis.

The barrage lies 4 km west up a clearly signed track. It cannot, however, be approached officially - the road sign says 'closed to civilians'. Further upstream, some 21 km, is a second barrage.

The road east climbs up to **Iouzioua Ounneine**, a settlement no longer than its name, over a pass of 1,050 m which provides good views to the southwest. Up here look out for restaurant *Noukia*, better than average, a good place for a coffee on a long journey.

Taliouine

Taliouine is a pleasant town, improved without doubt by the presence of a magnificent kasbah to the south of the road. Here you will find a pharmacy, post office, telephone, police, mechanics, taxis, cafés and hotels. There is petrol (*Ziz*) at the eastern end of town beyond the triumphal arches and a *Shell* in the centre, almost opposite the *Saffron Cooperative*. Note that the *Crédit Agricole* does not change travellers' cheques, but has more favourable rates for currency exchange than the *Hotel Ben Toumert*, which charges high commission. The pharmacy is on the western end of the main street near where the buses stop and a handful of cafés. Tour buses call in at Taliouine so photographs can be taken of the kasbah, also discreet shots of the women doing their washing in the *oued*, if this is your idea of the picturesque. Also a stop-off for tours is the 'best' hotel, *Ben Toumert*, for coffee or lunch.

Sleeping and eating **A** *Hotel Ben Toumert*, T048-535130, F048-535131. 100 rooms with bath, a/c and heating. Breakfast 39dh, lunch menus 112dh or 140dh, pleasant hotel, lovely surroundings, adjacent to recently deserted kasbah to the south of the road and east of the *oued*. Far cheaper is the *Hotel/Café Renaissance*. **E** ***Auberge-Restaurant Souktana***, T048-534075, on the north side of the road, west of the road junction to *Hotel Ben Toumert* and east of the *oued*. Small, pleasant garden surrounds it, also does camping. Recommended for good food, especially tagines, availability of guides, mules, tents for walkers etc for excursions up into the Jebel Siroua (see below). ***Hotel and Camping Siroua*** to south of road on west side of the town. ***Hotel de la Poste*** is to be avoided. **E** ***Auberge Askaoun***, T048-534017, just 1 km out of town towards Tazenakht, is better but kind of lonely.

Calling for rain

Close as they are to the Sahara, the farmlands of Morocco can on occasion suffer terrible drought, like other southern Mediterranean countries. In hard-pressed villages, when the wells and cisterns run dry, people gather for special ceremonies to call for rain. In some areas, the tislit n unzar, *'ceremony of the bride of the rain', is performed. Barley broth is prepared and ladled out to the group, and then a reed doll, whose head and arms are made of big wooden ladles (*taghounja*) is dressed as a bride. (In some regions, the fiancée is accompanied by a male doll swathed in a black cloak, representing the* anzar, *the rain clouds.) The* taghounja *doll is carried to a neighbouring lake or stream and cast into the water as an offering to the rain. The legend recounts how the Rain King desired a beautiful girl who would bathe in the stream. But he failed to conquer her heart, and in despair, dried up the water until she was given to him. After the ritual – which now certainly harks back to pre-Islamic times – the men of the village may walk barefoot to the local mosque or saint's shrine to perform the traditional prayers for rain. The* taghounja *rites are interesting as they mix mythical wedding ceremony, fertility and the idea of food and community – here symbolized by the shared spoon.*

Taliouine to Tazenakht

Taliouine is recognized as a starting point for walks into the Jebel Siroua

From Taliouine there is a road south to Irherm and a minor road north to Askaoun. Continuing east, the road climbs steeply out of Taliouine. Look back to the south and see the old deserted settlement right on the top of the hill. Northwards, you can see terraced slopes, tiny walls to hold back the soil, cereals and fruit trees. The pass provides good views down over the plain, intensive cultivation in valleys, usual oasis gardens behind the walls, cereals, olives, almonds, pomegranates, figs, vines taking advantage of the aspect and altitude which tempers the climate and takes away the fierceness of the summer heat. Beyond, on the top of the plateau, the soil is very thin and suitable only in places for dry farming, producing poor cereals. There is a small, not very special, café on top of this first climb out of Taliouine.

Between Taliouine and Tazenakht are two high passes, **Tizi-n-Taghatine** (1,886 m) and **Tizi Ikhsane** (1,650 m), with a small settlement of **Tinfat** boasting another imposing kasbah, midway between. The highest pass, Tizi-n-Taghatine, incorporates some of the nicest of the scenery on this route; a mixture of landforms, terracing with small trees, views on all sides, and the road, though not perfect, allows time for eyes to do a little wandering. In fact the journey is perhaps better going east to west as the snow-capped Atlas make a better backdrop, to the right and straight ahead.

The pattern of farming does not alter much. On some of the very straight sections between Taroudant and Ouarzazate, there are argan trees underplanted with wheat as far as the eye can see. There are a few long straight sections, though from the map these are not obvious. Some sections are in poor condition, the irregular surface being a little more than a car wide and sides dropping steeply away into mud that has been churned by heavy vehicles in the winter and has then baked hard.

Between the passes there is patchy shifting cultivation and little else. At the top of the lower pass, **Ikhsane**, there's a man with a small hut selling plain terracotta pottery. How's that for determination? Beyond Ikhsane after another very straight stretch of road is **Kourkouda**, by the well are a few stalls with pottery and fossils, another with a few carpets, painted rams' horns and sheets of selenite, a form of calcite.

Tazenakht & beyond

Tazenakht is at an important junction, though much of the town stands to the northwest of the road. Triumphal pillars announce the entrance to the town just before the junction off east to Foum Zguid. Adjacent to the arch is *Petrol Afrique* with a small clean restaurant. At this junction, grands taxis and petits taxis are on the left, bus station, pharmacy on right, *Café Essaadi*, *Hotel/Restaurant Senhaja*, basic rooms, very cheap, and telephone. Market Friday. *Hotel Etoile*, in the centre by the taxi stand, is a very run down motel, damp and unpleasant. *Hotel Zenaga* (T048-41032) is the only place fit to stay in, rooms vary and so do prices, hot water in evening only. The *Shell* petrol station is on the left by the *oued*, the triumphal arch which marks the far end of the town. Tazenakht also has a bank, a number of carpet shops, displaying wares produced by the local Ouzguita tribe - and very fine and geometrically designed they are too. There are the usual small shops for general supplies like fizzy drinks and biscuits, and a mosque.

After Tazenakht, the P32 road climbs up to Tizi-n-Bachkoum, 1,700 m. Nothing grows here in the very poor soil. There is, at the summit, a good view to the west and even a place to pull off. The inevitable group of small children could well be waiting.

Anezal stands by a large *oued* of the same name. Often tourist mini-coaches are parked at the café here, which is good for a rest and a drink. This has an important animal market.

To the right of the road between Anezal and Tiouine is a huge *oued* with tributaries which eventually lead into the barrage to the east of Ouarzazate. The road goes alongside this for 20 km, all the way to Tiouine. Here there is an old ruined fortress on the right and new buildings on the left. Manganese is mined in hills to the right. The road descends to cross the big Oued Iriri, just north of Tiouine. This *oued* also drains into the same large barrage of Mansour Eddahbi. There are two junctions where roads go north to Marrakech, which is 178 km away over the Tizi-n-Tichka. Beyond these the road is far busier. Roadside sales on this exceedingly straight road lined with eucalyptus trees include pottery, dyed desert roses, amathyst and polished stone. The village of Taborhat is at the junction where the road goes off southeast to Zagora. In this last stretch into Ouarzazate, the road climbs up and gives to those sitting on the right of the bus a lovely view down into the settlement of Taborhat below, views right into the square courtyards and across to the mosque.

Trekking in the Jebel Siroua

Colour map 1, grid C5, Jebel Siroua is best trekked in spring and autumn

As indicated above (see Talioune), the best starting point for Jebel Siroua treks is Taliouine. Rising to a twin-peak of 3,305 m, the Jebel Siroua is an arid, isolated region forming a sort of volcanic bridge between the High Atlas of Toubkal to the north and the Anti-Atlas to the south. As compared with the busy, even prosperous, Imilchil region, there are few trekkers for the moment. Communicating with locals can be a problem, unless you have fluent Tachelhit. Best trekked in autumn and spring, the Jebel Siroua is easily accessible from both Taroudant and Ouarzazate. From Marrakech, it is a long ride, nearly nine hours by the direct bus, depending on breakdowns and stops. Getting there from Marrakech, you could of course go for the Tizi-n-Test crossing to Taroudant, spectacular enough to make the slowness of the journey easily bearable.

Possible treks From Taliouine, there are numerous possibilities for trekking up into the Siroua. Richard Knight in his excellent *Trekking in the Moroccan Atlas* (Hindhead: Trailblazer Publications, 2001) gives an immense amount of useful detail on a nine-day round Jebel Siroua trek. If you have less time, the ***Auberge Souktana***, T048-534075, F048-231411, in Taliouine should be able to advise on short treks. Also try ***Jnène Remane*** in Taroudant, as they have excellent contacts in the region. (UK contact ***Naturally Morocco Ltd***, based at Hill House, Llansteffan SA33 5JG, Wales, T/F0044-1267-241999.) A number of European-based travel companies run treks into the Jebel Siroua, too. Another possibility might be to take a minibus from Taliouine up to **Akhfamane**, where many of the treks start. An irregular minibus service runs from the central *Shell* garage in Taliouine up to Akhfamane, although it is possible to walk this in about 5 hours. At Akhfamane, there are a rooms available and mules for hire.

Ouarzazate ورزازات

Colour map 1, grid C1

The very name Ouarzazate has a ring of the desert outpost. It spells Foreign Legion, austere mountains, wide open spaces and valleys of palm trees and tiny irrigated fields. The reality of Ouarzazate more or less conforms to this image: the town, once an isolated French outpost, remains essentially a garrison and regional centre, transformed by a graft of large new hotels. The primary attraction, however, is not in the settlement itself. Ouarzazate is to be seen as a base for exploring the Saharan regions, and as a transit point en route to the desert. For this, it is a pleasant enough place to stay.

Ins and outs

Getting there

See page 200 for further details

Taourirt airport is 2 km northeast of Ouarzazate. From there get a petit taxi to your hotel. Ouarzazate is well served by buses and grands taxis. By bus, the run from Taroudant takes 5 hrs, from Agadir 7½ hrs, from Marrakech hopefully under 5 hrs. In winter, the Tizi-n-Tichka col can be closed with snow. By grand taxi, Zagora to Ouarzazate takes 3 hrs, rather longer by bus. The *CTM* bus terminal is on a square on the main street, Ave Mohammed V, private line buses arrive at Place 3 Mars, and grands taxis on place Mouahidine.

Getting around Ouarzazate is a small place, really more of a base than anything else. You may want to get out to the spectacular kasbah at Aït Ben Haddou, which is awkward without your own car. You could club together with other tourists and hire a grand taxi, or you could get a bus going up the P31 Marrakech road, and get off at the turn off for the kasbah, and walk the rest. A few kilometres out of Ouarzazate, on the 'by-pass', is the well preserved kasbah of Tiffoultoute, easily reached by grand taxi. Another place you may want to get to from Ouarzazate is the oasis of Skoura, east along the Boumalne du Dadès P32 road, easily accessible by local bus.

History & background

The immediate vicinity of Ouarzazate is much in demand as a film location

Located at the confluence of three rivers, Ouarzazate is in a strategic location, and has been garrisoned since the Almohad period. A tribal war in the late 19th century left Ouarzazate in the hands of the El Glaoui family, and the kasbah became the power base from which they expanded control over the south. In 1926, the first airfield was built, and in 1928, a regular French military garrison was installed. Ouarzazate was henceforth the main administrative town for the region, the nerve centre for the Lyautey method of expanding French influence into tribal areas. A few buildings from this period straggle along the main street. Around and above them are the large hotels, built mainly in the 1980s. Today,

Ouarzazate is quite a solid (if sleepy) little town. Neat low-rise housing painted magenta brown with white trim is going up, there is a new bus station and the airport is increasingly busy with charter flights.

The epic *Lawrence of Arabia* was filmed at Aït Ben Haddou, and from then on the region, close to mountains and a variety of arid landscapes, was a popular director's choice. The *Atlas Studios* never seem to be out of work. (Look out for the mock Egyptian statues signalling the presence of the studios off the road north of the town.) Ouarzazate hosts a sedate handicrafts fair in May and the *moussem* of Sidi Daoud in September. It is popular as a base for birdwatchers. In spring, the town is at its best when the almond blossoms in the region and the snow still covers the summits of the High Atlas.

Sights

The town is proud of its mosque, the first stone of which was laid by King Mohammed V in 1958. The main days for the town market are Sunday and Tuesday, but beyond this the main point of interest in Ouarzazate is the **Kasbah Taourirt**, located east of the town centre along Ave Mohammed V. This was a Glaoui kasbah, built in the 19th century, reaching its height of importance in the 1930s. The kasbah would have housed the extended family of the chief, his servants and followers, as well as a community of tradesmen, artisans and cultivators, gathered together in a continuous area of building for common security. The kasbah is partly ruined, but is still occupied, on its rear side, by some of the poorest people in Ouarzazate in a maze of narrow passageways, small houses and shops. The area of the kasbah adjacent to the road has been maintained. This would have been the quarters of the family and immediate associates, and includes a courtyard and several reception rooms. Upstairs are a small dining room and salon. ■ *0830-1200 and 1500-1800 Mon-Fri, 0830-1200 Sat.*

Opposite the kasbah in the *Ensemble Artisanal*, there are a number of sculptors working on the premises, as well as a selection of local handicrafts. The local woollen carpets of the Ouzguita Berbers are worth looking out for. ■ *0800-1200 and 1300-1800 Mon-Fri, 0830-1200 Sat, T044-883449.* In the town centre there is also a *Coopérative Artisanale des Tissages de Tapis*, another fixed price shop. *Atlas Studios*, where film work is regularly in process, is open to public view (0800-2000), and is located 3 km from the centre, along the road to Marrakech.

Excursions

See page 201 for other excursions

To the east of town, on the Skoura road, the Barrage Al Mansour is a large man-made lake with the partly ruined **Tamdacht Kasbah**. To the north of Ouarzazate, off the P31 on the Zagora road, lies the **Kasbah Tifeltoute**, said to be over 300 years old. The present building is largely 20th century. Property of the Glaoui family, it is now used as a simple hotel, with adequate food and magnificent views, T044-882813. You can visit for a small fee and climb up to the roof terrace for views of the countryside and a stork's nest on one of the turrets. For those with four-wheel drive vehicles or hardy saloon cars, the oasis of **Fint** is a possible destination, a few kilometres off in the desert west of Ouarzazate.

Essentials

Sleeping
■ *on map*
Price codes: see inside front cover

If you are travelling by public transport, you will come into the *gare routière* on the Marrakech side of town. After a hot bus journey, you may want to take a petit taxi to run you into town, a couple of kilometres away. (*CTM* buses come into Ave Mohammed V.)

As Ouarzazate is basically a one-mule sort of place, a lot of streets have yet to get names

A *Hotel Kenzi Bélère*, 22 Ave Moulay Rachid, T044-882803, F044-883145. 270 rooms and 11 suites, a/c, pool, tennis, 4 restaurants, nightclub, cool, spacious, excellent facilities, helpful manager, 2nd best hotel in town. **A *Hotel Le Méridien Berbère Palace***, T044-883105, F044-883071. 211 rooms, well appointed with usual pool, bar, choice of restaurants, even a hammam, prices start at 1,400dh, 1 person, rising to the vizierial suite at 3,000dh a night, breakfast 110dh, evening buffet 270dh. **A *Hanane Club***, Ave Erraha, T044-882555, F044-885737. Part of the new hotels complex, 53 rooms including 7 suites, all have TV, telephone and minibar, a/c, restaurant has 200 spaces, Moroccan and international menus, pizzeria has 50 spaces, American bar, nightclub for 200-250, pool, hammam, tennis, shops. **A *Hotel Riad Salam***, Ave Mohammed V, T044-883335, F044-882766. 2 converted kasbahs, luxuriously equipped, 14 suites, 63 rooms, with TV, restaurant, bar, spectacular pool, as well as a sauna, massage, horse riding and tennis, shops, conference facilities, a bit overpriced. **C *Hotel Kenzi Azghor***, Blvd Prince Moulay Rachid, T044-886501/05. Above the town, a good place with 150 rooms, a restaurant, bar and pleasant pool, used mainly by tour-operator FRAM so often full. **C *Hotel Zat***, Aït Gief, T044-882521, F044-885550, 60 rooms, a quieter hotel on the outskirts, with an excellent restaurant, a bar and pool. **C *Hotel Oscar Salam***, on northern outskirts, at Tassoumaate, route de Marrakech, right next to the *Atlas Studios*, T044-882212, F044-882180. 64 rooms, a/c, pool.

D *Hotel la Gazelle*, Ave Mohammed V, T044-882151. A good option with 30 rooms, bar-restaurant, small pool, a little out of town on the Marrakech road. **D *Résidence Ouarda***, on Ave Mohammed V near Palais des Congrès, T06-1871499. 125dh 1 person, 150dh 2 persons, slightly mucky, decaying, last resort. **E *Hotel Amlal***, easily located on

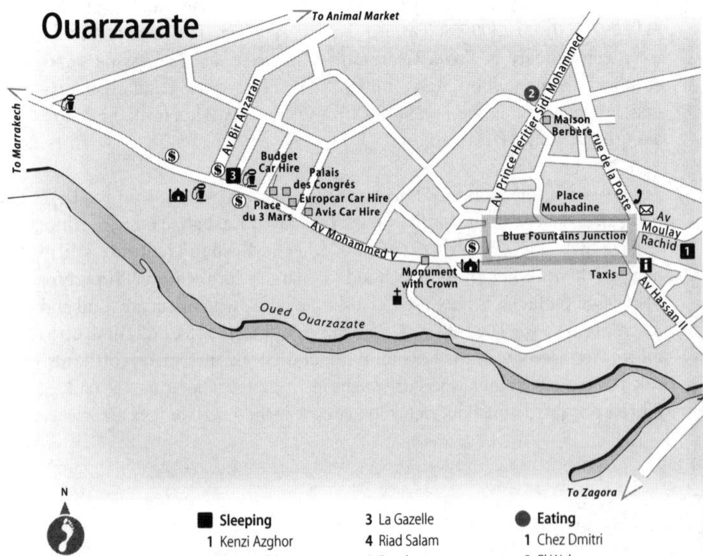

side street behind *Wafa Bank* and *RAM* office, signed, next to *Nekob Car Hire*, T044-884030, F044-884600. 100dh 1 person, 130dh 2 persons, clean rooms with showers, some rooms with 4 beds. Recommended. **E *Hotel Royal***, 24 Ave Mohammed V, T044-882258. A friendly place with good clean rooms with shower 90dh 2 persons, without 70dh 2 persons, some very basic rooms 30dh 1 person. Well located, fair prices, 1st floor rooms slightly better but hot in summer. A better option than the *Hotel Salam* almost opposite. **E *Hotel Salam***, opposite the BMCE on Ave Mohammed V, T044-882512, 3 floors, 55 rooms, many poorly ventilated, around long courtyard, rather like being in a large pink cake, fairly clean, requires payment in advance, with shower, 102dh 2 persons, 82dh 1 person, an option if all else fails. **F *Hotel Habib***, in low-rise building diagonally across waste ground from grand taxi station, T044-882024. 40dh 1 person, 65dh 2 persons, hot shower 5dh, clean. **F *Hotel Safsaf***, on left after Palais des Congrès as you come from Marrakech, T044-884121. 40dh 1 person, 70dh 2 persons without shower, 100dh 2 persons with shower, austere metal-bedstead-type hotel. Good value, central, used by tour-group drivers. **F *Hotel Atlas***, 13 Rue du Marché, T044-882307, behind the main street, cheap and more or less clean. **F *Essada***, Rue de la Poste, T044-883231, only has cheapness to recommend it.

Hayy Tabount There are a few hotels over the Tabount causeway on the west bank of Ouarzazate, including the highly recommended **D *Hotel La Vallée***, Zagora road, on left before causeway to east bank, T044-854034, F044-854043. 150dh 1 person, 200dh 2 persons, breakfast 20dh, meals 70dh. A very good option with 40 rooms, much used by tour groups for lunch, quiet in evening. **E *Hotel Saghro***, Zagora road, 2.5 km from centre, T044-8541365, F044-854709. Over 50 rooms, small pool. A bit noisy.

Tiffoultoute A pleasant, though basic option is the spectacular **D *Kasbah Tiffoultoute***, out on the Zagora by-pass, T044-885899. Only 6 rooms, 150dh 1 person, 300dh 2 persons, including breakfast. Clean rooms, possibility of sleeping out on roof in summer.

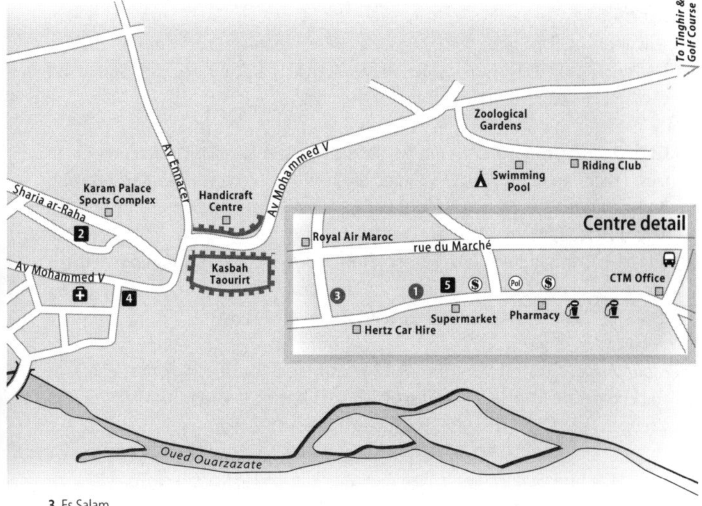

3 Es Salam

Camping *Camping Municipal*, T044-884636, is on the Tineghir exit of the town. A friendly place with running water, café and simple restaurant, pool next door, showers, electricity for caravans, grocery shop and petrol 800 m away, the site is small, only 1 ha, and a bit expensive, little shade, clean pitches. ***Camping Imlil*** has been recommended at 5dh pp and 10dh per tent.

Eating
● *on map*

Expensive *Complexe de Ouarzazate*, next to the campsite on the Skoura exit from town, T044-883110. Set menus from 130dh to 290dh, lots of groups, lots of traditional decoration and tents. ***Restaurant Waha***, T044-882354. Rather too far out of town for standard of food and price.

Mid-range Currently on the up is ***Chez Dimitri***, on Ave Mohammed V, in the town centre. Once the focus of Ouarzazate (as the bar of the Foreign Legion), the restaurant serves excellent European/Italian food, with a good lasagne; further out from the centre is the restaurant of the ***Hotel la Gazelle***, Ave Mohammed V, T044-882151. Try also ***La Kasbah***, opposite the Kasbah Taourirt, T044-882033, menu 100dh, no alcohol, good views if you eat outside, also ***La Datte d'Or***, on Ave Moulay Rachid, T044-887117, a new establishment with a menu at 100dh.

Cheap The cheapest places are along Rue du Marché and nearby streets. ***Restaurant Salam***, Ave du Prince Héritier Sidi Mohammed (and nothing to do with Hotel Salam), is a reasonable cheap touristy option for Moroccan food. ***Restaurant Chez Hellal***, 6 Rue du Marché, is a good choice. If passing through Ouarzazate, have lunch at the roast chicken restaurant almost opposite *Chez Dimitri*. Make sure you know what you're paying when you order. For breakfasts, try the ***Café du Sud***, on Ave Mohammed V towards the Kasbah Taourirt.

Bars The best place for a drink is obviously ***Chez Dimitri***, Ave Mohammed V.

Shopping Although much of the material on show is geared to the tourists who pass through each day to glimpse the kasbah, useful items like films, batteries for cameras, sun cream, writing paper and stamps can be obtained on Ave Mohammed V. In town there is the supermarket on Blvd Mohammed V, almost opposite *Chez Dimitri*, which even sells alcohol. On the same side of the street as the supermarket, look out for Abdallah Medkouri's shop sellling various local souvenirs and in particular pieces of *hizam*, a sort of carpet belt once worn by women in the region.

Sport **Golf** *Ouarzazate Royal Golf Club*, 9 holes, par 36, T044-882653, F044-883344. Green fees 150dh, open every day, a rather parched sort of course. **Go-Karting** With ***Kart aventure***, Ave Moulay Rachid, between the hotels ***Berbère Palace*** and the ***Kenzi Bélère***, T044-886374, F044-886216, full day's excursion in chunky off-road go-kart 1,700dh. **Riding Club** To east of town beyond kasbah. **Swimming** At major hotels and in particular the Complexe de Ouarzazate. That at the *Hotel Bélère* is very good, for around 50dh you can use pool as a non-resident.

Tour operators ***Ksour Voyages***, Place 3 Mars, T044-882840, turn left before the Palais des Congrès as you come from Marrakech; ***Palmiers Voyages***, place de la Poste, T044-882617; ***Top Voyages***, *Hotel Karam*, T044-883645, for excursions in the region.

Transport **Local** **Car hire**: ***Budget***, Ave Mohammed V, on the road to Marrakech, T044-882892. ***Hertz***, Blvd Mohammed V, T044-882048. ***Inter-Rent***, Place 3 Mars, T044-882035; other agencies around Place 3 Mars include ***Dani Car***.

Long distance Air There are flights from the Taourirt airport, T044-882383, north-east of the city, T044-882348, to **Casablanca** and **Marrakech** (4 a week) and **Agadir** (1 a week). International flights to **Europe** (mainly Paris) in season. For internal flights, whether you need to fill out a departure card is not entirely clear. ***Royal Air Maroc***, in Ave Mohammed V, can be contacted on T044-882348/044-883226.

Road Bus: To **Marrakech** cross the High Atlas by the impressive Tizi-n-Tichka pass. There are also several services a day to **Zagora**, east to **Boumalne**, **Tineghir**, **Er Rachidia**, and west to **Taroudant** and **Inezgane**. ***CTM*** buses, T044-882427, leave from the terminal on Ave Mohammed V, private line buses including ***SATAS*** from the *gare routière* outside town. ***CTM*** buses from Ouarzazate include: **Marrakech** 0830, 1130, 1230, 2100; **Agadir** 1200; **Casablanca** 2100; **M'Hamid** 1230; **Zagora** and **Agdz** 1230; **Er Rachidia** and **Tineghir** 1030. **Taxi**: From Place Al Mouahidine go to Skoura, Boumalne and Zagora amongst other destinations.

Directory

Airport T044-882345. ***RAM*** has an office on Ave Mohammed V, T044-885080. **Banks** ***Banque Populaire***, Ave Mohammed V. ***BMCE***, Ave Mohammed V and various others. **Communications** The PTT is on Ave Mohammed V. **Emergency numbers and addresses** Fire: T150. Police: Ave Mohammed V, T190. **Medical services** Chemist: ***Pharmacie de Nuit***, Ave Mohammed V, T044-882708, also on Ave Al Mouahidine. **Tourist offices** Ave Mohammed V, opposite the *CTM* bus terminal, T044-882485 (open 0900-1200 and 1430-1830 Mon-Fri). *Syndicat d'Initiative et du Tourisme*, Kasbah Taourirt.

Excursions from Ouarzazate

Mansour Eddahbi Dam

The best time to do this trip is spring or autumn

To the east of Ouarzazate, the Oued Draâ has been dammed to form a huge lake extending over 20 km in length and varying in width, as a number of tributaries such as the Oued Dadès and Oued Ouarzazate join the main valley. A few roads from the P32 lead down towards the northern shore. One is signed into a gated reserve, and another into the Golf Club. Access to the southern shore is more difficult and access to the dam itself is prohibited. Birdwatchers come here to see the wintering and migrating ducks and waders. Spoonbills and greater flamingoes make spectacular visitors, when there is sufficient water in the dam, that is. In recent years, water levels have fallen spectacularly, the golf course is a ghost of its former self, and the villas built as pricey lakeside retreats are now a fair way from the shore.

To get to the island in the barrage, contact Omar Aouzaale, BP206, 45000, Ouarzazate. He can also be contacted at *Club Med* on T044-890080. To get to the waterside at the gated reserve, just say you are a tourist or wave your binoculars and you should be able to go through.

Kasbah of Tiffoultoute

Take the road from Ouarzazate west across the causeway and turn right (north). After about 7 km you will come to the village of Tiffoultoute with a splendid kasbah built for the Glaoui family in the early 20th century. It stands alongside the Oued Igissi, the water from which is directed into a series of complicated irrigation channels. There are other kasbahs along this road, all interesting to see but none quite as spectacular as the first. At a main junction, take the road 5 km south back to Ouarzazate on the main Marrakech road.

Kasbah Aït Ben Haddou

Aït Ben Haddou is 30 km from Ouarzazate and its fame has spread far and wide. The kasbah sits on a dramatic hillside location and coach after coach drives up, pauses for a photograph to be taken and then returns.

The junction from the P32 after 22 km from Ouarzazate is clearly signed, and a large *marabout* with ridged cupola and crenellated edges on the tower is a prominent landmark to make sure you don't miss your way. The road, which is of fair quality, follows the valley, with the *oued* on the right. The first village is Tissergate, marked out in plots, the sandy soil growing cereals and onions, beans, citrus. A roadside seller takes advantage of the tour coaches and tries to sell large pieces of selenite. After a further 10 km the old kasbah comes into view on the right, in a bright green cultivated area. Quite a spectacular situation. The newer houses are set further away across the oued. The red towers of the kasbahs provide vantage points for views across the area and the old village also includes a large *agadir*, or store house, on the hilltop. Guides will show tourists around the kasbahs, which now figure on the UNESCO World Heritage List. Intricately decorated, they are relatively well preserved, no doubt thanks in part to film industry needs.

This was a strategic location on the old route from Marrakech to Ouarzazate from the 16th century. Few people live there now, however. The village is a must for tourists, both because of its intrinsic appeal and its role in the film industry, with *Lawrence of Arabia* and *Jewel of the Nile* filmed here, as well as *Jesus of Nazareth*, for which part of the settlement was actually rebuilt. Despite all the visitors, so far the area is not really spoilt.

Sleeping and eating As you drive up to Aït Ben Haddou on the metalled road, the hotels and restaurants are on your right, in the following order: ***Auberge Ben el Ouidane, Auberge La Kasbah, Restaurant Saghro, Auberge Al Baraka*** and ***Auberge Etoile Filante***, the latter being 400 m further on the left. At peak times of year, try to reserve accommodation in advance. **C/D** ***Auberge Ben el Ouidane***, T044-890312, F044-893737. 8 en suite rooms with view, 9 no view, all painted sandy brown. New rooms 1 person 270dh, 2 persons 280dh with breakfast, grey lino; old rooms 1 person 150dh, 2 persons 220dh. **C/D** ***Auberge La Kasbah***, T044-890302/08, F044-883787. 40 rooms, small, nice décor, 10 with shared bathrooms, 3 price categories: standard, 2 persons 320dh; without shower, 2 persons 260dh; and supérieur, 2 persons 480dh, a/c. Nice management, does car, mule and bike hire, pool, courtyard rooms hot in summer. Best choice here. **E** ***Auberge-Restaurant Al Baraka***, T044-890305, F044-886273. 80dh 1 person, 160dh 2 persons, a small place with a restaurant, ugly plastic tent out front and 5 fairly clean rooms, primitive washing arrangements, standards here are low, direct access to unprotected roof terrace extremely dangerous for children. **E** ***Auberge Etoile Filante***, T044-890322, F044-886113, 9 rooms at 100dh, set menu at 70dh. Nice welcome. A good cheap address.

To Tamdacht The road continues to the ford at Tamdacht, with accommodation at the gîte d'étape *La Kasbah* adjacent to the Oued Mellah (contact Abd el Aziz Taoufik on T044-890371) for 110dh a night. This is a splendid site. A bridge has been constructed, and with four-wheel drive you could carry on the 40 km or so remaining up to Tourhat along the Assif Ounila and then west to Telouet. The drive is described in more detail from the Telouet direction in the previous Jebel Toubkal chapter, and as stressed there, is not to be risked when there is lots of melt water or after late summer thunderstorms. Even the best off-road vehicle can be bogged down in the wet clay of the piste.

Gorges and kasbahs

The 'Road of the Thousand Kasbahs', as it is termed in the tourist blurbs, takes you from Ouarzazate up to Tineghir, via Skoura, El Kelaâ des Mgouna and Boumalne du Dadès, through arid plains and oases where the backdrop is one of harsh mountain landscapes, where semi-nomadic Berbers pasture their flocks. The modern world has arrived, however: tourist buses and four-wheel drives bring their flocks to the growing villages at the start of the spectacular gorges, and the new buildings replacing the crumbling kasbahs use concrete breeze blocks rather than pisé. Nevertheless, there is plenty of interest and walking opportunities along this route. Oases near to Ouarzazate like Skoura and El Kelaâ can be covered as day excursions, or you could do stop-overs while heading east to Er Rachidia. Those with four-wheel drive can try the bumpy mountain tracks leading into the Massif du Mgoun, from Skoura round to El Kelaâ via Toundout and Bou Thraghar, or the rugged gorge to gorge route from Boumalne to Tineghir, via Msemrir and Tamtatoucht.

As you set out travelling east of Ouarzazate on the P32, the land is flat and barren plain. To the north, outlying hills of the High Atlas become increasingly visible. To the right, signs indicate the presence of Al Mansour Eddahbi Barrage whose waters, in a good year, are just about visible from the road. No vegetation appears until the Oued Izerki provides water for cereals, olives and fruit trees. The golf course is a landmark. It has 'traditional style' villas beside the water and overlooking it and/or the green golf course.

The large oasis fed by the Oued Idelssan has irrigated gardens with palms, olives and cereals. The Oued Hajag crosses the road on the western side of Skoura. The small settlement here has a white square mosque with white cupola. The road rises up through the red clay-built houses and the oasis gardens.

Skoura oasis

The oasis is more interesting than the village at its centre: a large palmery surrounded by kasbahs and *ksour*. Before the village, to the left of the road, is **Kasbah d'Amerdihl**, the largest of Skoura's kasbahs. The village also includes two kasbahs formerly occupied by the El Glaoui family, **Dar Toundout** and **Dar Lahsoune**. Skoura village has a souk on Monday and Thursday, a few basic restaurants.

The older part of the town is to the north, providing all the usual services, petrol (*Ziz*), small shops in arcades on both sides of the road include bakers and pharmacy. If you stop, groups of children and youths will want to take you to the kasbahs. *Café Atlas* is clean and fairly welcoming and the *Café du Sud* is not too bad either. Since the construction of the by-pass road to the west, new buildings have filled in the space among the palm trees. There are plenty of kasbahs to walk around, some better than others. To get the maximum out of a wander round Skoura, you might as well take a local as a guide (50dh is a generous tip for a couple of hours). If by yourself, take care as it is sometimes difficult to see if a building is inhabited or not!

Sleeping and eating If you wish to stay, there is now an excellent option, just 3 km before Skoura proper, the **C** ***Kasbah Aït Ben Moro***, T/F044-852116. A beautifully restored building just a few metres off the main road. With so many concrete kasbahs around, it is splendid to find such a well restored building. Rooms are dark – as kasbah rooms had to be, décor is austere and elegant. From the roof terrace, views over the palm groves to the Kasbah d'Amerdihl. Prices 1 person 350dh, 2 persons 450dh, breakfast 40dh, meals 120dh. Capacity 24 rooms. Can organize horse riding, 350dh per day. Highly recommended, receptionist Aziz Sabir can be contacted T06-7194760 (mob). The alternative, some 200 m from the Kasbah d'Amerdihl, is **E** ***Chez Slimani***, a simple gîte-type place. And finally, at the bottom end of the market, there is the **F** ***Hotel Nakhil***, a primitive establishment for emergency use.

Imassine At Imassine, just east where the road crosses the Oued Dadès, there are two small places for a drink, the *Café des Amis* and the *Café Salam*. The number of new houses in **Aït Ridi** perhaps indicates money from abroad. This is the beginning of the rose-growing area. All the fields have hedges of roses, but there are no flowers to be seen because as soon as the bud opens the petals are picked.

El Kalaâ des Mgouna

Phone code: 044
Colour map 2, grid C2

Another ribbon-development sort of place, El Kelaâ des Mgouna, one hour 15 minutes drive from Ouarzazate, is the capital of the Moroccan rose-essence industry and centre of the Mgouna tribe. (The name means 'Citadel of the M'Gouna' and is also spelt Qalat Mgouna.) The former French administrative centre has become a sprawling town with banks, police, small shops for provisions, petrol and a Wednesday souk. The rose festival is held in late May/early June with dances and processions under a shower of rose petals. The children at the roadside will try to sell bunches of roses and garlands of rose petals, and there are plenty of shops selling rose water, *crème à la rose*, rose-scented soap and dried roses.

How is it then that El Kalaâ came to be a centre for this industry? A picturesque local legend runs that pilgrims travelling back from Mecca brought with them 'the Mother of All Flowers', the Damascus rose. It may be, however, that sometime in the 20th century, French perfumers realized that conditions in this out of the way part of southern Morocco would be ideal for the large-scale cultvation of the bushy Rosa Centifolia. Today, there are hundreds of kilometres of rose bush hedges, co-existing with other crops, and two factories, distilling rose essence. (The one in a kasbah-like building can be visited.) To produce a litre of good quality rose oil requires around five tonnes of petals, you will be told. The locals feel, however, that the price paid by the factories is too low, and prefer to sell dried rose petals on local markets. Pounded up, the petals can be used mixed with henna or other preparations. Rumour has it that Bulgarian rose growers are providing stiff competition for El Kelaâ.

Based in El Kelaâ, the energetic may want to head northwards 15 km up the M'Goun Valley to the Ksar de Bou Thrarar, at the entrance of the Mgoun Gorges. Less adventurously, there is a dagger-making co-operative on the eastern outskirts of the town. Trekking in the Massif Mgoun is covered in more detail in the chapter on the High Atlas of Azilal.

Sleeping & eating El Kelaâ does not have a vast range of accommodation – and you need to reserve if you are going to coincide with the rose festival (which in all honesty, is more for locals than tourists). **C** ***Hotel Les Roses de Mgouna***, T/F044-836007. 102 rooms, above the town at 1,927 m, a pure relic of the 1970s, with accommodation built around courtyards planted with bamboo and fruit trees. Reasonable restaurant, bar, nice pool with views of the Mgoun Massif. A sleepy sort of place, apart from the bar that is much used by locals. 1 person 250dh, 2 persons 300dh, breakfast 40dh. Prices negotiable out of season. **C** ***Hotel Rosa Damaskina***, pont d'Alnou, 6 km before El Kelaâ, to north of road, T044-836913, F044-836969. 2 persons 179dh with shower, 2 persons 130dh without, restaurant *Le Képi Blanc* (more memories of *la Légion*), beautiful views over river valley to poplar trees and ruined kasbah, small rose garden, tacky restaurant tent. An odd little place, fine for a night. **D/E** ***Kasbah Itren***, a tiny new auberge run by a Spanish-Moroccan partnership, up on a cliff on the road up into the Massif du Mgoun. 5 simple rooms, views of Kasbah Mirna to south and Kasbah du Glaoui to north, contact mountain guide Mohammed Taghada, T06-6161147, can organize treks for 350dh, 1 person night all in. **F** ***Hotel du Grand Atlas***, Ave Mohammed V, T044-836838. 12 rooms, basic and friendly. Communal showers. The owners can help you set up trekking into the nearby Massif du Mgoun.

Shopping

Apart from the ubiquitous rose products (best buy: large pink heart-shaped rose-flavoured soap), you could try the *Coopérative du poignard*, the Dagger Makers' Co-operative, on the right shortly after the centre. Making daggers is a craft tradition carried on from the now-departed Jewish communities in the region, and most of the artisans are concentrated in Azlague, south of the Co-operative. A good dagger, purely for ornamental use of course, may cost anything up to 400dh.

Sports

El Kelaâ is a good base town for trekking, call in at the ***Bureau des Guides de Montagne***, 1 km before the town centre, on south side of road, clearly signed, T044-836311. As elsewhere, the daily rate for a guide is around 200dh. The *Hotel du Grand Atlas* has plenty of contacts with guides. Ambitious walkers in late spring and summer may want to try to climb Irhil Mgoun, at 4,068 m one of the highest peaks in the central High Atlas. A good 7-day circuit would take you up to Amesker and back via Aït Youl.

Directory

Banks *Wafa Bank* and *Banque Populaire* right on main intersection. **Medical services** **Pharmacy** on left (east) after *Banque Populaire*, also on street leading to *Hotel Rose de Mgouna*. **Doctors**: Dr Brahim Charaf, T044-836118, home T044-850061.

El Kelaâ des Mgouna to Boumalne du Dadès

After El Kelaâ des Mgouna, the 20 km to Boumalne is heavily built up, in some places three blocks deep. As you leave El Kelaâ heading east, watch out for a bad bend marked by red/white crash barriers on the right. Much of the building is financed by locals who have emigrated to Europe and are putting up something for their retirement. Behind the houses is a string of prosperous oasis gardens, with dilapidated kasbahs popping up at intervals.

The Dadès and Todgha Gorges

Phone code: 044
Colour map 2, grid B3

Over the centuries, coming down from the High Atlas, the Oued Dadès and Oued Todgha have carved out narrow and spectacular gorges. These make attractive excursions from Boumalne (for the Dadès) and Tineghir (for the Todgha). Both gorges offer options for walking up into the mountains beyond. For the really rugged, it is possible to travel north up into the High Atlas to Imilchil and the Plateau des Lacs via remote Agoundal, and there is also a rough piste leading from Msemrir, on the Dadès round to Tamtatoucht, on the Todgha. However, most people choose just to walk in the lower gorges and enjoy the scenery from the pleasant vantage point of the restaurants located nearby. There are some fine opportunities for birdwatching.

Ins & outs

Both Boumalne (116 km from Ouarzazate), for exploring the Dadès Gorge, and Tineghir (170 km from Ouarzazate), for exploring the Todgha, are easily accessible by bus and grand taxi. Both places are on the P32 road linking Ouarzazate to Er Rachidia. There are grands taxis between Boumalne and Tineghir, taking about an hour. Tineghir is 5 hrs by bus from Ouarzazate. If in own car, note that when passing through ribbon settlements in this region in the evening you need to drive with care, watching out for small children, bicycles, mopeds and donkeys. There is quite a lot of four-wheel drive tourist traffic, too, which tends to race along too fast. Alternatively, you might approach Tineghir and Boumalne from the east, coming in from Er Rachidia or Erfoud via Tinejdad. On public transport, both Er Rachidia and Erfoud lie about 3 hrs from Tineghir.

Boumalne du Dadès

Colour map 2, grid B3

Boumalne is a small town (Wednesday market), with a reasonable selection of hotels. The town grew from a very basic settlement to its current size mainly in the second half of the 20th century. In the Muslim cemetery there is the domed shrine of one Sidi Daoud. He is commemorated in an annual festival, when bread is baked from flour left at the grave, and fed to husbands to ensure their fertility.

However, visitors really go to Boumalne for the landscape, harsh and rocky. From a high point above the town, a barracks and some hotels look out over the landscape. If you are a birdwatcher, you may well want to head off south to the Vallée des Oiseaux (the road from Boumalne to Iknioun). Otherwise, there are rewarding short walks up into the gorge. Msemrir, 60 km up the gorge, is a possible destination using local transport. Should you want to stay in the gorges, there is some basic accommodation at Aït Oudinar.

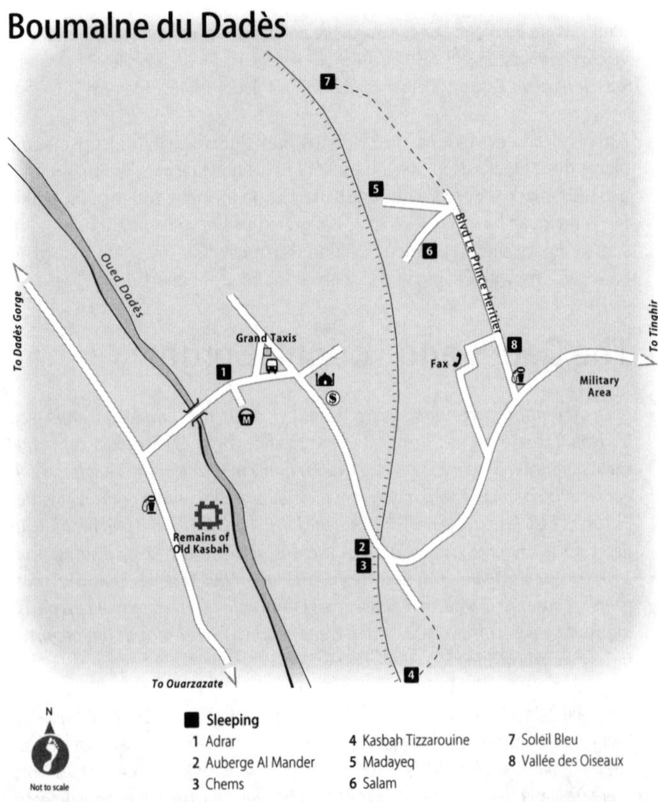

Approaching Boumalne from the west, note that there is usually a Gendarmerie royale check point at the intersection before the bridge, so slow down.

Sleeping

■ *on map*
Price codes: see inside front cover

C ***Kasbah Tizzarouine***, T044-830690/06134812, F044-830256. A largish hotel complex situated on the plateau, which overlooks Boumalne from the south (at top of slope, turn right just before large mural). There are fine views over the Oued Dadès and the mountains to the north. Accommodation includes fairly traditional buildings with all modern comforts, tiny underground rooms (troglodyte), cool in summer and cosy in winter, or even nomad tents kept cool by the breeze. Establishment is now too big with tent for entertainments and tour group lunches plus large conference rooms, pool under construction. A fairly well run address if lacking the personal touch. Prefer the *Kasbah Tomboctou*, Tineghir at this price, or the *Aït Ben Moro*, Skoura, slightly dearer. **C** ***Hotel Madayeq***, T/F044-830763. 100 rooms, comfortable, a/c, restaurant, bar and rooftop pool, only reception is very off-hand, once past them it is sunshine all the way. **D** ***Hotel-Restaurant Chems***, T044-830041, F044-831308. 10 double rooms and 5 single rooms, breakfast 20dh, at the top of the slope heading for Er Rachidia, on the right on the bend. Well maintained, nice reception, restaurant.

E ***Auberge de Soleil Bleu***, off to the right before the *Hotel Madayeq*, T044-830163. 12 rooms with bath, good restaurant, fine views, camping permitted, treks organized into High Atlas and Jebel Saghro by local guide Mustapha Najim. Popular with walkers and birdwatchers. **E** ***Hotel-Restaurant Salam***, T044-830762, near the *Hotel Madayeq*. A friendly and helpful place which provides free transport to Aït Oudinar in the gorge, and organizes skiing, trekking, 4WD, mountain bikes, contact Daoud in Boumalne, 15 rooms, shared showers, heating, rooftop terrace and restaurant with local food. Recommended. **E** ***Auberge Al Manader***, T044-830172, on the Er Rachidia road, near the *Hotel Chems*. 8 good clean rooms, 4 with bathroom, small restaurant, panoramic views as the name in Arabic suggests. **E** ***Hotel-Restaurant Vallée des Oiseaux***, T044-830764, on the Er Rachidia side of Boumalne, near the *Shell* station. 12 comfortable rooms and restaurant, can set up trips into the mountains, cheap rooms 70dh, with shower 110dh, open fire in winter. **F** ***Hotel Adrar***, opposite the souk, T044-830355. 27 rooms around a courtyard, with restaurant.

Eating

The best restaurant in town was once at the ***Hotel Madayeq***. Cheaper options include ***Hotel-Restaurant Salam*** and the ***Café Atlas***, in the centre, good for food or just a tea or coffee; just outside Boumalne, on the Er Rachidia road, ***Restaurant Chems*** is perhaps the best option with its pleasant terrace.

Gorges du Dadès

Colour map 2, grid B3

The 6901 leaves the P31 at Boumalne and follows the Oued Dadès through limestone cliffs, which form the striking Gorges du Dadès. The principal destination is the section of the gorges following Aït Oudinar, but the track continues up into the High Atlas, with public transport as far as Msemrir. There are very basic pistes into the mountains, and around into the Gorges du Todgha.

Just beyond Boumalne is **Aït Arbi**, where there is a series of striking *ksour* above the road. The road continues past areas of unusual rock formations, through Tamnalt and Aït Oudinar, where there is basic accommodation. The valley narrows after Aït Oudinar, creating the most striking area of the gorges, where the cliffs are in vivid shades of red. The road, now surfaced practically all the way, continues alongside the *oued* as far as Msemrir, just beyond which it branches. The right-hand branch turns into a difficult track, running east across the pass (2,800 m) and continuing to link with the 6902 through the

Gorges du Todgha, and up into the High Atlas. The gorges and crags offer a good environment for golden and Bonelli's eagles and lammergeiers, and the scree slopes for blue rock thrushes.

Back on the main P32 road, the track southeast which leaves the road just east of Boumalne gives easy access into the desert environment. It rises steadily to **Tagdilt** and provides an experience of the desert, and possibilities for spotting desert birds and, less likely, desert fauna.

Sleeping There are a number of small places to stay up in the Gorges du Dadès. However, standards of hygiene are variable, and the loos don't always seem to keep up with the influx of visitors. By the time of going to press, electricity should have arrived, which should lead to an improvement in food standards. When staying in simple places like these, make sure you know what you have to pay when you settle in. Note that Aït Oudinar makes a good starting point for a walking circuit.

Aït Oudinar In Tamnalt, some 14 km from Boumalne, accommodation and food are available at the **E *Hotel-Restaurant Meguirne*** and further on at the ***Hotel-Restaurant Kasbah***, 13 rooms and insufficient loos. 25 km from Boumalne is Aït Oudinar, with the **C *Auberge Chez Pierre***, T044-830267, a tasteful Belgian-run establishment with rooms and excellent food. Try also the **E *Auberge des Gorges du Dadès Aït Oudinar***, T044-831710, 25 rooms, restaurant, téléboutique. Variable reports on this. Facilities for campers and camper-vanners nearby.

Further on F *Auberge des Peupliers*, 27 km up in the valley, T044-831748, 4 rooms and camping, and the **E *Kasbah de la Vallée du Dadès***, about 27 km from Boumalne. Good reports. Most basic of all is the ***Auberge Tissadrine***, T044-831745, cheap and fairly clean. At Aït Hammou there is the simple **F *Café-Hotel Taghea***, with several rooms but no electricity. Basic accommodation is available at Msemrir (***Café Agdal*** and ***Hotel Ouarda***).

Boumalne du Dadès to Tineghir From Boumalne to Tineghir the road runs across a flat plateau land, between the southern side of the High Atlas, to the north, and the eastern end of the arid Jebel Saghro, to the south, forming a clear line. This is mining country, also a land of resistance to French forces. A track leads south to the 2,200 m Tizi-n-Tazazert shortly after Boumalne, and to Iknioun and Jebel Bou Gafer. The mining centre of **Imiter** is signed. At **Timadriouine** a track leads south to mines (silver) which can be seen from the road, and northwards to Arg Sidi Ali ou Bourek. A number of ruined *ksour* stand in the valley at Imiter, some quite tall. There is sparse pasture land between. 52 km from Boumalne, 166 km from Ouarzazate, **Tineghir** appears in the distance down a long straight stretch of road.

Tineghir الرشيدية

Colour map 2, grid B3

Once a tiny oasis settlement, Tineghir is a large, modern administrative centre, its population swelled by technicians and staff working for the local mining company. Tourism is taking on importance, and the town is an ideal overnight on the long road east to the Tafilalelt, the Gorges du Todgha being the sight to see. It also makes a good first night on a walking holiday.

Tineghir is an unexpectedly large place. There is the modern hub, now ribboning east and west along the P32. And then there are the older kasbah settlements, a few kilometres north from the town, overlooking an irrigated plain as one climbs out of the town towards the Gorges du Todgha. There is a stark contrast of magnificent barren mountains and verdant oases. For the rushed, there are views from the gorge road - otherwise you might explore on foot. Hire a guide for 40dh. You will find olive and fruit trees intercropped with cereals and vegetables, herds of sheep and goats out to pasture in the foothills. As elsewhere in the region, there is much new building along the roads, the old *ksour* partly abandoned to the side. The main population belong to the Aït Atta tribe. Try to visit the Kasbah El Glaoui. Although officially closed, it is normally possible to get in.

Sleeping

■ *on map*
Price codes:
see inside front cover

Nothing too complicated about Tineghir, which focuses on 2 squares, one with trees on the main road, and another a block back from the main street, sort of behind the post office. Town hotels are located around these 2 areas. The other option for accommodation is to head up into the gorges, taking a local grand taxi from the centre, or, with own transport, turn left before the low bridge on the eastern side of town (see below).

B ***Hotel Kenzi Bougafer***, Blvd Mohammed V, T044-833200/80, F044-833282. An early 1990s hotel 2 km west of town, comfortable, clean, good pool, alcohol, noisy with footsteps and door slamming echoing through building. **C** ***Hotel Saghro***, T044-834181, F044-834352, on the Ouarzazate road, with the appearance of a *ksar*. 62 comfortable rooms, a restaurant, bar and pool. **D** ***Hotel Tomboctou***, Ave Bir Anzane (take 1st major left coming into Tineghir from west), T044-834604, F044-833505. 250dh 1 person, 2 persons 300dh with loo, 1 person 89dh, 2 persons 156dh, no loo, 30dh breakfast, nice cool rooms in restored kasbah, small pool, 10dh extra for secure car parking. The Spanish owner is an authority on the region. Mountain bikes for rent, plus sketch maps of region. Best hotel. **E** ***Hotel l'avenir***, on the 2nd square, T044-834599. On 1st floor above a pharmacy, 12 small rooms, 1 person 60dh, 2 persons 100dh, 3 persons 130dh, very clean, good beds, roof terrace. Disadvantages: some rooms only open onto corridor, square below is noisy. Still the best cheap hotel. Bike hire. **E** ***Hotel Todgha***, 32 Ave Hassan II, T044-834249. 30 rooms, restaurant, over-priced. **F** ***Hotel El Fath***, Ave Hassan II, T044-844806. Next to the *CTM* bureau. Hot showers. Café-restaurant. **F** ***Hotel Houda***, Rue Moulay Ismaïl. A recent hotel, on a side street off Ave Hassan II. **F** ***Hotel Oasis***, Place Principale. Cheap, clean, central, welcoming, upstairs restaurant with good food and views over town. **F** ***Hotel Essalam***, on a side street behind the Place Principale. Basic, 1 person 25dh, hot foam mattresses. Acceptable if all else fails.

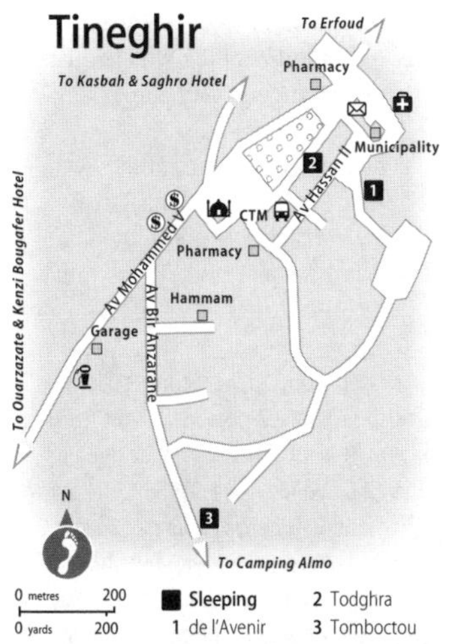

Camping *Camping Almo*, 8dh pp, is in centre of town, on south of road, very secure, with pool and shop, only open in summer. ***Camping Ourti***, south of road at western end of town beyond *Hotel Bougafer*, very secure, restaurant, bungalows, pool but quite a walk from town. All sites have electricity for caravans. Perhaps the best of the bunch.

Eating

No exciting gastronomic choices here. ***Hotel Saghro*** has a fair though expensive restaurant. ***Hotel Todgha***, 32 Ave Hassan II; and ***Hotel Oasis***, Place Principale, are a little cheaper. ***La Gazelle d'Or***, in the town centre, is also good. ***La Kasbah***, Ave Mohammed V, a friendly place with good food. A good café is ***Chez Habib***.

Shopping There is a Tue souk, behind the *Hotel Todgha*. The PTT is on the main square (the *Place Principale*), as are small shops, restaurants, cafés and grand taxi station, while the *Banque du Maroc*, along with other banks, are on the Ave Mohammed V. A welcome new addition to the Tineghir shopping scene is ***Chez Michelle***, T044-834668, a new supermarket (alcohol available), on your right after ***Ziz*** petrol as you come in from east. Look out for green façade.

Transport **Buses** and **grands taxis** to all locations, including **Ouarzazate**, **Boumalne** and **Er Rachidia**, leave from Place Principale. Grands taxis and vans run from Place Principale to the gorge. In some hotels, staff may organize trips to the gorge for 60dh. For locals, a place in a share taxi up the gorge costs 6dh, the whole taxi costing 36dh. Tineghir to **Boulmane** is 25dh by grand taxi, Tineghir to **Er Rachidia** 45dh.

Gorges du Todgha

Colour map 2, grid B3

The Gorges du Todgha are more spectacular than the Gorges du Dadès, particularly in the evening when the rocks are coloured in bands of bright sunlight and dark shadow. There are campsites and places to stay near the narrowest part of the gorge, a highly recommended break from the activity of the major towns.

The 14 km route is very narrow, and you will have to slow down for kids playing near the road. Also watch out for the tyre-splitting road edge when you move over for a bus thundering towards you. (Tourist buses and four-wheel drives head up to the gorge for lunch.)

Just north of Tineghir as the road climbs up is the village of Aït Ouaritane. There are many good views. The safest place to stop is generally picketed with camels, the most spectacular has the usual fossil and scarf sellers. Photocall for neat strips of crops in the oasis gardens and crumbling kasbah villages.

Some 9 km from Tineghir are campsites in an idyllic location in a palmgrove. About 6 km further on is the most visited section of the gorge, where the high cliffs leave just enough space for the road and river. As you might imagine, rocks, palm groves and river make this a good environment for birds. There are a couple of hotels (*La Vallée* and *Etoile des Gorges*) before the ford, and in the past there was a small toll to pay for taking one's car up beyond this point. Or someone would say that 'the gorges are closed', obliging you to park and pay them a car park fee. The ford should present no problems for ordinary cars, and you can carry on up to the next two hotels, *Les Roches* and *Yasmina*, which squat in the bogus kasbah-style under a spectacularly overhanging bit of gorge.

Sleeping There are plenty of options in the gorges, for all budgets, including campsites with facilities for campervans, and a number of hotels, some now quite substantial. In winter it gets pretty chilly at night up in the gorge hotels and campsites, and in late summer the river can swell suddenly after thunderstorms in the mountains, so choose your camping place with care.

D ***Hotel Amazir***, on your right after *Camping Des Poissons Sacrés*, stone building, T044-895109, F044-895050. Opened 2001, 1 person 170dh, 2 persons 300dh, with breakfast. 15 rooms (6 triple, 9 double), manager Omar Aït Chaoui very anxious to please. Recommended. **E** ***Hotel-Restaurant Auberge La Vallée***, T044-835580, on your left as you arrive. Small basic rooms, nice management. **E** ***Auberge Etoile des Gorges***, T044-835158. Another tiny, adequate hotel, 6 rooms, some with en suite hot shower. **D** ***Hotel Les Roches***, T044-834814, F044-833611, at the end of the road. Perfectly adequate, 30 rooms 1 person 129dh, 2 persons 200dh, 50dh to sleep out on terrace with mattress, lunchtime menu 90dh, tour group restaurant in plastic ceremonial tent. Why put such an ordinary building in such an extraordinary place? **D** ***Hotel Yasmina***, T044-895118, F044-833013. 2 persons 200dh, 1 person 110dh, breakfast included, amazingly kitsch shiny green bedspreads in new rooms, restaurant in tent for tour groups. Camping here by arrangement. Sleeping on roof (mattress provided) is 20dh per person and includes a hot shower. For these 2 hotels, hot water is only provided when the generator is working to produce light - so have your shower in the evening. Take a torch.

Camping As you head up into the Gorges, the first accommodation is a new campsite, 8 km from Tineghir, on your left. The better is *Hotel-Camping du Soleil*, aka *Chez Bernard*, T044-895111, open since Dec 2000, pool under completion, a bit lacking in shade, otherwise excellent, new loo block, washing machines, some rooms, 1 person 100dh without shower, 200dh with bath and loo, night under tent 25dh, restaurant 114 seats, meal around 100dh. Recommended, ably run by Bernard, formerly with the Légion, and Issa. The best option, although a fair way from the gorges. Can put you in contact with a local for mule rides in the region. Next door is the **E** ***Hotel Camping Azlag***, T044-896050, 5 nice rooms, 2 persons 80dh, small campsite out back with bamboo canopy, breakfast 15dh, meal 55dh. There are 3 camping sites on the right a bit further on along the road leading towards the gorges, all of which do rooms. First along is ***Camping Atlas***, **E** ***Hotel-Camping Atlas***, T/F044-895046. 6 rooms, 2 persons 90dh, 3 persons 140dh, just opposite téléboutique. Also camping 20dh, campervan 1 person 10dh, tent 15dh, car 15dh, hot shower included. Rooms are in small building overlooking site, meals to order 60dh, definitely the best of the 3, same management as *Hotel Amazir*. ***Camping du Lac***, T044-895005. Bar, restaurant, more expensive. Has rooms as well in building over the road, 2 persons 100dh. ***Camping des Poissons Sacrés ('Sacred Fish' campsite)***, T044-895139. 10 tent pitches, 5 rooms, faintly smelly, has a slightly dodgy feel to it. Management needs changing, basically. Have a look in to see the fish if you're nearby.

Tamtatouchte & around

The more adventurous will want to continue beyond the narrow confines of the Gorges du Todgha. The village of Tamtatouchte is a walk of about four hours considering the steady climb. The *Auberge Baddou*, the *Auberge Bougafer* and various other rudimentary establishments provide food and accommodation. A few lorries returning from the souk use this route and would provide a lift, which will prove to be a very slow, very dusty and very bumpy ride. With four-wheel drive many of the smaller villages to the north can be reached. By far the greatest danger to walkers are the fleets of Fronteras and squads of adapted motorbikes using these routes. With a good driver, connections can thus be made westward with the Dadès Gorge or northwards to Imilchil.

Gorge to Gorge route

Though rough, the 42 km west to **Msemrir from Tamtatoucht**, rising to a height of 2,800 m, is popular with the four-wheel drive brigade. It can be done in five hours, they say. This journey is best undertaken in a good four-wheel drive vehicle with reliable local driver. Ensure that tyre pressure is higher than normal, as tracks are very stony, and that you have a full tank. Find out about the condition of the piste before departure.

This route is best undertaken between May and September. At other times of year, potential flash floods make it dangerous. It is probably best to do this route starting at the Todgha Gorge so you do the most difficult pass, the one after Tamtatouche, 2,639 m, first. At **Msemrir**, a popular base village for treks, there are a couple of simple places to stay, including the *Auberge el Ouarda* and the *Auberge Agdal*.

Excursions south from Tineghir The village of **Aït Mohammed** is southeast of Tineghir and is clearly visible from the main road. It stands on the minor road which goes along the *oued* to **El Hart-n'Igouramène**. A track due south leads into the Jebel Saghro, aiming for the village of Iknioun which nestles under the central heights.

The road from Tineghir keeps to the south of the imposing Jebel Tisdafine. At 10 km from town a track to the right goes to Alnif (63 km) and a connection with the desert road from Erfoud to Zagora.

East from Tineghir to Er Rachidia

In terms of public transport, buses run from Tineghir to Er Rachidia, or from Tinejdad, en route, across to Erfoud. There are grands taxis from Tineghir to Tinejdad, Tinejdad to Goulmima, and Goulmima to Er Rachidia. Tineghir to Tinejdad takes about an hour on public transport. Er Rachidia is roughly two hours from Tinejdad, as is Erfoud.

Tinejdad East from Tineghir, the first major stop is Tinejdad, where the road forks and you have the choice of heading northeast for Er Rachidia or more directly east for Erfoud, Rissani and Merzouga. Tinejdad is a Berber and Haratine town in a large oasis, with some significant kasbahs, notably the **Ksar Asrir**; and the **F** *Hotel-Restaurant Tizgui*, with basic accommodation and food. There are an amazing number of bicycles in Tinejdad, every child seems to own one so be particularly careful when driving through. The central square offers a post office, the town gardens, town hall, telephones, taxis and *Total* petrol. There is a weekly souk. *Café El Fath*, *Café Assagm* and *Café Ferkla* are possibilities for refreshment. *Café Oued Ed-Dahab* stands north of Tinejdad at the junction with the road to Erfoud. It is a good place to stop offering cold drinks and juice, but you may find the place overrun with people from safari tours or even convoys of campervans.

The road from this Tinejdad junction goes due north, leaving the palms of the oasis gardens for dry farming cereals on the level plain and aiming for a gap in the scarp, a gorge cut by the Oued Gheris. This is an extension of the scarp through which the gorges of Dadès and Todgha are cut.

Goulmima Goulmima (not to be confused with Goulimine, aka Guelmime, south of Agadir) is one of a series of expanding small towns, mainly Amazigh in population, round the eastern side of the High Atlas. Er Rachidia, Rich and Midelt are others of similar ilk.

There is a lot of new property on the outskirts, well served with water, electricity and telephone. The centre of Goulmima is similar to Tineghir, and there are a large number of *ksour* out in the palm groves. Much of the town is to the north of the road in the main oasis.

Approaching the centre, after passing through the usual mechanics and carpenters on the outskirts, the road becomes wider. There are ministry buildings on both sides, a hospital on the left, village gardens on the right desperately in need of some attention. Opposite the garden is a bus station and a walled area for grands taxis, which extends about 200 m into town. *Agip* petrol station on the left before the market square. Market day Monday. Sleeping options include a guesthouse, **D** *Les Palmiers* (Franco-Moroccan management, rec), T055-784004, with 5 clean rooms and space for small tents in garden. More basic is the **F** *Hotel Gheris*, T055-783167, with 10 reasonable rooms, restaurant with good food. In this area are situated the pharmacy, telephone boutique and after 50 m *Petit Restaurant* advertising sandwiches, with chairs under the trees, all on the right. In the arcade of shops you will find another café, telephone, shop for stamps and postcards, *Restaurant Badou* and beyond up on the left the covered souk. *Camping Tamaris*, on a site of 4 ha, showers, petrol station 100 m.

Heading east out of Goulmima, the road sweeps up and over the *oued* after the *Ziz* petrol station. A high bridge indicates potential floods. The road climbs up sharply between the gardens, through the scarp (good views looking back).

Alternative routes from Goulmima

There is a road north from Goulmima leading to the villages of the High Atlas, only suitable for four-wheel drive. It is 'surfaced' for the 55 km to **Amellago**, from where it is possible to circle back to the Todgha Gorge and/or the Dadès Gorge. More handily, Amellago is on the recently surfaced Rich to Imilchil road, cutting right into the heart of the eastern High Atlas. There is a road southeast to **Gaouz** (4 km) and eventually to **Touroug** on the road to Erfoud.

The last 58 km to Er Rachidia are up on the plateau, where the Jebel Timetrout runs parallel to the road on the north side. It is very poor land, scrappy pasture for large flocks of sheep and goats and in places dromedaries herded by nomads with black tents. Changes in animal husbandry are under way. Shepherds sometimes ride motor bikes, while water is provided at evenly spaced drinking and penning areas. More spectacularly, livestock owners transport their flocks in lorries to find the best seasonal grazing.

Er Rachidia الرشيدية

Phone code: 055
Colour map 2, grid B5

Er Rachidia, previously known as Ksar Es Souk, was renamed after the first Alaouite leader, 17th-century Sultan Moulay Rachid, after independence. The Alaouites came from the Tafilalelt region. The present town was established by the French, initially by the Foreign Legion, as a military and administrative centre, a role it retains today. The town has little of interest for the visitor, beyond a 19th-century ksar near the Erfoud exit. It has the usual concrete architecture. Behind the new brown and red buildings, the older mud-walled dwellings still exist. Er Rachidia, however, is a convenient stopping point at the meeting of routes to Ouarzazate, Erfoud (south), Midelt and Meknès (north) and distant Figuig (east), and so has reasonable facilities and a relaxed atmosphere, with lots of people out strolling in the evenings after the heat of the day. Main market days in Er Rachidia are Sunday, Tuesday and Thursday.

Ins and outs

Getting there
See page 216 for further details

You will probably head for Er Rachidia by road. (There were no regular flights to the Aéroport Er Rachidia, T055-572350, in early 2001.) Should there be flights, a short taxi ride will take you into town. There are several buses a day for Erfoud and Rissani (2 hrs), Midelt (3 hrs), Tineghir (31/2 hrs), Fès (9 hrs) and Meknès (8 hrs), and one each morning to Figuig (8 hrs). There are frequent grands taxis to Erfoud and Meski, Goulmima and Tinejdad, from the taxi rank opposite the bus station.

Getting around

The grid iron street pattern, so typical of French garrison towns in the Sahara, makes orientation simple. The main road, Ave Moulay Ali Cherif, leads down to the new bridge over the Oued Ziz, after which it becomes the Ave El Massira. The *gare routière* (T055-572024) is on the right in the town centre as you head east.

Sights

Er Rachidia is not exactly blessed with myriad sights but architecture buffs may want to take a look at the historic **Ksar Targa**, about 5 km from the centre. Of passing interest are the **social housing developments** on either side of the Midelt road. Here the architects put new homes within neo-ksar type walls, painted a strong, Marrakech terracotta colour. As the largest town in the southeast, close to the Algerian frontier, it was clearly necessary for the modern Moroccan state to mark its presence by such projects.

Should you wish to get to the *Source Bleue* at Meski, 21 km south of Er Rachidia on the Erfoud road, you could take a grand taxi, paying the same price as for Erfoud - the *Source* and campsite are a few hundred metres from the road. Moving on from Meski, you might be able to get a bus, or (easier) hitch a lift with other tourists. Another option for a side trip are the hot springs of **Moulay Ali Cherif**, 42 km north of Er Rachidia on the P21 Midelt road - the first section, past the Barrage Hassan el Dakhil, through the Ziz Gorges past the village of Ifri and the Legionnaire's Tunnel, is truly magnificent.

Excursions

North through the Gorges of the Ziz

The P21 north to the Gorges of the Ziz is a superb route. For the first 20 km the road follows the Oued Ziz. Caves can be seen cut into the cliff, for use as storage. Then you come to the western shore of the Barrage de Hassan el Dakhil, completed in 1971. The dam ensures a regular water supply for Er Rachidia and the oasis gardens requiring irrigation, and limits the potentially destructive flash flooding of the Oued Ziz. The waters of the dam also provide a rest haven for migrating birds. Travelling this route in the evening, the sun accentuates the unusual landforms of the area, bands of hard rock with screes between. And then you come to the Gorges of Ziz, a spectacular ride in a narrow defile 2 km in length. At around 29 km from Er Rachidia,

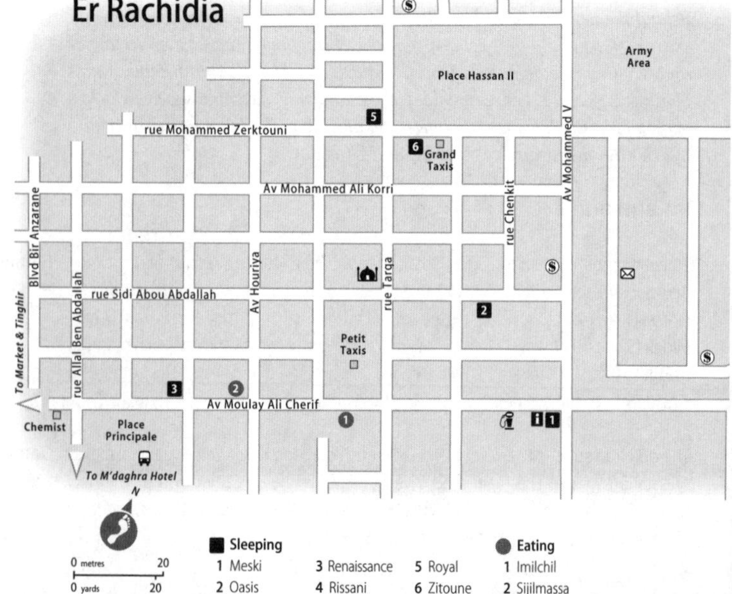

where a bridge crosses the river, there is a small settlement where picnicking and camping are possible. On the return journey take the road which goes to the dam wall, and follow it across the irrigation channels and through the oasis gardens of Tirhiourine. Keep to the surfaced road and eventually return to the P32 back to Er Rachidia.

If you are travelling north from Er Rachidia to complete a High Atlas circular tour, then the P21 can be followed on up to Midelt, the next major town where there is some fairly decent accommodation, 156 km from Er Rachidia.

Meski

The Ksar of Meski is around 500 years old and the ruins make an attractive silhouette

Heading for the Tafilalelt from Er Rachidia, you have 94 km to go before Rissani. Meski, lying to the west of the Erfoud road about 18 km south of Er Rachidia, is the first halt, famed for its *Source Bleue*. Developed by the Foreign Legion, Meski has a springwater pool surrounded by palms, and a popular camp site, the *Camping de la Source Bleue*, about 40dh for two with tent and car. Almost too lively in summer, the campsite (which had a poor reputation in the mid-1990s) is said to have improved considerably. Lots of fossil sellers nearby.

Continuing south on the P21 towards Erfoud, you could easily miss one of the most spectacular views in Morocco. Keeping an eye out, you will eventually glimpse the huge **oasis-canyon of the Oued Ziz** to the right (west). There is a track marked by a small cairn which goes across to the edge of the gorge. The view is magnificent - and you will probably see other tourist vehicles there admiring the scenery.

Essentials

Sleeping

■ on map

Kenzi-Rissani, Ave El Massira (de la Marche Verte), in the direction of Erfoud

Price codes: see inside front cover

There is not a huge choice of hotels in Er Rachidia, especially at top of the range. **B** ***Hotel Kenzi-Rissani***, Ave El Massira (de la Marche Verte), in the direction of Erfoud, T055-572184/86, F055-572585. Pleasant location on the town's outskirts, 60 rooms, restaurant, bar, disco, tennis and pool, open to non-residents for 50dh daily. Gets booked up by tour groups at peak times. **D** ***Hotel M'daghra***, Rue Allal ben Abdallah, T055-574047, F055-790864. Popular, try to reserve. If coming from west, turn left at *Café Lipton* on main drag, hotel 100 m down on right. 29 rooms, a little noisy, very clean, nice reception (goldfish), the best bet, have breakfast in café nearby. **D** ***Hotel Oasis***, 4 Rue Sidi Abou Abdallah, T055-572519. A modern place with 46 small hot rooms, lovely wallpaper, restaurant and bar, if stuck only. **E** ***Hotel Meski***, Ave Moulay Ali Cherif, T055-572065, near the intersection with the Midelt road. 25 rooms with uninteresting restaurant, café and small pool, streetside rooms noisy. **F** ***Hotel Ansar***, 34 Rue Ben Batouta, T055-573919. Clean, 14 rooms, on street leading away from main street behind bus station. **F** ***Hotel Renaissance***, 19 Rue Moulay Youssef, T055-572633. 15 none-too-clean rooms, people are helpful, restaurant, has limited choice but OK food. Close to bus station. **F** ***Royal***, 8 Rue Mohammed Zerktouni, T055-573068. 21 rooms, 31 beds, ask

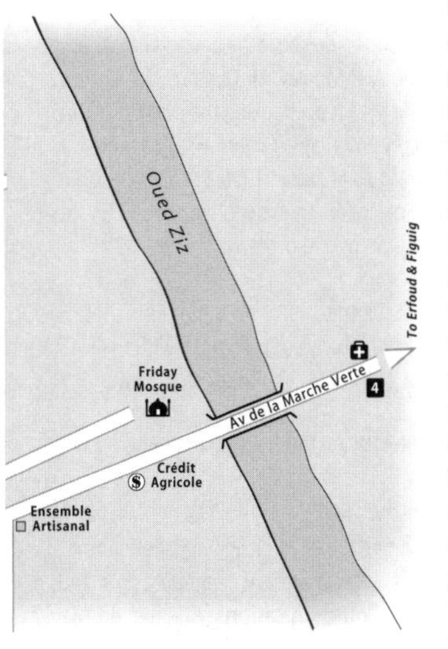

The mountain barred the way

When the French pushed roads out across southern Morocco in the late 1920s and 1930s, there was still much resistance to the outside world. Sometimes a local ruler made it impossible for a road to be built – witness Telouet. There Caïd Hammou el Glaoui was so anti-French that the road had to be taken over the nearby Tizi-n-Tichka rather than the easier Tizi-n-Telouet. Capable road builders were in short supply, too, so it was to the Foreign Legion that the task was often entrusted. Costs also had to be kept down, so there was no question of undertaking masses of slow tunnel building. Hence Atlas roads often snake down the mountain sides in breathtaking loops and hairpin bends. Take, for example, the routes over Jebel Afourer between Beni Mellal and Ouaouizaght. The hairpin tradition continues with the numerous new pistes – see the spectacular track running down from the Tizi-n-Tazazougart, southeast of Anergui in the High Atlas of Azilal.

Sometimes a tunnel was unavoidable. To complete the route round the eastern end of the High Atlas, linking Er Rachidia and Midelt via the Gorges du Ziz, the only option was to dig. 100 km south of Midelt, 56 km north of Er Rachidia, the Tunnel du Légionnaire is still in use today. Eight metres wide, 3 metres high, 60 metres long, it was built in 6 months by 40 légionnaires. Plaques at the entrances to the tunnel commemorated their achievement, but were destroyed after independence. One gave the names of the tunnellers, another read: "The mountain barred our way. The order to continue was given anyway. The Légion carried out the order. November 1927 – May 1928."

when you get to Place Hassan II. **F** ***Zitoune***, 25 Place Hassan II, T055-572449. 10 beds in 7 rooms, very basic, no hot water.

Camping The campsite is closed, the nearest possibility being at Meski, 18 km south-east of Er Rachidia.

Eating *● on map* ***Hotel Oasis***, 4 Rue Sidi Abou Abdallah, T055-572519. Serves Moroccan food and alcohol. ***Restaurant Lipton***, Ave Moulay Ali Cherif. Good food throughout the day and night - and handy for the bus station. ***Restaurant Imilchil***, Ave Moulay Ali Cherif, T055-572123. Moroccan standards served on a terraced establishment overlooking the main drag. The most economic place is ***Restaurant Sijilmassa***, Ave Moulay Ali Cherif, with a simple but good menu. ***Hotel-Café la Renaissance***, 19 Rue Moulay Youssef, T055-572633, is reliable, with excellent *couscous*. There are other cheap places along Ave Mohammed V. Try the *Café Bousten*, next to the bridge on right at the eastern end of town.

Transport **Air** From Er Rachidia, there used to be a weekly flight to Fès. At the moment, there is little traffic apart from the occasional private flight, usually emirs flying in with their falcons to hunt in the desert (Aéroport Er Rachidia, T055-572350). **Road** **Bus**: Leave from the bus station off Ave Mohammed V, T055-572760. The **Figuig** bus is a very early morning departure (0500, check time) - but then it's a very long ride to Figuig.

Directory **Bank** *Banque Populaire*, Ave Mohammed V. *BMCE* is on Place Hassan II. **Car parts** Renault and other vehicle parts, also tyre repair, at place opposite the *Hotel Meski*. **Chemist** Blvd Moulay Ali Cherif, open all night. Pharmacy near *Café Lipton* and next to bridge in same building as *Café Bousten*. **Communications** *PTT*, just off Ave Mohammed V, near the *Banque Populaire*. **Emergency services** Police: T190. Fire: T150. **Tourist offices** ave Moulay Ali Cherif, T055-572733 (open 0830-1200 and 1400-1800).

7 The High Atlas of Azilal and the Massif du Mgoun

The High Atlas of Azilal and the Massif du Mgoun

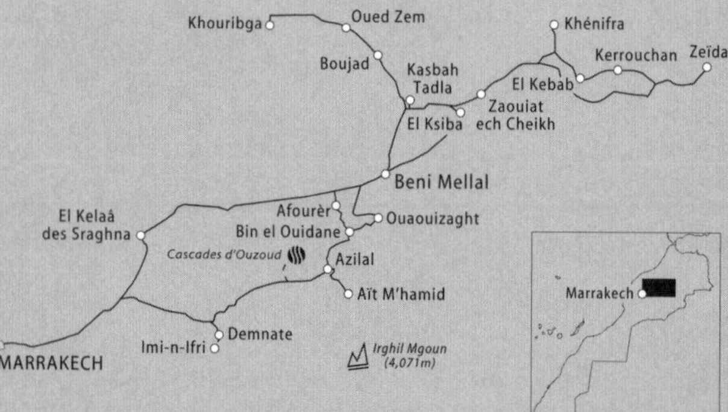

*The **High Atlas of Azilal** has some of the finest landscapes in Morocco. Just as green as the High Atlas of Toubkal, if not more so, the area is nevertheless of a very different character, due perhaps to the inaccessibility of its valleys, hidden away in the heart of the mountains. This part of the Atlas is a land of broad-shouldered mountains where the snow stays late – and where the deep valleys, set with fig trees and fields of barley, are green from the melt water. The people here are Tamazight speaking, and in many ways limited contact with mainstream Morocco has made them more conservative. Formal education has had little impact in the high valleys and it was only in the late 1990s that roads began to replace some of the landrover tracks.*

*Today, the region seems set to expand on its popularity with a small group of loyal walkers, helped by its proximity to Marrakech and the growth in adventure tourism. The high point is undoubtedly the **Vallée des Aït Bougmez** sometimes billed as a sort of Moroccan Tibet or Ladakh. You can enjoy gentle walking in the valley or climb the country's second highest mountain, the massive **Irghil Mgoun**. West of the Aït Bougmez are beautiful villages like **Ichbekane** and **Magdaz**. (Much of the beauty of the region comes from the architecture of the villages, as yet unspoiled by the charmless concrete constructions which have disfigured so many of the settlements in the High Atlas of Toubkal.)*

*For the less adventurous, the region has other draws in the form of the **Cascades d'Ouzoud** and the great natural grotto of **Imi-n-Ifri**, near **Demnate**. Its regional centres are **Azilal** and **Beni Mellal**.*

Marrakech to Azilal

The P24 Marrakech to Fès road runs northeast out of the Red City through flat countryside to **El Kelaâ des Sraghna**, and then eastwards to **Beni Mellal**, a large town of growing regional importance for both the rich irrigated areas of the Tadla Plain and a section of High Atlas hinterland to the south. Key places in this mountainous hinterland are **Azilal**, which gives access to the high valley of the **Aït Bougmez**, and **Ouaouizaght**, via which the mountain pastures of **Zaouiat Ahansal** can be reached. These areas are becoming increasingly popular with walkers, and rightly so. The landscapes are beautiful, accommodation is possible in village *gîtes*. Between Marrakech and Azilal, off the S508 road, other attractions include the natural grotto of **Imi-n-Ifri** near Demnate and the **Cascades d'Ouzoud**, Morocco's highest waterfall. North of Beni Mellal, still on the P24 heading for Meknès, the you pass through **Kasbah Tadla**. Here the P13 runs north and west via pilgrimage centre **Boujad**, and the phosphate towns of **Oued Zem** and **Khouribga**, the latter best known for its annual film festival.

Lac des Aït Aadel A short trip out of Marrakech is to the picturesque spot of Lac des Aït Aadel. Take the Fès road out of the city and at 16 km along that road, opposite the

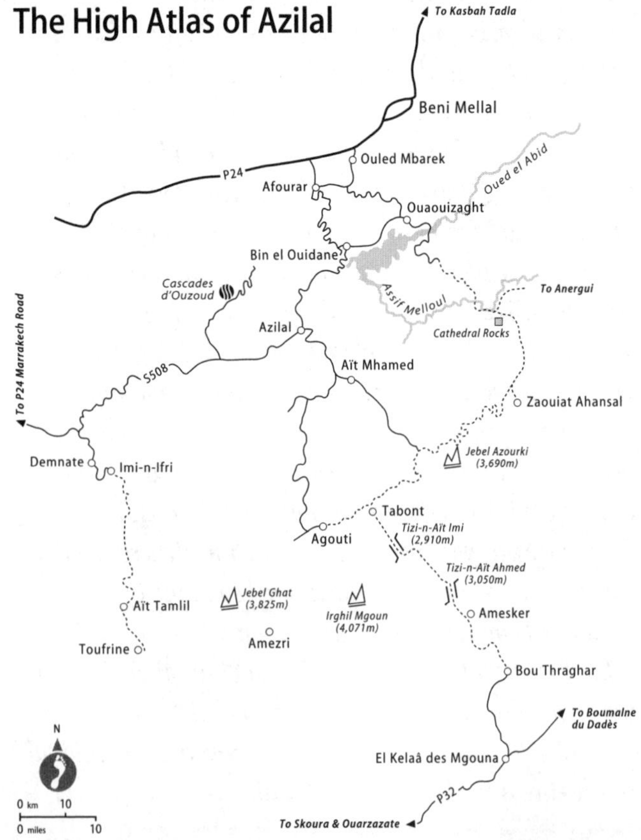

Five things to do in the Azilal High Atlas

- In spring, view the crashing waters of the **Cascades d'Ouzoud**.
- In summer, go for gentle hikes in the remote **Vallée des Aït Bougmez**, near Tabant.
- At **Abachkou**, west of the Aït Bougmez, find a guide to take you up to locate the prehistoric rock carvings near the Tizi-n-Tirghist.
- If you are lucky, see ***ahidous*** song and dance at a wedding after harvest time.
- For the very hardy: climb **Irghil Mgoun**, Morocco's second highest mountain.

road to Zaouia Bou Sassi, take the 6112 minor road through Sidi Rahhal to Tazzerte, which leads to Lac des Aït Aadel, aka Barrage Moulay Youssef. With the High Atlas as backdrop, the setting is attractive and popular with weekend picnickers. On the same trip, you could also travel on to Demnate where the Imi-n-Ifri, a large natural cavern, is another good side trip (see below).

To Azilal via Demnate and Ouzoud

Journey time from Marrakech to Azilal on this route is around three hours (with a 20-minute coffee stop), not allowing for side trips to Demnate and the Cascades d'Ouzoud. Take the P24 out of Marrakech heading for Fès. A few kilometres after Temelelt (watch your speed because of Gendarmerie checks here), take a right fork onto the S508 for Ettouia, a mushrooming town on the plain with a couple of good cafés. The landscape improves, with views of the High Atlas over to the south. About 50 km after Ettouia, the road rises, there are conifers and you are at the turn off for Demnate, some 10 km away.

Demnate

About two hours driving from Marrakech, Demnate, is worth a look. Only a 10-km detour of the S508, it was once a picturesque place – all whitewashed, if the old guide books are to be believed. It had an important Jewish community, now vanished. Unfortunately, Maréchal Lyautey's planners didn't do a good job on Demnate, and the crumbling kasbah, once set in the middle of olive groves, is surrounded by unsightly new building. There is also a chunky old minaret. So after a quick look round, continue up the much improved road to **Imi-n-Ifri** (lit 'the door to the cave' in Amazigh), a natural rock bridge formed by the partial collapse of a huge cavern. If you don't have transport, there are transit vans which do the short run up from Demnate. At Imi-n-Ifri, opposite the closed auberge of the same name, a path winds down to the stream bed. There is a small reservoir where local lads come to swim and camp. Concrete steps, partly gone, take you up to the grotto. Above your head, there are great sheets of calcareous rock, technically called dripstone. Mind you don't slip on the guano underfoot, created by cawing choughs (*alzoui* in Amazigh) circling overhead. You may also see the odd Barbary squirrel. All that is lacking are a few Barbary apes.

At the top, there is a small café with a lawn and fig trees. The road forks. The left fork takes you onto the black-top road all the way to

Market days in the Azilal and Imilchil regions

***Abachkou**: Saturday*
***Anergui**: Thursday*
***Azilal**: Thursday*
***Demnate**: Sunday*
***Imilchil**: Saturday*
***Tabant**: Sunday*
***Zaouiat Ahansal**: Monday*

Iouarden, where there are fossilized dinosaur footprints. Taking the right fork, the tarmac runs as far as Aït Imlil.

Sleeping and eating F *Hotel-Café d'Ouzoud*, T06-2239972 (manager), T06-1241099 (owner), on the main Ave Mohammed V. 24 rooms, 1 person/40dh, 2 persons/80d, shower 5dh, small clean rooms. At Imi-n-Ifri, taking the right hand fork past the café, there is a new ***gîte d'étape***, T044-456473, clearly signposted. Open only in summer.

Cascades d'Ouzoud

After visiting Demnate, return to the S508 which runs east to the signposted turn-off for the Cascades d'Ouzoud. (Many road-widening schemes under way in 2001.) For those without a hire car, a grand taxi from Azilal is an option if you get an early start. After the turn off, the road heads north through beautiful landscapes where the dominant colours are red earth, dark green thuya and the paler grey green of the olive trees. Arriving in the village of Ouzoud, various poor-looking local men will emerge, waving sticks, to help you park. For the cascades, head past the new riad, and a few metres of market garden land crossed by rivulets of fast flowing water lead you to the edge of the precipice (watch out for slippery clay). Look out for the traditional water-driven barley mills. There are various paths which will take you down to cafés on the rocks below the falls, and other walks are possible through the nearby olive groves. All in all, this is a most picturesque spot which is deservledy popular, particularly with young Moroccans camping in the summer. The word *ouzoud* comes from the Amazigh *izide*, meaning delicious, which is what bathing below the falls should be. (No diving, as the pool under the falls is very shallow.) Local blokes can be over-insistent in their desire to show you the ways down to the foot of the falls. You could give in, but agree on fee beforehand.

After visiting Ouzoud, return to the much improved S508 road and turn left. The main centre for the region, Azilal, is reached 21 km to the east.

There are some good options for staying here these days

Sleeping and eating C *Riad Cascades d'Ouzoud*, T023-459658. 6 most tasteful rooms, nice roof terrace, 2 persons, 500dh with breakfast, or 750dh half board. Check to be sure they're open. Try their traditionally milled couscous *balboula*. Can set you up with a guide for 150dh. In the village, the **D** ***Hotel de France***, T023-459017. Cheap but lacking in atmosphere, 2 persons, 150dh, 1 person/100dh, shower 8dh. **D** ***Hotel les Cascades***, above the téléboutique, noisy (in summer), slightly boozy post-hippy atmosphere. **D** ***Hotel Dar es Salam***, T023-459657, next to the car park. Mucky and best avoided. **Camping** is possible at various small sites, generally very noisy in summer and lacking in hygiene. Try ***Camping Cascades d'Ouzoud*** in 4 ha of land, first aid, nearest petrol 32 km.

Azilal

Colour map 2, grid B2

Sprawling west from a small core of kasbah and French military buildings, terracotta red Azilal is less of a one-mule place than it used to be. In fact, it is turning into a major town with the usual stilt-legged buildings, a big *gare routière* and a Thursday souk.

Accommodation and eateries can be found on the main street

Sleeping and eating Best option is the **D** ***Hotel Assounfou*** (which means 'relaxation' in Tachelhit), T023-459220, F023-458442, coming in from Marrakech, look out for the blue balconies on your right on main street. 29 rooms, 1 person 190dh, 2 persons 227dh, 2 suites, breakfast 24dh, satellite TV, everything very pink, solar-heated water, which only partly explains why it is generally cold. Nice management. Just as you arrive from Marrakech, on your right, look out for the basic **F** ***Hotel Dadès***, T023-458245,

Atlasaurus

She weighed 22.5 tonnes, was 15 m long and lived near Ouaouizaght, peaceful trailhead town in the High Atlas of Azilal. Unfortunately, a sudden flood got the better of the beast, and she was carried away, only to be washed up on a sand bank and covered in sediment, where her bones slowly fossilised. Her skeleton was found 165 million years later and studied by geologists. She was a sauropod, a large herbivorous dinosaur. Atlasaurus imalakei became her name.

It was in 1979 that Michel Monbaron and Philippe Taquet, geologists on a map-making expedition up at Ouaoumda, between Ouaouizaght and Tilouguite, spotted some dinosaur vertebrae poking out of the red Jurassic soil. Their immediate intuition? That there could well be a complete sauropod skeleton down there. Money was found and a dig organized in September 1980. Five months and much earth shifting later, the hunch was confirmed. Happily, as the giant lizard had got nicely wedged into the sand bank, the bones were not too dispersed. In fact, only a couple of vertebrae and the end of the tail were missing.

Then the problem was how to remove the bones. The physico-chemical process of fossilization turns bones into friable rock composed of millions of minute fragile cubes. The biggest bones were enormous, and might break under their own weight. The procedure was to consolidate them with glue, then cover them with a plaster shell. Small bones then travelled safely to the nearest road in mule-panniers; the heaviest pieces were airlifted out courtesy of a Gendarmerie royale Super-Puma helicopter. Quite a feat – and very much a nerve-wracking one, as only 10 or so complete herbivorous dinosaur skeletons have been found to date. (Some of the ones on display are assembled from different finds).

Analysed by experts from France and the USA, the Atlasaur's story became clearer. She was related to North American dinosaurs, as millions of years ago Africa and America were joined, and she was 15 million years older than her better known American cousins. Of the dinosaurs, only the Vulcanodon (205 million years old, also found in Morocco) and the Indian Barapasaurus (180 million years), are older. And today she can be seen in enthroned in the Ministry of Energy and Mines in Rabat. For the record, the Atlasaurus is just the most splendid of whole series of dinosaur fossil finds in the Azilal region. So keep your eyes open when out trekking.

3-bed concrete box room 50dh, hot showers 5dh. **F** ***Hotel Tanout***, T023-488281. 12 rooms, on your left next to the *Shell* station as you leave Azilal for Beni Mellal. Azilal has a tourist office on Ave Hassan II, T023-488334.

Transport Azilal is the transport hub for the regions of the High Atlas to the south, with a *gare routière* next to the main mosque. **Bus**: For **Marrakech** at 0600 and 1400, for **Casablanca** at 0700, and for **Beni Mellal** at 1400. **Grand taxi**: Landrovers (2 a day); Mercedes transit vans (2 a day) to **Tabant**; Landrovers for **Zaouiat Ahansal**, too, although for this destination it is probably best to get a Peugeot or Mercedes grand taxi to Ouaouizaght and then switch to the less comfortable Landrover.

Azilal to Tabant

From Azilal you have a slow, 2¾-hour drive over the mountains into the Aït Bougmez. In early 2001, all bar the last 17 km to Tabant, the main village in the valley, had been tarmacked. Works were well advanced on the last section. At the first major intersection, about 20 km from Azilal, you go right, taking the new route over and round to Agouti, to the west of Tabant, rather than the older, rougher route via Aït Mohammed. Drivers need to have their wits about them, your vehicle should have excellent brakes – which you will no doubt begin to smell as they heat up after particularly long descents such as the one down to Ighir where the Oued Lakhdar comes in from the west. Some 7 km further on, the piste turns east for Tabant. You should not start on this road if it looks like snow – you might find yourself cut off for a few days. The piste was just about manageable in a Fiat Uno – but remember, if you set out on rough tracks in an ordinary hire car with low clearance, the insurance will not cover any damage.

If you have already done the High Atlas of Toubkal south of Marrakech, the differences with the High Atlas of Azilal soon become apparent. Despite human pressure, there is more vegetation with conifer forests surviving at high altitude. If you go trekking, you will discover wide flat valleys, deep gorges and small rivers which can easily turn to flood after a rainstorm on the mountains. The highest mountain in the region is the long shoulder of the Irghil Mgoun, 4,071 m.

Vallée des Aït Bougmez

The Aït Bougmez is one of the most beautiful valleys of the High Atlas, so far unspoiled by breeze-block building. Electricity arrived in early 2001, and the completion of the black-top road will bring further changes. Hopefully, improved transport will not destroy the region's vernacular architectural traditions. The stone and pisé built villages above the fields of the valley bottom are fine examples of housing, perfectly adapted to local environment and needs.

One of the most isolated regions of the High Atlas, the Aït Bougmez was until very recently cut off by snow for part of the winter. The villagers had to be highly self-reliant, a factor in the local mind-set that explains the reluctance to abandon traditional crops such as barley, which can be cut for fodder and will sprout again to produce grain. Unlike Imlil in the Toubkal region, there is as yet no major switch to more profitable fruit trees. Though tourism in the form of small hiking groups is beginning to make a contribution to the local economy, life is still hard for most. Health-care provision is minimal. In the remotest villages over and beyond Jebel Wawgouzalt, women in particular are afflicted by thyroid problems due to the cheap, non-iodized salt used in cooking. The schools, teaching in formal written Arabic, make no allowances for the fact that children are Amazigh speakers. Of a primary school class of 40, barely four will make it through to the baccalauréat exam at the nearest lycée

in Azilal. For a beautifully illustrated personal account of a winter in the valley, look out for K Huet and T Lamazou's 1988 *Sous les toits de terre* ('Under the earthen roofs') published by Belvisi in Casablanca.

Tabant

Tabant, 1,850 m up in the Aït Bougmez, is the main administrative centre. There is even a new post office and a very handy téléboutique (no cyber-café as yet), also a number of basic shops. Down behind the téléboutique is a small café where the locals play bar billiards and table football, and for two hours every evening, when the generator kicks in, there is even Moroccan television. East of the village are the modern buildings of the *Centre de formation aux métiers de la montagne* (CFAMM), a vocational training school which trains mainly mountain guides.

Sleeping and eating *Gîte d'étape* is the best in the nearby village of Imelghas. Accommodation for up to 40, clean toilets and showers. Owned and run by Abdellah ben Saïd El Ouakhoumi, who can be contacted via the Tabant téléboutique on T023-459341, postal address Gîte d'étape Imelghas, Aït Bougmez, Tabant, 22480 Azilal. The upmarket option is ***Dar Hrane***, a fine *gîte* owned by Marrakech-based *Atlas Sahara Trek*, contact on T044-313901, F044-313995 atlassaharatrek@iam.net.ma Reservations via Marrakech office essential.

Options are limited in Tabant. In many villages in the valley there is simple sleeping-space in GTAM gîtes

Walking around the Aït Bougmez

The Aït Bougmez provides some excellent walking. The wide, flat-bottomed valley provides some excellent day walks out from Tabant for occasional walkers and those with young families. If you just want to relax in a calm mountain environment, you will be well served. You could find a local to walk you up to the dinosaur footsteps near Rabat. Tabant (or Imelghas) to Agouti is a very easy walk, say 8 km, along the valley road. Look out for the granary of Sidi Moussa up on a mound-like hill. There is another, rather longer walk (say 9 km), from Tabant to Ifrane along the old main piste to Aït Mohammed.

The valley can also work as an excellent starting point for hiking tours. Setting up a longish circuit with a local guide generally requires you to give a couple of months notice. The guide will need to have an idea of the group's walking experience and fitness levels. For setting up a trek, contact Saïd el Ouakhoumi at the Tabant téléboutique, T023-459341/42. A week-long trek with transfer to the valley from Marrakech airport will cost between 3,500dh and 4,000dh, meals excluded. A hiker consumes around 100dh worth of food and drink a day.

Maps and books Any properly organized guide will obviously have the maps necessary for hiking in the region. If you want to buy 1:100,000 scale maps, try *Chez Ali* in Marrakech (expensive) or, if you have lots to time in Rabat, the *Division de la cartographie* (see Essentials for contact details), where they are sold at 80dh a sheet. The eastern part of the Aït Bougmez is on the Zaouiat Ahansal sheet, ref NH-29-XXIV-4, as is most of the Irghil Mgoun. The western access to the Aït Bougmez, with most of the road from Azilal, Abachkou, administrative village of the Aït Bou Ouilli and Jebal Ghat, are shown on the NH-29-XXIV-3 Azilal sheet. Trekking south of the Irghil Mgoun, you will need the Qalaa't Mgouna NH-29-XXIV-2. The sheet west of this, the NH-29-XXIV-1, Skoura, shows Amezri and the Oued Tessaout. If you read French (and even if you don't there are some handy, small maps), in Marrakech you may be able to obtain a small publication called *Randonnées pédestres dans le Massif du Mgoun* ('Walking tours in the Mgoun Region').

Trekking in the Azilal High Atlas

There are great possibilities for hiking in the High Atlas of Azilal, and routes can be varied almost ad infinitum, depending on time of year, fitness of the group, time available – and of course, cash to cover costs of guides and mules. The region is now included by numerous hiking companies on their circuits, with the Aït Bougmez an increasingly popular destination. If you are not travelling on a group holiday purchased outside Morocco, it should be popular to set something up when you arrive. While the Aït Bougmez can function both as a base for longer treks up into the Mgoun Massif to the south, other shorter circuits are possible. Essentially, as elsewhere, your local guide will be able to advise you according to the fitness levels of your group.

A west to east, five-day valley trek

The non-technical, five-day trek described here takes you from **Aït Tamlil** (Souk el Tlata/Tuesday souk), over to **Tabant**, main village of the Aït Bougmez. If you are doing this under your own steam, you have to allow plenty of time for the slowness of public transport across the mountains. Described here as a west to east trek, it is equally possible to start at Azilal/Tabant, which means you are nearer Marrakech when you finish at Aït Tamlil. Starting point from the mountains is Demnate, then Imi-n-Ifri (see 'To Azilal via Demnate and Ouzoud' above). From here you take minibus or Landrover taxi up to Aït Tamlil, a distance of 60 km. The surface is metalled for the first 30 km, as far as Almesa (Wouggougene on map), although work is under way to extend it further up into the Tessaoute Valley. At Aït Tamlil, you have a small *gîte d'étape* and small shops.

Aït Tamlil to Toufghine

From Aït Tamlil, the **first stage** of this trek (15 km), takes you southeast to **Toufghine** (1,685 m) with some splendid views over the Tessaoute Valley on the way. You pass through the villages of Irkt, Takfast and Anfag, before

Toufghine to Abachkou & Jebel Ghat

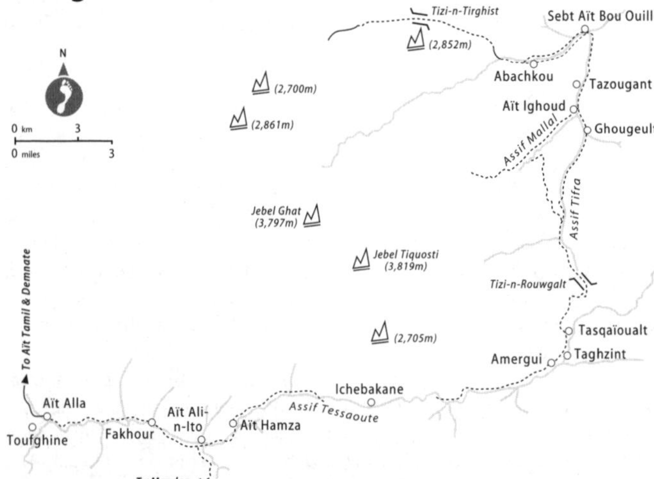

reaching Aït Alla Souk and then Toufghine. Here you have a *gîte* or the possibility of bivouacking. The **second stage** takes you east from Toufghine and on to **Megdaz**, along the Tessaoute Valley. You pass through the villages of Inbrar, Ifoulou and Fakhour (splendid square agadir). At Aït Ali-n-Ito, a well used track branches off right for Megdaz, about two hours walking south. You follow the Assif-n-Tifticht, then, where the valleys meet, head right (south) for Megdaz. With its magnificent natural setting of steep basalt and sandstone mountain and green orchards, Megdaz is one of the finest villages in the High Atlas. Its flat-roofed mud and stone houses are almost an archetype of traditional Tessaoute building. Here again there is a small *gîte d'étape*, also the possibility of finding accommodation in someone's home.

Megdaz to Amezri

From Megdaz, **stage three** on this hike takes you east from Megdaz via Aït Hamza and Ichbekane, another attractive village, to **Amezri**. You retrace your steps back down to Aït Ali-n-Ito, then head northeast for the first village, Aït Hamza (accommodation possible). You then drop down to the river valley, with well over two hours walk along a reasonable track through gorges east to the minor settlement of Talat-n-Tazart (2,530 m). To the south, you have the crest of Jebel Ouadaker (3,088 m), to the north, a high ridge. The double village of Ickhbekane is the next stop, set in an extraordinary rockscape. Continuing east, the gorge closes in, the vegetation disappears, and then, little by little, you come out into the Amezri-n-Aït Affan basin. There are bivouacking places at **Amezri** (or Amerzi, the maps differ on spelling here), also small shops selling the basics.

Amezri to Abachkou

From Amezri (2,250 m), **stage four** takes you north over the **Tizi-n-Rouwgalt** (2,860 m, 'Pass of the Storms') and on to another attractive village, **Abachkou**. With the col to climb up to, this is a much harder day's trekking than the previous day. You climb up from Amezri to the village of Tasgaïoualt, then up the west side of the valley to the col. From the Tizi-n-Rouwgalt, there are fine views back down to Amezri and north to the upper valley of the Assif-n-Aït Mallal and the upper Oued Lakhdar. You then drop down to the village of **Ifira** (2,286 m), wind down to the N-Doughour Canyon, after which comes the village of Ghougoult. The next village, **Tazegzaout**, is some two hours further on, after which Abachkou (1,750 m, Saturday souk) is just a short walk west. Here you have a *gîte* and a couple of small hanouts for soft drinks and the like.

Abachkou to Tabant

The final, rather long **fifth stage** on this trek runs east-northeast from Abachkou via Agouti and on to Tabant, 'capital' of the Aït Bougmez (shops, post office, téléboutique, *gîte d'étape*). There are no cols to cross, however, and the trails are clear. You pass through the villages of Taghia and Ighir-n-Ighrazene, Taghoulit and Aguercif and then Tighza, where you will intersect with the well used track coming in from Azilal to the north. This (by the time of publication), may have turned into a fully fledged road. After Tighza, the track takes you through **Agouti**, **Talsnant** (*gîte*) and **Aït Ziri** (*gîte*). You will pass under the cone shaped hill, atop which sits the fortified granary of Sidi Moussa, before the road forks left for Imelghas (*gîte*) or right across the wide flat valley for Tabant. Note that with a strong group of walkers, an experienced guide might suggest climbing up out of the valley, southwards, to the Tizi-n-Ougarmaghad to meet a path running high above the Jorro Gorges and along the slopes above the Assif Bougmez.

Around Tabant From **Tabant** (Sunday souk, cafés, small shops as mentioned above) you have to think about transport to get you back to mainstream Morocco. There are landrover taxis and Mercedes minibuses doing the 'run' (or rather, slow grind) on a daily basis to Azilal, whence you can take a bus or grand taxi back to Marrakech. It might, however, be good to spend an extra day enjoying the peace of the Aït Bougmez, climbing up to the granary of Sidi Moussa, perhaps. Another transport option, though slower, is to see what transport is going to Aït Mohammed, on the other access road to the valley. From Aït Mohammed, there are grand taxis down to Azilal. Expect to be packed in with lots of locals and their luggage.

Massif du Mgoun

Colour map 2, grid B2

With its alluring, extraterrestrial sounding name, the Mgoun is Morocco's second highest mountain massif. Although not the most aesthetically pleasing of mountains (no soaring peaks), it has the largest area of land above 3,000 m in the whole country. The best time to climb the mountain is probably summer or early autumn, for snow remains late into the year in these highlands. The easiest route to the summit is from the south side of the mountain, which either means starting from El Kelaâ des Mgouna (see chapter 6 in the Dadès Valley section). The alternative is to head south from the Aït Bougmez to approach the massif from the east. Taking this option, you will probably head south from Tabant over the Tizi-n-Aït Imi (2,905 m) to Tighremt n-Aït Ahmed, and thence west to the foot of the mountain along the course of the Assif Oulliliymt on a second day's trek. The actual ascent to the highest point (4,068 m) is not actually difficult. A good guide will ensure you avoid too much scree. Note that the summit is in some way sacred. In a survival of some obscure pre-Islamic tradition, the mountain's help (protection) may be asked, even today.

Other possible hikes

From Aït Bougmez south to Bou Thrarar and El Kelaâ des Mgouna One fairly popular, north-south hiking route takes you from the well watered Aït Bougmez, down to the arid south side of the High Atlas at Bou Thrarar on the Assif (river) Mgoun. After a toughish climb to the Tizi-n- Aït Imi (2,900 m) on the Jebel Wawgouzalt south of Tabant, and a first night's bivouac at Tighremt Aït Ahmed, the track takes you east along the winding course of the Assif Mgoun and down to Bou Thrarar. This is a six-day trip, with possible bivouacs at Tarzout, Aguerzka and Bou Thrarar. It will be up to your guides to break up the route as they see fit. Apart from the high pass on the first day, there are no huge climbs, and you will be walking for between six and seven hours a day.

Three canyons in the Azilal High Atlas A more difficult trip involving some real climbing is the so-called 'Three Canyons Trek', which takes in the gorges of Joro, Ouandras and Arous. The starting point is the Aït Bougmez – your guide will decide what order you do the gorges in. The Joro Gorges run south of Tiguelouene near Abachkou. (Possible bivouac near Amezri.) Next you head east along the Oued Tessaout, before heading north up the Assif-n-Arous to Agouti in the Aït Bougmez. Proper preparation, climbing kit and a qualified guide are necessary for this five-day trip.

Eight days walking: from the Tizi-n-Tichka to the Aït Bougmez If you have 12 days to spare, a west-to-east trek might go something as follows. Making an early start from Marrakech, by four-wheel drive vehicle you would head over the Tizi-n-Tichka (2,260 m), visit the kasbah at Telouet, and then drive on to the trek base at Tighza by early afternoon. Around two hours, 30 minutes walking would take you up the Ounila Valley to Anfergal, first bivouac site. The **Day 2** would begin with two hours uphill walking to Lac Aneghmar, followed by the Tizi-n-Timilitia (2,800 m) and down to bivouac site near village of Tamgrit, all in all approximately six hours walking, 800 m up, 800 m descent). An easy **Day 3** takes you down the Col de Fedghat, then through varied terrain to the Taouadja high pastures and the Tizi-n-Tagoukht. Descent to village of Tagoukht, bivouac. (Approximately five hours walking, 700 m descent, 300 m up.) **Day 4** would be over the Col de Megdaz (2,450 m), then down the valley to Aït Ali-n-Itto. Bivouac near the Oued Tessaout. (500 m up, 600 m down, six hours walking.) **Day 5** would be seven hours walking up the Tessaout Valley with a lunch stop at Ichbaken and bivouac near Amezri. **Day 6** is one of the longest days on this circuit with an early morning start for the Tizi-n-Asdrem and its magnificent views and lunch stop near a cave at the foot of the Jebel Tarkdit. Overnight bivouac is at the foot of the Irhil Mgoun at 2,900 m. (All in all 1,100 m up, 300 m down, seven hours walking.) **Day 7** is up the Mgoun for those in shape, while those feeling a little tired can opt to go round the massif via the Tizi-n-Oumsoud. Bivouac near the springs of Oulliliymt (1,200 m up, 1,600 m down to bivouac, eight hours walking for the summiteers, otherwise 600 m down, 500 m up, five hours walking for the rest). The final **Day 8**, would take you to Ifri-n-Oukhrif through varied landscape and up the Tizi-n-Aït Imi, 2,905 m. After a lunch stop, you then drop down to the springs of Aït Imi and into the Vallée des Aït Bougmez. Bivouac near Tabant or Imelghas. (800 m up, 1,000 m descent, seven hours walking.)

Other longer options If you want to do nine days walking, starting at Tabant, you could do a loop via the Aït Bougmez, Irhil Mgoun and the Tessaout Valley. Climbing the Irghil Mgoun (4,068 m) is the highlight of this circuit. If you want to see some prehistoric rock art, then head for the Jebel Ghat, southwest of Abachkou. You will need 5-6 days to do this region justice. Another longish trek (say 8-9 days), is a west-to-east trek from Imelghas to Imilchil in the eastern High Atlas. Lying some 30 km east of the Aït Bougmez as the mule trots, the Zaouiat Ahansal region with its high pastures and the Cirque de Taghia are relatively unexplored. Best vehicle access for Zaouiat Ahansal is via Ouaouizaght (see next chapter).

Beni Mellal بني ملال

Colour map 2, grid A2
200 km NE of Marrakech

This is one of the major centres of central Morocco, with a population of around 140,000, and an important souk on Tuesday. Like a number of other towns in the region (Fkih ben Salah, Zaouiat ech Cheikh), it has grown in size thanks to remittances from migrant workers in Italy. Main monuments include the **Kasbah Bel Kush**, built in the 17th century by Moulay Ismaïl, but heavily restored in the 19th century. The main thing to do in Beni Mellal is to walk up from the town to the small and quiet gardens below the ruined **Kasbah de Ras el Aïn**, perched precariously on the cliffside. There is a nice café in the gardens.

Coming from Marrakech, if you wish to avoid Beni Mellal go left for the bypass just before two petrol stations (*Somepi* on left, *Shell* on right).

Sleeping There are 1 or 2 good options in Beni Mellal. **C *Al Bassatine***, Route de Fkih ben Salah, T023-482227. 61 a/c rooms, pool, restaurant, TV, direct telephone, private parking and conference facilities. **C *Hotel Ouzoud***, Route de Marrakech, T023-483752/3. With restaurant, bar, tennis and pool. **C *Hotel Chems***, Route de Marrakech, BP 68, T023-483460, 77 rooms, with restaurant, bar, nightclub, tennis and pool, nice grounds. Could do with some renovation, has a 1970s air, far out from the centre. Has a certain run-down charm (some would say). In the new town, try **D/E *Hotel Gharnata***, Ave Mohammed V, easily located near *Petrom* station and the PTT, T023-483482. Must have been excellent in the 1950s, badly refurbished, 14 noisy rooms, cheapest 1 person/65dh, 2 persons/80dh, with shower 1 person/89dh, 2 persons/113dh. The **D *Hotel El Amria***, Ave des FAR, T023-483531. Simple. And the **D *Hotel de l'Aïn-Asserdoun***, Ave des FAR, T023-483493. A modern place with restaurant. Of the cheapish hotels near the *gare routière*, the best is probably the **D *Hotel Kamel***, T023-486941. Street-facing rooms noisy. In the older part of town, several good cheap options, the best being the **E *Hotel Tasmmet***, T023-421313, not very easy to find, but if you get onto the street which runs parallel to the main street behind the *CTM* offices you eventually see it down a side street to your left as you head towards the Kasbah. On the small square in the old town (reached by heading up the souk street which leads uphill to the right of the big ceremonial gates and square), 2 simple options with rooms around courtyards: **F *Hotel Marhaba***, T023-483991/023-420049, 1 person/40dh, 2 persons/70dh, 11 rooms, 27 beds, sleep on roof terrace for 25dh, and **F *Hotel El Fath***, no phone, opposite the *Marhaba*, 1 person/30dh, 2 persons/60dh, no shower, damp problems in some rooms.

Eating The best place used to be the ***Auberge du Vieux Moulin***, Ave Mohammed V. Try the restaurant of the ***Hotel de Paris***, T023-282245, a little way out of the town centre on Kasbah Tadla road. Serves alcohol. More decorously, try the ***Salon de Thé Azouhour***, 241 Ave Mohammed V. There are the usual *laiteries* and cafés along the main street.

Entertainment **Sports Gliding**: *Centre Royal de Vol à Voile de Beni Mellal*, T023-482095. Basically run for *RAM* employees.

Transport **Road** *CTM* buses leave from the terminal in the town centre. There are regular connections with Marrakech and 3 a day for Fès. From the all-company bus station it is a 10-min walk up Ave des FAR to the town centre. Note that in early 2001 it looked as though the *CTM* would suspend its Casablanca service. Grand taxis up to Ouaouizaght and to Azilal, whence you can pick up tougher transport to get you to the Aït Bougmez and Zaouiat Ahansal.

Directory **Tourist offices** A tourist office is located on the 1st floor of Immeuble Chichaoui, Ave Hassan II, T023-483981.

To Ouaouizaght via Bine el Ouidane

For those with a hire car and half a day to spare, there is a fine excursion out of Beni Mellal to the Bine el Ouidane dam lake. For those heading for Zaouiat Ahansal, Ouaouizaght (pronounced Wawizaght) is the place to pick up Landrover taxis. Head southwest out of Beni Mellal in the Marrakech direction on the P24. At Aouled M'barek there is a turn-off signed for Ouaouizaght. Continue on to the Afourer turn (left) onto the S508. At Afourer, there is a large, comfortable hotel, the **B** *Hotel Tazerkount*, T023-440101, F023-440094, much used by Italian and German tour groups, 1 person/550dh, 2 persons/750dh, breakfast a hefty 70dh, tennis courts, pool, can set up riding. You now have an amazing climb up to the top of the Jebel Tazerkount, superb views over the green Tadla Plain to the north, and into the High Atlas of Azilal to the south. The road, perfectly driveable even in a campervan, then winds down into spectacular gorges before approaching the Bine el Ouidane dam, 38 km south of the P24.

Supplying water for the great irrigated farming projects of the Tadla Plain, the **Bine el Ouidane dam** and lake is one of independent Morocco's star infrastructure projects. There is little sign of tourist development, however, apart from an unfinished holiday village belonging to the Moroccan post office. Note that visitors should beware of photographing the dam. The **E** *Auberge du Lac*, signed off the approach road east of the dam, should be a splendid place to stay but doesn't merit any recommendations.

Head east along the north shore of the dam (fine views) on the S508a to **Ouaouizaght**, which you would think was a small hamlet of flat-roofed stone and pisé dwellings. It turns out to have red-washed low-rise buildings and an almost up-beat air. There is a crumbling kasbah next to the new white mosque, two pharmacies, photo-labs, a cybernet and even a *Crédit Agricole* (no bureau de change). The only accommodation is the **F** *Hotel Atlas*, at the top of the village next to a téléboutique, T023-442042, with four rooms and a cool welcome. Ouaouizaght, accessible by Peugeot 504 taxi from the *gare routière* at Beni Mellal, 15dh, is the place to get a Landrover taxi on to **Zaouiat Ahansal** (Monday souk), 50dh per place, journey time about 3½ hours. It would be even better to do this route in your own four-wheel drive so you could stop to take a look at the cathedral rocks at Tilouguite. Information on walking in the Zaouiat Ahansal area from the *Bureau des Guides* on T023-459378. There are a couple of *gîtes*. For more details on this, see following chapter page 243.

Another possible option for tough walkers is to aim for **Anergui**, on the Assif Melloul, a feeder river for the Bine el Ouidane dam. This is one of the least visited areas of the High Atlas of Azilal, about 3½ days walking, or five hours of difficult piste driving. Note that Anergui has a new *gîte d'étape* (details in following chapter).

If you are just driving, complete the loop back from Ouaouizaght to Beni Mellal by taking a minor, recently surfaced road up over the top to Ouled M'barek (the turn off for which you passed on the P24 when outward-bound). There are superb views over the dam. On the north side the road loops down in hairpin bends to the Tadla Plain – views which the driver won't have much room to appreciate. Back on the P24, you are just 12 km west of Beni Mellal.

North of Beni Mellal

If you are on a circular tour with a hire car, possibly flying out from Casablanca, there are some minor places of interest as you head back coastwards from the mountains. Casablanca-bound from Beni Mellal and the High Atlas of Azilal, you take the P24 Casablanca road north from Beni Mellal to **Kasbah Tadla**, and then the P13 northwest to **Boujad** and **Oued Zem**. Here the P22 runs north to Rabat via **Rommani** and Aïn el Aouda. The P13 continues to the phosphate town of Khouribga across the Plateau des Phosphates, to intersect with the main P7 Marrakech to Casablanca road at **Berrechid**. Kasbah Tadla and Boujad are must visits for those doing their advanced Moroccan studies diploma.

Heading north out of Beni Mellal, a fast stretch of the P24 takes you through well irrigated orchards and olive groves and out into open grainlands. To your right are views of the northwestern side of the High Atlas. At a major junction (curious concrete monument over to your left), Kasbah Tadla comes into view. Head straight on for the town, its ramparts clearly visible above the Oum er Rbia, or go right past the closed *Hotel Bellevue* to continue on the P24 for Khénifra.

Kasbah Tadla

Kasbah Tadla doesn't really have enough attractions to be a stopover. Souk today is on Monday

Kasbah Tadla was founded in 1687 by the Alaouite Sultan Moulay Ismaïl, no doubt because it is ideally located more or less half-way between Marrakech and Meknès and Fès, the imperial cities of the Saïss Plain. The crumbling terracotta ramparts sit above the shrivelled course of the river. The view is little changed since its foundation, although a new housing project on the flood plain will change that. France developed Kasbah Tadla as a military garrison. On the plateau behind the kasbah is a rather derelict *jardin public*, splendid in a quiet sort of way when the purple jacarandas are in flower. Within the kasbah there are two mosques and a lot of self-built housing, put up by soldiers and their families. There are two mosques, one with the distinctive Almohad lozenge design on the minaret. The other has a Sahelian feel with poles protruding from the minaret. Hopefully, some lad will offer to show you into the courtyard building behind the mosque which was the Sultan's residence.

The best view of the kasbah is to be had from the austere monument to four resistance heroes on a low rise on the south side of the town. Four parallel concrete blades rise skywards. Unfortunately, there is no inscription to recall who the heroes were. Local youths sitting in the shade of the monument don't seem to know either.

Sleeping and eating Unfortunately, the ***Hotel Bellevue***, just outside the town off the P24 from Fès to Beni Mellal, is now derelict and there do not seem to be any plans to re-open. There are 3 very basic hotels in the centre: **F *Hotel des Alliés***, Ave Mohammed V, T023-418587, is perhaps the best though lacking in hot water. (Founded in 1921, it still has many of its original characteristics, albeit in desperate need of attention.) The other hotels are **F *Hotel El Atlas***, Rue el Majati Obad, T023-418046 and **F *Hotel Oum er Rbia***, 26 Blvd Mohammed Zerktouni, with no shower. There is a well run campsite ***Auberge des Artistes*** at El Ksiba, just 30 km east of Kasbah Tadla in 2 ha of grounds, showers, electricity for caravans, clean wash blocks, T02303415490. There are a few basic restaurants in the town centre. Try ***Restaurant Salem*** on the main drag. (**NB** The route from El Ksiba to Imilchil is dealt with under the High Atlas of Imilchil.)

Transport *CTM* **buses** leave at 1035 for **Fès**, 1145 for **Marrakech**, 1335 for **Casablanca** and 1705 for **Beni Mellal**, and private line buses from *Agence SLAC* for **Beni Mellal** at 1300, **Boujad** and **Oued Zem** at 1700, and **Rabat** at 0430, 0730 and 1300. These can all be caught from the bus-station on the Boujad side of town, ie the far side from the old kasbah.

Boujad

For the historic part of town, turn right off the P13 opposite the open ground used for the souk

Just a 25-minute drive from Kasbah Tadla, Boujad is something of a surprise. In recent memory, Boujad was an important town, essentially as a pilgrimage centre for the semi-nomadic inhabitants of the Tadla Plain. It gets plenty of coverage in guidebooks of the 1930s. The historic médina has an almost Mediterranean character with its arcaded square, whitewashed walls, shrines and paved streets and white houses. The main *zaouia* is a 16th-century foundation. Much of the town was destroyed in 1785. The key religious buildings are the **Zaouia of Sidi Othman** and the **Mosque of Sidi Mohammed Bu'abid ech Cherki**, the town's founder.

Sleeping, eating and transport There is one hotel on the main square, Place du Marché, the **F** ***Café-Hotel Essalyn***, and several cheap restaurants nearby. People on pilgrimages rent rooms in private houses near the shrines. Regular buses and grands taxis leave for **Kasbah Tadla** and **Oued Zem** from the main square.

Oued Zem

Oued Zem is interesting for those who like mining towns on arid plateau land, reached from Boujad on the P13. It has useful railway connections and a busy market in the centre. **F** *Hotel El Salam* is very cheap and central. The other option is **F** *Hotel des Cooperatives*, on Rue Rachid II. There are cheap restaurants in the centre. Trains to Casablanca leave at 0720, 0840 and 1500, and take between two and three hours.

Khouribga

35 km W from Oued Zem, just S of the P12

Khouribga is an important working town due to its central role in the phosphates industry. For the tourist, it is singularly lacking in any charm or appeal. There is one luxury hotel, the **A** *Hotel Safir*, T022-492013, F022-493013. With restaurant, bar, tennis and pool. The best cheap hotel is the clean **F** *Hotel de Paris*, 18 Ave Mohammed V, T022-492716. The only other is **F** *Hotel des Hôtes*, 1 Rue Moulay Ismaïl, T022-493030, a basic and unfriendly place. Around the market, just off the main street, are a number of basic restaurants. Trains to Casablanca, with connections to Marrakech, El Jadida, Safi, Rabat, Fès and Tanger, leave at 0757, 0923, 1540 and to Oued Zem at 1228, 1931 and 2239.

Kasbah Tadla to Khénifra

Leaving Kasbah Tadla in the Azrou/Fès direction, the P24 runs across fast, open corn lands. After about 22 km, the turn-off right to **El Ksiba**, the starting point for the north-south route to Imilchil, is reached (see next chapter). Next stop is **Zaouiat ech Cheikh**, best known for its roadside tagine restaurants. The road takes an increasingly winding route along the contours, so keep your speed down and watch out for wild-card grands taxis. **Aït Ishak** is signposted off to the left, and then you reach the junction with the P33, which will take you east to **Zeïda** and the P21 Azrou to Midelt road. For Midelt and Zeïda see next chapter, High Atlas of Imilchil. Distances between main towns as follows: Khénifra to Zeïda 110 km, Kasbah Tadla to Zeïda, 159 km, journey time to Midelt, 2¼ hours. If you need a pause, the roadside **C** *Hotel Transatlas*, T055-399030, 25 rooms, a/c, bar, small pool,

Kasblah Tadla to Zeïda & Midelt

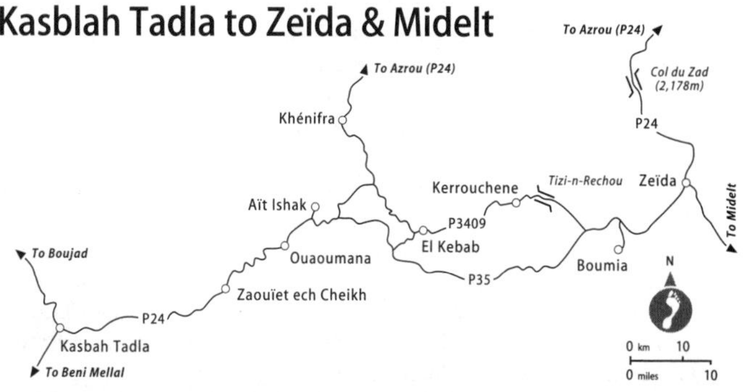

noisy in evenings, acceptable. There is certainly nothing much better until you reach Azrou.

After this junction, Khénifra is about 35 km further on. After 12 km, you reach the turn off for El Kebab and an alternative (and attractive) route across to Zeïda via Kerrouchen (26 km to El Kebab, 59 km from Khénifra). Details given below after Khénifra.

Khénifra Khénifra is another of the Middle Atlas towns that stood up to the French military in a big way, before becoming an important town in the colonial enterprise. In the late 19th century, Moha ou Hammou emerged as the dynamic leader of the Zaïane tribal confederation. (The region extending west from Khénifra to Rommani was once the sole domain of the Zaër-Zaïane tribes.) Hammou was named Caïd of the Zaïane by Sultan Hassan I – with whom he promptly broke, building up an independent power base. When the French arrived, the resistance was fierce, with the French using planes to bring the Zaïane to heel. In 1921, Hammou was killed fighting French forces.

Like Marrakech, it is a *ville rouge*. The locals have a tradition of horsemanship. Various kasbahs are sign-posted. There is an old bridge over the rubbish strewn bed of the Oum er Rbia. If you need a break from driving, have a drink at the *Café des Cascades*, on a rather minor precipice to your right as you head north out of town. (Views of people doing their washing in the 'rapids' below.) The most photogenic feature in Khénifra are probably the storks nesting on the chimneys and roofs of the 1930s houses. Otherwise, the town doesn't have too much to keep the traveller for more than 30 minutes, although you could check your emails at one of the cybercafés on the main drag.

In terms of accommodation there isn't much choice. Try **A** *Hotel Salam Zayyani*, T055-586020. Restaurant, pool, poorly maintained. **C** *Hotel Najah*, T055-588331, F055-587874 at 187 Blvd Mohammed Zerktouni, the main street, has simple clean rooms, 260dh per single, 320dh/2 persons.

The best cheap hotel has rather gone down **F** *Hotel-Restaurant de France* V, T055-586114, quartier des FAR, on the west side of the town. Restaurant overpriced. There are several new places on the main drag.

A picturesque route (P3409) to Zeïda via El Kebab & Kerrouchen Heading away from Marrakech, 12 km after the right turn for the P33 to Midelt, you reach another right turn onto the P3409, an alternative route east to the Midelt region. So, from this main Marrakech to Fès road, follow signs up to the hillside town of charmingly named **El Kebab**. Although the new building is unattractive, the views west are beautiful. The chunky lines of the table mountain behind Khénifra are clearly visible on the horizon. Down a narrow alley above the main street you will find a metal door set with a cross, the hermitage-house of *le Père*. For more than 30 years Father Albert Peyriguère (died 1959) lived here, providing basic medical treatment for the poor – and winning many friends in the region for his pro-independence stance. His successor, Père Michel Lafon, continued his work for many years. After El Kebab, the narrow P3409 follows the contour lines to the village of **Kerrouchen**, a village high above the valley. After rains, watch out for mud slides on the road. Villages of clay-red flat-roofed houses sit in olive groves above terraced fields. There is a steep climb up to the **Tizi-n-Ichou** (1,948 m). Here you reach the southern reaches of the cedar forests. Then the road descends to join the P33. Off right is the large rural town of Boumia. Eighteen km after the turn-off for Boumia, the approach to **Zeïda** (1,453 m), is across open plain with views of the Cirque de Jaffar in the eastern High Atlas away to the south. At Zeïda, you intersect with the the P21 Azrou to Midelt/Er Rachidia road.

Midelt, Imilchil and the Eastern High Atlas

Midelt, Imilchil and the Eastern High Atlas

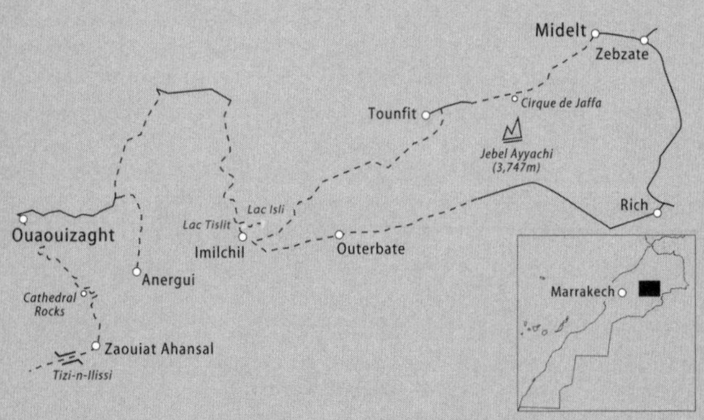

More arid, more remote, the Eastern or Imilchil High Atlas, taken here as the region between Midelt in the east and Zaouiat Ahansal in the west, is substantially different to the Toubkal High Atlas. Gone are the long deep winding valleys with their terraced fields. Here are long, shoulder mountains, snow-capped even in summer, and high pastures. While the western parts of the Atlas, easily reached from Marrakech, where widely visited in the late 19th and early 20th centuries, the east, resistant as it was to French 'pacification' was a different matter.

The eastern section of the region covered here includes the ***Jebel Ayyachi*** *and the high, bare plateaux of the* ***Imilchil*** *region. West of this, the deep gorges of the* ***Assif Melloul****, thick with vegetation, run west to* ***Anergui*** *and its confluence with the Oued Ahansal southeast of Ouaouizaght. While* ***Midelt*** *is a former mining town, which has a population with elements from all over Morocco, in the valleys east of Rich and around Imilchil, semi-nomad lifestyles still exist even today.* ***Tamazight****, as opposed to the Tachelhit variety of Amazigh found in the Toubkal High Atlas, is the main spoken language. Though men now mainly wear modern dress, the women in the Imilchil region can still be seen in their characteristic striped blanket-capes in some villages. The great attraction of this region is its wild openness, the great folds and striations of a remote geological past clearly visible. In early summer, the pale green of the poplars coming into leaf and the young barley on the terraced fields contrast with the creamy-brown nakedness of the rock faces above.*

Ins and outs

Getting around The P21 running north from Er Rachidia to Midelt, cutting through Ziz Gorges, across high plateau lands, and the Tizi-n-Taghamt, is one of the finest routes in Morocco. You can travel back up to the imperial cities of Fès and Meknès on this route. From Er Rachidia take the road north to Midelt, whence you can travel on up to Meknès and Fès via Azrou. An hour's drive south of Midelt is Rich, from where you can head west on the only metalled road (for the moment) up to trekking base Imilchil. Midelt, a small town with something of a reputation for carpets, is a base for exploring some out-of-the-way parts of the Middle Atlas, including the abandoned mines of Ahouli, the Cirque de Jaffar and the Jebel Ayyachi.

Rich

Colour map 2, grid A5 After the gorges, the landscape opens up, and the town of Rich is visible below the range to the west. To the east are some beautifully mysterious small mountains.

Sleeping Rich has 2 small, unclassified hotels, ***Hotel Salama***, 14 rooms, T055-579343; and ***Hotel El Massira***, 7 rooms, T055-579340.

Midelt

Colour map 2, grid A5 High on the plateau lands between Middle and High Atlas, Midelt (1,525 m) is a convenient stopping point en route from the Sahara, Er Rachidia (138 km) and Rich (75 km), to Azrou, Meknès and Fès. Despite high unemployment, the town has a calm, friendly atmosphere and a large **souk** on Sunday. The region's minerals and fossils are energetically sold on the street and in the shops.

Sights Apart from nice rocks, a possible buy for those in need of some shopping therapy are the town's carpets. These can be bought at a weaving school (*atelier de tissage*), the **Kasbah Meriem**, the local name for the monastery/convent of **Notre Dame de l'Atlas**, T055-580858, run by Franciscan sisters in premises off the road to Tattiouine. There is also a tiny community of Trappist monks here who relocated from Algeria. The sisters may be a source of information about the region. To find it, head north out of Midelt centre, take left turn onto track after bridge, follow track towards kasbah village, where you go sharp right and almost immediately left up the hill. After about 1 km, the Kasbah Meriem is signed left, down a dip and up again, its presence indicated by trees. The *atelier* is left of the large metal gate. Inside, there is a simple church with a small icon of the seven sleepers of Ephesus, symbol of a myth present both in Christianity and Islam.

The Franciscan sisters do lots of good work in the region, travelling into the countryside with mules and a dispensary tent. While recent undercover Protestant missionary activity, funded by US churches, has attracted criticism in the Moroccan press, the work of the Franciscans is much appreciated here.

For the record, Midelt also has a small Catholic church, near the *Hotel Ayyachi*, run by a Jesuit priest.

Strategically located on the Imperial cities to Tafilalelt road, next to magnificent mountains, Midelt looks as though it will have a good future as a base for hikers. For more on this, head for **Aït Ayach**, halfway between Midelt and Zeïda on the P21, where the *Auberge Timnay* can help (see below).

Five things to do in the Eastern High Atlas

- From Midelt, drive out to the abandoned mines of **Ahouli** in the Upper Moulouya Valley.
- From Midelt, take a 4WD excursion up onto the pistes of the **Cirque de Jaffar**.
- Camp out or spend the night in a faux kasbah near **Lac Tislit**, Imilchil.
- In a 4WD vehicle, travel the north route from Imilchil via **Tassent** to **El Ksiba** or **Aghbala**.
- The hardy can hike from Imilchil to Anergui, along and above the **Assif Melloul**.

Sleeping

Even remote Midelt seems to be getting in on the Moroccan tourist boom. Reservations are definitely a good idea in the spring

D ***Hotel Ayyachi***, Rue d'Agadir, a few minutes from the town centre, signposted behind the post office, T055-582161, F055-583307. Very 1930s, 30 big rooms with shower, 1 person 277dh, 2 persons 330dh, quiet, big restaurant, nightclub, safe parking and garden. Try to reserve, as sometimes it's full with tour groups. The old mining company hotel and best address. **D** ***Hotel Kasbah Asmaa***, on right on southern exit, the neo-kasbah building, T055-583945, F055-580408. 1 person 210dh, 2 persons 264dh, breakfast extra, 20 en suite rooms, nomad tents, garden, fireplaces, can set up treks. **E** ***Hotel Bougafer***, Ave Mohammed V, T055-583099. Up the hill round behind the bus station, best cheap option, en suite rooms and simple 3- and 4- bed rooms on top floor. Spotless, good food. Recommended. There are several more basic hotels, including: **E** ***Hotel Roi de la Bière***, T055-582625, near the southern exit. 1 person 110dh, 2 persons 150dh. Only 1 shower and loo. **F** ***Hotel Atlas***, Rue Mohammed Amraoui T055-582938. Small family run hotel. Very clean. **F** ***Hotel Mimlal***, T055-582266, on left as you come into town from north, 1½ km walk from bus station. Food fine, cheap rooms and 'suite' at 150dh. **F** ***Hotel Toulouz***, in the centre, behind the *Shell* station near the main roundabout. 4 rooms, you don't get more basic than this. You may be able to **camp** in the grounds of the *Hotel Ayyachi*, but the ***Timnay*** (see below) is really the best option for this.

Zaïda road D/E ***Auberge-Restaurant Timnay***, T055-583434, F055-360188, timnay@iam.net.ma 20 km from Midelt. This is an efficient set-up, with a range of accommodation, including simple rooms, camping, nomad tents and sites for campervans. There is a restaurant, shop and small pool, also rental of 4WD vehicles, with guide for exploring the region. For a 4WD, 4 people are necessary to cover costs. Possible circuits on offer include Zaouiat Sidi Hamza and the upper Taâraârt Valley (2 days, 415dh per person). A good day trip: Canyon de Tatrout.

Eating

Groups tend to use the restaurant of the ***Hotel Ayyachi***, perfectly acceptable, alcohol. Otherwise cheap options include: ***Restaurant de Fès***, 2 Ave Mohammed V, which has very good couscous; ***Excelsior***, also in the town centre, on the corner as you go uphill from central roundabout, alcohol, seedy inside, nice service; ***Brasserie Chez Aziz***, by the Er Rachidia exit. Plenty of cafés for breakfast opposite the central *gare routière*.

Excursions from Midelt

There are some excellent excursions from Midelt. Walkers will want to head for the mountains and the **Cirque de Jaffar**. For those with hire car, a good half-day adventure is to drive via **Mibladene** up to the abandoned mines at **Ahouli**. In the heart of the eastern High Atlas, **Imilchil** is now feasible as a long day trip on the metalled road via Rich. Note that as elsewhere in this plateau region, the winters are very cold and the summers very hot, so the best time to visit is the spring. Here the spring is later, and May or even early June are recommended for walking.

The Mines of Ahouli Another, shorter excursion north from Midelt goes along the S317 to **Mibladene** (10 km) and over the head of the Oued Moulouya to the abandoned mining settlement of Ahouli. The road is signed right a few metres north from the central, bus-station junction in Midelt. The first long straight section to Mibladene is badly potholed, then improves slightly after Mibladene, a former mining community, to the right of the road. You then wind into spectacular gorges. The road deteriorates after an Indiana Jones-style bridge, parts of it washed away by floods.

Ahouli, which once must have been a hive of industry, is an amazing sight. Copper and lead were the main products. The gorge is beautiful, with poplar, oleander and even the odd weeping willow. Mine infrastructure and housing clings to the cliffs. The community even had its own rather splendid cinema (now sanded up) and swimming pool. The lower floors of the houses had heavy metal doors, to keep out eventual flood water. There is a caretaker here, and he or his son may show you round.

After Ahouli, you can drive up out of the gorges on a well made track, turning left to more abandoned dwellings on the plateau. Turning left, and a couple of kilometres brings you to the small village and semi-abandoned ksar of **Ouled Taïr** next to the oued, reached by a wobbly footbridge. Few visitors ever come here. With a guide, there must be some superb hiking opportunities. The ksar village of **Ksabi** and the S329 road are only a few kilometres away in fact.

NB When driving out to Mibladene, men will try to flag your car down. Most will be selling fossils or stones of some kind. With all three mines in the region (Mibladene, Ahouli and Zaïda) now closed, there is a lot of poverty and selling stones is about the only thing left for many people to do .

The Aftis Plain & Jebel Missour A longer excursion, a round trip of 260 km, leaves the P21 just 15 km south of Midelt, taking the left turn, the S329 towards Missour and eventually to Guercif. This is the Aftis plain with orchards of olives, figs and tamarisk trees, among which are a number of *ksour*. Bee-eaters, nightingales and olivaceous warblers breed here. Jebel Missour gradually rises ahead to the left. From Missour, travel west rising up towards the Tazaouguart Pass, the bulk of Jebel Ouchilas (2,053 m) blocking the view south. For those with four-wheel drive a detour to the north to El Borj is possible, taking the rough road just after the *oued* cuts across the road. This road here is liable to be washed away after heavy rains. Beyond El Borj, the track is very unreliable and those determined to see subalpine and Orphean warblers must go carefully. The main road descends to Enjil after the pass, to the P20 and on to **Taouerda** and **Zeïda**, another poor former mining community located on Oued Moulouya. (For hard-core ornithologists, the area to the south is noted for hearing if not sighting the Dupont's lark at dusk.) More practically, at Zeïda you choose whether to take the P33 west to join the main P24 Marrakech-Khénifra-Azrou road, continue north on the P21 via the Col du Zad for Azrou, or simply go south back to Midelt.

Jebel Ayyachi Midelt it also the jumping off place for treks up to Jebel Ayyachi which at 3,747 m is eastern Morocco's highest mountain, an impressive 45 km stretch of solid mountain, unbroken by any peaks. The heights can remain snow-covered into late June. In the right conditions, on a long summer's day, the climb can be done in a day. Better, however, to take two days and bivouac out on the mountain. In the winter, sporty Morocco-based French ski-enthusiasts go in for some ski-touring on the mountain.

To tackle the Jebel Ayyachi, head first for **Tattiouine**, 12 km from Midelt (grand taxi transport available). Here it should be possible to find mules and a guide. For a fit party, the climb and back should take around 12 hours. Make sure you have plenty of water. Even in summer, it can be very cold at the summit. For information, the first ascent of the mountain was made in July 1901 by the Marquis de Segonzac.

Impressive and seemingly impenetrable with its snow-capped heights, the Jebel Ayyachi functions as a water tower for southeastern Morocco, its melt water feeding both the Moulouya to the north and the Oued Ziz to the south (and carving out the impressive gorges, see below, too). On the northern flanks, above 1,800 m, evergreen oak and juniper and even occasional patches of cedar forest survive. The south side is obviously far more arid. In the 17th and 18th centuries, the mountain was known as Jebel Sidi Hamza after a local holy man, founder of the Hamziya brotherhood. Later the mountain took on the name of the local Aït Ayyach tribe. Within living memory, caves in the cliffs were occupied by freedom fighters resisting the Makhzen and the incoming French. The last of such mountain strongpoints were only finally taken by the central authorities in 1932.

Cirque de Jaffar

One of Morocco's best known four-wheel drive excursions takes intrepid off-roaders up to the Cirque de Jaffar (map NI-30-II-3), one of the natural arenas hollowed out on the north side of the Jebel Ayyachi. In fact, in a good off-road vehicle it is just about possible to travel over from Midelt, via the Oued Jaffar to Imilchil, a distance of 160 km. The initial part through the Oued Jaffar gorges is the most scenic. The route is not to be attempted in winter, however, and certainly not risked in spring if there are April snows. Consult the Gendarmerie royale in Midelt or the people at *Auberge-Restaurant Timnay*, T055-583434, timnay@iam.net.ma, on the Zeïda road. At other times, the major problem on this route is the kids who come flying out of the villages as you drive through. Never get aggressive, take it easy – and remember, they can throw stones far better than you can. In the Oued Jaffar gorges, look out for the so-called 'Portuguese cave dwellings' up in the cliffs (see 'Art and Architecture' in the Background chapter). The basic four-wheel drive day trip option here is a 62 km round trip via Souk Aït Oumghar and the gorges.

Rich to Imilchil

Although geographically closer to Beni Mellal than to Rich, Imilchil is dealt with here via the easiest access route, the newly completed road from Rich (138 km, three hours). After crossing the wide Oudlalas plain to Amouguer, the road takes you up into the eastern High Atlas, through splendid landscapes with lots of geological convulsions clearly visible. Though good, the road is slow as it winds constantly, as befits a former mule track. There are straight bits where the temptation is to zip along, and then you meet sudden bends. Go carefully, especially when passing through villages. **Outerbate**, set among poplars and tiny fields, about 80 km from Imilchil, is the first major settlement, then you climb up towards the plateau regions.

Imilchil is famous for its annual *Moussem des fiançailles*, a sort of summer wedding festival which was an occasion for people from all over the region to get together. The *moussem* site is in fact at **Allamghou**, signed left off the route, some 20 km before Imilchil and near the meeting place with the mountain piste up from Tinghir. The local legend goes that two young people fell in love and wanted to marry. Their parents said no, and they cried so much that two lakes formed: Tislit for the girl, and Isli for the bridegroom. With such results, the parents could hardly continue to refuse and thus allowed their offspring to choose the partner of their choice. The *moussem* was a great occasion for locals to turn out in all their finery, and there were plenty of traditional dances and singing. In recent years, the occasion has suffered from the incursions of tourists – and drought. Being cancelled in 2000, the official explanation was that funds were unavailable. In all of Morocco's rural communities, weddings, expensive, once-in-a-lifetime occasions that they are, require a lot of available capital, always in short supply in drought years.

Nevertheless, in villages along the route to Imilchil, there is some new prosperity, lots of new building, for the most part using traditional packed-earth construction methods. In Imilchil itself, reinforced concrete has arrived, with unsightly new building ruining the area round the village's beautiful kasbah, sadly being allowed to crumble away by the owners.

Imilchil

Colour map 2, grid A3

The end of a slow drive up from Rich, the village of Imilchil does not exactly dazzle. There is a dusty, sloping main street, where you will find a couple of small cafés, the local dispensary and the entrance to the souk enclosure. The town's finest feature, the kasbah, is sadly sagging, its earthen walls deteriorating a little more with every passing winter. Apparently, descendants of the clan that built the kasbah cannot agree on what to do with their large earthen heirloom, which is really rather sad, as this used to be one of the most emblematic buildings in the Atlas. Still, the government has put in a new concrete administrative kasbah on a rise overlooking the village, and there are a couple of ersatz tourist kasbahs, too (and no doubt more on the way).

For walkers, a little information on possible treks can be obtained from the *Hotel Izlane* (see below), and the management may be able to put you in contact with a suitable local guide. Within the vicinity of Imilchil, a good long half day's walk would be to the settlement of **Iboukhennan** about 3 km from Imilchil on the route west, and then up the **Tissekt-n-Tamda** (3,022 m), a summit above the Tizi-n-Oughroum pass. Another, longer hike, also via Iboukhennan, takes you up the **Jebel Amandar** (3,037 m), the highest point in the range running northeast to southwest parallel to the Assif Melloul to the north.

As a trekking-base village, Imilchil has a number of accommodation possibilites, best of which is the **E** *Hotel Izlane*, clearly visible behind the Kasbah, T023-442806, run by mountain guide Khalla Boudrik. B&B 70dh, half-board 120dh, large restaurant, 15 rooms, 39 beds, three showers, four loos. Has regional maps and can advise on treks. Try also **E** *Café-Hotel Atlas*, T023-442828, ably managed by the volubile Moha Ougourar, 14 basic rooms, 1 person 40dh, 2 persons 80dh, breakfast 15dh, meals 55dh. There is simple dormitory accommodation elsewhere in the village. A good contact is Zayid the butcher (*el jazzar*), who speaks English and can put you in contact with guides and muleteers for a trek.

Towards Lac Tislit & Lac Isli

Just 5 km north of Imilchil lies Lac Tislit, an exquisite austere oval of blue ringed by reeds, and set in an arid hollow of the mountains. Unfortunately, the natural splendour has been marred by an unnecessary bogus kasbah, complete with plastic ceremonial tents and four-wheel drive park. Why, oh why are these things allowed to happen? Should you wish to stay, there is **D** *Auberge Tislit*, T055-524874 (Meknès office) T06-1251572, F055-527039. Half-board 165dh, loos could be cleaner. The other option, on the right a couple of kilometres between Imilchil and Lac Tislit, is the brand new **E** *Auberge-Kasbah Adrar*, BP 23, 52403 Imilchil, T/F023-442184, 1 person 100dh, 2 persons 200dh with breakfast, also 50dh with breakfast for night in nomad tent. Nothing authentic about this place, big, clean rooms. After Lac Tislit, the second, larger Lac Isli is an easy day's excursion by four-wheel drive.

North from Imilchil by road

Until recently, the easiest access to Imilchil was from the east, on the metalled road from Rich. The shorter, but much slower northern route, from either El Ksiba (see previous chapter, Azilal High Atlas for accommodation options) and Aghbala, difficult to metal in parts, was for four-wheel drive enthusiasts only. However with roadworks across Morocco advancing as the 2002 elections are in sight, Imilchil is getting steadily more accessible. Leaving Lac Tislit on the right, head north and up over the Bab ou Ayyad pass before dropping down to the Tassent Gorge. Here a 12 km section, in a difficult, frequently flooded section of valley (Tassent to Ou Ali ou Idir), is still track, almost guaranteed to take the bottom off a small car if you aren't a skilful driver. (A Peugeot 205 or Renault 4L should do it, with a lot of care.) From Ou Ali ou Idir, there is more tarmac to the junction at Sanslit-n-Ouzarghfal, where you can go right (east) for Aghbala (also spelt Arhbala) and on to the P33 or left (west) through to Naour. Shortly after Naour, the options are southwest to Ouaouizaght or north to El Ksiba (and the main P24), via the Tizi-n-Aït Ouirra. The completion of the last stretch of tarmac north of Imilchil will no doubt bring the region more into the main tourist circuit. Total distance between El Ksiba and Imilchil is 110 km, taking about five hours if the piste in the Tassent Gorge is not in too bad condition.

For the very hardy wishing to get to Imilchil from the south, there are lorries early on Monday mornings from Tineghir.

West from Imilchil to Anergui and Zaouiat Ahansal

One of the best treks in the Atlas takes you from the plateaux of the Imilchil region, via the Assif Melloul and the beautiful village of Anergui to the former pilgrimage centre of Zaouiat Ahansal. This route, part of the *Grande traversée de l'Atlas Marocain*, takes you through remote regions where knowledge of French (and even Arabic) will be rudimentary to say the least. Take a local, preferably Tabant-trained, guide who will be aware of conditions in terms of snow (if travelling outside summer) and water levels in the Assif Melloul. At Zaouiat Ahansal, you link in with further routes southwest to the Aït Bougmez and north to the so-called cathedral rocks of Tilouguite and Ouaouizaght.

From Imilchil to Anergui

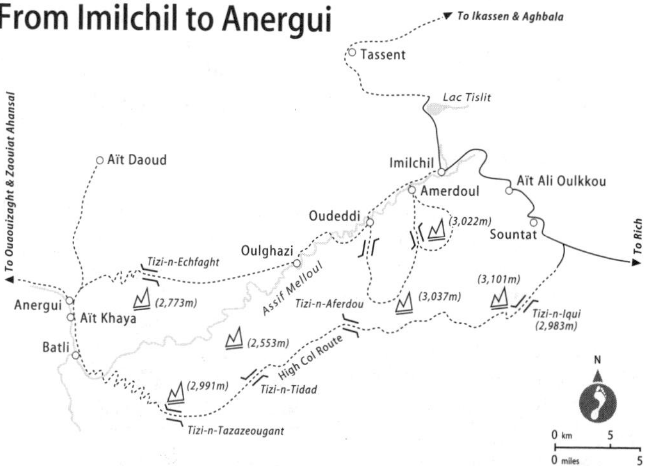

From Imilchil to Anergui There are various trek routes from Imilchil to Anergui, a distance of roughly 57 km. The route you take will depend on weather conditions. Some routes require better than average physical condition. If the Assif Melloul is not in flood, your guide will take you along the riverside route, which will involve some wading and goes via the small settlements of Oudeddi and Oulghazi. After Oulghazi, you may head up out of the river valley and head for Anergui via the Tizi-n-Echfart. The other option is a more perilous route high above the river. Note that the river will be in full flood in spring, and that ice in shady areas can make high paths perilous for both people and mules.

It is also said to be possible to do Imilchil to Anergui in a four-wheel drive vehicle, via the so-called 'High Cols' route. This means heading southeast from Imilchil to Bou Zemou. Thence you head more or less due west-southwest on piste taking you parallel to the Assif Melloul over four major cols, namely the Tizi-n-Igui, 2,983 m, the Tizi-n-Aferdou, 2,957 m, the Tizi-n-Tidad and Tizi-n-Tazazeougart. This last col is followed by an impressive series of hairpin bends dropping down 1,000 m in 9 km to the village of Batli. Ensure you get reliable local information on this route before setting out in vehicles.

With the green of its fruit and walnut trees, **Anergui** is one of the most beautiful sites in the eastern High Atlas. There is now a *gîte d'étape*, contactable via the café next to the Crédit agricole in Ouaouizaght. If you have time, it would be pleasant to spend more than just a night here. In fact, Anergui now has good accommodation, the *Wihalane* ('the right place'), capacity 24. For information, contact Lahcen Fouzal on T023-442331 via *Studio La Nature* in Ouaouizaght or via José Garcia, 17 Rue de Sermaize, 90000 Belfort, France, T0033-384266049. There is splendid walking out of Anergui, including a three-day excursion to the Gorges du Koucer, where there are old dwellings high in the cliffs. (For walking in the Anergui area, you will need the 1:100,000 scale sheets for Zaouiat Ahansal, Imilchil and Tinghir.)

From Anergui to Zaouiat Ahansal The Assif Melloul continues west from Anergui to meet the Assif ou Ahansal near the so-called 'cathedral rocks' near Tamga. A basic piste from Anergui to Zaouiat Ahansal can (just about) be done with four-wheel drive, a distance of around 92 km. For walkers, this route is one of the finest in the High Atlas, taking you through the beautiful gorges of the Assif Melloul. There is much vegetation, and here and there rather rustic wood and packed-earth bridges. Look out as well to see if there are any old, water-driven barley-mills still in use. Some 35 km from Anergui, you reach **Imi-n-Ouareg** and its metal bridge. Near here the Assif Melloul feeds into the Oued Ahansal. Here there are some good bivouac places in the pine forest. Some walkers may prefer to halt here for a couple of nights in order to have a day to explore the **Rocher du Cathédrale**, the celebrated **Amesfrane** (height 1,872 m) on the south bank of the Oued Ahansal. From the cathedral rocks, you have a further 58 km to go before reaching Zaouiat Ahansal, heading southwards along the valley of the Oued Ahansal.

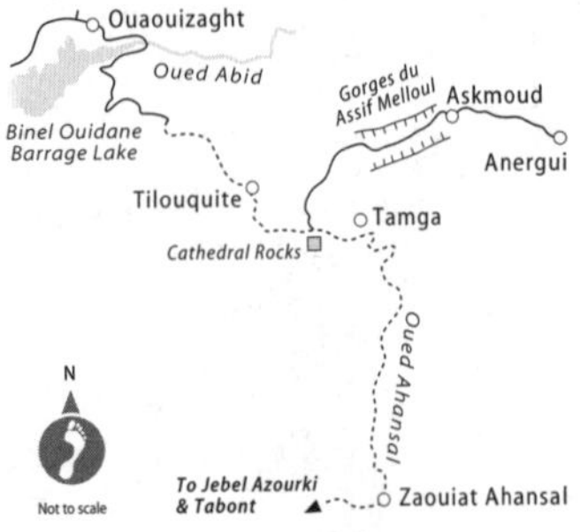

Zaouiat Ahansal

Colour map 2, grid B2

One time centre of the Ahansaliya brotherhood, the Zaouiat Ahansal (altitude 1,600 m) is renowned for its fortified granaries. In past days, the village became important due to its location at a meeting of the ways between the eastern and central High Atlas. For walkers, it is the base for spectacular treks into canyons such as the Akka Tazaght to the southeast. In terms of accommodation, there are a couple of *gîtes*. Note, however, that as in many poor, out of the way places, the children can be a bit trying.

The Ahansaliya

Back in the 17th century, Zaouiat Ahansal acquired its present name. One Sidi Saïd ou Youssef, scholar and soufi, achieved pre-eminence among the Ihansalen clan. But the Sultan of the day, the powerful Moulay Abdallah (he who had Essaouira fortified), captured Sidi Saïd during a punitive military expedition in 1729. The story goes that the leader of the Ihansalen was captured and tortured, his feet and hands chopped off and his body left out for the jackals. No possible alternative to the Alaouite dynasty with its impeccable religious credentials could be allowed to arise. For Sidi Saïd's followers, he had just 'disappeared'. The Ahansaliya and their zaouias, lodges where religious learning was dispensed and disputes settled, maintained their prestige, however, as did the the Ahansali lineage. When the French were taking over Morocco, there was much worry as to how to handle this region of difficult, isolated terrain. In the event, the leaders of some tribes, notably the Aït Mhamed, quickly made pacts with the French in the early 1920s, no doubt fearing that treatment at the hands of the rapacious Glaoui of Marrakech to the west would be far worse. Other Ahansaliya zaouias resisted and it was an Ahansali who led Aït Atta fighters in the early 1930s in their bid to maintain their freedom against overwhelming French firepower.

Azilal to Zaouiat Ahansal

The easiest way to Zaouiat Ahansal is from Azilal, a distance of 83 km. Much of the distance is now metalled. There are fairly frequent landrover taxis doing this run. About 17 km out of Azilal, a junction is reached where you either go right for the Aït Bougmez or left for Aït Mhamed (Saturday souk), 3 km further on. From here you have another 63 km to go to Zaouiat Ahansal. The tarmac runs out a few km out of Aït Mhamed. The track continues east-southeast towards the Tizi-n-Tsalli-n-Imenain (2,763 m, 50 km out of Azilal), in the shelter of the great Jebel Azourki (3, 677 m). A further col, the Tizi-n-Ilissi (2,600 m) comes 16 km further on, below Jebel Arroudane (3,359 m). Then comes the drop down to Zaouiat Ahansal.

Ouaouizaght to Zaouiat Ahansal

Another option, if starting from Beni Mellal, is to head for Ouaouizaght by grand taxi and then hope to pick up a landrover taxi to Zaouiat Ahansal (distance approximately 114 km). The surfaced road runs out some 30 km out of Ouaouizaght. Tilouguite (Saturday souk) is reached 42 km from Ouaouizaght, and 8 km further on are some good views of the cathedral rocks. About 55 km from Ouaouizaght the meeting of the Assif Melloul and the Oued Ahansal is reached near Imi-n-Ouareg. From here it is another spine-jarring 58 km to Zaouiat Ahansal.

Background

Background

History

The modern Kingdom of Morocco has a very particular geographic location – rather like its neighbour to the north, Spain – and this has undoubtedly been an important factor in shaping the country's history. Morocco is the westernmost country in the Muslim world, and for centuries it was 'the Land of the Farthest West', *El Maghreb El Aqsa*, to the Arabs. Despite being the closest Arab land to Europe, Morocco was the last to come under European domination. The Moroccans are highly aware of the particularities of their location, and are convinced that their history has given them a civilization which combines the virtues of the Arabs, Berbers, Andalucíans, Jews and Christians who converted to Islam.

Moroccan history can be conveniently divided into two major times: the distant **pre-Islamic past**, marked chiefly by Phoenicians and Romans, and the much better documented times of the **Islamic dynasties** – at their most brilliant during a period roughly equivalent to the European Middle Ages. From the 16th century into the 19th century, the rulers of Morocco were constantly fighting back the expansionist designs of the Iberian states – and later of France – under whose rule the majority of the Cherifian Empire, as it was called by the colonizers, came from 1912 to 1956. (The last area under colonial rule, the former Spanish Sahara, was regained in the 1970s.) The later 20th century saw the formation of the modern Moroccan State and its growing integration into the world system.

Pre-Islamic times

Human settlement in Morocco goes back millennia. Rock carvings in the High Atlas and Sahara and objects in stone, copper and bronze have survived from early times. Nomadic pastoralism is thought to have existed in North Africa from around 4000 BC, among a population today referred to as Libyco-Berber by historians, and thought to be part of the wider Hamito-Semitic group, which eventually sub-divided into the Egyptians in eastern North Africa, and the Berbers to the West.

The enterprising Phoenicians were to develop commercial interests in the Maghreb. Utica in Tunisia is thought to have been their first entrepôt in North Africa. Carthage (also in modern Tunisia) was founded in 814 BC, and was to develop an extensive network of trading posts along the Mediterranean and African coasts. Archaeological exacavations at Russadir (Melilla), and at Larache and Essaouira along the Atlantic coast have shown that these towns started life as Phoenician settlements. According to the *Journey of Hanno*, the Carthaginian expeditions were to undertake the careful exploration of the Mediterranean coast before preceding southwards along the dangerous Atlantic.

Lost in the mists of ancient times is the history of the Berber peoples of inland Morocco, referred to by the Romans as the Maures – hence the Latin name 'Mauretania' for the kingdom which seems to have taken shape in the fourth century BC over part of what is now Morocco. This early state, probably established by a federation of Berber tribes, may have had its capital at Volubilis, near Meknès, or possibly at Tanger or Rabat. It probably maintained close commercial links with the maritime empire of Carthage.

After the defeat and destruction of Carthage in 146 BC and the establishment of the Roman province of Africa (later to give its name to the continent), it was only natural that the empire of the Caesars develop an interest in the lands of the Maures – always a potential source of trouble. (Roman forces had had considerable trouble in putting down the revolts of the Berber kingdoms, the most difficult campaigns being in the eastern Maghreb against Jugurtha, from 109-105 BC.) To establish stable rule in northwestern Africa, Augustus was to entrust Mauretania to Juba II, son of Juba I, an enemy of Julius Caesar who had committed suicide after Pompey's defeat in the civil war between Caesar and Pompey.

Juba II proved to be a cultured monarch. He had grown up in Rome and had married Cleopatra Selene, daughter of the famous Cleopatra and Mark Anthony. From 25 BC, he reigned over much of what is now Morocco. He spoke Amazigh, Greek, Latin, and Punic, and travelled constantly through his domains. He had wide-ranging interests in the arts, sciences and medicine. His portrait in the form of a fine bronze bust was discovered during the excavation of the ancient city of Volubilis near Meknès.

Eventually, Rome was unable to tolerate the presence of the Mauretanian monarchy. The last king, Ptolomey, grandson of Anthony and Cleopatra, was put to death by the Roman emperor Gaius. The client kingdom was transformed into a Roman colony. In the early 20s AD, under Claudius, Roman northwestern Africa was reorganized as two provinces with capitals at Iol-Caesarea (Cherchell in Algeria) and Tingis, today's Tanger.

Roman administration and Latin culture were grafted onto Punic and Berber peoples. An important influence was the army (as was also the case in Roman Britain). Right down to 19 BC, there was fighting in North Africa and the army continued to extend its influence. A major Berber revolt, led by one Tacfarinas, took seven years to suppress.

Such tensions were probably generated as the Romans sought to extend agriculture into areas formerly occupied by nomads. Centurions were settled with grants of land. The wealth of Mauretania Tingitana was no doubt primarily agricultural, from olive and grain harvests. Army pay also brought money into the local economy. Although not as densely settled as the province of Africa (modern Tunisia), the towns had all the institutions and trappings of Romanized urban life, and were to flourish until the third century AD.

The third to eighth centuries AD are a somewhat hazy time in the history of northwestern Africa. There was a series of Amazigh insurrections, while the Romanized populations protested against the unfairly low prices of wheat, wine and olive oil supplied to the metropolis. Although Christianity became the official religion of Rome in 313 AD, it proved insufficient glue to hold the Empire together against the Germanic invasions. The Vandals swept down from Spain and across into the eastern Maghreb in the fifth century. Although the Byzantine Empire was to take back certain territories in the sixth century, its unity was undermined by struggles within the Church. Mauretania Tingitana was never effectively ruled again by a Roman administration.

The arrival of Islam

The key event in shaping Morocco's history was the conquest by the Muslim Arabs in the eighth century AD. Islam, the religion of the Prophet Mohammed, was born in the oases of Arabia in the seventh century AD. It gave the warring Arab tribes and oasis communities, formerly pagan, Jewish, and maybe Christian, the necessary cohesion to push back the Byzantine and Sassanian Empires, exhausted by years of warfare. Mesopotamia and Syro-Palestine, along with Egypt, were quickly taken – the population of the latter, Christian heretics in the eyes of Byzantium, welcomed the invaders. The first Arab conquerors of North Africa founded Kairouan (in present-day Tunisia) in 670 AD, and pushed on as far as the Atlantic.

In eighth century North Africa, Islam was welcomed by the slaves – who freed themselves by becoming Muslims – and by Christian 'heretics' who saw the new religion as simpler and more tolerant than Byzantine Christianity. In 711, therefore, it was an Islamized Amazigh army which crossed the Straits of Gibraltar under Tarik

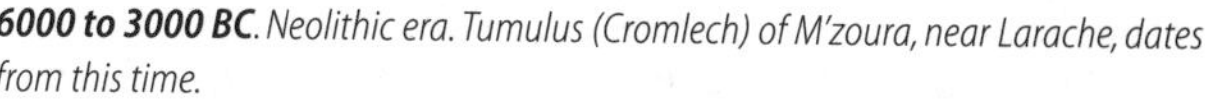

Quick chronology 1: ancient Morocco

6000 to 3000 BC*. Neolithic era. Tumulus (Cromlech) of M'zoura, near Larache, dates from this time.*
3000 BC onwards*. Proto-historic period. Bronze tools manufactured in Morocco, to judge from evidence of rock carvings.*
7th century BC*. First attested Phoenician presence in the form of trading posts in Morocco, notably near the sites of modern Essaouira and Larache.*
5th century BC*. Carthage establishes trading posts on the coast.*
4th to 3rd centuries BC*. Kingdom of the Maures established.*
146 BC*. Fall of Carthage to Rome. Northwest Africa (or* Mauretania, *as it is referred to by the Latin authors) comes under Roman influence.*
33 BC*. King Bocchus II leaves the Kingdom of the Maures to Rome.*
24 BC*. Juba II comes to the Mauretanian throne. Augustus rules in Rome.*
40 AD*. Ptolomey, son of Juba II and Cleopatra Selene, is assassinated on the orders of the Emperor Caligula.*
42 AD*. Northwestern Morocco becomes a Roman province as* Mauretania Tingitana *with its capital at Tingis, modern Tanger.*
3rd century AD*. Christianity appears in Morocco. Rome abandons the province south of the Oued Loukkos.*
4th century AD*. The elephant becomes extinct in northwestern Africa.*
429 AD*. The Vandals invade North Africa, but fail to establish a lasting presence in Mauretania Tingitana.*
533 AD*. During the reign of Justinian, the Byzantine Empire re-establishes control of the coastal cities of Ceuta and Tanger.*
Late 6th / early 7th centuries AD*. An obscure time.*

ben Ziyed, conquering the larger part of the Iberian peninsula. Along with North Africa, the southern regions of the peninsula, referred to as Al-Andalus (whence Andalucía), were to form a strong socio-cultural area until the 15th century.

Islam, which vaunts a spirit of brotherhood within a vast community of believers, and condemns petty clan interests and local loyalties, was to prove an effective base for new states based on dynastic rule, with central governments drawing their legitimacy from their respect for the precepts of the Koran and the Hadith, the codified practice of the Prophet Mohammed.

From the arrival of Islam, Morocco's history thus becomes that of the rise and fall of dynasties, often ruling areas far wider than that of the contemporary nation state. Putting things simply, these dynasties were the **Idrissids** (ninth century), the **Almoravids** (11th century), the **Almohads** (12th-13th centuries), the **Merinids** (13th-15th centuries), the **Wattasids** (15th-16th centuries), the **Saâdians** (16th century), and finally the **Alaouites**, rulers of Morocco from the 17th century to the present. All these dynasties were closely linked to the development of religious life, and in most cases, had sprung from politico-religious movements.

To return to the early centuries of Islamic rule in North Africa, the new religion took hold fairly slowly, as struggles between rival dynasties in the Middle East – the Umayyads and the Abbasids – divided the Islamic heartlands. The Islamic ideal was certainly not the only interest of the Arab conquerors and the governors sent out by the caliphs. Power was often exercised despotically, and exactions and repression led to a great revolt against the Arab rulers (740-780) in the name of Islam. The revolt was of Kharijite inspiration – the Kharijites considering that they practised the most pure and egalitarian form of Islam. The Kharijites rejected the split between Sunni and Shi'a Muslims and refused to submit to the authority of the caliphs of Damascus and Baghdad. Even at the end of the struggle between Umayyads and Abbasids in 750 AD, and the victory of the latter, central Islamic power was slow to reassert itself in the northwestern extremities of Africa, which remained, along with the northern Sahara, independent as the Berber Kharijite Kingdom of Tahert. Then, in the mid-eighth century, an Umayyad descendant of the Prophet, fleeing the Middle East, founded the first great Muslim dynasty in 788. Idriss I founded Fès in 808, while another Umayyad prince who had taken refuge in Cordoba was to build a kingdom in Al-Andalus.

The ninth and 10th centuries saw the development of the trans-Saharan caravan trade, notably in gold. There were routes leading up into what is now Tunisia and Libya, and other, longer routes across the western regions of the Sahara. The shorter, western route finished in the Draâ Valley and the southern slopes of the Atlas. Sijilmassa, close to today's eastern Moroccan town of Rissani, was to be the capital of this trade, the mustering place from which the caravans headed onwards to the Middle East and the Mediterranean ports. Sijilmassa was to be taken by a Shi'ite group who, thanks to their control of the gold trade, were able to found the Fatimid dynasty – named after Fatima, daughter of the Prophet and wife of Ali, considered by the Shi'ites as the legitimate caliph or successor of the Prophet Mohammed. This dynasty was subsequently to use Mahdiya, in Tunisia, as its springboard for the conquest of Egypt, heart of the Islamic world.

Tribal dynasties and religious causes

The Saharan gold trade, in the 11th century, was to be dominated by a nomad Berber group, based in fortified religious settlements or *ribat* – hence their name, *el murabitoun*, which transposes as **Almoravid**, the name of the dynasty, in English. Based in the northern Sahara, they founded a capital at Marrakech in 1062. Their empire was to expand to include much of Spain and present-day Algeria.

In the 12th century, the Almoravids were overthrown by the **Almohads**, *el muwahhidoun* or 'unitarians', whose power base lay in the Berber tribal groupings of the High Atlas. United by their common religious cause, the Almohads took Sijilmassa, the 'gold port', and their empire expanded to include the whole of present day Morocco, Algeria and Tunisia along with Andalucía. This political unity, lasting from circa 1160 to 1260 brought cultural and economic development. The cities expanded and distinctive mosques were built, along the lines of the Koutoubia at Marrakech. Trade grew with the merchant cities of Europe. Arabic took root as the language of the urban areas.

The Almohad dynasty disintegrated towards the end of the 13th century. The ruling tribal élite lost its sense of cohesion – and the feudal Christian lands of Spain were quick to react: Seville fell to the Christians in 1248, and Granada became a sort of protectorate. The Almohad Empire split into three separate kingdoms – roughly corresponding to the independent states of today's central Maghreb. Ifrikiya (presently Tunisia) was ruled by the **Hafsids**, who initially ruled in the name of the Almohads; the **Abdelwadids** ruled from Tlemcen in modern Algeria; in Morocco, the **Merinids** were to establish their capital in Fès.

The Merinids: from tribal to urban dynastic rule

What exactly made a nomadic tribal group, living on the fringes of the desert or in remote mountains, seek to rule all Morocco? In the case of the Almoravids and the Almohads, it was religious doctrine which gave them motivation, while tribal solidarity provided the necessary cohesion. The Beni Merini, rulers of Morocco from the mid-13th to mid-15th centuries, were not champions of any particular religious doctrine. Nomads from the Figuig region, migrating annually to the Mlouia Basin, they first appeared in Moroccan history in the late 12th century, and fought alongside the Almohads in Spain. In 1212, however, after the Almohad defeat at Las Navas de Tolosa, they re-entered Morocco. The first half of the 13th century was a turbulent time, with the Merinids ruling Taza, Fès and Ksar El Kebir in the 1220s, only to be defeated by the Almohads in 1244. But they had tasted power, and now wanted to rule.

In the 1250s, the Merinid forces took the main cities under Abou Yahya El Merini, and Abou Youssef Yacoub (1258-1286) consolidated their rule. The 14th and 15th centuries saw the Merinids build a state centred on Fès – but more or less constantly involved in struggles with mountain tribes and neighbouring dynasties – the Tlemcen-based Zayyanids, the Hafsids farther to the east, and the Nasrids to the north in Granada. The entanglements of late-mediaeval dynastic politics in North Africa are tortuous, to say the least. What, then, was the importance of the Merinids?

Merinid rule saw the emergence of Fès as an important urban centre. The city consolidated its position as a centre of religious learning. Having gained power in a land where political authority depended closely on religious credentials – as was the case for most mediaeval régimes – the Merinids tried to build legitimacy by sponsoring new theological foundations. *Medersas*, rather like the colleges of some early European universities, were founded at Fès and in other cities, providing teaching which reflected the religious mindset of the urban élite. Students, however, came from both town and country, and it may be that in attempting to build an educated group with theological and legal training, the Merinids were seeking to counter the influence of Sufi leaders in rural areas.

To an extent, the Merinids continued tribal traditions. Although there was a court and central administration in Fès, there was no civil provincial administration; regional governors came from the ruling house. However, the Merinids, unlike previous dynasties, were unable to establish their power on the basis of a single tribal element – probably because large settled communities of merchants and artisans were emerging. Thus it was that subsequent dynasties, although they had to use tribal support to achieve their initial aims, never maintained a single tribal affiliation. The European threat which emerged in the 15th century (Ceuta was occupied by the Portuguese in 1415) led to a resistance based on religious ideals, with leaders referred to as *cherifs*, claiming descent from the Prophet Mohammed. When the Merinids proved ineffective in fighting back the Europeans, these leaderships appeared, suitable symbols around which unity could be built due to Cherifian descent. The Saâdian dynasty is an example of one such movement.

Morocco and marauding Europe

The routes of the gold caravans linking sub-Saharan Africa to North Africa meant that any Moroccan dynasty had certain importance. However, as of the 14th century, new routes opened up, reducing the importance of the Maghreb. The Mamlouks in Egypt fought back the Christian kingdoms of Nubia, Spain and Portugal began the quest for maritime routes to the 'gold coasts'. The epoch of the great discoveries began as the Portuguese explored the Atlantic coast of Africa. In 1492, Granada, the last Muslim stronghold in Andalucía, fell to Ferdinand and Isabella – and Columbus sailed for America. The era of European imperialism had begun, and the Maghreb was first in the firing line as the Most Catholic monarchs attempted to continue the Reconquista into Africa. The two powers occupied strongpoints along the Atlantic and Mediterranean coasts (the Spanish *presidios* or garrison towns of Ceuta and Melilla date from this time). However, the Iberian powers' resources were soon to be taken up with the commercially more important development of far-flung empires in the Indies and the Americas. And the Arabo-Berber peoples of North Africa (and the terrain) put up solid resistance.

Quick chronology 2: medieval and early modern Morocco

***622**. Out in Arabia, the Prophet Mohammed is forced to leave unfriendly Mecca for Médina. His* hijra *('emigration') on account of his beliefs is the start of the Muslim era.*
***670**. Arab general Uqba ben Nafi reaches Tunisia.*
***681**. 'Uqba, the tradition says, sends his troops to conquer western North Africa.*
***703**. Moussa ben Nusayr conquers Morocco and begins the conversion of the Berbers to Islam.*
***704**. Tanger falls to the Muslim armies with the help of Count Julian.*
***711**. Tariq ben Ziyad crosses the straits which today bear his name (Jabal Tariq) to begin the conquest of Iberia, which lasts until 732.*
***740**. Berber revolt against central authorities in Damascus. Their heretic, Kharijite, brand of Islam leads to a political break with the Arab Near East.*
***786**. Idriss I, descendant of Caliph Ali and the Prophet's daughter Fatima, reaches Morocco fleeing the Abbasids of Baghdad.*
***788**. Idriss becomes religious leader of the Berber tribes of the Middle Atlas.*
***789**. Foundation of Fès.*
***791**. Idriss I poisoned at orders of Haroun Errachid.*
***803**. Idriss II on the throne.*
***809**. Fès refounded by Idriss II.*
***817-818**. Hundreds of Jewish and Muslim families move to Fès from Cordoba and Kairouan.*
***1048**. Abdallah ben Yassin, a religious reformer from Sijilmassa, creates a fortified settlement or* ribat, *home to warriors* (murabitoun) *– hence the name of the dynasty he founded, the Almoravids.*
***1070**. Youssouf ben Tachfine founds Marrakech (NB 1066 Battle of Hastings).*
***1086**. The minor kings of southern Spain appeal for help to the Almoravids who go on to beat Alfonso VI at the Battle of Sagrajas.*
***1125**. One Ben Toumert declares himself mahdi, 'the rightly guided one', at Tin Mal in the High Atlas. The purist Almohad movement is launched.*
***1126**. The Almohad Abd el Moumen ben Ali (ruled 1130-63) takes the title of caliph. Goes on to conquer North Africa and Iberia up to the Guadalquivir.*
***1143-47**. Collapse of the Almoravid Empire.*
***1148-97**. Construction of major mosques, including the Koutoubia in Marrakech, the Tour Hassan in Rabat and the Giralda, Seville.*
***1244-69**. Almohad Empire falls apart, having lasted barely one hundred years.*
***1248**. Fès falls to the Merinids. They begin the construction of Fès el Jedid.*
***1269**. Fall of Marrakech marks the beginning of the Merinid era.*
***1300s**. Merinid rule is at its height. (France and England are fighting the Hundred Years War.)*
***1400s**. Internal anarchy in Morocco. Merinid collapse in 1465.*
***1492**. Fall of Granada to the Catholic monarchs, Ferdinand and Isabella.*
***1509**. Spain takes Oran.*
***1525-1659**. Saâdian rule.*
***1578**. Battle of the Three Kings ends Portuguese threat to sultanate.*
***1578-1607**. Reign of Ahmed el Mansour ed Dahabi, contemporary of Elizabeth I.*
***1664**. Alaouite rule established at Fès under Moulay Rachid.*
***1672-1727**. Moulay Ismaïl, contemporary of Louis XIV, rules with an iron hand.*
***1757-90**. Sidi Mohammed ben Abdallah rules a stable country.*
***1817**. Corsairing is banned.*

In 1453, the last bastion of eastern Christianity, Constantinople, had fallen to the Ottoman Empire. Muslim resistance to the Christian powers in the western Mediterranean was led by corsairs who called on the Ottoman Sultan in Istanbul for support. By the end of the 16th century, the eastern part of the Maghreb had been divided into three *vilayet* or regencies, Algiers, Tunis and Tripoli. Morocco, however, remained independent, ruled by dynasties of cherifian origin, ie descendants of the Prophet Mohammed. The **Saâdians** (late 15th-16th century), sprang from the Sous region (Taroudant) and under Ahmed el Mansour ed Dahabi (1578-1607), destroyed a Portuguese army, re-established (for a short while) the gold trade, developed sugar cane plantations in the Sous and re-founded Marrakech.

The Alaouites and the foundations of the Cherifian State

After the decay of Saâdian power, a second cherifian dynasty, the **Alaouites**, originally from the oases of the Tafilalet (southeastern Morocco), came to power. The first sovereigns, Moulay Rachid (1664-1672) and Moulay Ismaïl (1672-1727), a tireless builder, restored order. As Fès and Marrakech had risen against him, he created a vast new capital at Meknès: with a large palace and four new mosques, he transformed a pleasant provincial town into a regal city.

There seem to have been major political and strategic motives behind the decision to centre Alaouite authority on Meknès. It enabled the sultan to avoid identifying himself too closely with the interests of either Fès or Marrakech. Meknès was very central, and better situated for campaigning against the Middle Atlas Berbers. It was also more distant than Fès from Turkish dominated lands further east.

Above all, however, Moulay Ismaïl's authority depended on a special army corps composed of black slave troops, the Abid Bukhari. By the end of his long reign, Moulay Ismaïl had a loyal force of some 150,000 men, ever ready to deal with Ottoman encroachment from Algeria, or rebellion amongst the Sanhaja Berbers. By 1686, the sultan's authority was complete, with only remote mountain areas outside his control. The maintenance of such a strong security force required considerable resources, however, and meant resorting to rather non-Islamic forms of taxation. Such economic repression could only lead to resentment in the already defiant urban communities, notably Fès.

After a period of chaos in the 1730s, the work of Moulay Ismaïl continued under Mohammed ben Abdallah (1757-1790). Stability was restored, and the influence of Moulay Ismaïl's Abid army was ended. Many of the *presidios* were re-taken, including Mazagan (today's El Jadida), while Essaouira was given splendid fortifications in 1765. In 1760, the port of Anfa (today's Casablanca) was fortified, and Christian merchants were exempted from duties to encourage them to settle. Morocco came to be respected by the European powers.

Mohammed ben Abdallah was also the first Alaouite sultan who was keen to gain the real support of the urban religious élite, the *ulema*. While previous sultans – and especially Moulay Ismaïl – had relied on their Cherifian lineage as an ideological prop for their rule, Mohammed ben Abdallah sought *ulema* support for his policies. He gained their support because of his own academic interests, and devoted time to developing scholarly activity, even initiating a reform of the curriculum at the Qaraouiyine Mosque. Thus the Moroccan State, although dependent on contingents of tribal soldiery, began to become identified with the interests and social attitudes of Morocco's city dwellers. This trend was accentuated under Mohammed ben Abdallah's successor, Moulay Suleyman (1792-1827).

The 19th century: colonialism held at bay

In 1798, Napoleon Bonaparte led an expedition to Egypt. The lands of Islam became aware of the newly acquired technological power of European armies. Modernization was essential, despite the high financial costs. The alternative was likely to be colonial rule of some kind. The European peace of 1815 was to establish favourable conditions for colonial expansion and France, anxious to re-establish lost prestige, looked towards North Africa. Algiers was taken in 1830, and French colonial expansion continued throughout the 19th century, with a settler population of Mediterranean origin putting down roots. European farming grew, thanks to the redistribution of land confiscated after revolts and modern land registration. New European-style cities were constructed. Although Algiers fell with little resistance, the central Maghreb was brought under French control at a terrible cost to the local population.

Due to the development of French Algeria, Morocco found itself isolated from the rest of the Islamic world – and subject to severe pressure from the increasingly confident European powers. France attacked Morocco for providing shelter to the Algerian leader, the Emir Abdelkader, bombarding Tanger and Mogador (Essaouira) and defeating the Moroccan army at the Battle of Isly in 1844. Great Britain forced the Moroccans to sign a preferential trade treaty in 1856, while in 1860, a Spanish expeditionary force under one Leopoldo O'Donnell took the key northern city of Tetouan. Sultan Abderrahman was forced to accept extremely unfavourable peace terms, with customs coming under foreign control by way of an indemnity and an ill-defined Saharan territory, the future province of Rio de Oro, was ceded to Spain. The departure of Spanish troops in 1862 left Morocco considerably weakened.

A reform policy had been launched, however, under a series of bright, dynamic sultans: **Abderrahman** (1822-1859), **Mohammed IV** (1859-1873) and **Hassan I** (1873-1894). Despite the latter's efforts to expand his power base with the support of the tribes of the High Atlas, further treaties were imposed by Great Britain, Spain and France. The country ran into increasing debt problems with foreign banks and the situation continued to worsen under the weak rulers who succeeded Hassan I.

At the end of the 19th century, with the vast majority of the African continent under colonial rule, Morocco, viewed from Europe, figured as something of an exception. The fact that Morocco was not under some sort of outside rule was due in part to the fact that the European powers could not agree as to who should get such a choice piece of territory. In 1906, the Conference of Algeciras brought 12 nations together to discuss the Moroccan debt. France and Spain were nominated acting representatives of the new *Bank of Morocco*. In 1907, following the killing of some Europeans during unrest, France occupied the key port of Casablanca. A new sultan, **Moulay Hafid** (great-uncle of the present king), was proclaimed the same year. In 1911, with Fès surrounded by insurgent tribes, he called in Algerian-based French forces to end the state of siege.

The last act came in 1912, when the Treaty of Fès, signed by France and Moulay Hafid for Morocco, established the French Protectorate over the Cherifian Empire. A subsequent Franco-Spanish treaty split the country into a northern zone, under Spanish control, a vast central area under French rule, and a southern zone, also assigned to Spain.

The Protectorate: separate development and exploitation

The full occupation of Morocco was to be an extremely arduous affair, with the tribes putting up heroic resistance in certain regions of the Middle and High Atlas and an area of the Rif (northern Morocco), establishing itself as an independent republic which threatened, for a while, the stability of the whole protectorate system.

Lyautey's Moroccomania

For Maréchal Lyautey, filled as he was with a love of tradition, France's role in Morocco was to bring that kingdom the best of modernity, and that only under the auspices of a Cherifian government. He ensured the survival of the monarchy, convincing Moroccans that Moulay Youssef was not 'the sultan of the French'. A real passion to see Morocco renewed motivated all his actions: he knew how to bring engineers and administrators together in a team, how to talk to the notables of Fès, the Paris bureaucrats, even the petits blancs *settlers of Casablanca. But, élitist at heart, he had a profound dislike of everything to do with French society following the 1789 revolution. Of the people of his adopted land, he wrote in 1919, "The Moroccan race is exquisite. It has remained a refuge of politeness, of good measure, of elegant ways, of noble fortunes, respect for social hierarchies, of all things which were such an ornament to us in the 18th century". But as the years passed, the ills of colonial rule took root, "Life here is becoming increasingly inept", wrote Lyautey in a letter to the Marquis de Castries, "not because of the sympathetic Muslims, loyal and gentlemanly, but because of the odious behaviour of French colonists ... what a race". But ironically, it was the organizing genius of Lyautey which made it possible for the whole of Morocco's Atlantic façade to become a laboratory for capitalism. A conservationist Swann in épaulettes, ever critical of the colonial world, he created the conditions for the rise of sprawling, industrious Casablanca and the great mining companies of the Moroccan south.*

The Lyautey system

The French protectorate in Morocco bore the imprint of the first French resident general, Maréchal Lyautey – and the work accomplished during his 12-year rule was to leave a long-lasting mark on the country. Lyautey, a Catholic aristocrat who had seen service in Algeria, Indochina and Madagascar – and witnessed at first hand what he considered to be the errors of the colonial system – was fascinated by Morocco. As something of a monarchist, he had great respect for the sultanate, and was thus not really disposed to intervene in the new protectorate's traditional life. (He saw the sultan as 'a crowned pontif', uniting the shifting, scattered nomad tribes, while the ancient cities were viewed as something akin to Florence under the Medicis. Aristomania aside, the problem was that a large country with such wild terrain could not be easily occupied, especially at a time when war was looming in Europe.

The policy of the Grands Caïds

In fact, when Lyautey took up his post as résident général in late May 1912, he found a full insurrection and total incomprehension on the part of the Court and notables. While Lyautey could say to the notables, "I have full respect for your faith, customs, institutions, your social ranks and protocol"; the Moroccans would merely reply, "Perhaps you do, but we know Algeria and what is happening there. You are the only Frenchman to think like this". On 6 September 1912, at Sidi Bou Othman north of Marrakech, Colonel Mangin's column managed to disperse the barely armed, ragged forces of one Ahmed el Hiba, a Saharan holy man who had proclaimed himself Sultan. While not exactly the Battle of the Pyramids, this clash did give France access to the whole of region from the Atlantic coast to El Kelaâ des Sraghna. But the mountains still remained to be taken. The easiest solution was to co-opt local Amazigh chiefs into the new system. Thus Marrakech and its region was ruled by a local potentate, Madani Glaoui, succeeded by T'hami Glaoui. This meant that large scale forces did not have to be committed at a time when they were needed elsewhere. Lyautey thought of this policy of using the Grands Caïds, as cheaper, more flexible, needing of fewer staff and ensuring better respect for customs and traditions. However, the new feudal lords of the western High Atlas did not go back to the time of

Quick chronology 3: modern Morocco

***1844**. Battle of Isly. Moroccan sultan's forces defeated by the French near Oujda.*
***1880**. Conference of Madrid, while recognizing Morocco as an independent kingdom, confirms the major European powers trade interests.*
***1905**. Kaiser William II visits Tanger and makes a speech proclaiming himself 'defender of Islam'.*
***1907**. France uses major riots in Casablanca as a pretext for sending in troops.*
***1908**. Deposition of Sultan Abd el Aziz by his brother Moulay Hafid with support of Madani el Glaoui. T'hami el Glaoui pacha of Marrakech.*
***1911**. French relieve Fès, besieged by rebel tribes. Sultan sacks T'hami el Glaoui.*
***1912**. 30 March. Proclamation of a French protectorate over central Morocco.*
***1912**. August. Pretender El Hiba besieges Marrakech but is defeated by Colonel Mangin's forces. French name T'hami el Glaoui pacha of the city.*
***1918**. Death of Madani el Glaoui. Pro-French T'hami el Glaoui supreme in Marrakech and the South.*
***1933**. Final pockets of Amazigh resistance crushed in High Atlas (Jebel Baddou).*
***1935**. French declare Morocco 'pacified'.*
***1942**. Allied landings at Casablanca (8 November).*
***1943**. Allied conference at Anfa, Casablanca.*
***1947**. Sultan Mohammed V calls for independence.*
***1953**. Mohammed V deposed and sent into exile, replaced by puppet ruler Mohammed Ben Arafa.*
***1956**. Moroccan independence.*

the Angevin kings. The French-supported Glaoui pachas of Marrakech proved rapacious and violent. Some High Atlas tribes preferred to submit to the *makhzen erroumi* (the French government) rather than come under Glaoui rule. But the so-called 'passive front' was useful to the Protectorate authorities. Though government forces managed to win control of Taroudant and the Sous Valley in 1916, it was well armed Glaoui bands which controlled the oases south of the High Atlas, from Ouarzazate to Tineghir, bringing violence of a new kind with them, that of a cruel feudal lord, Hamou el Glaoui, vulture of Telouet.

On Berber Island

In French colonial thought, the received wisdom about the Imazighen (Berbers) was that they were *bons berbères*. Analogies were made with the Kabyles of neighbouring Algeria, another Amazigh mountain people who were seen as being ready to form part of the French republic provided the veneer of Arab-Muslim culture could be peeled back to reveal a western core. "Let us be, among the Berbers, like Robinson Crusoe on his island", wrote Lyautey. And a decree of 1914 declared that tribes 'said to be Berber in custom' would remain administered by their own laws and customs, under the control of the authorities. This essentially meant that *izref*, Muslim law adapted to local tradition, would remain in force for the Amazigh communities. This absolute respect of custom was in keeping with the Lyautey administration's policy elsewhere. Every effort was made to keep Moroccans in their social roles: tribes and villages, professional guilds and ancient city neighbourhoods.

The Sultanate consolidated

Thus the first period of French rule saw local institutions consolidated, alongside the gradual occupation of the main cities and the coastal plains. The Sultan remained ruler, although executive and legislative powers were shared with the French resident general – and effectively only the latter could issue a *dahir*, a decree. Continuity was preserved: the Sultan had a mini-cabinet with a Grand Vizier, minister of justice and religious affairs. Mohamed El Mokri held the post of Grand Vizier for the entire French period of 44 years (dying shortly after independence, aged 105).

Modernizing Morocco

But exploitation of Morocco's natural wealth marked a break with tradition: it was a capitalist venture, rather than a settler one. Banks, like the *Banque de Paris et des Pays Bas*, financed public and private building works, and exploited mineral concessions through the *Compagnie Générale Marocaine* and the *Omnium Nord Africain*. A major new port was constructed at Casablanca. Rabat was chosen as the capital, and new neighbourhoods were built to house a modern national administration. In addition to this Franco-North African Canberra, other new towns were planned, using the most up-to-date techniques. Working closely with the planner Léon-Henri Prost, Lyautey ensured that Morocco's traditional cities were preserved – and carefully separated from the elegant new European quarters.

It was quickly realized too, that the lands controlled by the Sultan's government, the *bilad el-makhzen* (basically the coastal plains, along with the Fès, Meknès and Oujda regions), were the most fertile – hence the term *le Maroc utile*, 'useful Morocco'. An increasingly dynamic European community undertook to develop the country's resources to its own advantage, helped by various tax concessions.

Infrastructure development was impressive in the French zone. In 1911, a narrow gauge railway was completed between Rabat and Casablanca. In 1956, 1,600 kilometres of standard gauge track was in place, along with 43,000 kilometres of road, one third of it metalled. (The Spanish zone of the protectorate had barely 500 kilometres of road and hardly any agricultural settlers.) The European population reached 325,000 in 1951, with 5,000 people sharing the big fortunes.

But for Lyautey, Morocco was not to be a *colonie de peuplement*, a settler colony, like neighbouring Algeria where the French had shattered local society with such ferocity. Great efforts were made to understand Moroccan society – the rural areas were administered by the specially trained *officiers des affaires indigènes*, and special government departments were created to catalogue and restore Morocco's heritage of historic buildings and crafts. Unfortunately, the knowledge of French experts often only served would-be colonists' interests – take, for example, their calculations of the amount of land necessary for a nomad family's existence.

Fall of Lyautey

Ultimately, however, Lyautey may have been too 'pro-Moroccan' to satisfy a growing settler lobby. The fatal moment came in 1925. The uprising in the Rif led by the enterprising Abdelkrim El Khattabi imperilled the two protectorates. (In July 1921, the Rif armies had captured or killed around 15,000 Spanish soldiers at the Battle of Anoual.) Maybe Lyautey was felt to have hesitated – how could things have reached a point that the tribal army of the Rif Republic, led by a Muslim scholar, actually threatened Taza and Fès? Lyautey was recalled to France, replaced by Maréchal Pétain at the head of a large army which only finally defeated the Rifans in 1926 in co-operation with Spain. Fighting to defeat rebel tribes elsewhere in Morocco continued into the early 1930s.

An urban independence movement

Hardly had Morocco been 'pacified' than a nationalist movement arose, formed mainly of educated intellectuals from the great city families. A focal point for nationalist resentment was the so-called Berber *dahir* (decree) of 1933, which was basically an attempt to trace an artificial anthropological frontier between Morocco's two main ethnic components, Amazigh and Arab. Article Six of the decree said that crimes committed in Berber areas were to be judged by civil French courts (and not Muslim law). A huge storm of protest ensued, Article Six was abrogated – but the damage had been done. French colonial ethnography, source of the reasoning behind this project had made a fundamental miscalculation: Morocco could not be divided into Berbers versus Arabs.

The educated urban bourgeoisie demanded a reform programme in 1934, and with the Second World War, the international situation clearly shifted to favour independence. The urban élite formed the Istiqlal (Independence) Party in 1944 – with the goodwill of Sultan Mohammed V. Although closely watched by the French, the Alaouite Sultan had remained a symbol, and had come to be seen as an instrument of French policy, and certainly not a collaborator. This situation under which the sultan was to all intents and purposes the resident general's unwilling puppet was viewed by the influential religious leaders as an outrage.

Tension grew in the early 1950s – under T'hami el Glaoui, Pacha of Marrakech, contingents of tribal horsemen converged on Rabat to demand the deposition of the Sultan. In 1953, the resident general, in violation of the protectorate treaty, deposed Mohammed V and replaced him with a harmless relative. The royal family found themselves in exile in Madagascar, which gave the nationalist movement yet another point of leverage. The Sultan's return from exile was a key nationalist demand.

The 1950s: France withdraws The situation elsewhere in the French Empire was to ensure a fast settlement of the Moroccan question. France had been defeated in Indochina in 1954, and there was a major uprising in Algeria, considered as an integral part of France by Paris. Extra problems in protectorates like Morocco and Tunisia had to be avoided. The La Celle-St Cloud agreements of November 1955 ensured a triumphal return from exile for the royal family, and independence was achieved in March 1956, with Spain renouncing its protectorate over northern Morocco at the same time. (The issue of the southern desert provinces under Spanish rule, like Rio de Oro, was left to one side.)

Thus Morocco's independence was achieved under the leadership of the country's traditional ruler. The Istiqlal Party had fostered political consciousness in the Moroccan middle classes, and a confrontation between a colonial régime and the people had developed into a conflict between colonial rulers and Muslim ruler. Thus a medieval sultanate, which had been saved by a French colonial governor and had survived under foreign rule was to become an independent kingdom with a unique position in the Arab and Mediterranean worlds.

Modern Morocco

Morocco today is a rapidly changing country whose complexities are not easily dealt with in a few pages. In political terms, the country is one of the most interesting Arab states, with a degree of openness and debate (within certain limits), rare in the Maghreb and Middle East. With a young king on the throne since July 1999, new approaches are apparent in national policy. After a look at recent political history, the present section looks at the economy and contemporary society, touching on education and language, the media, daily life – and future prospects.

Recent history

In 1943, a 'national pact' was concluded between the monarchy and the leaders of the Istiqlal (independence) party. (In June 1943, at the Anfa Conference, Franklin Roosevelt, the Sultan Mohammed V and his son, the future Hassan II, had declared the colonial system out of date, and expressed their desire to see Morocco independent once the Second World War was over.) Much of the political history of contemporary Morocco is about the shifts in the power balance between palace and political groupings. An interesting phase began in 1998, when the left-wing opposition formed its first government. Note too that Morocco is a rarity among Arab states, a country where political

On crowns and things

The royal arms of Morocco (see dirham coins) feature a crown and two rather racy rampant lions. Despite this, the Atlas lion with its dark mane is probably extinct (though there is rumoured to be a pair in Cape Town zoo), and the kings of Morocco have no coronation regalia as such. The equivalent of the coronation is the bay'a, *a ceremony when all the leading figures of the kingdom, from politics and the judiciary, civil society, the armies and the Court, come to the palace to declare their allegiance. In a gesture of respect, all dignitaries incline to kiss the new king's right hand – as almost everyone does when they meet His Majesty, foreigners excluded. The* bay'a, *with almost everyone who counts in Morocco in cream-coloured, hooded robes, is an impressive demonstration of élite solidarity around the sovereign. Traditionally, the hand-kissing or baise-main is a traditional sign of respect for any senior person.*

Also important for Moroccan kingship are the first Friday prayers after the accession. To a wave of stentorian cries of 'May God bless our lord's life', His Majesty leaves the Rabat palace after the best manner of Buckingham Palace royalty, in the state coach, to travel the few hundred metres to the Mechouar Mosque. After prayers, the King returns across the palace enclosure on horseback. In oriental mode, the symbol of kingship, a splendid parasol, is held over His Majesty's head. (For the record, his late majesty, King Hassan II was very keen on vintage cars and thoroughbred Arabian horses, having the world's most fabulous collection of black Arabian steeds at his ranch at Bouznika.)

One Moroccan monarch did in fact acquire a crown. In the last years of the 19th century, shy Sultan Abd el Aziz, surrounded by lying viziers, was kept distracted from the affairs of state by an endless stream of gadgets from abroad. After Edward VII's coronation, someone thought that the Sultan should have a crown. When he objected that for a man to put gold and jewels on his head was contrary to the precepts of Islam, he was shown a picture of the new British monarch in his coronation gear, surveying the imperial horizon, a finger delicately placed on the summit of the bijou headgear. A crown was ordered from Paris.

Decades later, the uncrowned ruler of southern Morocco, T'hami el Glaoui, Pacha of Marrakech was invited to the coronation of Elizabeth II. He took with him presents of a gold and emerald crown for the new monarch and a dagger, for the Duke of Edinburgh. The offerings were declined, however. T'hami's motive in making such expensive gifts? He apparently wished for an English knighthood – as had been granted to Mehdi el Mnebhi, Sultan Abd el Aziz's Minister of War, back at Edward VII's coronation in 1902.

opposition exists openly and where flat consensus is openly contested in the newspapers. Parliamentary elections are due in 2002, the first to be held under the new monarch. Will they be more open and honest than in the past?

Independence in 1956 & after

After independence, the national pact was called into question by members of the urban élite. Their thinking was that it would be possible to push the monarchy aside – rather as had happened in Egypt, Tunisia and Iraq – and rule the country under a one-party system supported by the educated middle classes. The Istiqlal and USFP parties jockeyed for leadership, a revolt in the Rif was put down. The monarchy, however, proved remarkably durable, and after the death of Mohammed V in 1961, it built an alliance with the rural leaders which was to ensure the success of the constitutional referendum of December 1962 and the somewhat controversial parliamentary elections of April 1963.

The new monarch, Hassan II, was to prove a highly able player in the political game. Gradually, the army came to be guarantor of civil order – in particular after the Casablanca riots of March 1965. The Left lost its leader, Mehdi ben Barka, assassinated in Paris in November 1965. As of July 1965, the King was to rule without parliament.

The 1970s However, such a centralized system was fraught with risk, as was soon realized after two attempts on the King's life had been narrowly avoided – the Skhirat Palace attempted coup in 1971, and the attempt to shoot down the royal plane in 1972. Following these events, the King was to seek to rebuild a political system which would end the monarchy's relative isolation on the political scene – and still leave considerable room for manoeuvre. The 'Morocanization' of the remaining firms still (mainly) in French hands, launched in 1973, was part of the strategy, winning the support of the middle classes for the opportunities it offered their bright graduate offspring. Spanish-occupied Rio de Oro and Saquiet el Hamza were regained in the mid-1970s: the army was to be kept busy in these new Saharan provinces, fighting the Polisario, often at bonus pay rates. A number of key players emerged to second the King on the political scene. Foremost among them from the early 1980s was to be Driss Basri, Minister of the Interior. The dialogue between the King and Abderrahim Bouabid, head of the left-wing UNFP in the mid-1970s, was to give the opposition a chance to express itself – and represented a return to the methods used by Mohammed V after independence. In the 1990s, Parliament came to be dominated by the ruling conservative Wifak grouping and the opposition bloc, the Koutla. The early 1990s saw the King actively seeking to bring the opposition into government. In November 1997, Morocco was to elect a parliament with an opposition majority. Abderrahman Youssoufi, in his early 70s (like Hassan II), head of the socialist USFP, was entrusted with the task of forming a government.

1997: l'alternance or the opposition in power The arrival of the opposition in power in 1997 was the culmination of a process steered by the Palace. Hassan II wished to leave things in good running order for his son, Crown Prince Sidi Mohammed. (Some observers have drawn parallels with the transition to democracy in neighbouring Spain in the 1970s.) By the late 1980s, the Palace was clearly aware that the political élite born of the independence struggle was running out of steam – and that the opposition criticism of the inequalities in living standards (*la fracture sociale*, in Moroccan political parlance) had very good grounds. World Bank 'remedies', strenuously applied in the 1980s and early 1990s, have only helped to impoverish a large section of the population (although the OECD would argue otherwise). Drought and poor harvests accelerated the rural exodus, swelling the poorest districts of the major cities and rendering the split between poor and wealthy all the more visible. The first Youssoufi government of 1998 thus had a very clear remit to 'do something' – and quickly – for the poorest in Moroccan society. (Note that the Kingdom has a 60% illiteracy rate.)

Underlying the opposition's coming to power, however, was a very real fear that a large part of the *bidonville* population might be tempted by radical Islam. Viewed from a certain angle, this could be seen as the sole valid opposition now that the Left has been brought into government. Certainly, the middle classes have everything to lose should the country head towards an Algerian-type scenario, and the spectre of chaos and bloodletting just across the frontier from Oujda is felt by many to justify the sometimes strong-arm tactics of the authorities.

The elections of November 1997 unfortunately produced no clear majority. Youssoufi's USFP, with 18% of the votes, appeared as the leading party, closely followed by the Istiqlal (the two together took 102 seats). The right-wing Wifak took 100 seats – hence a coalition was essential, including centre-right parties such as the

Monarchs, battles and freedom fighters

The visitor to Morocco soon realizes that city streets draw on the same selection of names. The biggest avenue in any town will be named for ***Mohammed V*** *(1909-61). Third son of Sultan Moulay Youssef, the young Mohammed was chosen by the French to be Sultan because he was thought to be more malleable. In the event, he ruled Morocco from 1927 to 1961, seeing the country to independence in 1956. His son* ***Hassan II****, ruled 1961-99, also has many streets named after him, as does* ***Prince Moulay Abdallah****, the late king's younger brother. There are also streets named for dynasties (Avenue des* ***Almoravides****, des* ***Almohades****, des* ***Saâdiens****, des* ***Alaouites****) and for major monarchs (ninth century founder of Fès Idriss II, 16th century* ***Mansour ed Dahabi****, 'the victorious and golden'.*

In any self-respecting town, central streets also bear the names of freedom fighters and the battles of the resistance. ***Oued el Makhzen*** *was the battle in 1578 near modern Larache, where Mansour ed Dahabi wiped out the invading Portuguese. The* ***Amir Abdelkader*** *fought the French in Algeria in the 19th century, while* ***Abdelkarim el Khattabi*** *was the leader of the Rif rebellion that set up an independent republic in northern Morocco in the 1920s. At the* ***Battle of Anoual*** *in 1921, he won a famous victory over Spanish forces. In the 1950s,* ***Mohammed Zerktouni*** *lobbed a bomb into a market much frequented by French shoppers in Marrakech, thus ensuring his commemoration on numerous major boulevards. (Imprisoned, he took his own life to avoid torture.)* ***Allal al Fassi*** *was a political leader in the struggle for independence, which was requested on 11 January 1956 and granted on 18 November of the same year. On a more recent note, streets named* ***Al Massira al Khadhra*** *('the Green March') commemorate how thousands of Moroccans flooded southwards to reclaim the Spanish Saharan provinces on 6 November 1975. Streets named for the* ***Battle of Bir Anzarane*** *are a reminder of a major victory by Morocco's armed forces over Saharan separatists.*

RNI (46 seats). A moderate Islamist party, the MPCD, took 9 seats, as many as the communist PPS, which also joined the new ruling coalition.

The former opposition finally constituted a government in March 1998, but not until a number of compromises had been made with the powers that be, earning it the nickname of *la Gauche pastilla* (expression roughly equivalent to 'the Caviar Left' or 'Champagne socialists'). A number of major ministries remained in the hands of leading political figures, including home affairs, foreign affairs, justice and Islamic affairs. The much trumpeted *alternance* was thus initially seen as an attempt to open up the political game – and give the Left some real hands-on experience of government.

July 1999: a new reign

The equation changed sharply on the death of Hassan II on 23 July 1999. His eldest son, crown prince Mohammed, came to the throne as Mohammed VI. A spectacular funeral during which several hundred thousand people thronged the streets of Rabat went off without a hitch, a good sign for the new reign. Very quickly, a desire for change at official level became apparent. New areas, in particular the need to reduce social inequality, soon figured at the top of the royal agenda. And for the first time in decades, areas of the country never visited by the reigning monarch received a royal visit. In long-ignored Tanger and the north, ecstatic crowds turned out in the rain to welcome the King. In the palace, a new cohort of young, bright reform-minded counsellors, some of whom had studied with the King, joined the royal cabinet.

At the top

In public buildings, offices and shops all over Morocco you will see portraits of the country's royals, members of the ruling Alaouite dynasty which has been on the throne since the mid-17th century. Sometimes there is a triptych: a photograph of the late King Hassan II (ruled 1961-1999) flanked by the two princes, the then crown prince Sidi Mohammed and his younger brother, Moulay Rachid. On the death of Hassan II in July 1999, the crown prince came to the throne as Mohammed VI. Increasingly, his portrait as a sober-suited young technocrat is replacing that of the late king on public display. (Trendy clothes shops may have the king in ski-gear complete with woolly gnaoua cap.) In Hassan II's reign, shop-owners picked portraits appropriate to place: in a sports shop, there would be a picture of the king playing golf or in hunting gear while a crèmerie would have the picture of the king alongside a milkmaid; beauty salons favoured a picture of the king and one of his daughters fully made-up for her wedding day.

Hassan II had five children. Elegant Lalla Myriem, the eldest daughter, now in her late 30s, was married to the son of former prime minister Abdellatif Filali. She won much admiration for her courage in getting a divorce, apparently against her father's will. She is much involved in charity work, as are the younger sisters, Lalla Esma and Lalla Hasna. The princesses also accompany their brothers on official visits abroad. Their mother never appeared in public life, and in court protocol, as in the Gulf states, there was never any reference to 'the queen'. In October 2001, the Palace announced HM the King's forthcoming marriage (in early 2002) to Selma Bennani, a bright young IT engineer.

Hassan II also had a brother, the popular prince Moulay Abdallah who died young. By his Lebanese wife he had several children. The eldest, Moulay Hicham, has had an international career and was involved in the UN peacekeeping mission in Kosovo. When his cousin came to the throne, it was thought that his expertise would be brought in to help the new monarch.

For the moment, Morocco's royal family are a popular lot. The hard-working king is a jet-ski adept too, and is seen as being wa'er, *an almost untranslateable slang term meaning something like trendy or cool. The princesses are building themselves public profiles based on constant expression of their concern for the deprived. As an appalling Iranian-style upheaval looks unlikely, they seem set to carry on chairing committees, visiting hospitals and generally keeping the social deprivation issue in the public eye.*

Human rights & governance Described as "a liberal who knows how to listen to wise advice", the new king moved quickly to improve the human rights situation. Critical intellectual and one-time political prisoner Abraham Sarfaty was allowed to return, as were the families of General Oufkir (imprisoned for years before their escape to France) and assassinated left-wing politician Mehdi ben Barka. Former political prisoners and the families of those who 'disappeared' during the repression of the 1970s and 1980s began to receive compensation payments; the house arrest of a leader of an Islamist fringe party, Cheikh Yassine, was ended. The strongest sign of all was the replacement of long-standing Minister of the Interior, Driss Basri. In early 2001, the International Federation of Human Rights held its annual conference in Casablanca.

The replacement of Basri was held to herald an overhaul of the civil service and the security forces. Corruption would no longer be tolerated, local government was to be professionalized. In September 2001, Driss Jettou, a technocrat, became minister of the Interior – his predecessor, Ahmed Midaoui, was felt to have failed in his handling of a number of delicate issues, including the Sahara and relations with

War on kif

Back in the old days, every great Marrakchi home would have its patch of cannabis in the garden courtyard, often carefully tended by the master of the house himself. Things were all very artisanal, and local hash cookie variants were used to liven up dull wedding guests. Even back in the 1970s, with the Tanger on the trail of would-be Beats and other hippies seeking some cheap Nirvana close to Europe, the cultivation of kif (cannabis) was very much a home industry, out in the well watered northern mountains of the Rif. Then some moderately sophisticated technology was introduced to speed up the production of le shit. *As the 1980s advanced, things began to degenerate. The era of the top-of-the-range Mercedes and the drug baron had arrived. With demand fuelled by more permissive attitudes in nearby Europe, cultivation expanded and huge fortunes were accumulated, money being laundered in a rash of speculative building projects in Tanger and over the water in Spain.*

In 1992, the late Hassan II declared war on the drug trade in the northern reaches of his kingdom, the aim being to keep Morocco in the European Union's good books. Corrupt civil servants were sacked, local politicians were told to clean up their act, or else were unceremoniously removed from office. Equipped with four-wheel drives and helicopters, Royal Gendarmerie and customs officers searched the Rif for the drug barons' hideouts, powerful new motor launches combed the coast to identify export points. Behind the campaign was a fear that the Moroccan hash traffic might link in with more powerful Colombian and European networks specializing in hard drugs. By 1996, the authorities estimated that kif-cultivation had been limited to a 'mere' 65,000 ha. Though a number of big names were in prison, it was generally felt that many smugglers had slipped through the net.

Both Europe and Morocco realized that repression would not be enough. In 1996, the government set up the Agence du Nord *to steer through new policies. Spain and the Andalucían regional government pumped money into rural development projects. Slowly, the isolation of the region is coming to an end as electricity lines, better wells and new schools are put in. Ultimately, the idea is for cannabis to be replaced with other cash crops.*

However, this may be wishful thinking. In the late 1990s, yearly production of cannabis reached around 1,000 tonnes, generating a turnover of over 12 million pounds. An estimated million people in northwest Morocco derive some part of their livelihood from kif. The mountain people often have no choice but to supply the big drug barons: no other plant will produce such good crops on the Rif's steep slopes and poor soils. But ultimately the smallholders see little of the profits since they have no contact with European buyers. It is hardly surprising then that huge numbers of poorly qualified young men seek to leave the region, heading for nearby Andalucía. Nowhere else in the world is the wealth difference so great between two neighbouring countries: Spain is estimated to be at least 10 times wealthier than Morocco – and is short on labour. For the moment then, both kif growing and illegal emigration have a prosperous future.

Spain which had been tense due to the numbers of illegal immigrants filtering across the Straits of Gibraltar. Then, in October 2001, HM the King announced that parliamentary elections would be held in September 2002. There were great hopes that they would be fair and open, unlike those organized under the Basri ministry, characterized by extensive rigging and 'official' opposition parties. Officials at all levels were changed, the message went out that the impunity and corruption with which so many minor local *chefs* had operated would no longer be tolerated.

Gradual reform The task of the Youssoufi government was not an easy one. Even though it had legal and constitutional authority, it proved difficult to deal with deeply entrenched networks of economic influence. There was no spectacular wave of reforms, but rather a prolonged and general improvement. Most Moroccans realize that the habits of decades cannot be changed overnight. Reform will be gradual, and as they progress the improvements needed to encourage foreign investment will be made. The general feeling is that the post-2002 government will follow the present line, continuing the reform process in the civil service, security forces and justice, allowing the media more say, revising the labour code and taxation, bringing about an in-depth democratization of political life. Although the Islamists may achieve a greater presence in parliamentary life, they are unlikely to follow the path of their brethren further afield.

Issues and pressures

As a backdrop to the hoped for reforms are a number of issues, including the place of the Islamists, the future of the Saharan provinces, and relations with the European Union, the North African states and international lenders. There are pressures to be juggled with, including the demands of business, the liberal fringe of the middle class, unemployed graduates, the farming community and the shantytown dwellers. Eventually, the Youssoufi governments will be judged on how far they managed to satisfy the expectations of these disparate parties.

Demands & expectations The Conféderation générale des entreprises marocaines (CGEM), the Moroccan employers' organization, wants a reform of the civil service, which it sees as slow and inefficient. This organization has also been highly outspoken on the issue of corruption. The liberal middle classes, though fearful of a perceived Islamist threat, would like further reforms in the official news media – and a reform of the *Moudawana*, Morocco's code on the family and marriage (see 'Culture' below). Unemployed graduates, including many with post-graduate qualifications, want jobs suited to their qualifications – and have demonstrated vigorously for this. The farming community, including modern, mechanized agro-business, wants to preserve its subsidies. The shantytown dwellers and the rural poor want a decent standard of living, including access to education and health care.

The Youssoufi government has set ambitious targets, aiming to bring illiteracy down to 25% by 2007 and unemployment down to 5% from an official 19%. A Social Development Fund is to be created, with finance available for micro-projects. Basic education is to be available from age 6 to 15. Reforms are in the pipeline on land ownership, social housing and the mortgage system. Privatization is to be continued. The aim is an annual growth rate of 6 percent and a 25 percent GDP investment rate. The consensus it that only in this way can eventual political instability, arising from a growing Islamist influence among the urban poor be avoided.

Islamist pressures The question of Islamic revivalist movements (*les Islamistes*) is a complex one, however. The King of Morocco, as a descendant of the Prophet Mohammed and Commander of the Faithful, undoubtedly occupies the religious high ground. Religious legitimacy has always formed an important part of the monarchy's power base. In 1980, at the fall of the Shah of Iran, the King is said to have remarked that the Shah had attempted to rule by the sword, but without – or rather going against – the mosque, attempting to be a secular emperor in a land where Islam has a highly organized clergy. In Morocco, the *ulema* (experts on religious matters) have maintained their influence: their councils authorize new mosque building and religious studies graduates are trained at the Kénitra School to take up jobs in the Ministry of the Interior. The monarchy's religious profile is maintained by actions such as the

Hassanian Sermons (lectures by leading international Islamic scholars broadcast during Ramadhan), projects such as the Great Mosque at Casablanca, and the recognition achieved by the King as a leading Islamic leader. In 1979 he became president of the Al-Quds (Jerusalem) Committee.

The Islamists are active in poor areas, organizing funds to provide health care, ensuring children have the wherewithal to go to school, assisting families in difficulty. But they have been careful to avoid the violence which proved so counter-productive in Algeria. Their main figure, Abdallah Yassine, is more of a writer producing 'intellectual propaganda'; he is no charismatic Imam Khomeini-type figure. The Islamists might become important during urban riots. Their influence in parliament might grow as well, perhaps at the expense of the older conservative groupings. They now have nine deputies. Whatever, an Islamist current is a component on the Moroccan political chequerboard – but one which has been carefully managed so far.

The Saharan provinces

To jump to an area with more international implications, the issue of the former Spanish Sahara is now moving towards a definitive settlement. After independence from France and Spain in 1956, a number of pieces of Moroccan territory remained under Spanish rule – some enclaves in the North, notably Ceuta and Melilla (still held by Spain), Sidi Ifni (retaken by Morocco in 1969), and Rio de Oro, a large chunk of Saharan territory fronting onto the Atlantic. In 1974, with the Caudillo ailing in Madrid, the Moroccans launched their claims to the Sahara once more. In 1975, Franco died, and the moment seemed appropriate for action. Morocco and Mauritania moved into the Sahara, and in November 1975, the Green March, (*Al-Massira Al-Khadhra*), took place with 350,000 Moroccans marching southwards into the former Spanish colony. Underlying the issue was the question of resources – the Atlantic waters off the Saharan provinces are excellent fishing grounds, and there are phosphates. And there was also a fear that neighbouring Algeria might possibly sponsor a dummy republic. (Algeria has been perceived in political discourse as a rival nation able to dominate the Maghreb and possibly take over the whole Sahara.)

Algeria was to provide a rear base for the Polisario, an armed liberation group fighting for an independent 'Saharan' state. However, by 1987, the Moroccan army had completed seven earth ramparts to protect the Saharan provinces from armed incursion from across the frontier. In 1988, Algeria began to change its line on the Saharan issue. (In 1984, Libya had withdrawn financial help to the Polisario, and as of 1986, petrol revenues began to fall.) The Islamists had begun to appear as a major threat to the powers-that-be in Algiers. In February 1989, the Union du Maghreb Arabe treaty was signed at Marrakech – with North African leaders clearly agreed on the need to focus on the Islamist menace. (This only emerged in Morocco in the mid-1990s.) Morocco thus continued to invest heavily in the Sahara, developing Laâyoune and other towns. The Polisario ran out of steam – and Morocco agreed to a UN-sponsored referendum, originally to be held in 1992, on the future of the provinces. For the moment, with Algeria grappling with its ongoing internal crisis, the conflict has died down to the level of superficial tensions, and the provinces seem set to remain part of Morocco, possibly in a more regionalized set-up reminiscent of the Spanish autonomous regions or the German länder.

The Union du Maghreb Arabe (UMA)

The question of the Saharan provinces cannot be dissociated from Morocco's relations with the rest of the North African or Maghreb states, namely Algeria, Tunisia, Mauritania and Libya. A United Arab Maghreb, free of outside domination, was a dream back in colonial days. In February 1947 the Committee for the Liberation of the Maghreb was set up. Just over 40 years, later, a united Maghreb seemed to be on the way to becoming reality. At Marrakech, the leaders of the five states, King Hassan II of Morocco, President Chedli Bendjedid of Algeria, President Ben Ali of Tunisia,

Colonel Muammar Kaddhafi of Libya and President Ould Sidi Ahmad Al Taya of Mauritania signed the founding act of the Union du Maghreb Arabe, whose acronym, UMA, recalls the Arabic word *umma* or community. The new union was to be presided over by each nation in turn for six-month periods. In October 1990, a document was drawn up providing for the creation of a free exchange zone before the end of 1992 and the establishment of a customs union in 1995.

Very quickly, however, the new union ran into problems. With Bendjedid removed from power in Algeria, there was a cooling of Algero-Moroccan relations. Libya proved to be a difficult member of the team, and neither Morocco nor Tunisia were keen on weather-vane diplomacy à la Kaddhafi. The security situation deteriorated rapidly in Algeria, with guerrilla warfare and appalling massacres in certain regions. Thousands of Algerians began looking to emigrate. In 1994, after a terrorist attack on a Marrakech hotel, Morocco sought to limit any risk of Islamic fundamentalist contagion and introduced a visa for Algerian visitors. Algeria replied by closing the frontier. In response, Morocco put its activities in the UMA on hold. While relations between Algeria, Tunisia and Libya remained generally good, there was little move to develop things at UMA level. Tunisia was increasingly drawn into the orbit of the European Union, while maintaining good relations with Libya. The borders between the two countries were defined.

For the moment, the UMA is more or less stalled, although the bilateral contacts in 1998 and 1999 may get the machine going. However, if it is to succeed, any relaunch of the UMA will have to be based on the settlement of Algero-Moroccan differences over the latter's Saharan provinces. Without this, there seems little hope for any advance. In any case, for Morocco, like Tunisia, commercial relations with the European Union have taken on great importance.

Morocco & the European Union As of the late 1980s, Morocco opted to intensify its ties with Europe, and in 1987 the country requested membership of the EEC, perhaps more as a symbolic gesture than anything else. Although relations with Spain have been soured on occasion over the question of fishing rights, Europe and Morocco have too much in common for the two sides not to work together. Algerian gas transits over Moroccan territory on its way to the Iberian peninsula, European companies – and notably French and Spanish ones – are always on the starting blocks for major public works contracts in Morocco. The current privatization programme and the development of the Casablanca stock exchange will no doubt maintain European business interest. Morocco's credentials as a stable country, close to Europe, with a certain democratic openness will doubtless continue to make it favourable terrain for business relocation. The Euro-Mediterranean Partnership Initiative launched in 1995 (the Barcelona Process) will no doubt be important for the Moroccan economy.

Finance The most difficult issue facing the Youssoufi government, however, is that of finance. The IMF recently recommended a devaluation of the dirham, while Morocco wants help servicing its debt. For the moment, widening the tax base does not seem to be a viable option, and the government is counting on privatizations to raise the money to finance its social programmes. The Youssoufi government has found itself with a tightrope to tread: foreign investors have to be reassured that the liberalist rigour imposed by the IMF and the European Union (including bringing the public debt down to 3% of GDP) will be respected, while the local constituency wants jobs and social services. With foreign debt repayments absorbing a third of the budget, there is little room for manoeuvre for a Moroccan government, be it right or left wing.

Prospects Despite the financial constraints, the prospects for Morocco at the end of the 1990s are by no means black. (The next section on the economy explores this in more detail.) Serious social problems have been predicted. However, the poverty of the shantytowns of Casablanca is not as harsh as it was in the 1960s. The likelihood is that there will continue to be occasional outbreaks of urban rioting. The Moroccans are in many ways a patient lot, and people understand that it is impossible to achieve huge improvements overnight. But good results will have to be shown over the next few years. Ultimately, a lot of personal prestige is at stake. Neither the Palace nor the government coalition want to be seen to fail, as both have invested considerable time and effort in reaching a modus vivendi. With luck, this association between monarchy and government will give Morocco a greater capacity to tackle the big issues of social justice and fair economic development. In the final analysis, a new version of the national pact seems to be being worked out. It could be that a form of social democracy, USFP style, will facilitate the move towards democracy and eventually towards a more limited role for the monarchy.

Europe is seen as the principal foreign partner in this venture – and the Moroccans, rightly no doubt, feel that help and understanding should be forthcoming from the economic giant to the North. Little EU finance has been made available to assist southern Mediterranean economies such as that of Morocco – compared with the funds made available for the modernization of Greece, and more recently, for certain eastern European countries. Despite the growing populations of the southern Mediterranean, countries like Morocco feel they may be neglected while Germany directs finance and interest towards eastern Europe and the former Soviet lands.

Contemporary society

In late 1990s Morocco, institutions were being modernized, industry upgraded, the civil service reformed. Human rights were openly discussed, a critical press had emerged and was flourishing. After periods of political repression, Moroccans are proud of the changes taking place. Much is still to be done, however. Though parliamentary elections are free, open and multi-party, there are abuses. Though factories are getting their ISO 9000 certification, workers' salaries are rock bottom. Though there is a growing freedom of expression and civil liberties are respected, there are appalling and surprising exceptions. Moroccan society is in a period of change – and it can be difficult for the Moroccan to explain to the outsider the factors, both historical and social, which have led the country where it is today.

Education & language

The reform of the educational system is one area now opening up to debate. The state education system has been open to heavy criticism, seen by many commentators as costly and inefficient. However, when Morocco achieved its independence in the 1950's, practically nothing had been done by France to extend education to its Muslim Moroccan protégés. Everything remained to be done. While Tunisia (colonized by France in 1881) already had a small core of literate, educated women, the overwhelming majority of Morocco's women were illiterate, and male literacy was low too. Independent Morocco had to put a comprehensive education policy together. In the enthusiastic, public-spirited late 1950s, centres for fighting illiteracy (*muharabat al umiya*) were set up. However, over 40 years later, illiteracy remains high, touching around 65% of the population over 15.

The Moroccan school system divides into nine years' basic education, followed by three years of general secondary or technical education leading to the baccalauréat. Pre-school education is split between traditional Koran schools where the sacred texts are learned by rote, and modern private kindergartens. In 1990, 71% of primary school age children were in school (**NB** only 56% of girls). How to explain this low figure?

Getting girls into school is particularly difficult in rural areas, where girls are traditionally involved in household and agricultural tasks from an early age. Considerable distances have to be travelled to school, weather conditions are often difficult. Only a small number of schools have boarding facilities for children in isolated areas. In a rural area, when a school is close by, only one girl out of ten will complete basic schooling, one girl out of five complete two or three years schooling. Girls are just too important in the functioning of the rural economy to be left at school desks for long periods of time. Parental attitudes do seem to be changing, however.

Added to these factors, there is the nature of the school programmes. Education is very academic, books and equipment are often in very short supply – or quite simply beyond the means of many families. The teaching style often favours rote learning rather than developing creative skills and a critical mind. The language issue creates further problems.

The curriculum is in Arabic, with French, Spanish and English taught as foreign languages. The Arabic used is modern standard Arabic, a version of the Arabic of the Koran modernized in lexical terms in the 19th century. This means that children with a Berber language as mother tongue (circa 40% of the population) are faced with a foreign language at school. Children with Moroccan Arabic as a mother tongue have to learn a new range of verb and adjectival forms, rather as if the English speaking child had to learn to use Old English verbs with modern English vocabulary. This is basically manageable, although given translation problems, there is a severe shortage of reading material in Arabic.

However, the problem comes at university. All subjects are in French, bar family and criminal law and Arabic literature and some of the humanities. Hence parents with means put their children in bilingual primary schools with greater resources and more modern teaching methods. At secondary school level, the children with a bilingual background have much better chances of passing the baccalauréat. And after secondary school, private institutes providing training in secretarial skills, IT, management and accounting function exclusively in French.

The present system has been criticized for perpetuating Morocco's social divide, the gap between the bilingual middle classes, with their access to knowledge and wealth production, and the illiterate masses, using spoken Arabic and/or Berber in daily life. It remains, however, that both standard *fusha* Arabic and French are foreign languages for most Moroccan children going into primary school. No six-year-old speaks these languages as a mother tongue. But though Arabic is the official language of Morocco, nowhere is it specified that this is standard Arabic.

The media In the late 1980s, the Moroccan print media went through a difficult period. Some of the best and brightest titles went out of business, essentially for reasons of censorship. Among them were critical current affairs magazine *Lamalif*, women's magazine *Kalima* and the weekly *Al Massar*.

Since the early 1990s, however, the Moroccan news media has undergone major changes. Newspapers have been brightened up with new, more professional layouts, and a number of high standard leisure magazines have appeared. More interestingly, the tone of the press has become increasingly free and critical. Newspapers to look out for, if you read French, include the weeklies *Le Journal*, *La vie économique* and *Maroc-Hebdo*, *L'Economiste* (daily), and women's magazines *FDM* (*Femmes du Maroc*) and *La Citadine*. The French press, both news magazines and newspapers, continues to sell well in Morocco, proof that there is still plenty of room for improvement and a market for the local press to fill.

In terms of the audio-visual media, Morocco has two TV channels, the rather stodgy RTM and the dynamic, formerly private second channel, 2M. There is a huge demand for quality television – hence the massive sales of satellite dishes in Morocco, and proof again that the local television stations have a market waiting for them. The problem is partly a financial one. The RTM does not have direct control over its advertising revenues. With the Treasury setting tight limits on all forms of public spending, it is impossible for the RTM to produce and buy quality programmes. 2M does rather better – and may be returned to the private sector in the near future. The challenge is still there, however, for Moroccan TV professionals to produce programmes of real national and local interest. For the moment, satellite television, and pay channels such as Canal Plus Horizons, seem set to expand their share of the market.

Daily life

Morocco's population is moving towards a 60%/30% urban-rural divide. The land no longer provides the living it used to, expectations are higher, parents want their children to have some chance of an education – and this is most easily available in the towns. In the country, life is often hard, with women obliged to carry water, firewood and animal fodder over long distances.

In the cities, life is not easy either for the inhabitants of the *bidonvilles*. When it rains, the streets fill with water. The city, however, offers more opportunities. There are plenty of people with money to buy from a street-stall selling cigarettes, chewing-gum or fruit, there is occasional work on building sites and in factories and there is a chance of better housing, as government projects 'restructure' the shantytowns, bringing in water and electricity.

For the middle classes, opportunities have improved considerably, even though recruitment into government service has been cut back. There are, however, jobs in multinational companies, the banking sector and the new service economy. Compared with other Arab countries, there is a freedom in Morocco's cities. The streets, though increasingly traffic-ridden, are pleasant; there are cafés, bookshops, and cinemas. For those with salaries, there are car and home loans. Domestic help is available for two-career families, and there is a wide range of consumer goods. For the bright and energetic, the prospects are good – although family connections do help.

Outside the cities, life is improving, too, as even the most casual observer will notice. Mobile phones are making life easier, electricity is arriving in isolated mountain valleys. The ONEP has undertaken major infrastructure projects to improve drinking water provision. Always a sure sign of improving living standards, there is building everywhere. The ERACs (social housing authorities) are active in all major cities, putting up huge social housing schemes. Even in quite out-of-the-way places, much new building is in evidence, an indication that there is money in circulation and that there is a lot of work for unskilled and semi-skilled male labour. Though the official economic figures are often disappointing, Morocco's informal sector is undoubtedly extremely dynamic.

The wider picture

Morocco has changed enormously since independence. It is no longer, for the most part, a fragment of the Middle Ages anchored off the southern shores of Europe. There is, however, a striking stability and continuity in the political and social systems, looking back from the 20th-century reign of Hassan II to the reign of Hassan I. The question is whether the symbols of national unanimity – religion, the land, the people, the king – will continue to be sufficient under the new ruler. The palace is only too aware of the divisions in Moroccan society, the clans and competing family networks, the geographic and linguistic identities waiting to surface, and does its best to ensure that all groupings are able to influence events. Maybe the future of a more constitutional monarchy will be as a sort of ombudsman, arbitrating between influential groupings in society. Algerian-style military intervention in government affairs seems unlikely. The army is only too aware of the void it would create if it were to threaten the throne.

The rural world Moroccan rural areas will no doubt continue to depopulate. The countryside has changed hugely. In the 1960s, the caïds ran affairs, with authority over sharecroppers, shepherds and harvesters. By the 1990s, the caïds' descendants had become entrepreneurs, running mechanized farms. Seasonal workers have to get by on tiny smallholdings, or perhaps travel to cities to work as unskilled labour. Private landowners are doing well, especially in irrigated areas. The poorer parts of the countryside – the Rif and the Sous Valley – are no longer able to export their surplus labour to Europe, and drought years like 1980-1984 accelerated the rural exodus to Morocco's cities.

Economy & development In terms of the economy, Morocco has put its house in order. The rather adventurous financial policies of the 1970s are a thing of the past, and the budget deficit is now down to 1% of GDP. (It had been at 12% to 14% in 1982.) Debt repayments were rescheduled six times in the 1980s. Today, growth, with an average of around 5%, is above the birth rate. Nevertheless, there are some major difficulties: for sale of agricultural products, Morocco has stiff competition from Spain and Portugal; there are still large numbers of graduates coming onto the job market for whom there is no employment; in 1998, Morocco only came 125th out of 179 countries in the UNDP human development index, a fair way behind neighbours Algeria and Tunisia.

Challenges for the 21st century But such indexes do not take into account factors like the general political climate and levels of freedom of expression. Things have moved forward considerably since the 1970s, and on the whole, the situation in the early 21st century was a positive one. Morocco, with little oil resources, benefits from any fall in the price of oil, and its proximity to Europe and an expanding internal market make it an ideal base for relocating manufacturing industry. The question over the first decade of the 21st century will be how to reduce poverty and social inequality – and so avoid the risk of Algerian-type fundamentalist destabilization and strife. To create a more socially just, open Morocco, to create an investment-friendly climate, the upgrading of a slow and often poorly trained civil service will be essential. The opposition government elected in 1997 (and whatever government is elected in 2002) and the new king thus face considerable challenges. A strong desire for stability and consensus should allow much to be achieved.

Art & architecture

Morocco, as the visitor will quickly notice, has a wealth of characteristic buildings and craft forms. Though in certain areas, traditional architecture is giving way to less aesthetic – and less climatically adapted forms of buildings – there is a huge amount of interesting building to see. Regarding traditional crafts and art forms, some of the best examples can be found in museums in the major cities. Collections of traditional arts and crafts from recent centuries are held at the Musée Dar Saïd and the Maison Tiskiwine in Marrakech. Outside the region covered by the present book, both the Musée Dar Jamaï in Meknès and the Dar Batha in Fès also have good collections of traditional objects. The Musée archéologique in Rabat has the finest collection of objects from ancient times, however.

Prehistory

The earliest traces of human settlement in Morocco go back 800,000 BC. Towards 5000 BC, new populations, probably the ancestors of today's Berbers, are thought to

The Mosque: key features

In all Muslim countries, mosques are built orientated towards Mecca, as the believers must pray in the direction of their holy city. In Morocco's case, this means that the orientation is east-southeast. A large mosque has four main areas: prayer halls, courtyard and colonnade, minaret, and, in all likelihood, attached ablutions facility and hammam. Most mosques will have:

*1. the **qibla wall** (1), facing east-southeast, with a decorated niche or **mihrab** (2) in the middle, towards which the believers pray;*
*2. a colonnaded **prayer hall** (3), and a large **courtyard** (4), often with a fountain;*
*3. a **minaret** or* midhana *(5) from which the call to prayer is made five times a day;*
*4. an **entrance** (6), through which the non-Muslim visitor may glimpse the courtyard if there is no wooden lattice-work screen.*

On Fridays, there will often be so many people for the weekly midday prayers and accompanying sermon that latecomers, equipped with their rugs, will have to pray outside in the street.

Kasbah Mosque

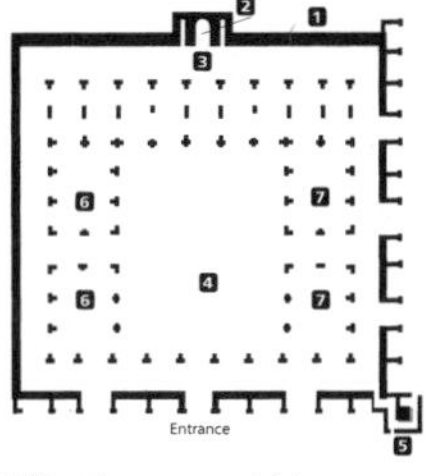

1 Qibla wall
2 Mihrab
3 "Recycled" capitals on 6 pillars around mihrab
4 Sahn
5 Minaret
6 Liwanat

have arrived. They brought with them a nomadic form of pastoralism. Morocco is particularly well endowed with early rock carvings, left behind by these nomads, which can be seen in the High Atlas, and Anti-Atlas, near Tafraoute, as well as in the southern oases of Akka and Foum Hassan. In the High Atlas, there are four main sites with carvings: the Yagour Plateau and Oukaïmeden (Toubkal region), at Tainant off the Tizi-n-Tichka road and below Jebel Ghat at the Tizi-n-Targhist (High Atlas of Azilal). The carvings at the Tizi-n-Targhist are particularly fine, there being lots of disc-shields, javelins and spears, and spry little spear-wielding horsemen. For those with a deep interest in such things, there exists a small research centre on the rock art heritage of the High Atlas, housed in Dar el Pacha at Bab Doukkala, Marrakech. (Ask for the Centre national du patrimoine rupestre.)

For completeness sake, note too that in northern Morocco, a stone circle survives at Mzoura, southeast of Asilah near Souk Tnine de Sidi el Yamami in northwestern Morocco. The locals call it 'Moroccan Stonehenge', which is stretching a point, as there is only one tall (8 m) menhir left standing.

Roman times

When Rome was founded in 753 BC, the coast of Morocco was on the trade routes of Phoenician merchants. Inland areas were inhabited by a people called the Maures by the Romans – hence the name Mauretania for the Roman province covering part of what is now Morocco. No doubt the land was divided into Berber kingdoms. From 25 BC to 23 AD, Juba II ruled Mauretania from Volubilis, today Morocco's best preserved Roman site, close to Meknès. Some of the finest Hellenistic and Roman bronzes extant from this site can be seen today at the Rabat archaeological museum, along with pottery and other objects from Roman times. Other Roman sites worth visiting, all in northwestern Morocco, include Thamusida (near Kénitra), Banasa (near Souk El Arba du Gharb) and Lixus (near Larache).

The buildings of Islam

In 682, the Arab general Okba ben Nafi and his army crossed the Maghreb, bringing with them a new revealed religion, Islam. This religion was to engender new architectural forms, shaped by the requirements of prayer and the Muslim urban lifestyle. The key building of Islam is of course the mosque, which evolved considerably from its humble beginnings as a sort of enclosure with an adjoinging low platform from which the call to prayer could be made. Mosques became spectacular buildings demonstrating the power of ruling dynasties, centring on colonnaded prayer halls and vast courtyards. The elegant towers of the minarets gave beauty and character to the skyline of the great Muslim cities.

Mosques cannot generally be visited in Morocco by the non-Muslim visitor, with some notable exceptions, including the Grande Mosquée Hassan II in Casablanca, the ruined mosque of the Chellah necropolis in Rabat, the restored Almohad mosque at Tin Mal in the High Atlas, and the so-called 'Spanish mosque', a ruin on a hilltop outside Chaouen. Minarets, visible from afar, are not always easy to photograph close to, being surrounded by narrow streets and densely built-up areas.

Minarets As an essential feature of the mosque, the minaret probably developed in the late 7th century. Islam had adopted a call to prayer or *idhan* rather than bells to summon the faithful. (Bilal, an Abyssinian slave, was the first muezzin.) The first minarets, no doubt built by local Christian builders, were adapted from the square towers of Syrian churches. Moroccan minarets are generally a simple square tower, with a small 'lantern' feature on the top, from which the muezzin makes the call to prayer. Older minarets tend to feature blind horseshoe arches and a small dome on the topmost 'lantern' room. On top of the dome is an ornamental feature resembling three metal spheres on a pole, topped by a crescent. This is the *jammour*, and tourist guides have a number of entertaining explanations for this, for example, that the spheres represent the basic ingredients of bread (flour, water and salt).There are unusual exceptions to the square minaret, however, including the round tower of the Moulay Idriss Mosque, covered in green ceramic tiles with Koranic verses in white, and the octagonal minaret of the Kasbah Mosque in Tanger. The great Almohad mosques – the Grand Mosque at Taza, Koutoubiya at Marrakech, the partially completed Tour Hassan, Rabat – are characterized by an interlinked lozenge pattern, executed in stone on their facades. (The Giralda tower of the Cathedral of Seville started life as an Almohad minaret, too.) One school of art history sees the proportions, arcades and decorative motifs of these buildings as setting trends eventually to be reproduced and transformed in European Gothic architecture.

Layout & decoration Mosques tend to have large covered prayer halls, comprising a series of narrow transepts, created by lines of arches supporting pitched roofs, generally covered with green tiles. There will be a main 'aisle' leading towards the *mihrab* (prayer niche) which indicates the direction of Mecca, and for prayer. The main nave in the traditional Moroccan mosque does not however have the same dimensions as the main nave of a Christian cathedral. Note that Islam does not favour representation of the human form, hence the use of highly elaborate geometric decorative motifs executed in ceramic mosaic (*zellij*), and on wood and plaster. There is no religious pictorial art. The same geometric motifs can be found in domestic architecture too. A mosque will also have an open courtyard, sometimes with a decorative fountain. Although all the usual decorative techniques can be seen, the 1990s Grande Mosquée Hassan II is an exception in layout, having just one major aisle, flanked by two narrower secondary naves.

Schools of religious science

The non-Muslim visitor can get a very good idea of Muslim sacred architecture by visiting one of the *medersas*, the colleges which were an essential part of the Moroccan Muslim education system from mediaeval times onward. One of the largest is the Medersa Ben Youssef in Marrakech, a 14th-century foundation entirely rebuilt in the 16th century. It has all the main decorative features: a courtyard with reflecting pool, ceramic mosaic, and densely carved stucco and cedar wood. The austere students' rooms come as something of a shock after the elaborate decoration of the courtyard.

Historic médinas

Perhaps the most easily photographed of the old mosques is the Koutoubia in Marrakech (and next to it, you can see the excavated remains of an earlier mosque). However, the Koutoubiya is an exception in that it stands apart from the city. Mosques and *medersas* are generally surrounded by buildings. The visitor to Morocco quickly has to learn to navigate through the narrow streets of the médina or old towns to reach the monument or museum to be visited.

In much 19th-century European writing, the médina of the Maghreb – and of the Arab world in general – were seen as chaotic places, which, although harbouring exotically clothed populations, were also home to disease and ignorance. The médina was taken as a metaphor for the backwardness of the *indigène*. In fact, the tangled streets of the average Moroccan médina are no more disorganized than many a European mediaeval town. Today's visitor will immediately be struck by the external walls in *pisé* (sundried clay, gravel and lime mix). Disorientation due to narrow alleys and high walls sets in later, perhaps after leaving the main souks.

The logic of the médina

The médina of Morocco do however obey a logic, satisfying architectural requirements arising from climatic and religious factors. The climate is hot in summer, but often very cold in winter. In the coastal towns, damp ocean mists roll in, while inland there are hot summer winds from the South. The city therefore has to provide protection from this climate, and networks of narrow streets are the ideal solution. Streets could be narrow as there was no wheeled transport, there being plenty of pack animals for carrying goods around. And narrow streets also ensured that precious building land within the city walls was not wasted.

For housing the Muslim family, the courtyard house was the ideal solution. This of course is an architectural model which goes back to Mesopotamia, Greece and Rome. For Islamic family life, with its insistence on gender separation in the public domain, the courtyard house provides a high level of family privacy. In densely built-up cities, the roof terraces also provided a place for women to perform household tasks – and to share news and gossip. The biggest houses would have several patios, the main one having arcades on two levels. Thus extended families could be accommodated in dwellings with large open areas. Old Moroccan courtyard homes are not easily visited however. In both Marrakech and Fès, there are houses which have been restored and altered to function as upmarket restaurants (see the late 19th-century *Dar Marjana* in Marrakech, for example, or the *Collier de la Colombe* in Meknès). In Marrakech, however, the visitor can discover a superb concentration of Moroccan craftwork in a lovingly restored patrician house, the Maison Tiskiwin, close to the Bahia Palace. You may well be invited into ordinary homes, however, where fridges and pressure cookers are in use alongside traditional braseros in the main courtyard.

Earthen architectures

The courtyard home is the most characteristic building in Morocco's cities, discreet and anonymous to all but a neighbourhood's inhabitants from the outside, spectacularly decorated in its patrician form on the inside. There are other, more rustic, building traditions in use, however, the best known being the kasbahs and ksours of the areas south of the High Atlas, the valleys of the Dadès, the Draâ and the Ziz. The visitor doing a trek will no doubt have the chance to appreciate vernacular architecture at close quarters, as walking groups are often accommodated in Atlas villages.

Mountain homes At strategic points in the mountain valleys, the villages of the Imazighen form compact masses of building. Houses are virtually wedged onto the hillside, slotting into each other, taking advantage of every bump and dip of the terrain. Built entirely with local materials, these *douar* merge perfectly with the reds, browns and greys of the landscape. With community interests predominant, individual houses are a rarity. Villages are generally located near a spring or an *assif* (river), although sometimes, as at Magdaz in the central High Atlas, defensive needs take priority. And as in the médina, the mosque is an integral part of the village, easily identifiable by its smooth and painted minaret. (In some communities, a large room in a house is reserved for prayer.)

Atlas houses are designed to accommodate both people and beasts. At its lowest level, the typical house will have a sort of corral, the *assareg*, for beasts, giving access to a ground-floor stable area, the *agrour*. From the *agrour*, stone stairs will lead upstairs to the *tigimmi*, the family living quarters. Generally, there are lots of rooms and sometimes a top level with a sort of gallery, much used for drying barley and other foodstuffs. With the roof terrace supported by a line of wooden pillars, these galleries give a characteristic touch to houses in the Aït Bou Oulli and the Aït Bougmez.

The heart of the house is the kitchen and its hearth. Generally, this is on the ground floor, as one or more fire-pits have to be dug out of the ground. The most noble room, the *tamsriyt*, used for receiving guests, will be on the first floor. Access will be such as to preserve the privacy of family rooms. The *tamsriyt* will often have a fine painted ceiling. In the old days, this would be in wood, and over the years, the wooden painted beams would acquire a patina. If changing the *tamsriyt*, the family would keep the ceiling beams for re-use in the new room. Nowadays, the trend is for the walls and ceiling of the reception room to be plastered and then painted by a local artist. With damp and cigarette and candle smoke, wall decoration is not as long-lasting as it was on wood.

Amazigh mountain houses evolve over time. If more space is needed, a new room can always be built on top. The use of the different spaces varies across the year. In the winter, with snow on the ground, the family will spend much time gathered in the warmest part of the house. In summer, with so much to do in the fields and possibly part of the family away in the mountains with the flocks, much less time is spent indoors. Terrace areas can be used for food preparation – or as a crèche area for keeping toddlers out of trouble. (They soon learn not to fall off.)

The **building techniques** used in the Atlas are more or less the same as they were centuries ago. In the early spring, work begins assembling stones. The best time for building is the spring, after the land has been ploughed but before the hard work of harvest time begins. The site of the new building is marked out with string and pickets. Foundation trenches, up to 2 m deep, are excavated and filled with stones. Very often, the first metre or so of building above ground will be a thick but carefully assembled stone wall. The main construction material throughout most of the Atlas is *toub* (French: *pisé*), a mix of damp clay, gravel and sometimes straw. In the upper mountains, where water is problematic, buildings – and in particular the fortified granaries – are entirely in stone. Building is supervised by a *maâlem*, a master builder. The technology consists of spades, wooden form work and posts, ladders and alfa baskets. Walls go up in short sections about 1.5 m long. With a system of vertical posts, an area about 70 cm wide and 80 cm high is enclosed with strong planks. This is filled in with the earth exacavated to make the foundations. Once the *toub* has been packed down by stamping or with a wooden tool, the form work is removed, and the process repeated. Once

Tadelakt

Sometime in the 1990s, the decorators of Marrakech rediscovered the advantages of a traditional wall rendering technique. Tadelakt *was originally used for the hammams (bath houses) of Marrakech as it kept the steamy damp out of mud-brick walls. The basis of* tadelakt *is burnt-lime powder, which, when sieved and put in water, becomes* jir *or slaked lime. The wall to which the* tadelakt *is to be applied is given a rough texture with a hammer. Then the gungy, limey paste is applied – but not too thickly, otherwise it falls off in chunks. After drying, the surface is evened out using the smooth flat surface of a heavy, convex stone. Then the rendering is waxed, some two months later, with olive-oil based* saboun beldi, *a traditional soap. The more sophisticated master craftsmen would put egg yolk in the* tadelakt *mix for extra fine binding. The craft is an ancient one of course, and similar facings are used in buildings in other dry arid climes, notably Rajasthan, India. The Italian wall rendering* marmorino, *to which finely powdered marble is added, is a relation to the ancient Marrakchi technique.*

Tadelakt *– basically reconstituted rock – can now be seen in the interiors of upscale homes, banks and travel agencies. It's silky coolness and local feel make it the ideal finishing touch for restaurants and hotel foyers seeking a note of character. Originally the colours were natural ones – beige, cream and Marrakech red. Architects now use the rendering in strong blues, greens and yellows, often to good effect, and should you want to take a souvenir home with you, the ever-inventive craftsmen of Marrakech make* tadelakt *candlesticks and vases.*

The renewed use of tadelakt *is not without its problems, however. The rendering was originally only used for small indoor areas like hammams.* Tadelakt *production on a large scale implies increased production of charcoal, which for the moment is a traditional industry consuming wood from Morocco's diminishing Atlas forests. Yet lime made using industrial charcoal does not produce the same irregular effects. Thus, for the moment, the popularity of this most local of building techniques is having a very un-ecological impact.*

a full circuit has been completed, the first chunk should be sufficiently hard and dry for form work to be set up on top and a new section of wall built. On the façades of the house, regularly spaced vertical grooves and lines of holes left by posts are the visible traces of the building process.

Particular attention is paid to the **roof terraces**. Poplar (in the eastern High Atlas) or walnut beams are placed to span the walls. Next, across these beams, comes a thick bed of reeds and woody artemisia. Care is taken to ensure that this overhangs on the outside to prevent melt water from running down the façades. This plant layer is then covered with tamped-down earth. Gutters made from hollowed out tree branches ensure that rain water drains off.

Careful maintenance is essential for the survival of the mountain pisé house. At the end of the winter, melting snow can easily turn a terrace to mud. Once the damp has penetrated the pisé walls, it is very difficult to get rid of.

In recent years, there have been **innovations in mountain houses**. The most noteworthy advance is the use of cement flooring, initially in guest rooms. Cement makes for more hygienic conditions, and greatly facilitates women's work. Sometimes special sleeping areas for hikers are added, including modern toilet areas. Windows are now widespread, and are broadly similar to those in traditional city houses. The lace-like window grills are held together with metal grips, there are no welded parts. A white painted surround gives a window extra impact. On a negative note, the once widespread carved wooden doors are increasingly being replaced by city-made metal ones. Unfortunately, the old doors (and the fine carved wooden columns of Anti-Atlas houses) find plenty of buyers in the antique shops of Marrakech. Still, the geometric motifs and bright colours of the metal doors do add a note of colour. For the moment, pisé and stone building seems to be just about holding its own, largely because it is far superior to concrete in terms of insulation from extremes of temperature.

Kasbahs The word kasbah probably derives from the Turkish *kasabe*, meaning small town. In contemporary North Africa, it is generally used to refer to the fortified strong point in a city. Morocco also has numerous kasbahs scattered across its territory, many erected by energetic 17th-century builder-ruler Moulay Ismaïl. (See for example the kasbah at Boulaouane, near Settat and the derelict Kasbah Tadla, near Beni Mellal.)

In the southern reaches of Morocco, the term kasbah is used to denote often vast fortified villages, with spectacular tower houses often several storeys high. Good examples can be found near Ouarzazate, at Aït Benhaddou (as used in part of Orson Welles' *Sodom and Gomorrah*) and up in the the High Atlas at Telouet, where a vast crumbling kasbah testifies to the power of the T'hami el Glaoui, ruler of Marrakech in the early part of the 20th century. There are a fair number of Glaoui kasbahs scattered across the southern valleys, and they tend to have decorative features of more urban inspiration than the kasbahs of the old Berber communities. There are good examples at Tamnougalt, south of Agdz in the Draâ Valley, and in the Skoura oasis (the Kasbah Amerhidl), Dadès Valley.

Ksours Ksour country is really the Ziz Valley (main towns Er Rachidia and Erfoud). The ksour sit surrounded by palm groves and walled market gardens. They house the families of the oasis dwellers, and like the kasbahs, are built in a defensive mode. Their smooth high walls, fortified with corner towers, and narrow windows enabled the inhabitants to protect their harvests. Back west again, in the mountains, the *tighremt* or *agadir*, the fortified grain store, held the same function. The ground floor was used for the animals, the first floor as a food store, and the top floor for family living space.

Spectacular and ecologically adapted though this traditional architecture is, it is very much under threat today. Vulnerable to the weather, it needs maintenance. In the past the labour force for this was available via the community *touiza* system. More seriously for the aesthetic appearance of the mountain villages and the southern valleys, reinforced concrete building is beginning to appear in areas where it was once entirely unknown. As roads and transport improve, it becomes a serious proposition in once remote valleys. It carries the prestige of being 'modern', signifying the wealth of home builders. However, in the Dadès Valley, there is a new wave of mock kasbah architecture. The crenellations, window slits and tapering towers of the ancient earthen buildings can now be found on hotels and electricity sub-stations, official buildings and in social housing (see the new estates north of Er Rachidia). The tourist industry may yet, however, fuel some sort of return to traditional – and more ecological – building typologies. See, for example, the kasbahs re-used as hotels, including the *Aït Moro* in Skoura and the *Tomboctou* in Tineghir.

Mountain Portuguese? On a more obscure note, if you venture up to the remote valley of the Assif Melloul, east of Tilouguite, west of Anergui in the Azilal High Atlas, you will see stone constructions situated in seemingly inaccessible locations. In recent times, some were used as granaries. But who built them? The local term for them is *ksqr bortgiz*, 'the citadel of the Portuguese' in Arabic, *ighrem-n-irrumiyine*, 'the Christians' granary' in Tamazight. Were these places built by Christians fleeing Islamic invasions or other foreigners seeking refuge from the great upheavals of the late Middle Ages? The term 'citadel of the Portuguese' at any rate indicates a foreign presence in the local collective memory.

Fortified ports

Still on the subject of the Portuguese and fortifications, on the coasts of Morocco can be found another form of defensive architecture, the military port of early modern European inspiration. In the 15th century, both Atlantic and Mediterranean coasts were targets for the expanding Iberian powers. Ports such as Agadir, Safi, Asilah and Tanger were occupied, all the better to control the lucrative trade routes to Asia and the Americas. In the early 16th century, Portugal was still at the height of its glory as an imperial power, and elaborate fortifications were erected at Azemmour, Mazagan (today's El Jadida), Safi, Mogador (today's Essaouira) and Agadir, equipped with all the most up-to-date features of the military architecture of the day. There were monumental gateways, cannon, watchtowers and round bastions. In the 18th century, the Portuguese were on the retreat. The sultan of the day, Sidi Mohammed ben Abdallah, had understood the importance of European military architecture. In 1764, he employed a French engineer, one Théodore Cornut, to lay out the new fortifications at Essaouira. This was to be the first example of modern urban planning on Moroccan soil.

Modern cities

The contemporary Moroccan city is very much an early 20th-century achievement, the work of two far-sighted people, Maréchal Lyautey and urban planner Henri Prost. France's first resident general in Morocco had been much impressed by Prost's plans for the re-design of Antwerp in Belgium – and was willing to give such schemes a chance in the new French protectorate. A Prost plan was characterized by a number of features that seemed particularly adaptable to the Moroccan context. Old walls were not demolished and re-used as development land, but kept as part of a buffer zone between old and new. The new areas had large open spaces planted with regular rows of trees, while a system of avenues within the city enhanced existing monumental buildings and linked in to a system of highways leading in and out of the city. The crucial point on which Prost focused was the preservation of the aesthetic face of the city without totally cutting it off from new forms of transport and infrastructure.

Prost, like Lyautey, was all for technological innovation. However, this position was balanced with a strong social conservatism: existing hierarchies were to be kept. In Morocco, 'respect for difference' was the justification for the strict zoning between old and new quarters, rich and poor.

In Morocco, Lyautey and his experts found themselves in an enviable position. They were able to appropriate land, levy taxes and develop a land-use policy with a freedom unthinkable in France. As they drew up plans for the *villes nouvelles*, their task was made all the easier by the fact that the watchwords of the French republic – liberty, equality and fraternity – were not applied in Morocco. Equality was out of the question. Although some lip-service was paid to fraternity, liberty to participate in decisions on the country's future was reserved to the technocratic élite around the Residency General – after a show of consultation with the sultan, of course.

The uses of urbanism

In Morocco Lyautey, wanted to apply the modern principles of 'the science of urbanism', and attempted to attract as many new architects as possible. With Algeria as the negative example of how the French had behaved abroad, Lyautey set out to promote a new system, the theatre of which would be the city. The crises of French and Algerian cities were to be avoided, the new urbanism was to be the showcase for the benefits of French rule. As Lyautey is reputed to have said in a famous dictum, 'a construction site is worth a battalion' (un chantier m'évite un bataillon).

The Moroccan notables, in many cases, wanted cleaner neighbourhoods with modern infrastructure – but separate from the new, impure Christian population.

(Spatial segregation by religion had been a feature in many of the older Moroccan towns.) However, the new European neighbourhoods were built close enough for there to be social contact. Where British colonialism had been based essentially on a structure of police intelligence, the French *villes nouvelles* of Morocco were to allow social meeting – or so the theory went. The urban planners faced a problem of how to integrate these social requirements into development plans – the Meknès plan, in particular, was criticized for the distance between the two communities. Speculation and building styles were to be strictly controlled, while new rail systems were planned and embedded into the city's structure.

Another French creation was the Fine Arts Department to ensure the protection of the main historic monuments. Sites for protection were selected, and the ground was prepared for tourism and a new historic awareness. Both Lyautey and Prost detested the kitsch of modern Algerian neo-Moorish architecture – and the banality of French suburban building. New construction was thus to follow principles valued by Lyautey and Prost, essentially simplicity of form and a high degree of functionality. Public buildings were to have simple lines, taking on the contours of traditional Arab building. Craft techniques were used for detailing, giving a 'Moroccan style' to otherwise modern buildings. Geometric public spaces made great use of fountains and vegetation.

The Prost plans laid the basis for the development of Morocco's cities for the 20th century, creating spacious urban centres which are still agreeable today, despite vehicle pollution. (Prost could hardly have been expected to imagine the huge growth in the number of noxious diesel vehicles by the end of the 20th century.) Most importantly, a tradition of planning and architectural innovation, along with respect for architectural heritage, was established. New official building across Morocco incorporates features of traditional architecture – green-tiled roofs, stone detailing, mosaic work – in a style referred to as Neo-Makhzen. Other building is often innovative and ambitious – take for example the dual towers of the TC (Twin Centre) in Casablanca, designed by Catalan architect Bofill.

Modern building in the Atlas

Up in the High Atlas, although it is the terraced villages and fortified granaries that catch the photo-seeking eye, there is other interesting building. Occasionally, especially in the southern regions, you may see an isolated fort, looking for all the world like something out of 'Beau Geste' – which is just what it is. As the mountain regions submitted to the French, the Foreign Legion built standard forts across the land. A large *borj* or fort would be a square enclosure 200 m by 200 m, with four watch towers. The walls were 1 m thick, 3 m high. In the middle of the enclosure was accommodation for the garrison, officers and some 200 troops. In such austere places lived the men who built mountain Morocco's first modern roads and engineered many a piste in the most difficult conditions.

There are other surprising survivals of French times in mountain Morocco. Here and there are *maisons forestières*, solid constructions looking like something out of the Vosges, built to house the personnel of the new forestry department. And then there are mining towns, some, like Midelt, much transformed, others like Ahouli in the gorges of the Upper Melouya, totally abandoned.

Contemporary painting

In terms of painting too, Morocco has proved a considerable bed of talent, perhaps surprisingly for a country that had no tradition of representing human and animal form. However, given the proximity of Europe, easel painting soon took root after the arrival

A Moroccan feast for the senses

The Western fascination with the vivid and diverse colours of Morocco has a short history, beginning with the first European travellers there in the 19th century. For a number of artists – not least Matisse – the Cherifian Empire was to be of prime importance. For the French romantic painter Eugène Delacroix, the scenes and colours witnessed during an early visit to Morocco were to shape his whole career.

Before his journey to Morocco, the well read Delacroix had travelled only in literature – apart from a brief stay in London in 1825, where he had become familiar with watercolour techniques. It was the speed and immediacy of watercolour that was to enable Delacroix to record so much of what he was to see in North Africa.

Delacroix arrived in Tanger in January 1832, a member of a diplomatic mission to the Sultan Moulay Abd Al-Rahman. (France had taken Algiers in July 1830, and one of the results had been a wave of resentment against French interests in Morocco.) In diplomatic terms the mission was a failure, with Morocco continuing to support the Algerian Emir Abdel Kader. But for Delacroix, the Moroccan notebooks, a rich mixture of watercolours, sketches and jottings, were to be a lifelong source of inspiration.

Shortly after arriving in Algiers, Delacroix wrote back to a friend, "We have landed in the midst of the strangest peoples ... At the moment I am like a man dreaming who sees things but fears that they will escape him." Delacroix sketched the town, the family of Abraham Benchimol, and the French consulate dragoman. In March, the Duc de Mornay's suite proceeded south towards Meknès to the meeting with the Sultan – later the subject of one of Delacroix's most important pictures, Le Sultan du Maroc entouré de sa garde *(1845). Mounted on a richly caparisoned horse, shaded by the imperial parasol, Moulay Abd Al-Rahman moves forward amidst a throng of courtiers and guards. In the background are the ramparts of Meknès. The painting is one of the earliest pictorial representations of a Muslim court – important given the reticence to portray the human form prevalent in Islamic art.*

In the 1820s, the youthful Delacroix had painted scenes of cruel carnage, inspired by the struggle for Greek independence. The six months of the Moroccan journey was to be his only contact with the Orient: his palette became warmer and lighter. "Come to Barbary," wrote Delacroix to a friend in 1832, "You will feel even more the precious and rare influence of the sun which gives each thing a penetrating life." He discovered what he was to call 'Living Antiquity', people who through their closeness to nature had all the nobility of the ancient Romans. (Contrasting the French delegation with graceful Moroccan dress, Delacroix wrote: "... in our corsets, our tight shoes, our ridiculous tight clothes, we are objects of pity.)"

Yet, despite the vivacity of the Moroccan notebooks – the lively realism of streetscapes and interiors – the Orient of the majority of Delacroix's great paintings is an Orient of cavalcades and bloody combats, of concubines lounging in cool harems – a world often cruel, sometimes erotic. Although memories of Morocco were a constant source of material for Delacroix, the vision that emerges is one of primitive nature, where cruel passions are played out – a world where painters freed themselves from constraints and morals of classicism, but never really sought to understand. That was left to later painters.

of the French protectorate. (A stay in Morocco had already been a popular source of inspiration for numerous European painters, for whom the kingdom was all exotic street scenes, cavalcades in movement, and sharp, often violent colour contrast.) A number of European artists settled in Morocco, the most important being Jacques Majorelle, 'the painter of Marrakech', best known for his scenes of the High Atlas,

The jeweller's craft

Jewellers must be masters of many crafts. Those in Morocco certainly are. The many types of metal and insets require great skill.

Engraved jewellery is very popular. Here the craftsman prepares his silvered plates and moulds them to the shapes required. He then smears them with 'jeweller's black', a preparation made from oil and darkened with smoke. When this is dried he removes with a dry tip the lines he intends to work on, and eventually the pattern emerges. He sets up his metal on a tripod called a h'mar el aoued, *or 'wooden donkey', and carefully chisels where he had previously drawn. This three-dimensional work is very skilful, particularly where the work is fine and the ornament small.*

Jewellers must also be masters of the art of gilding. In earlier days this process was done with veneers of thin gold leaves or powdered gold, mixed with fish glue which was then baked in a small wood-fired oven. Today the gilding is done with an amalgam of powdered gold and a mercury base. This is brushed on to the base metal and then heated, leaving a small film of gold. This process is repeated many times until the desired thickness of gold has been deposited.

Enamelled jewellery is very popular. Described simply, the shape for the decoration was scraped out of the metal and the liquid enamel was poured in. An alternative method was to place the powder in the desired shape and use fire to vitrify the enamel. In the southwest of the country and in the Meknès region, jewellers still prepare their insets in their traditional way. Small enclosures are constructed with silver wires by welding them to the surface of the ornament. These circular and geometric spaces are filled with a dough of enamel paste which is then exposed to heat, care being taken not to melt the silver surround. Colours are obtained from copper (green), lead (yellow) and cobalt (blue).

Edouard Edy-Legrand and Marianne Bertuchi. In the 1940s, a number of self-taught Moroccan painters emerged, sometimes directly imitating European styles, others, such as Moulay Ahmed Drissi, illustrating the rich heritage of oral literature. Jacques Azema produced fine frescoes – but is perhaps best known for his miniature line drawings, executed with finesse in biro.

After independence in 1956, a generation of Moroccan painters came to the fore, working in a number of registers – abstract, naïve, calligraphic. Many had received training at the fine arts schools set up in Tetouan in 1945 and Casablanca in 1950. Unfortunately, there is as yet no museum of contemporary art, but there are frequent exhibitions in galleries in Rabat, Casablanca and Marrakech. Major abstract painters include Ahmed Cherkaoui (d.1967), Jilali Gharbaoui, Saâd Hassani, Mohammed Kacimi, and Fouad Belamine. Mehdi Qotbi produces vast expanses of calligraphic signs, while Farid Belkahia works with wood, animal skins and natural pigments to produce objects and canvasses using ancestral symbols and archetypes.

Naïve painting has an important place in the Moroccan art scene. The Galerie Frédéric Damgaard in Essaouira has enabled many local artists to exhibit and live on their work, and an 'Essaouira school' of painting has emerged, filled with movement and joyful figures. Leading figures include Abdellah El Atrach and Rashid Amerhouch. Of Morocco's self-taught naïve painters, the best known is Chaïbia, who produces raw and colourful scenes of daily life. And then there is Saladi Abbès, a native of Marrakech, creator of an ironic universe, of trees and birds, orchards and chequerboards, and strange cyclops-like creatures. Naked, both male and female, shown in Egyptian profile, their faces tapering to muzzle-shape, Saladi's beings inhabit paradisiac gardens – or fly through the air with the birds. For some say that in Morocco, when a person dies, a bowl of water is left on their tomb for the birds. Coming down to drink, they may bear the soul of the deceased away to paradise.

Urban and rural crafts

Morocco has long had a reputation as a country with a vivid and imaginative craft industry, and the visitor will not be disappointed. The souks of the historic cities are full of vivid pottery and carpets, the delicate tracery of wrought iron, polished thuya wood and beautifully worked leather. Basically, the traditional arts divide into two categories, rural and urban. Urban crafts are generally taken to be more refined, displaying an Andalucían influence. Rural crafts, generally from the Berber-speaking regions, have provided a rich source of inspiration for contemporary designers.

But rural and urban crafts are in many ways very different. Rural craft items – carpets and woven items such as saddle bags and tent strips, pottery, jewellery – were, and still are to a great extent, produced in very different conditions from urban items. Rural craftwork is solid, practical, made to stand up to long years of use in places of harsh climatic extremes. Carpets and pottery are made by women, jewellery and metal utensils by men. The signs and symbols used to decorate these items are generally geometric, arranged in simple, repetitive combinations to pleasing effect. Lines, dots and dashes, lozenges and squares are combined to cover surfaces made from clay, metal and wool. Sometimes these decorative forms are linked to the tribal marks tatooed on women's faces and arms. The isolation of rural communities meant that the peoples of different areas could develop very individual styles of craftwork. This is apparent in weaving, clothing and women's jewellery. But given the fact that craft-made items were subject to harsh conditions of use, few pieces can be safely said to be more than a 100 years old.

Striking colour and form are often features of rural crafts. Made from thick wool, the carpets of the Middle Atlas, used both as mattresses and blankets, may have vivid red and deep brown backgrounds. Carpets from the Haouz Plain (Marrakech region) also have strong orange-red backgrounds. The jewellery of southern Berber communities was once made by Jewish craftsmen. It is always silver; necklaces include silver tubes and spheres, along with *tozra*, oversized orange copal beads. *Serdal*, silk headbands hung with silver coins and coral beads and *khalkhal* ankle bracelets are also worn. Simple enamel cloisonné work is another feature of southern jewellery. Pottery varies greatly from region to region, each area having very individual forms. With the spread of cheap plastic and enamelled utensils, many of the local forms are disappearing.

In contrast, urban craft items are generally produced by men, often working in structured corporations. While the women folk of nomadic tribes produced for their own use, men in towns were working to sell their produce. They did not, however, build up sufficient capital to develop production on a large scale. City craftsmen produced carpets, jewellery, pottery, leather items, and metal utensils. They worked the raw materials for their production. Urban jewellery is in gold, set with precious stones, and very finely worked. Pottery was enamelled and decorated with designs that were flowing and floral as well as geometric. The leather workers produced footwear (*belgha*) and high quality bindings for the sacred texts. Traditional copper work included chandeliers, lamps, kettles, trays and perfume sprinklers. Wooden items were often very elaborate – and still are, witness the workshops near the Kasbah des Oudayas, Rabat. There was a vogue for mosaic-type marquetry, with wooden furniture and other objects being inset with coloured woods and precious materials such as mother-of-pearl and ivory.

There was one area of craft production (excluding the arts of cooking) in which city women were highly active: embroidery. Each region had its characteristics. *Aleuj* embroidery, said to have been introduced by Christians converted to Islam, includes gold thread. Salé embroidery is sober and geometric, while Azemour women embroidered mythical beasts and birds. Sadly, many of these techniques and motifs now survive only in museum collections.

It is perhaps in dress that urban crafts have best resisted change. Although most Moroccans, both women and men, dress western-style in the cities, traditional dress is alive and well. A full-blown wedding requires the bride to be displayed to guests in various costumes – the most expensive and elaborate being rented. It is deemed more fitting for Moroccan men to wear a long, hooded garment to the mosque over their ordinary clothes. A stylish caftan, a long and elegant long-sleeved gown, generally decorated with brocade motifs, is essential in a woman's wardrobe. Fashions in caftans change from season to season, with new models created by couturières like Zineb Joundy and Tami Tazy much sought after. The *jallabah* is the most common woman's garment. In the 1930s, Moroccan city women began to abandon the *haïk*, the traditional wrap, too constraining for the new ways of living. They adopted the jallabah, a man's tunic with hood, as a garment that respected the need for modesty and was practical. Today the jallabah, in bright colours and synthetic fabrics, with fantasy embroidery is worn everywhere. Things have changed since 1939, when the bourgeoisie of Fès petitioned the pascha to outlaw the wearing of the jallabah by women.

Within living memory, Morocco's cities had very locally-specific forms of craft production. Today, certain craft items are mass produced for the tourist market. And very fine production it is too. However, older items can often be found in the antique shops of Marrakech and Casablanca, where they go for very high prices. The aesthetic qualities of Moroccan craftwork are much appreciated by collectors. Unlike the rest of the Maghreb, and Egypt and the Levant, for that matter, Morocco was never occupied by the Ottomans. Craft production hence retained a certain artistic independence, evolving in great isolation in the case of the mountain areas. As in building – see the 16th-century Saâdian tombs in Marrakech, or the kasbahs of the South – a sureness in aesthetic touch is the hallmark of the best craftwork, be it a Zaïane carpet, a pair of babouches with *khanjar* motif, or a simple blue and white bowl from Fès.

Culture

What makes Morocco tick? What makes Morocco so different from, say, its near neighbour Spain? In the travel brochures, it is a land peopled by men in flowing robes and camels, its cities full of winding streets, garden courtyards and sumptuous banquets. It is an Islamic country – but the women (who do not feature in the brochures) are not, on the whole, veiled. Standing back from the bright postcards and garden courtyards, the Arab-Amazigh dichotomy, the clichés about tolerance and eternal Moroccan civilization, what sort of a culture is this? Who are the Moroccans?

The Moroccan people

The population of Morocco was estimated in 1995 at 26.98 million. Although the crude birth rate has fallen sharply in recent years to 28 per 1,000 population, potential fertility is high. Better medical facilities have improved the child survival rate. At the same time, death rates are also down to six per 1,000 and life expectancy, now 69 years on average, will no doubt improve to swell the total population. The population is fairly young on average. More than 36% of people are under the age of 15, 50% are under 20 and a mere 6% over 60.

Which parts of Morocco are most populated, then? The coastal cities and plains are the key areas. Half the population now lives in cities, the great concentrations being in Casablanca with 2.9 million, Rabat-Salé with 1.2 million, Fès with 564,000 and Marrakech with 672,506, and Meknès, with 447,437 inhabitants. Areas of heavily settled land with 60-95 people per sq km are found round the Mediterranean and northern Atlantic coastal areas, notably in the Rif, Jebala, the Gharb Plain and the southern Sous Valley. Densities fall off rapidly as you go inland. Other than the great cities of Marrakech, Meknès and Fès, the inland regions have low population densities, averaging between 20-60 per sq km. The arid southern and eastern regions are sparsely settled with fewer than 20 people per sq km.

What does a typical Moroccan look like? The question is not an easy one to answer, as the population of contemporary Morocco is the result of a long history during which various settlers passed through the country. The earliest populations of northwestern Africa, the ancestors of today's Imazighen (Berbers) were probably of Hamitic stock (ie descendants of Biblical Ham, brother of Shem and Japheth). Since the Imazighen arrived, there have been numerous other inputs, including Phoenicians and Romans, and in particular the Arabs, who first occupied the region in the eighth century AD. Until the mid-20th century, there was an important Jewish community, originally part of the rural Amazigh population. This was reinforced, after the 15th-century Reconquista, by highly educated and talented groups of Iberian Jews. Many Jews left Morocco after the foundation of the State of Israel in 1948. As of the late 18th century, a European population settled in the coastal towns, and was particularly numerous in the mid-20th century. There is a sub-Saharan African component to Morocco's population, originally the result of the slave trade and the preference of 17th-century ruler Moulay Ismaïl for an all-black royal guard. In physical terms, then, an average roomful of Moroccans at, say, a business meeting will not look very different from Brazilian or Spanish counterparts.

There are, however, certain regional types. The inhabitants of cities like Fès, Meknès and Rabat tend to be pale skinned and slightly built, and have a distinctly Iberian look. There are certain faces which to the insider look very Fassi, and others which are distinctly Amazigh – something in the shape of the face, perhaps. The older generation of Moroccans, particularly the mountain people, are shorter than their European counterparts. Lifestyle for the urban middle classes differs little from that of southern Europeans. The rural regions, however, are vastly different, and there are still areas without electricity and other basic infrastructure, and in these regions life expectancy is lower.

Moroccans differ greatly from northern Europeans in the way their lives are focused. The family is of primary importance, determining a person's life chances to a great degree. Family loyalty is of great importance, with the father seemingly the dominant figure – although very often wives rule the roost. Islam is a strong force, laying down the limits of what can and cannot be done. The home is a private place – but strangers, when a friendship forms, are readily invited in. On the whole, however, men meet their friends in cafés, while women socialize in each others' homes.

Moroccan society is changing rapidly. Today, just over 50% of the population is urban. The main cities have expanded enormously over the last 20 years – Marrakech is a good example. Morocco's old families, and the brightest and best connected of the university-educated élite, have done very well for themselves since independence from France in 1956. The second generation urban populations have new aspirations, and expect some part of the national cake. Affluence is not for everybody at the moment and in 1998, the opposition won a majority in parliament with a remit to improve things, quickly (see section below, Modern Morocco). Despite the difficult international situation, Morocco's people have great hopes that a more egalitarian society will be achieved in the early years of the 21st century.

Language

Who speaks what language? when? and to whom? The visitor to Marrakech and southern Morocco will quickly become aware of the range of languages on offer.

Mauritania and Moors, Morocco and the Maghreb

Going way back into history, it seems likely that Mauritania, Morocco's neighbour to the south, takes its name from ***Mahour****, the ancient Phoenician word for the natives of the Mediterranean coast. This term then went into Latin to describe the tribes of the far northwest of Africa, the* ***Maures****. In 40 BC, the north of what is now Morocco became the Roman province of* ***Mauritania Tingitana*** *after the death of Ptolomey last king of the Maures and son of Cleopatra Selene and the cultured Juba II. In Spanish, the* ***Moros*** *were the Arab-Muslims who were eventually removed from the Iberian Peninsula when the Reconquista ended with the fall of Granada in 1492. The term* ***Moro*** *is used in Spanish, often disparagingly, for any North African – and in particular for the much-exploited Moroccan workforce of the plasticulture farms of the Ejido region. Until the mid-20th century, French writers used the term* ***Maure*** *for city Arabs in North Africa, as opposed to the nomads and the Berbers. In English, the term* ***Moor*** *was also much used by travel writers describing Morocco. Today, the term* ***Mauritania*** *is the name for the large desert republic between Morocco and Senegal. As for the origins of the word* ***Morocco****, variations of it passed into European languages in the 19th century. Prior to then, writers referred to Marrakech as* ***Morocco City****. In Arabic, Morocco is* ***Al Mamlaka al Maghribiya*** *(the Kingdom of Morocco), or more generally,* ***Al Maghreb****, which is also the term for Northwest Africa in western political jargon. A Moroccan is a* ***Maghrebi****, an adjective not to be confused with a* ***Magharebi****, Northwest African.*

Street signs and official notices are in Arabic and French, occasionally in English, people talk to each other in Arabic, Amazigh, French or even a mixture of all three.

Amazigh languages

Amazigh languages are spoken in the mountains, in scattered communities on the Atlantic plains – and in the poorer areas of the big cities. There are three main Amazigh languages: **Ta'rifit** spoken in the Rif mountains of the North, **Tamazight**, spoken in the Middle Atlas, and finally **Tachelhit**, the language of the High Atlas and the Sous Valley. While Tachelhit and Tamazight are fairly mutually comprehensible, Ta'rifit is a very different dialect. The Amazigh languages have a rich heritage of oral literature. Down in the Algerian Sahara, inscriptions in **Tamashek**, also an Amazigh language, can be seen written in Tifinagh characters. There is no great corpus of literature in Tifinagh, however. After independence, Amazigh gained a foothold in the cities as country people migrated. Although their language has no real presence in the school system, there is a new-found pride in the Amazigh identity. There are newspapers written in Amazigh using Arabic or Latin characters (*Tafoukt*, 'The Sun'), and Amazigh films and dramas circulate on video-cassette. It remains to be seen whether written forms of the Amazigh languages will gain currency, rather as the Celtic languages were revived in the British Isles. Unfortunately, there is much prejudice against them in official circles. Many urban Moroccans just dismiss languages of the Amazigh group as crude country 'dialects'.

The Arabics of Morocco

Arabic is a little like German in that it has a prestigious written version, generally called **Classical Arabic** in English, and numerous spoken dialects. Spoken **Moroccan Arabic**, *al darija al maghribiya*, is learned at home and is the everyday language of the cities, the dialects of Fès and Meknès being the most prestigious. *Fusha* (pronounce fus-ha) or formal written Arabic is the language of law, religion, official government activities and political speeches. It is learned, often with some difficulty, at school. In grammatical terms, there is a considerable gap between Classical Arabic and Moroccan. In some

Latin, Spanish and Arabic

*From the Muslim conquest in the early eighth century to the fall of Granada in 1492, much of Spain was under Muslim rule. Arabic was the language of the élite, of technology and letters, and as such left numerous traces in the rough Latin which was eventually to transform itself into Castillian, Catalan and the other languages of Spain. In particular, the Arabs left a huge number of places names: Valladolid (*Wilayat Walid*, the Province of Walid), Guadalquivir (*Wadi al Kabir*, the Big Wadi or River), and Gibraltar (*Jebel Tariq *or Mount Tariq) for the first Arab general to cross the straits in 710. In Portugal, the Algarve is the 'place in the west',* al gharb. *The Alhambra of Granada (and numerous cinemas across Britain) is short for* Al Qasr al Hamra, *the Red Palace, while the Alcazár of Segovia is just the Palace of the Seguia or irrigation channel.*

To agriculture, Muslim rule left words like noria *(from na'oura, water wheel),* algodón *(from qutn, cotton) and* azúcar *(sugar, from the Arabic sukar). Spanish cities would not be the same without the* alcalde *(mayor, from* al ca'id, *still very much present in Moroccan local administration).*

But the traffic in words was not all one way. In the Muslim Near East, the Arabs, a nomadic desert people, came into contact with the great civilizations of Sassanian Persia and Byzantium. From the latter, they acquired the words for money: dirham, *(Morocco's currency today) from the Greek* drachma; dinar, *from the Latin* denarius, *and* flous, *a corruption of the Latin* follis, *(lit. leaf), the smallest copper coins in use in the old Eastern Empire. And the Arabic* barid *(postal service) is the Latin* veredum *or* milepost *heavily transformed.*

quarters of academia, there have been calls for Moroccan Arabic to be made an official language – an unlikely possibility, since there is no standardized written form.

French & Spanish

Thus, for the time being, **French** is the language of business, science and higher education, while a mixed language, **Franco-Arabe**, is used by much of the urban educated élite on many occasions. **Spanish** – in part thanks to the availability of Spanish television – is spoken and often understood in the far north of Morocco. It has largely been replaced by French as the second language in the former Spanish Sahara. However, with Morocco's state schools continuing to decline and the French schools heavily oversubscribed, the Spanish schools have become very popular. With an eye to helping business interests, the Spanish government is showing signs of seeking to promote the language in Morocco, especially given Spaniards' general low level of ability when it comes to learning foreign languages.

A complex linguistic situation

The Moroccan language situation is complex – and changing. Behind the multi-lingual screen lie a range of personal attitudes and aspirations. How you get on in life is linked to your language ability, and few Moroccans have any doubt that mastery of at least one European language is essential for access to science and technology. French is certainly still vital for achieving a useful university degree. At the same time, there is a very strong tradition of learning in Arabic, cultivated in mosques like the Qaraouiyine in Fès by generations of *ulema* (scholars). The future of the Amazigh languages will be interesting to observe. From the mid-1990s, the lunchtime TV news was broadcast in all three Amazigh languages. It remains to be seen how these languages will develop in urban areas – or whether second-generation rural migrants will switch wholly to Arabic. And there is the question of whether the Amazigh languages will eventually achieve anything more than a symbolic presence in schools. After all, they are the mother-tongue of at least a third of Morocco's population. For the moment basic literacy

Berber manifesto

After the death of Hassan II in 1999, Amazigh militants discovered a new self-confidence. On 1 March 2000 came a major step forward with the publication of a so-called 'Berber manifesto', the result of two years debate among Morocco's Amazigh-speaking intellectuals. Signed by 229 leading figures, including lawyers, human-rights activists and a former minister, the manifesto makes some major demands. Firstly, the 'Berber question' is to be the object of a full national debate. Morocco's constitution is to be amended to make tamazight a national language, to be taught in schools and universities. The Manifesto also asks for institutes to be set up to develop written forms of Morocco's Amazigh languages and wants to see the official media make greater use of Amazigh, as well as the governmental bodies. (At the present time, certain civil servants refuse to register infants under traditional Berber names.) The Manifesto suggests that school curricula be reformed to take into account Morocco's Amazigh identity, and an end to the practice of systematically Arabizing the names of Amazigh historic figures and places. It also calls for greater support for Amazigh art and culture and for official recognition of Amazigh independent organizations to enable them to have access to public money. And finally, the Manifesto of 1st March 2000 wants to see the poorest – and generally Amazigh-speaking – regions of the country benefit from a priority economic development programme. It remains to be seen, however, if any of these demands will actually be met.

in Classical Arabic, the language of Islam, looks set to maintain its position in the education system. But there are new trends emerging. Parents with money put their children in bilingual schools as a matter of course. Written Arabic is important to many ideologically, but is of little use in a job market where technology and business skills are all.

Religion

The people of Morocco, and of North Africa for that matter, follow Islam in the main, a religion similar to Judaism and Christianity in its philosophical content. Muslims recognize that these three revealed religions have a common basis, and Jews and Christians are referred to as *Ahl al-kitab*, 'people of the book'. Even so, there are considerable differences in ritual, public observance of religious customs and the role of religion in daily life, and when travelling in Morocco it is as well to be aware of this. Note, however, that although the Islamic revivalist movement in recent years has been a force in neighbouring Algeria, in Morocco the situation, for historic and social reasons, is very different (see the section on 'Modern Morocco' below).

Islam is an Arabic word literally meaning 'submission to God'. As Muslims often point out, it is not just a religion, but a way of life. The main Islamic scripture is the Koran (often also spelt 'Quran' and 'Qur'an' in English), again an Arabic term meaning 'the recitation'. Islam appeared in the desert oases of western Arabia in the early-seventh century AD. The isolated communities of this region were Jewish, Christian or animist, existing on oasis cultivation and the trade in beasts of burden. There was considerable inter-tribal warfare. It was in this context that the third great revealed religion was to emerge. Its, prophet Mohammed, born in 570 AD, was a member of the aristocratic Meccan tribe of Quraysh.

The Koran Islam's holy book, the Koran divides into 114 *souras* or chapters, placed in order of length running from the longest to the shortest. Muslim and western scholars disagree on the nature of the Koran. For the true Muslim, it is the word of God, sent down via the Prophet Mohammed. The Koran appeared in this way in segments, some in Mecca, some after the Prophet was forced to leave Mecca for Medina in 622. The later *souras* tend to have a more practical content, and relate to family and inheritance law, for during the period in Medina, an embryonic Muslim community was taking shape. Western scholars, however, have opened up more critical approaches to the Koranic text and the way it was assembled. During the Prophet's lifetime, nothing was written down. After his death, fragments of the text, noted in simple script on parchment or flat bones, were assembled at the order of Abu Bakr, Mohammed's successor or *khalifa*. In fact, the Arabic script was not fully codified at the time. The language of the Koran was eventually to become the base reference point for the Arabic language. For most Muslim Arabs, the written classical form of the language can never escape this divine influence.

The Hadith

The Koran does not cover all aspects of the Muslim's life – and it became apparent to early Islamic rulers that they would need another source. The *hadith*, short statements which recount what the Prophet is supposed to have said about various issues, were assembled, providing crucial supplements to the main scripture.

Five pillars of Islam

The practice of Islam is based on five central points, the Pillars of Islam, namely the *shahada* or profession of faith, *salat* or prayer, *sawm* or fasting during the month of Ramadhan, *zakat* or giving charity, and the *hajj* or pilgrimage to Mecca which every Muslim is supposed to accomplish at least once. The mosque is the centre of religious activity. There is no clergy in Islam, although major mosques will have an *imam* to lead prayers. In principle, the *mesjed*, a small neighbourhood mosque, will have someone chosen from the area with enough religious knowledge to conduct prayers correctly.

The *shahada* is the testament of faith, and involves reciting, in all sincerity, the statement, "There is no god but God, and Mohammed is the Messenger of God." A Muslim will do this at *salat*, the prayer ritual performed five times a day, including at sunrise, midday and sunset. There are also the important Friday noon prayers, which include a sermon or *khutba*. When praying, Muslims bow and then kneel down and prostrate themselves in the direction of Mecca, indicated in a mosque by a door-sized niche in the wall called the *qibla*. The voice of the *muezzin* calling the faithful to prayer five times a day from the minaret provides Muslim cities with their characteristic soundscape. Note that a Muslim must be ritually pure to worship. This involves washing in a ritual manner, either at the hammam (local bathhouse) or the *midha*, the ablutions area of the mosque.

A third essential part of Islam is the giving of *zakat* or alms. A Muslim was supposed to give surplus revenues to the community. With time, the practice of *zakat* was codified. Today, however, *zakat* has largely disappeared to be replaced by modern taxation systems. The practice of *zakat al fitr*, giving alms at Aïd el Fitr, the Muslim holiday which marks the end of Ramadhan, is still current, however.

The fourth pillar of Islam is *sawm* or fasting during Ramadhan. The daytime month-long fast of Ramadhan is a time of contemplation, worship and piety – the Islamic equivalent of Lent. Muslims are expected to read one thirtieth of the Koran each night. Muslims who are ill or on a journey, as well as women breast-feeding are exempt from fasting. Otherwise, eating, drinking and sexual activity is only permitted at night, until "so much of the dawn appears that a white thread can be distinguished from a black one".

The *hajj* or pilgrimage to the holy city of Mecca in Arabia is required of all physically able Muslims at least once in their lifetime. The *hajj* takes place during the month of Dhu al Hijja. The 'lesser pilgrimage' to the holy places of Islam is referred to as the *umra*, and can be performed at any time of year. Needless to say, the journey to Mecca is not within every Muslim's financial grasp – fortunately, perhaps, as the mosques would probably be unable to cope with the millions involved, despite the extension works of recent years.

On prophets and revelation As mentioned above, Islam is a revealed religion, and God chose certain men to be **prophets**, his true representatives on Earth. In Arabic, a prophet is a *nabi*, while Mohammed is the messenger of God, *rasoul Allah*. The first prophet in Islam was Adam, and the last was Mohammed, 'seal of the prophets'. Major prophets are Sidna Nouh (Noah), Sidna Ibrahim (Abraham), Dawoud (David), Mousa (Moses), and 'Issa (Jesus). Yaqoub (Jacob), Youssuf (Joseph) and Ayyoub (Job) are all mentioned in the Koran. Prophets were recognized by their miracles, apart from Mohammed, who was to be the instrument via which the Koran was transmitted to humankind. Nevertheless, Mohammed's *mi'raj* or ascent to heaven on the winged horse, Al Buraq, may be considered as a sort of miracle.

The miracles performed by the prophets are not detailed in the Koran. **'Issa** (Jesus) is pictured in a particularly favourable light. While the virgin birth remains in the Koran, Issa is definitely not the son of God in Islam.

Sunna (standard Islamic practice) The Koran and the hadith also lay down a number of other practices and customs, some of which are close to the practices of Judaism. Sexuality, provided it is within marriage, is seen as positive, and there is no category of religious personnel for whom marriage is forbidden. Sensuality and seduction, between the married couple, are encouraged, without any guilt being involved. Eating pork is out, as is drinking alcohol and gambling. In the matter of dress, habits have changed hugely in recent years. Except in certain rural areas, young women no longer automatically veil their faces, rather, a headscarf and *jallabah* is the modern version of Islamic dress for women. However, Moroccan Islam is a long way from the more extreme forms practised in Saudi Arabia, where women are forbidden from driving and are all but invisible in the public sphere. While in traditional families the women's domain is most definitely the home, Islam does not stop Moroccan women getting themselves educated and into jobs once thought of as being exclusively for men

Gender issues

Despite the changes since independence, the status of women is likely to be an increasingly hot issue over the next decade in Morocco. For the moment, Tunisia is the most advanced Muslim country in terms of legislation aimed at removing discrimination against women – and is a model often referred to by Moroccans working for women's rights. The Tunisian *Code du statut personnel*, promulgated in 1956, abolished both polygamy and *talaq* (repudiation by the male partner), a step which the Moroccan women's movement would like to see taken in their own country. The Tunisian code did not however touch the issue of Islamic inheritance rules which favour male over female descendants, although laying down strict rules for the division of property.

The Moudawana The nature of women's status in Morocco is laid down in a code referred to as the *Moudawana*, passed in 1957 and revised in 1993. The *Moudawana*, like other codes in the North African states, affirms the importance of the family as the basis of society. The family is patrilinear, that is to say, takes its name from the father. Thus it is forbidden for a Muslim woman to marry a non-Muslim man. He must convert to Islam, even if this is only for form's sake, and the process is a long one. Non-Muslim women marrying Moroccans do not have to convert, however. Adoption, outlawed in the Koran, does not exist in Morocco. The marriageable age is 18 for men and 14 for women.

Much was expected of the 1993 revision of the *Moudawana*. Many activists, however, considered it as a mere rewriting of the existing code. At the very least, however, the demands of both women and civil society had been listened to. The arguments against polygamy are many. The *Moudawana* does specify that if there is a risk of injustice, the judge must refuse polygamy, and Moroccan women's rights groups argue that in its essence polygamy is unjust. A similar line of argument runs that Islamic repudiation is also to be abolished, to be replaced by fair divorce laws, given that a *hadith* or 'saying' attributed to the Prophet Mohammed runs that repudiation "is the permitted act which is most reproved by God".

A plan for change

In the late 1990s, Saïd Saâdi, Secretary of State for Family Affairs and Social Security, was entrusted with preparing a plan to improve the socio-legal conditions of Moroccan women. Resulting from co-operation between civil service departments and NGOs, the National Action Plan for Integrating Women into the Development Process was wide ranging and ambitious. Propositions included giving women a 33 % quota of seats in the parliament, raising the minimum marriage age from 14 to 18, ending the requirement for a male guardian's permission to be given to women before marriage, banning polygamy, and reforming divorce law. As at present, Islamic repudiation is in force; the Action Plan would have introduced divorce by judicial decree.

The reforms were not to be. Shortly after its unveiling in late 1999, the Plan for Integration was dropped in a storm of protest from reformists. It was much criticized by the Islamic fundamentalists as 'importing corrupt western values' and the old guard of parties in government like the Istiqlal were loath to be accused of being non-Islamic. Prime Minister Abderrahmane Youssoufi's coalition government felt it had other more pressing issues on the agenda, most notably the fight against poverty and educational reform.

Justifications of conservatism

With the number of educated women increasing year by year, attitudes will no doubt change. Long-established practices die hard, however, and the best thought-out family status code would have little effect without changes in mentalities. Morocco, like the rest of the Maghreb and much of southern Europe, is in many ways a macho land, and the young girls of the house are the object of jealous surveillance. Although the Koranic texts are basically clear on the principle of equality between men and women, certain *souras* and hadith stress women's weakness, the need for women to serve men, and mention the need for male protection. The way ordinary daily relations between the sexes run is the result of a long history in which economic, religious and traditional social factors are interlinked. While regulated by Islam, the nature of relations between women and men differs between social classes and regional groups. And very often, in traditional areas, it is the women who seem to be the most vigilant guardians of the status quo.

Expanding women's space

However, in this system, although women rarely have direct authority, they have very definite space of their own. All is not repression – far from it. While weddings are still very often a matter of alliances between families, loving marriages certainly develop in this traditional context. Women are now present in most areas of the country's economic and professional life. There are frequent television programmes on women who have succeeded in new domains, as train drivers, pilots and physicists, in stock-broking, advertising, the catering business and the like.

Moroccan women are clearly emerging into public life, too. They are to be found in key positions: Zoulikha Naciri, former Secretary of State for National Solidarity, is now part of the Royal Cabinet, Fathia Bennis heads the Casablanca Stock Exchange, Farida Belyazid makes successful films. They are *the* force in Morocco's dynamic (and influential) NGOs. Women head assocations working to help single mothers, battered women, the illiterate and street children, cancer and AIDs victims. They are active in promoting micro-business programmes for women. The UAF (*Union d'action féminine*) was one of the leading actors behind the government's Action Plan. Chabaka ('the net') brings together 200 NGOs supporting reform of the Moudawana.

Thus in the reformists' minds there is no doubt that women's status will have to change to keep up with women's responsibilities in society. The reduction of inequalities links in with the image which Morocco wishes to project for itself and for the outside world. Women's quest for new identities is a legitimate one – and probably inseparable from the evolving identity of the modern nation.

Culture of patriarchy

Despite Morocco's carefully nurtured image as one of the most tolerant, progressive Islamic nations, it remains a very conservative place in many ways. As one observer remarked, it is a Lampedusan quality ('everything must remain the same'). On close examination, the couplet 'tradition and modernity', a favourite in the tourist advertising, is problematic. In the late 1990s – and in particular since the accession of Mohammed VI to the throne in 1999 – reform-minded Moroccans have been calling for change. New forces are emerging – the Islamists, the so-called Berberists, democratic pressure groups – all advocating different forms of 'progress'. How the existing dominant forces in the system, the *makhzen*, (roughly translatable as 'government by the palace') and the political parties will evolve will be interesting to watch. Among some observers, the survival of traditional politics into the early-21 century leads to gloomy talk of insurmountable cultural factors to explain the obstacles to reform. In fact, one of the great fears of the reformers is that a strongman will rise to the top, taking control of the nation's destiny. The challenge now is for the country to move from government focused on a single personality to a more open, accountable system.

Patriarchs & strongmen

One view of Moroccan political, and indeed social, culture is strongly authoritarian. There are plenty of examples of despots and powerful henchmen in the country's recent history. In 1894, as Sultan Hassan I lay dying, the chamberlain Ba Hmad had the weakening monarch name his youngest son, Moulay Abdelaziz, his heir. When the sultan died out in the countryside, the chamberlain kept the news quiet for days until Moulay Abdelaziz could be safely installed on the throne. From then on, Ba Hmad ruled as he saw fit, putting his relatives in key positions, removing all opposition. The young sultan was kept quiet with a range of mechanical toys and other gewgaws supplied by a former British army officer, Caïd McLean. Later, during the French protectorate, the south was ruled by the Pacha of Marrakech, Thami el Glaoui, with a similar mixture of terror and clientelism. (Gavin Maxwell gives a fine account in his *Lords of the Atlas*).

Under the late king, Hassan II, the system focused immutably on the palace, as it had done for centuries. Prime ministers were generally (but not always) rather self-effacing men. Government was dominated by a strongman, often of modest origins, heading the security apparatus in one way or another. Until 1972, General Oufkir was the régime's policeman. It was Oufkir who as Minister of the Interior gave the order for the security forces to fire on unarmed demonstrators during the Casablanca riots of 1965. The abortive coup d'état at the Skhirat Palace in 1972 led to Oufkir's replacement by his shadow, Colonel Dlimi. For his effective leadership in the Saharan campaigns of the late 1970s, he was to rise to the rank of general before dying in obscure circumstances. His chief claim to fame was his role in the 'disappearance', yet to be fully explained, of key left-wing politician, Mehdi ben Barka. The 1980s saw the emergence of Driss Basri, who as Minister of the Interior operated for all the world like a Grand Vizier from some onion-domed oriental city. He started his career as a police inspector, rose to become the all-powerful figure in Morocco's

Moroccan family and first names

In the cities, Moroccan first names are almost always of Arabic origin. Many of the girls' names are poetic – Amel (Hope), Awatef (Emotions), Houriya (Spirit of Paradise), Kmar (Moon), Leïla (Night), Noura (Light), Raoudha (Garden), Sana (Radiance), Thouraya (Chandelier) and Zohra (Flower). Some suggest desirable characteristics Besma and Ibtissem (Smile), Emna (Serenity), Faïka (Outstanding), Latifa (Kindly), Nabiha (Distinguished), Rafia (Of great value), Wafa (Loyalty). Another, rather rare, set of first names have more exotic, Turco-Persian origins: Chiraz, Narimene and Safinaz.

First names referring back to the Prophet Mohammed's family are popular for girls: Aïcha was the Prophet's first wife, Khadija his second wife, while Fatima harks back to his daughter. Meriem is the Arabic equivalent of Mary, mother of the Islamic prophet Issa, (Jesus). Other male prophets who provide boys' names are Ibrahim (Abraham) and his son Ismaïl, Mousa (Moses), and Yacoub (Jacob). Returning to the Prophet Mohammed's descendants, Ali was Fatima's husband (fourth of the rightly guided caliphs who succeeded Mohammed), their sons were Hassan and Hussein. Omar and Othman were respectively Mohammed's second and third successors at the head of the Islamic community.

Some names come in male / female pairs, as in Aziz / Aziza (Beloved), Habib / Habiba (Beloved), Jamil / Jamila (Beautiful) Nabil / Nabila (Noble), Rachid / Rachida (Rightly Guided), Saïd / Saïda (Happy), and Zine / Zina. There are a number of variations around the root letters h-m-d, meaning praise: Ahmed, Hamid, Mahmoud and, of course, Mohammed, for men, Hamida for women.

Particularly popular in Morocco are men's first names often start with Abd (servant of God) and one of the 99 names of the divinity, ie Abd Allah, 'servant of god', Abd el Hédi, 'servant of the tranquil one', Abd el Karim 'servant of the noble one', Abdelatif, ('servant of the kindly one'), Abderrahman, 'servant of the compassionate one', etc. Among friends, these names are shortened to Abdou. Another type of male name ends in 'din' (pron: 'deen') meaning 'faith', as in Chemseddine (Sun of Faith), Kamareddine (Moon of Faith), and Noureddine (Light of Faith). Common men's names in Morocco include Adil (Just), Khaled (Eternal), Mahdi (Rightly guided), Mourad (Desired), Naji (Close friend) and Walid (Engendered).

In addition to Muslim first names, up in the mountains the Imazighen have their own selection of first names, of growing popularity. Boys may be named for kings who fought the Romans (Massinissa, Youba and Kouceila), while for girls there are names like Tilila (Freedom), Toudhart (Life), Tihiya and Rekkouch, Ijja, Itto and Iloudi. Other boy's names include Sifaw (Enlightening) and Ayyour (Moon), Lounès and the poetic Yaoufitri ('Better than a star').

Families actually living in France or where the mother is of foreign origin may choose names easily pronounced in French. For the boys, Karim, Khaled and Skander (Alexander), for the girls, Nadia and Sofiya, Sarra and Monia.

Family names tell a story, too. 'Ben' (Arabic) and 'Aït' (Amazigh) correspond to the Celtic 'Mc', 'son of'). Many indicate trades and professions: Haddad (Blacksmith), Meddeb (teacher in a Koran school), Najjar (Carpenter). Others are strong markers of a regional identity: Fehri-Fassi, Berrada, Ben Jelloun, and Cohen say 'family of Fassi origin'. The latter surname can be both Jewish and Muslim, as in the distant past many Fès Jews converted to Islam.

political life. Political opponents ran the risk of imprisonment after various forms of 'trial', torture went unmentioned. Election results were routinely falsified; with Basri's assistance, new political parties appeared as if by magic. Even potential democrats were corrupted. In short, the whole political and administrative machinery was gangrened with various forms of corruption. To universal sighs of relief, Basri was removed from office in late 1999 by the new King.

'Heads-down culture' Morocco, as run by patriarchs, necessarily had a strong culture of non-criticism. With any opponent (and their family and friends) running huge risks, things could not be otherwise. 'Heads down' was the only prudent way to act (until things began to loosen up in the mid-1990s). Leftist intellectuals found themselves in a double-walled prison: the right smothered the left, and the King smothered the right. The result was a law of doing what one wanted, covering one's tracks, and making loyal allies in the positions that mattered.

Towards the end of patriarchy? In the early 1990s, signs that political change was possible appeared. The first major breach in the patriarchal system was the new constitution of 1992, which brought in the rule that governments would be formed on the basis of a parliamentary majority. The new King, Mohammed VI has shown himself keen to reform the system. There is constant talk of 'a new concept of authority', the local administration is becoming more professional, the old guard are being replaced. The question is whether authoritarianism can be attacked while leaving the very cultural foundations of the monarchy intact. Traditionally, apparent servility went hand in hand with pumping the system for all it was worth. The rule was 'don't challenge your boss openly, screw him if you can', hardly conducive to the open, responsible management of people and institutions.

Might a new strongman emerge? Traditionally, Morocco's sultans governed alone, with the additional legitimating plus of strong religious charisma. On the downside, they ruled a land subject to frequent drought, where harvests failed, provoking difficult times in town and country alike. Thus (the theory goes) in a context where power could not be shared, a strongman was essential to handle the less gratifying aspects of being ruler: putting down incipient revolts, dealing with rising opponents. And perhaps the strongman's room for action was enhanced by a certain docility among the population. After all, the strongman was operating in the name of a monarch with unchallenged Islamic credentials.

So the question is really one of whether Morocco can move away from the system where one man mediated the patriarch's decisions, distributing favours and keeping the order in place. In the eyes of most Moroccans, a general or a minister with despotic powers, implementing programmes with little respect for the niceties of form, is a complete dinosaur. But is there enough of a new, open political culture to replace the old system of subservience to the patriarch? Technocratic government will not be enough to create a democratic system.

On the plus side, Morocco has strong institutions. Issues of government, accountability and corruption are widely debated in the press; the constitutional reforms of the 1990s were a major step, taken by the previous monarch, in the right direction. Political patterns, methods of management and deep-rooted behaviour seem to be changing, pushed by NGOs such as Transparency Maroc. Another sign of change was a major parliamentary enquiry into corruption and mismanagement of the country's biggest state-owned banks, the *CIH*. Though prospects for a fairer system of government seem good under Mohammed VI, for those in the grinding poverty of Morocco's fourth-world countryside, this is not much consolation. And if change is too slow, many of the best and brightest will be tempted to leave.

Entertainment

Still, all is not doom and gloom. Moroccans like to have a good time, as is evident if you happen to get invited to a wedding party. In their most elaborate form, weddings involve several days of festivities, and large sums are spent on ensuring that a good time is had by all (and that family status is maintained). There will be a jolly henna party at which the bride will have elaborate henna patterns done on her hands and feet by a relative or (preferably) an expert *nakkacha*. During the actual wedding party, bride and groom sit upon twin thrones before the assembled guests and receive their best wishes. Custom has it that the bride will appear in seven different costumes, generally hired. (The general logistics of this are handled by a *neggafa*.)

Also important, as they create opportunities for gatherings of family and friends, are the big religious holidays of the Muslim year. There is the Mouloud (celebration of the Prophet Mohammed's birthday, Aïd el Fitr, marking the end of Ramadhan, and Aïd el Kebir, aka Aïd el Adha, 'the Festival of the Sacrifice', two months later, when all right-minded families have a lamb to sacrifice to commemorate how Ibrahim nearly sacrificed his son, who was saved at the last minute when Allah sent a sheep as replacement. No matter how poor they are, it is absolutely vital. Of more pagan origin is the annual celebration of Achoura, a sort of Muslim Guy Fawkes day. Banging on small clay-pot drums, the kids run round the streets collecting small change to light bonfires (*el afiya*) in the street. Cheap and cheerful toys and especially firecrackers are on sale everywhere. On the actual morning of Achoura, you have licence to throw water at anyone you feel like. (Do not go out with important documents on the morning of Achoura.)

Music

What sort of music do Moroccans listen to? Walking past a cassette stall, your ears will be assailed by unfamiliar tunes and voices. With technology for the mass pirating of music so easily available now, Moroccan musical tastes have become increasingly catholic. Tapes are cheap too, between 12dh and 20dh. Among young women, top selling cassettes are by Arab singers, like the Iraqi Kazem Essaher and Diana Haddad, whose videos are shown on satellite TV. Algerian *raï* music is popular too (see below). Local *chaâbi* music had gone out of fashion by the late 1990s, only a few of the best known singers like Stati and Jadwane, and groups like Tagada are still popular. The 'politically committed' sound of the leading 1970s and 1980s groups still has its fans. You may want to buy tapes by Jil Jilala, Nass el Ghiwane or Lmachaheb. Another popular Moroccan sound is Gnaoua Jazz. Look out for tapes by the likes of Saha Koyo. Western music (*el gharbi*) is popular too, but mainly with the urban middle classes. Adolescents and students go for Bob Marley and Dr Alban, Madonna and The Spice Girls,or boy bands. 'Romantic' singers like Quebec's Céline Dion also have a following in Morocco.

An Andalucían taste: classical city music

There is of course a more classical taste in music. Moroccan urban music divides into a number of strands: *gharnati, el alat el andulsi* and *malhoun*. The latter is perhaps the most accessible form to the ear attuned to European sounds. In top bookshops you may find CD collections of these musical styles. On cassette, *malhoun* artists to look out for include the recently deceased Houcine Toulali from Meknès, Saïd Guennoun (Fès) and Mohammed Berrahal. In the late 1990s, writer Touria Hadraoui was the first woman to sing *malhoun*, and has produced a CD. In the evening, during Ramadhan, Moroccan television broadcasts music by the classical Andalucían-style orchestras. Maybe the violins and lutes, and the mix of solo and choral singing aids the digestion.

Middle Eastern divas and tenors

Also still popular in Morocco – as elsewhere in the Arab world – are the great Egyptian and Syro-Lebanese singers who had their heyday in the 1950s and 1960s. Um Kalthoum, a peasant girl from the Nile Delta who became a diva of the Arab world is popular everywhere. Her songs have probably done more for promoting classical Arabic poetry than any school book. Other great names you may want to look out for

Amazigh musical instruments

The musicians and dancers of the High Atlas make use of drums and tambourines, flutes and (occasionally) violons. The **agoual** *is a small pottery drum, shaped like a large wine goblet, used by taskiouine dancers. The* **allun** *(or* **tallunt***) is a large round tambourine, the skin stretched over a wooden frame, which has to be warmed over a fire before use. Sometimes an* allun *will have tiny cymbals attached to the frame. The* **ganga** *is a proper drum played with two curved sticks.* **Nuiqsat** *are tiny cymbals, attached to the fingers. The Imazighen also use string instruments. The violon or* **lekmenja** *is played vertically. Itinerant poet musicians favour the* **rribab***, a single-stringed violon-like instrument, or the* **lotar***, a three or four stringed lute. Apart from the human voice, the other essential element in Atlas mountain music are the hands. Rapid flat-palm clapping or* **r'sh** *gives life and soul to many an Amazigh evening.*

from this period include Druze princess Asmahane, Mohammed Abdewahab, Farid El Atrach, the Lebanese divas Fayrouz and Sabah, Najet Es Saghira and the brown nightingale, Abdel Halim Hafez, who died tragically young of bilharzia. Concerts by singers and musicians, both Moroccan and Middle Eastern regularly go out on the RTM, the national broadcasting company.

Music among the Imazighen

The oldest musical tradition in Morocco is undoubtedly that of the Imazighen, often displayed to visitors in packaged versions in the form of 1001 Nights Fantasia Spectacles at the likes of *Chez Ali* in Marrakech. The Imazighen have an ancient tradition of choral singing and dancing, relating mountain lives with nature and the agricultural year. The most famous dances, the **Ahouach** and the **Ahidous**, were performed on threshing floors once the harvest had been safely gathered in. These dances are often put on for visitors during the annual folklore festival held in Marrakech in June every year. (Organization is said to have been poor of late.)

For both main Amazigh communities in the High Atlas, the Chleuh or Ichlahiyen of the western High Atlas and the Berber of the central and eastern regions, music ties in closely with fertility and the ongoing life of the villages, to harvests and marriage. In isolated communities, the success of the various harvests – barley, nuts and fruit – is vital to survival. The quality of the barley harvest depends on the sun and the elements. Considered almost human in the way it grows, matures and dies, barley is held to have a *ruh*, a spirit, and must be protected against harmful winds, frosts and late snow. After the barley has been harvested (by women), threshing and then winnowing take place on the village *anrar* or threshing floor. The time of winnowing the grain has its songs, especially as the men often have lots of time to wait for the breeze to be right, enabling them to get to work.

And after the hard work of the agricultural season, May to mid-July, there comes time for celebration with weddings, circumcisions and visits to saints' shrines. This is the time for *Ahouach* and *Ahidous*, dances performed with twin swaying lines of dancers and tambourine-beating musicians. Numbers are important for these dances: the more participants, the stronger the impression. The men will be dressed in impeccable white capes and turbans, the women in heavy, richly-coloured robes with wide belts. Jewellery will be a mix of chunky silver and big, yellow bead necklaces. The head-dresses can be quite a thing, too. Moving between the two lines, a poet-singer with drum will launch verses taken up in singing by the women and men 'choirs'. Once he has finished, the drums start, to impressive effect, and the lines join to form an oval. On a really important occasion, the dances, Ahouach or Ahidous, will continue until late in the night.

Algerian & cross-over music: Raï

Though the musical traditions of the High Atlas are still very much alive, the guttural soaring voices of Algerian raï singers have gained quite a following, both in Morocco and among the Moroccan (and of course North African) diaspora in France, the Netherlands and elsewhere. Raï had its origins in the cabarets of Oran, a large nondescript port city in western Algeria (and setting for Albert Camus' *La Peste*). In former times, Oran had a large Spanish immigrant community and was known for its Iberian mores. The raï lyrics tell of impossible loves, of alcohol and *kif*, anger and regret. Sung by the likes of Chikha Remiti, her voice now a living monument, raï was considered too vulgar for Algerian, Moroccan and indeed other official Arab radio stations to broadcast. The erotic charge of raï singers' voices was too much of a challenge for the sugary sounds of the Middle East. And very quickly, as cheap cassette players reached every North African home in the late 1970s, raï found a huge audience with the likes of Cheb Khaled and Cheb Mami, now senior figures in the movement (if the term is applicable to this music). Eventually, raï broke through onto national airwaves, with videos making it onto TV. Popular today are the likes of Cheba Zahouania and Chaba Fadela, Cheb Hosni, Cheb Amro and Parisian-based Faudel, a boyband-type figure in raï. Mami and Faudel in particular have a big following in France. Although few raï singers actually do concerts in Morocco, as visas are a problem for Algerians, Moroccan raï-style music is beginning to emerge, and Algerian singers continue to be popular, as a visit to any cassette stall will show.

Sport

Morocco has its sporting heroes. Television, easily the most widely available form of popular entertainment, is much watched both at home and in cafés, with international football competitions being the big draw. The country has been particularly successful in international athletics. In 1984, Saïd Aouita won the 5,000 m at the Los Angeles Olympics, and went on to set five world records, ranging from the 1,500 m to the 5,000 m. Other Moroccan athletes went on to imitate his success, including Brahim Boutayeb, Olympic 10,000 m champion in 1988, Khalid Skah and Hichem Guerouj. Women's sport is catching up. At the 1984 Olympics, Nawal Moutawakil unexpectedly won the 400 m hurdles, the first major title won by an Arab woman in an international competition. Like Aouita, Moutawakil provides a model for aspiring Moroccan athletes to look up to. Events like the Marrakech marathon attract numerous participants and much media coverage.

***Koura* (football)**

But football remains the number one spectator sport. At age six or seven, the little lads are out in the street or on a piece of rough ground, kicking a football around. Their heroes are the Lions of the Atlas, the Moroccan national team which went to France in 1998, captained by mid-fielder Mustapha Hadji. Morocco had high hopes of its national team, which didn't however make the second round. In 2000, the country also had hopes that its enthusiasm for football would bring it the chance of organizing the next Mondial, and construction on a major new stadium was launched. This was not to be. Nevertheless, FIFA has promised that the World Cup after Germany will be held in Africa, and Morocco has great hopes of being the first African nation to host the event.

Land and environment

In their 1878 *Journal of a Tour in Morocco and the Great Atlas*, botanists Hooker and Ball noted that "up to the date of our visit, the Great Atlas was little better known to geographers than it was in the time of Strabo and Pliny". The rest of the country was only slightly better documented, the earliest accounts being produced by mysterious Polish counts (Potocki) and heavily disguised Frenchmen (De Foucauld). Despite the masses of geographical research since the 1920s, despite the recent push to develop the rural areas, on scanning the terracotta and beige expanses of the topographical maps, there remains the impression of isolated corners unknown to the outside world, places where benign rural lives go on much as they have done for centuries.

Today's Kingdom of Morocco has a surface area of 703,000 sq km and is thus the third largest country in northwest Africa, a region generally referred to in Arabic and French as the Maghreb. (The term derives from the Arabic *gharb*, meaning west, the Maghreb being 'the region of the west' for the Arab-Islamic lands. The Portuguese Algarve derives from the same word.) To the west, Morocco is bounded by the Atlantic, to the north by the Mediterranean, to the east and southeast by Algeria, and to the south by the Islamic Republic of Mauritania. The eastern frontiers with Algeria have yet to be precisely defined. (For completeness sake, the countries of the regional political grouping now referred to as the Maghreb, running east to west, are Libya, Tunisia, Algeria, Morocco and Mauritania.) Spain, just north of Tanger across the Straits of Gibraltar, is the closest European country to Morocco. Note too that Spain still has some colonial confetti in northern Morocco: the port-cities of Ceuta and Melilla plus miscellaneous rocky isles.

An African, Mediterranean country

With its great Saharan façade and long tradition of trade relations with the kingdoms of west Africa, Morocco is an African country. With its 450 km of Mediterranean coastline and its hot yet temperate climate, characterized by warm, often wet winters and hot, dry summers, it is also a Mediterranean country. (The old saying goes that Morocco is 'a cold country with a hot sun.) In fact, of the Maghreb countries, Morocco has the dampest climate, the most extensive forests and the longest, most regularly flowing rivers. The influence of the Atlantic explains the fact that the Sous region (centred on Agadir and Taroudant) has dense population and flourishing agriculture, even though it is at the same latitude as Saharan towns further east.

A hot temperate climate

Although there are wide regional differences, as is only to be expected in such a large country, the Moroccan climate can be described as 'hot temperate'. The average annual temperature only rises above 20° in the pre-Saharan and Saharan regions, although Marrakech and Kasbah Tadla are not far off. The winters are mild. In low-lying areas, only Meknès, Oujda and Figuig having monthly average temperatures below 10°. However, in the mountains, over 1,500 m, the monthly winter averages are below 0°. On the other hand, the summers, even in the mountains, can be very hot. For anything up to six months, the monthly averages are over 20°. In certain inland cities, notably Marrakech and Kasbah Tadla, average monthly temperatures in summer can reach 30°. Pre-Saharan and Saharan Morocco can experience maximum summer temperatures of over 40°.

On the whole, Morocco receives only modest rainfall. Although rainfall in parts of the Rif Mountains and certain summits of the Middle Atlas can reach 1,200 mm/annum, annual rainfall in most of Morocco is less than 500 mm/annum. The Atlantic plains get less than 300 mm, while south of the Anti-Atlas, the annual average is under 100 mm. Throughout the country, the summer is the dry season and

Nuts in September

In the middle reaches of certain High Atlas valleys, the **walnut tree** *provides welcome shade in the summer. Around the trail-head village of Imlil, conditions are just right for the walnut tree, which provides an extra source of revenue for village people: the wood, traditionally used in house building and for tools, is sold off to Marrakech craft carpenters, while the nuts are sold off in bulk – or used for afternoon snacks.*

Unlike the more recent cherry and apple tree plantations, no attempt is made to organize walnut orchards. The trees just sprout up from fallen nuts, along the stream beds, in rocky places where the creation of terraced fields is impossible. (Growing out of the tumbled rocks between Imlil and Arremd is a particularly impressive grove.) In any community, everyone knows whom the trees belong to, and individual trees can have quite a personality. Some, though small, produce good nut crops, others, more imposing, are left to grow for eventual felling as timber trees. Though the wood is in high demand for making bowls and marquetry work, the profits to be made from the sale of nuts mean that the Atlas people look after their trees as part of the family inheritance.

Unfortunately, the nut crop is somewhat irregular: late frosts destroy the newly opened flower buds, putting paid to a whole season's crop – and thereby pushing walnut prices up, if most valleys have suffered late frosts. If he has enough capital, a wily farmer will keep walnuts from a previous harvest back for such eventualities. Often, however, the crop is sold on the tree in June and July, when production estimates can be made. At this point in the year, the harvest is in, grain is at its cheapest, and villagers need cash to buy wheat and extra barley. The nuts are fully ripe in September. The owner of the trees then has to harvest and dry them in the sun, preparing them for transport by the buyer down to Marrakech. There in the médina, in Souk Semmarine, walnuts are on sale along with almonds, dates, raisins and the other healthy delights essential for the confection of Moroccan pâtisserie.

late summer rains, in the form of thunderstorms, rarely reach 25% of annual rainfall (more usually 10%). Most precipitation comes in the cold season, generally in November and March, with December and January also accounting for a good deal of rainfall. In mountain regions, precipitation takes the form of snow. Regions with good rainfall (70 days a year) include the Western Rif, the Middle Atlas and the Atlantic plains around Rabat; south of the Atlas, a year with over 20 days of rainfall can be described as a very wet year.

Although the Moroccan climate can be described as broadly Mediterranean, rainfall varies hugely from one year to another. The longer term pattern is one of a series of dry winters succeeded by rainy years, of cold winters succeeded by unusually hot winters. Unfortunately, there is no easily predictable pattern. The problem is that uncertain rainfall can play havoc with the harvests, especially in areas of traditional agriculture with no access to irrigation.

Along with geographical factors, such sharp climatic variations are in part responsible for the differences – of which the visitor soon becomes aware – between the wealthy, privileged areas and city enclaves of Morocco and the poverty of vast swathes of the countryside and segments of the urban population. The more favoured parts of the country lie between the Atlantic Ocean and the mountains of the Rif, Middle and High Atlas. Here the climate is more favourable to agriculture, the soils are richer and settlement is denser. These are regions well served by road, rail and air. Here agriculture is largely mechanised, there are concentrations of modern industry. Beyond the belt of mountains, however, to the east and the south, drought is endemic and the soil scant. Here nomad lifestyles and forms of transhumance over vast, arid landscapes provide the inhabitants with a sparse livelihood. Though change is in the air with extensive rural development programmes, the **contrasts of contemporary Morocco** are still sharp.

Marrakech and the High Atlas

Back in the 1920s, Louis Neltner, mountain enthusiast and one of the leading lights of the Club alpin français wrote of the High Atlas that "It is neither more or less beautiful than the Alps, it is simply different," which is a little sniffy as a summary of North Africa's major mountain range. Great chunks of certain Atlas massifs run at well over 3,000 m for considerable distances, their climate is unique given the closeness of the Sahara and the low latitude. Snow lies on the peaks for much of the year. The sublime summer green of the valleys contrasts with arid scree fall. More impressive still is the way the Amazigh have built their lives in such a harsh environment, making use of every stream and rivulet. In fact, the north facing valleys of the Atlas are extremely productive in human terms. And far below on the plains, sprawling Marrakech with its oases and olive groves remains very much the daughter of the Atlas, dependent on the rain and melt water coming down from the remote heights.

Marrakech & the Haouz Plain

Marrakech, capital of southern Morocco, discovered by tourism in the 1920s and 1930s, is a town with a long and noble past. One of the most important cities in Morocco, coming third after the Atlantic cities of Casablanca and Rabat-Salé in importance, it is located in south-central Morocco on the **Haouz Plain**, which extends north of the western High Atlas to a low range of hills called the **Jebilet**. To the west, the Haouz is closed off by the low hills of the **Haha** and **Chiadma** regions, to the east, it merges into the Sraghna Plain.

The problem of water on the Haouz Though essentially arid, the Haouz is blessed with good alluvial soil brought down by **the Oued Tensift** and its tributaries. Here and there, older, harder rock formations emerge, including notably the Jebel Guéliz just outside Marrakech and the Jebel Ardouz. Without irrigation, agriculture would be impossible on the Haouz: annual rainfall rarely rises above 300 mm, in summer a hot *chergui* wind blows off the desert.

The *khettaras* Nevertheless, in pre-modern times, highly sophisticated water-transfer and irrigation works enabled Marrakech to become a large and important city. Founded in the tenth century, Marrakech was able to grow thanks to a unique underground system of underground conduits, the *khettaras*, which captured the melt water running down from the Atlas Mountains. Happily for Marrakech, the Haouz Plain tilts slightly to the north, so the water could run for kilometres through the channels to great decantation pools outside the city. From there it could be distributed via open-air channels or *seguias* to the olive and palm groves and *arset* or market gardens. Evidently, such a system was the fruit of long periods of stability. It also required constant upkeep, which was undertaken by specially skilled tribes who would make an annual trip up from the Sahara to perform this job. Today, with the arrival of water pumped up from the water table or brought down by conduit from dams east of Marrakech, the *khettaras* are no longer maintained and used as they once were.

The *dir* lands At the foot of the High Atlas, the Tachelhit-speaking populations of the Ourika developed an elaborate system of irrigation channels to make maximum use of the water coming down from the mountains. In contrast with the *dir* or piedmont lands of the Tadla Plain, the valleys are narrow and the irrigable area fairly small. At the top of the *seguia* or irrigation channel systems, olive and fruit trees, including almonds and citrus are cultivated. Down towards the plain, cereal crops take over.

Modern irrigation Starting back in the 1950s, European colonial farmers and leading Moroccan landowners began to adopt modern irrigation methods for their estates. To the northwest of Marrakech, pumping stations were built, and a major dam, the Barrage Lalla Takerkoust (originally Cavagnac), was built on the Oued Nfis, partly to supply water for irrigation, partly to limit potentially disastrous floods and partly to supply some hydroelectric power. In recent years, low rainfall has kept the level of the lake well below par, just one indication of wider climatic change in the region – and possibly of future water-supply problems as the population and its demands grow.

The Jebilet, Plateau des Gantour & Rehamna

North of Marrakech, the **Jebilet** is a low mountain range rising to around 1,000 m (highest point, Jebel Tekzini, 1,060 m at the eastern end of this mini-range). Little goes on here apart from some goat-raising and barley cultivation. North of the Jebilet, comes the low-lying **Bahira Plain**, the **Gantour Plateau** and then the **Rehamna country**, characterized by *skhour*, rocky crests rising to 700 m. Hence Skhour des Rehamna, the lorry driver's favourite town for pulling over for barbecued lamb on the Casablanca to Marrakech run. Again, the Rehamna is a poor region where stock raising provides a supplement to modest barley, cactus and olive cultivation. Crossing the Gantour Plateau, heading for Safi, to the west of the Rehamna, one comes to Youssoufia, an important phosphate town.

The lower middle Atlantic plains

Despite the distances, the coastal cities of **Essaouira**, in the **Chiadma-Haha** country, and **Safi**, in the **Abda** country, are very much in the orbit of Marrakech. The Atlantic plains which form the hinterland of these towns are the lowest part of the central Moroccan tableland. East of Safi, the Abda plain narrows between the ocean and the Jebilet. From the mouth of the Oued Tensift, some 30 km south of Safi, to **Jebel Amssitene** south of Essaouira, the landscape for 15 km inland from the ocean is a series of limestone hills and valleys. Except in the immediate vicinity of Essaouira where the coastline is one of shifting dunes, the land ends in high and rocky cliffs. In the interior, in the Chiadma country, the land rises rapidly to over 700 m.

Both climate and vegetation in these coastal areas are more temperate than in the interior. In summer the Canary Islands current cools the coast. Whereas Marrakech has an average annual temperature gap of 18° (January average 11.2°, July average 29°), Essaouira has a gap of only 8.5° (January average 13.5°, July average 22°). Rainfall at around 300 mm/annum is just about enough for cereals. In areas closest to the coast, any shortfall is made up for by 'hidden precipitation', the term used to describe the impact of ocean mists and fogs. The high level of water vapour in the atmosphere is extremely beneficial to market garden crops.

The Tadla Plain

Heading east of Marrakech, aiming for Beni Mellal and Azilal with the Aït Bougmez your ultimate objective, you will cross the **Tadla Plain** which spreads, wide, fertile and forming a vast depression between the Plateau des Phosphates to the west and the Middle and High Atlas foothills to the east. In earlier times, the region was of huge strategic interest, as it was the easiest natural route between the imperial cities of Fès and Meknès and Marrakech, capital of the southern regions. Traditionally, the population lived in large villages or *douars*, deriving its livelihood from semi-nomadic stock-raising. In the *dir* or foothill regions, settled Amazigh populations made good use of the plentiful water, growing fruit trees in addition to cereals, cultivated mainly on the slopes where irrigating the trees would be impossible and the soil is thinner.

In the early 1930s, the transformation of the region through large scale irrigated cultivation began, thanks to the construction of a dam at Kasbah Tadla. After the

Selling stones

As you drive up into the Atlas from Marrakech, at the Tizi-n-Tichka pass and around Ouarzazate, you'll see trestle tables with impressive displays of minerals, fossils and tourist bric-à-brac. And at turns where the winding of the road forces you to slow down, you'll almost certainly see some individual waving a splendid mass of red-rock crystals at your vehicle. The truth is, Morocco is a geologist's paradise, and there are a good number of mines, both abandoned and working. In areas with rapidly growing population and little other source of a livelihood than subsistence farming, selling stones to tourists soon became a way of making some ready cash.

Back in the 1980s, things were authentic, and you could find real amethyst quartz geodes. But all the amethyst has long been sold. Then someone had the idea of tinting the white rock crystals with mauve dye. The effect was most convincing, and a new geological industry was born. And now you can get orange-red and green blocks of crystal too. Some have been surprised to find that the iron pyrites they purchased where in fact glued-together bits of khol, the shiny black lead-like stone used by Moroccan women to make eye-liner powder. But despite such deceptions, the demand for souvenir stones remained buoyant. So, after close market study, a bright spark down in Ouarzazate developed a new product: concrete balls which, when split open, reveal beautiful black crystals. Could such cobalt be the work of mother Earth or just electrolysis? Fossils too are much sought after, and when you chose yourself an ammonite or trilobite, be aware that its ribbed forms have just as good a chance of being carved as fossilized. Still, they are rather elegant and provide quite a frisson if you imagine such a creature swimming around off your local beach.

Second World War, the huge dam at Bin el Ouidane on the Oued el Abid went up, generating huge quantities of hydro-electric power and providing excellent salt-free irrigation for extensive new farms growing cotton, wheat and citrus fruit on the Tadla Plain. Heading northeast from Marrakech on the P24 for Beni Mellal, the visitor will be able to see the huge pipes bringing the waters of the **Ben el Ouidane Dam** spectacularly down to Afourer. The view of the irrigated plain from the road up and over to Ouaouizaght in the High Atlas is no less spectacular.

The High Atlas The High Atlas is the highest mountain range in North Africa. The range runs for over 700 km west-southwest to east-northeast from its Atlantic foothills to the eastern limits of Morocco. There are considerable contrasts between the damper, northwest facing side of the range and the Sahara facing southern and southeast slopes. Historically, the High Atlas separates the main body of Morocco from the more arid, pre-desert lands to the south. Within the range are a number of east-west valleys. Running eastwards from Agadir on the Atlantic to Figuig, the south-Atlas fault line separates the main body of the range from the Western Anti-Atlas and the Eastern Anti-Atlas, the latter including the arid **Jebel Saghro** (2,700 m) and the **Jebel Ougnate**. West of Ouarzazate, the **Jebel Siroua** (3,304 m) is a large tertiary volcanic massif linking High and Anti-Atlas.

In terms of climate, **rain and snow** in the High Atlas increase with altitude. Above 1,500 m on the northern slopes and above 2,000 m on the southern side of the range, precipitation takes the form of snow in winter. Above 3,000 m, the snow lasts several months, remaining longer on east and north facing slopes. Above 2,000 m, there will be many days with frost in the winter. And within living memory, there might be one or two days every winter on which the roof-terraces of Marrakech would receive a sugar-dusting of snow, much to the delight of the city's children. Climatic change seems to have produced milder winters, however.

The High Atlas divides into **three main areas**. Composed mainly of primary sandstone, with granite peaks and a cover of red Triassic sandstone, the **western High Atlas** is the highest part of the range with a number of peaks rising to well over 3,000 m. At 4,165 m, **Jebel Toubkal** is the highest summit, while Jebel Angour reaches 3,600 m. Certain summits are tabular in character, for instance the Tazaghart (3,900 m), others, like **Jebel Ouanoukrim** (4,080 m) were cut into peaks by glacial erosion. The deep well watered valleys, cut by streams which can quickly swell to floods after summer thunderstorms, contrast with the arid heights which nevertheless receive considerable snowfall in winter. The **Tizi-n-Test**, at 2,225 m one of the highest passes in the range, was historically one of the main routes from Marrakech to the Sous Valley. To the west, the western High Atlas drops down to undulating limestone plateaux lands, cut by wide valleys. Then, between high cliffs and wide bays, the land gives way to the Atlantic Ocean.

The walker in the High Atlas of Toubkal, in close and constant contact with the landscape, soon becomes aware of the gigantic processes of weathering going on in these remote places. Above 3,000 m, in the *adrar*, snow falls in late October and lasts through into April. Above 3,500 m, frost is a possibility all year round. Hence, the rocks, constantly heated and chilled, fracture and split, creating the vast areas of shattered rock called *felsenmeer* by the geologists. In summer, *chergui* winds create huge differences of temperature high in the mountains, creating great rainstorms which carry rock debris down the slopes, spilling loose rock and earth down into the valleys. Great spills of boulders (*talus*) and steep accumulations of small rock (scree) are features which walkers soon have to deal with in the higher areas. All this erosion is worsened by human action further down the valleys as the vegetation has been so heavily overgrazed and cut for firewood. It is thought that the original tree line was close to the 3,000 m mark. In the valleys, it is carefully constructed terraces protected by walnut trees which hold the land in place against the forces of erosion.

The **central High Atlas**, also referred to as the **High Atlas of Azilal** in the present handbook, begins to the east of the north-south route linking Marrakech and the Haouz to the Dadès Valley via the **Tizi-n-Tichka**, 2,250 m. Running eastwards to the Plateau des Lacs, this is a region of high, tabular limestone mountains and wide-floored valleys, such as that of the Aït Bougmez. At 4,071 m, the long mass of the **Jebel Mgoun** is the highest summit, closely followed by the **Jebel Azourki** to the north (3,685 m). To the south, impressive valleys and gorges such as those of the **Assif Mgoun** run towards the Oued Dadès. To the north, rivers such as the **Lakhdar** and **Tessaoute**, **Melloul** and **Ahansal**, tributaries of the Oum Errabia, Morocco's longest river, have cut deep valleys into the limestone.

The **eastern High Atlas** is lower and has more extensive forest cover, at least on its northern slopes. The climate, marked by sharper contrasts than, say, the western reaches of the Toubkal High Atlas, is definitely continental, with snow remaining longer into the summer on the highest ground. Beyond Imilchil and the **Plateau des Lacs**, **Jebel Ayyachi** (3,757 m) is the high point of this part of the range, dominating the upper plain of the **Oued Moulouya**, another major river which eventually reaches the Mediterranean near Oujda. The landscape is one of folded limestone rising up from depressions which sometimes widen out into real plains, as for example round Rich. At 1,900 m, the **Tizi-n-Talghemt** is the pass linking Midelt and the upper Moulouya and the plains around Rich. The southern part of the eastern High Atlas is formed of limestone plateaux crossed by gorges cut by small rivers such as the **Todgha**, the **Gheris** and the **Ziz**. Further east, the High Atlas gives way to chains of low hills, running west-east, which link in with the Saharan Atlas over the frontier in Algeria.

Thus, despite the oft-mentioned block-like character of the High Atlas (comparisons are often made with the Pyrénées), the landscapes are far from monotonous. In human terms, there is much of interest, for down the centuries the isolated

Intrepid explorers in the Atlas

Though the High Atlas have been known for centuries, neither the Arabs nor the Amazigh – a people with a primarily oral culture in any case – left any written accounts of ascents of the main summits of the Idraren Draren, 'the Mountains of Mountains'. In fact, it was not until 1922 that Toubkal was identified as the highest peak, its actual height (4,167 m) being determined in 1924 and a trig-point installed in 1931.

The first European explorers, generally dressed up in local gear, reached the region in the early 19th century. In 1804, the Spaniard Badia, adopting the name Ali Bey, visited the Atlas. The Saharan explorer René Auguste Caillié crossed the Atlas in 1828 on his way back from Timbuktu. Led by botanists JD Hooker and John Ball, the first scientific expedition visited the High Atlas in 1871, climbing Jebel Erdouz. In the early 1880s, French and German surveying parties began exploring the region in earnest.

The early 1900s saw exploration of the region by eminent geologist Louis Gentil (he who discovered the phosphates of present day Youssoufia) and the Marquis de Segonzac. In June 1923, the Marquis and his party reached the summit of Toubkal. As interest in southern Morocco grew, the 1930s saw frequent visits by French alpinistes like L. Neltner and T. de Lépiney. Along with the Italians, Poles and the British climber Bentley Beetham, they tested numerous new routes. In 1938, the first guidebook to the Toubkal region was published. The central and eastern High Atlas, however, remained largely unknown by Europeans, apart from the officiers des affaires indigènes *out in their remote postings.*

In 1948, Roger Mailly reached the limestone Aioui Cliffs near Zaouiat Ahansal. Ski mountaineering also developed at about the same time. In 1955, the great English traveller, Wilfred Thesiger, visited the Atlas, walking from Telouet to Zaouiat Ahansal. In the 1960s, there were large numbers of French teachers and technical experts in Morocco, many keen on outdoor sports. The realization grew that the High Atlas, though not exactly filled with diabolical K2-type peaks, had huge potential for trekking. In the early 1970s, an east-west high level walkers' route was mapped out by Michaël Peyron, covering a distance of 550 km from the Midelt in the east to the Moussa Gorges in the west. Thanks to enthusiastic locals and mountain experts like André Fougerolles, the development of Atlas trekking took a new step forward in 1984 with the creation of a centre for training mountain guides, the CFAMM, at Tabant in the Aït Bougmez.

Amazigh communities of the high valleys came to develop systems of agriculture and life perfectly adapted to their often harsh environment.

Flora and fauna

Flora

The gardens & palm groves of Marrakech The city of Marrakech stands at the heart of an immense palm grove, said to have been started by date stones which, dropped casually when Almoravid warriors finished their lunch, sprouted in the fertile ground. Today, with the urban area constantly expanding, the palm groves, mainly to the east and north of the city, are under a lot of pressure. The palmeraie is now prime land for upmarket villas, and many smallholders are selling up. In French times, every palm tree had a number, and it was illegal to cut down a date palm – or indeed, build higher than the topmost fronds. This legislation continues, just about, to be respected. Marrakech also has many street trees, including fine purple-flowering jacarandas and hardy evergreen ficus. Gardens of hotels such as the *Mamounia* have interesting shrubs from the Mediterranean and southern Africa.

Trees of the High Atlas

The High Atlas is characterized by tiers of vegetation, decreasingly dense with increasing altitude. Rainfall also has a major influence on vegetation. As the northern slopes generally receive between 700 to 800 mm of rain or snow per annum, evergreen forest can survive. Elsewhere aridity is the norm, with the valleys getting little more than 200 mm a year, although certain summits by virtue of their altitude receive up to 600 mm precipitation a year.

Of the mountain trees, the **evergreen oak** (French: *chêne vert*) is the most widespread tree, found in both the foothills and up to 2,200 m. At the upper limit of its range in the drier mountains, it becomes rather shrub-like. On the north side of the High Atlas, the evergreen oak grows alongside another evergreen tree, the **thuya**. Also in the High Atlas south of Beni Mellal, various sorts of **pine** can be found.

The pride of Morocco's forest is the **cedar**, which grows in the Rif and especially in the Middle Atlas, on the Plateau des Lacs around Aïn Leuh to the south of Azrou. In the High Atlas, cedars can still be found in the Jebel Ayyachi to the south of Midelt. With its wide platforms of foliage, the cedar is easily identified. Mature specimens can reach 50 m in height. However, as this is a tree which requires deep soil, extensive cedar forest is rare in Morocco's mountains. In earlier times, cedar wood was particularly prized for the construction of the gabled roofs of palaces on account of its strength and durability. Carved cedar panels were used for doors and ceilings to give a pleasant odour to a room.

One of the most extensive naturally occurring trees is the hardy **juniper thurifera** or silver juniper (Fr: *genévrier thurifère*). Capable of withstanding extremes of cold and drought, the juniper occurs at up to 3,000 m altitude. When snow covers the pasture, it is often used by shepherds to feed their flocks. The oldest specimens are said to be revered, and their trunks can reach 10 m in circumference.

Of the deciduous trees, the **weeping willow** and in particular the **poplar** are widespread in the valley bottoms of the eastern High Atlas. Poplar trunks and branches are used as beams in the flat roof terraces of village houses while the foliage makes good animal feed. In summer, the river beds are bright with pink and white flowering **oleander** (Arabic: defla). The grey-green foliage is highly poisonous to beasts, however.

In most of the High Atlas, though, the ground is either too steep or too arid to permit any form of forest cover. In certain high mountain areas, small spiny cushions of vegetation dominate, attractive in spring with mauve or yellow flowers. In certain areas, above 2,000 m, the ground remains damp in summer and there is seasonal pasture for the flocks. This is referred to as the **almou**, and there are strict customary laws about its use. To ensure the coming year's pasture, grazing only begins when the grass has seeded. At their eastern limit, the mountains fade away into wide steppe lands where **alfalfa** grass and sage bushes are the main vegetation.

Fauna

Morocco does not have a great number of observable large mammals. The once common lion of the Atlas, much in demand in the circuses of ancient Rome, seems to be extinct in the wild. However, out there in the countryside are genets, jackals, striped hyenas and wild cats. The desert is home to fennecs, gerbils and jerboas, as well as three species of gazelle, including the endangered Dorcas gazelle. A rare sighting in the High Atlas would be a mouflon (there are reserves between Amizmiz and Ouirgane and near Boumia). Wild boar are still common in the Rif, often wreaking havoc in the crops, while the forests of the Middle Atlas also harbour a few surviving leopards – watch how you go. With their nocturnal habits most of these animals evade casual visitors. You will, however, inevitably come across selections of animal pelts and horns at apothecaries' stalls in the médinas.

Perhaps the most easily observed of the wild animals are the Barbary apes (French: *magot* or *macaque de Barbarie*), which can be found in the Azrou area of the Middle Atlas, and at the Cascades d'Ouzoud, near Azilal, east of Marrakech. The Barbary ape can live for up to 20 years. It forages on the ground for food (leaves, roots, small insects), and has been known to enjoy yoghurt, bread and the occasional Flag beer contributed by passing picnickers.

Another observable mammal is the *anzid* or *sibsib*, known as the Barbary squirrel in English, chiefly found in the argan tree areas of the Anti-Atlas. In the Tafraoute region, you may see children at the roadside offering hapless rodents for sale. In Islam, animals have to be ritually slaughtered with the head turned towards Mecca. As the *sibsib* is said to have medicinal properties, it is licit and makes a delicious *tajine*.

Birdlife Morocco has the greatest diversity of birdlife north of the Sahara, with 460 species, of which 11 are threatened. For visitors to southern Morocco, bright coloured bee-eaters, blue rollers, and striped, crested hoopoes make distinctive sightings. The great cavern of Imi-n-Ifri near Demnate is famed for its flocks of wheeling chough, while in cities and mountain villages, storks can be seen nesting on ramparts and minarets.

Reptiles Morocco's reptilian fauna is among the richest in the Mediterranean region. While the whole European continent is home to a mere 60 species of reptile, the Kingdom has over 90 species. You will, however, see few lizards and very few snakes. Most are nocturnal and shun inhabited areas – or go skittering off into the brush at the approach of clumping people. Nevertheless, you will certainly see chameleons, live in small cages and dried on skewers, at apothecaries' booths in the souk. Vendors working for the tourist trade have also long been aware that tortoises and various lizards are a popular draw. (The latter are often painted by salesmen to make them more exotic.) Though tortoises are said to bring good luck to a home, and are often kept in Moroccan courtyard houses, they and other creatures are best left in the wild.

Insects Insects are much more easily observed than large mammals. As pesticides are not in widespread use in the countryside, being far beyond the means of most farmers, there are beautiful butterflies and a multitude of moths, both in evidence when the spring flowers are in bloom. There are flies both large and small, bees, wasps and mosquitoes, the latter tending to be too attentive in cheap hotels and at bivouacs late at night. In addition, there are scorpions, which can be attracted by the warmth of campfires and hikers boots, which should be shaken out in the morning.

10 Footnotes

Footnotes

Language in Morocco

Moroccan Arabic

For the English speaker, some of the sounds of Moroccan Arabic are totally alien. There is a strong glottal stop (as in the word 'bottle' when pronounced in Cockney English), generally represented by an apostrophe, and a rasping sound written here as 'kh', rather like the 'ch' of the Scots 'loch' or the Greek 'drachma'. And there is a glottal 'k' sound, which luckily often gets pronounced as the English hard 'g', and a very strongly aspirated 'h' in addition to the weak 'h'. The French 'r' sound is generally transcribed as 'gh'. Anyway, worry ye not. Moroccan acquaintances will have a fun time correcting your attempts at pronouncing Arabic. And for those with a little French and/or Spanish, the word lists after the Arabic section will be a handy reminder.

The language section here divides into three parts: Moroccan Arabic, a short section of Tachelhit Berber for the mountains (useful for reading topographic names), and a final section of French and Spanish. For Arabic and Tachelhit, the symbol 'í' is used to represent the English 'ee' sound. An apostrophe represents the glottal stop, as in the word *sa'a* (hour), for example. As mentioned above, Arabic has two sorts of 'h', and a capital H is used to represent the strongly aspirated sort.

Polite requests and saying thank you

excuse me, please – *'afek* (for calling attention politely) – عفاك
please – *min fadhlek* – من فضلك
one minute, please – *billatí* – بلاتي
(to call the the waiter) – *esh-sheríf* or *ya ma'alem* – الشريف / يامعلم
thank you – *teberkallah alík/Allah yekhallík* – تبرك الله عليك
thank you – *shukran* – شكرا

Saying hello (and goodbye)

Good morning – *sabaH el-khír* – صباح الخير
How's things? – *kí yedirkí dayir?* – كي داير ؟ كي يدير
Everything's fine – *el Hamdou lillah* (lit Praise be to God) – الحمد لله
Everything's fine – *kull shay la bas* – كل شيئ لاباس
Congratulations – *mabrouk* – مبروك
Goodbye – *bisslema* – بسلامة
Goodbye – *Allah ya'wnek* – الله يعاونك

Handy adjectives and adverbs

Like French, Moroccan Arabic has adjectives (and nouns) with feminine and masculine forms. To get the masculine form, simply knock off the final 'a'.
good – *mezyena* – مزيان
happy – *farhana* – فرحانة
beautiful – *jmíla, zwína* – جميلة
new – *jdída* – جديدة
old – *qdíma* – قديمة
cheap – *rkhíssa* – رخيسة

clean – *naqía* – نقية
full – *'amra* – عامرة
in a hurry – *zarbana* – زربانة
quickly – *dghiya dghiya* – دغية دغية
it doesn't matter – *belesh* – بلاش

Quantities

a lot – *bezaf* – بزاف
a little – *shwíya* – شوية
half – *nesf* – نصف

Numerals

one – *wahed*
two – *zouj or tnine*
three – *tlata*
four – *arba'*
five – *khamsa*
six – *setta*
seven – *saba'*
eight – *tmaniya*
nine – *ts'oud*
ten – *ashra*
eleven – *hedash*
twelve – *t'nash*
thirteen – *t'latash*
fourteen – *rb'atash*
fifteen – *kh'msatash*
sixteen – *settash*
seventeen – *sb'atash*
eighteen – *t'mentash*
nineteen – *ts'atash*
twenty – *'ashrine*
twenty-one – *wahed ou 'ashrine*
twenty-two – *tnine ou 'ashrine*
twenty-three – *tlata ou 'ashrine*
twenty-four – *'arba ou 'ashrine*
thirty – *tlatine*
forty – *'arba'ine*
fifty – *khamsine*
sixty – *sittine*
seventy – *saba'ine*
eighty – *temenine*
ninety – *t'issine*
one hundred – *miya*
two hundred – *miyatayn*
three hundred – *tlata miya*
thousand – *alf*
two thousand – *alfayn*
three thousand – *tlat alaf*
one hundred thousand – *miyat alf*

Days of the week

Monday – *nhar el itnayn* – نهار الأثنين
Tuesday – *nhar ettlata* – نهار الثلاثاء
Wednesday – *nhar el arba* – نهار الاربعاء
Thursday – *nhar el khemís* – نهار الخميس
Friday – *nhar el jema'* – نهار الجمعة
Saturday – *nhar essebt* – نهار السبت
Sunday – *nhar el had* – نهار الحد

A few expressions of time

today – *el yawm* – اليومة
yesterday – *el-bareh* – البارح
tomorrow – *ghedda* – غدة

day after tomorrow – *ba'da ghedda* – بعد غدة
day – *nhar* – النهار
morning – *sbah* – الصباح
midday – *letnash* – لاتناش
evening – *ashíya* – العشية
tonight/night – *el-líla/líl* – الليلة / الليل
hour – *sa'a* – ساعة
half an hour – *nes sa'a* – نصف ساعة

Miscellaneous expressions

Watch out! (as a mule comes careering down the street) – *balak! balak!*
No problem – *ma ka'in mushkil*
How much? – *bayshhal? aysh-hal ettaman?*
Free (of charge) – *fabor*
Look – *shouf* (pl *shoufou*)
OK, that's fine – *wakha*
Good luck! – *fursa sa'ída*

At the café

tea – *ettay* – التاي
weak milky coffee – *un crème* – قهوة بالحليب
half espresso, half milk – *nes nes* – نص نص
a small bottle – *gara' sghíra* – قرعة صغيرة
a large bottle – *gara' kbíra* – قرعة كبيرة
a bottle of still mineral water – *gara' Sidi Ali/Sidi Harazem* – قرعة سيدي علي
a bottle of fizzy mineral water – *gara' Oulmes/Bonacqua* – قرعة اولماس
ashtray – *dfeya, cendrier* – طفاية
do you have change? – *'indak sarf/vous avez de la monnaie?* – عندك الصرف

At the restaurant

bill – *l'hseb* – لحساب
fork – *foursheta, lamtíqa* – فورشتة / لمتيقة
knife – *mous, mis* – موس
spoon – *mu'allaka* – معلقة / عاشق
glass – *ka's* (pl *kísan*) – كاس / كيسان
bowl – *zellafa* – زلافة
plate – *tobsil* – تبصيل
could you bring us some more bread – *afak tzídna khubz*– عفاك تزيدنا الخبز

Food and drink

bananas – *mouz* – موز
beef – *lham bagri* – لحم بقري
butter – *zebda* – زبدة
bread – *khobz* – خبز
chicken – *djaj* – دجاج
chips – *btata maklya, frites* – بطاطة مقلية
egg – *bíd* (sing *bída*) – بيض / بيضة
fruit – *fekiha* – فواكه
mandarins – *tchína* – تشينة

mutton – *lham ghenmí*– لحم غنمي
milk – *hlíb* – حليب
olive oil – *zít zítoun* – زيت زيتون
oranges – *límoun* – ليمون
rice – *rouz* – روز
tomatoes – *ma'tísha* – مطيشة
vegetables – *khudra* – خضرة
water – *ma* – ماء

At the hotel

room – *el-bít/la chambre* – البيت
bed – *tliq, farsh* – تليق / فراش
mattress – *talmíta* – طلميتة
shower – *douche* – دوش
without shower – *bila douche, sans douche* – بلا دوش
key – *es sarrout/la clef* – السروت
blanket – *ghta'/couverture* – غطاء
sheet – *izar/le drap* – ازار
corridor – *couloir* – كولوار
noise – *sda'* – صداع

At the hotel – a few requests and complaints

Can I see the room, please? – *Afak, mumkin nshouf el bít* – عفاك ممكن نشوف البيت
The water's off – *El ma maktou'a* – الماء مقطوع
There's no hot water – *El-ma skhoun ma ka'insh* – الماء سخون ماكاينش
Excuse me, are there any towels? – *Afak ka'in foutet* – عفاك كاين فوطاط
Could you bring us some towels? – *Mumkin tjíbilna foutet* – ممكن تجيب النا فوطاط
The washbasin's blocked – *El lavabo makhnouk* – الافابو مخنوقة
The window doesn't close – *Esh sherajim ma yetsidoush* – الشراجم مايتسدوش
Can you change the light bulb? – *Mumkin tebedil el bawla* – ممكن تبدل البولة
The toilet flush doesn't work – *La chasse ma tekhdemsh* – لاشاس ماخدامش
There's a lot of noise – *Ka'in sda' bezef* – كاين صداع بزاف
Can I change rooms? – *Mumkin nebedil el bít* – ممكن نبدل البيت

On the road

Where is the bus station? – *Fayn kayin maHata diyal kíran?* –
فين كاين المحطة ديال الكران
Where is the *CTM* bus station? – *Fayn kayin mHata diyal Saytayem?* –
فين كاين المحطة ديال الستيام
road – *tríq* – طريق
street – *zanqa* – زنقة
neighbourhood, also street – *derb* – درب
bridge – *qantra* – قنطرة
straight ahead – *níshan* – نيشان
to the right/left – *ila l-yemin/sh-shimal*– الى اليمن / الى اليسر
turn at the corner – *dour fil-qent* – دور في القنت
wheel – *rwída* – رويدة

Public transport

aeroplane – *tayyara* – الطيارة
bus – *tobís, Hafila* – طوبيس / حافلة
inter-city bus – *kar* (pl *kíran*) – كار / كيران
customs – *díwana* – ديوانة
express service – *sarí', mosta'jal, rapide* – سريع
luggage – *Hwayaj, bagaj* – حوايج
porter – *Hamal* – حمال
ticket – *bitaqa*, also *warqa* (lit 'paper') – ورقة
train – *qitar* – قطار
How much is the ticket? – *Aysh Hal taman diyal warqa?* – ابش حال الثمن ديال ورقة ؟
I didn't understand – *Ma fehimtiksh* – مافهمتكش
Speak slowly please – *Tekellem bishweyya min fedlek* – تكلم بشوية من فضلك
Could you write that down please? – *'Afak, uktebhu liya* – عفاك اكتب لي

Tachelhit

A few handy expressions to help you function in a village in the High Atlas, plus some topographic words to help you understand the maps. Note that Arabic and French words for numbers are generally understood.

Greetings and things

How are you? (woman/man) – *La bes darim? La bes darik?*
Fine thanks – *La bes*
Please – *Allah yarhum el welidín/'afek /mardi el welidín*
Thank you – *Barak Allaw fík*
thanks (responding to congratulations) – *el agoub alík*
Yes – *ayer, wakha*
No – *oho*

Travelling around

Is Aremd near here? – *Aremd iqarreb zeghí?*
near/far – *iqarreb/yagoug*
It's on the right/on the left – *foufessí/fozlemad*
On your right/on your left – *foufessínek/fozelmadnek*
Go straight ahead – *Zayid goud/níshen*
On foot – *Fudár*
How far is it on foot? – *Mishta nugharas aylen fudár?*
How long will it take me to get there on foot? – *Mishta el waqt ayikhsen afade adrouHagh fudár?*
30 mins/one hour/two hours – *nus sa'a/sa'a/sa'atayn*
Where is Mohammed the guide's house? – *Mani eghtilla teguemí en Mhamid le guide?*
Can you take me to Mohammed's house? – *Izd imkin aystitmellet?*
mule – *asserdoun (m), tasserdount (f)*
How much is it to rent a mule? – *Mishta izkar lekra nesserdoun?*
When does the minibus leave for Marrakech? – *Melouqt arrifough minibus ne Maraksh?*
In an hour? In two hours? – *Zeghík yan sa'a? Zeghík sa'atayn?*
How long does it take? – *Mishta fra naruh?*

In the village

Can we camp here? – *Izd imkin enkhayim ghí?*
Can we find a room to rent here? – *Izd imkin anaf kra la chambre ghí?*
How much for the night? – *Mishta iyad?*

In the shop

Please, do you have – *'afek, íz daroun*
Do you have – *kre (particle to make question)*
Can we buy – *'afek, íz imkin edsagh*
Please give me – *'afek, fkíyí*
bread – *aghroum*
eggs – *tiglay*
Sidi Ali bottled water – *amen Sidi Ali*
salt – *tisent*
meat – *tifiyí*
onions – *azelim*
potatoes – *betata*
tomatoes – *ma'tísha*
almonds – *louz*
walnuts – *guirga'a*
a little – *ímík*
a lot – *agoudí*

Expressions of time

today – *ghassa*
dawn – *zíg sbaH*
tomorrow – *azga*
day after tomorrow – *nefouzga*
next week – *símana yedísoudan*
yesterday – *idgam*

Some numbers

one – *yen*
two – *sín*
three – *krad*
four – *koz*
five – *smous*
six – *sddes*
seven – *sa*
eight – *tem*
nine – *tza*
ten – *mrawet*
eleven – *yen de mrawet*
twelve – *sín de mrawet*
twenty – *ashrínt*
one hundred – *míya*

Landscape words

Tachelhit is given first to help you identify the meanings of the terms found on the maps
adrar – mountain
afella – summit
agdal, aguedal – grazing land (also a garden in Marrakech)
agharas – path, track
aghbalou (pl *ighboula*) – spring (*taghbalout* – small spring)
aghoulid – steep slope

agrour – enclosure
aguelmane – lake
aït – lit 'the people of'
ahir (pl *iheren*) – slow flowing spring
almou – pasture
amen – water
aourir – hill
aserdoun – mule
asif – river which dries up in summer
azaghar – plateau (pl *izghwar*)
azib – shepherd's shelter
azrou – rock
douar – village
ifri – cave
ighil – arm, by extension long mountain
ighir – shoulder, rocky shoulder of mountain
ighzer – ravine
imi – mouth, hole
kerkour – cairn
moussem – annual festival
taddart – house
tagadirt – fortified granary
talat – ravine
tamda – lake
targa – irrigation channel
tighermt – fortified house
tiguimine – house
timzguida – mosque
tizi – moutain pass
taourirt – (pron tawrirt) hill
taslit – fiancée
unzar – rain

And finally, some words for beautiful: *ífulkí* (m) *tfulkí* (f)

French and Spanish

English	French	Spanish
hello	salut	hola
good morning	bonjour	buenos días
good afternoon/evening/night	bonsoir/bonne nuit	buenas tardes/noches
goodbye	au revoir/ciao	adiós/chao
see you later	à tout à l'heure	hasta luego
Pleased to meet you	enchanté	encantado
how are you?	comment allez-vous?	¿qué tal?
fine, thankyou	très bien	muy bien
yes	oui	sí
no	non	no
please	s'il vous plaît	por favor
excuse me	s'il vous plaît/excusez-moi	con permiso
I do not understand	Je ne comprends pas	No entiendo

English	French	Spanish
Speak slowly please	Parlez lentement s'il vous plaît	Hable despacio por favor
Do you speak some English?	Parlez-vous un peu l'anglais?	¿Habla usted un poco el inglés?
What is your name?	Comment vous? Appellez-vous?	¿Cómo se llama?
How do you say XX?	Comment est-ce qu'on dit XX?	¿Cómo se dice XX?
What is this called?	Comment ça s'appelle?	¿Cómo se llama esto?

Some basic vocabulary and phrases

Toilet/bathroom	les toilettes/la salle de bain	los retretes/el baño
where are the toilets?	où sont les toilettes?	¿dónde está el baño?
police/policeman	la police	la policía
hotel	hôtel, auberge	el hotel, la pensión
youth hostel	auberge de jeunesse	albergue turístico juvenil
restaurant/fast food	le restaurant/le snack	el restaurante
post office	les PTT, la poste	los correos
stamps	des timbres poste	los sellos
corner grocery	l'épicerie	la tienda
market	le marché	el mercado
bank	la banque	el banco
ATM machine	GAB guichet automatique	
bureau de change	bureau de change	la case de cambio
notes	billets de banque	los billete/
coins	pièces de monnaie	las monedas
do you have change?	est-ce que vous avez de la monnaie?	¿tiene de la moneda?
cash	du cash/du liquide	el efectivo

Meals

breakfast	petit déjeuner	desayuno
lunch	le déjeuner	el almuerzo
dinner	le dîner	la cena
meal	le repas	la comida
without meat	sans viande	sin carne
drink	la boisson	la bebida
mineral water	l'eau minérale	el agua mineral
fizzy drink	une boisson gazeuse	la gaseosa/cola
wine	le vin	el vino
beer	la bière	la cerveza
dessert	le dessert	el postre
without sugar	sans sucre	sin azúcar

Some useful adjectives

French and Spanish adjectives have masculine and feminine forms, which correspond to noun genders

cheap	pas cher	barato/barata
expensive	cher	caro/cara
ready	prêt/prête	listo/lista
near	proche, près	cerca

English	**French**	**Spanish**
far	loin	lejos
hot	chaud	caliente (liquid) hace calor (temperature)
cold	froid	frío
That's great	C'est super	¡Qué maravilla!
beautiful	beau/belle	hermoso/hermosa

Travelling around

on the left/right	à gauche/à droite	a la izquierda/a la derecha
straight on	tout droit	derecho
first/second street	la première/deuxième rue	la primera/segunda
on the right	à droite	calle a la derecha
to walk	marcher	caminar
bus station	la gare routière	la terminal
town bus/inter city coach	le bus/le car	el bus/el autobus
city bus stop	l'arrêt (des buses)	la parada
ticket office	le guichet	la taquilla
train station (Morrocan railways)	la gare (de l'ONCF)	la estación del ferrocarril
train	le train	el tren
airport	l'aéroport	el aeropuerto
airplane	l'avion	el avión
first/second class	première/deuxième classe	primera/segunda clase
ticket (return)	le billet (aller – retour)	el billete (de ida y vuelta)
ferry/boat	le ferry/le navire	el ferry/el barco
a hire car	une voiture de location	un coche alquilado

Accommodation

room	une chambre	el cuarto, la habitación
I'd like to see the room	J'aimerais voir la chambre	Me gustaría ver el cuarto
with two beds	avec deux petits lits	con dos camas
with private bathroom	avec salle de bain	con baño
hot/cold water	de l'eau chaude/froide	agua caliente/fría
there's no hot water	il n'y a pas d'eau chaude	no hay agua caliente
noisy	bruyant	ruidoso
(there's a lot of noise)	(il y a beaucoup de bruit)	(hay mucho ruido)
to make up/clean the room	arranger/nettoyer la chambre	limpiar el cuarto
sheets/pillows	des draps/des oreillers	las sábanas/la almohadas
blankets	des couvertures	las mantas
clean/dirty towels	des serviettes propres/sales	toallas limpias/sucias
loo paper	du papier hygiénique	el papel higiénico

Health

English	French	Spanish
chemist/all night chemist	la pharmacie/ pharmacie de garde	la farmacia
doctor	le médecin	el médico
Do you have the number of a doctor ?	Est-ce que vous avez le numéro de téléphone un médecin?	¿Por favour, tiene el número de teléfono de un médico?
emergency medical services	la SAMU	las urgencias
where does it hurt?	Où est la douleur?	¿Dónde está el dolor?
stomach	l'estomac	el estómago
fever/sweat	la fièvre/la sueur	la fiebre/el sudor
diarrohea	la diarrhée	la diarrea
blood	le sang	la sangre
headache	un mal de tête	un dolor de cabeza
condoms	les préservatifs	les preservativos
contraceptive pill	la pillule	la píldora anticonceptiva
period/towels	les règles	la regla/las toallas
contact lenses	les lentilles de contact	las lentes de contacto

Numbers

one	un	uno
two	deux	dos
three	trois	tres
four	quatre	cuatro
five	cinq	cinco
six	six	seis
seven	sept	siete
eight	huit	ocho
nine	neuf	nueve
ten	dix	diez

Days of the week

Monday	lundi	lunes
Tuesday	mardi	martes
Wednesday	mercredi	miércoles
Thursday	jeudi	jueves
Friday	vendredi	viernes
Saturday	samedi	sábado
Sunday	dimanche	domingo

Expressions of time

today	aujourd'hui	hoy
yesterday	hier	ayer
tomorrow	demain	mañana
tomorrow morning	demain matin	mañana por la mañana
day	le jour	el día
morning	le matin	la mañana
midday	midi	mediodía
evening	le soir	la sera
night/tonight	la nuit/ce soir	la noche/esta noche

English	**French**	**Spanish**
hour	une heure	una hora
in half an hour	dans une demie heure	después de media hora
later	plus tard	más tarde

Months

January	janvier	enero
February	février	febrero
March	mars	marzo
April	avril	abril
May	mai	mayo
June	juin	junio
July	juillet	julio
August	août	agosto
September	septembre	setiembre
October	octobre	octubre
November	novembre	noviembre
December	décembre	diciembre

Less educated people will not know the names of the months in Morocco, and will use expressions like 'le mois trois' or 'le mois huit'

Glossary

All terms are Arabic or French, unless marked (Amz) for Amazigh. The spellings generally used in Morocco are given. Note that 'ch' in this system is generally pronounced 'sh', and that 'ou' often represents 'w', ie 'mechoui' is pronounced 'meshwi'.

General background

Achoura The first day of the Muslim (or Hijra) year, a lunar month after 'Id El-Kabir, 3 months and 10 days before the Mouloud, the Prophet Mohammed's birthday.

Adrar (Amz) Mountain

Agadir (Amz) Fortified granary in the Anti-Atlas

Agdal, pl. **Aguedal** Garden

Aguelmame (Amz) Natural depression where run-off water collects.

Aghroum(Amz) Bread

Agrour (Amz) Ground floor level of the traditional house in the High Atlas. Used to accommodate animals and as storage space for tools and sometimes grain.

Ahidous Group dance in the villages of the Middle and eastern High Atlas (Tamazight-speaking regions).

Ahouach Group dance in the villages of the High and Anti-Atlas (Tachelhit-speaking regions).

Aïd (usual English spelling 'Id) Islam has two major religious holidays or 'ids, the first, the 'Id as-saghir, ends Ramadhan, the month of fasting. 'Id al-Kabir, a lunar month later, celebrated with the sacrifice of a sheep, commemorates how Allah sent down a heavenly sheep for sacrifice to Ibrahim, who was about to sacrifice his son Ismael.

Aïn Spring

Aït (Amz) 'Sons of', ie tribal grouping

Alaouite (pron. 'Alawite') The ruling dynasty in Morocco today.
Amarg (Amz) Several meanings: 1. Poetry sung by and for women; 2. Nostalgia; 3. Poetry sung by itinerant musicians.
Amdyaz, pl **Imdyazen** (Amz) Itinerant troubadours in the High Atlas.
Amghar (Amz) Broadly speaking 'leader'. Term used in many contexts in Amazigh society. An amghar may be appointed to direct the tribal council or jema'a, also to oversee access to irrigation water in a village.
Almohads (lit trans. 'Unitarians) Berber dynasty which sprang from the Atlas Mountains in the 12th century.
Almoravids First (and short lived) Muslim Berber dynasty, arose in the eleventh century.
Almou (Amz) Summer pasture in damp hollows at high altitude.
Alpinisme Mountain climbing in French.
Amazigh Singular adjective of Imazighen, (Berbers).
Andalucía The South of Spain, from the Arabic 'al-Andalus', the Land of the Vandals, who occupied the area before the Arabs.
Andrair (Amz) Traditional threshing platform in the High Atlas.
Anedam (Amz) Poetry
Aqilous (Amz) Pointy hood with multi-coloured cords.
Arganier The Argan Tree. A spiney, drought resistant tree. The kernels produce a high quality oil. Species unique to southwestern Morocco.
Arset Orchard – in Marrakech and the South (from the Arabic *gharasa*, to plant)
Aserou (Amz) Ditch
Assareg (Amz) Forecourt, enclosed by dry-stone walls, located in front of the ground-floor stable area of a house in the High Atlas. Used for goats and sheep in the winter.
Assif (Amz) River in the High Atlas, often seasonal.
Astara (Amz) Shoulder-trembling dance performed by women.
Attarine Perfumers, as in 'Souk el Attarine'.
Azib (Amz) Seasonal mountain shelter, originally for animals.
Azm'ou (Amz) Valley floors in the High Atlas, used for fodder crops, subject to flooding during thunder storms.

B

Bab Gate, door.
Bahja From Marrakech.
Balgha Soft leather slippers, generally referred to in English as 'babouches'.
Bali (as in Fès el-Bali) Old – for a city area.
Baraka Divine quality inherent in all living beings. Especially present in certain chosen individuals. Holy people like the seven saints of Marrakech and Sidi Chamharouch near Jebel Toubkal have exceptional powers of baraka.
Baydhaoui From Casablanca
Bayoud Fungal infection of the palm tree which has ravaged the oases of North Africa.
Bejmet Small ceramic enamelled bricks.
Bendir Drum
Beni 'Sons of', tribal grouping.
Berber Term used by ethnographers to designate the Tamazight-speaking peoples.
Bildi From the bled, (countryside), local, indigenous, and by extension traditional. Contrasts with *roumi* (foreign, modern). There are *bildi* and *roumi* versions of many vegetables and fruit.
Bidonville Shanty town. From the French 'bidon', tin can, the main roofing material.
Bir Well
Bkhour Incense. Sba' bkhour, mixture of seven types of incense with strong powers.
Bled Hometown, countryside.
Borj Tower, bastion
Bou Ughanim (Amz) Lit. 'the flute player'. Clown figure who plays the clarinette in a group of Imdyazen.

C

Caïd Local government official, often with considerable power.
Calèche Horse-drawn carriage.
Cercle Rural administrative unit.
Cheikhate Female dancer-musicians.
Cherif (pl. Chorfa) Descendants of the Prophet Mohammed.
Chergui Hot, dry, stifling and dusty wind blowing out of the southeast, especially in summer, raising temperatures to the 40° mark.
Chikhat Women singer dancers in the Beraber lands, performing accompanied by professional musicians (*chikh*). In Atlantic Morocco, term refers to popular women singers with a sulphurous reputation.
Chleuh French term for the inhabitants of the western High Atlas and Anti-Atlas (see Ichelhiyn).
Choukara Leather bag

D

Dahir Royal decree
Dar House – and by extension, the family.
Darak al-malaki The Royal Gendarmerie – highway patrols and police in rural areas.
Dayat Freshwater lake
Dechra Hamlet
Derb Street (in an old city), also neighbourhood.
Dhikr From the Arabic to remind or recall. Religious chanting invoking Allah and the Prophet, essential part of trance ceremonies.
Diffa Ceremonial banquet
Dikka In Marrakech, chanting accompanied by tambourines, often performed for Achoura.
Dir Fertile lands at the foot of the mountains, created where sediment washed down from the mountains fans out onto the plain. Dir lands lie along the foot of the northern slopes of the High Atlas.
Douar Village

E

Empire chérifien Term used for Morocco during the late 19th century and under French rule.
Erg Sand dune region of the desert.

F

Fantasia Military exercise involving charging tribal cavalry and spectacular feats by riders. Now often performed for tourists.
Fassi From Fès. Things Fassi are held to be of higher quality – hence a certain snobbery among those with Fassi origins.
Fasqiya Pool with fountain.
Faux guide (lit. False guide) Anyone from a student hoping for a tip for showing you the town to an all-out hustler. Now heavily repressed by the *Brigade Touristique*.
Fondouk (From the Greek 'pandokeïon', hostelry) Merchants hostel in the city, now often used for craft manufacture.
Fkih, also spelt **fqih** Person learnèd in the religious sciences.

G

Gaouri European. See also nasrani.
Gare routière Bus station
Glaoua Major tribal confederation which dominated Marrakech for the first half of the 20th century from the mountain stronghold of Telouet.
Gnaoua (from Guinea?) Mystic cult found principally in Marrakech and Essaouira.
Grand taxi Inter-city private shared taxi. Fast and sometimes dangerous.
Guembri Three-corded lute used by the Gnaoua.

H

Habous Land or property held under a system akin to the medieval 'morte-main', ie managed as a sort of perpetual endowment to benefit a family or a charitable cause.
Haïk Long cloth wrap for women.

Hamada Stoney plain
Hammam Bath house
Harkous Elaborate geometric henna designs on hands and feet.
Hendira Thick, wool tunic worn by men, especially in the Rif.
Henna Vegetable dye used for hair and hands.
Herz Talisman, amulet – also called 'hjab', 'jedoual', 'ktab'.
Hizam Belt

I

Ichelhiyn (Amz) Inhabitants of the western High Atlas, Sous Valley and Anti-Atlas.
Idraren Draren (Amz) 'The Mountains of the Mountains', local name for the High Atlas.
Idrissid Early Moroccan Muslim dynasty (eighth century), founders of Fès.
Ighs (Amz) Bone, and by extension, family lineage.
Imam Essentially, the senior religious figure in a mosque.
Imazighen Lit. 'the free men'. Original Hamitic inhabitans of North Africa. There are three main Amazigh groups in Morocco, speaking respectively Ta'rifit (Znatiya) in the North, Tamazight (Middle Atlas) and Tachelhit (southern areas). The Kabyles and Chaouïa of Algeria are also Amazigh, as are the Touareg of Mali and Niger.
Imi (Amz) Gateway, mouth
Irhil (Amz) Mountain massif, also spelt Irghil.
Itouizi (Amz), **Touiza** (Ar) Co-operative labour in a mountain village.

J

Jellabah Long flowing tunic.
Jema'a Community council in the High Atlas.
Jinan sing. **Jenna** Garden. Jenna is also the Arabic for Paradise.
Jamaâ (often spelt Djam'i) Mosque. From the Arabic root 'jama'a', to gather.
Jebel (pl. Jibal) Mountain (Jeblaoui, mountain dweller).
Jobbana Traditional cheese pot

K

Kasbah Fort, citadel
Khabiya Traditional amphora pot
Khattara Underground water channel
Khayma Tent
Kilim Flat weave carpet
Kif Hashish
Kissaria Market specializing in clothes and fabrics.
Ksar (pl. Ksour) Palace, also fortified village.
Kufic Early Arabic script, often without the dots of later Arabic writing.

L

Lalla Madame. Title of a female saint.
Lila Night. Lila ed-derdeba, nightime Gnaoua ceremony.

M

Ma'alem Master craftsman
Ma'arouf Village ritual in the High Atlas, taking the form of the sacrifice of one or more beasts, a collective meal, and the auctioning of the remaining meat.
Magana Public clock
Maghreb (lit. Land of the West, al-Gharb) North Africa, as opposed to the Machrek, (Land of the East), the Near East. (Al-Maghrib = Morocco; Al-Mamlaka al-Maghribiya = Kingdom of Morocco.)
Makhzen Term used to designate 'the authorities' in a general sense. People with power and influence close to the Palace are said to be 'makhzen'.
Maktoub Lit. 'written', used to refer to an event pre-ordained by God and therefore unavoidable. Concept helpful for overcoming grief and adversity.
Malekite The main rite of Sunni Islam in North Africa.
Maqsoura Compartment or enclosure
Marabout French term used for saint in North African context. In Arabic the term is 'wali salih' or 'sidi' (pl. sadat).
Maristan Hospital
Mechouar Royal parade ground, enclosure near the palace.
Médersa College dispensing education in the Islamic legal and religious studies.

Médina City
Mellah Jewish quarter
Merinids Major dynasty in Morocco, held sway c.1248-1420.
Mihrab Prayer niche in a mosque indicating the direction of Mecca.
Minbar Pulpit in a mosque
Moulay Arabic honorific, 'sir', 'my lord'. Polite form of address.
Mouloud Celebration of the Prophet Mohammed's birthday.
Moussem Annual festival, of religious origin, often centred on a pilgrimage to a saint's tomb. Practice falling out of use in late 20th century.

Nasrani Christian (lit. 'follower of the man from Nazareth'), and by extension European.
Nécropole French term for ancient cemetery.
Neggafa (pl. 'neggafat') Women responsible for preparing the bride for her wedding.
Nekkacha (pl. 'nekkachat') Women specializing in doing henna designs on the skin.

Ottoman Turkey-based Muslim Empire, 13th to early 20th century.
Ougoug Small dam for diverting irrigation water.
Ouled (lit. 'Sons of') Tribal grouping.

Pisé Sundried earth used for building, Arabic 'toub'.
Piste Rough track, generally accessible by all but the lowest slung cars.
Politique des grands caïds French policy of indirect rule in southern Morocco based on support for dominant clans (the Glaoua and Goundafa). Practice similar to British rule through maharajahs in India.

Qibla Wall of mosque facing towards Mecca.

Ramadhan Month of fasting in Muslim calendar.
Rays (Amz) (pl. rwayes), Lit. leader, designates poet-singers among the Chleuh. Plural indicates the whole troop of musicians.
Reg Rock desert
Roumi (lit. 'from Rome). Adjective designating things foreign or modern, especially with regard to food and recipes. Used in opposition to things 'bildi', indigenous and traditional.

Saâdian Dynasty ruling from Marrakech, 1554-1659.
Sabil Public fountain.
Sidi Honorific. Mr, also refers to a saint.
Sunni Mainstream Islam, as opposed to Shi'a Islam, prevalent in Iran.

Taghounja (Amz) Lit. wooden spoon. Ceremony to bring rain.
Taghwrit (Amz) High pitched ululations made by women to express joy, called 'tzagrit' in Arabic.
Takhemt (Amz) Nomad tent
Tamazgha (Amz) Amazigh lands
Tamghart (Amz) 'She who runs' (about numerous tasks), ie the mature woman in a High Atlas village.
Tamghra (Amz) Wedding rituals among the Chleuh.
Tamsriyt (Amz) Reception area, an upper room, often elaborately decorated in a house or kasbah, used by women and men separately for gatherings.
Targa (Amz) Irrigation ditch (Ar. 'seguia')
Tifinagh Oldest form of writing in Amazigh, predates the Greek alphabet by six centuries. Essentially used by the Touareg in the Sahara.
Tighremt (Amz) Fortified granary in the High Atlas. Once a central institution of the Amazigh communities, symbol of their ability to survive.
Tigimmi (Amz) House, living area above the stabling or 'agrour'.

Timzguida (Amz) Mosque
Tit (Amz) Spring
Tizi (Amz) Col, mountain pass

U

'Ud Lute
'Ulema (sing. alim) Persons learnèd in the religious sciences
'Urf Customary law
Villes impériales French 20th century term used to designate the cities where the sultan established his temporary capital, ie Fès and Meknès, Marrakech and Rabat.

W

Wali Provincial governor; 'wali salih', a holy man

Z

Zanka Street, as opposed to 'derb', a residential street.
Zakat Islamic tithe
Zaouia Saint's shrine, generally a domed, whitewashed building containing tomb of a wali salih (holy man) or woman.
Zellige Elaborate ceramic wall mosaics
Zenata Tribal confederation, ruled northern Morocco in late tenth century.
Zerbia Carpet
Zriba Hut

Food and cooking

B

Briouet Filo pastry envelopes, filled with crushed nuts and basted in olive oil, then dipped in honey.

C

Chermoula Marinade sauce.
Couscous Steamed semolina heaped with meat and vegetables.

F

Fliou Peppermint, also used in tea preparations.

H

Harira Chickpea and mutton soup, especially popular when breaking the fast in Ramadhan.

K

Ka'b el-ghizal Gazelles' horns Traditional marzipan filled pastry.
Kahoua Coffee
Kefta Meat balls.

L

Luiza Verbena herbal tea.

M

Mahchi (or **mo'ammar**) Stuffed (chicken, vegetables, etc)
Mechoui Barbecued meat.
Mqali Meat dishes gently simmered with sauce reduced rapidly on high flame at end of cooking.
Mouhallabiya Milk pudding.

N

Na'na Mint, essential for preparing tea The best mint is produced in Meknès.

O

Orz bil-bahiya Paëlla

P

Pastila Elaborate sweet and sour pie. made of alternating layers of filopastry and egg, pigeon, and crushed almonds. Speciality of Fès.
Pessara Bean soup

Q

Qa'ida Tradition – vital to any meal prepared for guests in a Moroccan home.

Index

Footnotes

Shorts

Maps

Updates

We try as hard as we can to make each Footprint Handbook as up-to-date and accurate as possible but, of course, things always change. Many people email or write to us – with corrections, new information, or simply comments. If you want to let us know about your experiences and adventures – be they good, bad or ugly – then don't delay; we're dying to hear from you. And please try to include all the relevant details and juicy bits. Your help will be greatly appreciated, especially by other travellers. In return we will send you details about our special guidebook offer. Why not contact via our **website**:

www.footprintbooks.com
A new place to visit

alternatively email Footprint at:
mar1_online@footprintbooks.com

or write to:

Elizabeth Taylor
Footprint Handbooks
6 Riverside Court
Lower Bristol Road
Bath
BA2 3DZ
UK